Industrial Relations

Industrial Relations
Theory and Practice

SECOND EDITION

Michael Salamon

Bristol Business School
University of the West of England

Prentice Hall
New York · London · Toronto · Sydney · Tokyo · Singapore

First published 1992 by
Prentice Hall International (UK) Ltd
Campus 400, Maylands Avenue
Hemel Hempstead
Hertfordshire, HP2 7EZ
A division of
Simon & Schuster International Group

Typeset in 10½/12pt Garamond
by Keyset Composition, Colchester
Printed and bound in Great Britain at
the University Press, Cambridge

Library of Congress Cataloging-in-Publication Data

Salamon, Michael, 1944–
    Industrial relations : theory and practice / Michael Salamon. –
2nd ed.
        p.   cm.
    Includes bibliographical references and index.
    ISBN 0-13-457433-8
    1. Industrial relations.   2. Industrial relations – Great Britain.
I. Title.
HD6971.s137   1992
331—dc20   92-12390
                                                               CIP

British Library Cataloguing in Publication Data

A catalogue record for this book is available from
the British Library

ISBN 0-13-457433-8 (pbk)

---

1 2 3 4 5   96 95 94 93 92

To my wife (Barbara) and children (Leesha, Joanne, James and Philip) for their forbearance during the long writing of this book.

To Mike Goddard and Ian Grayston for their friendship, support and inspiration at different points in my career.

To Mark Anstey in the hope that the tensions of transition will give way to a better future.

Contents

Preface

Objectives

This book is intended for students studying industrial relations on under-graduate, postgraduate or post-experience courses. It seeks:

- to provide a framework of knowledge relating to the concepts, theories, institutions and practices of industrial relations in Britain; and
- to present that knowledge in a way which facilitates the student's learning.

The knowledge and understanding gained from this book may then be further developed and refined through the student's reading of more specialised books and articles and the lecturer's use of lectures, seminars, tutorials, exercises, etc.

Structure

The subject matter of Industrial Relations may be presented in many different ways. However, whatever approach is adopted, it soon becomes apparent that the multi-disciplinary nature of the subject combined with its complex interrelationships mean that it is difficult to comprehend fully one aspect of the subject without reference to other aspects. The framework and sequence adopted within this book owes as much, if not more, to the student's need for knowledge to be presented in a structured and segmented way as it does to any intrinsic academic logic.

The book is divided into four parts:

- Part A (Perspectives) introduces the student to a range of concepts and approaches which are central to a study and understanding of industrial relations.

- Part B (Participants) examines the function, organisation and problems of the three main participants within industrial relations – trade unions, management and the government.
- Part C (Processes) examines the range of processes used by the participants in the conduct of their relationships.
- Part D (Practices) examines a number of industrial relations activities undertaken at the organisational level.

Presentation

The book seeks to aid the student's learning in a number of ways. Each chapter:

- commences with a *definition* section which identifies the parameters of that topic area;
- uses *diagrams*, wherever possible, to help explain concepts, institutions, relationships, influences, etc.;
- concludes with *summary propositions* which both highlight significant points and provide areas for discussion;
- provides a short list of *further reading* on that topic.

The use of the terms 'production', 'productive' or 'operations' in this book is intended to cover both manufacturing and service situations. The issues covered by this book are just as relevant to service situations, whether private or public sector, as they are to manufacturing.

Acknowledgements

I should like to express my appreciation to all those people with whom I have worked in different aspects of industrial relations over the past twenty-five years and whose thoughts and insights have helped me to clarify and refine my own perceptions of industrial relations both as an area of study and as a practical activity. In particular I should like to express my thanks to my colleagues in the Bristol Business School (notably Ian Grayston) for their thoughts and discussions over the years; and to Cathy Peck and Julia Helmsley (Prentice Hall International) for their support during the revision of this book. Some of their comments have been included in this book, others have had to be excluded because of the pressure of space.

Finally, it is important to recognise that the success and value of this book owes as much to the thoughts and efforts of many other writers and researchers over the years as it does to my own.

All extracts from HMSO publications are reproduced courtesy of the Controller of Her Majesty's Stationery Office.

Michael Salamon
January 1992

Abbreviations

ABS – Association of Broadcasting Staffs (merged with NATTKE in 1984 to form BETA)

ACAS – Advisory, Conciliation and Arbitration Service

ACTAT – Association of Cinematograph Television and Allied Technicians (merged with BETA in 1990 to form BECTU)

ACTTS – Association of Clerical, Technical & Supervisory Staffs (white collar section of T&GWU)

AEU – Amalgamated Engineering Union

APAC – Association of Patternmakers & Allied Craftsmen (merged with TASS)

APEX – Association of Professional, Executive, Clerical & Computer Staff (merged with GMB in 1989)

ASBSB&SW – Amalgamated Society of Boilermakers, Shipwrights, Blacksmiths & Structural Workers (merged with GMWU in 1982 to form GMB)

ASLEF – Associated Society of Locomotive Engineers & Firemen

ASTMS – Association of Scientific, Technical & Managerial Staffs (merged with TASS in 1987 to form MSF)

AUFW – Amalgamated Union of Foundry Workers (merged with AEU in 1960s)

BECTU – Broadcasting, Entertainment & Cinematograph Technicians' Union

BETA – Broadcasting and Entertainment Trade Union (merged with ACTAT in 1990 to form BECTU)

BIM – British Institute of Management

BMA – British Medical Association

CAC – Central Arbitration Committee

CBI – Confederation of British Industry

CEU – Construction Engineering Union (merged with AEU in 1960s)

CIR – Commission on Industrial Relations

COHSE – Confederation of Health Service Employees

CPSA – Civil & Public Servants Association

CSEU – Confederation of Shipbuilding & Engineering Unions

CSU – Civil Service Union (merged with SCPS in 1988 to form NUCAPS)

DATA – Draughtsmen & Allied Technicians Association (merged with AEU in 1960s to form TASS section)

EAT – Employment Appeals Tribunal

EEF – Engineering Employers' Federation

EEPTU – Electrical, Electronic, Plumbing & Telecommunications Union
ETU – Electrical Trades Union (now EETPU)
GCHQ – Government Communications Head Quarters
GMB or **GMBATU** – General, Municipal, Boilermakers & Allied Trades Union
GMWU – General & Municipal Workers Union (merged with ASBSB&SW in 1982 to form GMB)
GPMU – Graphical, Paper & Media Union
ICFTU – International Confederation of Free Trades Union
ILO – International Labour Organisation
IPM – Institute of Personnel Management
IPMS – Institution of Professionals, Managers & Specialists (formerly Institution of Professional Civil Servants)
ISTC – Iron & Steel Trades Confederation
JCC – Joint Consultative Committee
JIC – Joint Industrial Council
JSSC – Joint Shop Stewards Committee
JUNC – Joint Union Negotiating Committee
MSC – Manpower Services Commission
MSF – Manufacturing, Science & Finance Union
NALGO – National and Local Government Officers' Association
NATTKE – National Association of Theatrical, Television & Kine Employees (merged with ABS in 1984 to form BETA)
NBPI – National Board for Prices and Incomes
NCB – National Coal Board
NEC – National Executive Committee
NEDO – National Economic Development Office
NGA – National Graphical Association (merged with SOGAT in 1990 to form GPMU)
NJC – National Joint Council or Committee
NJIC – National Joint Industrial Council
NUAAW – National Union of Agricultural & Allied Workers (merged with T&GWU in 1981)
NUCAPS – National Union of Civil & Public Servants
NUDB&TW – National Union of Dyers, Bleachers & Textile Workers (merged with T&GWU in 1981)
NUFLAT – National Union of Footwear, Leather and Allied Trades (merged with NUHKW in 1990 to form NUKF&AT)
NUHKW – National Union of Hosiery and Knitwear Workers (merged with NUFLAT in 1990 to form NUKF&AT)
NUKF&AT – National Union of Knitwear, Footwear & Apparel Trades
NUM – National Union of Mineworkers
NUPE – National Union of Public Employees
NUR – National Union of Railwaymen (merged with NUS to form RMT)
NUS – National Union of Seamen (merged with NUR to form RMT)
NUSMWCH&DE – National Union of Sheet Metal Workers, Coppersmiths, Heating & Domestic Engineers (merged with TASS)
NUT – National Union of Teachers
NUTGW – National Union of Tailors & Garment Workers (merged with GMB)
PBR – Payment by Results
POEU – Post Office Engineering Union (now called National Communications Union)

RCN – Royal College of Nursing
RMT – National Union of Rail, Marine & Transport Workers
SCPS – Society of Civil & Public Servants (merged with CSU in 1988 to form NUCAPS)
SJIC – Statutory Joint Industrial Council
SOGAT – Society of Graphical & Allied Trades (merged with NGA in 1990 to form GPMU)
TASS – Technical & Supervisory Section (merged with ASTMS in 1987 to form MSF)
T&GWU – Transport & General Workers Union
TSSA – Transport Salaried Staffs Association
TUC – Trades Union Congress
UCATT – Union of Construction, Allied Trades & Technicians
UCW – Union of Communication Workers
UMA – Union Membership Agreement
USDAW – Union of Shop, Distributive & Allied Workers

PART A

Perspectives

Chapter 1

The context of industrial relations

1.1 Definition

An industrial society is a highly complex and dynamic arrangement of differentiated groups, activities and institutional relationships intertwined with a variety of attitudes and expectations. Consequently, any specific social phenomenon, such as industrial relations, cannot and should not be viewed in isolation from its wider context. The 'context' of industrial relations may usefully be divided into three major elements (see Figure 1.1).

- *The industrial relations 'system'*. The roles, relationships, institutions, processes and activities which comprise the phenomena of industrial relations exist both in a wide variety of industries and services and at a number of levels ranging from the suborganisational (workgroup, section or department) and organisational (site or company) levels through the industry level to the national level. This inevitably creates a pattern of internal influences both horizontally (between different organisations/industries) and vertically (between different levels). Consequently, the industrial relations system, in terms of the attitudes and activities existing within it at any point in time, provides its own context or climate for the individual industrial relations situations.

- *Other segments of social activity*. Industrial relations is only one segment of a society's structure and activity and as such is influenced by, and in turn influences, other segments of the society's activity. The economic, social and political segments are of particular importance in this respect. Actions or changes in these areas may directly stimulate or constrain specific industrial relations activities as well as indirectly influence the attitudes of the participants. It is important to recognise that these environments exert an influence at all levels of industrial relations and therefore, as Fox argues, 'organisational issues, conflicts and values are inextricably bound up with those of society at large' [1].

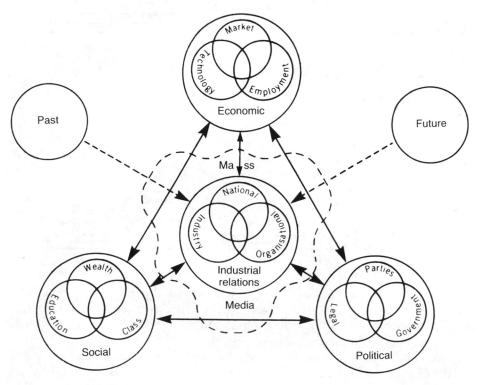

Figure 1.1 *The context of industrial relations*

• *Time*. The present is only part of a continuum between the past and the future; consequently, current industrial relations owes much to its past (whether last week, last year, the last decade or even the last century) and the participant's goals and expectations for the future. At the micro level, the time context may be evidenced in two ways: (a) today's problem stems from yesterday's decision and its solution will, as the environments change, become a problem in the future, and (b) the attitudes, expectations and relationships manifest by the participants are, at least in part, the product of their past individual and collective experiences. At the macro level, industrial relations as a whole is subject to adjustment and development as society, expressed through changes in the economic, social and political environments, itself changes and develops.

At the same time it is important to recognise that the 'mass media' provide an additional, and very significant, context for industrial relations by virtue of their role in shaping attitudes, opinions and expectations. Any individual, whether as a manager, trade unionist or part of the 'general public', has only a partial direct experience of the full range of activities present in a society. Most knowledge and appreciation of economic, social, political and industrial relations affairs is, therefore, gained indirectly from the facts and opinions disseminated through newspapers and television.

1.2 Economic, social and political environments

Each of the environments (economic, social and political) which surround industrial relations is composed of a number of interactive elements and interrelates with the other environments and industrial relations. For example:

1. The economic environment (principally the market and employment elements at both the macro and micro levels), social expectations regarding the distribution of wealth and government economic policy interact through industrial relations in the determination of wage structures and levels.
2. The growth of female employment, and its importance for industrial relations, is closely bound up with changing social patterns and expectations in respect of education, work and family arrangements, changes in industrial structure, technology and the level of economic activity and the introduction of legislation directed towards reducing sex discrimination in employment.

It is not the intention of this section to provide a comprehensive analysis of the interactive development of British society but rather to highlight a number of the more important changes which have taken place in these environments over the post-war period.

Economic environment

In 1982 Taylor argued not only that Britain in the 1980s was 'suffering its worst economic slump since the years between the two world wars', but also that 'the first industrial proletariat in the world is fast disappearing with hardly a whimper' [2].

The decline in British manufacturing industries
This decline has been both in terms of the manufacturing industries' level of output and employment and in terms of their contribution to Britain's economy. Whilst their declining contribution to the balance of payments has been offset by Britain's role as an oil exporting country and by increases in invisible earnings from banking and insurance, tourism, shipping and income from overseas investments, the increased activity in these other segments of the economy has not offset the reduction in employment in manufacturing

industries. There has been a shift in employment to the service sector from the mid-1980s, but these industries (such as financial services, tourism, retail and distribution, catering, etc.) are themselves beginning to decline at the end of the decade as they face a recession perhaps just as severe as manufacturing at the beginning of the decade. The economic conditions of the 1960s provided the highpoint for British manufacturing industries. Since then they have, in general, suffered from a declining share of the world market – a market which since the late 1970s has been itself contracting due to world recession. At the same time the strong home consumer market developed during the 1960s has been weakened by Britain's recession and by strong competition from abroad. The competition in both the home and world markets has come from: (i) other industrialised countries (such as the USA, Japan, Sweden, Germany, etc.) whose lower inflation and higher productivity rates have given them an advantage over British manufacturers, and (ii) developing countries whose low wages have allowed them to virtually take over certain British markets, such as textiles, and whose governmental support for their own industrialisation, in such sectors as iron and steel, and car manufacture, has reduced overseas markets for British products.

The cause of Britain's decline in this area has been variously ascribed to management's lack of investment in new plant and new ideas, to trade unions pushing up wage levels and resisting measures aimed at increasing production, and to the inevitable de-industrialisation of Britain and other western industrial countries in the wake of Third World economic development. Whatever the precise cause, one result has been to focus attention on **governmental policy towards the management of the economy**. Post-war economic growth was closely associated with what is often referred to as **Keynsian economic management**. The social objective of full employment was regarded as both of central importance and a governmental responsibility to be maintained, if necessary, by direct action on the demand side of the economy – recession and consequent unemployment was counteracted by deficit government budgeting and increased public expenditure. During the 1960s and 1970s this was frequently accompanied by formal incomes policies in an attempt to contain inflation resulting from either internal or external pressures and governmental support for struggling firms or industries whether in the public or private sector ('lame duck' policy).

However, since the election of the Conservative Government in 1979 the direction of economic policy has shifted to a **monetarist approach** which regards the control of inflation and the achievement of a competitive international position to be of central importance. The Government's policy has been directed towards reducing public sector expenditure by 'privatisation', 'rate capping' local authority income, low pay increases, etc. This action is intended to allow the Government to reduce its borrowing and taxes and thereby reduce interest rates and divert national resources into investment in the private sector. Within this approach high unemployment is seen as a necessary, but hopefully temporary, prelude to improved productivity and competitiveness which will result in sustained economic growth. The public and private sectors are seen in 'competitive' rather than 'complementary' terms. The Government's approach has been supported by management strategies aimed at securing more competitive performance orientated and flexible organisations.

Growth of non-manual employment and technology

Non-manual employment now accounts for virtually 50 per cent of the employed workforce and has resulted from the growth of service industries in both the public and private sectors and the growth of technical, professional, administrative and managerial work generally. This process of employment restructuring is now clearly associated with the increasing rate of introduction of **new technology** based on computers and the micro chip. The new technology is being applied to both manual and non-manual work and has the potential to revolutionise the work situation: in the manual area it has created the possibility of robotic factories serviced by a small number of technicians, whilst in the non-manual area the development of information handling technology may allow individuals to work from home via a computer link with their organisation without the need to come together with other employees in an office. This trend away from manual work, certainly of an unskilled or semi-skilled level, is reflected in the unemployment rate amongst manual workers being 2½ times greater than amongst technical, professional and other non-manual groups. However, the creation of new employment opportunities amongst the new 'high technology' industries which supply the micro chips, computers and new technical systems is too low and of the wrong type to compensate for the rate of job losses in the other industries introducing the new technology.

Employment

An examination of Britain's **employment** figures shows a significant change over the post-war period. Throughout the **1950s and most of the 1960s** Britain experienced stable and 'full' or 'overfull' employment. The annual average rate of unemployment fluctuated, in line with the business cycle, between 1 and 2 per cent whilst the underlying unemployment trend remained static. Apart from a small core of 'unemployable' labour (those physically or mentally incapable of working), most unemployment was of short duration because a buoyant economy provided a steady demand for labour. Indeed, there were periods of labour shortage (more job vacancies than the number unemployed), particularly amongst skilled workers, which provided an impetus for both wage competition between employers as they sought to attract the required labour and the development of productivity bargaining as organisations sought to expand their production by making the most effective use of a scarce resource (labour).

However, in 1979–81 Britain was hit by soaring inflation. Deaton's [3] examination of unemployment over this period (see Table 1.1) shows that

Table 1.1 *Employment trends, 1966–81*

	1966–1979 (millions)		1979–1981 (millions)
Working population	+0.7		−0.5
Male	−0.7		−0.2
Female	+1.5		−0.3
Employed	−0.3		−2.0
Manufacturing	−1.4		−1.3
Public services*	+1.1		−0.1
Others*	−		−0.7
Unemployed			
Number	+1.0		+1.6
Rate (%)	1.5–5.5		5.5–11.5
Participation rates† (%)	*1966*	*1979*	*1981*
Overall	77.3	77.6	75.3
Male	97.7	90.4	87.8
Female	55.4	63.6	61.5

All figures rounded to nearest '000.
* Public services includes only central and local government, health, education and the armed forces. Others include nationalised industries and private services.
† Participation rate is the working population as a percentage of the population of working age (15–59 for women and 15–64 for men).

Source: D. Deaton, 'Unemployment' in G. S. Bain (ed.), *Industrial Relations in Britain*, Blackwell, 1983 (Table 10.1, p. 239).

the rise between 1966 and 1979, both low points of unemployment in the business cycle, was two-thirds attributable to an increase in the size of the working population and one-third to a decrease in the level of employment. However, the changes were not uniform. Whilst the numbers remaining at school beyond the statutory leaving age or entering tertiary education mainly accounted for the decline of 700,000 in the male working population, the same trend amongst females was more than compensated for by others seeking employment (particularly those over 25) to give a net increase in the female working population of 1.5 million. At the same time, the relatively small decrease in the level of employment disguised a considerable fall in manufacturing employment and almost equal increase in employment in the public services.

After 1979 the picture changed significantly. The numbers employed in manufacturing continued to decline, so that by the end of 1981 there were 2.6 million (31 per cent) fewer than in 1966, whilst the earlier expansion of the public services became a small decrease. In addition, employment also fell in other industries and services by 700,000. The reduction in the size of the working population, both male and female, at a time when the population of working age continued to rise (400,000 between 1979 and

1981), is regarded by Deaton as 'a consequence of the recession itself as people withdraw from the labour force because of the lack of job opportunities' and 'suggests that there is considerable hidden unemployment in addition to the registered unemployment recorded in the statistics' [4].

The UK has experienced **a continuing high rate of unemployment** throughout the 1980s (see Figure 1.2) with a peak of 13 per cent in 1981 (over 3 million people), remaining above 10 per cent until 1987, falling to a 'low' of 6 per cent in 1990 and then rising to nearly 9 per cent by the end of 1991 and projected to rise further to nearly 10 per cent again in 1992 (2.8 million). The official figure is based on the number of people who claim unemployment related benefits and therefore is 'vulnerable to changes in coverage whenever there are changes to the administrative procedures' [5] and during the 1980s there have been some twenty-eight changes which have, in the main, removed people from the 'claimant count' (for example, unemployed men over 60 and young people on Government training schemes). It is difficult to calculate precisely how much these changes have reduced the figure but Lawlor and White have identified that the UK count in 1990 was 350,000 lower compared to using the ILO basis of calculating unemployment. However, the aggregate number or rate of unemployment do not, on their own adequately reflect the full extent and nature of the unemployment problem:

1. **Average duration of unemployment** has risen from 3 weeks in the 1950s to 16+ weeks in the 1980s.

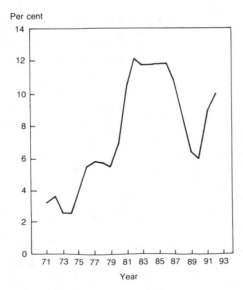

Figure 1.2   *UK rate of unemployment, 1971–92 (% of working population)*

2. **Long-term unemployed** (those unemployed for more than 52 weeks) in the 1980s is 3–4 times the *total* unemployed in the 1950s and early 1960s and account for 26 per cent of all unemployed. The long-term unemployed includes those who lack the qualifications, skill, experience or personal attributes which are sought by potential employers; those for whom there is no work in their area; and those whose personal confidence and attractiveness to employers has been undermined by their experience of long unemployment.

3. Unemployment amongst **young people** in the early 1980s was also particularly high and unemployment amongst ethnic minority groups is significantly higher than amongst white males [6].

Deaton notes that over the post-war period the aggregate flow onto the unemployed register has remained fairly consistent at some 4–4.5 million people per year with increased redundancies during recessions being offset by a reduction in voluntary resignations. He argues that 'the picture of unemployment that emerges is one of a large number of people joining the register, with the state of demand affecting their probability of re-employment and hence their duration of unemployment' [7]. Similarly, Hunter believes that 'unemployment has mounted by reason of inadequate outflow' [8].

The extent and nature of unemployment is affected not only by the level of economic activity (boom or recession) and changes in the industrial and occupational employment structure (demand), but also by changes in the workforce (supply). Several trends in the **structure of the workforce** are particularly important:

1. **Increase in the proportion of females**: between 1971 and 1988 the population of working age, that is all people over 16 and under retirement age (labour supply), increased by 2.5 million; but whilst the male labour force remained relatively constant at approximately 15.5 million, the female labour force rose from 9.3 million to 11.8 million (+2.5 million) and it is projected that virtually all of the expected increase in labour supply to 2000 will be among women who will comprise 44 per cent of the labour force [9].

2. **'Demographic timebomb'**: there will be some 25 per cent less people in the 15–19 age group in 1995 than there were in 1985 and although it will start increasing after 1995 it will not reach the 1985 level until well into the next century. In seeking to respond to this anticipated shortfall in traditional new entrants management has encouraged female 'returners' [10].

3. **Part-time and/or temporary work**: the proportion of part-time workers has increased from 4 per cent in 1951 to 22 per cent in 1984 [11] and, whilst it is not by any means an exclusively female phenomena, nevertheless a substantial element are women. The development of

increased part-time work has not simply been in response to the needs of those (males or females) who wish, for whatever reason, to combine work with their domestic life but has, along with casual work, temporary contracts, etc., been an integral part of some management's strategies to develop numerical flexibility within the organisation (i.e. to be able to 'hire and fire' as needed by their labour demand). Thus although the total number of people employed may have increased during the 1980s, many of these jobs are not full-time permanent jobs.

All these developments raise issues for the nature of the relationships between the employee, management and unions. Certainly, the change in the composition of the workforce, combined with the decline in union membership has led trade unions to focus more on the distinct needs of women and part-time workers both in their recruitment strategies and in their negotiations with management.

Social environment

Britain's society is generally described, using economic and political terminology, as an **industrialised capitalist democracy** based on the principles of individual freedom of thought, expression and association. Within this society the economic activity of work is supported by social values (often referred to as the 'Protestant work ethic') wherein, as Tawney argued, 'the conscientious discharge of the duties of business is among the loftiest of religious and moral virtues' [12]. Certainly, it is the principle of one individual working for another and accepting superior authority which has given rise to the complex arrangement of economic and social divisions within a modern society.

However, society has changed over the post-war period. The initial period after World War II is perhaps best characterised by the idea of reconstruction – not just of the buildings and economy but also the social order. The creation of the **modern welfare state** embodied the beliefs that the strong within society should support the weak and that the state should accept responsibility both for the provision of education, health and other social services and for ensuring that equality of access should prevail rather than access being dependent on the ability of the individual to pay. In the economic environment, the state took responsibility for maintaining full employment and, through nationalisation, the management of certain key industries which it was felt should operate in the interests of the economy and society as a whole rather than the interests of profit for the shareholder. Society became more 'socialist' in its outlook and based on a mixed economy.

The effects of these changes, particularly in areas such as education, were not fully felt until the 1960s. The 1960s saw the **demise of the deferential**

society and a challenge to previously accepted values, attitudes and institutions. Although to some the existence of the welfare state coupled with the state's acceptance of responsibility for the maintenance of full employment stifles individual initiative by creating a belief that 'society owes the individual a living', to others it represents the achievement of independence and an expansion of opportunities for the individual. Certainly, the provision of social benefits in respect of unemployment, sickness, family circumstances, etc., reduces the individual's dependence on the work situation for determining his/her standard of living and the existence of full employment reduces his/her reliance on any particular employer. In this way the individual becomes less constrained to accept low pay, bad working conditions or harsh management. At the same time an expansion of educational opportunities not only increases the individual's awareness of the surrounding world and willingness to question, but also opens up occupational and social possibilities which previously had been denied. Consequently, the 1960s' developments in education coupled with economic prosperity, employment stability and the creation of a consumer market through advertising created a population and workforce which had increased expectations in respect of both material rewards and participation in the decisions at work and outside which affected their lives.

However, despite presenting an appearance of a more egalitarian society in terms of the distribution of both material rewards and decision making, Britain remains essentially a **class based society**. The possibility of upward social mobility generated by increased educational opportunities and the overlapping material lifestyles between 'manual' workers and the 'professional' or 'middle' classes created by economic prosperity has not removed the fundamental divisions within society. An individual's position within the economic hierarchy is still an important factor in determining perceived status relative to others within society. In order to gain wider support for the capitalist ethos, the Government has encouraged individual share-ownership in its privatisation of parts of the public sector. Although it is estimated that there are some 10 million individual shareholders (about the same number as are trade union members), most only have a small holding acquired under the preferential terms offered by the Government privatisation plans. Real wealth and power, both economic and political, still remain unequally divided and largely in the hands of a small number of individuals, organisations and financial institutions. In reality, it is a society of inequalities.

The decline in economic growth and prosperity experienced during the late 1970s and 1980s has negated much of the social development of the 1960s. Consistently high unemployment and reductions in public expenditure on benefits and social services at a time when, due to the recession and unemployment, more people are in need of such support has **heightened the divisions within society:** between those who have work and those who do not; between economic deprivation in inner city and traditional manufacturing areas and relative prosperity in the suburbs and south-east of England;

between those who can purchase private medicine and education and those who have to rely on the declining standards of the public services. Within this environment there is evidence to suggest not only an increasing polarisation of attitudes and values within society but also increasing frustration of the 'have nots' at their apparent inability to influence governmental policies and achieve change through the normal political processes.

High unemployment has also undermined a number of traditional assumptions associated with the 'Protestant work ethic': for example, 'providing an employee does a "fair day's work", he or she has nothing to worry about'; 'there are three generations of the same family working here'; 'get a trade or skill and you'll always have work'; 'the pay may be low to start with, but there's a good pension at the end'; and 'I'm looking on this as a long-term career'. The reality is that few, if any, jobs have permanent job security.

Whilst the Industrial Revolution acted as a catalyst for a major social change by drawing people into factories to work machines and thereby created an urban industrialised society based on the sale of labour, high unemployment and the 'technological revolution' may create an equally severe social change by removing people from the 'paid work' situation.

Political environment

It has been suggested that the political environment 'is in many ways the most complex and the most difficult to handle, both because of its impact on the other environments and because of its roles within and without the system' [13] of industrial relations. Certainly, it is difficult to define **what is meant by political environment.** The term 'political' is used colloquially with either a small 'p' or capital 'P'. The former usually refers to the power–authority nature of an organisation's decision making process or the attitudes and actions of a person within that process. When used with a capital 'P' it is intended to refer to society's system of government. Thus, there are two levels of political environment: the internal organisational decision making process which is part of industrial relations and the external society system of government. The remainder of this section is concerned with the latter.

The political environment encompasses both **the means by which society organises itself in order to express and achieve the goals and aspirations of the people and the nature of these goals and aspirations.** It comprises not only the formal system of political parties, Parliament and government at the national level but also local authority government, Quangos (Quasi-Autonomous Non-Governmental Organisations with financial support from and senior appointments made by government) and a range of informal pressure groups which seek to influence the decisions of the formal system. However, it is the political parties and government, and their underlying ideologies, which are, perhaps, the most important and active elements within the political environment, for it is they which ultimately determine the direction, policies and actions of the governmental process.

Political differentiation, and consequently differential government policies and actions is determined by differences in view regarding the nature of the society which it is intended to create or at least encourage [14]. In Britain the type of desired society has tended to be differentiated on the basis of the extent to which it should be **individualistic or corporatist** orientated on such issues as the respective roles of the state and the individual in the creation and distribution of economic wealth; the role of the state in the management and control of the economy; the approach and priority afforded to social welfare; and the nature and authority of 'political' decision making and regulation at all levels of the society. Over the nineteenth and twentieth centuries there have been significant shifts in the dominant ideology between these two approaches.

During the nineteenth century a **liberalist or *laissez-faire* ideology** dominated the emergence of the new social order based on capitalism. The emphasis on an economic regulation of society was closely associated with the concept of individualism. Economic and social matters were perceived as being determined by contracts made between individuals who were equals and responsible for their own destiny. In the economic sphere it was believed that individuals should act alone and not distort the operation of supply and demand forces within the labour market by seeking to combine with others to increase economic power. This approach found expression in the legal doctrines of 'restraint of trade' and 'conspiracy' which, in industrial relations, constrained the development of trade unions until they were granted immunity in the Trade Union Act (1871) and Trade Disputes Act (1906).

These enactments were a reflection of the shift in dominant political ideology from the 'liberal individualists of 1830' to the 'democratic socialists of 1905' [15]. The growth of collectivism amongst the 'working classes' and its resultant pressure for industrial, economic and social reform led to a realisation that the Government could not and should not ignore the social problems arising from industrial capitalism but rather should accept responsibility for greater intervention to protect and improve people's quality of life. This corporatist or interventionist ideology is founded on the principle of integration rather than separation of the political, economic and social aspects of life and the involvement of 'capital' and 'labour' in the process of government. This provided the basis for the apparent 'consensus politics' of the post-war period when both Conservative and Labour Governments were committed to the maintenance of full employment and the welfare state and to the involvement of trade union and employer representatives in tri-partite discussions on a wide range of economic and social issues, including incomes policy. Indeed, it was a Conservative Government which both established the National Economic Development Office (NEDO) in 1961 as the main forum for these discussions and confirmed the TUC's predominance by refusing to grant representation to non-affiliated unions. However, this apparent consensus over objectives did not preclude differences of emphasis in government policies or differences in strategy for the achievement of these objectives.

Within all political parties there are both **fundamentalists** who assert the importance of maintaining party philosophy and doctrine and **pragmatists** who assert the importance of acceptability to the electorate and practicability of implementation. (These are more commonly, but perhaps erroneously, referred to as 'extremists' and 'moderates'.) Under a broadly two party political system, the fundamentalists in the Labour and Conservative Parties appear to have exerted influence primarily when the party was 'out of office' and as part of the process of party re-identification in preparation for the next election, whilst the pragmatists have exerted the major influence when the party was 'in office' – again enhancing the appearance of governmental consensus. The polarisation of political ideologies is clearly reflected in what are perceived to be the **political issues**; indeed, it may be argued that a political issue cannot arise unless there are differences of view about:

1. the government's responsibility for creating and/or resolving the high unemployment level;
2. the balance between public and private sectors (privatisation);
3. the nature and extent of the power that trade unions may be allowed to exercise within industry and society;
4. the 'rule of law', maintenance of 'law and order' and the role of the police in 'social' actions such as strikes and picketing;
5. the extent to which government policy and decision making should be conducted within a framework of public debate and involvement.

Contrary to this model, the election of Mrs Thatcher in 1979 brought a return to the more fundamentalist doctrine of the Conservative Party – one involving a *laissez-faire* individualism reminiscent of the early nineteenth century and marked by 'free enterprise, open markets, deregulation, individualism, privatisation' [16] as well as monetarist rather than Keynesian demand management economic policies. No longer were trade unions seen as 'joint managers' *with* Government of the industrial and economic system but rather a barrier to the achievement of Government objectives and therefore needing to be curtailed through legislation (one Act every two years progressively reducing union rights and power).

It seemed in the early 1980s that the creation of the Social Democratic Party (by disaffected Labour Party members) and its alliance with the Liberal Party (subsequently merged to form the Liberal Democrats) would, given the apparent polarisation between Thatcherism in the Conservative

Party and Militant Tendency in the Labour Party, take over the so-called middle ground of politics. However, the removal of Mrs Thatcher and Labour's shift to a 'democratic socialist' ideology has reduced, to some extent, the polarisation between the two parties.

However, a more important development in the political environment, so far as industrial relations is concerned, has been the development of the **European Community**. There is little doubt that Due *et al.* are right when they state that 'the interesting feature of EC co-operation is the emergence of quite new actors in industrial relations, such as the EC Commission and the European Parliament – actors whose roles are essentially supra-national' [17]. However, currently, there is a fundamental **conflict of political ideology** between the UK Conservative Government and its EC partners. The 'social democratic' ideology of most European countries (based on a corporatist social partnership between government, capital and labour) is reflected in the aims of the Social Charter which are at variance with the *laissez-faire*/individualism' ideology of the UK Government. The question is which will dominate and have most influence on the development of UK industrial relations?

1.3   Development of industrial relations

The present structures of industrial relations in Britain are the result of an unplanned evolution over the past 125 years. Although it is possible to identify different stages in this development it is important to realise that each stage did not supersede and replace the previous stage but rather supplemented and modified it. Furthermore, the rate and strength of these developments have varied from industry to industry and, therefore, the present industrial relations system in each industry is a unique mixture of these developments.

Early development

During the latter part of the nineteenth century trade unionism and collective bargaining were largely confined to the skilled trades and piecework industries. In the former the workers had the industrial strength, through mutual insurance and their control over entry into the trade, to seek employer acceptance of the 'union's rules', whilst in the latter both workers and employers had an interest in controlling wage competition. Although many trade unions were already organised on a national basis, this early collective bargaining was conducted almost exclusively on either an organisational or district basis. Wherever trade unions had sufficient organisation and strength they sought the establishment of a 'common rule' to ensure that different employers within a local labour market applied the same terms of employment. The workers' common interest centred primarily on their immediate geographical locality.

Flanders [18] argued that the main impetus for the development of collective bargaining at the national or industry level came during World War I. In some industries nationalisation presented the trade unions with the opportunity to negotiate with a single employer, whilst in others labour shortages and the consequent enhancement of trade union power led employers to seek national agreements as a protection against being 'played-off' one against another. At the same time, inflation coupled with the introduction of a system of compulsory arbitration resulted in a large measure of uniformity in both the wage claims presented on behalf of different groups and the wage increases granted. Perhaps most importantly for the long-term development of national level bargaining, the Whitley Committee (1916) recommended the establishment of Joint Industrial Councils (JICs) with formal written constitutions and functioning at national, district and work levels. As a result of this recommendation some 73 JICs and 33 Interim Reconstruction Committees (which were intended to become JICs) were set up between 1918 and 1921.

During the 1920s and early 1930s the economic depression and more repressive attitude of employers and government was reflected in a decline in trade union membership (from a high of 8.3 million in 1920 to a low of 4.4 million in 1932/1933), wage cuts and a high incidence of industrial action. At the same time over half of the JICs established after the war were disbanded, particularly in industries which were susceptible to foreign competition. Significantly, and largely as a result of government policy, they survived in industries such as gas, electricity, water, national and local government. However, in many of the JICs which did survive the emphasis was firmly centred on their role in developing national collective bargaining and the district and works levels remained non-existent or underdeveloped. Improving economic conditions prior to World War II and the need for employee and trade union co-operation in the war effort provided an impetus for increased unionisation and a resurgence of industrial relations activity.

Since World War II industrial relations in Britain has developed through a number of overlapping phases: increased pressure, particularly on the industry-level part of the system; voluntary reform; increased governmental and legislative intervention; confrontation; and possibly a new realism.

Increased pressure

Hawkins suggests that in the immediate post-war period it was assumed that 'the great industrial conflicts of the past had been resolved by the gradual development of a framework of voluntary institutions'; that the role of trade union leaders 'was to direct industrial conflict into the established framework of industry-wide procedures where peaceful solutions could be found with the minimum disorder', and that 'the more integrated the unions became in the system, the more committed they would be to its success and the more responsibly they would behave' [19]. However, this assumption of an orderly system of industrial relations based on industry-level agreements soon came under pressure.

The **main pressures** came from both employees and management. On the employees' side, full employment, the welfare state and changes in society resulted in rising aspirations in respect of both material rewards and greater involvement in managerial decision making. Trade union membership expanded, particularly amongst non-manual employees, and maintained a density of approximately 45–50 per cent of the working population. At the same time, management's attention was focused increasingly on changing working practices and improving productivity within the organisation; initially to meet rising demand and subsequently to improve its cost competitiveness. However, industry-level bargaining and agreements in the main provided only basic terms of employment (wage rates, hours, holidays, etc.) and had little role in respect of regulating the work relationship and the exercise of authority and decision making within the organisation. Inevitably, the attention of both sides was directed towards collective bargaining at the organisational level.

The consequence of this **shift in the locus of regulation** was increased fragmentation and tension within many segments of the industrial relations system. The development of organisational bargaining, and its associated increase in the power of work groups and the greater involvement of the shop steward in negotiations with management on the workgroup's behalf, increased the gap between the 'grass roots' union organisation (members and shop stewards) and workplace issues and the 'official' union organisation (regional and national officials, NEC and delegate conference) and wider policy issues. Evidence of this could be seen in the demise of the branch as the focus of the interface between member and union and its replacement by the shop steward, and in an increase in 'unofficial' industrial action (action determined by the members and shop stewards rather than by the NEC or officials of the union). On the management side, a similar tension arose as many organisations sought to act independently by conducting their own negotiations rather than acting collectively with other organisations through their employers' association at the industry level. Thus, in 1967, Flanders described organisational level collective bargaining as 'largely informal, largely fragmented and largely autonomous' [20].

A central part of the Donovan Commission (1968) [21] analysis of industrial relations was the **conflict between organisational- and industry-level collective bargaining** and their respective underlying assumptions. On the one hand, the formal system of industry-level bargaining assumed that:

1. it was possible to negotiate and resolve most, if not all, industrial relations issues in a single written agreement which could then be applied throughout an industry;

2. the central organs of the trade unions and employers' associations had the capacity to ensure that the terms of any agreement were observed by their members; and

3. the function of the industrial relations system at the organisational level was primarily one of interpreting and applying the industry agreement and providing a basis for joint consultation between management and employees.

The informal system of organisational bargaining, on the other hand, assumed that:

1. many industrial relations issues were specific to the organisation and could be regulated by informal arrangements or 'custom and practice' at the workplace;

2. both management and union members at the workplace had a relatively high degree of autonomy to reach decisions independently of their central organisations; and

3. the distinction between the processes of joint consultation and collective bargaining, and therefore between which issues were appropriate for which process, was blurred.

In their view, the operation of the informal system at the organisational level reduced, if not undermined, the regulatory effect of agreements reached in formal industry-level bargaining – particularly in respect of the determination of wage levels. However, the conflict between the two systems could not be resolved 'by forcing the informal system to comply with the assumptions of the formal system' [22] but only by management and trade unions accepting the reality and importance of the organisational level and developing it on a more formal and orderly basis.

Voluntary reform

It is important to realise that the Donovan Commission's recommendation was, in part, a reflection of a process of reform which had already started amongst some companies in the early 1960s. However, the Commission's recommendation did provide a stimulus for a more widespread and conscious strategy on the part of most managements to formalise and co-ordinate their bargaining arrangements within the organisation. In Hawkins' view the recommendation 'strongly reflected the view that the key to a better system of industrial relations lay in the reform and extension of collective bargaining by management *initiative* and trade union *agreement*' [my italics] [23]. The **onus and responsibility for reform was placed on management.**

There were a number of elements to the reform. Perhaps the most important, and certainly the one most open to management initiative, was the **systematic development of formal substantive and procedural agreements at the organisational level.** The review of substantive agreements often involved a reform of payment structures and systems (including the removal of piecework or bonus systems, a reduction in the number of grades/jobs, and a linking of such reforms (and pay increases) to changes in working arrangements) as a means for management to regain a measure of control over wages and reduce 'wage drift'. At the same time, the introduction or reform of procedural agreements provided a clearer identification of not only the procedures and institutions through which industrial relations issues were to be processed but also the various roles and responsibilities for handling such issues. As part of this process it became necessary for **employers' associations** to re-examine and, if necessary, adjust their role. The shift in emphasis of industrial relations regulation to the organisational level has meant that, in many instances, their role has become more of an advisor/co-ordinator of such activities than a regulator and, consequently, the national agreement has become a minimum to be built upon and expanded at the organisational level.

At the same time, **trade unions** were involved in their own process of reform. In one direction, the structure of British trade unionism has been 'simplified' during the post-war period through the process of mergers – the reduction in the number of trade unions has, in many cases, simplified collective bargaining arrangements and, in some, made the introduction of new working arrangements easier by reducing the boundary between workgroups. In another direction, the internal organisation and government of trade unions have been amended to bridge the gap with their membership. This has taken many forms including the establishment of plant-based branches more able to deal with the workplace issues of most concern to the membership; drawing the shop steward more into the formal organisation through regular committee meetings with full-time officials; creating separate committees/conferences at local and national levels to deal with the problems of particular industries; and the increased use of postal balloting for the election of the NEC and others rather than relying on the membership attendance at the branch. In addition, trade unions have sought to increase their expertise through the employment of more specialists and the training of shop stewards.

However, the process of voluntary reform has not precluded greater government involvement in industrial relations or, more importantly, attempts to impose greater legal control.

Government and legislative intervention

Although both trade unions and management expound the notion of 'voluntarism' and their freedom to determine the nature and content of their relationship, there is no doubt that the extent of voluntarism has been reduced by government intervention. The existence of a more corporatist ideology until 1979 meant that the government sought the involvement of trade unions and management, but particularly the trade unions, in discussions regarding the **management of the economy** as part of its strategy to achieve their active support for the government's policies. This presented a major dilemma for trade unions since much of government policy was directed towards controlling inflation; often through a formal incomes policy. Trade unions had the choice of protecting their members' interests either indirectly by co-operating with government economic policies or directly through the collective bargaining process with management. In so far as the trade unions did support government policies of restraint it not only reduced the basis of 'voluntarism' in industrial relations but also widened the gap between the unions and their membership at a time when the memberships' autonomy had already been increased by the development of organisational level bargaining.

The 1970s also saw an **increased legal intervention** into industrial relations. Despite the Donovan Commission's emphasis on the benefits that could be achieved from a voluntary reform of industrial relations it was clear that even a Labour Government was 'displeased by the absence of any positive recommendations in favour of using the law to deter unofficial strikers in sensitive areas of the economy' [24]. In January 1969, only some six months after the publication of the Donovan Commission report, the Government published a White Paper setting out their policy for industrial relations which would 'help to control the destructive expression of industrial conflict' [25] and which proposed changes in the law to give the Secretary of State the power to order a 'cooling off' period in unconstitutional strikes (i.e. those where the disputes procedure had not been exhausted and which were, in most cases, also unofficial strikes) and to order a ballot where an official strike involved a serious threat to the economy or public interest. Pressure from the trade unions led to the withdrawal of the Paper and replacement by a TUC undertaking to use its authority and influence to secure industrial peace.

Hawkins suggests that the Labour Government's withdrawal of its legislative proposals 'simply reinforced the determination of the Conservative Party to enact their own proposals for reforming industrial relations' [26]. This they did in the **Industrial Relations Act (1971)**. However, their attempt at establishing a greater legal control of trade unions, in particular unofficial industrial action, also failed – but not without a number of court cases [27] which resulted in the brief imprisonment of seven dockers, fines being imposed against trade unions, their funds being sequestrated to pay the fines and 'a growing anxiety about the extent to which [the Act's] provisions could be operated in practice' [28].

However, on its return to power in 1974, the Labour Government adopted a different approach which, McIlroy notes, had at its centre 'an accord between government and unions which was projected as the basis for a new social contract' [29]. The unions, on their part, agreed to consider the needs of the economy in their wage bargaining whilst the Government agreed, in addition to pursuing socially desirable policies, to support trade unions through legislation. Thus, the repeal of the Industrial Relations Act by the Labour Government's **Trade Union and Labour Relations Act, 1974 and 1976,** did not herald a withdrawal of legal intervention but merely a change in direction. The **Employment Protection Act (1975)** not only established a number of employee rights but also provided positive support for trade unionism and collective bargaining by establishing rights in such areas as disclosure of information, consultation in a redundancy, time off for trade union duties, etc. This positive support for trade unionism was reflected also in the terms of reference of the Bullock Committee on Industrial Democracy (1977) which required it to accept 'the need for a radical extension of industrial democracy in the control of companies by means of representation on boards of directors' and 'the essential role of trade union organisations in this process' [30].

Confrontation

However, the 'winter of discontent' (1978/1979) arising from, Taylor argues, a 'desire for "more money now" after three years of voluntary pay restraint' [31] and the subsequent election of a Conservative Government in 1979 once again changed the direction of legislative intervention. The Government's strategy has been to impose, in stages, increasingly greater legal control and restrictions on the activities and affairs of trade unions. The legislation (**Employment Acts 1980 and 1982, Trade Union Act 1984, Wages Act 1986 and Employment Acts 1988 and 1990**) has:

1. removed the statutory recognition procedure and the closed shop (Union Membership Agreement) – undermining the union's ability to organise;
2. removed immunity completely from secondary industrial action – removing any support from other trade unionists in a dispute;
3. required unions to ballot on industrial action; made them responsible for unlawful actions authorised by the union's officers, committees or shop stewards unless they repudiate such actions; given individual members the right not to be disciplined by their union for not undertaking industrial action (even if lawful and supported by a majority vote in favour); and made it easier for the employer to dismiss strikers (particularly in an unofficial strike) – all potentially weakening the union's 'strike weapon';

4. required unions to elect their NEC, General Secretary and President by direct secret ballot with independent scrutineers, and given individual members legal rights to inspect the union's accounts and challenge unlawful actions – regulating the union's organisation;
5. restricted the scope of Wages Councils as part of its strategy to 'price people back into jobs' – the only statutory support given to bargaining in a number of poorly organised and low-paid industries.

Significantly, it would appear that the Labour Party does not intend, if returned to power, to repeal all this legislation, but rather may introduce a more positive 'right to strike' (which would reduce the employer's ability to dismiss strikers) and introduce legislation which would strengthen the unions' collective bargaining role and right to be involved in organisational decision making.

The Government also 'confronted' the established role of unions by abolishing some of the tripartite bodies on which the TUC was represented (e.g. MSC), down-graded the importance of others (by, for example, reducing the frequency of NEDO meetings), and no longer regards the TUC as the body which has the exclusive right to nominate the 'employee' repesentatives to bodies such as Industrial Tribunals and ACAS. At the same time, as an employer, it has been prepared to withdraw bargaining rights from teachers and replace it with a review body and confront trade unions in its own disputes: for example, POEU privatisation dispute (1983), GCHQ withdrawal of right to belong to a union (1984), NUM/NCB pit closure dispute (1984/5), ambulance pay dispute (1988).

However, confrontation has not been the sole province of the Government. At times it appeared that confrontational 'macho management' and the enforcement of the new legal rights might be the standard for industrial relations as some managements in the private sector endured long disputes to 'force through' the major work changes they regarded as necessary to maintain their competitiveness and used the courts to weaken the union's opposition – for example, News International at Wapping (1986) and P&O/NUS (1989). It might also be argued that trade unions have been similarly confronted by the need to accept a 'single union agreement' almost on management's terms as an alternative to non-unionism in some high-tech 'greenfield' sites; alternatively, this can be seen as part of the 'new realism' which the Government has sought to engender in industrial relations.

New realism

The so-called new realism in industrial relations is not a single cohesive strategy which has been applied uniformly across all organisations but, as during the previous periods of development, different strands have taken place in varying degrees at different speeds in different organisations for different reasons. The major strands of this development are as follows:

1. **Management**: taking a more proactive approach to industrial relations to ensure that it supports and is integregated with the achievement of business objectives (be it improved competitiveness, quality or customer care).
2. **Process relationship**: shifting from negotiation and agreement to communication and consultation (strengthening managerial 'prerogative'), from 'disclosure' of information to unions for bargaining to 'dissemination' of information to employees and from union 'participation' to employee 'involvement' to secure the individual's identification with and commitment to the organisation and its goals.
3. **Structure of bargaining**: continuing to shift from the national 'multi-employer' level to the 'single-employer' organisational level (to better relate pay with work and to take advantage of local labour market conditions); rationalisation of recognition to a 'single table' or 'single union' basis' ; replacing industrial action with 'pendulum' arbitration.
4. **Workplace:** becoming more flexible in numerical (differentiating between core and periphery employees), task and time terms.
5. **Basis of pay**: placing more emphasis on organisational or individual performance and less on uniform rate for the job.
6. **Union response**: recruiting in employment growth areas (women, part-timers, service sector, etc.); developing individual member services ('plastic card' unionism); selling themselves to the employer rather than employees.

The new realism of the 1980s appears to be based not on a joint acceptance of management's and union's respective rights or any spirit of positive co-operation between them, but rather on an employee/union acceptance that economic circumstances coupled with government attitude have curtailed their influence. Certainly, Brown and Sisson believe that the new realism 'is likely to be as ephemeral in the face of economic recovery as were the attitudes of the 1930s when wartime restored job security' [32].

1.4 The mass media

Beharrell and Philo argue that the mass media of newspapers and television 'play a crucial role in the battle of ideas, over what is held by people to be important, necessary or possible within society' [33] and consequently 'never simply gives "the news" but always offers us a way of understanding the world' [34]. In their view the mass media's projection of industrial relations is 'a world populated by inflationary wage claims, strikes and disruptions, and the perpetual battle between the responsible majority and the small minority who always want to spoil everything for the rest' [35]. It is, therefore, perhaps not surprising that trade union leaders and active trade union members are suspicious of the mass media and, as Seaton notes, fear 'that the long-term political and social role of the unions is being eroded and distorted by the effects of increasingly hostile reporting' [36].

Extensive research by the Glasgow Media Group [37] shows that the media's reporting of industrial relations is both **selective and subjective.** This is reflected in a number of areas.

What constitutes 'news' which should be presented to the public?

In one sense, Beharrell and Philo point out, the answer is tautological – news is news because it is in a newspaper or on television. However, the fact that something is presented as 'news' inevitably creates a mass media impetus as journalists seek to enhance the item by inviting people in authority roles, whether government, trade unions or management, to comment on the validity and importance of the original item. This process is seen clearly in what is often referred to as 'negotiation through the mass media' as journalists seek information and comments from both sides and outsiders at each development, or supposed development, in a dispute. On the other hand, it may be argued that the mass media can only report what they are given and therefore 'news' is, at least in part, determined by what the participants want to have reported. In this respect, the trade unions' public and press relations appear to be much less positive and successful than those of either government or management – particularly the management of large corporations. Management is better able to project, through the mass media's reporting of industrial, economic and financial matters, its values of a basic consensus between employees and itself and the need for organisational productivity, competitiveness and profitability.

Imbalanced reporting

Although the mass media seek to project an image of balanced reporting, in reality their reporting is imbalanced by virtue of the 'slant' or 'wording' of the item. This can be seen in a number of ways:

1. Most 'front page' items relating to industrial relations, and therefore of greatest impact on the public, report disputes, conflicts and failures to agree rather than the successful situations. Indeed, quite often the resolution of a dispute goes unannounced or is reported as a small item of news, whilst the conflict generated during the dispute has received wide coverage. The successful industrial relations situations, when they are reported, are usually found as serious items on the business pages or

in current affairs programmes and even then are presented as examples which the rest of 'strike-torn' industries ought to be copying.

2. In reporting industrial relations disputes there is a tendency for 'normal' production to be equated not only to 'strike free' production but also 'full' production thereby ignoring the fact that 'normal' production may not equal 'full' production because of material shortages, machine breakdowns or lack of capital investment.

3. There is an imbalance in respect of the coverage and treatment afforded to different individuals and groups. In television interviews, the interviewer may often adopt a more 'challenging' line of questioning towards a trade union representative than towards government or management representatives.

4. There is also a tendency, in the words used by the reporter or interviewer, to personalise and politicise a situation by the use of phrases such as 'left and right wing', 'militant', 'bid for power', etc. Some may argue that this is simply good journalese, but its influence is great. It was the media which applied phrases such as the 'winter of discontent', 'flying pickets', and 'secondary picketing' to industrial relations; some of which have 'since passed into political mythology and in fact have come to form the basis for legislation' [38].

Incomplete reporting of the facts

Perhaps most importantly, the mass media do not present a complete reporting of the facts and issues because of either a shortage of space/time or the complexities of the situation. No industrial relations situation is ever simple and yet they are generally projected as such – more often than not related to pay. At the same time the reporting of 'facts' is often enmeshed in the **expression of opinion** by the reporter. Frequently, the journalist will 'read between the lines' of a statement or situation and offer his/her own interpretation rather than the views and thinking of the participants. This is, in effect, suggesting that the statement is untrue, or at least not telling the complete truth, and therefore tends to discredit both the content of the statement and the person making it in the eyes of the other participants as well as the public. Even a statement of 'no comment' will be interpreted in some way by the reporter or interviewer. Finally, it is not just the reporting of 'industrial relations' situations which influences people's perceptions of industrial relations but also its almost throwaway inclusion in other items. For example, Beharrell and Philo refer to the inclusion of the phrase 'strikes permitting' in a television news item dealing with the launch of a new British Leyland car [39].

Whether or not the selectivity and subjectivity of the mass media are parts of a conspiracy against trade unions or simply the result of the process of gathering and disseminating news is a matter of personal judgement.

1.5 Summary propositions

- The development of British industrial relations has been significantly influenced by the developments in its economic, social and political environments.
- The mass media, perhaps unintentionally, exert a perverse influence on the perception of industrial relations.

Further reading

- R. Taylor, *Workers and the New Depression*, Macmillan, 1982. A readable examination of the labour market in the 1980s including such areas as training, productivity, wages and strikes.
- K. Hawkins, *British Industrial Relations 1945–1975*, Barrie & Jenkins, 1976. This book traces the development of British industrial relations up to the mid-1970s with particular emphasis on relations between trade unions and the government in the development of legislation and incomes policy.
- P. Beharrel and G. Philo, *Trade Unions and the Media*, Macmillan, 1977. A useful examination of not only the influence of the mass media on industrial relations but also the operation and control of the mass media.

References

1. A. Fox, *Man Mismanagement*, Hutchinson, 1974, p. 4.
2. R. Taylor, *Workers and the New Depression*, Macmillan, 1982, pp. vii and 199.
3. D. Deaton, 'Unemployment' in G. S. Bain (ed.), *Industrial Relations in Britain*, Blackwell, 1983, pp. 237–62.
4. *ibid.*, p. 239.
5. J. Lawlor and A. White, 'Measures of unemployment: the claimant count and the LFS', *Employment Gazette*, November 1991, p. 618.
6. 'Unemployment and ethnic origin', *Employment Gazette*, June 1984, pp. 260–64.
7. D. Deaton, *op. cit.* p. 240.
8. L. Hunter, 'Unemployment and industrial relations', *British Journal of Industrial Relations*, vol. 26, no. 2, 1988, p. 204.
9. *Social Trends 20*, HMSO, 1990, Table 4.3, p. 69.
10. J. Atkinson, 'Four stages of adjustment to the demographic downturn', *Personnel Management*, August 1989.
11. J. MacInnes, 'Why nothing much has changed: recession, economic restructuring and industrial relations since 1979', *Employee Relations*, vol. 9, no. 1, 1987.

12. R. H. Tawney, *Religion and the Rise of Capitalism*, Penguin, 1961, p. 239. Reprinted with permission of John Murray (Publishers) Ltd.
13. 'Political and legal environments' (Unit 8B, *Industrial Relations*), Open University Press, 1976, p. 7.
14. C. Crouch, *Class Conflict and the Industrial Relations Crisis*, Heinemann, 1977.
    D. Strinati, *Capitalism, the State and Industrial Relations*, Croom Helm, 1982.
    C. Crouch, *The Politics of Industrial Relations* (2nd edn), Fontana, 1982, p. 145.
15. Prof. J. Griffith, 'The collective unfairness of laissez-faire', *The Guardian*, 14 June 1990.
16. *ibid*.
17. J. Due *et al.*, 'The social dimension: convergence or diversification of IR in the Single European Market?', *Industrial Relations Journal*, vol. 22, no. 2, 1991, p. 88.
18. A. Flanders, 'Collective bargaining' in A. Flanders and H. A. Clegg (eds), *The System of Industrial Relations in Great Britain*, Blackwell, 1960, pp. 276–278.
19. K. Hawkins, *British Industrial Relations 1945–1975*, Barrie & Jenkins, 1976, pp. 18–19.
20. A. Flanders, *Collective Bargaining: Prescription for Change*, Faber & Faber, 1967, p. 28.
21. Report of *Royal Commission on Trade Unions and Employers Associations* (Donovan Commission), HMSO, 1968 (Chapter III).
22. *ibid*, p. 36.
23. K. Hawkins, *op.cit.*, p. 63.
24. *ibid.*, p. 80.
25. *In Place of Strife*, HMSO, 1969, p. 5.
26. K. Hawkins, *op. cit.*, p. 82.
27. *Heaton Transport* v. *T&GWU* (1973); *Midland Cold Storage* v. *Turner* (1972); *Con-Mech (Engineering)* v. *AUEW* (1973).
28. *Trade Union Immunities*, HMSO, 1981, p. 20.
29. J. McIlroy, *Trade Unions in Britain Today*, Manchester University Press, 1988, p. 9.
30. *Report of the Committee of Inquiry on Industrial Democracy* (Bullock), HMSO, 1977, p. v.
31. R. Taylor, 'The trade union "problem" since 1960' in B. Pimlott and C. Cook (eds), *Trade Unions in British Politics*, Longman, 1982, p. 206.
32. W. Brown and K. Sisson, 'Industrial relations in the next decade – current trends and future possibilities', *Industrial Relations Journal*, vol. 13, 1982, p. 20.
33. P. Beharrell and G. Philo, *Trade Unions and the Media*, Macmillan, 1977, p. ix.
34. *ibid.*, p. 1.
35. *ibid.*, p. 4.
36. J. Seaton, 'Trade unions and the media' in B. Pimlott and C. Cook (eds), *op. cit.*, p. 273.
37. Glasgow University Media Group, *Bad News* (1976); *More Bad News* (1977); and *More Bad News*, vol. 2 (1980), Routledge & Kegan Paul.
38. TUC Media Group, *A Course for Concern*, TUC, 1980, p. 29.
39. P. Beharrell and G. Philo, *op. cit.*, p. 7.

Chapter 2
Approaches to industrial relations

2.1 Definition

The term 'industrial relations' denotes a specialist area of organisational management and study which is concerned with a **particular set of phenomena associated with regulating the human activity of employment**. It is, however, difficult to define the boundaries of this set of phenomena, and therefore the term itself, in a precise and universally accepted way. Any more specific definition must, of necessity, assume and emphasise a particular view of the nature and purpose of industrial relations – consequently, there are as many definitions as there are writers on industrial relations. For example, the two most frequently used terms of 'industrial relations' and 'employee relations' are, in most practical senses, interchangeable; yet they have very different connotations. The former, more traditional, term reflects the original historical base of unionised manual workers within the manufacturing sector of the economy whilst the latter has come into greater use with the development of less unionised white collar employment and the service and commercial sectors of the economy.

The way we perceive the overall nature of this area of organisational study (our frame of reference) determines to a very large extent not only how we approach and analyse specific issues and situations within industrial relations but also how we expect others to behave, how we respond to their actual behaviour and the means we adopt to influence or modify their behaviour. In examining the different approaches it is useful to differentiate between those approaches which are concerned with the general nature of employment organisations and those which specifically deal with the industrial relations system itself (see Figure 2.1).

However, it is important to bear in mind that:

(i) they are primarily analytical categorisations rather than causative theories or predictive models, and

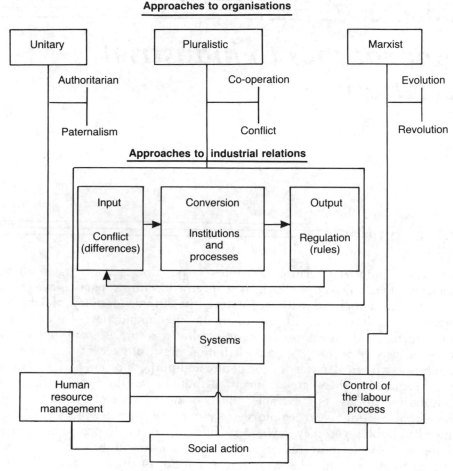

Figure 2.1   *Approaches to industrial relations*

(ii)   there is no one 'right' approach; rather each approach emphasises a
particular aspect of industrial relations and taken together can provide a
framework for analysing and understanding the diversity and
complexity of industrial relations (i.e. the complexity of the human
aspect of work organisations).

2.2 The nature of employment organisations

There are three major views of employment organisations:

1.   The unitary perspective, which emphasises the organisation as a coherent
and integrated team 'unified by a common purpose' [1].

2. The pluralistic perspective, which emphasises the organisation as an amalgamation of separate homogeneous groups – 'a miniature democratic state composed of sectional groups with divergent interests over which the government tries to maintain some kind of dynamic equilibrium' [2].
3. The Marxist perspective which emphasises the organisation as a microcosm and replica of the society within which it exists.

However, it is important to recognise from the outset that there is as much **variation within each perspective** as there are differences between them:

1. The unitary perspective can encompass either an authoritarian or paternalistic approach to the role of management.
2. The pluralistic perspective can emphasise co-operation between the parties as well as conflict.
3. The Marxist perspective may advocate either an evolutionary or revolutionary approach to the desired social change.

Unitary perspective

The unitary perspective is based on the **assumptions** that the organisation is, or if it is not then it should be, an integrated group of people with a single authority/loyalty structure and a set of common values, interests and objectives shared by all members of the organisation. Management's prerogative (i.e. its right to manage and make decisions) is regarded as legitimate, rational and accepted and any opposition to it (whether formal or informal, internal or external) is seen as irrational. The organisation is not, therefore, regarded as a 'them and us' situation – as Farnham and Pimlott put it, there is 'no conflict between the interests of those supplying capital to the enterprise and their managerial representatives, and those contributing their labour . . . the owners of capital and labour are but complementary partners to the common aims of production, profits and pay in which everyone in the organization has a stake' [3]. The underlying assumption of this view, therefore, is that the organisational system is in basic harmony and conflict is unnecessary and exceptional.

This has two important implications:

● *Conflict (i.e. the expression of employee dissatisfaction and differences with management) is perceived as an irrational activity*. Fox, the most prominent writer in the unitary, pluralistic, radical debate, has argued that the 'conviction of the rightness of management rule and the norms issuing from it may create difficulty for [the manager], not simply in acknowledging the legitimacy of challenges to it, but even in fully grasping that such challenges may at least be grounded in legitimacy for those who mount them' [4]. Any transgression of management's rule is viewed as aberrant rather than non-conformist behaviour – that is, the individual recognises that 'he is only being required to do what at a considered level he knows to be right' [5]. Farnham and Pimlott argue that the existence of factionalism within the organisation may even be regarded as 'a pathological social condition' and collective bargaining as 'an anti-social mechanism' [6] since they are founded on the premise of the existence of conflicting interests. Conflict, when it does arise, is believed to be primarily frictional rather than structural in nature and caused by such factors as: clashes of personalities within the organisation; poor communication by management of its plans and decisions; a lack of understanding on the part of the employees that management's decisions and actions are made for the good of all within the organisation; or by agitators.

Consequently, management's approach to resolving such conflict is often based on an authoritarian and/or paternalistic style. The **use of coercion** is regarded as a legitimate use of managerial power. Management does not perceive any need, given the legitimacy of its prerogative, to obtain the consent of its employees to any decisions or changes through the process of negotiation. This attitude is often also reflected in its view of the **role of law** in industrial relations. Fox argues that managers who adopt the unitary perspective are likely to believe that 'increased legal intervention can and should take the form of regulating men's behaviour directly and enforcing this regulation by direct punitive legal sanctions' [7]. This approach has been evident in the legislative changes in the 1980s aimed at reducing the incidence of trade union actions which are regarded as disruptive and disorderly. At the same time, management may concentrate on a human relations approach (improving interpersonal relations and ensuring that the communications system within the organisation is adequate) or make appeals to the loyalty of the employees (the 'lets pull together, we're all in the same boat' syndrome).

• *Trade unions are regarded as an intrusion into the organisation from outside which competes with management for the loyalty of employees.* Many managers perceive trade unions as little more than an historical anachronism that had a role within the framework of nineteenth century employer/ employee relations but, with enlightened management in the twentieth century, are no longer necessary to protect the employees' interests – these will be taken fully into account, alongside other factors, in management's decision making. Whilst management may be prepared to accept the existence of trade unions in the determination of terms and conditions of employment (market relations), they are certainly reluctant to concede any role for trade unions in the exercise of authority and decision making within the organisation (managerial relations). In this latter area trade unions are likely to be seen as little more than a political power vehicle used by a militant minority in order to subvert the existing and legitimate political, social and economic structure of society. The existence of trade unions and collective bargaining, therefore, is suffered rather than welcomed and is to be resisted wherever possible.

The unitary perspective is found predominantly amongst managers – particularly line management – and therefore is often regarded as a **management ideology**. Fox has argued that management clings to this view for the following reasons:

1. It legitimises its authority role by projecting the interests of management and employees as being the same and by emphasising management's role of 'governing' in the best interests of the organisation as a whole.
2. It reassures managers by confirming that conflict (dissatisfaction), where it exists, is largely the fault of the governed rather than management.
3. It may be projected to the outside world as a means of persuading them that management's decisions and actions are right and the best in the circumstances and that any challenge to them is, at best, misguided or, at worst, subversive.

Although Fox believes that this view of organisations 'has long since been abandoned by most social scientists as incongruent with reality and useless for purpose of analysis' [8], other writers believe it should not be discarded too lightly. Maitland, for example, argues that surveys of employee attitudes show an underlying consensus that management and employees are 'on the same side'. He attributes the failure of this consensus to come to the fore, and the resultant industrial disorder, to 'a breakdown of "government" – both management and labour representation – in the workplace. Without effective government the consensus simply could not be administered or *its terms imposed on recalcitrant minorities*' [my italics] [9]. This latter phrase suggests that the consensus is by no means universal. Yet, even where managers appear to consciously reject the unitary perspective as unrealistic, it still provides the subconscious foundation (the 'right to manage') for their seeking to maintain a clear distinction between those issues on which they are prepared to negotiate and those issues on which they are prepared only to consult.

Pluralistic perspective

Fox believes that this view of the organisation 'probably represents the received orthodoxy in many Western societies' [10] and is often associated with a view of society as being 'post-capitalist': that is, that there is a relatively widespread distribution of authority and power within the society, a separation of ownership from management, a separation of political and industrial conflict, and an acceptance and institutionalisation of conflict in both spheres. This perspective is based on the **assumption** that the organisation is composed of individuals who coalesce into a variety of distinct sectional groups, each with its own interests, objectives and leadership (either formal or informal). The organisation is perceived as being multi-structured and competitive in terms of groupings, leadership, authority and loyalty, and this, Fox argues, gives rise to 'a complex of tensions and competing claims which have to be "managed" in the interests of maintaining a viable collaborative structure' [11]. The underlying assumption of this approach, therefore, is that the organisation is in a permanent state of dynamic tension resulting from the inherent conflict of interest between the various sectional groups and requires to be managed through a variety of roles, institutions and processes. The implications of this view for the nature of conflict and the role of the trade unions are very different to those of the unitary approach.

● *Conflict between management and employees*. Kornhauser *et al.* define this as not just industrial disputes and strikes but 'the total range of behaviour and attitudes that express opposition and divergent orientation between industrial owners and managers on the one hand and working people and their organisations on the other hand' [12]. Such conflict **is seen to be both rational and inevitable**. It results from industrial and organisational factors (structually determined) rather than from individual personal factors. The primary source of this organisational conflict stems from the differing roles of the managerial and employee groups. The managerial group is responsible for the efficiency, productivity and profitability of the organisation and for co-ordinating the activities of others to achieve these objectives (this is the basis on which the success of both individual managers and management in general is judged). However, the only formal organisational responsibility of the employee group is 'to do' and their main industrial concerns are more likely to be perceived in personal terms, such as higher pay, better working conditions, greater job security, more meaningful work, etc.

Consequently, conflictual behaviour may arise in respect of both specific situations and general 'management principles'. Clearly, the closure of a high-cost operation is intended to meet management's objectives of increased profitability but will clash with the employees' objective of greater job security. The same will apply in the context of the introduction of new technology – its introduction will meet management's objective of greater productivity and profitability but may create de-skilling and less meaningful work for the employees and, possibly, feelings of job insecurity. At the same time conflict may stem from different perceptions of 'general principles'. For example, management will, wherever possible, seek to keep its labour costs to the minimum necessary to attract and retain the labour it requires and to maintain it competitiveness, whilst employees will always seek to maximise their wages (income) in order to maximise their standard of living. Equally, there may be clashes over the principle of productivity which is a group objective amongst the managerial group but not necessarily within employee groups. (Even where a bonus scheme exists the employee objective is to

increase wages rather than increase productivity (management's objective).)
Management will seek also to maintain the maximum degree of power/
authority in order to control the organisation's activities whilst employees
will seek to establish safeguards against arbitrary management actions and
decisions.

Fox has argued that, within the pluralistic perspective, 'the degree of
common purpose which can exist in industry is only of a very limited nature'
[13]. The mutual dependence of the sectional groups exists only in so far as
they 'have a common interest in the survival of the whole of which they are
parts' and this is, at best, only a 'remote long-term consideration' [14].
However, at the same time as emphasising the conflictual nature of industrial
organisations, the pluralistic perspective also assumes that 'the normative
divergencies between the parties are not so fundamental or so wide as to be
unbridgeable by compromises' [15]. Consequently there is, within industrial
relations, a basic **procedural consensus** founded on the belief that 'managements and unions will always and everywhere be able ultimately to negotiate
comprehensive, codified systems of regulation' [16]. Such a consensus
implies, first, that 'there can and should be, or indeed even is, a balance of
power as between the principal interest groups' [17] within the organisation
(that trade unions provide a countervailing power to management) and,
secondly, that each group is prepared to limit 'its claims and aspirations to a
level which the other party finds sufficiently tolerable to enable collaboration
to continue' [18].

Thus, the **resolution of conflict** is characterised by an emphasis on the
need to establish accepted procedures and institutions which achieve
collaboration through negotiated compromises. Within the pluralistic perspective, Clegg argues that there can be 'no definitive decisions by final
authorities; only continuous compromises' [19] and Ross believes the
concern of management should be 'not to unify, integrate or liquidate
sectional groups and their special interests in the name of some overriding
corporate existence, but to control and balance the activities of constituent
groups so as to provide for the maximum degree of freedom of association
and action for sectional and group purposes consistent with the general
interest of the society [the organisation]' [20]. There has to be an acceptance
of the need for shared decision making between management and employee
representatives. The legitimacy of management's role is not automatic but
must be sought and maintained by management itself ('management by
consent' rather than 'management by right'). As far as the **role of the law** is
concerned, Fox argues, the pluralistic perspective accepts that '"interests"
have rights of free association and, within legal limits, of asserting their
claims and aspirations' [21]. The role of law becomes primarily one of
defining the limits of socially acceptable collective actions and use of power.

- *A positive role for trade unions*. The pluralistic perspective accepts that it
is legitimate for employees to combine in formal organisations in order to

express their interests and to seek to influence management decisions and achieve their objectives. Fox believes such legitimacy is founded, not just on industrial power or management acceptance but, 'on social values which recognise the right of interest groups to combine and have an effective voice in their own destiny' [22]. It accepts, also, that employees, through their horizontal linkage with similar employees in other organisations, will owe loyalty to authority structures other than their own management and may pursue not only narrow organisational interests but also wider fraternalistic interests. Trade unions and their representatives are as much an internal part of the organisation and its managerial processes as they are an external body to the organisation. They do not, of themselves, cause the conflict within organisations but 'simply provide a highly organised and continuous form of expression for sectional interests which would exist anyway' [23]. It is, therefore, 'inappropriate for management to experience "guilt" at "surrendering" their "proper functions"' [24].

However, some critics argue that the 'post-capitalist' notion of society which underlies the pluralistic perspective is wrong and that the issue of the nature of organisations and industrial relations should be approached from a more radical perspective.

Marxist perspective

The Marxist perspective concentrates on the nature of the society surrounding the organisation. It assumes, and emphasises, that the organisation exists within a **capitalist society** where, Hyman argues, 'the production system is privately owned . . .; profit . . . is the key influence on company policy . . .; and control over production is enforced downwards by the owners' managerial agents' [25]. The Marxist general theory of society argues that:

1. Class (group) conflict is the source of societal change – without such conflict the society would stagnate.
2. Class conflict arises primarily from the disparity in the distribution of, and access to, economic power within the society – the principal disparity being between those who own capital and those who supply their labour.
3. The nature of the society's social and political institutions is derived from this economic disparity and reinforces the position of the dominant establishment group, for example through differential access to education, the media, employment in government and other establishment bodies, etc.
4. Social and political conflict in whatever form is merely an expression of the underlying economic conflict within the society.

Within this analysis:

- *Industrial conflict*. This is seen as a reflection of not just organisational demands and tensions but also, and perhaps more importantly, the inherent nature of the capitalist economic and social system. All conflict is believed to stem principally from the division within society between those who own or manage the means of production and those who have only their labour to sell and, therefore, is continuous and unavoidable: industrial conflict is synonymous with political and social conflict.

- *The growth of trade unionism*. This is seen as an inevitable employee response to capitalism. The organisation of employees into trade unions not only enhances their collective industrial power by reducing competition between individual employees but also provides a focus for the expression and protection of the interests of the working classes. The fraternalism developed within trade unions can then be converted into class consciousness within the social and political systems. From the Marxist perspective, trade unionism and industrial relations may be viewed as political activities associated with the development of the working classes; they are part of the overall political process for achieving fundamental changes in the nature of the economic and social systems. Therefore, unless this is recognised by the union's members, and acted upon accordingly through the policies and decisions of their organisation, they will not be fulfilling the primary purpose of trade unionism.

Those who favour the Marxist perspective criticise pluralism for maintaining an **illusion of a balance of power** between the various interest groups which hides the reality of imbalance in social power despite claims from its supporters, such as Clegg, that it does 'accommodate shifts in the aims and interests of the diverse groups . . . and in the distribution of power between groups' [26]. Fox [27] has suggested that the apparent balance of power which is perceived to exist in industrial relations results from two factors:

1. Employers do not need to exercise their full industrial power by closing plants and withdrawing their capital; the implicit threat that they have such power is sufficient to balance any direct collective power exercised by employees and trade unions.
2. The social and political institutions within the society support the intrinsic position of management; employees, through the influence of education and the mass media, become socialised into accepting the existing system and role of management.

Trade unions, as Marchington points out, 'do not restore the balance but merely mitigate the imbalance' [28]. Thus, Fox argues, employment organisations are not really a form of coalition government because the employees and trade unions are no more than a permanent opposition which neither seeks nor is able to be an alternative management controlling the organisation. Industrial relations is, at best, concerned only with marginal issues and power (relative distribution of pay between employees and the exercise of management's operational authority) rather than fundamental issues (the distribution of wealth and control within the society).

The Marxist perspective perceives the establishment of **processes and institutions of joint regulation** within the organisation as an enhancement rather than reduction in management's position. Management is able, by projecting a pluralistic perspective and institutional forms, to achieve its objective of greater organisational effectiveness – as Fox argues the 'satisfaction of their [the employees] marginal aspirations strengthens the legitimacy of the system' [29]. Collective bargaining acts only as a limited and temporary accommodation process for the inherent and fundamental divisions within capitalist-based work and social structures. Indeed, Marchington has suggested that the attention of management, trade unions and employees is directed towards the maintenance of the system of regulation to such an extent that 'procedural principles may be elevated above substantive outcomes' [30] – stability through compromise is preferable to a polarisation of conflicting interests and objectives which could destroy the system. Thus, trade unions and collective bargaining become an established, accepted and supportive part of the capitalist system rather than a challenge to it. However, Clegg argues that, in fact, 'pluralism implies that an acceptable compromise is not always and inevitably available' [31] because negotiation, to have meaning, must imply the possibility of a failure to agree.

The **legal contractual relationship** between the employer and employee is projected, in capitalist economies, as being one freely entered into between equals. However, from a Marxist perspective, the nature of the economic and social system within capitalist economies challenges the notions of both 'freedom' and 'equality'. The application of the law in respect of the contract of employment is perceived as being asymmetrical. As Hyman points out 'the obligations undertaken by the employer are relatively precise and specific' whilst 'the obligations on the worker . . . are imprecise and elastic' [32]. In return for the employer's 'payment' of the substantive terms of the contract (such as wages, hours, holidays, etc.) and the maintenance of reasonable conditions of working, the employee is required to provide honest and faithful service, obey all orders and do nothing harmful to the employer's interests. Hyman believes that in the eyes of the law '"equality" of the employment relationship is one which gives the employer the right to issue orders, while imposing on the worker the duty to obey' [33]. Hence, from the Marxist perspective, the reality is that the law is supportive of management's interests and position rather than being an independent referee between competing interests.

The Marxist perspective, therefore, views and analyses industrial relations not in organisational job regulation terms but in social, political and economic terms.

2.3 The nature of industrial relations

The approaches to industrial relations, deriving from these different perspectives, can be divided broadly into two groups. First, there are the 'input–output' and 'systems' approaches which derive from the pluralistic concept that employment organisations are comprised of sectional interest groups and consequently there is a need within the organisation to manage the different and possibly divergent interests of management and employees. Secondly, there are the 'human resource management' and 'control of labour process' approaches (derived from the unitary and Marxist perspectives respectively) which, it may be argued, represent opposite forms of analysis of the same phenomenon – control of the human activity of paid work.

Input–output model

The input–output model regards industrial relations primarily as a process of converting conflict into regulation. The genesis of industrial relations must be the **existence of conflict**; if it did not exist regulation would be simple, automatic and imposed. Certainly Margerison believes that the emphasis of much of the industrial relations literature appears to be 'more concerned with studying the resolution of industrial conflict than its generation' [34], and Barbash argues that in reality 'conflict, latent or manifest, is the essence of industrial relations' [35] and equal consideration must be given to its nature and development. However, whilst Barbash sees the conflict being generated by the inherent tensions within the organisations ('technology, scale, organisation, efficiency and uncertainty – the essential features of industrialism' which 'necessarily generate tensions ... of command and subordination, competitiveness, exploitation, physical deprivation at work and economic insecurity' [36]), Fox perceives it to stem from the surrounding capitalist society ('industrial conflict may be rooted in a clash of values as well as a conflict of interests' [37]). Thus, the latent conflict of interest which provides the core of industrial relations can arise from either the micro level of the organisation (the economic exchange (wage/work bargain) and the managerial systems of authority and government) or the macro level (the fundamental divisions and differing values in society).

It is important to recognise that the **transformation of latent conflict into manifest conflict** may take different forms – all of which are the subject matter of industrial relations in one way or another:

1. It may be expressed in a relatively hidden, unorganised and individual way through low employee morale, high labour turnover, absenteeism, etc.
2. It may be expressed in an overt, constitutional form, on an individual and/or collective basis, through the established procedures and institutions of industrial relations (e.g. the grievance procedure and collective bargaining machinery).
3. It may be expressed in the form of industrial pressure (e.g. strikes and other forms of industrial action) – for most people this is commonly, but wrongly, what is meant by conflict in industrial relations.

Clearly, the expression of conflict in either of the latter forms requires both a will to change the situation and often, on the part of the employees, a collective consciousness.

The expression of conflict, including the use of industrial action, may be regarded as **legitimate and functional** in identifying the differences of interest as a prelude to resolving them so as to maintain stability and equilibrium within the social structure. However, for Barbash there is 'a point beyond which conflict becomes "aberrant", "abnormal", "dysfunctional" or "pathological"' [38] because it may destabilise, if not destroy, the social structure. He suggests conflict is dysfunctional when it involves violence, a major social disorganisation of the community, civil disobedience or the extinction of either management or union. However, Hyman regards the function of conflict as being 'a total transformation of the whole structure of control . . . within the organisation of work and in social and economic life more generally' [39]. From this perspective the seeking of order and stability in industrial relations is a constraint on the function of conflict.

The remainder of the input–output model derives from the acceptance that, to be functional, the **conflict of interest has to be reconciled through some form of processes and institutions**. Thus, Laffer regards industrial relations as being 'concerned with the bargaining explicitly or implicitly between and amongst employers and employees . . . and with the factors which affect this bargaining' [40]. He postulates a simple bargaining exchange (demand–supply) model as the basis for understanding industrial relations – but not one just concerned with economic matters. The same model can apply equally to less tangible social and organisational issues which may be affected more by the different cultural values of the various participants. Within this model the relationships between the parties are adjusted through the use of 'accommodation' processes – collective bargaining, conciliation/arbitration and the law. This perspective of industrial relations emphasises the conversion processes that may be used to transform the conflict of interest into rules regulating the organisation. It concentrates, therefore, on the nature and variety of interactions which may appropriately be utilised as conversion processes. The processes may vary through a spectrum from unilateral management decision making (discipline), unilateral employee decision making (restrictive practices) or unilateral government decision making (law, incomes policy); through joint management/union processes (joint consultation, collective bargaining and employee participation); to tripartite processes involving management, unions and government (incomes policy).

Collective bargaining, therefore, may be regarded as simply one method of conflict resolution and rule making. However, it is the most common method and the one whereby, through trade unions, the employees' collective power is used to counterbalance the power of the employer. It is from this basis that Flanders [41] has described the process of negotiation as the diplomatic use of coercive power; collective bargaining as a pressure group activity; and collective agreements as compromise settlements of power conflicts. The importance of the ability of employees to exercise some countervailing power if they are to be successful in conducting an exchange based on 'bargaining' has led Lumley to suggest that 'in the absence of any organised countervailing force outside an organisation's managerial hierarchy to provide a check on unilateral management decision making over employment relationships, the study of the process of rule making and interpretation is one of administrative procedures and management decision making processes' [42] and therefore outside the scope of industrial relations study. By implication 'industrial relations' only exists if employees are collectively organised and joint processes are used. This is too rigid an approach because: (i) it ignores the 'collective' intent and application of many of the unilateral rules imposed by management and employees, and (ii) it appears to suggest that there is some level of power which must reside in the hands of the employees before a situation comes within the scope of industrial relations, whereas in reality power is a matter of varying degree. Both of these areas may reasonably be considered part of the study of industrial relations.

So far as institutions are concerned, industrial relations has been defined by Flanders as 'a study of the institutions of job regulation' [43]. However, this relatively narrow and static approach to industrial relations has been criticised most often because it emphasises the formal, institutional or structured relationships at the organisational and industry levels (and their interface) to the exclusion of the less formal, personal or unstructured relationships which exist between the participants and which are important in terms of understanding actual behaviour. Certainly, Clegg, in his examination of trade unions and collective bargaining in different countries, found that the differing structures of collective bargaining in the various countries was 'the main, major, foremost and principal influences on trade union behaviour' [44]. However, it is perhaps more useful, as Bain and Clegg suggest, to include within the study of industrial relations 'all aspects of job regulation – the making and administering of the rules which regulate employment relationships – regardless of whether they are seen as being formal or informal, structured or unstructured' [45].

The **regulatory output** of industrial relations is generally seen to be 'rules'. This perspective of industrial relations emphasises the fundamental consensus which must exist between the parties within the organisation regarding both the need to establish and maintain a system (processes and institutions) through which they may resolve their differences and the need for both sides to reach, and abide by, outcomes from that system. It stresses the general stability generated by the rule making system. Concentration on the rules themselves has been criticised by Lumley because it seems 'to emphasise the output of the system – the web of rules – at the expense of the rule making process' [46]. However, Goodman *et al.* [47] have justified such a concentration on the rules because of the need for an organised social structure to establish formalised 'norms' of behaviour amongst its members. Certainly this approach allows a structured consideration of the **types of rules** which may exist within industrial relations. There are a number of bases on which the rules may be differentiated:

1. The **authorship** of rules in terms of the process used for its determination – in particular whether it is unilateral (management or employees), joint or imposed by government.
2. **Substantive and procedural rules**: substantive rules may be regarded as defining the rights and obligations of employer and employee in the contractual wage/work bargain; procedural rules, on the other hand, seek to define the conduct of the relationship by specifying the means to be adopted within the organisation for handling specified issues (e.g. Grievance, Discipline, Redundancy, Work Changes, Union Recognition, Joint Consultation, Collective Bargaining, etc.). Many of these rules may be regarded primarily as a regulation of the two collective parties (management and unions) and only indirectly as a regulation of the relationship between individuals.
3. Whether the rules are determined **within the organisation or externally**. This distinction is important in terms of specificity and ease of change of the rule. External rules, such as the law and national agreements, apply to more than one organisation and place a limitation on the freedom of action and decision making of those at the organisation level. Consequently, the rules tend to be more general in nature and can only be changed if the proposed change is acceptable to the majority of the managements and unions covered by the national agreement. Internal rules can be more easily tailor-made to the specific needs and situation of the organisation and may be abandoned, modified or replaced at the convenience and wish of the management and unions within the organisation. It is common to find that the rules covering an

organisation, both substantive and procedural, are derived from both levels – which may, itself, present 'interface' problems.

4. Differing **degrees of formality** in the determination and recording of the rules. At one extreme the rules may be codified within formal written agreements. Such formality allows for a more universal application although the rule may require to be interpreted in the light of varying circumstances (the development of formal 'case law' on which to base future interpretations). At the other extreme the rules may be found in 'custom and practice' which often has its base in obscurity. Custom and practice may arise, perhaps most importantly, from management acceptance of informal unilateral work practices developed by workgroups or from an isolated management decision which employees regard as binding on future decisions in similar circumstances. The characteristics of custom and practice are that it is informal and unwritten, developed in the immediate work situation (largely through the actions of management and employees) and is separated from the formal mechanisms of rule regulation. Thus, there is often a conflict between the two processes of rule making with the formal process, generally at the instigation of management, seeking to exert control over the informal process.

Although the complexities of industrial relations can be seen through the input–output model, the model suffers from the major defect that it does not provide an adequate framework for understanding either the integrative nature of the parts which comprise 'industrial relations' or its relationship to the wider society within which it operates. To do this, it is useful to examine the systems approach.

Industrial relations system

Dunlop, who originated the application of the systems concept to industrial relations in 1958, sought to overcome the relative fragmentation of the subject and produce a broad-based integrative model which would both allow the study of the interrelationships between the parts and justify the subject as a separate discipline for study. He sought, through the development of a **general theory of industrial relations**, 'to provide tools of analysis to interpret and gain understanding of the widest possible range of industrial relations facts and practices' and 'to explain why particular rules are established in particular industrial relations systems and how and why they change in response to changes affecting the system' [48].

Although Dunlop's work has, over the years, been subject to a variety of interpretations, uses and criticisms, few writers have suggested its abandonment. Certainly, Wood *et al.* believe that, in terms of theory development,

Dunlop's system approach may be regarded as a conceptual categorisation which 'does not represent any real conceptual departure from previous work, and much writing both before and since may be seen as "fitting comfortably" within Dunlop's framework' [49]. It will soon be evident that the input–output model duplicates major elements of the systems approach.

Dunlop started his analysis by distinguishing industrial relations as a subsystem of society – distinct from, but overlapping, the economic and political subsystems. He suggested that the **industrial relations system could be divided into four interrelated elements** 'comprised of certain actors, certain contexts, an ideology which binds the industrial relations system together and a body of rules created to govern the actors at the workplace' [50]:

1. The **actors** can be divided into three main groups: the hierarchy of management; the hierarchy of non-managerial employees and their representatives; and specialised government agencies concerned with industrial relations.
2. The decisions and actions of the actors are influenced and constrained by the **contexts** emanating from other parts of society. Dunlop highlighted three particular contexts – the technological character of the organisation; the market or budgetary constraints affecting the organisation; and the locus and distribution of power within society.
3. There has to be an **ideology** (a set of common beliefs) within the system which acts as an integrating force through not only defining the role of each actor or group of actors but also defining the view that each actor has of the role of the other actors in the system – only if the views of the roles, one with another, are compatible is there a stable industrial relations system; if the views are incompatible then the system is unstable.
4. The **rules** generated within the system are developed by a variety of processes and presented in a variety of forms.

However, there have been a number of **significant criticisms** of the systems approach:

1. Banks [51] has argued that the management hierarchy, as set out by Dunlop, ignores the influential role of the **owners of the business** which should be accommodated by including them as an actor on the management side and their property ownership interest as a context impinging on the operation of the industrial relations system.
2. It appears to emphasise **roles rather than people** and consequently, as Jackson points out, 'ignores such behavioural variables as human motivations, perceptions, and attitudes' [52]. Industrial relations appears to be structurally determined and underestimates the effects and

importance of personal leadership in determining the outcomes of industrial relations situations.

3. Perhaps most importantly, the belief that it is possible to have a common ideology amongst the actors which integrates the system has been criticised because it implies that the industrial relations system is, or should be, **naturally stable and orderly**. Hyman argues that by concentrating attention on 'how any conflict is contained and controlled rather than on the processes through which disagreements and disputes are generated' an image is projected that 'the various institutions and procedures are compatible and well integrated; and that conflict is therefore largely self-correcting' [53]. The functional view of industrial relations (to produce order) appears to skate over the fact that what constitutes order is a matter of belief and perception of individuals and that the existence of order is a matter of degree rather than an absolute. Certainly, Schienstock argues that the system's apparent 'concentration on the stability issue should . . . not be represented as though it presupposes an imminent tendency towards stability in the industrial relations system' [54]. It is for this reason that Jackson has suggested that the systems approach is only of value 'if it incorporates the existence of contradictory processes and forces and therefore treats instability and stability as of equal significance as "system outcomes"' [55] and Eldridge has argued that 'the sources of conflict and cooperation, order and instability must have an equally valid claim to problem status' [56] in the study of industrial relations.

4. Associated with (3), it has been argued that the systems view does not adequately reflect the **real nature of the wider society**. Winchester has argued that the system view of industrial relations fails because it 'assumes multiplicity of individual and group interests (both broader class forces and structures), focuses in its analysis on an empirical conception of power at the workplace or organisational level (not the less visible impact of social power) and develops a restricted definition of workers' interests and trade union purpose that concentrates attention largely on the institutions and procedures in collective bargaining (not broader mechanisms for the distribution of power and rewards in society)' [57]. He cites, as a justification for adopting this wider perspective of the industrial relations system, the fact that much of the debate and controversy in industrial relations, certainly in the last two decades, has stemmed 'from policy makers' (especially governments') definitions of social problems or in response to potential or actual policy developments' [58]; for example, Donovan Commission, Bullock Committee, industrial relations legislation and government policies. Wood argues that Dunlop's view of the industrial relations system prefers 'to take the analysis of it [society] as given, presumably leaving it to the other disciplines of the social sciences' [59]. However, industrial

relations must of necessity interrelate with wider social, economic and political issues.

These criticisms do not themselves invalidate the systems approach to examining industrial relations but rather highlight the need for accommodation and refinement. Perhaps the most constructive **modification of the systems approach**, which can incorporate these criticisms, has been put forward by Wood *et al.* and provides the basis for Figure 2.2.

The starting point for Wood *et al.* in reconstructing the systems approach is the **meaning and purpose of an industrial relations system** (I.R.S.). The crucial issue, in their view, is whether the central feature of the industrial relations system should be the rules (output) or rule making (process). They are in no doubt that 'rule-making action (i.e. those "aspects" of behaviour directed towards rule making), as opposed to the totality of worker–management–government interaction, is central to the concept of the I.R.S.' [60]. Stemming from this they believe that it is therefore important that 'an analytical distinction can be made between the system which "produces" rules (i.e. the I.R.S.) and the system which is "governed" by such rules (i.e. the production system)' [61]. This in turn provides a framework for distinguishing between:

1. rules which are an output from the industrial relations system to 'govern' behaviour within the production system (substantive rules and, possibly procedural rules for regulating the interpretation and application of the substantive rules); and
2. rules which are established for the internal regulation of the conduct of the industrial relations system (procedural).

This distinction, however, may not be as clear as Wood *et al.* suggest because the need to interpret and apply substantive rules can be seen as conflict generation (the feedback loop in the input–output model) and therefore the procedures for regulating such activities may more appropriately be classified as part of the rule making process. Nevertheless, the differentiation between the two systems has a significant impact on the **perceived purpose** of the industrial relations system. Dunlop argued that the objective of the system could be seen primarily in terms of stability and ultimate survival of the industrial relations system itself – hence his concern for the common ideology amongst the actors within the system. Wood *et al.* believe that it would be more useful and appropriate to regard 'the goal of the I.R.S. as satisfying the functional need for order within the production system' [62] and, in this context, order may be assumed to be a matter of degree and therefore a variable. Certainly this view of the purpose of the industrial relations system accords with the empirical evidence of the management attitude towards industrial relations – that industrial relations is seen to be supportive of business objectives rather than an end in itself.

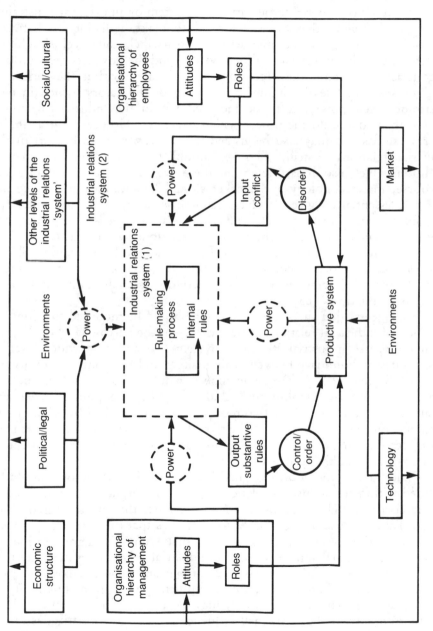

Figure 2.2 *The system of industrial relations*

The second crucial issue presented by Wood *et al.* in their development of the systems view is the **location of the contexts** in relation to the industrial relations system. Dunlop was somewhat ambiguous as to whether they were to be considered to be part of the system or an external constraint. Wood *et al.* believe that there is a need to make a distinction between Dunlop's technological and market contexts (which they feel should be located outside the industrial relations system) and the power context (which in contrast to Dunlop they feel should be located within the industrial relations system). Clearly, if the organisation of the actors, which in part determines their power, is to be included within the industrial relations system, then so should the power which it creates. However, on a similar but reverse basis, it may also be argued that if 'power' is to be part of the industrial relations system, then so should the technology or market conditions which also in part determine the power. It may be counterargued, of course, that technology and market should be located outside because they are, essentially, 'givens' which cannot be changed by the industrial relations system in order to meet industrial relations needs – or at best can only be marginally affected. The industrial relations system has to adapt to the constraints of these contexts rather than vice versa. Certainly, Shalev believes that 'the social, economic and political environment can be more fruitfully seen as interacting with, and therefore as analytically inseparable from labour relations' [63].

This suggests that the system approach should be modified to allow for the study of industrial relations at two levels – at the narrow level of the rule making process (Industrial Relations System (1)) and at a wider level to incorporate the boundary between rule making and the contexts (Industrial Relations System (2)). At the same time it would be useful to expand the contexts set out by Dunlop to include, at least, the political/legal and social/cultural contexts. These two modifications are implied by Wood *et al.* when they argue that the other levels of the industrial relations system to that under examination at the time should be regarded as a context affecting the narrow rule making process.

In addition, Wood *et al.* recognised that **behavioural factors** should be included within the industrial relations system but argued that such factors are exercised through 'roles' on a structured rather than unstructured basis. Indeed, Dunlop's use of the term 'actors' implies that they are acting a role. At the same time Wood *et al.* recognised that Dunlop's 'defocalisation' of **power** to an external influence on the industrial relations system (derived largely from public policy towards trade unions and collective bargaining) is too narrow. Power, in terms of ability to influence through the possibility of inflicting a 'loss' on the opposition, may be focused on the rule making process from any of the contextual influences as well as the attitudes of the participants. Hence, the systems approach has to accept a **variety of ideologies**, which may or may not be congruent, rather than one. Ideology is as likely to produce conflict within the rule making process as it is to produce consensus, and therefore the rule making process is often involved in reconciling these differing ideologies in the rules it generates.

Control of the labour process

Thompson defines **the labour process** as 'the means by which raw materials are transformed by human labour, acting on the objects with tools and machinery; first into products for use and, under capitalism, into commodities to be exchanged on the market' [64]. This definition immediately raises two questions:

1. Does the labour process only exist in manufacturing situations? This concept is just as relevant to the private service sectors such as retail, banking, etc., as it is to manufacturing because they are an integral part of the process whereby 'products' are transformed into 'commodities to be exchanged' and the organisations in these industries seek to make a profit.
2. Does it only apply to the private sector? It might appear at first sight that the public sector, by its very nature, is not concerned with 'commodities to be exchanged on the market'. However, the public sector does exist within a capitalist society and therefore must, to some extent, be influenced by that particular set of values, ethics, etc. Furthermore, the Government has, during the 1980s, imposed capitalist mechanisms and systems on the management of the public sector (privatisation, cash limits, competitive tendering, performance related pay for senior managers, etc.) which then directly impact on its methods of operation.

Thompson argues that the core of **theory of the labour process** rests on the fact that 'the social relations which workers enter into to produce useful things becomes a capitalist labour process when the capacity to work is utilised as a means of producing value' and 'therefore on the unique characteristics of labour as a commodity' [65]. Four elements stem from this core:

1. The labour-capital relationship is essentially one of exploitation wherein surplus value from work activities accrues to capital.
2. The 'logic of accumulation' requires capital continually to develop the production process and cheapen the costs of production.
3. Continual development of the production processes requires the establishment and maintenance of both general and specific 'structures of control';
4. The resultant 'structured antagonism' relationship includes systematic

attempts by capital to obtain co-operation and consent and 'a continuum of possible and overlapping worker responses, from resistance, to accommodation on temporary common objectives, to compliance with the greater power of capital, and consent to production practices' [66].

Braverman [67] argued that the fundamental industrial relationship during the twentieth century has been one of **management exploitation and degradation of labour** by deskilling work through the use of scientific management techniques (Taylorism) to support the achievement of capital's objective. The application of work study techniques facilitated the break down of work into its component tasks which could then be allocated to separate individuals (specialisation). Management thereby cheapened the individual's input value to the production process (the task required less training, skill and/or responsibility and therefore arguably less reward), tied the individual more directly to the technical system (in particular the assembly line) and made the individual or group capable of being subjected to production output controls (bonus payments, quota levels, etc.). Braverman argued that this process was as applicable to non-manual clerical and administrative work as it was to manual production work and consequently many non-manual employees should be regarded, and might come to regard themselves, as part of the 'working class' because they were subject to the same type of work controls and working conditions as manual workers.

However Nichols [68] points out that this general analysis has been criticised and developed in two main ways. First, it does not appear to take sufficient account of **employee resistance** to the introduction of scientific management; yet there is clear evidence (the existence of so-called restrictive practices) that employees have, in different situations and to varying degrees, resisted or modified scientific management approaches and exerted some influence or control over their work situation. Secondly, it does not take account of **other mechanisms of management control over labour**. Nichols argues that 'the exploitation of labour, though a necessary condition of existence for a capitalist mode of production, always takes place in a particular historical situation, which *inter alia* has its own specific political and ideological components' [69]. Whilst scientific management and deskilling may, in the past, have provided the main plank for management control of labour, management's approach to controlling the labour process has not remained static. He identifies two aspects which have concerned more recent approaches to control of the labour process:

1. The concept of **segmented labour markets** divides 'core' or 'central' employees (whose role, skill and expertise are required for the long-term viability and profitability of the organisation) from 'peripheral' or 'marginal' employees (where there is less commonality between the employee's role/function and the organisation's long-term needs). Such a division in management thinking and organisational strategy can lead to

a real or perceived segmentation of interests between these groups and consequently a less effective resistance to management control ('divide and rule').

2.   Management has at its disposal a variety of mechanisms, apart from scientific management techniques, to 'control' labour. Friedman [70], for example, differentiates between 'direct control' exercised through the application of scientific management from **'responsible autonomy'** forms of management control over labour. This latter approach involves expanding or enhancing the employee's job or work situation so that it *appears* to allow the employee some degree of 'self control' but only in areas and in a direction which support the achievement of management objectives and increase organisational effectiveness and efficiency. In practice employees are required to adopt and pursue management objectives and ideals as an integral part of their job and working situation. Edwards [71] identifies two forms of managerial control which supplement scientific management's technical or production control of the individual: (i) simple, direct, **personal control** arising from the superior's responsibility for the work and activities of subordinates; and (ii) **'bureaucratic' control** stemming from the policies, procedures and rules within the workplace.

Sisson suggests that the significance of this approach, apart from directing attention to the specific mechanisms of 'control' within the workplace, has been to recognise that 'the policies, processes and procedures typically involved in the management of people are to be seen, first and foremost, as instruments of management control' [72] and clearly subordinate to management's needs in the production/technical system.

Human resource management

The term 'human resource management' (HRM) has become increasingly used in Britain during the 1980s (both in the literature of personnel/ industrial relations and in management job titles). However, like the term 'industrial relations', there is no one universal definition of 'human resource management'. The term has been applied to a diverse range of management strategies and, indeed, sometimes used simply as a more modern, and therefore more acceptable, term for personnel or industrial relations management. Its importance for understanding industrial relations lies in its association with **a strategic, integrated and highly distinctive managerial approach to the management of people**.

Armstrong [73] points out that the **roots of human resource management** can be found in the 1950/60s human relations concepts and approaches of writers such as McGregor, Maslow and Hertzberg combined with the organisational development movement of the 1960/70s. The distinctiveness of human resource management, Torrington and Hall argue, lies in the fact that it is 'directed mainly at management needs for human resources (not necessarily employees) to be provided and deployed . . . greater emphasis on planning, monitoring and control, rather than on problem-solving and mediation . . . totally identified with management interests, being a general management activity, and is relatively distant from the workforce as a whole' [74]. Guest has sought to identify a specific and distinctive **model of human resource management**. The underpinning of the model lies in combining established elements of organisational psychology (both what he terms the 'softer' elements of leadership, culture and commitment and 'harder' elements of selection methods, job redesign, goal setting and performance monitoring) with strategic management to provide 'a coherent and distinctive set of propositions about an approach to management – human resource management – which seeks . . . to promote positive organisational outcomes' [75]. Storey believes 'it implies something different from the proceduralized approach to handling labour . . . it eschews the joint regulative approach . . . places emphasis on utilizing labour to its full capacity or potential . . . HRM is therefore about (and the term is used neutrally here) *exploiting* the labour resource more fully' [76]. This is echoed by Legge who suggests that 'our new enterprise culture demands a different language, one that asserts management's right to manipulate, *and* ability to generate and develop resources' [77].

However, for some writers human resource management should perhaps be re-titled **human resource manipulation**. Fowler, for example, questions whether supporters of HRM are 'genuinely concerned with creating a new, equal partnership between employer and employed, or are they really offering a covert form of employee manipulation dressed up as mutuality' [78]. Certainly, the range of personnel practices frequently associated with human resource management (such as psychological testing, appraisal, performance related pay, individual contracts, quality circles, team briefings, etc.) are regarded by some as 'HRM policies designed to influence workers attitudes' and 'the use of psychological pressure and group discipline' is seen as 'management by stress' [79]. Storey suggests that there is 'a view of HRM which puts the emphasis on the "resource management" element, with overtones of the dispassionate acquisition, deployment and disposal of resources and an abandonment of the "caring" and empathetic elements in some traditional personnel practice' [80]. Such an approach would seem almost to ignore or dismiss the centrality of people [human beings] in the the study of this aspect of organisations. It may be argued that the development of human resource management strategies and approaches during the 1980s provides the evidence of modern management exploitation of labour required by the 'control of the labour process' approach.

Human resource management approaches certainly emphasise individualism and the direct relationship between management and its employees. Quite clearly, therefore, it **questions the collective regulation basis**

of traditional industrial relations. Indeed, it may be argued that an essential part of a human resource management approach is that negotiations with trade unions, as the representative of employees, and other such industrial relations activities are to be avoided, removed or, at least, minimised. Storey believes that perhaps the central question, from a human resource management perspective, is 'can industrial relations be transformed from an adversarial, rule-based institution into a cooperative, commitment-inducing process?' [81]; in other words, does human resource management have to equate to a non-union individualistic model of 'industrial relations' or can there be a form of 'dualism' within the organisation where human resource management co-exists with industrial relations?

Social action

This approach to the study of industrial relations has its base within sociology. Bain and Clegg believe that it 'emphasises the actors' definition of reality' [82], while Jackson notes that it 'stresses the way in which man influences the social structures and "makes society"' [83]. It is the actors' perception and definition of their reality which determines their behaviour, actions and relationships. In this respect it is important to recognise that people's orientation to work is as much the result of their extra-organisational experiences as their experience within the workplace. However, over concentration on the individual's ability to choose and determine his/her own situation has the danger that the individual is not always aware that choice is being restricted by structural factors. The essential nature of the relationship between these two elements is that structures may limit the choice of action, but the action chosen will itself produce a change, however small, in that social structure or relationship. The extent to which it will produce any change is, in part, dependent on the choices made by others. The importance of this view of industrial relations is that it weakens the fatalism of structural determinism and 'stresses that the individual retains at least some freedom of action and ability to influence events' [84] in the direction that he/she believes to be 'right' and 'desirable'.

2.4 Summary propositions

- The systems approach to industrial relations does not explain industrial relations issues or events, it simply allows us to analyse and understand them better.
- The 'human resource management' and 'control of labour process' models of industrial relations represent opposing analyses of the same phenomenon – control of the human activity of paid work.

2.5 Author's note

It is important in any book on industrial relations that the reader is aware of the author's perspective of the subject:

1. Organisations are composed of sectional groups which have different, and frequently divergent, interests and whose members' expectations, perceptions and attitudes are the product of a combination of both social and organisational factors and differences. Within this framework management is simply one of the sectional groups – but one which perceives itself to be the embodiment of 'the organisation' and which has privileged access to power through its control of information and resources within the organisation and its linkage to the 'establishment' within society.
2. Any consensus between the participants in respect of their need to establish and maintain institutions, processes and rules to regulate their relationships requires *all* parties to be prepared to accept compromises in resolving problems or issues between them (i.e. not fully to achieve their aspirations and objectives). However, this apparent need to reach some agreement in order to maintain the relationship is not always paramount nor overrides the pursuit of sectional interests. There will be occasions when one side will pursue a strategy of imposing a solution against the felt goals or wishes of the other party.
3. Within the rule making processes of industrial relations both management and employees have an equal and legitimate right to seek to protect what they perceive as their interests and to secure their objectives – including the right to exert pressure through industrial power if it is felt by them to be necessary. The relative power relationship between the participants is never 'right' or 'in balance' but constantly varying, dependent on organisational and societal factors. Finally, there is never a universally 'right' solution to an industrial relations problem or situation. The only 'right' solution is that which is acceptable to the parties involved.

Further reading

- A. Fox, 'Industrial relations: a social critique of pluralist ideology' in J. Child (ed.), *Man and Organization*, Allen & Unwin, 1973. This provides a very useful discussion of unitary, pluralistic and radical frames of reference.
- J. T. Dunlop, *Industrial Relations Systems*, Holt, 1958. Although dated, this must be the definitive work on systems from which all other works have started and developed.

- R. Hyman, *Industrial Relations: A Marxist introduction*, Macmillan, 1975. A leading, and very readable, book which approaches and explains industrial relations, and particularly the role and problems of trade unions, from a clearly Marxist perspective.
- P. Thompson, *The Nature of Work: An introduction to debates on the labour process* (2nd edn), Macmillan, 1989. This provides a concise and comprehensive introduction to a range of debates on the labour process.
- J. Storey (ed.), *New Perspectives on Human Resource Management*, Routledge, 1989. A very readable discussion of both the overall concept of HRM and the various elements within such an approach.

References

1. A. Fox, 'Industrial Sociology and Industrial Relations', *Royal Commission Research Paper No. 3*, HMSO, 1966, p. 2.
2. *ibid.*
3. D. Farnham and J. Pimlott, *Understanding Industrial Relations* (2nd edn), Cassell, 1983, p. 52.
4. A. Fox, 'Industrial relations: a social critique of pluralist ideology' in J. Child (ed.), *Man and Organization*, Allen & Unwin, 1973, p. 189.
5. *ibid.*
6. D. Farnham and J. Pimlott, *op. cit.*, p. 53.
7. A. Fox (1973), *op. cit.*, p. 188.
8. A. Fox (1966), *op. cit.*, p. 4.
9. I. Maitland, 'Disorder in the British workplace: the limits of consensus', *British Journal of Industrial Relations*, vol. XVIII, 1980, p. 361.
10. A. Fox, *Man Mismanagement*, Hutchinson, 1974, p. 10.
11. A. Fox (1973), *op. cit.*, p. 193.
12. A. Kornhauser, R. Dubin and A. M. Ross (eds), *Industrial Conflict*, McGraw-Hill, 1954, p. 13.
13. A. Fox (1966), *op. cit.*, p. 4.
14. *ibid.*
15. A. Fox (1973), *op. cit.*, pp. 195–6.
16. *ibid.*, p. 196.
17. *ibid.*, p. 199.
18. *ibid.*, p. 196.
19. H. A. Clegg, 'Pluralism in industrial relations', *British Journal of Industrial Relations*, vol. XIII, 1975, p. 309.
20. N. S. Ross in E. M. Hugh-Jones (ed.), *Human Relations and Modern Management* (1958), quoted by Fox (1966), p. 4.
21. A. Fox (1973), *op. cit.*, p. 193.
22. A. Fox (1966), *op. cit.*, p. 7.
23. *ibid.*, p. 8.
24. *ibid.*, p. 7.
25. R. Hyman, *Industrial Relations: A Marxist Introduction*, Macmillan, 1975, p. 19.
26. H. A. Clegg, *op. cit.*, p. 310.

27. A. Fox (1973), *op. cit.*

28. M. Marchington, *Managing Industrial Relations*, McGraw-Hill, 1982, p. 47.

29. A. Fox (1973), *op. cit.*, p. 210.

30. M. Marchington, *op. cit.*, p. 48.

31. H. A. Clegg, *op. cit.*, p. 24.

32. R. Hyman, *op. cit.*, p. 24.

33. *ibid.*

34. C. J. Margerison, 'What do we mean by industrial relations? A behavioural approach', *British Journal of Industrial Relations*, vol. VII, no. 2, 1969, p. 273.

35. J. Barbash, 'Collective bargaining and the theory of conflict', *British Journal of Industrial Relations*, vol. XVIII, 1980, p. 86.

36. *ibid.*, p. 87.

37. A. Fox, *A Sociology of Work in Industry*, Collier Macmillan, 1971, p. 28. Reprinted with permission of the publisher.

38. J. Barbash, *op. cit.*, p. 88.

39. R. Hyman, *op. cit.*, p. 203.

40. K. Laffer, 'Is industrial relations an academic discipline?', *Australian Journal of Industrial Relations*, 1973, p. 72.

41. A. Flanders, 'Collective bargaining: a theoretical analysis', *British Journal of Industrial Relations*, vol. VI, 1968, pp. 1–26.

42. R. Lumely, 'A modified rules approach to workplace industrial relations', *Industrial Relations Journal*, vol. 10, no. 3, 1979, p. 49.

43. A. Flanders, *Industrial Relations – What's Wrong with the System?*, Faber, 1965, p. 4.

44. H. A. Clegg, *Trade Unionism under Collective Bargaining*, Blackwell, 1976, p. 10.

45. G. S. Bain and H. Clegg, 'Strategy for industrial relations research in Great Britain', *British Journal of Industrial Relations*, vol. XII, 1974, p. 95.

46. R. Lumley, *op. cit.*, p. 49.

47. J. F. B. Goodman, E. G. A. Armstrong, A. Wagner, J. E. Davis and J. J. Wood, 'Rules in industrial relations theory: a discussion', *Industrial Relations Journal*, vol. 6, no. 1, 1975, pp. 14–30.

48. J. T. Dunlop, *Industrial Relations Systems*, Henry Holt Ltd, 1958, pp. vi and ix. Reprinted by permission of CBS College Publishing.

49. S. J. Wood, A. Wagner, E. G. A. Armstrong, J. F. B. Goodman and J. E. Davis, 'The "industrial relations system" concept as a basis for theory in industrial relations', *British Journal of Industrial Relations*, vol. XIII, 1975, p. 293.

50. J. T. Dunlop, *op. cit.*, p. 7.

51. J. A. Banks, *Trade Unionism*, Collier Macmillan, 1974.

52. M. Jackson, *Industrial Relations* (2nd edn), Croom Helm, 1982, p. 20.

53. R. Hyman, *op. cit.*, p. 11.

54. G. Schienstock, 'Towards a theory of industrial relations', *British Journal of Industrial Relations*, vol. XIX, 1981, p. 172.

55. M. Jackson, *op. cit.*, p. 22.

56. J. E. T. Eldridge, *Industrial Disputes*, Routledge & Kegan Paul, 1968, p. 22.

57. D. Winchester, 'Industrial relations research in Britain', *British Journal of Industrial Relations*, vol. XX, 1983, p. 104.

58. *ibid.*, p. 105.

59. S. Wood, 'Ideology in industrial relations theory', *Industrial Relations Journal*, vol. 9, no. 4, 1978/1979, p. 45.

60. S. Wood *et al.*, *op. cit.*, p. 295.

61. *ibid.*
62. *ibid.*, p. 296.
63. M. Shalev, 'Industrial relations theory and the comparative study of industrial relations and industrial conflict', *British Journal of Industrial Relations*, vol. XVIII, 1980, p. 26.
64. P. Thompson, *The Nature of Work: An introduction to debates on the labour process* (2nd edn), Macmillan, 1989, p. xv.
65. *ibid.*, p. 242.
66. P. Thompson and E. Bannon (1985), quoted in P. Thompson, *op. cit.*, p. 245.
67. H. A. Braverman, 'Labour and monopoly capital: the degradation of work in the twentieth century', *Monthly Review Press*, 1974.
68. T. Nichols, *The British Worker Question*, RKP, 1986.
69. *ibid.*, p. 31.
70. A. Friedman, *Industry and Labour: Class struggle at work and monopoly capitalism*, Macmillan, 1977.
71. R. Edwards, *Contested Terrain: The transformation of the workplace in the twentieth century*, Heinemann, 1979.
72. K. Sisson, 'Personnel management in perspective' in K. Sisson (ed.), *Personnel Management in Britain*, Blackwell, 1989, p. 7.
73. M. Armstrong, 'Human resource management: a case of the emperor's new clothes?', *Personnel Management*, August 1987.
74. D. Torrington and L. Hall, *Personnel Management: A new approach*, Prentice Hall, 1987, p. 14.
75. D. Guest, 'Personnel and HRM: can you tell the difference?', *Personnel Management*, January 1989, p. 49.
76. J. Storey (ed.), *New Perspectives on Human Resource Management*, Routledge, 1989, p. 9.
77. K. Legge, 'Human resource management: a critical analysis' in J. Storey (ed.), *op. cit.*, p. 40.
78. A. Fowler, 'When chief executives discover HRM', *Personnel Management*, January 1987.
79. 'HRM – human resource manipulation?', *Labour Research*, August 1989, p. 8.
80. J. Storey, 'Developments in the management of human resources: an interim report', *Warwick Papers in Industrial Relations*, no. 17, November 1987, p. 7.
81. *ibid.*, p. 9.
82. G. S. Bain and H. Clegg, *op. cit.*, p. 95.
83. M. Jackson, *op. cit.*, p. 24.
84. *ibid.*, p. 27.

Chapter 3
Concepts and values in industrial relations

3.1 Definition

Industrial relations is not an 'objective' science. Indeed, it may be argued that there are no simple objective facts in industrial relations. For example, before it is possible to calculate the number of trade unions in Britain it is necessary to define what organisational characteristics are appropriate for determining whether or not an organisation may be classified as a 'trade union' and the characteristics which are chosen will depend on what is *believed* to be the purpose and nature of a trade union. More importantly, as Hyman and Brough point out, 'the arguments of those involved in industrial relations are shot through with essentially *moral* terminology' [1]. Perhaps the most important issues and debates in industrial relations, apart from that concerning the conflictual/consensual relationship of the participants, centre around such concepts as fairness/equity, power/authority and individualism/collectivism. However, as Kerr and Siegal argue, these concepts 'are not subject to discovery by any purely technical explanation but must be defined by the exercise of value judgements' [2]. Therefore, **industrial relations is concerned with subjective, value judgements about concepts for which there are no universally accepted criteria**. Different individuals and groups have different perceptions of what is 'good/bad', 'right/wrong' or what power may be exercised legitimately and when. It is these differing perceptions which provide the underlying dynamic tension within industrial relations. The inherent problem with any value laden concept is trying to understand what is meant by the term and its limitations.

3.2 Fairness and equity

Although the concept of 'fairness' or 'equity' implicitly underlies the entire conduct of industrial relations, it is explicitly most frequently associated with considerations of payment structures/levels and dismissals. However, there are many who would argue, perhaps cynically, that nothing in life is ever fair and therefore appeals to fairness are little more than attempts to provide a semblance of justification or legitimacy for actions and decisions which might otherwise appear to be simply expedient. Others, such as Brown, argue that the use of the concept is 'more than an ideological whitewash, to be applied ex post to provide an appearance of rationality' [3] and certainly Hyman and Brough believe that 'the commitment of one side or the other to a particular notion of fairness often appears to exert a significant influence on the actual course of industrial relations' [4].

The use of the term is confused perhaps by its close association, in many people's mind, with the term **equality**. In this way anything which creates or sustains inequality may be perceived as being 'unfair'. However, the concept of 'fairness' or 'equity' does not automatically imply equality; equality is only one value or belief set that may be used to judge the existence and extent of fairness. There are many who would argue that the existence of social inequality is both inevitable and fair because of differences in individual personal attributes. Certainly there is no doubt that inequalities exist both within society and the organisation: for example, unequal distribution of wealth, incomes and ownership; variations in benefits such as job security, nature of work, status, education, health, etc.; differential access to power, authority and control. Indeed, the dominant values and ethos within a capitalist society, extolled through the virtues of individualism and competition, support the creation and maintenance of such inequalities and thereby legitimise their fairness. However, from a Marxist perspective based on more egalitarian values it is the existence of such inequalities at the macro level of society (the absence of 'social justice' in respect of the distribution of wealth, power, rights and duties) which renders the concept of 'fairness' at the micro level of the individual or organisation almost meaningless. Any notions of fairness held by the subordinate which differ from those of the dominant may be seen as destabilising and, if recognised and accepted, a threat to the dominant's position.

Zweig has suggested that 'the idea of fairness is linked strongly with the best customs and traditions and the best social rules' [5]. However, this more abstract approach immediately raises problems of how to identify what is 'the best'. The values to which one person attaches the highest priority and greatest concern may not be the same for other people. This has led many, consciously or unconsciously, to adopt a **utilitarian or democratic notion of fairness** (that which is in the interests of or acceptable to the majority) in the mistaken belief that it is demonstrably impartial and fair and will therefore dispel feelings of unfairness amongst the minority. However, the outcome of majority rule, even though it is legitimised by the nature of the process, will not automatically be considered to be 'right' or 'fair' by the minority who have different values and expectations to the majority.

Some people might go even further to suggest that certain activities rise above personal values and provide an **impersonal technical notion of fairness**: for example, market forces, job evaluation or the legal process. However, even the proposition that 'the free interplay of market forces should be allowed to determine wage levels' is a value judgement and, certainly, any suggestion that in the process of job evaluation it is the system which independently and impartially determines an individual's pay ignores the fact that it is people who, subjectively, both allocate the weightings in the scheme (i.e. determine which attributes are to attract the highest measure) and evaluate the individual's job against those criteria. So far as the legal process is concerned, again it is people who make, invoke, interpret and apply the law in the light of their values and notions of fairness.

Fairness is perhaps most usefully seen as a **relative and variable concept** with which to examine the conduct of human relationships. In this respect it may be used in three ways:

1. It may imply, as Hyman and Brough suggest, that 'in an exchange there should be reasonable reciprocity or balance between the parties concerned' [6]. (An exchange or relationship may be either a monetary one (wage bargaining) or, more often, non-monetary (from trade union recognition, redundancies, etc., to individual grievances, discipline and work changes).) However, difficulties arise in determining what are the relevant criteria by which to judge the **reciprocity of the exchange** – should they relate only to the outcome (the costs/benefits to each party) or should they include some assessment of the quality of the process by which the outcome is achieved (collective bargaining v. unilateral imposition)? Ultimately, whether or not reciprocity exists can only be determined by reference to the values of the participants and *their* view of the nature and quality of their exchange. It is 'fair' if the participants consider it to be fair.

2. In a wider context, fairness may imply that a particular exchange is **consistent with other exchanges** undertaken elsewhere. It is in this context that it is possible to have 'fair' inequalities; but this requires a wide measure of agreement regarding both the criteria for determining similarities and differences between situations and the evaluation of their relative importance. An exchange is only 'fair' if others, outside the direct participants, consider it to be fair in relation to themselves or other individuals and groups.

3. Fairness may, particularly in respect of non-monetary exchanges, imply **equality of treatment and consideration** in the conduct of different relationships and within the same relationship over time. There is an expectation that the same types of criteria and standards of judgements should apply in similar circumstances; that relationships should be conducted, and therefore may be judged, according to an accepted code. It is 'fair' if it is consistent.

Finally, because fairness is relative, it is **not constant**. As situations and environments change so the participants' notion of what is fair may change. For example, in wage bargaining, it is to be expected that during recession management's notion of a 'fair' wage increase will decrease because its major reference point (ability to pay) changes whilst the employees' notion of a 'fair' increase may remain unchanged because their major reference points (cost of living, comparability, etc.) are less affected by recession. Equally, if one group of employees perceive other groups to achieve better wage increases through the use of industrial action and/or they become more aware of their own industrial power, so they are more likely to perceive it as being 'fair' for them to seek the same levels and/or use the same means.

3.3 Power and authority

The concepts of 'power' and 'authority' occupy a central position in industrial relations – particularly with respect to its collective aspects. People frequently make value judgements regarding trade unions having too much or too little power in relation to management and government; or trade unions having little authority or control over their membership; or management having too little authority within its own organisation. In practice the two concepts are inextricably linked: authority is achieved through power and vice versa.

There is no universally accepted definition of **power**. For Koontz and O'Donnell 'power implies force' [7]; for Hyman it is 'the ability of an individual or group to control his (their) physical and social environment; and, as part of the process, the ability to influence the decisions which are or are not taken by others' [8]; while in purely operational terms, for example in negotiations, Magenau and Pruitt regard it simply as the 'capacity to elicit concessions from the other party' [9]. Clearly, therefore, power has different meanings and it is useful to differentiate between the following:

1. Power meaning the ability to **control** or impose, i.e. to direct or regulate a situation or person(s) despite any desire or attempt to influence from another individual or group. Certainly Kirkbride and Durcan argue that 'power . . . is inherently entwined in the very fabric of social life and its processes . . . "domination" is where there is an asymmetry of resources and one actor is thus much more "powerful" than the other' and power is 'not "a" resource, but instead resources are the means through which power is exercised and by which structures of domination are reproduced' [10].

2. Power meaning the ability to **influence** and thereby secure some modification in another party's decision or action; this may be subdivided between:

    (a) the ability to force a change in the other party's decision, usually after it has been made, by the **explicit** expression or threat to express that power; or

    (b) the ability to generate an **implicit** influence which will form an integral part of the environment which has to be taken into account by the other party in its decision making process.

This latter distinction is recognised by Magenau and Pruitt when, in the context of negotiations, they distinguish between strategic power which 'consists of all the elements of the situation that allow one party to influence the other' and tactical advantage which consists of the 'successful use of distributive tactics for enhancing one's influence' [11].

Hyman argues that whilst power is used *for* a purpose, which in industrial relations is 'primarily as a resource . . . in the service of collective interests' [12], it can only serve this purpose if it is exercised *over* people. Consequently, the **source of power** must be sought within the industrial relationship itself. French and Raven [13] identified five major interrelated sources of power:

1. *Reward* – having control or influence over the achievement of some goal or benefit which is desired by another.
2. *Coercion* – having the ability to inflict some punitive measure against another (this may be linked to the denial of reward or the formal roles which the people hold).
3. *Legitimised* – occupying a role which is formally designated as containing a superior direction or regulation of others.
4. *Referment* – having the personal attributes which lead others to defer in their decisions or opinions.
5. *Expertise* – having particular knowledge or experience which is considered to be superior to that of others (this may be linked to the role occupied by the person or their personal attributes).

More importantly, Magenau and Pruitt highlight that power can only exist and be exerted if there is a **reciprocal perception of power**. In the context of bargaining negotiations, they argue that 'when I feel stronger than you, this is no guarantee that you will feel weaker than me or, feeling weaker, that you will accept my contention that you should concede' [14]. From this they conclude that:

1. Perceived power equality between the parties provides for an easy agreement and high value outcome.

2. Perceived low power inequality provides for a difficult agreement and low value outcome.
3. Perceived high power inequality provides for an 'easy' agreement and high but biased value outcome.

This latter situation equates to control or imposition through power and is always likely to be perceived as 'unfair' by the 'losing' party. It is because of the need to establish a reciprocal perception of power, and thereby determine the relative power relationship between the parties, that power needs to be demonstrated explicitly – at least occasionally.

At the same time, because of the collective nature of industrial relations, it is important to recognise that the concept of power over people has an **internal as well as external dimension**. Any collectivity, whether a work group, trade union or management, exercises internal power and authority over its individual members in the establishment and achievement of the collectivity's objectives. Without the exercise of such power and authority the collectivity lacks direction and control (i.e. is not a collectivity). It is the exercise of this internal power and authority which, to a large measure, provides the real source and extent of the power which the collectivity may direct towards influencing others and controlling their situation.

Authority is usually defined in terms of the legitimate use of power. Hence, Koontz and O'Donnell regard it as 'the right inherent in a position to utilize discretion in such a way that [organizational] objectives are set and achieved' [15], and Fox defines it as 'the right to expect and command obedience' [16]. If the concept of 'authority' rests on the **legitimisation of power** then it is important to examine the basis of this legitimacy. An important part of legitimisation comes from the general process of **socialisation**. At the society level Fox points out that 'as children we are urged to obey parents, teachers, policemen, and public officials simply *because* they are parents, teachers, policemen and public officials . . . We also learn that if punished for transgression we are receiving no less than our just desert. These are lessons in the behaviours appropriate to subordination. . . . By the time [the majority] take up employment they are trained to accept that they . . . come under a generalized expectation that they will accept the orders of persons appointed to govern them' [17].

At the organisational level this process of socialisation is reflected in the notion of **managerial prerogative**. Hyman regards this as a natural privilege or 'right accorded to management in capitalism to direct production and to command the labour force' [18], whilst Fox believes that 'in entering into a contract of employment, the employee legitimises the employer in directing and controlling his actions . . . and legitimises, too, the employer's use of sanctions if necessary to maintain this obedience' [19]. In this way, Torrington and Chapman argue, 'the individuals who become employees of the organisation surrender a segment of their personal autonomy to become relatively weaker, making the organisation inordinately stronger' [20].

Management's inherent authority is based, therefore, on society's infrastructure legitimising its role and power in the operation of the economic system. Consequently, it is argued, it has little need to utilise overtly coercive power in exercising this authority because the subordinates it seeks to control accept the values on which its power and authority rests. However, if necessary, the mechanism of coercion legitimised by society (the law) will support its authority.

The notion of power being legitimised through authority has a number of important implications for industrial relations:

1. It induces a perception that the **use of power is unacceptable** (wrong/bad) **whilst the exercise of authority is acceptable** (right/good). This is often accompanied by a belief that power should not be used for sectional goals or purposes but only in the furtherance of 'society' goals (i.e. those determined by the dominant values within society). Hence, the existence of a belief that the trade union organisation, through its officials, should act responsibly and if necessary become a 'social police force' to ensure that its members' demands or actions do not threaten to disrupt society.

2. The process of socialisation which induces an acceptance of orders from those appointed to 'govern' (i.e. those in superior social or organisational roles) has produced the so-called **conflict of loyalty** between the individual's role as an employee and a trade union member. The growth and legitimisation of trade unions within both society and the organisation has meant that the individual's shop steward and union official are just as likely to be perceived as authority roles as management.

3. The **rights or entitlements of subordinates** are closely bound up with the exercise of power and authority – or, more particularly, its control. Some subordinate rights are formally legitimised by direct management acquiescence through the process of collective bargaining. Through this process the exercise of managerial power and authority becomes, in certain areas, subject to the subordinates' formal acceptance and agreement and may involve at least a partial accommodation between dominant and subordinate values. The precise nature and extent of these rights will vary depending on the power relationship between the parties involved in the negotiation. Other subordinate rights may be created and supported by society through the law imposing an external control on the exercise of managerial power and authority (for example, dismissals). Such rights are universal and not, as in collective bargaining, directly dependent on the power of subordinates to influence their management. However, they are dependent on the wider power of the subordinate groups as a whole to influence society's decision making process (i.e. the government). Equally, of course, the law may maintain or extend managerial power and authority and even negate subordinate rights

which have been obtained through collective bargaining (for example, the introduction of legal restrictions on the operation of Union Membership Agreements). Finally, other rights (such as the 'right' to strike) appear to rest on management's informal condonation of such actions by surbordinates (i.e. the preparedness of management not to exercise their socialised or legal rights against such actions). Such a process requires no formal concession to the subordinates' values and continues only so long as the action does not present a serious threat to the dominant's position or values.

3.4 Individualism and collectivism

A frequently expressed value throughout much of a modern industrialised society is the importance of the individual. In the employment sphere this is reflected in a belief that people should not be lumped together simply as units of a factor of production or treated impersonally as a number on a clockcard. Rather they should be seen as individual human beings each with his or her own aspirations, attitudes and attributes and each, in their own sphere of work, able to make a unique and significant contribution to the successful operation of the organisation. This philosophy appears to be at variance with the collective nature of much of industrial relations. Certainly, a number of very important aspects of industrial relations centre on the question of how much freedom should be allowed to the individual or how far the needs of a collective system should predominate.

In the UK context, waged work in industry was regarded in the beginning as little more than a continuation of the individual master/servant relationship associated with the earlier 'feudal' type agriculture and domestic work situation. It was in response to this harsh, coercive or, at best, paternalist subordinated individual relationship that employees combined together to redress the power imbalance and secure a less asymmetrical relationship. However, it would be too simplistic to equate the management–employee relationship with 'individualism' and the management–union relationship with 'collectivism'. It is important to realise that the inputs of both management and unions into the industrial relations system contain elements of both individualism and collectivism. It is this interrelationship between individualism and collectivism which lies at the heart of industrial relations. Perhaps the real issue in respect of the balance between the two is not one of an absolute freedom or constraint of the individual employee *per se* but rather the degree to which the individual is, or should be, (a) responsible and subordinated to, (b) regulated by, and/or (c) protected against either or both of the two collectivities with which he/she has dealings – the employing organisation and the union.

It is important to recognise that **the terms 'individualism' and**

'collectivism' may be used to refer to different aspects of industrial relations. For example, they may refer to the extent to which:

1. Management is free to deal with *its* employees as *it* sees best without any intermediary constraint or filter of a trade union; *or* trade unions, as the collective representative of employees, regulate the work situation on an equal and joint basis with management.
2. Employees are treated differentially: for example, individuals doing the same work receive different pay dependent on their individual attributes, abilities or performance (individual contract); *or* employees receive the same terms and conditions of employment (common collective contract) irrespective of their individual attributes, abilities or performance.
3. The individual perceives his/her economic or social well-being to be a matter for his/her own efforts independent of any peer group (the concept of egotism); *or* the individual perceives a bond with fellow employees and believes that individual needs can only be met via collective action (the concept of fraternalism).

It is often argued that the fundamental basis of a democratic society is the **freedom of the individual**; the freedom to choose and make decisions in respect of the conduct of the individual's life. However, there is no such thing in any society as total freedom to do as one wishes: 'individual freedom' is a relative not absolute concept. At the society level, it is generally accepted that the individual has freedom of action only where that action does not harm others or interfere with the 'rights' or 'freedoms' of others. However, from a Marxist perspective, it may be argued that these 'rights' or 'freedoms' are determined by the dominant values within society and, therefore, any change in the basis of society can be achieved only by actions which will be regarded as a challenge to those dominant values and harmful to or an interference with the existing 'rights' of others. At a lower level, whenever an individual joins an organisation – whether it is a company, trade union, political party or even a social club – he/she agrees, explicitly or implicitly, to abide by the objectives, rules and decisions of that organisation and, in so doing, relinquishes the 'freedom' to act independently for the period of membership. If at any time the decisions of the organisation or the restrictions placed on the individual's freedom are considered to be unacceptable, then he/she may choose between seeking change whilst remaining a member of the organisation or resigning from the organisation.

An important element of the debate, at least in industrial relations, appears to centre on **whether or not the act of joining an organisation and the associated relinquishing of individual freedom is voluntary**. For example, it has been argued that if trade union membership is not voluntary (i.e. if the individual is coerced into membership without the opportunity to exercise choice) then it is an unacceptable use of power and negation of individual freedom which requires legal intervention to restore and protect the individual's 'rights'. Indeed, some distinguish between the individual's relationship to the trade union (which may appear involuntary where there is either a Union Membership Agreement or pressure from work colleagues to join the union) and the individual's relationship to the employer (which appears to be voluntary in that the individual may choose whether or not to work for a particular organisation). Yet, is an individual's acceptance or continuation of employment at a low wage during times of high unemployment when the employer 'can always get someone else' any more or less of a voluntary act, any more or less coerced, than an individual being required to join a trade union as part of his/her acceptance or continuation of employment? All decisions involve elements of voluntariness and coercion or pressure.

A **collective basis to the employment relationship** exists because it meets certain needs of both management and employees. On the management side, a modern organisation encompasses a variety of specialised tasks and roles which require to be integrated, co-ordinated and regulated to achieve the effective operation of the organisation. Thus, management defines the tasks and responsibilities of each role (through job descriptions, organisational planning, operating procedures, etc.) and plans its work arrangements and the numbers of each specialism (through work study, manpower planning, etc.). Each employee fits within this **systematised arrangement of tasks, roles and operations** as part of a particular department, category of employee or operational activity – whether process worker, technician, clerk or manager. The creation of groups of people with similar tasks/roles within the organisation is generally accompanied, even without trade unions and collective bargaining, by similar treatment in respect of the reward system and other conditions of employment. Thus, management's own arrangement of its operations induces the development of a collective basis to the employment relationship. The collective basis is enhanced when, with the advent of trade unionism within the organisation, it becomes formalised through written agreements and procedures.

On the employees' side, the fact that the individual is a member of a group subject to the same controls and terms and conditions of employment means that, for most individuals, any **improvements in their personal situation can be achieved only by improving the group's situation**: individualism has to be replaced by collectivism. The individual, by combining with others, not only establishes the means to protect his/her interests and improve terms and conditions of employment but also increases his/her power vis-à-vis management and is able to secure a more favourable outcome than by acting as an individual. The individual is no longer one person who may easily be replaced by another person but part of a collectivity for which it is more difficult for management to find a substitute – certainly at short notice. However, the power and ability of the employees' collectivity to further the individual's interests rests largely on its internal **fraternalism/solidarity**: that is, the extent to which the individual members are prepared to subordinate personal aspirations to the collective needs, goals and decisions of the group. The individual is free to dissent and oppose during the decision making process but once the collective decision has been made he/she is expected to support it and, if necessary, display collective solidarity. The collectivity must ensure the organisation, control and compliance of its members.

The emphasis on collectivism in the determination of the employment relationship is closely associated with the notion of **voluntarism**: that is, the freedom of the parties to organise themselves, to determine the nature and content of their relationship and to regulate it without governmental or legal intervention. Within this principle both management and trade unions, as the parties responsible for the conduct of collective relations, have an interest and responsibility to ensure that individuals on either side do not, through their actions, challenge or undermine the operation and authority of the collective system. There is certainly an expectation that individual managers and union members will comply with collective agreements made on their behalf. Thus, it may be argued, the foundation of 'voluntarism' in industrial relations is the control of individuals – if necessary by coercion.

Individual subordination to collective interests appears to clash with society's notion of 'freedom of the individual'. However, **the law** treats the employer/employee relationship differently to the trade union/member relationship. In the former, even though there has been some legislative restriction of management's exercise of control over its employees (e.g. Unfair Dismissal), the common law still supports the corporate power position of the organisation (management) by assuming the individual's contract of employment to be one made voluntarily between equals and by establishing an asymmetrical set of rights and obligations which clearly favour management over the individual. In the latter, particularly as a result of the 1980s legislation, the law is directed towards supporting individualism by allowing the individual to exercise freedom in respect of not joining a trade union or not taking part in industrial action. Such protection or advancement of the rights of the individual at the expense of the collectivity must weaken the solidarity, and therefore the power, of the trade union. Clearly, therefore, the issue of individualism versus collectivism is closely bound up with perceptions regarding what is the legitimate exercise of power and authority within the employment relationship.

3.5 Rights and responsibilities

A '**right**' is generally defined as 'a just or legal claim or title' or 'that which is due to anyone by law, tradition or nature' and appears to rest on two distinctive groups of concepts. First, there are concepts (such as 'freedom' and 'entitlement') which seem to imply a positive approach wherein the 'right' is regarded as being fundamental in nature and universally applicable to all – for example, a right to freedom of speech. However, such freedom may not be absolute and without constraint where it impinges on the right or freedom of others – for example, the constraints placed on freedom of speech in respect of libel, slander, incitement to racial hatred, etc. Secondly, there are concepts (such as 'privilege' or 'immunity') which suggest a negative approach wherein the 'right' is regarded as a special advantage not given to others or an exemption from a general obligation or duty – for example, the 'right to strike' in Britain is based on providing immunity from a tort claim for damages. It is important to recognise that such an immunity does not remove the 'wrong'; it is only the sanction for committing that 'wrong' which is waived. It is this latter notion which gives rise to the idea that a 'right' is something which has to be earned.

Perhaps one of the most fundamental 'rights' issues in industrial relations is that of **'managerial prerogative'** or **'management's right to manage'**. 'Prerogative' is often defined as 'an *exclusive* right or privilege held by a person or group especially an hereditary or official right'. Managerial prerogative has been characterised by Storey as representing 'an area of decision making over which management believes it should have (and acts as if it does have) sole and exclusive rights of determination' [21] and by Marsh as carrying with it 'the implication that there are actions or areas for action so essential to management that these must remain unilaterally the property of management if management itself is to continue to exist' [22]. The idea of the existence of a managerial prerogative has been derived initially from the pre-eminence given to management's agency relationship to the owner (provider of capital) within the capitalist system and more latterly from its perceived monopoly of expertise to make the right organisational judgements and decisions. Arguably, it is against this perceived fundamental right that the rights of employees have to be judged. Perhaps management needs no more than an acceptance of its general socialised 'right to manage' whereas employees need a myriad of specific legislated rights if there is to be any sort of balance.

The term **'responsibility'** is defined as 'a duty, obligation or burden' or 'having control over something'. Again, the definitions seem to imply two very different views of the effect of a 'responsibility' on the individual. On the one hand it seems to imply a constraint on the individual's freedom to act (the concept of accountability – 'I have a responsibility to'), whilst on the other hand it seems to imply having the freedom or discretion to make decisions and exercise judgement (the concept of control – 'I have responsibility for'). Responsibility *to* and responsibility *for* are often interlinked – a manager may have a responsibility *to* (accountable) his/her superior *for* (control) the effective and efficient operation of a part of the organisation, whilst trade union leaders have a responsibility to their members *for* protecting their interests, maintaining and improving their terms and conditions of employment and maintaining the integrity, continuity and strength of the union as an organisation. It is important to recognise that a 'responsibility' may be either internally generated from within the individual's own personal perceptions and beliefs or may arise from the external expectations of others in a positive way (*given to* the individual) or negative way (*forced on* the individual).

The 'rights' and 'responsibilities' within a social relationship are not determined by one role unilaterally (unless that role has power to impose its expectations on others) but rather result from an interaction between different role expectations. It is the range, balance and **interaction between 'rights' and 'responsibilities'** and the extent to which these are implicitly or explicitly stated and accepted or challenged which demonstrate the nature and quality of social relationships. They reflect our social values and beliefs about the way we expect people to behave and relate to each other, what degree of freedom and/or control they have and what degree of accountability we expect in return. Ideally, perhaps, there should be congruence between the perceptions the different roles have of their respective rights and responsibilities but there is always bound to be potential conflict between the idea that 'I should have the right' and 'we allow you the right' and between the responsibility a person seeks and that which is expected of them. At the same time, the rights and responsibilities of one will impinge on the rights and responsibilities of others.

So far as industrial relations is concerned, the explicit statement of 'rights' and 'responsibilities' may be codified and enforced within the bipartite rule making of the industrial relations system as well as being set out in society's legislation. The industrial relationship is more than just a simple individual wage/work exchange (economic) or contract of employment (legal): it is also about the power and authority relationship between groups within the workplace. The fact that the interaction is, at least in part, determined by the perceived relative power relationship means that **the existence of 'rights' and 'responsibilities' is inextricably linked to the concepts of 'power' and 'authority'**. It might be argued that the law is simply an impartial expression of accepted social expectations about human behaviour and that the legal underpinning of rights is a reflection, codification and demonstration of society's willingness to provide protection and enforcement for those whose right is being infringed or restricted by others. However, much of the law in industrial relations may not be universally or even widely accepted but may result from the views of a sectional interest within society predominating within the political system. Therefore, the explicit statement of 'rights' and 'responsibilities' within legislation may be little more than the use of State power to impose the beliefs and expectations of one group on others.

There appears to be some interesting **perceptions of the relationship between 'rights' and 'responsibilities'**:

1.   Must a 'right' carry with it some equal and opposite 'responsibility'? For

example, does the right to strike also imply a responsibility to exercise that right with discretion (in particular not to inflict irreparable harm to the employer or harm 'innocent' bystanders) and should that responsibility be codified in law (so curtailing or redefining the right)? This view is based on the belief that the 'right' is a 'privilege' which can be withdrawn if the behaviour in exercising that right is deemed by others to be unacceptable.

2. Does the existence of a 'right' imply a responsibility on the part of others to ensure that the right can be exercised effectively? For example, it can be argued that the basic right of employees to associate and organise can only have real meaning and effect if a responsibility is placed on the employer to recognise and bargain with the employees' association and the employees have the further positive 'right' to withdraw labour temporarily without fear of losing their jobs.

3. Can responsibility, in terms of accountability, only be invoked if there is the right to control? For example, reference is frequently made to both management's *responsibility* to secure the future well-being of the organisation and management's *right* to manage the organisation. Does the same then also apply in respect of a union's leadership?

4. Are references to 'rights' and 'responsibilities' used simply to help justify (legitimise) particular perceptions and beliefs? For example, during the 1980s the Government espoused the view that 'unions have a responsibility to represent the views and interests of *all* their members', that a union's leadership and policies do not reflect the wishes of the 'silent majority' (who do not participate in union affairs) and, therefore, the union leadership should moderate its demands in order to secure the future prosperity of the organisations for which its members work and so protect the long-term interests of its members – the Government's perception of what is responsible union behaviour!

3.6 Integrity and trust

Although the phrase 'it's a matter of principle' is heard frequently in industrial relations, there are many who perceive it to be largely a matter of *ad hoc* expediency based only on the principles of subterfuge, opportunism and 'wheeler-dealing'. However, the conduct of the personal relations which underpin industrial relations is very much concerned with the values of integrity and trust – whether between employee and supervisor; between shop steward and member, full-time official or manager; between industrial relations manager and other managers; or between negotiators.

Integrity must be defined in terms of **the individual acting in accordance with his or her personal values and beliefs (ethics)** rather than in terms of the individual acting according to some 'universally accepted' code of conduct. Thus, a Marxist shop steward seeking through his/her actions to overthrow capitalism and managerial authority is acting with as much integrity as the manager seeking to maintain them. The essential quality of integrity (honesty) is that the individual's words and actions should be seen by others to coincide and express a consistent set of values. A problem may arise for the individual where personal values and beliefs do not coincide with the organisational demands placed on the individuals' role. In such a situation the incumbent must, if he/she is to maintain integrity and cannot change the organisational demands, either refuse to meet those demands and face any consequences or resign. If personal integrity is compromised (i.e. present statements or actions conflict with the values perceived by others to underlay previous statements or actions) then the trust and respect of others will be lost. It may be argued that the only 'matter of principle' in industrial relations is the maintenance of personal integrity.

Trust may be established only between people rather than between organisational collectivities called 'management' and 'union': inter-organisational trust stems from interpersonal trust. At a general level, but equally applicable to the interpersonal level, Fox [23] differentiates between 'high trust' employment relationships, in which management and employees are prepared to accept an informal 'give and take' basis to their relationship, and 'low trust' relationships where there is greater formalisation of the control within the relationship. Interpersonal trust exists where the individuals have confidence in, and feel able to rely on, one another not to seek actively, or even passively, to harm each other. In industrial relations 'trust' does not require that the individuals will be completely 'open and frank' with each other because within their relationship each recognises that the other may be seeking maximum gain in a situation where there are competing interests and objectives. Rather, the establishment of trust requires the individual not to seek to subvert the other's position or relationship with third parties; to keep his/her word and agreements; to keep confidences or 'off the record' information; and, above all, to accept the legitimacy of the other's role and objectives. Finally, it is important to remember that it is difficult to establish trust but easy to lose it and that, because trust is based on interpersonal relationships between individuals, it is not automatically transferable to new role incumbents.

3.7 Summary proposition

- Perception of industrial relations is individual and value laden: it is based primarily on a belief of what is 'right' in respect of 'fairness' and the exercise of 'power' and 'authority'.

Further reading

- R. Hyman and I. Brough, *Social Values and Industrial Relations*, Blackwell, 1975. This examines the role of values and ideologies in industrial relations and the notion of fairness (particularly in respect of wage bargaining).
- A. Fox, *Beyond Contract: Work, power and trust relations*, Faber, 1974. This examines the nature of power and authority in industry and its effect on the employment relationship.

References

1. R. Hyman and I. Brough, *Social Values and Industrial Relations*, Blackwell, 1975, p. 1.
2. C. Kerr and A. Siegal, 'The interindustry propensity to strike – an international comparison' in A. Kornhauser, R. Dubin and A. M. Ross (eds), *Industrial Conflict*, McGraw-Hill, 1954, p. 204.
3. W. Brown, 'Social determinants of pay' in G. M. Stephenson and C. J. Brotherton (eds), *Industrial Relations: A social psychological approach*, John Wiley & Sons, 1979, p. 122.
4. R. Hyman and I. Brough, *op. cit.*, p. 1.
5. F. Zweig, *The British Worker*, Penguin, 1952, p. 194.
6. R. Hyman and I. Brough, *op. cit.*, p. 8.
7. H. Koontz and C. O'Donnel, *Essentials of Management*, McGraw-Hill, 1974, p. 36.
8. R. Hyman, *Industrial Relations: A Marxist introduction*, Macmillan, 1975, p. 26.
9. J. M. Magenau and D. G. Pruitt, 'The social psychology of bargaining' in G. M. Stephenson and C. J. Brotherton (eds), *op. cit.*, p. 197.
10. P. S. Kirkbride and J. Durcan, 'Bargaining power and industrial relations', *Personnel Review*, 1987.
11. J. M. Magenau and D. G. Pruitt, *op. cit.*
12. R. Hyman, *op. cit.*, p. 26.
13. W. L. French and S. Raven, 'The basis of social power' in D. Cartwright (ed.), *Studies in Social Power*, Michigan, 1959.
14. J. M. Magenau and D. G. Pruitt, *op. cit.*, p. 198.
15. H. Koontz and C. O'Donnell, *op. cit.*, p. 36.
16. A. Fox, *A Sociology of Work in Industry*, Collier Macmillan, 1971, p. 34. Reprinted with permission of the publisher.
17. *ibid.*, pp. 45–6.
18. R. Hyman, *op. cit.*, p. 97.
19. A. Fox, *op. cit.*, p. 40.
20. D. Torrington and J. Chapman, *Personnel Management* (2nd edn), Prentice Hall, 1983, p. 220.
21. J. Storey, *Managerial Prerogative and the Question of Control*, Routledge & Kegan Paul, 1983, p. 102.
22. A. Marsh, *Concise Encyclopedia of Industrial Relations*, Gower, 1979.
23. A. Fox, *Beyond Contract: Work, power and trust relations*, Faber, 1974.

PART B

Participants

Chapter 4

Trade union development and function

4.1 Definition

Trade unions have been described as 'organisations of workers set up to improve the status, pay and conditions of employment of their members' [1], and 'associations of workers who by means of collective bargaining endeavour to improve their working conditions, and economic and social position' [2]. However, the **functional approach** underlying these descriptions will include any organisation which adheres to these purposes irrespective of its 'unionateness'.

Blackburn defined **unionateness** as the extent to which an organisation 'is a whole-hearted trade union, identifying with the labour movement and willing to use all the power of the movement' [3]. He postulated seven characteristics by which to judge unionateness:

1. The organisation regards collective bargaining and the protection of its members interests, as employees, as its major function.
2. It is independent from any influence by employers, particularly in relation to collective bargaining.
3. It is prepared to be 'militant' – use industrial action.
4. It declares itself to be a 'trade union'.
5. It is registered as a trade union.
6. It is affiliated to the TUC.
7. It is affiliated to the Labour Party.

However, (2) and (5) have become bound together through legislative changes.

The concept of 'unionateness' presents serious problems if used to define what constitutes a trade union:

1. There will be differences of opinion as to the criteria which should be

included (e.g. Blackburn's inclusion of affiliation to the Labour Party as evidence of the organisation's commitment to the wider 'labour movement').

2. The inclusion of relative criteria relating to the extent and method of the organisation's representational role requires the identification of some point along a continuum at which 'trade unions' may be divided from other, lesser organisations – and this point will be an arbitrary one. As far as the TUC and its members are concerned, affiliation to the TUC is the crucial criterion and it is only they who are bona fide trade unions!

Any general definition of a trade union must encompass a variety of organisations, with varying degrees of unionateness, ranging from traditional 'manual unions' through 'white collar unions' and 'staff associations' to some 'professional associations'. Three elements are crucial to any definition which distinguishes trade unions from other organisations: the nature of their membership, their purpose, and the means they employ to achieve their purpose. A trade union may, therefore, be defined as:

> **any organisation, whose membership consists of employees, which seeks to organise and represent their interests both in the workplace and society and, in particular, seeks to regulate their employment relationship through the direct process of collective bargaining with management.**

The **legal definition** makes no reference to 'means'; it simply defines a trade union as 'an organisation, whether permanent or temporary, which consists wholly or mainly of workers of one or more descriptions and is an organisation whose principal purposes include the regulation of relations between workers of that description and employers or employers' associations' (S.28, Trade Union and Labour Relations Act (1974)). In addition, the law recognises various gradations of trade unions:

(i)   **Registered Trade Union** – registration provides the trade union with certain advantages in the handling of its financial affairs.

(ii) **Independent Trade Union** – a registered trade union may apply to the Certification Officer for a declaration that it is 'not under the domination or control of an employer and not liable to interference by an employer (arising out of the provision of financial or material support)' (S.30, TULRA (1974)).

(iii) **Recognised Trade Union** – a union which is recognised by management as representing all or part of the workforce for the purpose of collective bargaining.

It is important to note that the purpose of the organisation need not be confined exclusively to employment or industrial matters. The **inclusion of political or social objectives** does not negate an organisation being classified as a trade union. Indeed, the trade union's role in representing its members' interests outside the workplace requires it to participate in 'political' activities. Towers believes that trade unions are 'much more than engines for converting bargaining power into improved pay and conditions for their members . . . they are an integral and important part of the system of checks and balances which compose capitalist, liberal democracies' [4].

4.2 Trade union development

Trade unionism may be seen as a **social response to the advent of industrialisation and capitalism**. The earlier, largely agrarian, semi-feudal society relied primarily on a 'benevolent' state [5] and trade guilds to provide limited protection for peasants and artisans. The development of a new society based on the principle of a paid contractual relationship between 'employer' and 'employee', the emergence of a range of industrially based 'wage earning' classes, together with the withdrawal of the state from the determination of the terms of the new relationship, required 'employees' to create new institutions for their collective protection. The drawing together of individuals, as 'employees', into similar circumstances within new industrial organisations provided the focus for their collective interest. However, as Pelling points out, it is important to remember that the development of trade unionism is not simply the result of structural determinism, nor just a catalogue of dates, events and Acts of Parliament, but is 'concerned with the aspirations and the fears of ordinary people, with their endeavours and their struggles, with their modest successes and their setbacks' [6].

This section briefly examines trade union development in three inter-related areas: organisational, legal and political (see Figure 4.1).

Organisational development

It is difficult to identify the precise origins of the modern trade union organisation. Tannenbaum [7] argued that trade unions should be regarded as an extension and development of the craft guilds because of their similarity of concern for industrial and employment matters (including pay). The difference between the types of organisation reflected the differing social and technological systems of the periods within which each existed; therefore, trade unions represent an organisational development rather than an organisational innovation. The Webbs [8], however, argued that it is the uniqueness of their membership being confined to employees which makes trade unions qualitatively different to the guilds and, therefore, a separate distinct organisational category. Although there is some evidence of trade

80

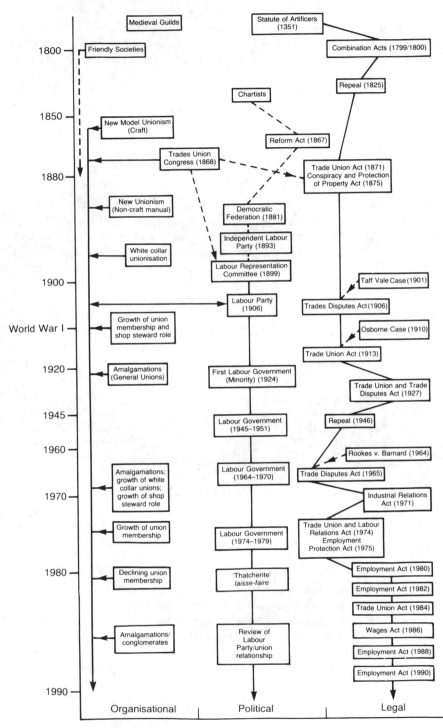

Figure 4.1 *Trade union development*

unionism as early as the 1660s [9] there is no evidence of any continuity of organisation from the craft guilds to these or later embryonic trade unions.

The real beginnings of trade unionism lie in the **Friendly Societies** established by craftsmen in the late eighteenth century. Members contributed a small amount each week and were entitled to receive benefit in the event of sickness, retirement, unemployment or death – **mutual insurance.** These societies also provided a forum for discussing wages and other employment matters which, on occasions, led to the formulation of a 'wage claim'; however, these were generally couched in a subservient manner and processed not through recognised channels of collective bargaining with the employer but in the form of a petition to the employer or Parliament. Sometimes these societies established a loose co-operation to provide assistance to members who were 'on the tramp' – this included providing lodgings, help in seeking work and finance to move on to the next town if work was not available. Less often the co-operation involved financial or other help to a society whose members were in dispute with their employers. Co-operation was not permanent and might be withdrawn because of a shortage of funds or the rivalries which existed between societies.

Following the repeal of the Combination Acts in 1824, workers could openly organise trade unions rather than under the guise of Friendly Societies. Attempts were made to establish trade unions on a more national basis and to widen their employment range. However, these organisations encountered many difficulties and often existed for only a few years. They relied on the officers of one of the member societies to provide the secretariat for the whole organisation and were, therefore, subject to the rivalry, and even hostility, which existed between the local societies. Attempts were also made to establish **one consolidated trade union** to represent all workers irrespective of their trade or locality as part of a process of mobilising the 'working classes' on a collective basis to press for political and social reform. Perhaps the best known example is the Grand National Consolidated Trade Union (1834). Organisationally, the GNCTU was a matrix federation of separate trade or industry sections linked together at the district level. Like similar organisations of the period, it only lasted for a short period because its limited funds were soon drained by a series of strikes.

In the mid-nineteenth century the first modern trade unions were founded amongst craftsmen – **new model unionism**: (the Amalgamated Society of Engineers (now AEU) in 1851). Apprentice-served craftsmen not only had the ability to read and write, which was essential for the development and maintenance of an organisation, and were better paid and in more regular employment than other workers, but, importantly, also had industrial strength derived from their possession of a scarce skill. The new model involved an organisational hierarchy from national to branch level with a separate head office and full-time General Secretary rather than relying on the officers of a dominant branch or society to carry out this function as in earlier attempts. Despite the apparent move towards a bureaucratic form of organisation they relied heavily on their lay membership to administer and govern the union. As these unions achieved the permanency lacking in earlier national societies, so it became possible for them to secure recognition from employers and undertake collective bargaining.

During the second half of the nineteenth century **trade union co-operation** became established at the local and national levels, initially to represent their views to government and seek reforms in legislation. Although trade unions previously had worked together on a transient basis, they now joined with other types of organisations which sought to represent the 'working classes' on a more formal, permanent basis in local **Trades Councils**. In 1868 a congress of Trades Councils representatives, called to discuss issues of concern to the trade union movement, laid the foundation for the present **Trades Union Congress** (TUC). Although no formal organisation was established at that time, further congresses were held involving trade union representatives and, in 1871, a Parliamentary Committee with a full-time secretary was established as the executive body of Congress to provide a focus for political pressure (this committee became, in 1920, the General Council of the TUC). In 1895 significant changes were made within Congress: the exclusion of Trades Council delegates and the introduction of the 'block voting' system (i.e. vote in proportion to the union's membership size). From that point the TUC's membership was confined solely to trade unions.

During the 1880s non-craft manual workers began to organise on permanent basis – **new unionism**: (gas workers' and dockers' unions were formed in 1889 which provided the forerunners of the modern GMBATU and T&GWU respectively). These unions organised the semi-skilled and unskilled, poorer-paid workers and had to rely heavily on organising large groups as their source of industrial power because, as Lovell notes, 'it was only in times of exceptionally high employment that the mass of workers possessed any bargaining power' [10]. Cole also notes that as a result they 'dispensed with friendly benefits altogether, and concentrated on the possession of funds for use in strikes and lockouts and in the expenses of organising and administration' [11]. Furthermore, because of their largely illiterate membership, they relied more heavily than the earlier craft unions on the use of outsiders to organise and run the union – a feature which is reflected today in their different organisational arrangements. At the same time **white collar unionism** was also being established (the National Union of Elementary Teachers in 1870 (now NUT), the Clerks Union in 1890 (later APEX) and the Municipal Officers Association in 1894 (now NALGO)).

Thus, by the end of the nineteenth century the foundations of the modern trade union movement had been laid – permanent organisations representing a wide range of manual and non-manual employees with the TUC providing a focal point for co-ordination.

The increase in union membership and a change in management and government attitude towards trade unionism in order to secure co-operation during World War I resulted in the increasing **appearance of shop stewards** who, as Pelling notes, 'had existed before the war, but they had received little general notice, and their activities were often curbed by intolerant employers' [12]. The period was closely associated with the political growth of the Shop Stewards Movement and syndicalism which, although confined to a small number of major engineering, shipbuilding and munitions factories, sought to mobilise the rank and file union movement to secure the workers control of industry. Although the shop steward role declined during the inter-war period, its re-emergence from the 1960s, as a consequence of full employment and the reform and formalisation of industrial relations at the organisational level, led Turner *et al.* [13] to adopt the phrase 'parallel unionism'; that is, a focal point for the membership and industrial relations activity and a possible challenge to the formal, official union organisation.

During the twentieth century there has been a **significant reduction in the number of trade unions** from a peak of 1,384 in 1920 to 309 in 1989 (Appendix 1). This reduction has been associated with the process of union amalgamations which, although continuous, accelerated in the 1920s, the late 1940s and since the mid-1960s. This resulted in the **evolution of 'open' general or conglomerate unions** through reducing membership homogeneity. This, in turn, has led unions to reconsider their internal organisation so as to better reflect and represent the differing needs and aspirations of diverse groups within their membership. The variety of sectional interests displayed in earlier periods by a multiplicity of trade unions is now reflected within the unions' internal organisational arrangements. The significant growth in union membership displayed during the 1970s was primarily due to an **increase in white collar unionisation**. Price and Bain [14] show that between 1968 and 1979 manual union membership rose by 14 per cent against a decline in potential membership of 9 per cent whilst white collar unionisation rose by 67 per cent against an increase of only 24 per cent in potential membership. The importance for the trade union movement of this growth in white collar unionisation is that it now accounts for half of trade union membership and therefore exerts a greater influence in trade union thinking. In organisational terms, its importance has been reflected in the creation of separate white collar sections in most major manual unions. The substantial decline in union membership since 1979 and the consequent desire of trade unions to recruit more women, part-time employees and black employees has led some unions to amend their organisational arrangements to be more representative of their interests and so encourage more of them to join (for example, reserved places on the NEC and other committees for women and the call for unions to establish 'black' sections).

Legal development

The legal rights of trade unions reflect the attitude of the government of the day. However, even where legislation is established it has to be interpreted by the courts and whilst the trade union movement may be able to influence the nature and extent of legislation, its influence on the interpretation of that legislation by the courts is very limited.

The **Combination Acts (1799/1800)**, rather than being the first trade union legislation, were the last in a line of legislation (originating in the Statute of Artificers (1351)) which sought to restrict the freedom of people to combine in organisations to further their interests and which might be used to subvert the process of government and act as a cover for rebellion. Certainly, Pelling [15] has questioned their significance in repressing the development of trade unions. The combinations affected by these Acts were already illegal under both common law and other statutes and the penalties which could be imposed by the courts under these Acts were, in fact, less harsh; for example, the maximum penalty was two months imprisonment compared to seven years transportation given to the Tolpuddle Martyrs in 1834 under the Unlawful Oaths Act (1797).

The basis of a restrictive approach towards trade unions was founded on the **civil doctrine of restraint of trade** (any agreement which restricted trade or competition was void and unenforceable) and the **criminal offence of conspiracy**. These concepts were to play an important part in the legal development of trade unions. The attitude of the courts was clearly seen in 1855, after the repeal of the Combination Acts, when it was argued that to treat a trade union as anything other than an illegal agreement in restraint of trade 'would establish a principle upon which the fantastic and mischievious notion of a "Labour Parliament" might be realised for regulating the wages and the hours of labour in every branch of trade all over the empire' with 'the most disastrous consequences' [16]. This restrictive approach was seen also in the individual employee's contractual position. Since 1351 employees had been guilty of a criminal offence if they failed to fulfil the terms of their contract of employment. Wedderburn notes that 'in 1854 over 3,000 workers were imprisoned for leaving or neglecting their work' whilst in 1872, despite revisions in the Master and Servant Act (1867), 'the figure reached 17,100 prosecution and 10,400 convictions' [17].

The Combination Acts were repealed in 1824/1825. However, Hawkins argues that the effect of this was to provide 'a legal freedom to organize but no corresponding freedom to pursue the objectives of trade unionism' [18]. Certainly, Wedderburn points out that even when the criminal offences relating to intimidation and threats were amended by the Molestation of Workmen Act [1859], so as to exclude peaceful persuasion of employees to strike from criminal liability, 'many of the judges' decisions scarcely registered this amendment' [19]. It was not until the 1870s that there were the beginnings of a real change in the legal status of trade unions.

The **Trade Union Act (1871)** and the **Conspiracy and Protection of Property Act (1875)** established that trade unions were not to be regarded as criminal conspiracies simply because their purpose was in restraint of trade and that two or more persons acting in contemplation of furtherance of a trade dispute could not be considered a criminal conspiracy unless the act undertaken would be criminal if committed by one person. At the same time, the Employers and Workmen Act (1875) removed criminal liability from the employee for breaching the contract of employment. However, the Conspiracy and Protection of Property Act maintained criminal sanctions for gas and water workers who, by striking, deprived consumers of their supply – this provision was extended in 1919 to include electricity workers and was not removed until the Industrial Relations Act (1971).

However, the legislation still left trade unions open to legal claims based on **civil, as opposed to criminal, liability for conspiracy**. In 1901 it was held that union officials organising a boycott amounted to a conspiracy to injure (*Quinn* v. *Leathem*) and that damages could be enforced against the funds of a union (*Taff Vale Railway Co.* v. *Amalgamated Society of Railway Servants*). This meant that if, during an industrial dispute, the union was successful in exerting economic pressure on the employer then the union or its officials could be liable to reimburse the employer's loss through a claim for damages. It is not surprising, as Vester and Gardiner pointed out, that the 1871 Act 'began to be regarded by many trade unionists as the most oppressive of all the oppressive legislation that had encumbered the growth of their unions, while some blamed the courts for having robbed them of the immunities Parliament had intended to give them' [20]. The position was remedied by the **Trade Disputes Act (1906)** under which:

(i)   trade union funds were protected from civil claims for damages;
(ii) acts done in contemplation or furtherance of a trade dispute were no longer civil conspiracy;
(iii) persons acting in a trade dispute could no longer be liable for inducing a breach of contract of employment; and
(iv) peaceful picketing became lawful.

In 1910 a further omission came to light (*Osborne* v. *Amalgamated Society of Railway Servants*) when it was held that it was *ultra vires* (outside their constitution), and therefore unlawful, for a trade union to raise funds for or contribute to a political party. This was a severe constraint on the unions' ability to further their members' interests by actively assisting in the development of the newly founded Labour Party. The position was reversed by the **Trade Union Act (1913)** which allowed trade unions to participate in political activities providing they established a separate political fund to finance such activities and individual members had the right and opportunity to opt out of contributing to such a fund.

Thus, by the beginning of World War I trade unions had been removed from both criminal and civil liability for actions in pursuit of an industrial dispute and were free to support political parties.

The inter-war period was characterised by not only economic recession but also a regression in the legal status of trade unions. The **Trade Disputes and Trade Union Act (1927)** (following the General Strike in 1926):

  (i)   restricted sympathetic strikes to disputes within the trade or industry of the strikers;

  (ii) made illegal any strike which sought to coerce the government either directly or by inflicting hardship on the community;

 (iii) declared various forms of industrial action to constitute 'intimidation' and therefore illegal;

 (iv) amended the rules relating to political funds by introducing 'contracting in' to replace 'contracting out'.

  (v) prohibited crown servants from joining trade unions which had political objectives or were affiliated to 'outside' bodies such as the TUC; and

 (vi) prohibited local authorities and other public bodies from operating closed shops.

The Act represented a severe curtailment of trade union legal rights; certainly, the introduction of 'contracting in' to the political fund reduced trade union affiliation to the Labour Party by about a third. The Act was repealed in 1946 under the Labour Government.

The period from the end of World War II until the 1970s was virtually free of trade union legislation. However, in *Rookes* v. *Barnard* (1964) it was held that a threat to induce a breach of contract by going on strike could amount to conspiracy to intimidate. Grunfeld points out that 'what startled the trade union world was that, after . . . more than half a century of case law . . . there still remained coiled in the common law the possibility of an action against union officials for crushing damages and costs for threatening strike action in breach of contracts of employment' [21]. The situation was quickly remedied by the **Trade Disputes Act (1965)**.

Since 1971 trade union legislation has passed through a number of fundamental shifts in orientation. The Conservative Government's **Industrial Relations Act (1971)** sought to balance some positive gains for trade unions (statutory recognition procedure, rights to disclosure of information, etc.) against a comprehensive redirection of the law to bring trade unions under greater statutory regulation and public accountability (in particular, protecting the individual in a closed shop and subjecting it to periodic review; regulating union rules through the registration procedure; restricting immunity only to official industrial action and providing for compulsory strike ballots and 'cooling off' periods in certain major strikes; and presuming collective agreements to be legally enforceable). Although the Act was only in effective existence for some two years it provoked extensive hostility and active resistance from the trade union movement and resulted in court cases involving the imprisonment of shop stewards and the sequestration of union funds [22]. In 1974/5 the Labour Government sought to support trade unions and collective bargaining by not only restoring trade union immunities to the pre-1971 position and extending them to include breach of commercial as well as employment contracts (**Trade Union & Labour Relations Act (1974)**) but also confirming the union's right to disclosure of information and adding the right to be consulted in a redundancy; time off for trade union activities and the right to refer a claim to the CAC that an employer was not observing the recognised or general terms and conditions (**Employment Protection Act (1975)**).

In marked contrast, the Conservative Government's strategy during the 1980s, based on a liberalist/*laissez-faire* ideology, has been to redress the perceived power imbalance in favour of trade unions and allow management to re-exert its prerogative, promote 'responsible' trade unionism and protect individual members against union 'tyranny'. The legislation was introduced in stages (**Employment Acts 1980 & 1982, Trade Union Act 1984, Wages Act 1986 and Employment Acts 1988 & 1990**) and has:

1. restricted and then removed immunity from secondary industrial action and made secondary picketing unlawful;
2. required unions to ballot on industrial action and made them responsible for any unlawful actions authorised by the union's officers, committees or shop stewards unless they repudiate such action;
3. given individual members the right not to be disciplined by their union for not undertaking industrial action (even if lawful and supported by a majority vote in favour);
4. made it easier for the employer to dismiss strikers (particularly in an unofficial strike);
5. restricted and then removed the closed shop (Union Membership Agreement);
6. required unions to elect their NEC, General Secretary and President by direct secret ballot with independent scrutineers;
7. given individual members legal rights to inspect the union's accounts and challenge unlawful actions;
8. restricted the scope of Wages Councils.

Like the 1920s, its introduction coincided with economic circumstances and management strategies which weakened trade unionism. Despite the fact that it was initially resisted by trade unions (including a number of major disputes where, through employer action to enforce these new rights, unions were fined for contempt of court and had their funds sequestrated), nevertheless it appears that trade unions have now resigned themselves to having to work within this legal regulation. Certainly, it would appear that the Labour Party does not intend, if returned to power, to repeal all this legislation, but rather may introduce a more positive 'right to strike' (which would reduce the employers' ability to dismiss strikers) and introduce legislation which would strengthen the unions' collective bargaining role and right to be involved in organisational decision making.

Political development

The nineteenth century was a period of considerable political as well as industrial change. It started with two major political parties (Conservative and Liberal) and finished with the emergence of a third (Labour) representing the interests of the 'working classes'. During the twentieth century this party developed to replace the Liberal Party as the viable alternative to the Conservative Party and provided the government for almost half of the post-war period. However, this situation has been challenged by the creation of the Social Democratic Party, largely from disaffected Labour supporters, and its subsequent merger with the Liberal Party.

In their early years trade unions enlisted the support of radical members of existing parties to lead their agitation for industrial reforms and act as their voice within Parliament. Pelling notes that even during the period of the **Chartists Movement**, 'which, confused and inchoate though it was, nevertheless had ambitious national aims based upon the belief in the identity of interests of the entire working class' [23], there were no formal direct links between it and the developing trade union movement. Indeed, he suggests that whilst the development of trade unionism was greatest in times of booming employment and amongst those groups of workers who were relatively unaffected by the industrial changes of the nineteenth century, the impetus for political reform and action came from those who were suffering the greatest effects of these changes and during periods of economic slump.

Even after the Reform Act (1867), which gave urban workers the vote, most trade union leaders supported the Liberal Party and favoured political action within the established political system rather than the creation of a new party. However, by the late nineteenth century organisations with socialist orientations had been formed to give political expression to the 'working class movement'. Finally, in 1893, the **Independent Labour Party** was formed which sought to adopt a middle-of-the-road stance by both opposing collaboration with the Liberal Party and rejecting the revolutionary policies of the socialist parties. Although trade unions had already achieved representation in Parliament (11 union MPs in 1885) they either sat as Liberals or were prepared to co-operate closely with them. A reconciliation between the leadership of the major unions and the socialists concerning the approach and form of political representation, was eventually achieved in 1899 when the TUC Parliamentary Committee agreed to convene a special congress of interested organisations to examine how to improve labour representation in Parliament. This resulted in the establishment of the **Labour Representation Committee (LRC)**.

The initial response of the trade unions was mixed; less than half of the TUC's membership was represented at the special congress. In the 1900 general election the LRC managed to secure the election of only two MPs but in 1906 it won 29 seats and officially changed its name to the **Labour Party**. The relationship between trade unions and the Labour Party has since developed to the extent that the trade unions provide 80 per cent of its annual income and sponsor almost 50 per cent of its MPs. However, it would be wrong to assume that there is overwhelming support for the Labour Party amongst all trade unions or trade unionists. Only about 50 per cent of the unions affiliated to the TUC are also affiliated to the Labour Party; for example, NALGO, NUT and CPSA are not (partly because of the wide spectrum of political views of their membership and party because of their perceived relationship to government at the local and national levels); the level of membership 'contracting out' of the political levy in affiliated unions is 50 per cent or more in some unions; and 'a majority of trade union members no longer vote for the trade unions' party' [24].

Furthermore, the trade unions have found that, in spite of their significant role in the establishment and maintenance of the Labour Party, their special relationship does not result in a subservient Labour government. As early as 1924 the trade unions found that there was 'a permanent difference in point of view between the government on the one hand and the trade unions on the other ... the trade unions had different functions to perform than the functions of government' [25]. The trade union movement has, certainly until 1979, recognised the need and desirability for working with and seeking to influence any government irrespective of its political party. Nevertheless, the underlying affinity between the trade union movement as a whole and the Labour Party, coupled with the reluctance of the Conservative Party to accord trade unions a special role in its deliberations, has resulted in the trade union movement being prepared to give more sympathetic consideration to the problems facing a Labour Government than a Conservative one.

Trade union membership

During the twentieth century there has been a substantial increase in aggregate trade union membership from 2.6 million (15 per cent density) in 1910 to 13.5 million (56 per cent density) in 1979. (**Trade union density** is actual trade union membership as a percentage of potential union membership (those employed, excluding employers, self-employed and the armed forces, plus those unemployed [26].) However, this growth has been neither steady nor continuous; there have been three periods of significant increase in union membership (1911–20, 1934–48 and 1969–79), two followed by a decline in membership (1921–33 and post-1979) and the other followed by a period of slow growth (see Appendix 1 and Figures 4.2 and 4.3).

The level of unionisation is influenced by a number of factors:

1. **Strategic variables** such as changes in the nature and structure of the labour force as between well-organised and less well-organised segments and changes in social values as expressed through government policies [27] and management attitudes and actions.

2. **Economic variables**; Bain and Elsheikh [28] and Disney [29] have put forward a model of union growth related to changes in prices, wages, unemployment and union density:
   (a) **prices** – an increase in the rate of change in retail prices may induce employees to unionise as a means of maintaining or improving their standard of living (positive effect);
   (b) **wages** – a rise in the level of money wages may be perceived not only as an improvement in living standards but also the result of union efforts (positive effect);
   (c) **unemployment** – whilst the threat of redundancy may stimulate an increase in union membership in that organisation (positive effect), a rise in the general level of unemployment affects aggregate union membership to the extent that the unemployed relinquish their membership, those in employment reduce their propensity to organise through concern for their job security, and management becomes more resistant to union claims and even unionisation itself (negative effect);
   (d) **density** – initially, as union density increases, the trade unions' ability to persuade more employees to join also increases and management's ability to resist decreases (positive effect). However, a point may be reached when, through saturation, non-unionists become fewer and more difficult to recruit as a result of organisational or ideological isolation (negative effect).

3. **Organisational variables** such as size, socio-demographic characteristics of the employees and the nature of the union and its leadership may help to explain micro level variations in trade union membership and growth.

It is from the first two groups of variables that Price and Bain conclude that 'the "membership explosion" of 1969–70 [+6.7 per cent] was caused not by economic factors alone but by the favourable conjunction of these factors with greater public support for union recognition and the extension of collective bargaining' [30]. Their analysis of the expansion of trade union membership between 1968 and 1979 showed:

1. female membership increased by 69 per cent compared with 14 per cent

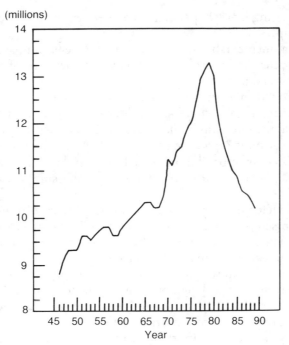

Figure 4.2 *Trade union membership, 1946–89*

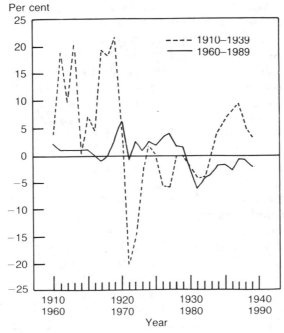

Figure 4.3 *Trade union membership (yearly % change), 1910–39 and 1960–89*

for males (rising from 23 per cent to 30 per cent of total trade union membership);

2. non-manual membership increased by 68 per cent compared with 14 per cent for manual (rising from 31 per cent to 40 per cent of total trade union membership);

3. public sector membership increased by 42 per cent;

4. manufacturing membership increased by only 25 per cent (although non-manual membership in manufacturing increased by 180 per cent it accounted for only 7 per cent of total trade union membership in 1979);

5. private services membership increased by 58 per cent but accounted for less than 10 per cent of total trade union membership in 1979.

They conclude that there was a 'duality' in the pattern of union growth: 'in the well organised sector [public services and manufacturing] economic factors, employer policies, and public support for union recognition combined to produce a major expansion and consolidation of union membership and organisation' whilst 'in the poorly organised sector [particularly private services] neither economic factors nor public support for unionisation was sufficiently strong to overcome hostile employer policies and . . . unfavourable structural characteristics' [31].

This duality is equally important in the context of the **decline in trade union membership since 1979**. Union membership has declined by 3.1 million between 1979 and 1989 (wiping out the gain made during 1968–79) (see Figure 4.2) and there is little evidence, as Bain and Price believed, that union recognition gained during the 1970s would 'act as a ratchet which will prevent union membership slipping away on the scale which . . . occurred during the mass unemployment of the inter-war years' [32]. Indeed, as Figure 4.3 shows, the drop in union membership since 1979, although significantly lower in terms of the yearly rate of loss than the dramatic reversal of union recruitment from +21.5 per cent in 1919 to −20.5 per cent in 1921, has perhaps been more persistent and there is little sign that the trend will be significantly reversed (although a change in the political climate and greater acceptance of trade unionism might help to halt the decline). Much of the reduction, particularly in the early 1980s, resulted from the rapid and substantial decline in employment in the manufacturing sector. In addition, other factors such as reduced inflation, very high and persistent unemployment and government/management strategies aimed at reducing trade union power have combined to reinforce the effect of the change in the composition of the workforce. However, **union density** when measured simply in terms of the proportion of *employees* [33] remains at over 50 per cent in establishments employing more than 25 people in both the manufacturing and service sectors although there are significant variations between sectors, between manual and non-manual and between full and part-time employees (see Figure 4.4). The greatest scope for union recruitment appears to lie not amongst full-time manual (and particularly male)

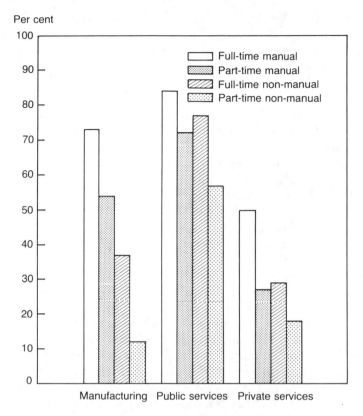

Figure 4.4 *Union density by industry group, 1984, in establishments*
with 25+ employees
Source: N. Millward and M. Stevens, 'Union density in the regions',
Employment Gazette, May 1988, pp. 286–95

employees in manufacturing and public services because they are already 'saturated', but rather amongst part-time, non-manual (particularly female) employees in both manufacturing and private service industries (although there is some scope to increase unionisation amongst full-time manual employees in private service industries).

These are the very areas where trade unions, with the support of the TUC, have been concentrating their **recruitment strategies**. However, they are also the very industries and groups of employees where organisational variables (small and often dispersed establishments) and employer attitudes mitigate against increasing union membership. Their approach can be divided into three strategies [34]:

1.   Improving recruitment literature and strategies (including undertaking local labour market surveys and joint recruitment campaigns in particular localities) aimed at particular groups such as service

organisations, women, part-timers and young people (although Payne points out in respect of young people that their low unionisation 'is due more to their overrepresentation in poorly unionised jobs than to apathy or antagonism towards unionism' [35]).

2. Developing services for individual members (such as legal advice, pension and insurance arrangement and credit cards) which it is felt will appeal to many of these employees who have no 'tradition' of unionism (i.e. do not display the 'fraternalist' attitudes normally associated with unionism).

3. Seeking to establish sole recognition agreements with employers (particularly in 'high-tech' and/or 'greenfield' sites even before employees have been recruited).

However, Mason and Bain criticise the unions for 'little evidence to show that unions have developed *systematic and coherent* strategies' [my italics] and point out that they need to 'shift resources towards recruitment so that the union's aims can be prioritised and implemented' [36].

Willman believes that, in the absence of an aggregate increase in union membership, the relative importance of organisational variables increases and trade unions are essentially **competing for a share of two markets**: in the **membership market** they compete to provide representation, insurance and other services to individuals whilst in the **employer market** they compete to become the bargaining agent and 'voice' of employees in the organisation. He argues that whilst the two 'markets' are normally interrelated – recognition usually depends on sufficient membership, and recruiting and maintaining membership depends on recognition – nevertheless the 'employer market' is to a certain extent independent of the 'membership market', in so far as the model suggests that unions will avoid membership market competition in 'difficult and expensive pre-recognition situations where the employer is hostile' but the 'unorganised or greenfield site employer can "deliver" his workforce into membership quite cheaply" [37]. Unfortunately 'competition in both the employer and membership markets . . . may lead in the long term to further impoverishment of unions and greater dependence on employers' [38].

However, this competition may be mitigated by two factors. First, the TUC has always sought to minimise and regulate conflict between unions over recruitment and has amended the Bridlington Principles to take account of the recent development of 'single union agreements'. Secondly, the continuing decline in the number of unions through amalgamations has been associated with an **increasing concentration of union membership** in a relatively small number of unions (see Table 4.1). In 1989 80 per cent of trade union membership was concentrated in 23 unions over 100,000 members and many have predicted that by the year 2000 there will be only some 10 'giant' conglomerate unions. Whether this will reduce or intensify competition, in the absence of any change in the strategic or economic

Table 4.1 *Distribution of unions and union membership by size, 1939–89*

Size of union	1939			1959			1969			1979			1989		
	Number of unions	% of unions	% of union members	Number of unions	% of unions	% of union members	Number of unions	% of unions	% of union members	Number of unions	% of unions	% of union members	Number of unions	% of unions	% of union members
Under 1,000	680	67.5	2.5	358	55.0	0.9	311	55.0	0.8	244	53.7	0.5	140	45.3	0.3
1,000–10,000	246	24.4	13.8	201	30.9	6.1	165	29.2	5.2	125	27.5	3.0	98	31.7	2.9
10,000–100,000	68	6.8	32.8	75	11.5	25.5	67	11.9	21.8	58	12.8	14.9	48	15.5	16.4
100,000–250,000	13	1.3	50.9	10	1.5	17.7	13	2.3	17.9	16	3.5	19.2	13	4.2	20.0
Over 250,000	–	–	–	7	1.1	49.3	9	1.6	54.2	11	2.4	62.4	10	3.2	60.4
Total	1007			651			565			454			309		

Source: Ministry of Labour and Department of Employment *Gazette* (no category of Over 250,000 given separately for 1939)

factors to increase the level of aggregate union membership, only time will tell.

4.3 Trade union function

An organisation's function may be defined as **the role or task it is required to perform and the means employed to carry it out**. However, it is difficult to consider the function of an organisation without, perhaps misleadingly, ascribing personal attributes to the organisation itself. Hyman emphasises that 'organisations do not perform actions or take decisions: rather, certain people decide and act in the name of the organisation' and '"institutional" needs or interests makes sense only if interpreted as a metaphor for the considerations and priorities motivating those with power within organisations' [39]. The objectives, policies and actions displayed by trade unions derive from the 'leadership's' perception of its function and may be at variance with the perception of individual members or distinct classes of membership. Those charged with leadership and decision making within the organisation may become as much concerned with organisational matters, such as the maintenance of an effective organisation *per se*, as ensuring that the policies and actions of the organisation serve the needs of the membership and fulfil the purpose for which it was established.

Trade union objectives

It often appears attractive to ignore the complexities of trade unions and summarise their function in a single phrase. However, such approaches emphasise only one aspect of trade unions to the exclusion of others and assume that all trade unions see their role in the same light. Thus, the Marxist approach, primarily concerned with the role trade unions might play in developing a socialist society, places emphasis on their being an **expression of class consciousness**, albeit sectional and incomplete, which requires to be mobilised within a 'revolutionary' political party if its full potential is to be achieved. At the other end of the spectrum, there are those concerned about the effects of trade union action on the existing capitalist economic, social and political system and who believe that, above all, the function of a trade union is to conduct its activities in a **socially responsible** manner (i.e. discourage its membership from demanding high wage increases and resorting to industrial action and encourage them to co-operate with management in improving productivity). There are also those who concentrate on the process of collective bargaining employed by trade unions and emphasise their **job regulation and rule making** role in the negotiation of terms and conditions of employment for their membership.

At the same time, comparisons are drawn between the general approach of British trade unions to the performance of their role and that adopted by trade unions in other countries. British trade unions are often referred to as having a **welfare orientation**: that is, they look beyond the narrow economic and industrial interests of their immediate membership and concern themselves with general social, economic and political issues. In contrast, trade unions in the USA are perceived to adopt a more **business orientation** and to be reluctant to question or seek to change the economic, social or political system within which they operate. Their reliance on the use of the collective bargaining process to achieve improved health and welfare provisions for their membership from the employer instead of seeking a general improvement through the political system is a reflection of this general stance. European unions, on the other hand, appear to have a more **political orientation**. This may be attributed, in part, to the significant role played by political parties in their early development. Whilst in Britain trade unions developed first and were instrumental in establishing the political party, in Europe the process was reversed and as a result trade unions are often regarded as the industrial wing of the political parties. As with the USA, the general stance of European unions is reflected in the means adopted in obtaining improvements for their membership – in this case, a greater reliance on statutory regulation.

The function of British trade unions is in reality a mixture of all these approaches. Whilst it is true that trade unionism developed as a countervailing force to the power of management in the labour market and the workplace, and this continues to be the principal area of their activity, nevertheless as Roberts pointed out 'there are few subjects of social significance with which trade unions do not concern themselves' [40].

Whilst the overall role of a trade union may be seen as representing the sectional needs and interests of its membership, it is possible to identify five distinct aspects of their function (see Figure 4.5).

1. **Power**: protect and support the individual by providing a collective strength to act as a countervailing force to the employer and a pressure group within society.
2. **Economic regulation**: maximise the wages and employment of their members within the framework of the wage/work contract of employment.
3. **Job regulation**: establish a joint rule making system which both protects their members from arbitrary management actions and allows them to participate in decision making within the organisation for which they work.
4. **Social change**: express the social cohesion and aspirations or political

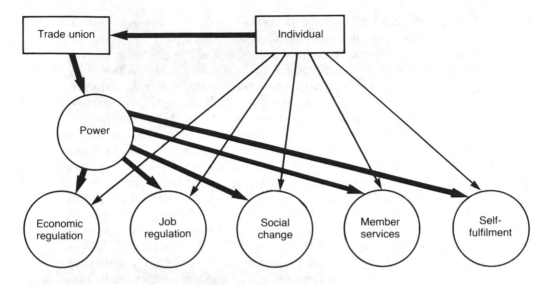

Figure 4.5 *Trade union function*

ideology of their membership and seek to develop a society which reflects this view.

5. **Member services**: provide a range of benefits or services to the individual member.
6. **Self-fulfilment**: provide a mechanism whereby individuals may develop outside the immediate confines of their jobs and participate in decision making processes.

Power

Although **the power function of trade unions is a latent one**, manifest only in the exercise of its other functions, nevertheless Hyman argues that 'a trade union is, first and foremost, an agency and a medium of power' [41]. Without an organisation to represent them, individual employees are at a serious power disadvantage in their relationships with management. Not only do they lack resources in terms of knowledge and expertise to negotiate their terms and conditions of employment on an equal basis, but also the individual is one out of many potential employees who may, as a source of labour, be more easily substituted by management than he/she may substitute the employer as the source of wages. However, by acting in concert, management is less able to treat employees as individual, replaceable units of a commodity but rather is required to regard them as one collective and indivisible unit.

It is the acquisition of power through the collective strength of its membership which, to a large measure, determines the success of the trade union in carrying out its other functions. However, as Perlman has pointed out trade unionism is both '*individualistic* in the sense that it aims to satisfy the individual aspirations . . . for a decent livelihood, for economic security and for freedom from tyranny on the part of the boss' and '*collectivistic*, since it aspires to develop in the individual a willingness to subordinate his own interests to the superior interests of the collectivity' [42]. Whilst most employees join a trade union for instrumental reasons (protection and benefits in improved terms and conditions of employment), this can be achieved only through the power the trade union derives from the collective strength and solidarity of its membership. The power the trade union is able to exert in carrying out its economic and job regulation functions is dependent on its ability to secure concerted and controlled collective responses from its membership. This, in turn, is dependent on the preparedness of the members to forego their individual freedom and recognise the need for collective decision making and action. Hyman points out that 'it is only through the power *over* its members which is vested in the trade union that it is able to exert power *for* them' [43].

Perlman has argued that the **preparedness of the membership to express this collective solidarity** will vary – 'the more distinct the trade identity of a given group and therefore the clearer the boundaries of its particular "job territory", the stronger are normally the bonds which tie members together in a spontaneous solidarity' [44]. The increasing heterogeneity of many trade unions means that the 'bond' of common interest, and therefore collective solidarity, may not encompass the whole union's membership but be restricted to only a section. This is perhaps most pronounced in the union's collective bargaining function where the varied industrial, occupational and organisational composition of its membership may be reflected in different needs and aspirations and may lead, in some situations, to conflict rather than solidarity between different groups of members within the same union. The 'bonding' is most likely to encompass the whole membership, or even the entire trade union movement, only where the membership perceive an overriding commonality of interest (e.g. if government 'incomes policy' is perceived to be affecting all collective bargaining) or where the union as an organisation is perceived to be under threat (e.g. government legislation to restrict trade union activities). Even then, this may be only a tenuous solidarity. Furthermore, collective solidarity is not confined solely to members of the same union. Often there is greater solidarity between members of different unions at the same workplace and experiencing the same work problems than between disparate sections of the same union.

Bain and Price [45], in examining the level of union membership as an indictor of union power, suggested that trade unions seek to exercise power (influence) in three directions:

1. **Within the labour movement** – here a union's power may be related to its size relative to other unions, but other factors such as leadership 'quality' and alliances between unions are also likely to be important.
2. **Towards government** – here union power is not so dependent on the level of aggregate union membership as the government's perceived dependence on trade union support for the achievement of its policies (although, it may be argued, as union membership increases so does the government's perception of their importance and the need for their co-operation).
3. **Towards employers** – here it is not the absolute level of membership but rather union density ('completeness of organisation') which provides the basis of union power; but this may be enhanced or weakened by economic, technological and political factors.

Thus, the external power of trade unions is derived from not only intrinsic factors such as their numerical strength, the importance of the members in the employer's productive process and the degree of collective consciousness amongst the membership, but also the extent to which extrinsic factors such as economic conditions and public policy allow such power to be exercised. It is in this context that the freedom to undertake industrial action is important to trade unions.

Economic regulation

Most rank and file members would emphasise the **collective negotiation of wages and other monetary terms of employment** (including hours and holidays) as a major, if not *the* major, function of a trade union. The importance of this function extends well beyond those union members or employees who are the direct recipients of the improvements negotiated by a trade union. For example:

1. The level of wages and other rewards negotiated in areas where trade unionism is strong often become, through a process of comparison, the benchmarks for wages in areas of weak unionism and even for non-union groups of employees and non-union firms.
2. The level of wages resulting directly or indirectly from collective bargaining is a major input into the economic system and may be significant in determining not only employment levels and production costs but also overall demand in the economy, inflation, the balance of payments and economic growth.

Economists, such as Mulvey [46], argue that a trade union, in carrying out its economic regulation function, is seeking to behave in a rational economic manner by maximising some aspect of the wage/employment relationship.

However, it is necessary to refer first to the individual employee. The traditional economic view is that **the individual's wage policy** is to maximise satisfaction (utility) in respect of income and leisure. It is argued that the individual will seek, where possible, to work up to a point where the 'cost' of foregoing an additional hour's leisure equates to the value placed on the wages received for that hour. However, this assumes that the individual may expand working time until this point is reached. Clearly this is untrue for most employees with a fixed working week and, at best, only a limited opportunity to work extra time. It is perhaps better to regard the individual as seeking to maximise earnings against a personal notion of an acceptable standard of living.

The **union's wage policy** is regarded as seeking to maximise satisfaction (utility) in respect of wages and employment ($U_1, \ldots U_n$, for different levels of labour demand in Figure 4.6). However, because trade unions do not unilaterally determine wage levels but do so through the joint process of collective bargaining, the *actual* level of wages and consequent level of employment will be determined by the relative bargaining power of the parties involved and may be different to the *optimum* preferred by the union. Nevertheless, Mulvey argues, the future wage policy of the union will still be closely linked to its utility function. This is depicted by line *YXZ* which links the union's maximisation points for different levels of demand. The change in angle at point *X* indicates 'that unions will vigorously resist wage

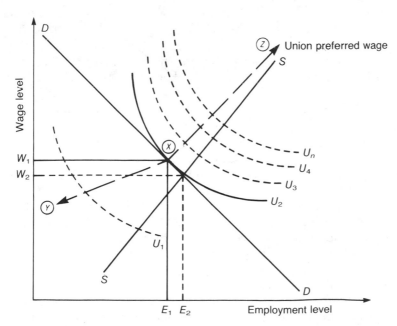

Figure 4.6 *Union wage policy – an economic model*

reductions and trade away employment to do so when demand falls, whereas when demand rises they will tend to divide the demand increases more equally between wage increases and employment growth' [47]. Finally, the implication of the supply curve of labour (S–S) in relation to the union's wage preference line (YXZ) is that a union will always seek to maintain a level of wages higher than the level that would result simply from the unrestricted interaction of supply and demand even though if left to market forces the level of employment might be higher. Thus, by seeking a wage level (W_1) above the market level (W_2) the union is prepared to accept a level of employment (E_1) below the market level (E_2).

Robertson and Thomas have gone further and suggested that the objective of trade union wage policy is 'to secure the maximum "real" wage consistent with full (or "high") employment of a union's membership . . . and consistent with the members' leisure–income choice' [48]. The introduction of the concepts of 'real' wages and 'full' employment as opposed to 'money' wages and 'maximising' employment, whilst certainly relevant, makes it even more difficult to convert the theory of union wage policy into practical action. If it is difficult for a trade union to assess the impact of a change in wage levels on the employment level of its membership, it is even more difficult for it to determine, with any precision, what effect a given increase in money wages (which is the core of any wage bargaining) will have on members' real wages or full employment without a degree of certain knowledge regarding other factors which impinge on these objectives (e.g. interest rates, cost of living, taxation and government policies on employment). In the absence of such knowledge the trade union can only rely on maximising money wages as the means of maximising real wages. The equation is made more complex if the union's maximisation of wage and employment levels is to be consistent with the minimisation of the working week which economists assume to be inherent in the members' leisure–income choice. However, it is made easier if it is assumed that the individual is seeking to maximise income – which, from pressure to continue working overtime even when there is unemployment amongst the membership, appears to be the case. Finally, this approach is deficient in not identifying whether it is the present or potential membership for which the union is seeking to maximise wage levels and employment and whether it is seeking to do so in the short term or long term.

On the other hand there are those, such as Ross [49] as early as the 1940s, who emphasise the **political nature of the union's wage policy** and argue that it is the result of a reconciliation, by the leadership, of conflicting priorities amongst a generally heterogeneous membership. In their view, the policies and actions of trade unions in wage bargaining do not represent the results of rational economic decisions. Certainly, Mulvey accepts that in practice 'most trade unions formulate their wages policy with an eye to the wage policy they expect or observe other unions to follow' [50]. This may be due partly to the difficulties of applying an economic maximising approach and partly to the existence of perceived relationships between the wages of different groups of employees. These perceived relationships may be based on:

1. **comparability** or 'horizontal equity' between similar work in different organisations or industries; or
2. **differentials** or 'vertical equity' between different work or levels within the same organisation or industry.

The effect of this is to establish a wage and salary structure with a relatively high degree of rigidity which reflects neither the relative bargaining power of different groups or trade unions in different industrial or economic circumstances nor the supply and demand for different categories of labour. Through this mechanism the bargaining strength of a few significant groups may determine the general wage level for the majority.

It is difficult to assess the **effect of the trade unions' economic function** in isolation from other factors such as changes in technology, productivity, demand for labour and government monetary and fiscal policies. There is little doubt that the general standard of living has increased; certainly, figures relating to the **distribution of national income** show that the share accruing to labour has increased from 55 per cent in 1910 to 78 per cent in 1976 with significant increases during both World Wars [51]. However, Jackson attributes this to 'increases in salaries, not wages, and because salary earners are now a much larger section of the workforce' [52]. Certainly, Hawkins believes that 'while a trade union can negotiate wage increases which raise its members' real incomes, the effect will fall mainly on some other group of workers whose real wages will decline' [53] and Phelps Brown, who believes that 'the major cause of the rise in real wages . . . over the last hundred years has been the raising of productivity' [54] rather than trade union strength through collective bargaining, has argued that collective bargaining is 'between different groups of employees for the distribution of the national income between them as a whole and the inactive population' [55]. It may be argued that the trade unions' economic function achieves little more than an internal redistribution of labour's share of the national income. Whether or not the trade unions' economic function has *achieved* a redistribution of national income towards labour, it is the *pressure* for such a redistribution which is seen as a cause of inflation.

There are two different theories regarding the effect of the trade unions' economic function on **inflation and unemployment**:

1. **Cost–push** – wage increases are a direct primary cause of inflation and unemployment by increasing production costs and reducing profits, investment and competitiveness.
2. **Demand–pull** – expansive demand management policies of post-war governments seeking to maintain full employment are the major cause of inflation, lack of competitiveness and unemployment.

Trade union wage bargaining activity is primarily reactive, but, as Hawkins points out, this 'does not . . . imply that particular wage agreements do not contribute to the upward movement of money wages' but rather that the trade unions' economic function is not 'an independent cause of inflation or unemployment' [56].

Since 1979 government monetarist policies have sought to reduce the demand–pull effect whilst economic factors such as recession and high unemployment have resulted in management becoming 'tougher' in wage bargaining in an attempt to reduce the cost-push effect. Nevertheless, apart from the early 1980s when some organisations imposed small wage cuts or a pay standstill, wage rates during the later 1980s have continued to increase faster than inflation. Even the management strategy to decentralise pay bargaining from national to organisational level so that pay may be more related to local labour market conditions as well as organisational profitability or productivity does not appear to have resulted in lower wages but rather an increase in areas of labour shortage (such as the south-east). However, it is perhaps management strategies to shift the emphasis of the 'reward system' from a common 'rate for the job' basis to an individual ability or performance related basis (including individual contracts for some staff), and thereby re-establish personal differentials within groups of employees, that may have the greatest effect on the union's economic function. Certainly, some unions see a new 'wage bargaining' role in assisting such employees in their individual bargaining by providing information, advice and guidance.

Job regulation

The emphasis given in the definition of a trade union to their regulatory function covers much more than purely economic matters. Flanders argues that it also includes the 'creation of a social order in industry embodied in a code of industrial rights' [57]. Within this job regulation function the trade union is principally concerned to **protect its members in the employment relationship**. Whilst management wishes to retain the maximum degree of freedom of power, authority and decision making in managing the business, so employees wish to protect themselves against the adverse effects of such decisions. The trade union seeks, on behalf of its members, to limit management's power by not only challenging their decisions and actions but also, wherever possible, establishing 'joint' regulation. In so doing, the power and authority structure within the organisation based on managerial prerogative is replaced by a system of jointly determined rules, particularly procedural, which regulate not only the employer/employee relationship but also the organisational relationship between the company and the trade union.

The growth of 'informal' collective bargaining at the organisational level and, more importantly, its formalisation since the mid-1960s has provided the basis for an **expansion of the job regulation function**. Full employment coupled with expanding but competitive markets led management to become increasingly concerned about the effective use of their scarce labour resource – particularly skilled labour. This involved negotiating changes in working arrangements and payments outside the framework of existing national level negotiating machinery and agreements. As a consequence trade union involvement in job regulation has, in most organisations, become codified in a range of jointly agreed procedures covering recognition, including the provision of shop steward facilities; the provision and scope of consultative and negotiating machinery; and the handling of grievances, disciplines, redundancy, introduction of work study and work changes, safety, etc. It is the strengthening of the trade union's bargaining role at the organisational level which effectively provides their job regulation function.

The job regulation role of the trade union has been **supported by legislation**; for example, requiring management to consult recognised independent trade unions in a redundancy. However, in the main, such statutory provisions have not introduced a new trade union 'right' to participate in a particular aspect of job regulation but merely given legislative backing to a right which had already been secured from many employers through the process of collective bargaining. The traditional attitude of British trade unions towards securing such rights through collective bargaining is important in two respects:

1. By obtaining these rights directly from the employer through their own power and efforts makes them, in the opinion of many trade unionists, more secure – what Parliament gives, Parliament may take away.
2. The process of achieving these rights directly from management is itself both a recognition by management of the importance of the trade union and a means for employees to participate in decisions affecting their working lives.

Certainly, Flanders believes that 'a worker through his union has more direct influence in what rules are made and how they are applied than he can ever exercise by his vote over the laws made by Parliament' [58].

However, this function has come under **pressure during the 1980s**. Management has become increasingly concerned to re-exert its authority within the organisation. It has sought to do this not only by adopting a 'tougher' stance in negotiating with trade unions but also, and perhaps more importantly, by bypassing union representatives and appealing direct to its employees when it has been unable to reach a satisfactory conclusion to negotiations over pay or work changes and by establishing greater 'employee involvement', as opposed to 'trade union participation', within the organisation through strengthening communication and joint consultation arrangements and introducing direct forms of employee involvement. The trade union's role as the representative of employees in jointly regulating the employment relationship is being challenged by management attempts to establish direct links between itself and its employees.

At the same time, trade unions have sought to expand the scope of job regulation in areas such as training (to ensure that their members are equipped to meet changes in work resulting from new technology) and, perhaps most important for strengthening their recruitment appeal amongst women, equal opportunities (such as maternity career breaks, childcare provisions, job sharing, equal rights for part-time employees, sexual harassment, etc.) [59].

Political (social change)

The trade union movement came into existence and experienced its initial phase of development at a time when the **segregation of society between 'capital' and 'labour'** was perhaps most marked and when the political aspiration of the working classes was first manifesting itself through the newly won rights to participate in the political system. Thus it is that van de Vall believes 'political action in the class war has always provided the union with *latent* macro-social functions' [60] and Jackson notes that trade unions 'aim to change or help to change the nature of society' [61]. However, Anderson argues from a radical perspective that trade unions, because of their sectional approach to representing the interests of the working classes, 'do not *challenge* the existence of society based on division of classes, they merely *express* it' [62]. Indeed, it has been argued that changes in society have modified the trade union's social change function. Certainly, van de Vall believes that 'societal class conflict has been reduced to a merely industrial, or microsocial, conflict' (**institutional isolation of social conflict**) and the early political, revolutionary approach displayed by some trade unions has given way to a more conservative approach based on evolution within the existing industrial and political system: 'the war between two industrial classes has gradually been succeeded by a system of labour–management accommodation' [63].

This accommodation does not mean, however, that trade unions are no longer 'socialist' in their orientation. Most still seek, through their policies and actions in both the industrial and political spheres, to attain a more egalitarian society based on broadly socialist principles. The 'consensus' or 'corporatist' political climate for most of the post-war period produced a panoply of government supported institutions in the area of industrial and national economic planning through which trade unions sought to **influence government economic and social policies** (see Figure 4.7). However, the involvement of trade unions, even indirectly, in the process of national economic planning presents them with a **dilemma** – by entering into this accommodation they also share, in varying degrees depending on the

107

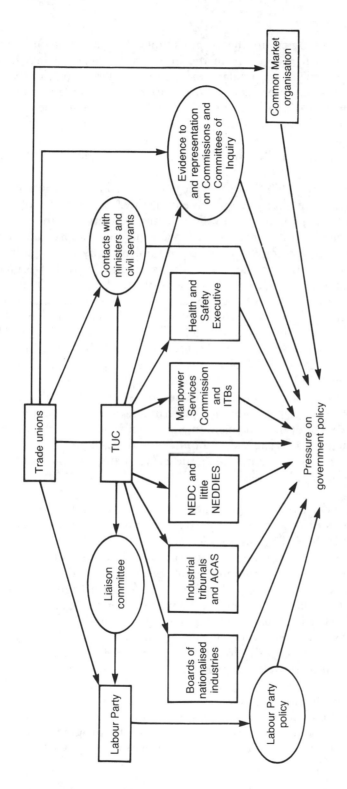

Figure 4.7 *Trade union influence in industrial and economic planning*

political party in power, in the responsibility for the decisions reached. These decisions, whilst arguably in the interests of society as a whole and wage/salary earners in particular, may, nevertheless, conflict with the sectional demands and interests of their members. Thus, trade unions have to balance directly protecting their members' interests, through their economic and job regulation functions in the collective bargaining process with management, with indirectly influencing government to adopt or modify policies which may equally affect their members' standard of living, job security, etc.

The period since 1979 has seen recession, declining economic growth and prosperity, increasing unemployment, greater polarisation of political ideologies and a heightening of divisions within society. At the same time, the abandonment by the Conservative Government of the previous 'consensus' or 'corporatist' ideology has severely diminished any potential influence unions might exert through the TUC's direct contacts with Government or indirectly through its involvement, on a tripartite basis with management and Government, in NEDO etc. Indeed, the Government has not only abolished some of these bodies (e.g. MSC) but has also downgraded the importance of others (by, for example, reducing the frequency of NEDO meetings) and no longer regards the TUC as the body which has the exclusive right to nominate the 'employee' representatives to them (including Industrial Tribunals and ACAS). Perhaps, not surprisingly, this has been accompanied by frustration amongst many trade unionists and others arising from a perceived inability to persuade the government to take greater positive responsibility by adopting 'demand management' policies which, in their view, would help to alleviate the economic situation.

There are intriguing contrasts in the **relationship of the trade union movement to political parties**:

1. **Labour Party**: Taylor regards trade union involvement as 'the only real counterweight to combat the negative extremism of the constituency rank and file' [64]. This suggests a conflict between the accommodation strategy of trade unions and the polarisation of political ideology within the Labour Party with the trade unions providing a 'moderating' influence. Nevertheless, Drucker notes that *both* the 'right' and 'left' are critical of the unions' influence in the party: the right 'claim that the Labour Party is the creation of the union bosses' and 'think that Britain's social and economic problems cannot seriously be tackled by a party dominated by institutions which are themselves part of the problem', whilst the left complain 'that the unions are, if not inevitably social democrats, necessarily conservative' and that 'their attempts to protect their members stifle a revolutionary consciousness' [65]. However, the Labour Party leadership's 'purge' of Militant supporters in constituencies and its adoption of a more 'centre' programme of policies (including not repealing most of the Conservative industrial relations

legislation), coupled with the constitutional changes to reduce the role of unions within the party, not only avoids this conflict but loosens the previously tight relationship between the Labour Party and unions thereby allowing each to develop its own policies and strategies with more freedom.

2. **Conservative Party**: Taylor notes that 'at no time in their history have Conservative leaders made a deliberate and sustained effort to provide an active role for trade unionists in their ranks' [66], rather it encourages its supporters who are members of trade unions to become active in their union as a counterbalance to the perceived more traditional 'left wing' activists.

3. **Communist Party**: Taylor suggests that 'militant' behaviour is seen as a way of 'bringing pressure to bear on established union leaders and making them pursue policies that reflect the mood of the rank and file' but that 'party shopfloor workers accept that there is a wide gulf between economic issues and political ideology' [67]. The high degree of active involvement of Communists in trade unions is inevitable given their belief in the establishment of a social system and government based on the pre-eminence of workers as a group. However, this active involvement, coupled with examples of concerted malpractice such as the ETU ballot rigging in 1961 [68], has tended to produce a 'reds under the bed syndrome'; a tendency to interpret the industrial actions of trade unions, particularly major disputes, solely as a means calculated to achieve political ends.

Clearly, even if trade unions wished to stay out of politics, political parties do not want to stay out of trade unions. However, any political activity must be funded from a separate **political fund**. Under the **Trade Union Act (1984)** trade unions wishing to maintain a political fund must:

1. conduct a ballot of the members every ten years (S.12);

2. have the rules for the ballot and notification of the members' right to be exempt from contributing to the political fund approved by the Certification Officer (S.13(4));

3. conduct the ballot by postal voting (Employment Act 1988, S.14) with independent scrutiny (Employment Act 1990, S.5);

4. where the majority of those voting do not support the maintenance of a political fund:

    (a) cease making payments from its political fund within six months (S.15(1)); and

    (b) cease collecting contributions from the members as soon as is reasonably practicable (S.15(3)).

In addition, members who 'opt out' of the political contribution may, if their union dues are deducted from wages by the employer, inform the employer not to deduct any contribution in respect of the political contribution (S.18). The member may seek a court order where the employer fails to comply with this or refuses to deduct only the 'normal' union dues (i.e. seeks to get the employee to make his/her own arrangements to pay union dues). Furthermore, any union member may apply for a court order where the union fails to comply with 4(b) above.

As Leopold points out 'one of the few successes recorded by the trade union movement under recent Conservative governments was the campaign to retain political funds' [69]. All thirty-eight unions which had a political fund obtained large majority votes in favour (averaging 84 per cent) as a result of a co-ordinating campaign amongst these unions emphasising that the ballot was about being able to undertake 'political' activities not about affiliation to the Labour Party. Perhaps more significantly, the 1984 Act amended the definition of 'political activity' so that union campaigns against government policies (such as NALGO's campaign against public service cuts) could be construed as political activity, certainly if (as NALGO's campaign did) it coincides with an election. As a consequence a number of public sector unions, which had generally sought to avoid any perception of being 'political', felt it necessary to establish political funds for the first time in order to safeguard their campaigning activities. All seventeen unions which established a political fund for the first time (of which twelve were public sector unions) also gained a resounding 'yes' vote (averaging 78 per cent). However, perhaps the real test will come in the mid-1990s, when the unions have to re-ballot their membership to continue the fund, as to whether they will be able to achieve the same degree of membership interest and support.

Member services

In their early days, before the advent of the welfare state, unions often provided a range of **'mutual insurance'** benefits not only to cover loss of pay during a strike but also in the event of the member's unemployment, sickness, injury or death. The emphasis was on the 'mutality' of these benefits in that they were provided from the subscriptions of the members themselves and unions would often call for an additional levy from working members to support others involved in a strike or during periods of prolonged unemployment. Thus, these benefits helped to strengthen the union's collective role by making members less dependent on their employer's 'benevolence'. During the course of the twentieth century these benefits have generally become an insignificant aspect of the union's activity as the state has taken over the providing role.

However, during the 1980s many trade unions have turned to the provision of more **modern 'member services'** (similar to the services provided by many companies to their employees) as part of their strategy to appeal to new potential recruits who do not have a 'tradition' of unionism. As Towers points out, such services have 'long been a feature of professional, managerial and white-collar unions' [70] but a recent survey [71] found that two-thirds of the seventeen unions surveyed provide a package of discounted financial services, including insurance, mortgages and personal loans, and 70 per cent provide legal assistance for non-work related matters. The TUC has supported this development through the establishment of a Unionlaw scheme (in conjunction with the Law Society) and Unity Financial Services (through the Unity Trust Bank which was formed in 1984 by trade unions to handle union funds and investments). It is the offer of credit cards by some unions as part of this package which has given rise to the term 'plastic card unionism'.

The term 'member services' may apply to 'any union facility which is of benefit to members *individually* [72] [my italic] and it is the **individual basis** of these modern services which some believe may detract from the fundamental nature of trade unionism. Some unions which have adopted this strategy believe it is 'easier to appeal to a potential member's self-interest than to explain the more traditional industrial relations benefits associated with a union' [73], and Mason and Bain note that 'in some cases, advocates of services have been associated with the view that potential members are put off from joining unions by industrial action' [74]; hence they regard it as an alternative to union 'militancy'. However, McIlroy argues that 'unless the unions can continue to effectively assert and extend their essential roles as successful wage bargainers, credit cards, Filofax and videos are unlikely to reverse their present decline' [75]. Certainly, if people join a union *only* or *primarily* for the personal benefits they gain from these services (as opposed to the alternative instrumental reason of gaining its protection in the workplace), they are likely to weaken the basis of the unions's 'fraternalist' ideals and 'collective consciousness' and, thereby, its ability to carry out its economic and job regulation function.

Self-fulfilment

The importance of the trade union, in terms of the individual's self-fulfilment, lies primarily in its **role in decision making**. It is through this that the member is able to develop outside the normal confines of his or her daily work. Its role in decision making operates within three interrelated systems:

1. The union's own **internal system of government** wherein the member is encouraged to attend the branch and become involved in the administration of the organisation as well as participate in the discussion

and decision making associated with the development of union policy on a range of social and political issues as well as economic and industrial matters.

2. The **collective bargaining system**, in making decisions which affect the members' terms and conditions of employment.
3. The **political representational system**, in seeking to influence government policies and actions.

The individual member may become actively involved in these systems by being appointed or elected to positions of responsibility and authority such as shop steward, branch official, delegate to local or national committees/ conferences or full-time official. Through this process individuals may become involved in areas of decision making far removed from their immediate work situation.

In their early years trade unions were, in the absence of educational, political or other opportunities, an important, and sometimes the sole, **vehicle for the advancement of those with ability**. Indeed, membership participation was frequently encouraged by fining members who failed to attend branch meetings or by operating a form of 'organic democracy' which required each member to take a turn in holding office within the branch or union and thereby actively sharing the responsibility for the government of the union. In the post-war period, however, the growth of educational opportunities coupled with greater job opportunities in the technical and managerial fields has created other avenues whereby the individual may achieve greater self-fulfilment and, as a result, has diminished the role of the union in this area.

Nevertheless, this aspect of trade unionism is still important in trying to understand why people become active within trade unions and are prepared to give up their own time, with the consequent social cost to themselves and their families, to attend meetings and to stand out from the mass to act as the representative of their fellow workers or union members. It is too simplistic to state that they have a desire for 'power' and that these roles within a trade union provide them with the opportunity to acquire and exercise such power. It is perhaps better to say that any 'activist' within a trade union, whether simply a member or a shop steward, branch official or other officer of the union, is active because of some social commitment to improving employees' working lives. Thus, by taking an active part within the union the individual achieves a generally more satisfying role in life than he/she would otherwise do.

It must be remembered that the mass of the rank and file members join a trade union for its economic and job regulation functions on their behalf and therefore the number of members who seek self-fulfilment by playing an active role in the union (committed trade unionists) is always likely to be limited. However, although it is these active members who take the major part in determining union policies and actions, they must always have regard to the aspirations of the mass of passive membership who, in the final analysis, will not let the active membership go beyond a point that they consider acceptable.

4.4 Summary propositions

- Trade unions have developed from small localised organisations into complex national institutions which play an integral and influential role in society; but this development has been hindered by periods of legislative and political restriction.
- The strength of a trade union depends on the 'collective consciousness' of its membership and the preparedness of the individual to subordinate his/her personal aspirations to those of the group.
- Trade unions cannot adequately represent the interests of their membership by confining their activities to direct economic and job regulation with management; trade unions are, by their nature, 'political' organisations.
- Trade union power and influence has been weakened in the 1980s by declining membership, economic recession and high unemployment and, most importantly, the withdrawal of government support.

Further reading

- H. Pelling, *A History of British Trade Unionism*, Penguin, 1976. A very readable account of the historical development of the trade union movement in Britain.
- W. E. J. McCarthy (ed.), *Trade Unions* (2nd edn), Penguin, 1985. This provides a selection of readings on trade unions – Part One (Union Objectives and Methods), Part Five (Factors Affecting Union Growth) and Part Six (The Economic Effects of Trade Unionism) are particularly relevant.
- B. Burkitt and D. Bowers, *Trade Unions and the Economy*, Macmillan, 1979. A good analysis of the economic function and impact of trade unions.
- B. Pimlott and C. Cook (eds), *Trade Unions in British Politics*, Longman, 1982. This examines the development of the trade unions' political role and its relationship to both the Labour Party and governments.
- J. T. Ward and W. Hamish Fraser (eds), *Workers and Employers*, Macmillan, 1980. Contains extracts from documents relating to trade unions and industrial relations from the eighteenth century onwards and

thereby provides the reader with an insight into the actual words and attitudes of the past.

- J. McIlroy, *Trade Unions in Britain Today*, Manchester University Press, 1988. An up to date account of the issues facing trade unions during the 1980s and into the 1990s.

References

1. ACAS, *Industrial Relations Handbook*, HMSO, 1980, p. 39.
2. W. Hirsh-Weber quoted in M. van de Vall, *Labor Organizations*, Cambridge University Press, 1970, p. 53.
3. R. M. Blackburn, *Union Character and Social Class*, Batsford, 1967, p. 18.
4. B. Towers, 'Trends and developments in industrial relations: derecognising trade unions: implications and consequences', *Industrial Relations Journal*, vol. 19, no. 3, 1988, p. 184.
5. For example, the Statute of Artificers (1563) which allowed JPs to fix wage rates in their locality.
6. H. Pelling, *A History of British Trade Unionism*, Penguin, 1976, p. 8. Reprinted by permission of Penguin Books Ltd. ©Henry Pelling, 1963, 1971, 1976.
7. F. Tannenbaum, *The True Society: A Philosophy of Labour*, Cape, 1964.
8. S. and B. Webb, *History of Trade Unions*, Longman, 1896.
9. B. C. Roberts, *Trade Unions in a Free Society*, Institute of Economic Affairs, 1959, p. 54.
10. J. Lovell, *British Trade Unions 1875–1933*, Macmillan, 1977, p. 21.
11. G. D. H. Cole, *A Short History of the British Working Class Movement 1789–1947*, Allen & Unwin, 1966, p. 246.
12. H. Pelling, *op. cit.*, p. 151. Reprinted by permission of Penguin Books Ltd. ©Henry Pelling, 1963, 1971, 1976.
13. H. A. Turner, G. Clack and B. Roberts, *Labour Relations in the Motor Industry*, Allen & Unwin, 1967.
14. R. Price and G. S. Bain, 'Union growth in Britain: retrospect and prospect', *British Journal of Industrial Relations*, vol. XXI, no. 1, 1983.
15. H. Pelling, *op. cit.*, p. 26.
16. *Hilton* v. *Eckersley* (1855) quoted in K. W. Wedderburn, *The Worker and the Law*, Penguin, 1971, p. 86. ©K. W. Wedderburn, 1965, 1971.
17. K. W. Wedderburn, *op. cit.*, p. 76. ©K. W. Wedderburn, 1965, 1971.
18. K. Hawkins, *Trade Unions*, Hutchinson, 1981, p. 40.
19. K. W. Wedderburn, *op. cit.*, p. 310. ©K. W. Wedderburn, 1965, 1971.
20. H. Vester and A. H. Gardiner, *Trade Union Law and Practice*, Sweet & Maxwell, 1958, p. 11.
21. C. Grunfeld, *Modern Trade Union Law*, Sweet & Maxwell, 1966, p. 439.
22. *Heaton Transport* v. *T&GWU* (1973); *Midland Cold Storage* v. *Turner* (1972); *Con-Mech (Engineering)* v. *AUEW* (1973).
23. H. Pelling, *op. cit.*, p. 42. Reprinted by permission of Penguin Books Ltd. ©Henry Pelling, 1963, 1971, 1976.
24. J. McIlroy, *Trade Unions in Britain Today*, Manchester University Press, 1988, p. 56.

25. W. J. Brown (1925 TUC Congress) quoted in H. Pelling, *op. cit.*, p. 170. Reprinted by permission of Penguin Books Ltd. ©Henry Pelling, 1963, 1971, 1976.
26. J. Kelly and R. Bailey, 'British trade union membership, density and decline in the 1980s: a research note', *Industrial Relations Journal*, vol. 20, no. 1, 1989.
27. R. Freeman and J. Pelletier, 'The impact of industrial relations legislation on British union density', *British Journal of Industrial Relations*, vol. 28, no. 2, 1990.
28. G. S. Bain and F. Elsheikh, *Union Growth and the Business Cycle*, Blackwell, 1976; see also G. S. Bain and R. Price, 'Union growth: dimensions, determinants and destiny', in G. S. Bain (ed.), *Industrial Relations in Britain*, Blackwell, 1983.
29. R. Disney, 'Explanations of the decline in trade union density in Britain: an appraisal', *British Journal of Industrial Relations*, vol. 28, no. 2, 1990.
30. R. Price and G. S. Bain, *op. cit.*, p. 59.
31. *ibid.*, p. 61.
32. G. S. Bain and R. Price, 'Union growth: dimensions, determinants and destiny', in G. S. Bain (ed.), *op. cit.*, p. 33.
33. N. Millward and M. Stevens, 'Union density in the regions', *Employment Gazette*, May 1988, p. 287.
34. B. Mason and P. Bain, 'Trade union recruitment strategies: facing the 1990s', *Industrial Relations Journal*, vol. 22, no. 1, 1991.
35. J. Payne, 'Trade union membership and activism among young people in Great Britain', *British Journal of Industrial Relations*, vol. 27, no. 1, 1989.
36. B. Mason and P. Bain, *op. cit.*, p. 44.
37. P. Willman, 'The logic of "market-share" trade unionism: is membership decline inevitable?', *Industrial Relations Journal*, vol. 20, no. 4, 1989, p. 263.
38. *ibid.*, p. 269.
39. R. Hyman, *Industrial Relations: A Marxist introduction*, Macmillan, 1975, p. 66.
40. B. C. Roberts, *op. cit.*, p. 4.
41. R. Hyman, *op. cit.*, p. 64.
42. S. Perlman, 'Labour's "home grown" philosophy' in W. E. J. McCarthy (ed.), *Trade Unions*, Penguin, 1972, p. 28.
43. R. Hyman, *op. cit.*, p. 65.
44. S. Perlman, *op. cit.*, p. 30.
45. G. S. Bain and R. Price, *Profiles of Union Growth: A comparative statistical portrait of eight countries*, Blackwell, 1980.
46. C. Mulvey, *The Economic Analysis of Trade Unions*, Martin Robertson, 1976.
47. *ibid.*, p. 35.
48. N. Robertson and J. L. Thomas, *Trade Unions and Industrial Relations*, Business Books Ltd., 1968, p. 39.
49. A. M. Ross, *Trade Union Wage Policy*, University of California Press, 1948.
50. C. Mulvey, *op. cit.*, p. 42.
51. B. Burkitt and D. Bowers, *Trade Unions and the Economy*, Macmillan, 1979, Table 5.2, p. 62.
52. M. Jackson, *Trade Unions*, Longman, 1982, p. 109.
53. K. Hawkins, *op. cit.*, p. 228.
54. E. H. Phelps Brown, *The Growth of British Industrial Relations*, Macmillan, 1960, p. 366.
55. E. H. Phelps Brown, 'New wine in old bottles: reflections on the changed working of collective bargaining in Great Britain', *British Journal of Industrial Relations*, vol. XI, no. 2, 1973.

56. K. Hawkins, *op. cit.*, p. 222.
57. A. Flanders, *Management and Unions*, Faber & Faber, 1970, p. 43.
58. *ibid.*
59. 'New bargaining agenda for unions', *IRS Employment Trends*, no. 479, January 1991.
60. M. van de Vall, *Labor Organizations*, Cambridge University Press, 1970, p. 54.
61. M. Jackson, *op. cit.*, p. 143.
62. P. Anderson, 'The limits and possibilities of trade union action', in R. Blackburn and A. Cockburn (eds), *The Incompatibles*, Penguin, 1967, p. 264. Reprinted by permission of Penguin Books Ltd. ©New Left Review, 1967.
63. M. van de Vall, *op. cit.*, p. 55.
64. R. Taylor, *The Fifth Estate*, Pan, 1980, p. 100.
65. H. M. Drucker, 'The influence of the trade unions on the ethos of the Labour Party' in B. Pimlott and C. Cook (eds), *Trade Unions in British Politics*, Longman, 1982, p. 258.
66. R. Taylor, *op. cit.*, p. 114.
67. *ibid.*, pp. 124–5.
68. C. H. Rolph, *All Those in Favour?: The ETU Trial*, André Deutsch, 1962.
69. J. W. Leopold, 'Moving the status quo: the growth of trade union political funds', *Industrial Relations Journal*, vol. 19, no. 4, 1988, p. 286.
70. B. Towers (ed.), *A Handbook of Industrial Relations Practice*, Kogan Page, 1989, p. 25.
71. 'Union services: the way forward?', *IRS Employment Trends*, no. 457, February 1990.
72. *ibid.*, p. 6.
73. *ibid.*, p. 12.
74. B. Mason and P. Bain, *op. cit.*, p. 37.
75. J. McIlroy, *Trade Unions in Britain Today*, Manchester University Press, 1988, pp. 220–1.

Chapter 5

Trade union structure and the TUC

5.1 Definition

The term 'structure' refers to **the classification of unions by their recruitment patterns or memberships' job territory**. It is not concerned with how individual unions organise their internal administration and government (although this may be influenced by the particular structural type) but with how trade unions, as independent and autonomous organisations, have been conceived and developed in order to promote the process of recruiting, organising and representing employees across the diverse range of industries and occupations that exist in an industrialised society.

Most writers on British industrial relations have referred to the apparent haphazard and illogical recruitment pattern of its trade unions and the resultant state of multi-unionism involving competition between unions for both members and jobs. Farnham and Pimlott described it as giving an 'impression of irrational heterogeneity' [1], whilst Hawkins points out that it has been 'criticized for its baffling complexity and apparent lack of rationality' [2]. Certainly Bell argued that 'only a classification with as many separate categories as there are major individual unions could do justice to the diversity which exists' [3].

5.2 Multi-unionism

Definition and extent

The term 'multi-unionism' is used to describe **the existence of more than a single union in relation to the collective bargaining structure**. On this basis it is possible to identify two distinct forms of multi-unionism:

TYPE A –   where each distinct bargaining unit in an organisation or
industry is organised and represented by a different union

TYPE B –   where there is more than one union competing to organise
and represent a distinct group within the organisation or
industry

Multi-unionism is likely to remain a feature of British industrial relations despite the relatively small number of 'single union' agreements established during the 1980s. Millward and Stevens' survey of workplace industrial relations in 1984 found that multi-unionism was 'especially common for manual employees in large manufacturing plants and for non-manual workers in the public sector" [4] (see Table 5.1). However, only 6 per cent of private manufacturing establishments recognised more than four unions for manual employees whilst 26 per cent of public sector establishments recognised more than four unions for non-manual employees. The fact that, except for private manufacturing non-manual employees, the proportion of establishments recognising more than one union was substantially higher than the proportion having more than one bargaining unit suggests that Type B 'competitive' multi-unionism is still significant. Where there are two or more unions for the same group of employees, however, they generally negotiate jointly with management rather than separately.

The problem

As early as the 1950s and 1960s writers [5] criticised Britain's trade union structure for being outdated, lacking in industrial unions and giving craft unions a predominant role, thereby creating a conservative and reactionary trade union movement reluctant to accept technological change. However, Hyman took the opposite view and argued that 'the fact that multi-unionism may cause certain problems for managerial control should not be accepted as

Table 5.1   *The extent of multi-unionism*

	Private Manufacture (%)	Private Services (%)	Public Sector (%)
Manual:			
More than 1 union	42	20	38
More than 1 bargaining unit	29	11	17
Non-manual:			
More than 1 union	31	37	74
More than 1 bargaining unit	35	25	45

Table 5.2   *The effects of multi-unionism*

	TYPE A 'Bargaining Units'		TYPE B 'Competitive'	
	Group A Union A	Group B Union B	Group A Unions A and B	Group B Unions C and D
Demarcation of work	Reinforced by boundary of work being coterminus with union boundary		Members of the different unions carry out the same work	
Inter-union conflict	1. Demarcation disputes 2. Poaching disputes as members transfer from one work to another		1. Recognition disputes 2. Poaching disputes as members transfer from one union to another	
Complicates collective bargaining	1. Comparability claims 2. Leapfrogging wage claims		Need to co-ordinate approach to management; establishment of joint negotiating arrangements	
Duplication and dilution of union efforts	Less duplication		More duplication	
Role of shop steward	Inter-union committee for matters of general concern		Inter-union committee for most matters	
Union outlook	More likely to be introvert		More likely to be extrovert	
Individual choice	No choice		Limited initial choice	

a valid base for criticism of union structure' [6] – trade unions exist to represent the diverse sectional interests of employees as they perceive them. Certainly, the effects of multi-unionism may be seen in a number of areas of industrial relations (see Table 5.2).

Demarcation of work

Demarcation problems are essentially concerned with which group of workers in an organisation is to carry out a particular task or operation. They may arise at the boundary between work groups or within groups, between members of the same union or members of different unions. Although Clegg believed that 'union boundaries are not the cause of demarcation rules' [7], if the groups disputing the work are members of different unions the problem takes on an institutional character involving an element of conflict between organisations as well as people and therefore becomes more complex and difficult to resolve. The amalgamation of the unions concerned may ease the problem because it becomes an intra-organisational rather than inter-organisational issue.

Inter-union conflict

The existence of more than one union in an organisation or industry can create:

1. **recognition disputes**: whether a union should be recognised as having a right to represent a particular group;
2. **poaching disputes**: where one union seeks to take into membership people who are already members of another union or who are in a group of workers for whom another union is already recognised.

Management often perceives itself as the 'innocent bystander' in such a dispute; powerless to solve it in spite of the effect it may be having on production. The conflict cannot be resolved by a managerial decision alone but can only be resolved by an accommodation being reached by the unions and employees involved.

Complicates collective bargaining

The greater the number of parties involved in the collective bargaining process the more complex it becomes. In a situation where there is only one union in the organisation the collective bargaining process is a direct interaction between that union and management. In multi-unionism Type B there has to be an intermediate step where each union has to reconcile its objectives with those of the other unions before they are able to present a united face to the management. Multi-unionism Type A creates, or at least reinforces, differences between groups in the terms and conditions of employment. The existence of a number of separate 'bargaining units' represented by different unions institutionalises the problems of differentials and can lead to comparability claims and leap-frogging wage negotiations. As a result, both trade unions and management face difficulties in developing and maintaining a comprehensive and integrated approach to industrial relations.

Duplication and dilution of union effort

Many trade unionists believe that unions competing amongst themselves diverts attention away from the unions' real purpose of confronting the employer and allows management the opportunity to use 'divide and rule' tactics in their dealings with unions. There can be little doubt that multi-unionism leads to a duplication of effort by trade unions in servicing their respective memberships in an organisation or industry. The opportunity cost of this duplication is the dilution of the unions' efforts to provide a better service to their membership and to recruit new members into trade unions.

Strengthens the role of the shop steward

Multi-unionism in an organisation or industry presents the unions with the organisational problem of how to co-ordinate their activities. The result has been the creation of joint shop stewards' committees to integrate the approaches of the various unions at the organisational level; and, because these committees comprise shop stewards from different unions, no single union or union official has authority over their actions or decisions. These committees may amount to an alternative parallel form of union organisation and represent a potential weakening of the official's position both with the membership and management.

Union outlook

One advantage of multi-unionism is that trade unions are constantly brought into contact with each other in a wide range of industries, organisations and occupations and are, therefore, forced to take a wider perspective of their role and the interests of their members within the larger trade union movement. A single union, without any competition, may well become introvert in character and concentrate on the affairs and interests of its industry or occupation to the exclusion of others. However, many employers would applaud and encourage an 'introvert' union concerned more with the affairs of the organisation or industry than with the affairs of the wider trade union movement.

The solution

The problem of multi-unionism and any inherent inter-union conflict is not resolved simply by the amalgamation of unions, but is partly the result of an absence of a proactive managerial strategy on trade union recognition in the past. The adoption of a logical and orderly approach to trade union recognition within an organisation can, at least, avoid multi-unionism Type B and mitigate the effects of multi-unionism Type A and may lead to 'single table bargaining' or a 'single union agreement'.

5.3 Structural classification

Problems of classification

Over the period of its development the structure of the British trade union movement has been influenced by a number of factors which complicate any attempt at classification.

The important common factor in the origin of any union is the need felt by individuals to combine together for mutual protection and to deal with common problems. The initial members were able to determine the **basis of common interest** of their union thereby providing the union's sense of identity and common purpose. However, today when employees combine together at the workplace for the first time they will probably seek to join an existing union which they feel best meets their needs and aspirations rather than create an entirely new organisation. The range and variety of 'types' of union seen in Britain today are the result of not only, as Clegg noted, 'the state of technology and industrial organization at the time of their birth and growth' [8] but also, as Jenkins and Mortimer pointed out, an evolution 'in response to the needs and wishes of its members' [9].

However, in spite of frequent debates within the TUC and the trade union movement regarding trade union structure, at no time has there been a significant conscious move to reform along one line as opposed to another. In marked contrast to other countries, **British trade unions have determined their own membership patterns without any systematic intervention from the TUC.** In Germany, for example, there was a need to reconstruct the trade union movement at the end of World War II and the opportunity was taken, under the auspices of the British TUC, to re-establish it on an industrial basis. In the USA, despite the clash of ideologies, both the AFL (craft) and the CIO (industrial) (and the combined AFL–CIO after 1955) have delineated and, to some degree, controlled the occupational/ industrial membership of individual unions by granting charters to their constituent unions.

The problem of classification has been further compounded by the need for trade unions to modify their recruitment patterns in response to changes in the industrial and technological environments and the associated changes in jobs, skills and occupations. The reduction in the number of unions and the consequent increasing size of many unions implies an **increasing heterogeneity of membership** and weakening of the bond of common interest displayed by the early trade unions.

It is important to remember that the approaches set out below should not be seen as identifying separate categories within which unions have to be fitted but rather concepts against which unions can be analysed to judge the extent to which they comply with or deviate from one or more of these principles.

Traditional classification

The origins of this classification can be found in the development of the trade union movement during the nineteenth and early twentieth centuries, particularly in the context of the doctrinal debate between craft, industrial and general unionism. It is, therefore, based on the pattern of trade union membership as it was some one hundred years ago rather than as it is today. Nevertheless, it is a useful analytical tool for understanding the origin or early development of a trade union (which may still exert an influence on the trade union's ethos today).

Occupational union

Bell noted that this type of union 'seeks to unite all workers of a particular craft, trade, occupation or grade of skill, irrespective of the industry in which they happen to be engaged' [10]. Within this organising principle it is the work performed by the individual and their location in the industrial hierarchy which provides the unifying force (common interest). These unions may, alternatively, be classified as **horizontal in character** in that they generally spread across a number of industries. Within this category there are a number of subgroups.

- *Craft union.* These may be distinguished from other occupational unions on the basis of a qualitative difference resulting from their exercise of control over entry into the trade and their concern for the skill basis of that trade. In spite of it being the earliest form of union in Britain there are few, if any, 'pure' craft unions remaining (i.e. unions which will take into membership only apprentice-served 'craftsmen' of a single trade). Some of the single-craft unions amalgamated to form **multi-craft unions** whilst others have become **craft and allied occupation unions**. The inclusion of less skilled employees has arisen as a consequence of technological change. Initially they were there not to represent their own interests but in order to better protect the interests of the skilled membership. However, as the proportion of unskilled and semi-skilled members increased within these unions, so the character and structural type has changed. Subsequently, many craft unions sought to recruit upwards into the supervisory and managerial levels; again, initially, as a means of protecting the lines of promotion of their skilled membership.

- *Promotion union.* This refers to unions, in industries such as cotton spinning and iron and steel, which covered skilled manual workers who were not apprentice-served 'craftsmen'. The skill was acquired not from a formal apprenticeship but from on-the-job experience and a system of internal promotion from the most junior to the most senior, and highly paid, work within the group. It was this promotion linkage which provided the impetus to organise a number of 'related occupations' into one union. However, as the skills and promotion linkage were limited to a given industry, these unions tended also to take on an industrial as well as occupational character, thus making them difficult to distinguish from an industrial union.

- *Semi-skilled/unskilled union.* These unions came about as part of the 'new unionism' of the late nineteenth century and concentrated on organising semi-skilled and unskilled workers in those industries which already had unions catering for the skilled workers. Subsequently, a number of these unions provided the nucleus, through the process of amalgamation, for the creation of 'general' unions or combined with 'craft' or 'promotion' unions in the same industry to produce 'industrial' manual unions.

● *Non-manual (white collar) union.* A significant feature of British trade union structure has been the organisation of non-manual employees into separate unions or virtually autonomous sections of manual unions. However, those unions which are wholly non-manual may be regarded as 'occupational' in that their area of recruitment is confined to 'non-manual' categories of work. Whilst some restrict their membership to a **single occupation**, others take a much wider perspective and are **multi-occupational** and, in some cases, prepared to take into membership a very wide range of non-manual employees irrespective of industry or occupation; some confine their membership to a **single industry** or a **single employer**. An added complication is the existence of **professional associations** which, in addition to their role of maintaining professional standards, carry out collective bargaining on behalf of their members.

Industrial union

An industrial union, according to Bell, is one which 'seeks to unite all workers engaged in a particular industry irrespective of their individual crafts, trades, occupations or grades of skill' [11]. This organising principle requires the union to abandon any occupational barrier to its recruitment within the industry and implies that the individual members will perceive a greater bond of common interest with fellow employees performing different work than with other people applying the same craft, skill or occupation in other industries. An industrial union is therefore **vertical in character** in so far as it seeks to encompass the organisational hierarchy.

Within this category Jackson identifies two different forms of industrial union: 'one is the "*monopoly industrial union*" which organises all workers in one industry, while the other is the "*single industry union*" which does not organise all of the workers in an industry, but restricts its recruitment to that industry [12] [my italics]. In Britain there is no monopoly industrial union – unlike the sixteen industrial unions in Germany. However, there have been a number of unions which have adopted this principle (e.g. COHSE, ISTC, NUM and NUR) but in all these industries there are other unions seeking to organise specific groups of workers. Hughes [13] suggested that this form of unionisation would have the greatest appeal where:

1. the production or service processes require knowledge or skills that are special to that industry and cannot easily be transferred or applied in other industries;
2. the product or service establishes a unique working environment not fully understood by those outside the industry, thus isolating the employees from those in other industries;

3. it is possible for employees to progress through the organisation by promotion to more senior levels;

to which may be added:

4. where all, or at least a significant proportion, of the industry is within single, often public, ownership.

General union

Hughes argued that the organising principle underlying this type of union 'implies no limitation of recruitment, either occupational or industrial' [14]. Whilst general unions, such as the T&GWU and GMB created in the 1920s, represent a modification of the nineteenth century division between occupational and industrial unions, nevertheless the idea of a general union without either occupational or industrial boundaries pre-dates even the craft unions of the mid-nineteenth century. However, it is important to differentiate the earlier **politically inspired** attempts to create on general union (the Grand National Consolidated Trades Union of 1834) from the **structurally evolved** general unions which exist today. The unions which might be classified as general unions today did not originate as general unions but developed into such by virtue of amalgamations between unions which themselves were organised on occupational or industrial lines. Each has tended to adopt the occupational and industrial pattern provided by the amalgamating unions as its major sphere of organisation, and each new amalgamation has produced a shift in that sphere of organisation.

More dynamic approach

Many qualifications have to be made to the simple three category traditional approach if it is used to examine current trade union structure. It is necessary to use words such as restrict, confine, exclude, and boundary as a means of delineating the recruitment pattern of the various types of union. The very fact that trade unions have changed from the simple occupational/industrial concepts of the nineteenth century illustrates Hyman's point that trade union structure 'is not a fixed phenomenon but a process' [15] involving constant adaptations. Therefore, in order to analyse trade union structure it is necessary to adopt more dynamic concepts.

Hyman argues that in the area of trade union structure 'two contradictory forces have operated: on the one hand towards breadth, unity and solidarity; on the other towards parochialism, sectionalism and exclusion. The one encourages unionism which is open and expansive; the other, unionism which is closed and restrictive' [16]. It was to accommodate the tension between these two forces that Turner [17] originally developed the terms **open** and **closed** to refer to the relationship between the union and control of entry into the trade or occupation and from that the resultant recruitment pattern of the union's membership. 'Closed' delineated those unions which had the ability to restrict entry into the trade or occupation and as a result maintained an exclusive approach to their membership pattern and had little interest in recruiting outside their area of control. 'Open' unions, on the other hand, lacked the ability to control entry into the trade or occupation and therefore relied on the numerical strength of their membership to provide their bargaining power. Subsequently, the terms 'open' and 'closed' have been used simply as a method of categorising unions on the basis of the scope and direction of their membership patterns and no longer necessarily imply a qualitative judgement in respect of a union's attitude towards controlling the labour supply.

However, the extremes of any classification present little difficulty: the extreme forms of 'open' and 'closed' unions may be equated to the extreme forms of 'general' and 'craft' unions in that a closed union will maintain very tight limits on its area of recruitment whilst a completely open union will have no limits at all. The importance of these concepts, therefore, lies in analysing and understanding the **hybrid unions** which form the bulk of trade unions and which are open in certain directions and closed in others. It also provides a useful tool for examining the changes in a union's structural type which have taken place in the past and/or may take place in the future.

The majority of unions in Britain use both **occupational and industrial boundaries** to delineate their membership recruitment interests. However, in other countries different boundaries may be extremely important in determining a union's membership. For example, British trade unions have not attempted to use race or political and religious beliefs as boundaries. In contrast, political and religious beliefs form important boundaries for union membership in Italy, France, Belgium and The Netherlands where separate Communist, Socialist, Christian Democrat and Catholic trade union groupings exist.

However, Undy *et al.* believe that Turner's open–closed typology does not 'distinguish sufficiently between the various dimensions of development in union job territory' [18]. In their view, the full dynamics of changing union structure can only be understood if the relative openness of the union's recruitment boundaries is related to two other important factors:

1. **The membership market:** it is necessary to have regard to not only whether the union exists in an expanding or declining employment area but also the **degree of inter-union competition for membership** within that area. In this respect Undy *et al.* differentiate between a **sheltered** environment where the union has sole recognition and an **exposed** environment where the union competes for membership with other recognised unions.
2. **Union orientation to recruitment:** unions with the same degree of openness and existing within similar membership markets may,

nevertheless, display different policies and strategies towards the recruitment of members. Undy *et al.* distinguish between a **passive** approach, wherein membership expansion is not afforded a high priority, and a **positive** approach, where the union consciously seeks to expand its membership within its existing market and/or expand into new markets.

On this basis Undy *et al.* identified that the General and Municipal Workers Union (now GMB), whilst open in terms of its scope of recruitment and exposed in terms of inter-union competition for membership, nevertheless was passive in its orientation to growth. ASTMS now (MSF), on the other hand, whilst 'intermediate' in respect of both its scope and recruitment and inter-union competition for membership, was very positive in its policy towards growth and expansion of its membership.

Finally, it has become useful to adopt the wider concept of a **sectorial union** to replace the narrower concept of an industrial union. Hughes applied the term to those unions 'which are by historical origin or "principle" of organisation, concentrated in a particular section of the economy, but prone to take an "open" approach to the definition of that sector and ready to extend into "allied" fields' [19]. The term is used to denote a union which is prepared, at least in part, to recruit from a significant range of occupations across a number of related industries.

Rationalisation of union structure

Industrial unionism

The original concept of industrial unionism was closely bound up with the **socio-political principle** of reordering society and was seen as the means whereby the working classes could take control of both their workplace and society. If workers are to control their workplace and industry, including the election of those who manage it, it is axiomatic that trade unions should adopt similar boundaries for their organisational pattern. The idea of industrial unionism as an **organisational principle of structural reform or rationalisation** has been a recurrent item on the agenda of the Trades Union Congress. Yet, its greatest advocates have been those unions which already have a clearly identified industrial base. Three major **advantages** are often put forward for industrial unionism:

1. It would **strengthen the unity of trade union membership and organisation** by:
   (a) removing competition between unions;
   (b) spreading the bargaining strength of strong groups, such as skilled workers, across all employees; and

       (c) removing the need for shop stewards to form unofficial joint committees at the workplace and therefore allow for them to be formally integrated into the union organisation.

2. It would **simplify collective bargaining** by:
       (a) making union structure correspond to the normal arrangements of employers' associations;
       (b) allowing for better integration between industrial and organisational level bargaining; and
       (c) making sectional claims and demarcation disputes easier to resolve.

3. It would **facilitate the process of economic planning** by creating a greater sense of affinity between the trade union and the industry it represents.

However, a number of factors make the achievement of industrial unionism **highly unlikely**:

1. The **industrial system does not divide neatly into discrete industries with clear boundaries** and, even if it were possible to define the boundaries of industries and 'allocate' areas to specific unions, these boundaries are constantly changing and therefore there would need to be an updating of the allocation to take account of new techniques, processes and industries. There would be a need for a central agency (presumably the TUC) to be given, or to take, the power not only to determine which union should organise which industry but also to set up new unions and undertake initial recruitment drives. In addition, the establishment of industrial unionism would still leave the multi-industry employers, of whom there are a substantial number, having to deal with multi-unionism at the company or group level.

2. As the Donovan Commission recognised in 1968, the establishment of a trade union movement based on industrial unionism would 'involve a drastic upheaval in the structure of almost every major union in the country' [20]. In the case of the so-called general unions (such as the T&GWU and GMB) it would mean their virtual dismantlement. More importantly, there would be problems at two levels:
       (a) At the union organisation level, there would be a need to integrate the policies, institutions, practices and officers, as well as membership, from a number of very different unions with the possibility of friction as to which philosophy should predominate.
       (b) At the membership level, some of the membership might feel that their sectional interests are likely to be overridden by those of the majority.

3. Industrial unionism could produce **tensions in those industries which were, or became, in decline**. Representational influence and efficiency is,

in part, dependent on the size of the union. A union based on a declining industry would suffer diminished influence and effectiveness at the very time when perhaps they are needed most. In the end the union will reach a situation where it is no longer able to carry out its function of representing the membership's interests.

In spite of these organisational problems, the possibility of industrial unionism still exists. However, it will take place as an **individual development in union structure in certain appropriate industries rather than as part of a planned overall reform.**

Federations

Given a number of unions in an industry, it is inevitable that they will need to **co-operate and co-ordinate** their activities. In some industries this was achieved through a **formal federation** of the unions involved. The TUC recognised that this arrangement could provide 'a loose form of industrial unionism . . . where the industrial, craft or general workers unions, who are concerned in any industry, may get together to pursue jointly the problems affecting the industry with which they are concerned' [21]. Thus, the Federation may be viewed either as a structural form in its own right, halfway between autonomous unions acting independently and full amalgamation into an industrial union, or as a necessary prelude to industrial unionism. However, it presents certain **issues** for the unions involved:

1. The **balance of power and decision making between the Federation and its individual constituent unions**. In some, decisions on such issues as wage bargaining, industrial action, etc. remained with the individual unions, whilst in others they were centralised within the control of the Federation.
2. The **relationship between the Federation and the membership of the individual unions**. In some unions the membership of the individual unions were linked to the Federation by Federation branches which dealt with collective issues at the organisational and local level. However, Federation policy and decisions were determined by officials representing individual unions who were accountable for their actions and decisions to their membership in the normal way. The Federation provided a structural framework for the co-ordination of unions as organisations rather than the integration of their membership.
3. The **varying membership of the individual unions**. For some unions the Federation occupied a central place in their thinking because the bulk, if not all, of their membership was within that industry; for others the Federation was more marginal because only a small proportion of their membership came within the industry concerned.

The Confederation of Shipbuilding and Engineering Unions (CSEU) is the most significant union Federation in the private sector, whilst the Council of Civil Service Unions (CSSU) is the largest within the public sector. Both of these represent a halfway structural form and are the main union negotiating bodies in their respective industries.

Role of the TUC

The TUC approach to trade union structure is perhaps best summed up in the 1964 Report which recommended that, instead of trying to draw up a comprehensive structural blueprint for the future, the TUC should consider 'how best to stimulate and guide the process of piecemeal and ad hoc developments by which changes have come about in the past' [22]. Thus, the role of the TUC is essentially to act as a **catalyst** to draw together unions with a common interest and be available if needed to aid the process of merger. Through its role as a **mediator in inter-union disputes**, the TUC is in a position to be able to influence union structure. However, Clegg has described the Bridlington principles as being 'principles of good relations, not of structural design, and the case law is intended to preserve established rights' [23], whilst Lerner argued that 'in its jurisdictional disputes awards, the TUC's premise has become that a union's rights to retain its members is supreme over the member's rights to change his affiliation in all cases in which the two come into conflict' [24].

This attitude is also reflected in the TUC's concern to ensure that the creation of **breakaway unions** does not fragment and weaken the movement [25]. Most recently the trade union movement has seen secessions from the NUM and the creation of the Union of Democratic Miners, and the creation of a small number of organisations/groups founded on the principle of 'professionalism' and the preclusion of industrial action (e.g. the Association of Professional Teachers (APT) and the Nationally Integrated Caring Employees (NICE) in the NHS). These organisations, although small, present a potential problem in respect of the fragmentation of both the trade union movement and collective bargaining. Certainly, the government's recognition of APT at the national level within the Burnham negotiating machinery has led to disputes between the APT and the other established TUC affiliated unions (including court action).

Mergers and amalgamations

During the twentieth century there have been a number of waves of union amalgamations – the first between 1917 and 1922, the second in the early 1940s and the third since the early 1960s. Buchanan [26] noted that these waves followed changes in the **law relating to union amalgamations**. There are legal differences between **merger by amalgamation** and **merger by transfer of engagement**: either method may be used where two unions merge by one losing its identity within the other; but where they merge to form a totally new union only merger by amalgamation may be used. Under the Trade Union Amendment Act (1876) merger by amalgamation could only take place if not less than two-thirds of the total membership of each union agreed. This was relaxed by the Trade Union (Amalgamation) Act (1917) which allowed a merger by amalgamation to take place if (a) at least 50 per cent of the membership of each union voted and (b) those voting in favour of amalgamation exceeded those voting against by 20 per cent or more. This was followed by the first wave of mergers which included the creation of the T&GWU and GMWU. However, as unions increased in size it became more difficult, if not impossible, for the unions to meet the first requirement of at least 50 per cent of the membership participating in the ballot. This problem was overcome, in the first instance, by the Societies (Miscellaneous Provisions) Act (1940) which applied to mergers by transfer of engagements: this required only the transferring union, which was often a small union, to undertake the ballot. Subsequently, in the Trade Union (Amalgamation) Act (1964), the voting requirement was relaxed still further to a simple majority of those voting in both types of merger.

There appears to be a difference of opinion as to the **effect of these amalgamations on British trade union structure**. Robertson and Thomas believe that since 'amalgamations usually consist of "like joining like", they seldom change the basic pattern [27], whilst Clegg believes 'they have strung together groups of members and areas of recognised bargaining rights in ever more incomprehensible confusion' [28]. All that can really be said is that for two or more unions to merge there has to be some common element of interest or purpose on which to build, but that the common element varies between different mergers.

It is important to recognise that union mergers are a **response to some perceived change in the union's environment**. Buchanan's [29] analysis of the post-war pattern of union mergers shows that not only was there an acceleration in the annual average rate of mergers from five per year during 1949–62 to fifteen per year during 1963–79 but also that the earlier period was characterised by mergers involving small manual unions whilst the latter saw more larger mergers and mergers involving white collar unions. He explains this increased merger activity not only in terms of changing technology and employment affecting unions' recruitment patterns but also in economic terms. 1963–79, like 1917–22, was a period of increasing inflation in which rising prices and falling real incomes 'create financial difficulties for small unions . . . and may also emphasise the need to protect living standards by a powerful union negotiating with employers or government' [30]. This situation has remained during the 1980s and, at the same time, there have been more mergers of the medium-sized unions.

Undy et al. [31] have similarly argued that union mergers are a response to the need to **maintain financial and/or organisational viability**. They suggest that the desire to merge is related to some aspect of the union's size. They concluded from an analysis of a number of union mergers during the

1960s and 1970s that a decline in absolute membership or an increase in the demands on the union's services, resulting from such developments as more sophisticated bargaining, increased legislation or incomes policy, may prompt a **defensive merger** in which the union, usually the minor union in the merger, seeks organisational security by joining with a larger organisation. However, for the dominant union the merger may be primarily a **consolidatory merger** which confirms its position as the dominant union in the industry.

In contrast, Undy *et al.* regarded the approach of both the T&GWU and ASTMS as primarily one of **aggressive mergers** wherein they 'generally outbid their competitors for the privilege of rescuing minor unions from extinction' and thereby 'make effective inroads into the minor merging unions' new and relatively unorganized job territories – or, on the other hand, to prevent the better organized areas of job territory falling to some other competitor organization' [32]. Indeed, Undy notes an interesting contrast in union approach to mergers in that 'while the TGWU successfully negotiated 15 mergers between 1968 and 1974 . . . the GMWU did not complete any mergers of note' [33] – a reflection of their differing passive/positive approaches to recruitment.

A number of significant points arise from the studies of trade union amalgamations:

1. The **attitudes of the unions' leadership** is of crucial importance. Undy *et al.* noted that whilst natural growth of a union's membership 'can be determined by factors outside the control of the national leaders', mergers and amalgamations 'cannot be experienced by the union without a positive act by the national leadership' [34]. It is they who determine the suitability of potential and actual merger partners; and suitability is measured not simply in terms of industrial/occupational 'fit' of the respective unions' memberships but involves other factors such as the proposed internal governmental arrangements for the new union (including arrangements for the existing officers of the merging union) and the 'political' stance of the unions.

2. Amalgamations between unions are **not generally a simple 'once and for all' integration of two organisations** but, as Hughes pointed out, are 'a process involving structural changes, and changes in trade union organisation and attitudes extending over a number of years' [35]. External changes in trade union structure are closely associated with, and may indeed be the cause or effect of, internal organisational change. In some cases organisational changes have been a prerequisite for amalgamation to be acceptable whilst in others it has been left to be dealt with after the amalgamation. At the same time, Undy *et al.* noted that the dynamic nature of the union mergers had the potential to create a merger movement in so far as 'a merger stimulated by absolute size reasons disturbed other unions' relative size considerations' who then 'in turn, sought mergers in order to restore the status quo' [36].

3. Any amalgamation involves **some degree of loss of identity**, particularly
    for the smaller union. Upton noted that for many union activists 'they
    may be asked to merge with another union which has often been
    regarded as a nuisance, a rival or even a downright bogey' [37]. The
    extent of any loss of identity will depend on the organisational
    arrangements made for integrating the different sets of membership,
    officers and institutions. This problem has been eased to the extent that
    most major unions have developed internal organisational arrangements
    which allow a degree of separate identity through trade or service
    sections (amounting almost to internal 'federations'). When the
    NUAAW merged with the T&GWU in 1981 it, in effect, took over the
    T&GWU's existing agricultural section. However, as Upton points out,
    it is important to recognise that 'however much autonomy is promised
    within its own province a small union which goes in with a larger
    partner does have a lesser pull on the resources of the organisation and is
    only a minority sectional interest in the new union' [38].

Overall, the process of amalgamation during the post-war period has
resulted not only in fewer unions but also in larger sectoral or conglomerate
unions with increasingly diverse memberships. Figure 5.1 shows the development of the modern Amalgamated Engineering Union (AEU), based on the
old strength of manual labour in manufacturing, and Manufacturing, Science
& Finance Union (MSF), based on the new strength of non-manual
employment, service industries and new technology. The Amalgamated
Society of Engineers was conceived in the 1850s as an amalgamation of local
societies representing apprenticed craftsmen in the engineering industry. As
other industries developed and more machinery was needed, so engineering
craftsmen and the ASE's craft membership spread into these other non-
engineering industries. Subsequently, the union recruited downwards into
the semi-skilled and unskilled grades and upwards into the supervisory
grades – principally in the engineering industries. In these industries it
became a craft and allied occupation union. Further amalgamations in 1920
and the change in its name to the Amalgamated Engineering Union indicates
its movement away from a narrow occupational basis of engineers to an
industrial basis of engineering.

In the early 1960s the AEU (1 million) had unsuccessful discussions with
the T&GWU, GMWU and ETU about forming a conglomerate union which
would be pre-eminent in the trade union movement. Instead, it looked to
smaller unions in its own sphere of activities to secure a **consolidatory
merger** which would increase its size and create a dominant **sectoral/general
union** in engineering. For the smaller unions (Union of Foundry Workers
(UFW – 68,000) and Constructional Engineering Union (CEU – 27,000)) it
provided a **defensive merger** giving increased security and influence as part
of a bigger organisation. Although the Draughtsmen & Allied Technicians
Association (DATA – 90,000 non-manual members) saw merit in closer
collaboration with its manual counterparts it was unhappy at losing its

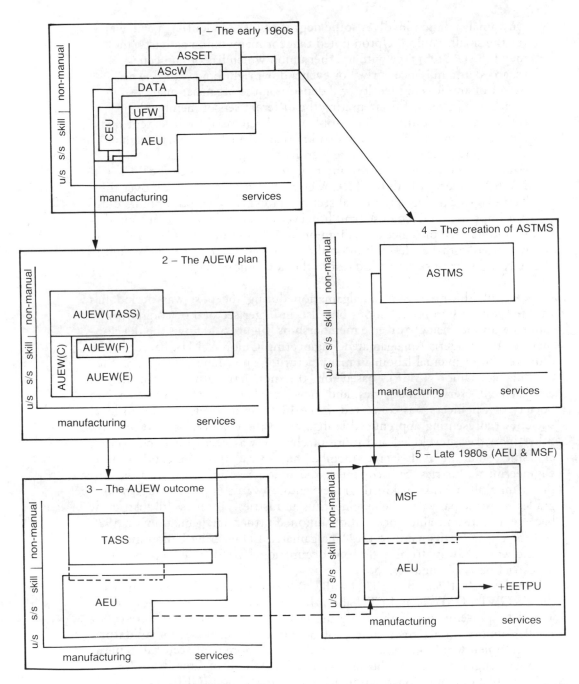

Figure 5.1   *Development of the AEU and MSF*

independence and identity as a junior partner in the new union. To facilitate the merger process:

1. The four unions were initially to retain their individual identity through separate sections (with internal self-government) within a federal union which would eventually become a single unified organisation.
2. The non-manual members of the original AEU were combined with the DATA membership and renamed Technical & Supervisory Section (TASS).

During the 1970s the AEU continued, again unsuccessfully, to try to further consolidate its aim of one sectoral/general union in the engineering/ metal industries through merger discussions with the National Union of Sheet Metal Workers, Coppersmiths, Heating & Domestic Engineers (NUSMWCH&DE) (which eventually merged with TASS), National Union of Vehicle Builders (which merged with T&GWU), Amalgamated Society of Boilermakers, Shipwrights, Blacksmiths & Structural Workers (which merged with GMWU) and the Iron & Steel Trades Confederation. TASS's differences with the AEU about the process of union government and its different political outlook meant that it resisted attempts at final unification of the four sections – to the extent of, unsuccessfully, using legal action to try to stop the merger of the other sections. In 1984 the other sections formally united in one union (1 million) and reverted to the name AEU. The original plan of one sectoral/general union had become divided into two quite separate unions with the AEU returning to primarily a craft/allied occupation union. However, TASS had exerted its independence by also merging with unions (the Association of Patternmakers & Allied Craftsmen, NUSMWCH&DE and Tobacco Workers Union) which were, primarily, manual and therefore went beyond the boundary established by the AEU's plan (i.e. it was no longer purely a non-manual union).

At the same time as the AEU's plan for a sectoral/general union, the Association of Scientific Workers (AScW – 50,000) and Association of Salaried Staffs, Executives & Technicians (ASSET – 21,000) merged in 1967 to form the Association of Scientific, Technical & Managerial Staffs (ASTMS). This opened the boundaries of the union and ASTMS adopted a strategy of **aggressive mergers** by outbidding competing unions to acquire, in particular, staff associations in insurance, building societies and other private sector companies. The union also increased by natural growth as the high profile image of the union, and in particular its General Secretary (Clive Jenkins), attracted many of the new technical staffs, professionals, administrators and managers (71,000 in 1967, 147,000 in 1969 and 496,000 in 1979). However, the pressures of the 1980s affected even an aggressive recruiter like ASTMS and its membership declined. In 1988 ASTMS (390,000) and TASS (241,000) merged: both were of the same 'type' (non-manual, mainly private sector), shared a similar 'political' outlook and for both it represented a

consolidatory merger to help secure a position as the premier union for non-manual employees in the private sector. Significantly the new name of Manufacturing, Science & Finance Union denotes a further opening of the union's main areas of recruitment interest.

The six 'traditional' relatively closed unions of the 1960s have become two quite different 'modern' unions. The AEU, despite its grand plan, lost its future potential base of membership growth (non-manual members) and has had to re-create a non-manual section and appears to be looking to a merger with the EETPU (both originally craft unions) but, first, will have to overcome the problem created by the EETPU's expulsion from the TUC. MSF, on the other hand, has steadily built up its position based on technical, professional and managerial employment, service industries and new technology.

A number of interesting trends appear in other mergers during the 1980s (membership figures as at 1989):

1. A number of the mergers appear to be directed towards the creation of a stronger **industrial/sectoral** basis in industries facing strong competition, declining employment and/or management rationalisation strategies; but have not always achieved completeness. For example:
   (a) in printing the NGA (125,000) has merged with SOGAT (176,000) to form the GPMU [39];
   (b) in television BETA (32,000 and formed in 1984 from a merger between the ABS and NATTKE) has merged with the ACTAT (30,000) to form BECTU. However, a 'breakaway' from ACTAT (the Television & Film Production Employees Association) merged with EETPU;
   (c) in the clothing sector whilst NUH&KW (39,000) has merged with NUFLAT (29,000) to form a new union NUKFAT, the larger NUT&GW (73,000) has merged with GMB;
   (d) in transport, although a Railway Federation of Unions was established in 1983 by the NUR and ASLEF (19,000) which it was hoped TSSA (36,000) would eventually join, subsequently the NUR (103,000) merged with the NUS (20,000) to form RMT;
   (e) in the civil service NUCAPS (116,000) was formed in 1988 from a merger between the CSU and SCPs and subsequently has sought merger with the CPSA (128,000);
   (f) most significantly, COHSE (21,000), NALGO (750,000) and NUPE (605,000) are to merge into a single primarily public sector union.

2. The continued development of **conglomerate** unions. For example:
   (a) the GMB (823,000) was formed in 1982 by the merger of the GMWU with the ASBSB&SW to which has been added APEX (83,000), NUT&GW (see (1(c)) above) plus a series of small textile unions;

Table 5.3   *Transfers of engagement of EETPU, 1989 and 1990*

1989:
1. Association of British Professional Divers
2. Ministry of Defence Staff Association
3. Springfields Foremans Associations
4. Nelson & District Power-Loom Overlookers Society
5. National Association of Senior Probation Officers

1990:
1. Nationally Integrated Caring Employees
   (breakaway from health service unions)
2. National Association of Fire Officers
3. Prison Service Union
   (breakaway from POA)
4. Institute of Journalists
5. Television & Film Production Employees Association
   (breakaway from ACTAT)
6. Haslingden & District Power-Loom Overlookers Society
7. National Association of Power-Loom Overlookers

Source: *Annual Report of the Certification Officer*, 1989 and 1990

(b) the T&GWU (1,271,000) has absorbed the NUDB&TW, NUAAW and several small manual industrial unions and there is the possibility that it will absorb the NUM (59,000);

(c) the EETPU has recently absorbed a range of unions which have no relationship to its principal industrial base and whose merger with the EETPU appears to be more 'politically' based (certainly three are 'breakaways' from other, TUC affiliated, unions) (see Table 5.3).

3. A blurring of the **public/private sector boundary**. For example, the public sector Health Visitors Association (16,000) has merged with MSF, whilst the private sector National Unilever Managers Association (3,000) has merged with IPMS (formerly the Institution of Professional Civil Servants).

5.4 Trades Union Congress

The Trades Union Congress (TUC) is the central co-ordinating organisation of the trade union movement in Britain. However, the term may be used in two quite distinct, but related, ways:

1. **The institution as a whole**, encompassing, as with trade unions, the entire organisational arrangement of annual conference, General Council and secretariat including the General Secretary;
2. Only the **annual conference of delegates** from affiliated organisations.

[Throughout this section the terms TUC and Congress will be used to refer to the complete organisation and the annual delegate conference respectively.]

Function

When considering the **relationship between the TUC and its affiliated organisations**, it is important to remember that, like employers' associations, it is a second degree grouping comprising organisations rather than individuals and it is 'inevitably distant from the branch room and from the shop and office' [40] and, as Taylor points out, it is 'a loose confederation, not a centralized monolith' [41]. A trade union is not required, on joining, to surrender its sovereignty or autonomy – particularly in carrying out its economic and job regulation functions in pursuit of the interests of its membership. The TUC has stated that its authority over affiliated members must 'be defined in terms of influence, not of power' derived from 'the willingness by unions, and by their members, to abide by decisions to which they are parties' [42] and that it would be meaningless for them 'to be given powers to direct and instruct unions unless unions in their turn have the same power over their members' [43]. However, affiliated organisations are expected to conform to TUC policies.

The potential **power and authority of the TUC** is enhanced by, as Clegg notes, the fact that 'there are few British trade unions of any size or importance which remain unaffiliated' [44]. The only major organisations outside the TUC are professional associations such as the British Medical Association, the Royal College of Nursing and the Assistant Masters and Mistresses Association. Furthermore, as Jackson points out, the TUC has 'been able to prevent the major rifts developing between sections of the union movement that are a characteristic of some other countries' [45]. Whereas in these other countries there is more than one central co-ordinating body providing a focal point for national trade union activity (France, Italy and The Netherlands divided on political and religious lines; Sweden and Australia divided between manual and white collar unions), the TUC in Britain has all types of unions within its membership. At its peak of membership (1979) the TUC, through its affiliated organisations, represented 50 per cent of the total workforce; however, this has decreased with the decline in trade union membership since 1979.

It may be argued, taking a **narrow constitutional view**, that the TUC's function is to represent the interests of the organisations which are its direct members and not the individual trade union members who are indirectly linked to the TUC through their union's affiliation. However, in a more general sense, the TUC may be regarded as the only organisation which is representative of all trade unionists and the trade union movement as a whole, and indeed is often regarded as being the spokesman for all wage and salary earners irrespective of whether they are unionised or not. This dichotomy is reflected in the **objectives of the TUC** which include:

1. 'To do anything to promote the interests of all or any of its affiliated organisations or anything beneficial to the interests of past or present individual members.
2. To assist in the complete organisation of all workers eligible for membership of its affiliated organisations and . . . to assist in settling disputes between the members of such organisations and their employers or between such organisations and their members or between the organisations themselves.
3. Generally to improve the economic and social conditions of workers in all parts of the world and to render them assistance' [46].

The TUC itself distinguishes between its internal functions within the trade union movement and its external function on behalf of the movement. Its **internal function** is primarily concerned with developing policy, co-ordinating the activities of its affiliated organisations, stimulating trade union activity in those areas and on those issues where it is needed; and trying to ensure that its affiliated organisations 'take into account the interests of other unions, and the broader interests of trade unionists as a whole' [47]. Whilst it is true, given the retained autonomy of affiliated organisations, that the TUC cannot instruct its membership, either individually or collectively, to pursue a particular course of action, nevertheless Congress has delegated to the General Council certain powers over affiliated organisations. In particular, the General Council has, through its Disputes Committee, the **power to adjudicate** in respect of inter-union disputes relating to recognition or membership rights and the **power to suspend from TUC membership** any affiliated organisation which does not abide by the policies determined at the annual Congress or whose activities are detrimental to the trade union movement. However, the **power to expel from TUC membership** is clearly retained by Congress.

As Hawkins has pointed out, the essential dilemma for the TUC is that 'if [it] ever found itself in the position of having to expel two or three major unions which have seats on the General Council, its own credibility as a representative body would be damaged' [48]. However, on two occasions the TUC has found itself in this dilemma. Some twenty unions, although none of them major ones, were expelled from the TUC for non-compliance with its policy of opposition to the Industrial Relations Act (1971). Following the repeal of this legislation the unions were re-admitted. In 1985, there was a confrontation between the TUC and the AEU and EEPTU, with potential expulsion and suggestions of forming an alternative 'TUC', regarding their acceptance of public funds to support the use of ballots which, at that time, was against the policy of the TUC. The issue was resolved by a change in TUC policy. However, the expulsion of the EEPTU in 1988 for failing to abide by a Disputes Committee decision requiring it to terminate two of its single union recognition agreements presented a more serious threat to the 'completeness' of the TUC's coverage. Although there was again the possibility of the EEPTU providing the nucleus around which other non-TUC unions might group to form an alternative focus of representation this failed to materialise; rather a handfull of small associations of similar 'political' and industrial outlook (some 'breakaways' from TUC affiliates) have merged with the EEPTU.

The **external function** of the TUC is to represent 'the movement to the government and other outside organisations, asserting the independence of the trade union movement and the right of trade unionists to a share in decisions which affect them, accepting the corresponding obligations and reminding unions of those obligations, and when necessary defending particular unions against external bodies' [49]. It is important to note that it has **no direct collective bargaining role**; whilst Congress may adopt policies in respect of wages, hours, holidays, retirement age and general working conditions, it is up to the affiliated organisations to translate these policies into reality, through their negotiations with companies and employers' associations. This is in marked contrast to other countries, such as Sweden and The Netherlands, where the central union organisations have accepted the responsibility of periodically negotiating national 'umbrella' agreements with the government and central employers' organisations. However, under the corporatist political ideology of the 1960s and 1970s the TUC became 'increasingly involved in the actual administration of the industrial system, nominating representatives of the trade union movement to a great variety of public committees, councils, boards and other organisations' [50]. During the period of the 'social contract' (1974–77) the TUC agreed to, and supported, an incomes policy with the Labour Government in return for their commitment to a range of economic and social policies and, as Hawkins points out, in the 1973/1974 mining dispute which immediately preceded this, the TUC went so far as to make an offer to the Conservative Government 'which committed the General Council to dissuade affiliated unions from quoting an exceptional miners' settlement, if such a settlement was allowed, in support of their own wage claims' [51]. However, the shift in political ideology after 1979 towards a 'free market' orientation has substantially reduced the TUC's role in tripartite discussions with Government and employers regarding economic and industrial issues.

Much of the TUC's effort in the late 1980s has been directed towards **reducing the decline in trade union membership**. Part of the TUC's Special Review Body report in 1988 was concerned with examining how the TUC might support and co-ordinate individual trade union activity in a number of areas. For example:

1. Pooling resources to undertake local labour market surveys and joint recruitment campaigns in particular localities.

2. Improving recruitment literature and strategies aimed at particular groups such as women, young people, part-timers, etc.
3. Developing joint services for individual union members (e.g. legal advice, pension and insurance arrangements and credit cards).
4. Creating a positive image for trade unionism.

At first sight it may appear that the **weakness** of the TUC is its lack of ability to pursue a firm, positive role on behalf of the trade union movement because of its limited power and authority over its affiliated members and its lack of active participation in the process of collective bargaining. However, these may also be seen as the source of its **strength**. The TUC is a voluntary federation of trade unions and therefore it believes it has to be seen to retain a substantial degree of impartiality if it is to aid the process of 'reconciling the special interests of particular unions, or groups of members, with the general interests of the trade union movement and of deciding when which set of interests should prevail' [52]. Thus, its decisions and policies have to come from a large measure of internal consensus within its membership rather than be imposed by the TUC as one organisation on the other organisations which are its members.

Organisation

The **function of Congress**, which meets annually, is as follows:

1. To consider the annual report of the General Council on the activities of the TUC during the previous year.
2. To debate and vote on resolutions submitted by member trade unions and the General Council.
3. To approve/elect the General Council for the forthcoming year.

It is the debates and votes on the General Council report and the various resolutions which determine the TUC's policies. The **relationship between Congress and the General Council** is complex. On the one hand, the General Council appears to have significant influence on both what is debated and the outcome of such debates. For example:

1. It has the right to submit resolutions for debate and, because its members are drawn from the major unions, any initiation of policy or action on its part is almost certain to gain the support of Congress.
2. The members of the General Council are able, at their own union conferences, to exert influence on the content and approach of their union's resolutions to the TUC Congress.
3. They are also considerable, or even majority, contributors to the Congress debates themselves.

Indeed, Clegg commented that 'the council dominates Congress' and that 'unless the council is divided, it is not easy for Congress to initiate policy' [53]. On the other hand, Congress is not completely powerless to check the activities of the General Council and Clegg also noted that Congress is able to exercise a degree of control over the General Council by 'referring back' sections of its report for further consideration which 'is almost invariably followed by a modification of the council's line'[54].

It would be wrong to regard Congress as an opportunity for rank and file members to participate in what may be considered the supreme policy making body of the trade union movement. Many unions do not send their full quota of delegates. In part, this may be due to the relatively high costs incurred by unions in sending their full quota of delegates. However, the main reasons are to be found in the **voting arrangements** at Congress and the **nature and composition of the delegations** themselves:

1.   The availability and use of the card 'block' voting system on important issues means that a union does not need to send its full quota of delegates for its influence to be commensurate with its size – at the extreme it only needs one delegate to cast the union's card vote.
2.   It is preferable that the delegations should be composed of representatives with the authority to speak on behalf of, and commit, their organisation, and this constrains how many, and who, should form the union's delegation. Certainly many delegations include a significant proportion of senior full-time officers and NEC members.
3.   The delegations are generally mandated on most issues (and therefore controlled by their membership) by virtue of the policies and decisions previously determined by their own annual conferences.

The **duties of the General Council** include that they shall:

1.   'keep a watch on all industrial movements and, where possible, coordinate industrial action;
2.   watch all legislation affecting labour and initiate such legislation as Congress may direct;
3.   endeavour to adjust disputes and differences between affiliated organisations;
4.   promote common action by the Trade Union Movement on general questions, such as wages and hours of labour, and any matter of general concern that may arise between trade unions, or between employers and trade unions, or between the Trade Union Movement and the Government, and shall have power to assist any union which is attacked on any vital question of trade union principle;
5.   assist trade unions in the work of organisation, and shall carry on propaganda with a view to strengthening the Trade Union Movement' [55].

Until 1983 the General Council was elected annually by Congress. The **process of election** was based on the division of the affiliated members into trade groups each of which had one or more General Council members. Whilst each union could nominate candidates to serve as General Council members for their particular trade group, the actual voting was not conducted on an exclusively trade group basis but spread across the entire membership of Congress. Thus, all unions were involved in the election of the General Council members for each of the trade groups. The intention underlying this system was to produce General Council members who were responsible not to a particular union or trade group but to Congress as a whole.

However, in practice, this method of election was open to criticism in two directions:

1. Changes in the allocation of General Council seats was slow to reflect changes in the membership levels between trade groups.
2. The bigger unions tended to predominate. In some trade groups there was only one union and therefore their candidates were automatically 'elected' without any contest, and, Hawkins argued, 'election to represent any trade group is virtually impossible without the support of one or more of the giant unions' and 'candidates from the smaller unions must be politically acceptable to the leaders of the large unions' [56].

The arrangement for selecting the General Council was changed in 1983 to one based on an **automatic right of representation dependent on size**:

1,500,000 members and over	5 seats
1,000,000–1,499,999 members	4 seats
750,000–999,999 members	3 seats
500,000–749,999 members	2 seats
100,000–499,999 members	1 seat

Eleven seats were allocated for unions with less than 100,000 members to be elected at Congress from within that group of unions. The number of seats to represent women workers was increased to six; also on an elected basis. The effects of this arrangement are significant when, due to declining membership, a union drops below the 100,000 mark and thereby loses its right to a General Council seat. Certainly, the size of a union's affiliated membership, which in some cases has been questioned in the past, is now important not just in respect of the size of the block vote but also in respect of the right to a General Council seat. It is possible that this 'right' based on size has provided an additional stimulus for amalgamations. Perhaps most importantly the change to 'representation by right' has weakened the constitutional relationship between the General Council and Congress.

The **General Secretary** is perhaps the only role within the TUC's organisation which may truly be said to **represent the whole TUC** and trade union movement. Unlike the members of the General Council who are only part-time representatives of the TUC, and for the remainder of their time represent their individual unions, the General Secretary is employed full-time on behalf of the TUC. Although the General Secretary's role may be regarded as an executive one subordinate to both the General Council and Congress, nevertheless it plays a significant part in influencing the direction of the TUC's affairs and policies. Not only is the General Secretary a member of Congress and the General Council and its key committees, but is also invariably a member of TUC delegations to government, employers and other bodies and often acts as the leader and chief spokesman of such delegations. However, as Taylor points out, it must be remembered that although the General Secretary 'symbolizes the TUC, acting as its collective spokesman to the outside world . . . he has no big battalions to mobilize in his own support' [57] and can only exercise influence through persuasion.

Trades Councils have a longer history than the TUC and were instrumental in its establishment in 1868. Constitutionally the 435 Trades Councils are not affiliated members of the TUC but simply registered with it. Their function is, primarily, to provide a focal point for trade unions in their locality and any branch of a TUC affiliated union may affiliate to its local Trades Council. However, their importance and influence within the trade union movement has been reduced. Whilst it is the policy of the TUC and many unions to encourage union branches to affiliate to their local Trades Council, the TUC reported in 1980 that 'only approximately 4 million trade unionists are members of branches affiliated to Trades Councils' [58]. Nevertheless, on many occasions Trades Councils are able to play an important role in mobilising rank and file trade union support for both local and national issues.

The TUC does have eight **Regional Councils** in England and a Welsh TUC whose functions are 'to represent the TUC at regional level, to assist in gaining support for TUC policies, to monitor the implementation of these policies and as far as possible service trade union members of statutory and other related bodies' [59]. The membership of these Regional Councils comprises officials (either full-time or lay) nominated by those unions which have membership in the region with, in addition, 25 per cent of the members being appointed by the County Associations of Trades Councils (CATCs) within the region. The Welsh TUC, however, is structured more closely on the national institutions of the TUC itself with an annual delegate conference and a General Council. The TUC believes this regional organisation 'provides a better operational structure for the TUC to involve active trade unionists in its work' [60].

In addition, Scotland has its own, completely separate **Scottish TUC**. The STUC was established in 1897, following the decision of the 'English' TUC to exclude Trades Councils from membership. Its organisational arrangements reflect the duality of its membership, although trade unions have the predominant position. It has some 80 affiliated unions (of which a few are exclusive to Scotland). The STUC works in close collaboration with the 'English' TUC but is the trade union movement's representative on Scottish employment, industrial, economic and social matters – particularly to government.

Inter-union relations

The extent of the TUC's ability to involve itself in the affairs of its affiliated organisations is limited by the fundamental principle that each union retains its independence to protect and pursue the interests of its members and is responsible ultimately only to its own members for its actions. However, by affiliating to the TUC a union also accepts that this right is tempered by the need for it to conduct its affairs in a way which is not detrimental to either another affiliated member or the trade union movement as a whole. Thus, there is provision within the TUC's constitution for the General Council, in certain circumstances, to play a role in regulating such relationships.

Industrial disputes

All affiliated organisations should inform the General Secretary of 'matters arising between them and their employers and/or between one organisation and another, including unauthorised and unconstitutional stoppages of work, in particular where such matters may involve directly or indirectly large bodies of workers' [61]. Once informed, the TUC will not intervene unless invited to do so by the member organisation concerned and so long as there is the prospect of the dispute being resolved through the normal industry disputes machinery. If this is not the case, the General Secretary or General Council may simply inform other affected organisations of the circumstances of the dispute or, if the members of other affiliated organisations are likely to be involved in the stoppage or otherwise affected, formally consult with representatives of the organisations concerned and offer advice for the solution of the problem. The General Council may also organise 'such moral and material support as the circumstances of the dispute may appear to justify' [62].

It is difficult to assess the precise degree of TUC involvement under this heading. Certainly it has rarely used the full extent of its powers to organise active support from affiliates for a member in dispute. The most notable occasion being the 1926 General Strike when affiliated organisations were formally called upon to support the miners in their resistance to a wage cut. However, this presented a major constitutional problem – who should control the conduct of such a dispute including, most importantly, the negotiations? The TUC felt that the miners, in requesting such support, had effectively transferred responsibility for negotiations and the determination of the final settlement to the TUC. The fact that the final settlement agreed to by the TUC was unacceptable to the miners largely because it included wage cuts (indeed there was no miners' representative on the TUC Negotiating Committee) did not stop the TUC from calling off the General Strike. When similar situations have arisen more recently, as in 1984 GCHQ and mining disputes, the TUC's call for support was confined to an exhortation for moral and financial support from the trade union movement generally and seeking more active support only from those unions closely associated with the main dispute. However, the removal of legal immunity from secondary industrial action (Employment Act 1990) means that any call for supportive industrial action would open unions and their members to injunctions and possible claims for damages.

At the level of **consulting and offering advice**, either on their own initiative or at the request of the organisation involved in the dispute, the TUC's activities are more extensive, but at the same time less obvious, because much of this work may be conducted informally. Nevertheless, the TUC through the General Secretary and/or representatives of the General Council, has participated in a number of disputes in the past (particularly in the public sector). During such initiatives, which have involved meetings with government ministers and the chairmen or chief executives of nationalised industries and major companies, the TUC has sought not only to put the union's case more forcefully to the employer but also to conciliate between the two sides in order to reach a settlement without recourse to a strike. In this respect the TUC's efforts have often been complementary to, and supportive of, the work of ACAS. However, during the 1980s the Government has been unwilling to meet the TUC during disputes.

Inter-union disputes

An affiliated organisation should not authorise an official stoppage of work by its members over an inter-union dispute relating to recognition, membership, demarcation of work, etc., until the dispute has been referred to and considered by the General Secretary and/or the Disputes Committee. In addition, if there is an unofficial stoppage by its members, the union is required to take 'immediate and energetic steps to obtain a resumption of work' [63]. The Disputes Committee, comprising a chairman from the General Council and two senior trade union officials, is empowered, after investigation and hearing evidence from the unions involved, to make an award which is binding on all affiliated members.

In exercising its role as a conciliator or arbitrator in inter-union disputes, the TUC has been guided by the **Bridlington principles** first established in 1939. Apart from seeking to encourage unions to develop arrangements on closer working and spheres of influence, the Bridlington principles deal specifically with two areas:

1. **Poaching**: before a union may take into membership applicants who are or have been members of another union, their standing with the previous

union has to be cleared and the previous union may decline to 'release' them if, for example, they are in arrears of contribution or in the process of being disciplined for a breach of the union's rules.

2. **Organising**: a union should not attempt to recruit employees at any place where another union already has members and is recognised for that group of employees.

The importance of the TUC's role in helping to regulate relationships between trade unions is demonstrated by the number of cases dealt with each year. During 1980–89 722 disputes were referred to the TUC of which only 128 were formally referred to the Disputes Committee. Clearly, the application of these principles has become increasingly important in the context of the growth of more open recruitment patterns amongst many unions and, in particular, the development of 'single union agreements'. Consequently, the Bridlington Principles were amended in 1988 [64] to require a union not to enter into a single union agreement which might deprive other union(s) of existing recognition and/or negotiation rights without their agreement. Furthermore, a Code of Practice requires a union to notify the TUC when it is 'in the process of making' a single-union agreement (irrespective of whether other unions have recognition or negotiation rights) so that the TUC may offer advice taking into account whether another union has significant membership or is recognised else-where for a similar group of employees and/or the same employer. In this way the TUC may be able to both regulate and minimise inter-union conflict over single-union agreements. At the same time, the Special Review Body raised the possibility of introducing procedures 'whereby a union or group of unions wishing to organise a particular undertaking, establishment or grade could apply for sole organising rights for a period of one year' or 'under which particular industries or sectors could be accorded "protected status" with the result that access to them would be restricted to those unions already there' [65]. However, the Government's proposal [66] to give employees a legal right to join whichever union they wish 'will undoubtedly serve to fragment union membership and increase inter-union competition' [67] and certainly make any TUC attempt to regulate the pattern of union recruitment potentially unworkable.

Conduct of affiliated organisations

The General Council has the power to investigate the conduct of any affiliated member whose activities may be detrimental to the interests of the trade union movement or contrary to the declared principles or declared policy of Congress' [68] and may instruct the union to cease such activities; if the union does not comply, it may be suspended or expelled. The only time that this rule has been invoked in the recent past against a union for its internal activities was in 1961 when the Electrical Trades Union was expelled as a result of ballot-rigging by Communist elements within the union [69].

There was an obvious reluctance on the part of the TUC both to become involved in the internal affairs of a member organisation and to proceed with the expulsion of a major union which could reduce its solidarity and representative nature. In seeking to implement this, the TUC must always have regard to how far they should rely on persuasion to reform the behaviour of an affiliated organisation before resorting to the ultimate sanction of expulsion.

In 1976, in response to pressure concerning the power of trade unions to expel or refuse membership in a **Union Membership Agreement (closed shop)** situation, the TUC established an 'independent review committee' to which an individual could appeal. However, the number of appeals heard by this committee was small (53 cases between 1976 and 1983 with 23 formal hearings) and there was no provision for any financial compensation to be awarded. The existence of the committee was not sufficient to avoid the introduction of legislation in the Employment Act (1980).

International relations

The TUC's external role is not confined to Britain. The TUC also plays a very active and important part at the international level in both trade union and 'state' organisations. It is a member of the European Trade Union Confederation (formed in 1973) which covers eighteen countries and some 40 million trade unionists both inside and outside the EC and has representatives on the Economic and Social Committee of the EC and a range of specialist advisory committees. At the worldwide level the TUC was instrumental in the formation of the International Confederation of Free Trade Unions (ICFTU) in 1949 as an alternative to the Communist dominated World Federation of Trade Unions. (There is a third international federation of trade unions, the Christian-based World Confederation of Labour.) The ICFTU therefore has in membership social-democratic trade union organisations from some 80 countries with a combined membership of approximately 60 million. The TUC also provides Britain's worker representative to attend the annual conference of the International Labour Organisation (UN agency) and is represented on a number of its industrial committees. At the same time, the TUC has encouraged its affiliated members to play an active part in international affairs through their own industry based international federations (such as the International Metalworkers Federations [70].

Throughout its international activities the TUC has sought not only to represent and pursue the interests of British trade unionists and workers but also to aid and support trade union organisations and workers in those countries where trade unionism is weak or under threat from either employers or government. In particular the TUC, and the British trade union movement generally, has been concerned to establish trade union co-operation at company, industry and national levels to counteract the growth in power of multinational corporations. Although there are many obstacles to the creation of either a genuinely international trade union or international collective agreement, nevertheless there have been attempts by trade unions and employees to move towards similar terms and conditions of employment and to initiate active international action in support of an industrial dispute in one country. However, the major task at the international level has been to resist directly, and indirectly through influencing governments, the ability of multinational corporations to move their production and investment to those areas where wage costs are low and trade unionism weak.

5.5 Summary propositions

- The present structural arrangement of British trade unions is the result of a variety of influences over the past 150 years and the effect of the diversity of structure has been to produce competition between unions over both membership and jobs and to complicate the collective bargaining process.
- The process of amalgamation has not resulted in the predominance of one form of trade union but has created, and is likely to continue to create, larger open unions with a diversity of membership interests which have to be accommodated and reconciled within the internal organisation of the union.
- The function of the TUC is not to decide and direct the affairs of the trade union movement but to provide a focus for the expression of its collective view to employers, government and society and act as a forum for resolving inter-union problems.
- The authority of the TUC over its member organisations rests on their willingness to accept and abide by such authority; ultimately each member organisation is a sovereign body.

Further reading

- R. Undy, V. Ellis, W. E. J. McCarthy and A. M. Halmos, *Change in Trade Unions*, Hutchinson, 1981. Chapters 3, 5 and 6 provide a useful insight into changing trade union structure.
- W. E. J. McCarthy (ed). *Trade Unions* (2nd edn), Penguin, 1985. Part Three (Trade Union Structure) provides three useful readings.
- P. Taylor, *The Fifth Estate*, Pan, 1978. Part 2 is a useful source of

information on a relatively wide range of unions (although some of the information is now out of date as a result of subsequent union mergers).

- J. Lovell and B. C. Roberts, *A Short History of the TUC*, Macmillan, 1968. This provides a concise account of the history and development of the TUC.
- *TUC Reports*. The annual reports of the TUC provide an up-to-date insight into the range of work carried out by the TUC and the policy debates of the annual Congress.

References

1. D. Farnham and J. Pimlott, *Understanding Industrial Relations* (2nd edn), Cassell, 1983, p. 82.
2. K. Hawkins, *Trade Unions*, Hutchinson, 1981, p. 107.
3. J. D. M. Bell, 'Trade unions' in A. Flanders and H. Clegg (eds), *The System of Industrial Relations in Great Britain*, Blackwell, 1960, p. 138.
4. N. Millward and M. Stevens, *British Workplace Industrial Relations 1980–1984*, Gower, 1986, p. 73.
5. M. Shanks, *The Stagnant Society*, Penguin, 1962, and A. Shonfield, *British Economic Policy Since the War*, Penguin, 1958.
6. R. Hyman, *Industrial Relations: A Marxist introduction*, Macmillan, 1975, p. 59.
7. H. A. Clegg, *The Changing System of Industrial Relations in Britain*, Blackwell, 1979, p. 193.
8. H. Clegg, *Trade Unionism under Collective Bargaining*, Blackwell, 1976, p. 39.
9. C. Jenkins and J. E. Mortimer, *British Trade Unions Today*, Pergamon Press, 1965, p. 1.
10. J. D. M. Bell, *op. cit.*, p. 138.
11. *ibid.*
12. M. P. Jackson, *Industrial Relations* (2nd edn), Croom Helm, 1982, p. 49.
13. J. Hughes, 'Trade Union Structure and Government', Research Paper 5 (1), *Royal Commission on Trade Unions and Employers' Associations*, HMSO, 1967.
14. *ibid.*, p. 4.
15. R. Hyman, *op. cit.*, p. 41.
16. *ibid.*
17. H. A. Turner, *Trade Union Growth, Structure and Policy*, Allen & Unwin, 1962.
18. R. Undy, V. Ellis, W. E. J. McCarthy and A. M. Halmos, *Change in Trade Unions*, Hutchinson, 1981, p. 74.
19. J. Hughes, *op. cit.*, p. 6.
20. Report of *Royal Commission on Trade Unions and Employers' Associations* (Donovan Commission), HMSO, 1968, p. 180.
21. TUC Report on Trade Union Structure and Closer Unity, 1947.
22. TUC *Annual Report*, 1964.
23. H. Clegg, *op. cit.*, p. 38.
24. S. W. Lerner, 'The future organisation and structure of trade unions' in B. C. Roberts (ed.), *Industrial Relations: Contemporary problems and perspectives*, Methuen, 1962, p. 94.

25. S. W. Lerner, *Breakaway Unions and the Small Trade Union*, Allen & Unwin, 1962.
26. R. T. Buchanan, 'Merger waves in British unionism', *Industrial Relations Journal*, vol. 5, no. 2, 1974.
27. N. Robertson and J. L. Thomas, *Trade Unions and Industrial Relations*, Business Books Ltd, 1968.
28. H. Clegg, *op. cit.*, p. 32.
29. R. Buchanan, 'Mergers in British trade unions 1949–79', *Industrial Relations Journal*, vol. 12, no. 3, 1981, Table 1, p. 41.
30. *ibid.*, p. 48.
31. R. Undy *et al.*, *op. cit.*
32. *ibid.*, p. 215.
33. R. Undy, 'Twenty years of change in British unions', *Personnel Management*, May 1981, p. 35.
34. R. Undy *et al.*, *op. cit.*, p. 61.
35. J. Hughes, *op. cit.*
36. R. Undy *et al.*, *op. cit.*, p. 216.
37. R. Upton, 'Trade union marriages – the reasons and the rites', *Personnel Management*, September 1980, p. 39.
38. *ibid.*, p. 38.
39. J. Gennard and S. Dunn, 'The impact of new technology on the structure and organisation of craft unions in the printing industry' *British Journal of Industrial Relations*, vol. XXI, 1983, pp. 17–32.
40. 'Trades Union Congress Structure and Development', *Interim Report of the General Council*, TUC, 1970, p. 2.
41. R. Taylor, *The Fifth Estate*, Pan, 1978, p. 71.
42. 'Trades Union Congress Structure and Development', *op. cit.*
43. *TUC Annual Report*, 1975.
44. H. Clegg, *Trade Unionism under Collective Bargaining*, Blackwell, 1976, p. 35.
45. M. Jackson, *Trade Unions*, Longman, 1982, p. 4.
46. *TUC Rules and Standing Orders*, TUC, 1978, p. 3.
47. 'Trades Union Congress Structure and Development', *op. cit.*
48. K. Hawkins, *Trade Unions*, Hutchinson, 1981, p. 102.
49. 'Trades Union Congress Structure and Development', *op. cit.*
50. K. Hawkins, *op. cit.*, p. 100.
51. ACAS, *Industrial Relations Handbook*, HMSO, 1980, p. 44.
52. 'Trades Union Congress Structure and Development', *op. cit.*
53. H. A. Clegg (1979), *op. cit.*, p. 336.
54. *ibid.*
55. *TUC Rules and Standing Orders*, *op. cit.*, p. 6.
56. K. Hawkins, *op. cit.*, p. 97.
57. R. Taylor, *op. cit.*, pp. 78–9.
58. 'The Organisation, Structure and Services of the TUC', TUC Consultative Document, 1980, p. 8.
59. *ibid.*, p. 7.
60. *ibid.*, p. 8.
61. *TUC Rules and Standing Orders*, *op. cit.*, p. 8.
62. *ibid.*
63. *ibid.*, p. 9.
64. P. James, 'The TUC Bridlington Principles: a suitable case for treatment', *IRS Employment Trends*, no. 496, September 1991.

65. 'TUC special review body reports', *Industrial Relations Review & Report*, no. 420, July 1988, p. 9.
66. *Industrial Relations in the 1990s*, HMSO, 1991.
67. P. James, *op. cit.*, p. 6.
68. *TUC Rules and Standing Orders, op. cit.*, p. 10.
69. See C. H. Rolph, *All Those in Favour? The ETU Trial*, André Deutsch, 1962.
70. See ACAS, *Industrial Relations Handbook, op. cit.*, pp. 68–78, and A. Marsh, *Trade Union Handbook*, Gower, 1979, pp. 63–72 for details of international organisations.

Chapter 6

White collar unionism

6.1 Definition

It is extremely difficult to define precisely the term 'white collar' [1]. Most attempts at an **objective definition** concentrate on such factors as the employees' type of dress, method of payment or place and nature of their work. In addition to the term 'white collar' as opposed to 'blue collar' (which differentiates employees according to their working clothes), alternative terms frequently used include 'staff' as opposed to 'industrial' (which emphasises differences in terms and conditions of employment); 'office' as opposed to 'works' (derived from differences in the location and physical working conditions of the employees); and 'non-manual' as opposed to 'manual' (based on a distinction between the cerebral and manual content of work).

However, these approaches produce results which are often contradictory or inappropriate in the context of modern industry and technology. Both the copy typist in an office and tracer in a drawing office would commonly be regarded as 'white collar' (non-manual), yet the work which they carry out is low in diagnostic and discretionary skills (cerebral content) but high in manual dexterity skills and therefore, it may be argued, primarily manual in nature. It is equally difficult, and perhaps wrong, to seek to distinguish a maintenance craftsman (traditionally classified as a manual employee) from a maintenance technician (often regarded as a white collar employee) simply because it is possible to identify a difference in one set of criteria (such as payment system and job title) whilst there may be little if any difference under other criteria (such as type of work or the conditions under which it is carried out).

An **alternative subjective approach**, adopted by Bain [2], is to seek to distinguish white collar employees from manual employees by reference to the organisation's authority system and, therefore, include within the white collar category those groups which, because of their association with the management decision making process, 'generally see themselves as belonging more with management than with manual workers, and are generally regarded by manual workers as one of them rather than one of us, and by employers and managers as part of staff rather than part of the works' [3]. On this basis Bain included supervisors; scientists, technologists and technicians; clerical and administrative workers; professionals; commercial travellers and shop assistants; government administrators and executives; and special creative groups such as artists, musicians, etc. However, whilst this approach provides some insight into the nature of white collar employees and their position in the organisation, nevertheless it is open to criticism.

Bain's exclusion of managers in private industry, because he believed they performed the function of employer by exercising control over employees and therefore should not be regarded as potential recruits for trade unions, is unsound not only because they are also employees and have in many situations felt the need to become unionised, but also because even if they are not a potential for trade unionism this does not negate their being considered as white collar employees. More importantly, the three elements of subjective perception used by Bain to distinguish white collar from manual employees do not apply with equal force to all members of the same group and may, in some cases, even be absent. Whilst some clerical, secretarial, technical and professional staff working closely with decision makers at middle or senior management levels may, as a consequence, identify with the decision making process and therefore regard themselves as part of management, this is much less likely to be true for the mass of these staffs undertaking routine duties in general offices. It may be argued that these people, like manual workers, are divorced from the decision making process.

Thus, there is no clear-cut basis on which to define the term 'white collar'. Certainly, Wedderburn believes that technological change and the complex stratification of both work and society cannot be easily accommodated within 'the limitations of traditional occupational groupings (and certainly the limitations of a simple two-fold division)' [4]. Rather, as Bain and Price concluded, the common perception of what is meant by white collar appears to rest on a process of **assimilation by association** in which 'a group whose work possesses characteristics which have become symbolically associated with the possession of, or proximity to, authority may become assimilated to the white-collar group by its association with those symbols' [5] – the symbols being the work-based factors of type of dress, terms and conditions of employment or place and nature of the work.

Despite the difficulty of defining white collar, the development of white collar unionism is an important facet of British industrial relations in terms of its relatively late development during the 1960s and 1970s, its importance for the future development of trade unionism and, in particular, its potential impact on the character of the trade union movement.

6.2 Growth and importance of white collar unionism

The importance of unionisation amongst white collar employees is evident from the **significant changes in the structure of the labour force** which have occurred in Britain during the twentieth century. The proportion of the workforce classified as white collar has risen from under 20 per cent in 1911 to over 50 per cent by 1981. The growth in the numbers of white collar employees has been in marked contrast to the slow rate of growth, stagnation and then decline of manual employment and may be explained by two major industrial changes over this period:

1. There has been a significant development of tertiary industries which employ a much higher proportion of white collar employees than manufacturing industries (insurance, central and local government and service industries generally).
2. Within the manufacturing industries there has been an increase in the numbers of clerical, administrative, technical and professional employees as the result of organisational and technological growth.

The growth in white collar employment in the post-war period has been reflected in the figures for **trade union membership**. Bain and Price's analysis of trade union growth shows that whilst white collar union membership increased by a third in the sixteen years between 1948 and 1964 (2.1 per cent per annum), it increased by a similar proportion again in the six years between 1964 and 1970 (5.8 per cent per annum) [6]. In addition, Bain pointed out that in the period 1948–64 'almost the entire expansion of the TUC ... has been due to the increase in its affiliated white-collar membership' [7]. This expansion of union membership amongst white collar employees at a time of stagnating membership amongst manual workers meant that by the late 1970s white collar union density reached 43 per cent and represented 40 per cent of total trade union membership (as opposed to 21 per cent in 1948).

Model of white collar union growth

In seeking to explain the growth of aggregate white collar unionisation Bain [8] put forward a two-part functional equation:

1. the density of white collar unionisation is a function of the degree of white collar employment concentration and the degree to which employers are prepared to recognise white collar unions; and
2. the propensity of employers to recognise white collar unions is itself a

function of white collar union density and the extent to which government is prepared actively to promote the recognition of white collar unions.

Thus, he argued that three factors were crucial to the development of white collar unionism – employment concentration, employer reaction and government stimulus.

Perhaps the most significant factor within the work situation to influence the growth of white collar unionisation has been the **increasing concentration of white collar employees and the consequent change in their employment relationship with the employer**. Whilst in the early stages of the development of white collar employment it was possible for management to maintain a relatively personal and individual relationship with most of their white collar employees, this approach had to be modified once they became concentrated into bigger groups. The creation of an administrative system to manage these groups more effectively involved:

1. The intervention of supervisory/managerial roles between the individual white collar employee and the 'employer'.
2. A more specific definition of their work role through the development of job descriptions, job evaluation, management by objectives, etc.
3. Perhaps most importantly, the introduction of corporate payment structures and employment policies.

These developments tended to place more emphasis on the role than the role holder and as management began to regard the individual employee as simply a member of a group of similar employees subject to common terms and conditions of work, so the employees began to develop a group identity and loyalty. Indeed, Kleingarten argued that 'white collar employees are subject to a "reign of rules" in the same way and for the same reason as manual workers' [9].

Consequently, the individual employee's opportunity to influence his/her terms and conditions of employment was diminished in favour of corporate determination by senior management as part of their 'policy making' role. In such a situation, white collar employees are forced, if they wish to improve their personal situation, to do so through a mechanism of improving the situation of the group as a whole. Management's **standardised administration** provides the stimulus for white collar employees to act in a collective manner, despite any personal desire to act in an individual manner. The two pressures are mutually interactive in that whilst standardisation of terms and conditions of employment may encourage white collar employees to seek collective representation and protection through trade unions in the determination of these terms, this, in turn, leads to further standardisation of the relationship between management and white collar employees.

Some degree of **recognition by the employer** is vital to the development of white collar unionisation within an organisation. Without such recognition it is difficult for any union, but particularly white collar unions, to establish the necessary processes of joint regulation by which to demonstrate to members and non-members alike that it has the capacity to represent their interests. White collar unionisation is unlikely to progress beyond an embryonic stage unless management demonstrates its preparedness to recognise and negotiate with such unions. However, management has frequently sought to restrict the development of white collar unionisation:

1. At the lowest level, through what has been termed **peaceful competition**, management has tried to reduce the attraction of joining a trade union by:
    (a) establishing pay levels higher than those being paid in unionised organisations;
    (b) making pay increases at the very time the union is actively recruiting members, thereby seeking to demonstrate to employees that they do not need a trade union to bargain on their behalf to achieve pay increases; and
    (c) in some cases creating, or aiding staff to create, their own separate 'staff association'.

2. At the other extreme, through what has been termed **forcible opposition**, management has taken positive action to discourage employees from joining or becoming active in a union by:
    (a) ensuring that such active union members do not progress within the organisation in either pay or promotion;
    (b) insinuating management representatives (spies) into union meetings to note what is said and who is present; and
    (c) in some cases, dismissing those employees whom it believes are active leaders of the movement towards unionisation.

White collar employees generally lack the industrial strength to secure recognition from a recalcitrant employer and therefore **government policy** and action has been important in supporting the growth of white collar unionisation. Clearly, the high level of white collar unionisation in the public sector may be related directly to positive government policy since World War I. In addition, the government's preparedness to recognise and negotiate with unions representing its white collar employees may have influenced private employers to recognise white collar unions in their own organisations. However, it was not until the 1970s that the government took more active steps to restrict the employer's resistance to recognition. The Industrial Relations Act (1971) established a statutory recognition procedure (repealed in 1980) whereby a trade union refused recognition could invoke an investigation by the Commission on Industrial Relations (CIR) who would then make a recommendation on whether or not the union should be recognised. Despite the limited formal usage of the procedure, it nevertheless provided a positive backcloth which could not be ignored by management – particularly the principle that a union did not have to have a majority of the employees in membership nor even majority support amongst employees in any ballot before the CIR was prepared to recommend recognition. In effect, government policy recognised that if white collar unionism was to grow then white collar unions had to be recognised in order to be able to demonstrate their effectiveness. In addition, the legislation declared many of the actions which management had used to coerce employees into not joining a trade union to be Unfair Industrial Practices.

The implication of Bain's model is that the growth of white collar unionism had been restricted by the reluctance of management to accept union representation for their white collar employees – particularly in the private sector. However, Price points out that during the period 1968–79 'well over one-half of the total increase in white-collar membership occurred in industries and sectors where recognition had been achieved for the unions concerned many years previously'[10]. Price argues that whilst organisational factors relating to work concentration and employer acceptance are necessary for the development of white collar unionisation, so is the existence of a perceived **material interest** which may be served by collective organisation. In his view the economic pressures of rapidly rising prices and wages during the 1970s provided an impetus for both initial unionisation in many areas and an expansion of unionisation in areas where recognition had already been achieved.

It is often argued that the traditional **wage differential** between white collar employees and manual workers is eroded by strong unionisation amongst manual workers, and as a consequence white collar employees have themselves become unionised in order to restore their position. However, this argument requires to be treated with a degree of caution for the following reasons:

1. There has never been a time when there was a clear differential between manual wages as a group and white collar salaries as a group; there has always been an overlap between the earnings of the two groups as a result of the manual workers' ability to enhance their earnings through paid overtime, bonus payments, etc., and the fact that many of the lower paid white collar jobs are occupied by women or young people.
2. The variation in the level of white collar unionisation between industries does not appear to correlate with either the absolute level of white collar salaries or the degree of the erosion of their differentials over manual workers.
3. The pay relativity with manual workers may be seen by many white collar employees as a less significant reference point than their pay comparability with other white collar employees performing similar work.

However, this is not to say that white collar employees did not perceive themselves to be in a situation of **relative deprivation**. The frequent intervention of incomes policy during the late 1960s and 1970s not only limited increases in pay and reduced living standards but also, through the application of 'flat rate' increase formulae, had the effect of reducing differentials. Whilst this erosion affected the internal differentials of both manual and white collar groups, it was also perceived as an erosion of the differential between the groups. At the same time, manual workers tended to benefit more than white collar employees from the productivity schemes which management introduced and which provided pay increases above the policy norm. It was a frequent complaint of supervisors that they had to administer such agreements and schemes without any additional payments and that as a consequence the people under them were earning more than themselves.

Furthermore, white collar employees often found that the additional **fringe benefits** they received in the form of a shorter working week, longer holidays, pension and sick pay rights (which in part provided their status differential over manual workers) were also being eroded. Similar benefits were provided for manual workers either because management was pursuing a positive policy of 'harmonisation' or 'single status' within their organisation or because both management and manual trade unions saw it as a way to provide improvements outside the restrictions of incomes policy.

It was also a period during which white collar employees began to realise that the **job security** which traditionally had been associated with their type of employment no longer applied. It is significant that in many organisations the major impetus for white collar unionisation came when there was a threat of redundancy and white collar employees realised that manual workers, through the collective approach of their unions, were able to obtain better treatment and terms than they could achieve as individuals.

Importance to management

In the past management regarded its relationship with white collar employees, even on issues such as pay, as primarily an individual one; unlike the collective relationship more generally developed with manual workers. Consequently, white collar unionisation has tended to be regarded by management as unnecessary in that white collar employees must, as a result of their position within the organisational hierarchy, realise that management looks after their interests without the need for recourse to **external representation** on their behalf. At the same time, the advent of unionisation may be perceived as a restriction on management's prerogative to make decisions and an intrusion into its special relationship with white collar employees which might result in a clash of loyalties for their staff. These attitudes are perhaps best summed up in management's own words [11]:

1. 'It is our company's policy . . . that all employees have the right to approach management direct with any complaint or query which may arise, and which might affect the cordial relationship which exists between us. I cannot see any purpose, therefore, in our meeting to discuss the introduction of a third party into the relationship.'
2. 'A few of my staff may be members of a trade union and I do not interfere with their right to do so. Conversely I do not expect them to interfere with my rights to decide to run my business as I think fit, consistent with any duties I may have as a good employer.'
3. 'I do not see how management or a part of management such as foremen can be part of an anti-management organisation such as a trade union, and still be an effective member of the management team.'
4. 'If staff members are encouraged to join trade unions they must inevitably be liable to a conflict between their loyalty to the company and their responsibility to the union.'

Such attitudes have resulted in white collar employees often feeling reluctant either to join a union or, more importantly, to actively encourage other employees to join for fear of incurring management disapproval. However, as Bain points out, such management attitudes towards white collar unionisation appear to ignore the fact that 'regardless of how fair-minded or accessible to his employees an employer may be, he will not always be able to make decisions which are in his employees' best interests' [12]. Fox argues strongly that 'the legitimacy and justification of trade unions in our society rests . . . on social values which recognise the right of interest-groups to combine and have effective voice in their own destiny' [13]. In this context, white collar employees represent a distinct interest group, or series of subgroups, and the importance to management of their unionisation lies in the fact that the recognition of a trade union to negotiate on their behalf involves not only a change in the mechanism for determining their substantive terms of employment but also a **fundamental shift in the authority relationship between management and white collar employees.**

Importance to trade union movement

The shift in employment structure, coupled with the possibility that the trade union movement might fail to attract white collar employees into membership in sufficient numbers, led in the 1960s to McCarthy pointing out the danger to the trade union movement of 'concentrating on the least dynamic group in modern society' [14] and Bain suggesting the possibility of the trade union movement becoming 'the increasingly outdated representatives of a declining industrial minority' [15]. However, the growth of white collar union membership during the 1970s has meant that the trade union movement has avoided these dangers.

Whilst manual trade unions still exert considerable influence within both the trade union movement and the industrial relations system as a whole, the **balance is shifting towards those unions which represent white collar employees** because of both their increased numerical strength and their being the most obvious line for any future expansion of trade unionism. If white collar employees' attitudes towards such issues as industrial action, incomes policy and the role of trade unions in general are significantly different to those of manual workers, because of their different social and work stratification, then this is likely to be reflected eventually in a change in the attitudes and policies of the TUC and trade union movement as a whole. If, on the other hand, the increased unionisation amongst white collar employees is indicative of a change in what is often referred to as their 'middle class' attitudes, then the likelihood of any change in the general outlook of the trade union movement is much less.

The growth of white collar unionisation has certainly had an **impact on union structure**. White collar employees may belong to two types of union:

1. unions whose membership is exclusively or primarily white collar employees (MSF or NALGO); or
2. unions whose membership includes manual as well as white collar employees (AEU, T&GWU or GMBATU).

In the former, it is the employee's distinctive position in the occupational hierarchy which provides the basis of common interest and, as a result, such unions claim they are in a better position to represent the special interests of these employees. The fact that a person is a clerk or technician is considered to be more important than the type of firm or industry in which he/she works. The advantage claimed for the latter is that, by bringing together allied groups of workers in the same firm or industry within the same union, it is better able to provide a unified approach to management and at the same time use the strength of its manual members (who are generally the majority within the union) to support its relatively weaker white collar members.

However, the distinction between these two types of union will become increasingly unrealistic in the future with the continuing amalgamation of unions (of various types) into a very small number of conglomerate unions. As Bowen *et al.* point out, 'claiming to represent both manual and non-manual workers in the same industry must contain inherent instabilities arising over the latent conflict between rival interest groups' [16]. As a consequence the major manual unions which have significant numbers of white collar members have created **distinct white collar sections** within their organisational arrangements. The separation of the two groups has gone as far as the white collar 'section' having its own committees, conferences and full-time officers as well as having a separate name – for example, ACTSS (T&GWU). The degree of institutional separation means that these 'sections' are often in effect distinct unions in their own right, combining with their manual colleagues only to develop general policy for the whole organisation.

It has been suggested that white collar unionisation is, in some way, incompatible with **affiliation to the TUC or Labour Party**. Certainly, a number of white collar unions, principally in the public sector, did not affiliate to the TUC until the early 1960s. Nevertheless, there is no evidence to suggest that a union's affiliation to the TUC has detracted from its ability to attract and recruit white collar employees. Most white collar employees appear to accept the argument put forward by NALGO's leadership in the early 1960s that 'so long as NALGO remains outside the TUC it must become a powerless spectator on the sidelines. Only inside the TUC has it any hope of influencing national economic and wages policy and adequately protecting its members' [17]. Thus, the growth of white collar unionisation has not resulted in a split in the trade union movement. Significantly, all the public sector unions which balloted to *establish* a political fund for the first time in the mid-1980s because of potential restrictive definition of political activity were white collar and achieved substantial majorities in favour.

6.3 Character of white collar unionism

The character of white collar unionism may be examined at the macro level in terms of its relationship to the trade union movement and at the micro level in terms of white collar employees' attitudes towards trade unionism.

Union character

Price describes the concept of 'union character' as 'a shorthand phrase for conveying some of the differences between unions in goals, policies and activities' [18]. Discussions of the character of white collar unionism appear to be closely tied to comparisons with manual unions and, through this, assumptions about the nature of economic and social stratification within society and the role of trade unionism within that stratification. Two major approaches can be differentiated within this framework – one based on the notion of class ideology and the other based on the notion of status ideology (see Figure 6.1).

Prandy *et al.* argue that all theories of trade unionism, whether Marxian based or not, assume a **class ideology** approach which incorporates the 'conception of class based upon the market position of labour in the production of commodities, and of trade unionism as the pursuit, however limited, of class interests' [19]. Certainly, within a Marxian analysis, it may be argued that white collar employees form part of a middle class distinct from the working classes of manual workers and that it is manual workers who provide the impetus, because of their lack of status and power within

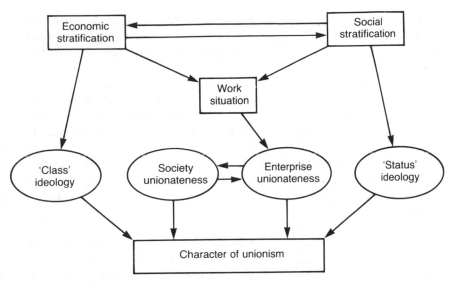

Figure 6.1 *Character of white collar unionism*

society, for the development of trade unions to protect their interests. The early absence of white collar unionisation may then be explained by reference to the values and perceptions on which trade unionism was founded being alien to white collar employees and their avoidance of such institutions as a means of maintaining their social differentiation from manual workers. The reluctance of white collar employees to join trade unions, or the development of a distinctive character to any organisation which they do join, is frequently attributed to their maintenance of a 'false class consciousness'.

However, many people believe that whilst a class analysis may have been appropriate in the nineteenth century (and even that is questionable in view of the existence of permanent white collar unions as early as the 1880s/ 1890s), it is no longer valid within a modern industrial society. As evidence they cite the difficulty of distinguishing between classes on the basis of such factors as income, education, social origin, access to social power, etc., because manual workers have gained many of the attributes often associated with the middle class (higher and more regular income, greater material rewards, increased job security and status and improved access to education and political influence) whilst white collar employees have seen their differentials in these areas eroded or removed altogether. At the same time, trade unionism has become involved in the operation and even management of the 'capitalist' system rather than a challenge to it and represents sectional rather than more general class interests.

It is the development and changes in unionisation during the twentieth century which has led a number of authors to question the applicability of the **concept of unionateness** as a basis for comparing and contrasting the character of white collar and manual unions. The criteria put forward by Blackburn [20] for judging the unionateness of an organisation involves:

1. determining the organisation's ability and willingness to pursue its members' interests by having regard to the extent to which it regards collective bargaining as its primary function, its degree of independence from employer influence and its preparedness to utilise industrial action, and
2. determining the organisation's commitment to the principles and ideology of a trade union movement by having regard to whether it considers itself a trade union and is affiliated to the TUC and Labour Party.

When applied in the context of the 1960s many white collar unions rated lower than manual unions on some or all of these criteria (particularly preparedness to use industrial action and identification with the wider trade union movement) and therefore could be considered as less unionate and clinging to a 'false class consciousness'. However, both Bain *et al.* [21] and Price criticise the applicability of unionateness not only at an operational level in terms of the ambiguity and relevance of the criteria, the difficulty of measuring them and the outcome variability as much within manual and white collar union groupings as between the groups, but also at a more fundamental level. As Price points out it is based on an 'assumption that the manual union "ideal-type" advanced . . . to measure white-collar unionateness is itself a measure of a class-conscious form of worker organization' whereas the 'sectionalism, instrumentalism and accommodation to the capitalist control of industrial and state power' [22] displayed by manual unions suggests this is not the case.

However, Prandy *et al.* believe that the underlying notions of 'class interest', 'class consciousness' and 'unionateness' are relevant to an understanding of the character of trade unionism, and particularly white collar unionism, providing it is recognised that 'class consciousness varies . . . in terms of the particularity or generality of interests' [23] which are identified and acted upon. Consequently, they feel it is necessary to distinguish between **enterprise unionateness** and **society unionateness**. The former refers to a collective pattern of behaviour within the workplace which seeks change in the immediate employment situation based on instrumental and sectional interest with no requirement for an ideological commitment. The latter refers to collective behaviour patterns which recognise a commonality of interest with other groups and organisations outside the immediate work situation and a need to act at the society level to achieve the desired change, and, therefore, contains an ideological element. They argue that both forms of unionateness 'reflect "class" action, in that they are concerned with strategies for bringing about changes in the distribution of rewards. The distinction between them is a result of the fact that they relate to strategies within different distributional structures, or rather different aspects of the same structure' [24].

By approaching this issue of unionateness from an examination and measurement of the attitudes of white collar employees rather than the institutional behavioural characteristics of the union as an organisation, Prandy *et al.* identify a number of **influences on the degree of unionateness**. Amongst both private and public sector white collar employees the prime determinant of 'society unionateness' appears to be the social origin of the employee, in particular whether or not the employee's father was a member of a trade union, although unionateness is also stronger amongst lower-paid, longer-service employees. 'Enterprise unionateness', on the other hand, appears to be influenced in the private sector by the employee's attitude to management (negative or positive) linked to the employee's degree of job attachment, promotion expectations and self-estrangement. Amongst public sector white collar employees, however, enterprise unionateness appears to be unrelated to such workplace factors. However, Prandy *et al.* recognise that the development of enterprise unionateness depends not only on changes in employee attitudes but also the employer's response and therefore it may be argued that the situation in the public sector reflects an employer response at an early date in advance of the development of unionateness. Whilst in the public sector enterprise unionateness appears to have only a marginal effect on the development of 'society unionateness', in the private sector the interrelationship between the two appears to be stronger with society unionateness exerting a greater influence on enterprise unionateness. This leads Prandy *et al.* to conclude that these are 'two different but related aspects, rather than totally distinct variables' [25].

Bain *et al.*'s approach to the character of white collar unionism is to differentiate the social and economic stratification elements within society and concentrate on the **status ideology** generated by the social stratification rather than the economic labour/capital division which underlies the 'class ideology' approach. In their view 'status is concerned with a person's position in the hierarchy of prestige in the society at large' and 'the workers' position in the social stratification system generates a certain picture or image of industry and the wider society which shapes their attitudes to trade unionism' [26]. It may be argued that 'status ideology' also implies an acceptance of the hierarchical stratification and the authority structure it represents as being both valid and internally compatible. Thus, because of the inherent 'middle class' values of individualism associated with the higher social position, unionism will only arise when white collar employees perceive their social position to be threatened by activities within the industrial environment (relative deprivation). Further, it may be expected that white collar unionism, when it does arise, will display different characteristics and have less in common with manual unionism.

Certainly, this view of the different character of white collar unionism was prevalent in the 1950s and early 1960s. Strauss, for example, argued that white collar employees joined unions 'not because they reject middle class aspirations, but because they see unionism as a better way of obtaining them' [27]. At the same time Mills argued that 'in so far as white collar claims for prestige rest upon differences between themselves and wage workers, and in so far as the organisations they join are publicly associated with worker organisations, one of the bases of white collar prestige is done away with' [28]. As Price points out, this approach views white collar unionism as 'a means of keeping ahead of manual workers rather than an expression of unity with them in fighting for a common cause' [29]. Within this analysis the development of a common cause with manual unionism or the display of similar collective behaviour patterns must imply a change in the social imagery which white collar employees have of both the social/authority stratification and their position within it. Arguably this has happened since the 1960s with white collar unions playing an active role within the TUC and trade union movement and white collar employees being more prepared to utilise industrial action to secure their interests.

The varying character of white collar unionism is reflected in the existence of not only trade unions but also staff associations and professional associations which may represent the interests of white collar employees. A combination of the unionateness concept (class identity) and social imagery (status ideology) may be utilised to examine the nature of these organisations within industrial relations.

It may be argued that a **staff association** is a form of 'false class consciousness'. However, this ignores the variation that exists within this group of associations in respect of their attitudes and activities. Certainly, Prandy et al. [30] argue that whilst society unionateness provides a basis for differentiating staff associations in general from unions in general, nevertheless staff associations can be internally differentiated in respect of enterprise unionateness – some occupying a communication/consultation role while others may undertake full negotiating with management. However, even when undertaking full negotiating their 'enterprise unionateness' is likely to be less than that of a union in so far as their members are generally not prepared or perceive themselves unable to support such negotiations by industrial action. The propensity of different groups of white collar employees to seek a staff association rather than union may also be explained. Technicians in manufacturing may adopt a class ideology perspective because of their close association with the production process and its obvious division between labour and capital and therefore prefer a union, whilst bank staff may adopt a status ideology perspective because of the nature of their industry and job and therefore prefer a staff association. It is important to note that a significant number of staff associations, some created in the 1970s as an alternative to trade unions, have subsequently transferred their engagements to TUC affiliated trade unions.

Prandy *et al.* regard **professional associations** primarily as associations for the regulation of prices rather than wages or job regulation because they have a client rather than employer orientation. Certainly, professional associations appear to embody the opposite class consciousness to that of trade unions but are strongly allied to the concept of status ideology. Thomason [31], on the other hand, regards them as associations of workers controlled through a corporation established and supported by the state. However, the position is complicated by the existence of different forms of professional association. It is the 'occupational association' within Millerson's four categories which is of importance in industrial relations – the others being prestige associations, study associations and qualifying associations. Whilst it is primarily the protective association subcategory (such as the BMA and other health service professional associations) which seeks to provide 'an organised means of exercising pressure to protect and improve the working conditions and remuneration' [32] of its members, the co-ordinating association subcategory may also provide a forum for specialist professions to discuss and act upon issues which are of common concern.

The **protective associations** may be distinguished from unions on the basis that their members do not generally regard their association as a trade union or themselves as trade unionists and are, through the maintenance of the status of the profession as a whole, primarily seeking to maintain their own personal status. As a consequence of their high status ideology, their society unionateness is virtually non-existent although, within the NHS, they have links between themselves. Their involvement in industrial relations activities has arisen primarily because their membership, or substantial parts of it, have become employed rather than being self-employed. Some associations (BMA) have taken the necessary steps to become legally recognised as trade unions and may be regarded as such in so far as the protection of their members' interests is a major function and they participate in collective bargaining on their behalf. However, their degree of enterprise unionateness may be regarded as low as a result of their reluctance, whether because of 'professionalism' or other reasons, to undertake industrial action in support of their sectional interests and because the principles underlying such associations still embody the acceptance of competition rather than co-operation between members.

Although the current professional/union mix in protective associations such as the BMA has come about in a move *away* from a purely professional association basis, a similar mix is being sought by other white collar employees in a movement away from trade unionism and *towards* professional association (for example, the Professional Association of Teachers and Association of Polytechnic Teachers in education). This development may be explained not only in terms of a simple rejection by such individuals of the strike 'weapon' or the 'politicisation of unions' but also, and more importantly, in status ideology terms. By publicly projecting an image of 'responsibility' and 'professionalism' these individuals and organisations are seeking to enhance the status of their occupation in the eyes of employers, government and the public. However, it may be argued that whereas the BMA has only to conform and reinforce the current social status of its members within society these others are seeking to create that status.

Clearly, no one theory adequately explains the complex nature and character of white collar unionism. The variation in the type of organisation adopted and the variety of attitudes displayed by these organisations suggests that the attitudes of white collar employees, like those of manual workers, result from a mixture of status ideology and class ideology which is not constant between different groups or even within the same group over time.

Member attitudes

Runciman [33] points out that employees who are dissatisfied with their work situation may react in either an **egotist/individual or fraternalist/collective manner**. In the former, they will seek to improve their economic or social status by their own individual efforts, but in the latter they combine with others in a similar position to exert greater pressure to improve the position of the group as a whole – and thereby improve their own position. It is often argued that egotism is the characteristic of white collar employees whilst fraternalism characterises manual workers and trade unionism. It would appear that in joining a union a white collar employee will be required to forsake individualism in favour of fraternalism. However, in reality the two are not incompatible. Roberts *et al.* found that white collar employees, like manual employees, are prepared 'to support either individualistic or collective action, or a combination of both, depending upon the strategy that best fits their situation' [34].

At the same time, it is often suggested that, because of their lower perceived society unionateness, white collar employees join a trade union primarily for **instrumental reasons**. They may join for the 'insurance policy' which the union provides should they, as individuals, require its assistance in any problem they encounter with their employer which they cannot handle or even for the discounts, cheap insurance or mortgage which the union is able to arrange for its members. However, as Mercer and Weir point out 'it would perhaps be accurate to characterize them as displaying a limited instrumentalism, a "conditional assent" not to the *values* necessarily, but to the possible *efficacy*, of trade unions in obtaining tangible benefits for their members' [35]. Whilst white collar union members may not display the attributes of commitment through their union to the trade union movement as a whole, nevertheless they perceive unionism to have advantages for them in protecting their interests. The implied criticism of unions adopting too 'political' a stance outside the industrial environment was noted by Nicholson *et al.* [36] in their study of a NALGO branch.

Finally, there appears to be a preference amongst white collar employees for **co-operation rather than conflict** with management. This co-operative approach, coupled with the integration of individualism with collectivism, may be seen in their greater preparedness to be involved in management systems such as work study, job evaluation, merit rating, etc., which allow for individual advancement within a collective framework. Furthermore, white collar employees are often perceived to be less inclined to utilise industrial action and to be more prepared than manual unions to accept no-strike clauses and arbitration. However, it must be recognised that white collar employees, particularly in the public sector, have increasingly displayed a preparedness to use industrial action although their propensity for such action may well be less than that of manual workers. It is debatable whether this lower propensity stems from a status ideology/individualism perspective or from a realism that, in general, they do not have the capacity to inflict a quick and serious economic loss on the employer.

In short, white collar union members appear to display the same range of behaviour patterns as those found amongst manual workers.

6.4 Summary propositions

- The relatively late development of substantial unionisation amongst white collar employees may be primarily due to their status-based social imagery and their perceived special relationship with management.
- Although white collar employees appear to be more status/egotist orientated than manual workers, nevertheless their unions appear to display a similar degree and range of unionateness as manual unions.

Further reading

- R. Hyman and R. Price (eds), *The New Working Class? White-Collar Workers and their Organizations*, Macmillan, 1983. A very useful collection of readings drawn from a variety of authors relating to both the nature of white collar labour and the development and character of white collar unionism.
- K. Prandy, A. Stewart and R. M. Blackburn, *White-Collar Unionism*, Macmillan, 1983. A detailed discussion of the 'class ideology' base to union character. (See also Chapter 6 in *White-Collar Work* by the same authors; Macmillan, 1982.)
- G. Bain, D. Coates and V. Ellis, *Social Stratification and Trade Unionism*, Heinemann, 1973. A comprehensive survey of the literature relating to social stratification, social imagery and union character.

- G. S. Bain, *The Growth of White Collar Unionism*, Clarendon Press, 1970. Although somewhat dated, this provides a useful examination of the factors which have influenced white collar union growth.

References

1. G. S. Bain and R. J. Price, 'Who is a white collar employee?', *British Journal of Industrial Relations*, vol. X, 1972, pp. 325–39.
2. G. S. Bain, *The Growth of White Collar Unionism*, Clarendon Press, 1970.
3. *ibid.*, p. 4.
4. D. Wedderburn, 'The conditions of employment of manual and non-manual workers' in *Social Stratification and Industrial Relations* (SSRC Conference), SSRC, 1969, p. 9.
5. G. S. Bain and R. J. Price, *op. cit.*, p. 338.
6. G. S. Bain and R. Price, 'Union growth and employment trends in the UK 1964–1970', *British Journal of Industrial Relations*, vol. X, 1972, Table 10, p. 378.
7. G. S. Bain, 'Trade Union Growth and Recognition', Research Paper No. 6, *Royal Commission on Trade Unions and Employers' Associations*, HMSO, 1967, p. 18.
8. G. S. Bain (1970), *op. cit.*
9. A. Kleingarten, 'The organisation of white collar workers', *British Journal of Industrial Relations*, vol. VI, no. 1, 1968.
10. R. Price, 'White-collar unions: growth, character and attitudes in the 1970s' in R. Hyman and R. Price, *The New Working Class? White-Collar Workers and their Organizations*, Macmillan, 1983, p. 156.
11. Quoted in G. S. Bain (1967), *op. cit.*, pp. 74–7.
12. *ibid.*, p. 75.
13. A. Fox, 'Industrial Sociology and Industrial Relations', Research Paper No. 3, *Royal Commission on Trade Unions and Employers' Associations*, HMSO, 1966, p. 7.
14. W. E. J. McCarthy, *The Future of the Unions*, Fabian Society, 1962, p. 4.
15. G. S. Bain (1967), *op. cit.*, p. 29.
16. P. Bowen, V. Shaw and M. Shaw, 'The attachment of white-collar workers to trade unions', *Personnel Review*, vol. 13, no. 3, 1974, p. 29.
17. Quoted in Volker, 'Nalgo's affiliation to the TUC', *British Journal of Industrial Relations*, vol. IV, no. 1, 1966.
18. R. Price, *op. cit.*, p. 163.
19. K. Prandy, A. Stewart and R. M. Blackburn, *White-Collar Unionism*, Macmillan, 1983, p. 2.
20. R. M. Blackburn, *Union Character and Social Class*, Batsford, 1967, p. 18.
21. G. Bain, D. Coates and V. Ellis, *Social Stratification and Trade Unionism*, Heinemann, 1973.
22. R. Price, *op. cit.*, p. 166.
23. K. Prandy *et al.*, *op. cit.*, p. 13.
24. K. Prandy, A. Stewart and R. M. Blackburn, *White-Collar Work*, Macmillan, 1982, p. 153.
25. *ibid.*, p. 171.
26. G. Bain *et al.*, *op. cit.*, pp. 8–9.

27. G. Strauss, 'White-collar unions are different', *Harvard Business Review*, vol. XXXII, Sept/Oct, 1954, p. 81.
28. C. Wright Mills, *White Collar*, Oxford University Press, 1951, pp. 311–12.
29. R. Price *op. cit.*, p. 163.
30. K. Prandy *et al.* (1983), *op. cit.*, pp. 33–4.
31. G. Thomason, *A Textbook of Industrial Relations Management*, Institute of Personnel Management, 1984, pp. 135–6.
32. G. Millerson, *The Qualifying Associations*, Routledge, 1964, p. 39.
33. W. G. Runciman, *Relative Deprivation and Social Justice*, Routledge & Kegan Paul, 1966.
34. K. Roberts *et al.*, *The Fragmentary Class Structure*, Heinemann, 1977, p. 134.
35. D. E. Mercer and D. T. Weir, 'Attitudes to work and trade unionism among white-collar workers', *Industrial Relations Journal*, vol. 3 (summer), 1972, p. 57.
36. N. Nicholson, G. Ursell and P. Blyton, *The Dynamics of White Collar Unionism: A study of local union participation*, Academic Press, 1981.

Chapter 7

Trade union organisation and government

7.1 Definition

The terms 'organisation' and 'government' refer to **the institutions and processes whereby trade unions arrange their internal administrative, representative and authority systems**. The central issue is how to combine *efficiency* (i.e. act as a countervailing power to management in the performance of the economic and job regulation functions) with *democracy* (i.e. being representative of, and ultimately controlled by, the membership). Hyman argues that trade unions 'explicitly incorporate a *two-way system of control*. Union officials are accorded specific powers of leadership and of discipline; in appropriate situations they are legitimately entitled to exert control over the members. But at the same time they are the employees and servants of the members, who are thus in appropriate situations entitled to exert control over *them*' [1].

7.2 Trade union organisation

Although each trade union is unique in terms of the precise role and relationship between the various organisational segments, in particular the relationship between officers and the institutions which comprise elected members and the degree of autonomy given to the local and intermediate levels, nevertheless all unions display the same basic pattern of institutions (see Figure 7.1).

The branch

Roberts argued that the branch was 'the primary unit of trade union organisation, and on it is based the whole pyramid of administrative and

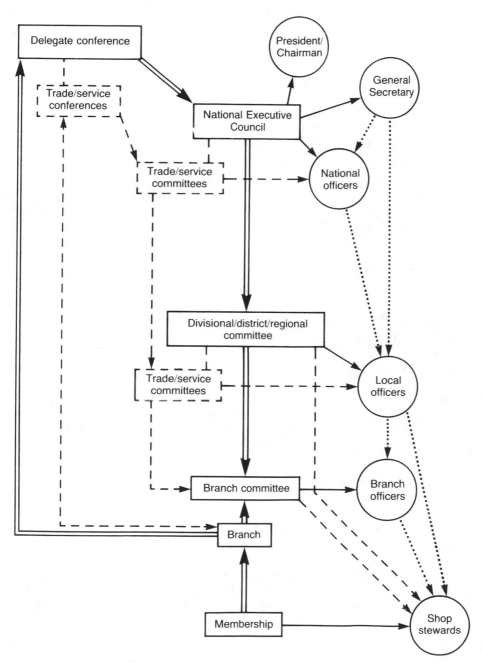

Figure 7.1 *Trade union organisation*

governmental structure' [2]. Certainly the branch is the formal institution within the union for the **regular meeting of the rank and file membership** to discuss matters of common concern and to directly participate in union affairs. It acts as:

1. a channel of communication between leadership and membership to convey the views of the membership upwards and disseminate union policy and instructions downwards;
2. an agency for the election of delegates to various union committees and conferences, and to submit resolutions and instigate changes in the union's rules;
3. a formal entry point for admitting members.

However, this has been reduced by the increasing role of the shop steward in servicing the union's membership at the workplace and the use of the check-off system, whereby union contributions are directly deducted from wages by the employer. Whilst guaranteeing the union's income, this also removes the need for the member to attend the branch in order to pay contributions.

The **size** of the branch may range from a handful of members to several thousand and the **frequency** of meetings may range from once a fortnight to only once a year (the Annual General Meeting). Whilst the majority of branches are administered by lay members elected each year, a number of larger branches, particularly in the general and white collar unions, are managed by full-time paid appointed secretaries. The branch may be:

1. **geographically based**: membership drawn from a given geographical area irrespective of the industry or company for whom they work; or
2. **plant based**: membership drawn entirely from a single employer.

A major problem facing trade unions is one of very **low attendance at branch meetings**: often not more than 10–15 per cent of the membership. Although it may be argued that this reflects a general feeling of satisfaction amongst members with the way the union is conducting its affairs on their behalf, nevertheless it means that the policies and actions of the union at all levels can only reflect the views of a minority who are interested and active enough to attend branch meetings and become delegates to the various committees and conferences. Whilst it is possible to attribute this low attendance to people's general apathy and dislike of meetings, the timing and manner of conducting branch meetings, or specific factors relating to the membership pattern of the union (in particular women and part-time workers), part of the explanation also lies in the **changing role of the branch within the union**. In the early local societies the branch and union were one indivisible institution with the membership directly participating in its affairs. However, as trade unions grew both in size and geographical coverage the branch became only one out of a number of units within a larger organisation and, with the advent of national bargaining, the union's collective bargaining function was transferred to full-time officers at the intermediate and national levels.

The subsequent movement of collective bargaining, in many instances, away from national level to the plant or company level has resulted in the **branch being bypassed in favour of the shop steward** as the focus of this activity. Therefore, because the majority of members join a trade union for instrumental reasons relating to wage bargaining and job regulation, it is perhaps inevitable that the membership should regard the relationship with their shop steward, who acts as their representative to management, as being more important than the relationship with their branch. The branch has become, in the eyes of many members, simply concerned with the internal government of the union and of marginal value in determining the policies and actions of the union in those areas they consider to be most important.

However, it is important not to overstate the problem of membership apathy in attending branch meetings:

1. It is not new – the Webbs stated in the 1890s, 'only in the crisis of some great dispute do we find the branch meetings crowded' [3].
2. If non-attendance at branch meetings is the result of effective union organisation and representation at the workplace then it is not necessarily to be deplored – rather, it may be argued, the link between the shop steward and the membership should be integrated within the union's formal organisational arrangement.

Intermediate organisation

Most unions, apart from the very small, have some form of intermediate organisation variously entitled Area, District, Division or Region. The **role** ranges from one of purely administrative convenience to one where, Roberts argued, because of their 'considerable degree of autonomy they provide an important check on the power of national executives and national officers' [4]. The relationship between the branch and these intermediate levels also varies in respect of the **election or appointment of delegates to the committee**. In some unions each branch has the right to its own representative, thus providing for direct participation and feedback by the branch in the affairs of these committees. In others the branch only has the right to nominate a candidate for election by the entire membership of the District, etc., to one of a limited number of places, thus resulting in some branches having no direct representation or link with the committee.

The relative **power and autonomy** of the intermediate level in some unions is perhaps as much a result of their historical development as it is of a conscious decision to create a system of power separation within the union's constitution. For example, the relative autonomy of the Area level in both the NUM and NACODS is reflected in their still seeking separate listing by the Certification Officer; the AEU's District Secretary's and Committee's power stems from the time when they were responsible for negotiating 'district' agreements; and, until the 1980s, the Regional Secretaries of the GMWU (formed from unskilled and semi-skilled workers of the nineteenth century who often enlisted 'outsiders' to help form and run their union) were automatically a substantial and important element of the union's National General Council and Executive Committee. Some unions (e.g. T&GWU and NALGO) make provision for distinct trade or service committees at the regional level to provide a co-ordinating link between members and branches in the same industry.

National executive council

Roberts argued that trade unions seek, wherever possible, to adopt the principle that 'policy making should be carried out by lay members responsible to the general membership, while the execution of the policy should be in the hands of full-time officers' [5]. The NEC may fall into both categories. In theory, the overall function of the NEC is to **administer and control the union between delegate conferences** and ensure that the policies determined by the delegate conference are carried out. In practice, however, the division of responsibilities is not clearly adhered to; the NEC cannot avoid being involved in **making policy**, as well as executing policy determined by the delegate conference, at least in so far as it has to interpret and apply what is often a generally worded policy and respond to events and developments which occur between delegate conferences.

There are, or have been, significant variations, in the composition and system of election of NECs:

• *Size and type of NEC*. At one extreme NALGO has a large part-time NEC of lay members (although some are virtually full-time as a result of their extensive subcommittee commitments), whilst at the other extreme the AEU has a small full-time NEC. The argument in favour of a part-time NEC is that, by still continuing to work at their normal job, the members are able to retain a close contact with rank and file members and thereby are better able to reflect their views. A full-time NEC, on the other hand, may identify more with the full-time officers of the union and become part of the administrative establishment. Nevertheless, a full-time NEC is better able to exercise control over the activities of the full-time officers whilst a part-time NEC, because of its infrequent meetings, may leave many, perhaps important, decisions in the hands of the full-time officers. This illustrates the essential dilemma between efficiency and democracy within union organisation.

- *Method of election*. The majority of trade unions have always elected their NEC on the basis of a membership ballot based on regional or divisional constituencies. However, in a small number of unions the NEC was elected by the delegates at the annual conference. The argument in favour of the latter approach centred on the desirability of confirming the supremacy of the delegate conference by ensuring that the NEC was accountable to that body and no other. It has been argued that in the AEU, where there is an extensive system of direct membership election of NEC members, national and local officers, the authority of the delegate conference is reduced by each segment of the organisation being able to claim to have the support of the same power base (i.e. the membership); thereby increasing the likelihood of conflict in the decision making process. However, the Trade Union Act (1984) and Employment Act (1988) require that all members of the union's principal executive committee, the General Secretary and President must be directly elected by the membership by means of, where reasonably practicable, a secret postal ballot.

- *Special provision based on distinct interest groups*. A number of trade unions, in addition to establishing national trade or service committees to deal with specific matters relating to these groups, have also made provision for these groups to be represented on the NEC alongside the more normal geographically-based constituencies. During the 1980s many trade unions have, as part of a policy of positive discrimination to stimulate greater participation, established a proportion of 'reserved' places on the NEC for women. McIlroy [6] notes that as a result NUPE, in 1987, reported a majority of women on its NEC but also notes that unions have not, as yet, been prepared to apply a similar strategy for black members.

Delegate conference

In the early years of their development trade unions were small enough to be able to adopt a form of 'primitive democracy' by convening a meeting of the entire membership as the supreme policy making body. However, as trade unions grew in size such an approach became impossible and it has been replaced by a 'representative democracy' body: the Delegate Conference. Its function is as follows:

1. To **determine the policy of the union** through resolutions from either the membership through their branches or the NEC.
2. To act as the **controlling body** to which both the NEC and national officers of the union are accountable.

Roberts regarded it as the 'device of trade union government by which ultimate authority is returned to the members' [7]. However, Hawkins notes that union conferences 'tend to discuss policy issues only in very general terms' [8], whilst McIlroy argues that the NEC can always 'interpret conference decisions to their own satisfaction, or argue that changed circumstances have rendered their realisation redundant and weather the storm at the next conference' [9].

The most noticeable variation between unions is in terms of the **size and type** of Delegate Conference. The National Committee of the AEU comprises 92 members, whereas the Biennial Delegate Conference of the T&GWU comprises approximately 1,100 delegates. Whilst the T&GWU approach affords a greater opportunity for rank and file members to be part of the governmental process of their union at the highest level, the effectiveness of this participation is reduced by the limited opportunity for any single delegate to voice his/her views on the issues before the conference. The T&GWU arrangement only allows for a limited number of speeches, many from the NEC or officers of the union, before delegates have to vote. The AEU arrangement, on the other hand, facilitates a more detailed discussion and scrutiny of union policy and actions by all the delegates. The smaller conference also has the advantage that it may be reconvened quickly for the NEC to seek its guidance and authorisation for a change in union policy or actions in the light of external developments during the period between normal conferences.

Many large unions incorporate additional **trade or service delegate conferences** which generally precede the general delegate conference and are confined to issues which relate specifically and exclusively to that trade or service, particularly terms and conditions of employment and the annual wage claim. Such an arrangement provides a more effective means of representing and discussing sectional interests and a more efficient means of servicing a heterogeneous membership than could be achieved within a single conference.

The **content** of delegate conferences is fairly uniform in that it ranges over social and political issues as well as industrial and economic. It is also noticeable that the union establishment is rarely defeated on any issues of importance. Whilst speakers at the conference may express criticism of the union's policy or leadership, the leadership is generally able, through appeals to unity and informal discussions with interested delegates, to ensure that the motion to be debated is composited or drafted in such a general way that it does not preclude the policy or course of action they are recommending.

The conference may also perform the function of a **Final Appeal Court** (to consider any claim by a member against disciplinary action, including expulsion, or complaint against the actions of the NEC or officers), or as a **Rules Revision Conference**.

Full-time officers

The **number of full-time officers** in Britain is generally lower than in other countries. The Donovan Commission estimated that there was one full-time officer to every 3,800 members in Britain compared to one to 800 members in West Germany [10]. Certainly, the ratio varied amongst the major unions from one to 1,726 members (UCATT) to one to 16,758 members (UPW) [11]. It is also important to note that the number of **female full-time officers** is much less than would be justified by the proportion of female membership within the union. In 1988, of the ten unions with the largest female membership, NUPE, with 66 per cent female membership, had only 9 per cent female full-time national officials; USDAW, with 61 per cent female membership, had only 13 per cent female full-time national officials; and only COHSE, with 83 per cent female membership, had 50 per cent female full-time national officials [12]. Significantly, perhaps, in 1984 SOGAT elected the first female general secretary, but there are still significant perception and organisational barriers to increasing the proportion of female full-time officers at all levels [13].

Whilst lay union officials are invariably elected to their posts and secretariat staff appointed, both methods are used in the selection of full-time officers. At one extreme, the AEU elects all its full-time officers by direct membership election and, at the other, NALGO appoints all its officers. The operation of these methods vary between unions:

1. Within the **election** method the votes may be cast by branch block voting, individual voting at the branch or individual postal voting.
2. Within the **appointment** method the candidates may be restricted to the membership group which the officer will represent or, more widely, to the membership of the union as a whole, or there may be no restriction and the post advertised widely thus allowing non-members to apply and be considered.

However, the variation within each method is perhaps less important than the variations between them in their effect on union government. Whilst the election method will be defined within the union rule book and therefore subject to ultimate control by the membership through the Rules Revision Conference, the same is generally not true of the appointment method which Hughes argued is 'merely treated as a function of Executive authority' [14]. This lack of **potential membership influence** is also manifest in three other respects:

1. The election method allows the membership to initiate the process by expressing their preference through the formal nomination, or supporting the nomination, of a particular candidate. The appointment

method, on the other hand, relies heavily on the individual candidate desiring office and therefore initiating the process.

2.   Although under both methods the full-time officer is nominally responsible to a lay committee, nevertheless under the election method, he/she is also likely to perceive a responsibility downwards to the electorate, whilst under the appointment method he/she is more likely to perceive a responsibility upwards to a superior office-holder in the union hierarchy.

3.   The appointment method contains the constant danger of the creation of a self-perpetuating, like-minded group of office-holders, whereas with the election method the membership may always initiate a change in leadership style and direction by selecting candidates prepared to challenge the current, established leadership.

In reality the **apparent benefits for the election method are distorted**:

1.   The incumbent office-holder has in-built advantages over any challenger in respect of being better known to the electorate and having legitimate access to the formal channels of communication. For example, the right of a candidate to campaign by addressing branch meetings is often restricted; however, the incumbent often has to attend branch meetings of the membership during the normal course of his/her duties.

2.   The actions of the full-time office in the period preceding an election may become more militant, particularly in respect of negotiations with employers, to justify the electorate's support and gain re-election. Indeed, some would argue cynically that it is only during this period that the election method makes the full-time officer any more responsive to the membership's wishes than an appointed full-time officer.

7.3 Trade union government

The popular perception of trade union government displays a dichotomy regarding the expected relationship between the membership and the leadership. The leadership is often regarded as too powerful and unrepresentative of the wishes of the membership, especially when calling on members to undertake industrial action; yet, when the rank and file pressurise their leadership to take action or themselves take unofficial action, the leadership is then criticised for exercising too little control over its members. It would appear that, as far as popular opinion is concerned, there is no constant ideal form of union government but only a pragmatic approach wherein the preferred governmental arrangement is that which is most likely to produce a moderate union stance at that point in time.

However, trade unions are complex organisations and, therefore, it would be too simplistic to state that they are, or should be, always controlled either from the top or the bottom; in reality the processes of communication, representation and control need to be constantly exercised in both an upward and downward direction.

Bureaucracy and forms of union government

Traditional approaches to examining the process of trade union government have centred on two themes.

- *The administrative, bureaucratic nature of trade union organisation.* This, as Hyman argues, concentrates on the 'role of the leaders and other full-time officers as guardians of organisational efficiency' [15] and uses Michels 'iron law of oligarchy' [16] as its starting point. Michels concluded that all voluntary democratic organisations, within which may be included trade unions, will, because of the need to develop an effective system of internal administration, tend towards an oligarchical style of government involving the creation of a hierarchical bureaucracy with power and influence concentrated in the formal office holders (particularly at the apex of the organisation). He observed that these roles:

1. have greater access to knowledge and information than the rank and file members;
2. are able to exercise a considerable degree of control over the organisation's formal means of communication and decision making; and
3. are strengthened by the personal organisational and political skills of the incumbent office-holder coupled with the general apathy and low level of participation of the membership.

Thus, it is argued, the goals and decisions of the organisation are more often a reflection of the leadership's views than they are of the membership's views. The belief that such a situation is not only inevitable but also perhaps desirable has been expressed by a number of writers. For example, Ross suggested that in the process of wage bargaining, where it might be argued that the membership would, and should, have the greatest say and control, 'trade union wage policy is inevitably a leadership function . . . it alone is in possession of the necessary knowledge, experience, and skill to perform the function adequately' [17].

- *The form of trade union government.* This, Turner argued, 'depends on the relationship between three groups: its full-time officials, that proportion of its lay members which takes an active part in the union's management and the usually more passive majority of the rank-and-file' [18]. He identified three major categories:

1. **Exclusive democracy**: characterised by a 'closed' occupational boundary; a high level of participation by the membership; and a relatively small number of full-time officers invariably drawn directly from the ranks of the membership. This form of government is generally associated with the smaller craft unions.

2. **Aristocracies**: characterised by a dominant group with a high level of participation (for example, the skilled apprentice-served craftsman in craft type unions, the face worker in the NUM and the Co-op worker in USDAW); sometimes a restriction on the participation of other 'ancillary' groups; and full-time officers generally drawn from the dominant group. This form of government is often associated with 'closed' craft unions which have become more 'open' through the recruitment of semi-skilled ancillary groups or 'promotion' unions and where, Hughes believed, the election of full-time officers may 'serve to confirm the predominance of the "aristocratic" group in union government' [19].

3. **Popular bossdom**: characterised by an 'open' membership recruitment policy across a range of industries and occupations but generally amongst unskilled and semi-skilled workers; the absence of a clearly dominant group; a generally low level of participation by the rank and file members; and the establishment of a 'professional' full-time officer group, often with the dominant role in union affairs at the national level being taken by the General Secretary. Clegg believed that this form of government is most noticeable amongst the general unions where 'because there is less common interest between the various groups of members . . . the union is therefore cemented together by its relatively small body of officers' [20].

Whilst these approaches provide some insight into the nature of trade union government they are, nevertheless, deficient in that they categorise in a static format what is in reality a dynamic process capable of great variety and subtlety of form, and imply that democracy is unobtainable or, at best, possible only in small homogeneous unions.

Organisational democracy

Stein regards trade unions as 'philosophically and traditionally a democratic institution which differs from other types of association . . . in the degree to which it emphasises internal democracy' [21] and Hyman believes that 'all forms of governmental arrangements reflect some recognition of the principle of democratic control' [22].

The **ideals of democracy** are perhaps best summarised in the words of Abraham Lincoln – 'government of the people, by the people, for the people'. This highlights three essential ingredients for democratic government:

1. The members of the government should be drawn from the people they are to govern.
2. The process of government should seek to involve the people themselves.
3. The output of the governmental system should meet the needs and interests of those governed.

Those who place the greatest emphasis on the third element of democratic government appear to centre their concern on the **efficiency of the organisation in achieving its objectives**. Certainly, Allen has argued that 'trade union activity is to protect and improve the general living standards of its members and not to provide workers with an exercise in self-government' [23] whilst Taylor believes that 'the exercise in democratic self-government is only a by-product, a safeguard against an entrenched oligarchy ignoring rank and file opinion' [24]. The weakness, or even absence, of the democratic basis to the governmental process is not important so long as the leadership is able, overall, to satisfy the needs of the membership and protect their interests. Indeed, Hawkins argues that because the members regard their union as an instrumental collective 'they are not unduly disturbed if the union is led by individuals whose political outlook is at variance with their own' [25]. It is argued that any dissatisfied members have the ultimate democratic sanction of leaving what is, at its core, a voluntary organisation. However, the members' ability to 'vote with their feet' is restricted by the development of fewer unions and the limiting of union 'poaching' by the TUC's Bridlington Principles. However, sometimes groups of members will 'breakaway' to form their own organisation because of dissatisfaction with union policies, action or leadership. Certainly, the Government's proposal [26] to give employees a legal right to join whichever union they wish would facilitate members being able to move to another union.

However, Fox has suggested that the membership is able to **express its democratic will outside the normal governmental decision making processes** without leaving the union and cites many examples of where the membership has 'withdrawn legitimacy and vested it in the unofficial leaders of low-level collectivities' [27]. In most instances it is the shop stewards who are perceived as the 'unofficial' leaders in these cases. However, shop stewards may equally be regarded as part of the dispersed, but nevertheless official, leadership role within trade unions and therefore in these situations the membership is not withdrawing its support from the leadership as such but is transferring the emphasis of its loyalty to that segment of the leadership role which is not only closest to them, and therefore likely to better understand their needs, but also subject to a more direct and immediate control by the membership.

The critical ingredient of any democratic government for writers who emphasise the **democratic quality of the decision making process** is 'popular power, the active involvement in decision making of the ordinary members' [28]. Certainly Hughes has argued that the active participation of the membership in the affairs of their union is important for the following reasons:

1. Given that a trade union is a voluntary association seeking to represent the interests of its membership to management and government, its power and influence is proportional 'to the extent to which its actions and demands are known to represent the felt interest and active concern of its members' [29]. A low participation by the membership may allow employers and government to argue that the demands and policies put forward by the union are not genuinely representative of the majority of members and may therefore be disregarded.
2. If the trade union is to succeed in translating the instrumental desires of individual members into an organised collective solidarity then active participation by the membership in the decision making process is vital 'for building up wider loyalties and a more comprehensive view of what is of collective concern' [30]. Nowhere, perhaps, is this more important than in industrial action, where, Hughes argues, 'if conformity is required, and minorities coerced, the democratic basis of union decisions has to be clearly in evidence for union actions to retain moral force [31].
3. In the absence of a large number of full-time officers, the 'recruitment, retention and servicing of members are all heavily dependent on active and reliable lay participation' [32].

Organisational democracy involves two quite distinct but interrelated elements: **participative democracy** (direct membership involvement in discussions relating to policy formulation and decision making) and **representational democracy** (involving the election of representatives to positions of 'government' or leadership and membership ballots on specific issues). Bray notes, that the so-called Right/Left factions within unions perceive the basis of democratic government in different ways: to the Right 'it is a representative process dependent upon an electoral technique designed to maximise the turnout of votes', whilst to the Left 'it is the regular participation of members in the affairs of their union' [33]. The persistent low attendance at branch meetings precludes the achievement of direct participation in discussions on policies and decisions amongst a wide range of the membership. However, the absence of substantial levels of participation at the branch or in elections does not inevitably imply an absence of democracy but rather that many members do not exercise their democratic rights. Consequently, much of the debate on union democracy has centred on the election/ballot mechanism.

Many writers on union government have emphasised the **opposition/ choice elements** which are integral to any notion of democracy. As early as the 1950s Goldstein argued that 'an election, to have meaning to an individual in a free society, must provide an opportunity for making a choice. Choice, to have meaning, must imply the right of opposition. The right of opposition, to have meaning, implies the right and opportunity of a free exchange of and easy access to information and ideas that any member of the society might consider relevant to an informed discussion' [34]. Lipset *et al.* also argued that 'democracy is most likely to become institutionalized in organizations whose members form organized or structured sub-groups which while maintaining a basic loyalty to the larger organization constitute relatively independent and autonomous centers of power within the organization' [35]. This approach led Martin to postulate that the extent of democracy within the trade union organisation may be gauged by the degree to which there are 'constraints inhibiting union executives from destroying internal opposition' [36], and Edelstein and Warner to suggest that 'the effectiveness of opposition . . . may be manifest in the closeness of votes' [37].

The model of organisational democracy developed by Edelstein and Warner accepts the **oligarchical nature of trade unions** but rejects any assumption that it inevitably means an undemocratic abuse of power. Rather, they view oligarchy as an organisational form of decision making which retains democratic principles as long as choice exists for the electorate. They believe that organisational democracy exists provided 'consistently effective opposition results from competition between equally powerful potential competitors and their supporters' [38]. Thus, their notion of democracy rests on the twin concepts of majority rule prevailing in both the formulation/ implementation of policies and decisions and the selection of officials to govern the organisation and the right of the minority to organise opposition through formal and informal channels and, where the minority is substantial enough, to be represented within the decision makers. From this they developed a range of factors relating to the status hierarchy of officials, the existence of local centres of autonomy and the election/voting procedures which might allow the development and expression of opposition and thereby produce close votes. They concluded from their survey of British and American unions that the formal union organisation could itself constrain any abuse of power from the development of oligarchy by stimulating competition within the union – particularly amongst the lower level officials seeking to rise within the union hierarchy.

Dickenson also has noted the **importance of factionalism** within unions in terms of developing potential leadership ability, informing the membership, providing choice and making the current leadership more aware and possibly responsive to the membership. However, she believes that it is important to differentiate the 'factionalism' evidenced amongst British trade unions from the 'party system' which Lipset *et al.* examined in the American International Typographical Union. Whilst these factions are more than simply a transient response to specific issues and may, particularly in the case of the left wing factions, be based on a common ideological belief amongst its members, nevertheless they generally lack sufficient formal organisation to ensure their continuity and have 'to depend more on personal leadership and may disintegrate when key personalities leave the scene' [39]. Taft, on the other hand, has taken the view that 'mutually warring factions are a luxury most unions cannot afford, and the result is a gradual elimination of open differences, and the growth of compromises between influential groups' [40]. Certainly, Dickenson recognises that factions tend to focus attention on the internal affairs of the union and, indeed, may provide the 'evidence' of both 'political motivation' amongst certain segments of the membership and polarisation within the union.

It is possible to argue, therefore, that trade unions are democratic organisations in that their governmental arrangements are intended to provide both the means of membership participation and membership control. However, whether or not the outcomes of the governmental process are an expression of the popular will depends on the desire of the membership to use these institutional opportunities to exert their influence and control. Hyman certainly believes that 'a system of checks and balances, while ensuring that control is not concentrated in the hands of key individuals, does not guarantee that it is widely distributed' [41].

Legislated democracy

The only legislation, prior to the 1980s, affecting the unions' decision making process was the requirement to ballot members on the initial establishment of a political fund (Trade Union Act 1913) and amalgamations (Trade Union Amendment Act 1876 as amended). However, during the 1980s the Government has given statutory support to the representational concept of democracy in order to, in its terms, promote 'responsible' unionism, 'return the union to its members' and protect the individual member against union 'tyranny'.

First, public **financial assistance** was made available for expenditure incurred in conducting secret ballots and elections (Employment Act 1980). Initially, TUC policy was not to take advantage of this offer; however, following a major confrontation with the AEU in 1985, the policy was abandoned and, in 1990, 74 unions (of which 47 were TUC affiliates) received £2.6 million for 557 elections/ballots [42]. In addition, management was required, when requested by an independent recognised union, to permit its premises to be used to provide a convenient opportunity for the union members to vote. This facility was only available for the election of officers or delegates and for ballots in respect of negotiations and/or industrial action and not for determining more general union policy. Subsequently, the Employment Act (1988) has required that elections of the union's principal executive committee and ballots for a political fund must be conducted by **postal voting**. The underlying assumption was, as McIlroy notes, 'if the silent majority were able to participate through secret postal ballots, insulated from the "intimidation" of union meetings, the Conservatives felt that there would be a move to the right and improved industrial relations' [43]. However, he argues, 'if we are simply interested in increasing turnout then *workplace* ballots would appear to represent the best bet, as can be seen from the ballots in the NUM, which regularly passes the 70 per cent turnout mark' [44] and that 'members are in a better position to take decisions when they have listened to the arguments and made their own contribution' [45]. There is no legal requirement for industrial action ballots to be conducted on a postal basis – although many unions do, in fact, use postal balloting for securing membership decisions on negotiations and industrial action.

Secondly, legislation on **ballots and elections**, starting with the Trade Union Act 1984, has required that:

1. the union's 'principal executive governing body' [the NEC] must be directly elected by the membership; extended by the Employment Act (1988) to the union's General Secretary, President and any non-voting members of the NEC and gave candidates in all these elections the right to prepare an election address and have it circulated with the voting papers at no cost to the candidate;
2. the maintenance of a political fund must be balloted every ten years; and
3. industrial action must be supported by a majority vote in a ballot of the membership concerned if the union is to retain immunity.

The Employment Act 1988 added a requirement that there must be independent scrutiny of political fund ballots and elections of the executive committee, and the Employment Act 1990 requires that the identity of the scrutineer must be printed on the voting paper.

However, Hawkins argues that a major 'criticism of the electoral process is that in most unions it has consistently failed to attract the participation of more than a tiny minority of the electorate' [46]. Certainly, Fatchett's examination of the use of postal ballots in several unions during 1981/1982 suggests that there is neither a substantial participation by the membership nor is there a 'regular silent majority waiting to support moderate candidates' [47]. He found that the turnout ranged from 12.6 per cent to 47.9 per cent – these figures are in line with the experience of the EETPU and AEU who have used postal ballots for the election of officers and where the turnout has been generally around 30–35 per cent. Significantly, the ballot results regarding political funds in the mid-1980s showed a turnout of over

60 per cent. It must be remembered that trade unions, particularly the large unions, have a major administrative problem in maintaining an up-to-date list of members and their home addresses – they have to rely on the members themselves, shop stewards and branch officers to supply them with the necessary information.

Thirdly, the Government established (Employment Act 1988) **legal rights for individual members** to:

1. challenge expenditure from general funds for political purposes (Trade Union Act, 1984);
2. inspect the union's financial records, take copies or extracts and be accompanied by an accountant;
3. challenge the trustees of the union if they have or intend to use the union's funds or property unlawfully;
4. challenge use of funds to indemnify member or officer against court penalty for offence or contempt;
5. seek a court order restraining the union from proceeding with industrial action which might affect the member where it is not supported by a properly conducted ballot;
6. protection against unjustifiable disciplinary action by the union in certain circumstances (including where the member does not support industrial action – even where it is lawful and supported by a majority in a properly conducted ballot);
7. in limited situations, apply to the court for a legal determination of a grievance the member may have with the union.

The effect of these provisions is to give the individual the right to question, challenge and even ignore decisions which have been made by the active membership through the appropriate union mechanism (participatory democracy).

Perhaps most significantly, the Employment Act 1988 also established a new **Commissioner for the Rights of Trade Union Members** (CRTUM) to assist members who wish to take legal proceedings against their union under these statutory rights. In deciding whether or not to provide assistance, the CRTUM may take into account whether the case raises a question of principle, involves a matter of substantial public interest and/or it is unreasonable to expect the individual union member to deal with the complexities of the case. The CRTUM's assistance may take the form of either bearing the costs of any advice or assistance provided by a solicitor or barrister or representing the individual in 'out of court' proceedings. The CRTUM will not directly represent the individual but is required, where proceedings result from its assistance, to indemnify the individual against liability for costs or expenses which might arise from a court judgement. The Employment Act 1990 has extended the CRTUM's role to cover allegations of breach of the union's rulebook as well as the individual's statutory rights.

No such statutory body exists to support employees in legal challenges to the actions of their employer!

The process of union government

As Hyman argues, 'the two-way power relationship which is central to the trade union function forms the ever present context of the internal control processes within trade unions' [48]. It is important to view the relationship between the full-time officers and the active and passive membership within a framework which differentiates between the representative (legislative) and administrative (executive) subsystems that constitute the process of government. Furthermore the terms 'full-time officers' and 'leadership' should not be regarded as synonymous and require clarification.

Although there are obvious differences in role, and therefore power and authority, between the various categories of **full-time officers** within a union, such distinctions are less significant in the process of government than the major division between full-time officers as a group and the ordinary members. The term 'full-time officers' may be taken to include all those who, irrespective of their specific role and whether they are elected or appointed, are employed full-time by the union to act in a representative capacity on behalf of the union and its members at the local, intermediate or national levels – this does not include purely administrative or secretariat staff.

The term **leadership** is frequently used in such a way as to imply that it is located exclusively at the national level or, indeed, is embodied in a small group (the NEC) or a single role (the general secretary or president). However, in reality a trade union is not a monolithic entity with a single focal point of leadership. It is composed of an array of subgroups administered and represented, at national and company levels, by a mixture of full-time officials and active lay officials. The leadership role within trade unions is therefore diffuse. Whilst in the national context the general secretary and the NEC may be regarded as the union's principal leadership, at the company level this role is performed by shop stewards, convenors, branch officers as well as by the local full-time officer. Thus, the term 'leadership' should be taken to include all those roles within the union organisation which may be deemed, either individually or collectively, to have the power and authority to speak, make decisions and act on behalf of the union and its members. It will include not only full-time officials at all levels but also lay officials such as shop stewards, branch officers, NEC members and even delegates to the various union committees and conferences.

The **union's governmental cycle** therefore involves an interaction between the rank and file members and a range of leadership roles at all levels of the union through the representative and administrative subsystems

190

of the union organisation (see Figure 7.2). As Child *et al.* point out, the organisational rationality which underlies each of the subsystems may produce conflict within the union's governmental process in that 'administrative rationality is . . . the logic of a goal-implementation or operational system, while representative rationality is the logic of a goal-formation or policy-deliberation system' [49].

The function of the union's **administrative subsystem** is to ensure that the goals of the organisation are achieved in the most efficient and orderly manner and is generally founded on the following principles:

1. There is a formal designation of decision making roles with ultimate power, authority and control being vested in the formal leadership at the apex of the organisation.
2. Decisions and instructions are communicated downward through a formal organisational hierarchy for implementation by the designated role holder at the appropriate level.

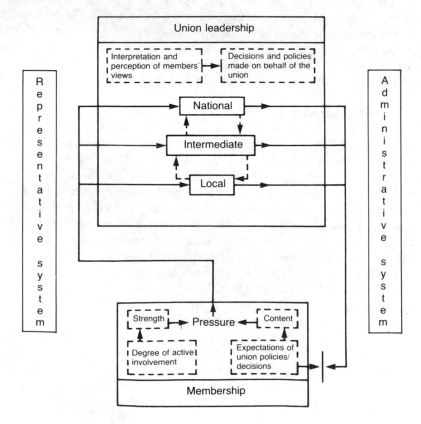

Figure 7.2 *Cycle of union activity*

3. Subordinates are accountable to the leadership for the successful achievement of the tasks set.

The objective of the **representative subsystem**, on the other hand, is to ensure that the policies and decisions of the union represent the wishes of, and are acceptable to, the membership and necessitates the adoption of the following principles:

1. Ultimate power, authority and control are retained by the rank and file membership itself.
2. There is effective representative communication upward within the organisation.
3. The decision making process should be flexible and responsive to the varying needs of the multitude of subgroups within the union.
4. Decisions made in one part of the organisation may be challenged by the membership through other institutions within the organisation.
5. It is the leadership which is accountable to the membership for the successful achievement of the tasks set.

Perhaps the most critical stage in the cycle of government lies in the generation of **membership pressure** on the leadership. The nature of the pressure, in terms of its content and strength, results largely from a combination of the membership's expectations with regard to how the union will conduct its affairs on their behalf and the extent of their active involvement in the union's management. The varying interaction between these two element has been used by Child *et al.* to produce a typology of **membership attachment** which identifies four major types:

1. Amongst the smaller group of active membership:
    (a) the **stalwart** for whom the union's policies, decisions and general approach are very much a reflection of the member's own perceptions and aspirations and therefore is prepared to maintain and uphold the status quo within the union, thereby legitimising the union's leaderships;
    (b) the **trouble-maker**, for whom there is a divergence from the union's approach on at least some, if not all, issues and therefore seeks to influence the leadership and modify its policies and decisions.

2. Amongst the much larger group of inactive members:
    (a) the **card-holder**, for whom the union serves an instrumental function in respect of wage bargaining and job regulation and therefore is content to remain passive so long as these needs are met;
    (b) the **alienated member**, whose expectations of the union, in instrumental and/or ideological terms, diverge from the actual achievements of the union but who is not prepared to actively seek to change the union's approach.

It must be remembered that such a categorisation is dynamic. Once the trouble-maker has achieved the change in policy or approach he/she is likely to become a stalwart, prepared to defend that policy or approach, whilst the original stalwart may become a trouble-maker seeking to reverse the decision and reinstate the previous policy or approach. Equally, the card-holder may, if the union no longer meets his/her instrumental needs, become an alienated member or possibly enter the trouble-maker category by actively seeking to change the policies and actions of the union.

The other crucial stage in the governmental cycle involves **the interpretation and translation of the membership pressure into action** by the union's leadership. This is normally achieved through the variety of organisational institutions (branches, committees, conferences, etc.). However, a critical issue centres on whether it should be regarded as a process of direct representation, involving the membership in expressing their views to the leadership for their implementation, or whether it should be equated with a meeting of different segments of the union's leadership (with the process of direct representation having been carried out previously between the membership and these delegates). For example, is the union's delegate conference to be viewed as a meeting between the membership and the leadership or a meeting of different levels of the leadership role? If the term 'leadership' is restricted to only the formal union hierarchy of office holders then the representative subsystem may be viewed as a direct interaction between the views of the membership and the leadership of the union; but if, as has been suggested, the term is defined more widely to include shop stewards and the delegates to such committees and conferences then the subsystem has to be regarded as a process of decision making within the leadership rather than representation and control by the membership.

The effectiveness of the representative subsystem is affected by the **size of the union and the heterogeneity of its membership**. As a union increases in size and becomes more diverse in its membership, the administrative subsystem is likely to become more formalised and bureaucratic and the representative system will face increased difficulties in ensuring that the differing views of disparate groups are brought to bear on decision making. Many unions have sought to mitigate the effects of size and heterogeneity of membership by segmenting their membership into more homogeneous, almost autonomous, units based on the nature of the members' work and by decentralising certain aspects of the decision making and policy formulation process (particularly in relation to wages and terms and conditions of employment) to a series of mirror institutions at all levels – specialised branches, trade/service committees, conferences, etc.

The complexity and variety of styles and methods of internal decision making within trade unions led Undy *et al.* to develop an **analytical framework** which distinguished between centralised and decentralised government on a vertical axis and diffused or concentrated decision making at each level on a horizontal axis and which also distinguished between decision making relating to bargaining and non-bargaining issues (see Figure 7.3). They found, from their examination of a number of unions, that 'many unions experienced a *de facto* externally determined downwards shift in bargaining levels' which 'did not itself bring about immediate and direct major *de jure* changes in non-bargaining systems of government' [50]. However, this change did provide a stimulus for factionalism and a source of power for opposition to the national leadership. It would appear that the major factors which stimulated a *de jure* change arose out of union mergers or a change in the national leadership. However, Hawkins believes that 'while lay involvement in collective bargaining and the use of "reference back" procedures has strengthened the position of the minority of shop stewards and activists, the membership as a whole is no more involved in unions affairs' [51].

The other major influence on the interpretative stage is the **nature of the leadership role** itself. Any union leader, at whatever level in the union hierarchy, would argue that the role is not simply to carry out the membership's wishes without question but to interpret them in the light of the external environments within which the organisation exists and to determine what is 'feasible and realistic'. To a large extent, the maintenance of the leadership's power, and the power of the union, is dependent first on the leadership's ability to 'deliver the goods' for its members, and secondly, on the continuation of an organisation which is believed by others, particularly employers and government, to have power. Therefore, the leadership will always seek, through its influence or control of the representative subsystem, to ensure that the 'goods' which are formally demanded by the membership are achievable and that the union's efforts and

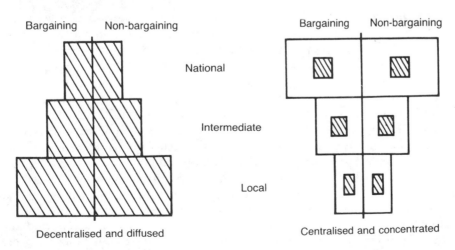

Figure 7.3 *Analytical framework of union government*
Source: R. Undy *et al.*, *Change in Trade Unions*, Hutchinson, 1981, p. 42

resources are not dissipated on issues which cannot be achieved and which will eventually diminish the power of the union in the eyes of those it seeks to influence.

Thus union government is, in practice, much more complicated than a simple relationship between a homogeneous mass of members and a single leader. On the one hand, the leadership role is dispersed throughout all levels and institutions of the union and, on the other hand, the nature of the membership's involvement in the management of the union is not constant. Van de Vall has suggested that trade unions are **polyarchic organisations**. Within this form of government the active membership and lay officials, 'by their two way communication within the organisation (controlling from members to leaders and informing from leaders to members), . . . act as its democratic core. The larger and the more active this group, the closer the organisation approaches the ideal of the democratic theorists. The smaller its number and strength, the more the organisation moves towards the oligarchic pole' [52].

7.4 The shop steward

A shop steward may be defined as:

> **an employee who is accepted by both management and union as a lay representative of the union and its members with responsibility to act on their behalf in industrial relations matters at the organisational level.**

Other terms, such as 'staff or departmental representative' may be used and branch officials may carry out the 'shop steward' role (particularly amongst non-manual employees or in the public sector). Moore [53] notes that the uniqueness of the shop steward role lies in the individual being employed by one organisation but acting as an officer and representative of another organisation; consequently, the individual occupies a dual status role of employee (low status) and union representative (high status).

The **development of the shop steward role** is closely associated with periods when the workplace has become the focus of collective bargaining and industrial relations activity. In the mining industry a shop steward role had been established under the Coal Mines Regulation Act (1887) which allowed miners to elect and pay a 'checkweighman' to check the weight of each miner's output (a matter of vital concern because of their piecework payment system) and, in the engineering industry, employers reported the existence of shop stewards responsible for ensuring that craft practices were enforced as early as the 1890s. Goodman and Whittingham have argued that this development 'originated in the change in industrial techniques and workplace management, especially the introduction of piece rate, incentive schemes, and high speed machine tools' [54]. The first major impetus for a more general development of the shop steward role came during **World War I** when government and employers were anxious to secure changes in working methods and maximise the war effort. The need to consult and negotiate over new production arrangements and the dilution of labour increased the need for the unions to be represented by a person who was familiar with the working methods of the particular factory and had the direct support of the employees involved. The importance of the shop steward as a negotiator on behalf of the union and its members was recognised when the Whitley Committee Report (1917) recommended the establishment of joint committees at the workplace and the Engineering National Agreement accepted shop stewards and work committees as the first level of negotiation.

During this period, however, the shop steward role also provided an alternative focus of industrial activity and power to the official trade union organisation. The **Shop Stewards Movement**, in addition to co-ordinating trade union activity at the workplace to deal with dilution of labour, new working arrangements, etc., sought to mobilise the rank and file of the trade union movement to demand increased industrial democracy through the workers' control of industry. Its strength declined with the end of World War I and during the inter-war period the shop steward role reverted to one of 'minimum' union administration.

World War II, and increased economic activity immediately prior to it, again provided a stimulus for a resurgence in the shop steward's role. However, whereas the economic recession following World War I reduced their importance, the **post World War II period saw a maintenance and growth of their role**. Their growth, particularly during the 1960s and 1970s, may be attributed to three main factors:

1. 'Full employment' and a shift in the emphasis of collective bargaining away from the national level and full-time officers and to the workplace and shop stewards.
2. The formalisation of this informal and fragmented bargaining through the development of written policies, procedures and agreements at the workplace level which necessitated the increased involvement of shop stewards and a further strengthening of their role.
3. The growth in the size of trade unions and positive attempts to decentralise power and authority to where most members have the greatest interest in union affairs – the workplace and the shop steward.

The growth in the shop steward's role is reflected in the number of shop stewards. A CIR study in 1971 [55] estimated that there were between 250,000 and 300,000 shop stewards nationally. Millward and Stevens [56] found that over 75 per cent of all establishments which recognised unions reported 'shop stewards' or 'union representatives' present at either the immediate workplace or elsewhere in the organisation. The higher proportion of non-manual union representatives reported as being 'elsewhere in the organisation' probably reflects the fact that the role is undertaken by branch officers.

In the 1980s the shop steward role has once again come under pressure as a consequence of recession, declining trade union membership and power, and management actively seeking greater employee identification with, and commitment to, the interests and objectives of the organisation. However, it may be argued that the very same factors are also heightening the importance of the shop steward role as a focus for the maintenance of trade unionism amongst employees.

The shop steward role has not, in most unions, been created as part of a conscious organisational arrangement but evolved over a period of time to fill a gap made apparent by the shift in emphasis of collective bargaining to the workplace level. Consequently, **the role tends to lack precision and formality**. Whilst the shop steward epitomises the primary trade union function of protecting and furthering the interests of the members in their relationship with management, there is, nevertheless, an inherent dilemma within the role. The T&GWU, for example, point out that the shop steward is often regarded as 'The Union' by the members, but go on to exhort their shop stewards to 'remember first of all you *represent on behalf of the Union* its members at the workplace' [57] [my italics]. Although the prerequisite for a shop steward is to be elected by the members at the workplace, the official status of the role is dependent on the shop steward being formally accredited as such by the union and accepted by management.

It is useful to follow the approach adopted by Warren [58] and examine the shop steward's role in terms of its relationship to the other parts of the role set – namely the union, the rank and file members who form the steward's 'constituency' and the management with whom the steward has to deal (see Figure 7.4). However, as Warren points out 'for any focal person, there is not only a sent role, but also a received role' [59] consisting of the individual's perceptions and understanding of what was sent, and the role itself.

Shop steward and the union

There are two sources for the expectations placed on the role:

1. **Formal expectation** expressed in its rule book, policies and other official documents.
2. Superimposed **informal expectations** derived from the particular full-time officer(s) with whom the shop steward deals.

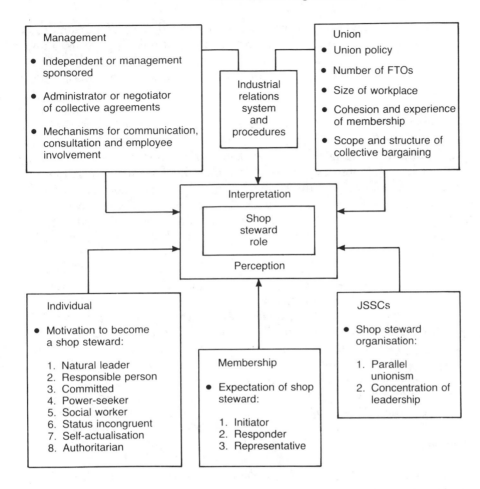

Figure 7.4 *Influences on the shop steward role*

The latter are likely to be more powerful in influencing the actual behaviour of the shop steward because not only are the expectations more immediate and direct but they are also continually being reinforced through the interaction between the steward and full-time officer(s). Therefore, even within the same union the expectations of their role perceived by shop stewards may vary.

Most studies of union rule books have commented on the lack of formal definition and regulation of the shop steward role compared with the other roles within the union organisation. Certainly, union rule books tend to emphasise the **administrative part** of the role on behalf of the union: the recruitment of new members, collection of subscriptions, inspection of union cards, ensuring that national and other agreements are applied at the workplace and acting as a communication link between the union and its membership.

So far as the **representative part** of the shop steward's role is concerned, whilst union rule books may state, as COHSE's does, that 'the function of the steward shall be to organise and represent the membership within his department, to investigate any complaints or difficulty raised by those members, and make representation to the immediate departmental head' [60], neither the rule book nor the shop steward's handbook specify the precise authority the shop steward has in exercising this function. The vagueness displayed in respect of this part of the shop steward's role is both understandable and inevitable given the variety of situations within which the role is carried out. The shop steward's representational role may only be determined in the light of the circumstances within which he/she is expected to carry out the role and with due regard to the expectations of the full-time officer(s), members and management.

In their examination of the **relationship between the shop steward and the full-time officer** Boraston *et al.* concluded that there are 'varying degrees of interdependence ranged along a continuum, approaching complete independence at one end and verging on complete dependence at the other' [61]. From their study of fourteen unions they identified a number of factors which might affect the degree of shop steward independence from, or reliance on, the full-time officer:

- *The union itself.*

1. **Policy of the union** towards the concept of shop steward independence. However, a change in policy towards one of encouraging greater independence at the workplace level may not, on its own, be sufficient to achieve such independence in practice without associated changes in trade union organisation – for example, the creation and strengthening of workplace branches.
2. **Lack of sufficient full-time officers** to adequately surpervise their activities. The smaller the number of full-time officers and the more their time is devoted to trade union administration and to aiding smaller, weaker branches or workplaces, then the more the shop stewards at well-organised workplaces will have to rely on their own resources to represent the membership's interests at the workplace, thereby increasing their independence. However, Boraston *et al.* found that the full-time officer, even when available to become more involved in the industrial relations activity at the workplace, may be kept out by the desire of the shop stewards to maintain their independence.

- *The workplace and nature of the collective bargaining system.*

1. **Size of the workplace**. A large workplace may provide not only a management which has greater delegated authority to resolve its own problems but also more issues to be resolved between union and management, allowing the shop stewards a greater opportunity to gain experience in handling industrial relations problems.
2. **Cohesion and trade union experience of the union's membership**. A labour force with considerable experience of, and commitment to, trade unionism is likely to try to ensure that management's actions are subjected to trade union scrutiny and agreement.
3. **Scope and structure of the collective bargaining system**. Where terms and conditions of employment are 'tightly' regulated at the national level there is less scope for shop stewards to develop an independent collective bargaining role at the workplace level. However, Boraston *et al.* found that even where there was only a limited scope for workplace bargaining, shop stewards could nevertheless achieve a marked degree of independence from full-time officers in their handling of these issues. Thus, the structure of the collective bargaining system may limit the effect of shop steward independence by confining it to what are, perhaps, less critical issues, but it does not necessarily limit their desire or ability to act independently of their full-time officer or their union.

In assessing the **extent of independence** exercised by the shop steward role it is necessary to make a **qualitative as well as a quantitative** judgement. Shop steward independence is not just a function of how often they, as opposed to the full-time officer, act as the union's representative in meetings with management but also a function of the type and importance of the issues over which they have authority to reach agreement with management without reference to the full-time officer. If shop stewards negotiate with management on such fundamental issues as new pay rates then their independence may be considered to be greater than if they are confined simply to handling members' grievances. However, the fact that the full-time officer is not present does not automatically mean that shop stewards are acting independently for they may already have consulted with the full-time officer and may indeed be following instructions. Furthermore, the relationship between the shop steward and full-time officer is not constant and may well change over time. For example, the advent of negotiations over a major productivity agreement may lead in the initial 'working party' stages to an increased role for shop stewards in discussing and agreeing new working practices, followed by a predominant role for the full-time officer in the negotiation of the new pay rates, and subsequently a relatively independent role for the shop stewards in the implementation and administration of the new agreement.

Goodman and Whittingham believe that a further major factor in the relationship between shop stewards and their full-time officers has been 'the nature of relationships *between* stewards and the influence of the organisations they have formed' [62]. In their study of the motor industry, Turner *et al.* commented that 'to be fully effective ... shop stewards of different unions have to be brought together to compare wages and conditions in their respective constituencies within the plant, to formulate joint policies on workshop issues, and to make common agreements with their employers' [63]. **Multi-unionism** in many workplaces inevitably requires some form of inter-union co-ordination within the workplace. To meet this need shop stewards established a range of different committees:

1. At the plant level it is quite common for the shop stewards to establish a **Joint Shop Stewards Committee** (JSSC) to consider matters of common concern to all unions. The status of the JSSC is enhanced if it is also associated with a **Joint Union Negotiating Committee** (JUNC) which collectively negotiates terms and conditions of employment.

2. At the company level the shop stewards may establish a **combine committee** which brings together representatives from the JSSCs at different sites. Lerner and Bescoby [64] argued that only where site bargaining is well developed are combine committees likely to develop from informal committees which simply transfer information on rates and earnings between the different sites into bodies which seek to co-ordinate shop steward activity and develop policies to be applied across the organisation. They believed that any further development required the committee to achieve recognition from both management and unions. However, Willman [65] criticises this view because it assumes that strong JSSCs at the site level are an essential prerequisite, that shop stewards are actively seeking to establish greater uniformity across the organisation and that once the committee is recognised and accommodated by management and/or union its independence is lost. He suggests that combine committees may also develop to provide mutual support to site-level shop steward organisations which otherwise would be weak and isolated; or, through direct management support, develop as part of a strategy to establish company-level negotiations and thereby become part of the formal negotiation and consultation machinery; or develop as part of a union's initiative to better represent the differing interests and needs of a diffuse membership.

There is little doubt that it is difficult, if not impossible, for any individual union, or indeed the trade union movement as a whole, to control these combine committees because their membership and activities cross the traditional intra-union boundaries of geographical or industrial areas as well as inter-union boundaries. At best a union may only control the activities of those shop stewards who are its members. Indeed, it may be argued that the central dilemma for the official union organisation is that if they seek to curb the activities of shop stewards and these committees they will, in effect, be restricting their own ability to pursue their primary function of maintaining and improving the terms and conditions of their members. Boraston *et al.* argued that 'if a greater concentration of authority at high levels of union organisation is thought to be desirable, it cannot be achieved by attempting to reduce self-reliant workplace organisations to dependence on their full-time officers in the conduct of workplace business' [66].

However, the institutionalisation of the shop steward's autonomy and power through such committees may reach the stage of what Turner *et al.* termed **parallel unionism** where the union members identify with fellow unionists and shop stewards within their work organisation, irrespective of their union, rather than with fellow members of their specific union outside. It is significant to note that such parallel unionism is also subject to the same internal pressures as the official union organisation. Turner *et al.* argued that within such combine committees 'senior stewards, like the full-time officials before them, are forced to assume something of the role of buffer between the employer and the operatives' and 'its leaders are obliged to balance a variety of group interests against the particular sectional claims with which they are confronted' [67].

Trade unions have sought to accommodate the growth of the shop steward role by amending their organisational arrangements to provide for greater shop steward involvement in both collective bargaining and general policy decisions. However, England [68] concludes that management's incorporation of the shop steward role within a more formalised industrial relations system at the organisational level has presented a major obstacle to union attempts to incorporate the role within its policy making arrangements and thereby secure their active commitment to the achievement of such policies. Indeed, Brown has argued that the problems of trade union structure, coupled with the declining regulatory effect of national agreements and management strategies at the organisational level which isolate employees from the labour market, is likely to produce a form of **enterprise unionism,** that is 'a union organisation whose commitments, loyalties and resources effectively extend no further than the enterprise itself' [69]. Such a development on any significant scale would further divorce the shop steward role from the remainder of the trade union organisation and its policies.

Shop steward and union members

The workplace link between shop steward and union members is of crucial importance given the general apathy amongst rank and file members in attending branch meetings. Although this apathy in union affairs has carried over into the workplace in that some 75 per cent of shop stewards take up their position unopposed, nevertheless the steward is, in theory at least,

elected by the union members at the workplace and therefore, Warren argues, 'remains accountable to those who have elected him ... since without their support, even if it is expressed merely as apathetic non-opposition, he is impotent' [70]. Certainly, Schuller and Robertson believe that the absence of a formal contested election does not indicate the absence of membership involvement in the selection process in that the selection may be made informally by the members so that there is only one nomination for the official election. Nevertheless, they observe that the absence of formal approval, if only by an unopposed 'election', can result in the steward feeling 'less able to claim the active support of his members' and 'this may diminish his confidence in dealing both with management and with his members' [71].

The essential quality of the shop steward role, and the real source of its power and influence, lies in being a **lay official** who continues to work amongst, and experience the same day-to-day problems as, the people who elected him/her. Thus, the steward has considerable opportunity, particularly on an informal basis, to discuss both workplace and union affairs with the membership. Stewards represent not only their constituents to both management and the union but also the union, and the trade union movement as a whole, to constituents and management. Consequently, the role is crucial in the development and maintenance of unionateness amongst the membership – particularly, in the 1980s, in the face of recession, declining trade union membership and power, and challenge from management.

However, it would be wrong to assume that the shop steward role is simply a formalisation of the natural **workgroup leadership**. First, although it is difficult to define the precise boundaries of primary workgroups, the shop steward's constituency often contains more than one such group. Goodman and Whittingham argue that 'it is more plausible to count shop stewards as leaders of work *groups* rather than as work-*group* leaders' [72]. Secondly, the existence of the shop steward role does not remove the need for, or likely existence of, informal group leaders amongst these primary workgroups. These informal leaders often act as the focus of primary workgroup pressure on the shop steward and may even, in certain circumstances, provide a positive opposition and challenge to the shop steward.

If shop stewards wish to 'lead' their members they must do so by argument and persuasion because they have no sanction which may be applied against the members collectively. The members, on the other hand, may apply the ultimate sanction of removing stewards from office if they fail to respond to their wishes. Thus, shop stewards have to conform to the broad expectations of their members, although they have some freedom to interpret these in the light of union policy or their own assessment of the situation.

Certainly, there has been considerable discussion of the extent to which shop stewards exercise a **leadership role**. Pedler [73] has suggested that the shop steward performs three functions on behalf of the union members:

1. **Initiator**: to identify problems and issues of concern to the group, to formulate ideas and possible solutions and, if necessary, to provide a lead to the group.
2. **Responder**: be aware of, and to take account of, the collective aspirations and feelings of the members and to seek to attain their goals wherever possible.
3. **Representative**: act as their spokesman in any dealings with management, union or other workgroups.

Pedler concluded, therefore, that 'it is an oversimplification to term the union representative either a 'delegate' or a 'leader' – typically his role varies with the issue and with the work group involved' [74].

Batstone *et al.* [75] have put forward a **shop steward typology** which combines the steward's relationship to the members in formulating decisions with the steward's pursuit of trade union principles within the decisions made (see Figure 7.5). In their view the 'nascent leader' is a transient type which will develop into either a 'leader' or 'popularist'. A 'leader' adopts a

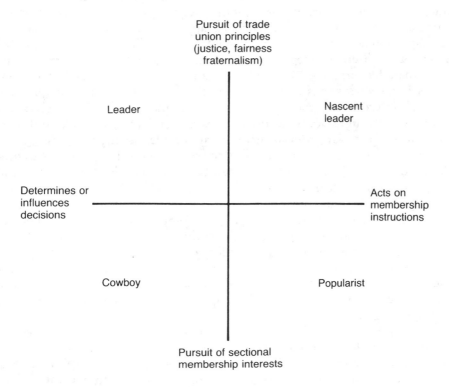

Figure 7.5 *Shop steward typology*
Source: E. Batstone *et al.*, *Shop Stewards in Action*, Blackwell, 1974, p. 34

positive initiator role in decision making and seeks to achieve decisions and strategies which are supportive of trade union principles. Such a role is closely associated with the development of shop steward 'networks' and possible élitism. Thus, it may be argued that 'leadership' is a function of not only individual personality but also the degree of authority afforded to the role by the structure and institutions of the industrial relations system. Both the 'popularist' and 'cowboy' place greater emphasis on the pursuit of sectional interests but, whereas the 'cowboy' adopts a positive initiator role in identifying and supporting situations or strategies which will enhance this objective, the 'popularist' acts only in response to direct expressed membership wishes.

However, Willman [76] suggests that this approach suffers from two major weaknesses. First, the definition of 'trade union principles' in terms of generalised subjective value concepts such as 'justice' and 'fairness' cannot easily be related to the specific actions or policies adopted by shop stewards and that success in leadership requires to be judged in relation to the achievement of more specific issue-related policies. Secondly, it does not allow for the impact which management may have had through promoting the shop steward role. He suggests that 'management sponsored' and 'independent' shop steward organisations may display quite different policy characteristics and as a consequence 'an apparent "cowboy", in a management sponsored organisation, might be pursuing policies convergent with a 'leader' in a different independent one: he may simply be in "opposition" rather than "government" within the organisation' [77]. Certainly, Batstone et al.'s framework seems to imply not only that trade union principles and sectional interests are incongruent but also that left to themselves the members will pursue only sectional interests and therefore it requires an 'initiator' shop steward to lead them towards trade union principles.

Schuller and Robertson noted that shop stewards spent more time talking to each other than talking to their constituents. They suggest that this could arise from a **strategic concentration of leadership** as part of a strong union presence within the organisation or from a **defensive cohesion** as shop stewards take 'refuge in each other's company in the face of member apathy or even hostility' [78]. Significantly, most of the shop stewards' contact with members was undertaken in the context of dealing with individual or workgroup problems and very little time was spent discussing union policy. Indeed, 29 per cent of the shop stewards surveyed never held formal meetings with their membership and 37 per cent only held such meetings irregularly.

Terry [79] noted a similar situation in local government. Management pressure to develop joint consultative arrangements to further the introduction of work changes, in a situation characterised by a relative absence of organisational bargaining on terms and conditions of employment and an often fragmented and dispersed workforce, resulted in the development of a **key stewards role**. The individuals who occupy the role are mobile and have access to a range of both membership and management; however, their contact with the members is again primarily on an individual or small workgroup problem related basis, and they lack support from a strong shop steward committee or organisation. Thus, it would appear that any leadership displayed by shop stewards may be more significant in the area of the specific instrumental needs of the membership than in the area of the developing unionateness and trade union principles amongst the membership.

Certainly it would appear, at least amongst some non-manual shop stewards, that there is an absence of any desire on their part to develop unionateness and union principles amongst their membership. Nicholson *et al.*'s survey of NALGO stewards found that in terms of **political socialisation** some 37 per cent of the shop stewards described themselves as centre right or right and that 'these more conservative stewards tend to espouse the "spokesman" rather than the "leader" role for stewards', 'had fewer close links with their fellow stewards either within or outside their own departments' and adopted 'a less committed and more oppositional stance towards [the union]' [80]. This reflects Batstone *et al.*'s findings [81] that shop stewards representing manual workers saw their role as primarily protecting their members and improving their pay and working conditions, whilst shop stewards representing non-manual employees placed the greatest emphasis on acting as a communication link with the membership and ensuring harmonious relations with management.

Shop steward and management

The development of the shop steward role took place largely outside any organised framework of management policy on industrial relations. Flanders, referring to the growth of the shop steward's role during the 1960s, suggested that 'by making ad hoc concessions to pressure, when resistance proved too costly, [management] fostered guerilla warfare over wages and working conditions in the workplace and encouraged aggressive shop-floor tactics by rewarding them' [82]. Hyman, seeing the development more in terms of strong workplace organisation than weak management, believed that 'sophisticated and inventive workplace representatives have been able to exploit the discontinuities between the individual firm and its employer's association, play on the internal divisions and weaknesses of management, and generalise concessions won in positions of strength' [83].

It is evident, from the general range of issues over which shop stewards negotiate, that the growth of the role has been, at least in part, due to management's willingness to allow or even encourage such a development. It is significant that, despite the popular perception of shop stewards being active militants as compared to the responsible approach of union full-time officers, most managers have preferred to negotiate with shop stewards and believe that they aid the resolution of industrial relations problems. As Hawkins points out, this apparent contradiction is generally explained by reference to shop stewards being 'employees of the firm, they know how their members are likely to react to a particular proposal, they are likely to have detailed knowledge of problems on the shop floor, and they have to maintain an effective, day-to-day working relationship with management' [84]. Certainly, the involvement of the full-time officer may present the appearance of intervention by an external body (the union organisation) in the affairs of the firm and a challenge to the process of management, whilst reconciling issues and differences with shop stewards (the employees' representatives) may be seen as part of the process of management in modern industrial organisations.

The extension and formalisation of collective bargaining at the organisation level in the 1960s and 1970s resulted in a greater codification of the shop steward's role and authority. The role moved away from being a passive one of acting as the union's guardian of collective agreements negotiated between union full-time officers and employers' associations at the national level to one of **positively seeking to protect and improve the terms and conditions of the members by direct negotiations with management**. Surveys of workplace industrial relations show that the shop steward became an active negotiator on a wide range of issues, including:

1. Grievances relating to the application of collective agreements and management policies.
2. Defending members when disciplinary action is taken against them by management.
3. Negotiating payment-by-results schemes, abnormal working arrangements, changes in working practices and the introduction of new technology (including changes in manning levels and redundancy) as well as physical working conditions (health and safety, canteens, toilets, etc.).

In addition, shop stewards may be consulted by management on a range of general issues relating to the state of the business, future orders, etc. However, in spite of this increased role, shop stewards are not generally responsible, on their own, for the negotiation of basic rates of pay, hours, holidays, etc., even where such items are determined at the organisational level. These matters are normally still the formal province of the full-time officer although, where the shop steward organisation is strong, they may play an influential, if not controlling, role in the formulation of claims and negotiating strategy and the full-time officer may feel constrained to act in accordance with their wishes and those of their members.

However, Schuller and Robertson concluded from their survey that shop stewards remain **primarily administrators rather than negotiators of collective agreements**. They found that the majority of stewards 'did not engage in negotiation in the sense of taking part in the making of agreements' and therefore 'were very little concerned with the making of rules, and spent the vast bulk of their time as representatives in their interpretation and application' [85]. More importantly, they identified a need to differentiate between the role of convenors and 'ordinary' shop stewards in the negotiating/rule making process. They noted that negotiation, in the sense of making agreements, was conducted either outside the organisation at national or company level by full-time officers or at the organisational level by full-time officers and/or convenors often supported by a small number of senior stewards. This would indicate that the convenor or senior steward element of the shop steward organisation does play a significant role in the negotiation of agreements. Furthermore, the ordinary shop steward may be involved, and even influential, in the determination of claims, strategy and outcomes through membership of the shop stewards committee and participation in its affairs.

Whilst the close involvement of shop stewards with management in resolving industrial problems may be desirable, it also presents certain dangers. The day-to-day interaction between shop stewards and managers may allow them to develop a better understanding of each other's attitudes and views, but it may also present the appearance, to the union members, of the shop steward becoming **socialised into an acceptance of management's views**. Shop stewards may, through their involvement with management in the implementation of agreements, take on quasi-managerial responsibility in ensuring their members' compliance with the provisions of such agreements. This is a particular problem faced by full-time convenors who, because of their high interaction with industrial relations specialists and senior management, may easily become divorced from both the union members and the other shop stewards.

Furthermore, it is important to take account of Willman's differentiation between **independent** and **management sponsored** shop steward organisations [86]. An independent shop steward organisation arises through the employees'/union's bargaining power and is characterised by an emphasis on policies, decisions and actions which maintain employee control over the work situation and extend employee influence over management decision making. Management sponsored shop steward organisations, on the other hand, develop with the direct or indirect support of management and are characterised by the pursuit of policies allied to 'the rationalisation of personnel administration' within the organisation. Willman suggests that the development of management sponsorship of shop stewards may be related, at least in timing, to the development of regulatory legislation (dismissals, health and safety, equal pay, maternity rights, etc.) and management efforts aimed at labour rationalisation; hence the involvement of shop stewards in management systems and procedures such as work study, job evaluation, etc. Certainly, Willman believes that the differences displayed by these two types of shop steward organisation distinguish, in the common perception, between militant and moderate shop steward behaviour – for example, he notes that with independent shop steward organisations 'restrictive practices may be protected, rather than sold under productivity bargaining, and allegiance to the technology upon which job control practices rely may encourage opposition to technological change' [87].

However, it would appear that in many organisations management's support, or even acceptance, of the shop steward role has **diminished** during the 1980s. There has been evidence of management going directly to employees to obtain approval of their proposals when an impasse has been reached in negotiations or the union has threatened industrial action, as well as withdrawal of union recognition, seeking to reduce or withdraw shop steward facilities or curtailing their time-off for union duties. At the same time management, more generally, has presented a challenge to the shop steward role through developing direct forms of employee involvement and placing emphasis on the dissemination of information to employees rather than disclosure of information to shop stewards and trade unions. Any enhancement of managerial 'prerogative' represents a challenge to both the shop steward role and trade unionism.

Shop steward – an individual

In view of the varying nature and vagueness of the expectations placed on the shop steward by the other 'actors' in the role set, it is perhaps not surprising that the shop steward role suffers from both role ambiguity and role conflict. The shop steward, as an individual, also has expectations of the nature of the role. Moore [88] identified eight reasons which are frequently put forward to explain the **motivation of individual members to become shop stewards**:

1. **Natural leader** – inherent 'leadership' qualities are evident in the normal working relationships.
2. **Responsible person** – feels a responsibility to take on a role which no one else will do or perceives the only candidate(s) to be poorly qualified for the role.
3. **Committed individual** – is committed to opposition to the capitalist/ management system and regards the role as a means of expressing/ furthering that opposition.
4. **Power-seeker** – accepts a role because of the power contained in that role.
5. **Social worker** – wishes to serve the needs of others.
6. **Status incongruent** – seeks to enhance his/her status by occupying a role of higher status than the one currently occupied.
7. **Self-actualisation** – regards the role as an opportunity to utilise and develop his/her abilities and so enhance job satisfaction.

8. **Authoritarian** – regards the role as providing a position of authority over others.

Moore found from his survey of shop stewards that none of these explanations were satisfactory. He concluded that 'perhaps the greatest single characteristic . . . underlying the motives of the respondents in becoming shop stewards, was the inability to stand the stress of the disorganisation that results from ineffective or non-existent shop-floor leadership' linked to 'a sense of responsibility mainly to self, but partly to others' and 'a desire to have some measure of control over the matters which are of immediate personal concern in the workplace' [89]. It would appear, therefore, that the main motivation to become a shop steward is that the individual is a committed trade unionist.

7.5 Summary propositions

- The essential objective of trade union organisation is to combine efficiency in carrying out its external economic and job regulation functions with democratic government of its internal affairs; not to maximise one at the expense of the other.
- Trade unions are democratic institutions if their organisation provides the opportunities for the membership to participate in their affairs and allows the membership or segments of the leadership to express and organise opposition.
- The shop steward role developed because the formal union organisation was not able to cope with the change in emphasis of collective bargaining to the organisational level.
- The shop steward is expected to represent both the members' interests and union policy to management and secure acceptance of union policy amongst the membership and is vital to the maintenance and development of unionateness amongst the membership.

Further reading

- J. D. Edelstein and M. Warner, *Comparative Union Democracy*, Allen & Unwin, 1975. Part 1 and Chapter 7 in Part 2 provide a very useful discussion of oligarchy, organisational democracy and the role of opposition and factions.
- R. Undy *et al.*, *Change in Trade Unions*, Hutchinson, 1981. Chapters 4 and 8 provide a very useful examination of internal decision making in a number of unions.

- W. E. J. McCarthy (ed.), *Trade Unions* (2nd edn), Penguin, 1985. Part Four provides a number of readings on trade union government.
- J. McIlroy, *Trade Unions in Britain Today*, Manchester University Press, 1988. Chapter 5 provides a useful discussion of union democracy issues.
- I. Boraston, H. Clegg and M. Rimmer, *Workplace and Union*, Heinemann, 1975. This study, covering some fourteen unions, concentrates on the relationship between shop stewards and full-time officers.
- E. Batstone, I. Boraston and S. Frenkel, *Shop Stewards in Action*, Blackwell, 1977. A study of manual and non-manual shop stewards in one company.

References

1. R. Hyman, *Industrial Relations – A Marxist introduction*, Macmillan, 1975, p. 73.
2. B. C. Roberts, *Trade Union Government and Administration*, Bell, 1956, p. 80.
3. S. and B. Webb, *The History of Trade Unionism* (1920 edn), Longman, p. 465.
4. B. C. Roberts, *op. cit.*, p. 113.
5. *ibid.*, p. 133.
6. J. McIlroy, *Trade Unions in Britain Today*, Manchester University Press, 1988, p. 147.
7. B. C. Roberts, *op. cit.*, p. 160.
8. K. Hawkins, *Trade Union*, Hutchinson, 1981, p. 112.
9. J. McIlroy, *op. cit.*, pp. 135–6.
10. *Report of Royal Commission on Trade Unions and Employers' Associations*, (Donovan Commission), HMSO, 1968, p. 188.
11. R. Taylor, *The Fifth Estate*, Pan, 1980, p. 63 (Table 1.10).
12. 'Working for equality in the unions', *Labour Research*, March 1988.
13. E. Heery and J. Kelly, 'A cracking job for a woman – a profile of women trade union officers', *Industrial Relations Journal*, vol. 20, no. 3, 1989; S. Ledwith *et al.*, 'The making of women trade union leaders', *Industrial Relations Journal*, vol. 21, no. 2. 1990.
14. J. Hughes, 'Trade Union Structure and Government', Research Paper 5 (2), *Royal Commission on Trade Unions and Employers' Associations*, HMSO, 1968, p. 45.
15. R. Hyman, *op. cit.*, p. 74.
16. R. Michels, *Political Parties*, Free Press, 1966.
17. A. M. Ross, *Trade Union Wage Policy*, University of California Press, 1948, p. 39.
18. H. A. Turner, *Trade Union Growth, Structure and Policy*, Allen & Unwin, 1962, p. 289.
19. J. Hughes, *op. cit.*, p. 12.
20. H. A. Clegg, *General Union*, Blackwell, 1954, p. 342.
21. E. Stein, 'The dilemma of union democracy' in J. M. Shepheard (ed.), *Organisational Issues in Industrial Society*, Prentice Hall, 1972.
22. R. Hyman, *op. cit.*, p. 73.
23. V. L. Allen, *Power in Trade Unions*, Longman, 1954, p. 15.
24. R. Taylor, *op. cit.*, p. 196.

25. K. Hawkins, *op. cit.*, p. 115.
26. *Industrial Relations in the 1990s*, HMSO, 1991.
27. A. Fox, *A Sociology of Work in Industry*, Collier Macmillan, 1972, p. 123. Reprinted with permission of the publisher.
28. R. Hyman, *op. cit.*, p. 76.
29. J. Hughes, *op. cit.*, p. 5.
30. *ibid.*, p. 6.
31. *ibid.*, p. 5.
32. *ibid.*
33. M. Bray, 'Democracy from the inside: the British AUEW(ES) and the Australian AMWSU', *Industrial Relations Journal*, vol. 13, no. 4, 1982, p. 91.
34. J. Goldstein, *The Government of a British Trade Union*, Allen & Unwin, 1952.
35. S. M. Lipset, M. A. Trow and J. S. Coleman, *Union Democracy*, Free Press, 1956, p. 15.
36. R. Martin, 'Union democracy: an explanatory framework', *Sociology*, vol. 2, 1968, p. 205.
37. J. D. Edelstein and M. Warner, *Comparative Union Democracy*, Allen & Unwin, 1975.
38. *ibid.*, p. 339.
39. M. Dickenson, 'The effects of parties and factions on trade union elections', *British Journal of Industrial Relations*, vol. 19, no. 2, 1981, p. 198.
40. P. Taft, *The Structure and Government of Labor Unions*, Harvard University Press, 1954.
41. R. Hyman, *op. cit.*, p. 81.
42. *Annual Report of the Certification Officer 1990*, Appendix 9.
43. J. McIlroy, *op. cit.*, p. 150.
44. *ibid.*, p. 153.
45. *ibid.*, p. 154.
46. K. Hawkins, *op. cit.*, p. 112.
47. D. Fatchett, 'Postal ballots – some practical considerations', *Industrial Relations Journal*, vol. 13, no. 4, 1982, p. 15.
48. R. Hyman, *op. cit.*, p. 67.
49. J. Child, R. Loveridge and M. Warner, 'Towards an organizational study of trade unions', *Sociology*, vol. 7, no. 1, 1973, p. 78.
50. R. Undy, V. Ellis, W. E. J. McCarthy and A. M. Halmos, *Change in Trade Unions*, Hutchinson, 1981, p. 119.
51. K. Hawkins, *op. cit.*, p. 122.
52. M. van de Vall, *Labor Organizations*, Cambridge University Press, 1970, p. 153.
53. R. J. Moore, 'The motivation to become a shop steward', *British Journal of Industrial Relations*, vol. XVIII, 1980, p. 91.
54. J. F. B. Goodman and T. G. Whittingham, *Shop Stewards*, Pan, 1973, p. 28.
55. CIR Study No. 2, *Industrial Relations at Establishment Level: A Statistical Survey*, HMSO, 1973.
56. N. Millward and M. Stevens, *British Workplace Industrial Relations 1980–1984*, Gower, 1986, p. 80 (Table 3.12).
57. T&GWU, *Shop Stewards Handbook*, 1970, pp. 5–6.
58. A. Warren, 'The challenge from below: an analysis of the role of the shop steward in industrial relations', *Industrial Relations Journal*, autumn 1971, pp. 52–60.
59. *ibid.*, p. 54.
60. COHSE, 'Rule Book', 1979, p. 28.

61. I. Boraston, H. Clegg and M. Rimmer, *Workplace and Union*, Heinemann, 1975, p. 153.
62. J. F. B. Goodman and T. G. Whittingham, *op. cit.*, p. 126.
63. H. A. Turner, G. Clack and B. Roberts, *Labour Relations in the Motor Industry*, Allen & Unwin, 1967, p. 206.
64. S. W. Lerner and J. Bescoby, 'Shop steward combine committees in the British engineering industry', *British Journal of Industrial Relations*, vol. IV, 1966, pp. 137–53.
65. P. Willman, 'The growth of combine committees: a reconsideration', *British Journal of Industrial Relations*, vol. XIX, no. 1, 1981, pp. 1–13.
66. I. Boraston *et al.*, *op. cit.*, p. 199.
67. H. A. Turner *et al.*, *op. cit.*, p. 222.
68. J. England, 'Shop stewards in Transport House: a comment upon the incorporation of the rank and file', *Industrial Relations Journal*, vol. 12, no. 5, 1981, pp. 16–29.
69. W. Brown, 'Britain's unions: new pressures and shifting loyalties', *Personnel Management*, October 1983, p. 48.
70. A. Warren, *op. cit.*, p. 57.
71. T. Schuller and D. Robertson, 'How representatives allocate their time: shop steward activity and membership contact', *British Journal of Industrial Relations*, vol. XXI, 1983, p. 333.
72. J. F. B. Goodman and T. G. Whittingham, *op. cit.*, p. 89.
73. M. J. Pedler, 'Shop stewards as leaders', *Industrial Relations Journal*, winter, 1973, pp. 43–60.
74. *ibid.*, p. 59.
75. E. Batstone, I. Boraston and S. Frenkel, *Shop Stewards in Action*, Blackwell, 1977.
76. P. Willman, 'Leadership and trade union principles: some problems of management sponsorship and independence', *Industrial Relations Journal*, vol. 11, no. 4, 1980, pp. 39–49.
77. *ibid.*, p. 44.
78. T. Schuller and D. Robertson, *op. cit.*, p. 340.
79. M. Terry, 'Organising a fragmented workforce: shop stewards in local government', *British Journal of Industrial Relations*, vol. XX, 1982, pp. 1–19.
80. N. Nicholson, G. Ursell and P. Blyton, 'Social background, attitudes and behaviour of white-collar shop stewards', *British Journal of Industrial Relations*, vol. XVIII, 1980, p. 236.
81. E. Batstone *et al.*, *op. cit.*, p. 25.
82. A. Flanders, *Management and Unions*, Faber, 1970, p. 196.
83. R. Hyman, *Industrial Relations – A Marxist introduction*, Macmillan, 1975, pp. 154–5.
84. K. Hawkins, *A Handbook of Industrial Relations Practice*, Kogan Page, 1979, pp. 183–4.
85. T. Schuller and D. Robertson, *op. cit.*, p. 339.
86. P. Willman (1980), *op. cit.*
87. *ibid.*, p. 45.
88. R. J. Moore, *op. cit.*, p. 92.
89. *ibid.*, p. 97.

Chapter 8
Management and employers' associations

8.1 Definition

The term 'management' may be applied to both a process and a distinct group of roles within the organisation. The **process of management** has been described most often in functional terms of planning, organising, staffing, directing and controlling the activities of the organisation in order to achieve its designated objectives [1]. All definitions of **management as a group** stem from this. The CIR considered that the term 'manager' should encompass 'all levels of management . . . insofar as they perform management functions' [2]. Clearly such a definition is too vague to be practically useful. Mansfield uses an alternative definition based on the existence of a hierarchical superior/subordinate authority relationship through which organisational control is exercised; namely, that a manager is 'anyone who by virtue of their organizational employment may legitimately . . . give orders to subordinates' [3].

However, this appears to ignore the fact that some managers who do not have subordinates whom they may instruct may nevertheless play an important part in the management process (e.g. industrial relations specialists). It is, therefore, perhaps more useful to concentrate on the decision making process itself, and in particular the act of committing the organisation to the decisions arrived at, as the basis for delineating those who should be included within the group called management. From this it is possible to define management as:

> **those roles where the holders have, and are accepted by others in the organisation to have, a formal role and authority to make decisions which can be regarded as binding on the organisation.**

The characteristic which then delineates management from other roles in the organisation is that through the formal authority structure of the organisation they represent, make decisions and act on behalf of the organisation as an entity.

8.2 The role of management

Traditionally management is, from a legalistic or labour/capital frame of reference, equated to the employer. Conversely, managers are often at pains to point out that they are employees like anyone else in the organisation. However, both these views are too simplistic; few managers are either the owners of capital (although they are generally perceived by many to represent that interest) or the personal employer of other people. In terms of its role in organisational decision making, management as a group is distinct from the owner (shareholder), employer (the impersonal organisation) and, certainly, other employees. However, recent management 'buy outs' in a number of organisations may well create a greater personal feeling of being the owner and employer amongst the management concerned.

Consequently, the perceived basis of management's legitimacy to manage has tended to move away from the 'agency' principle, where its authority stems solely from it being the appointed representative of the organisation's owners, in favour of the 'possession of expertise' principle, where its authority derives primarily from a belief and acceptance that it has the requisite knowledge and ability to direct the affairs of the organisation. This growth of **managerialism** has reached the point where it is possible to see management as a distinct group not only within the organisation but also, perhaps, within society. Certainly, there is some evidence [4] to suggest that whilst a significant proportion of managers may come from a socio-economic background where their fathers were skilled manual or low level white collar, nevertheless, because of increased access to education and greater formalisation of career entry to management and the managerial professions (e.g. graduate entry), they are less likely than their predecessors to have started their working careers in manual or clerical work (i.e. to have worked their way up the organisation to a managerial position).

However, it is also important to recognise that the management group is heterogeneous. It would be wrong, in examining the role of management within the industrial relations system, to include only those managers involved directly in making 'industrial relations' decisions because, as Simpson argues, to do so 'says more about the power of management as a whole to limit the actual context of industrial relations discussion, than it does about the nature and effects of managerial decisions on the interests of workers' [5]. Certainly, some writers [6] have emphasised the importance of the organisation's strategic decision making both in determining the scope, level and control of collective bargaining and in providing the impetus and context for industrial relations problems.

The growth of managerialism has been reflected in an increased **specialisation within management** on both a functional and hierarchical basis. The **functional** division is particularly noticeable between 'line' or 'general' management and 'functional specialists'. It is often argued that the traditional role and authority of the 'line/general' management have been eroded not only by the growth of trade unions but also by the increased complexity and sophistication of modern organisations based on 'functional specialisms' – research and development, marketing, finance, production control and, perhaps most importantly in the industrial relations area, management services (work/method study) and personnel. The organisational division between functional specialist and line/general management roles remains an important one despite the trend towards greater flexibility, in individual manager career development, both between different specialisms and between specialisms and line/general management. The line/general management group is often regarded as the only group within management responsible for the organisation in some holistic sense; whilst the 'functional specialist' is responsible only for narrow technical decisions or advising line/general management in the exercise of wider responsibilities.

The **hierarchical** division within management, with its inherent differentials in authority and scope for decision making, also has important implications for the management of industrial relations. The policies and broad organisational strategies determined by directors and senior management are implemented through the operational decisions of those lower in the organisational hierarchy. This has led some to limit the term management to those at the top of the organisation (directors and senior management) who may be perceived as the appointed agents of the owner/employer, whilst those at the bottom of the hierarchy (supervisory management) are regarded as little more than a subgroup of employees because of their virtual removal from the organisation's decision making process. The tendency in the 1970s for supervisory, junior and even middle levels of management and the technical/professional groups to become organised in collectivities, whether through trade unions or other bodies such as staff or professional associations, was seen as evidence to further justify the exclusion of these groups from both the managerial decision making process and the group termed management.

Fox believed that the **development of a collective consciousness amongst management groups** and their 'pursuit of some degree of collective security by imposing discretion-reducing rules or understandings, upon top management' [7] demonstrated the existence of a 'low trust' relationship within the management structure. However, in response to this situation, many senior managers have sought to enhance the managerial role of these groups and draw them back into the decision making process. Clearly, the process of managing industrial relations within an organisation comprises an interrelated mixture of decisions at both the policy/strategic and operational levels – the lower groups within the organisational hierarchy certainly perceive themselves, and are perceived by other employees, to be part of management. For these reasons, they should be regarded as an integral part of the management control structure, and therefore of the management of the industrial relations system.

In analysing the role of management in industrial relations it is useful to examine (see Figure 8.1):

1. the interrelationship between 'constraints' and 'choices' which, it is argued, shape managerial strategy in industrial relations;
2. managerial objectives and alternative styles of industrial relations management;
3. certain aspects of the industrial relations system which impinge on the development and execution of managerial strategies; and
4. management strategies in the post-war period and possible future developments.

'Constraints' and 'choices'

Poole [8] suggests that management's decisions and actions in industrial relations can only be appreciated fully if it is recognised that they result from an **interaction between constraints and choices**. The constraints which surround management, stemming from economic and political pressures within the organisation's environment, 'set boundaries to the probable strategic choices', 'place certain identifiable limitations upon the total amount of control vested in members of the enterprise' and 'tend to direct choices along particular channels while curtailing other modes of initiative' [9]. However, Poole argues, it would be wrong to adopt a purely deterministic view of management decision making and strategy develop-ment – to do so would mean that the 'crucial role of choice in the formulation of strategy tends to be "organized out"' when 'the very conception of strategy incorporates at root the idea of an overall design within social action and a considerable measure of rationality and calculus' [10] in its determination and achievement. Thus management's strategies and decisions in industrial relations are not simply imposed by circumstances but are the result of conscious choices.

Poole identifies two major **environmental constraints** which appear to have a significant influence on management's strategy formulation:

1. Both Marxists and capitalists often argue that the **free enterprise market ideology** imposes a fundamental limitation on managerial discretion which mitigates against the implementation of policies and strategies which are employee-centred rather than production-centred (i.e. meeting the needs and aspirations of employees in preference to satisfying the economic and productive needs of management). The predominance of the capitalist ethos within society directs management towards policies which will minimise the organisation's wage costs and maintain output. At the same time, the changeable and unpredictable nature of the organisation's market environment 'induces an excessive caution in the formulation of advanced labour policies' [11].

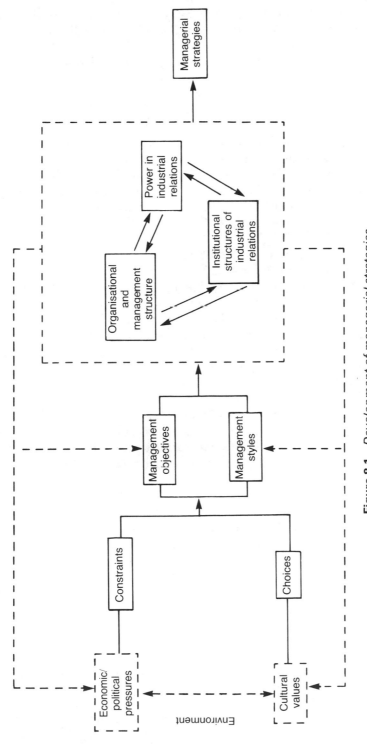

Figure 8.1 *Development of managerial strategies*

Derived from: M. Poole, 'Management strategies and industrial relations',
in M. Poole and R. Mansfield (eds), *Managerial Roles in Industrial Relations*, Gower, 1980

2. **Governmental concern for the management of the economy**, whether directly through a corporatist political ideology or indirectly through a *laissez-faire* one, imposes some restriction on managerial freedom and initiative at the organisational level. In industrial relations this has led to an increasing expression of concern for order (through the control of wages, industrial action and industrial power) and unity (through increased co-operation between management and employees).

Despite these constraints, management is still able to exercise **choice** in how it responds to these general pressures and the more specific pressures resulting from the organisation's particular market and technological position. Poole suggests that there are **three types of rationality** which may, individually or in combination, determine management's perception and choice of strategies:

1. Rationality based on **material interest** which will tend to favour those strategies and decisions which are perceived to best serve management's economic, productive and power interests; for example, strategies intended to minimise wage costs and maximise productivity.
2. Rationality based on **moral idealistic values** which regard certain issues to be 'a matter of principle' and a particular strategy to be intrinsically 'right' in terms of achieving an ideologically based goal; for example, strategies to avoid, resist or remove trade union recognition or the expansion of collective bargaining and thereby support management's 'right to manage'.
3. Rationality derived from **technocrat values** which support the adoption of strategies which appear to take account of all variables and provide a satisfactory outcome with the least harmful repercussions; for example, strategies based on an algorithmic approach which satisfy the criterion of logical reasoning.

Wilson suggests that the **social responsibility** of industry, which is 'a concept involving consideration of ethics . . ., power and authority' [12], is a crucial area in which 'constraints' and 'choices' have to be reconciled by management. It implies that management should give consideration, within its decision making, to the values, expectations and interests of the external society. This may be applied in two distinct directions dependent on whose interests it is believed should be taken into account:

1. **Internal responsibility**, which is directed towards accommodating the interests, expectations and satisfaction of the organisation's employees.
2. **External responsibility**, which is directed towards accommodating the needs and expectations of the surrounding community and society.

Whilst the former has been the focus of much of industrial relations and personnel thinking for some considerable time (extending management accountability through employee participation) the latter has achieved prominence only more recently. It has become an increasing focus of attention primarily because the scale of organisations and the interrelated complexities of industry and society have meant that decisions made in one organisation have significant effects outside the organisation – both in other organisations and society itself. Consequently, it has been argued, management must take a less parochial perspective and consider the results of their strategies and decisions in a wider setting.

Social responsibility may be incorporated into managerial decisions for different reasons:

1. There may be a **tradition or custom** within the management of the organisation, based on ideological values, which accepts the notion of social responsibility (for example, in the nineteenth century a number of Quaker companies recognised and implemented social responsibility through the medium of employee welfare).
2. It may be incorporated purely out of **management self-interest** – by appearing to accommodate a measure of social responsibility within its actions and decision making management can more easily gain acceptance of its actions and achieve its primary economic and productive goals.
3. Management may incorporate it simply because it is required to do so, to varying degrees and on some issues, by **external conventions or law** emanating from society itself (i.e. social responsibility is an externally imposed constraint).

(2) and (3) may be interrelated – only by incorporating social responsibility into its decision making can management maintain the greatest discretion in its authority and control. However, those who adopt a radical perspective might argue that in a modern industrial society management's authority and legitimacy is **dependent** not just on the employees' acceptance of management's role and strategies but also society's acceptance.

Management objectives

So far as management is concerned, the primary purpose of industrial relations is to support its objectives and strategies in the financial and productive aspects of the business. Consequently, **management's basic objective in industrial relations is to ensure the most effective operation of the organisation**. This may be achieved through two very different approaches to the management of industrial relations. On the one hand, management may seek to maintain unilateral control of the organisation through safeguarding, and if possible extending, its 'managerial prerogative', that is, the widest possible freedom and discretion to act as it sees best in operational decisions. Alternatively, management may seek to include employees and their representatives in the decision making process and 'manage by agreement', that is, accept the principle of joint regulation of the organisation's operations through the mechanisms of the industrial relations system.

The notion of **managerial prerogative** or the 'right to manage', whether derived from management's agency relationship to the owners or its perceived monopoly of expertise to make the 'right' organisational judgements and decisions, is still deeply ingrained in the thinking and behaviour of management. Storey argues that it represents 'an area of decision making over which management believes it should have (and acts as if it does have) sole and exclusive rights of determination and upon which it strenuously resists any interference' [13]. Despite an apparent acceptance of the pluralistic perspective, many managers remain irritated by what they regard as restrictions placed on 'their ability to do their job' by trade unions, collective bargaining and the industrial relations system. The requirement to consult or negotiate about organisational changes is often perceived as an imposition which diverts time and attention away from their primary task of maintaining the productivity and efficiency of the organisation. Consequently, it may be argued that there is a constant underlying pressure within management both to resist any extension of joint regulation and to restore unilateral regulation wherever and whenever circumstances allow.

However, McCarthy and Ellis believe that management's 'pursuit of what might be termed a "hard-line", insisting on their so-called managerial prerogatives, would involve them in using their economic power to the full' [14] and would, in a context where trade unions and collective bargaining are already established, create deep-seated conflict. The confrontational attitudes engendered by the forceful re-exertion of managerial prerogatives cannot realistically provide a foundation for the creation of a long-term co-operative relationship between management and employees. The **management by agreement** approach is founded on the principle that management can only effectively manage the organisation's operations by sharing power, authority and decision making through the joint regulatory processes of the industrial relations system.

Gospel, for example, has argued that in addition to profit optimisation there is a further major, but often unstated, management objective to optimise the long-term security of the organisation – in this context security means 'the desire for control over, and for regularities in, the firm's environment' [15] (including its labour environment). He differentiates between two areas of security which are important to management – market and managerial security. Market security is concerned with the need to maintain balanced and continuous operations, whilst **managerial security** 'is concerned with the distribution of power, control and decision making' [16]. The achievement of security in either area requires management both to recognise the existence of other interest groups and then to seek 'to build up a series of interdependent relationships, explicit or tacit rules and under-standings' [17] with them. In the same way that management seeks long-term agreements with its customers and suppliers to aid its market security, so, through the industrial relations system and the creation of jointly agreed rules, management is able to establish an interdependent relationship with its workforce which aids managerial security by reducing uncertainty and creating a more stable and predictable industrial relations environment. The notion of 'interdependence' implies that management is prepared to seek and agree to compromises which may only partly meet their objectives, but which at the same time partly meet the needs of employees, rather than pursue its objectives at the expense of its employees aspirations and interests.

The potential clash between management seeking to maintain its prerogative and employees/unions seeking more management by consent is clearly demonstrated in Perline and Poynter's survey of union research directors and corporate executives in charge of labour relations in the USA in which they sought to discover 'if disagreement over the issue of managerial prerogative was likely to deter a more co-operative relationship between labour and management in the USA' [18] (i.e. the extent to which the parties agreed or disagreed on the fundamental basis for determining issues which arose in the workplace). The results of this survey (see Table 8.1) show that whilst there was broad agreement between both sets of respondents that a range of corporate policy or strategic decisions should be regarded as managerial decisions there was also wide disagreement over many other issues. On ten items relating to significant areas of work control (including items such as 'business location', 'size of workforce' and 'means of manufacture') over 75 per cent of the managers felt these should be management decisions whilst, in all items except one, a majority of the union respondents felt these should be joint decisions. On a further five items (including 'job content' and 'assignment of work') whilst two-thirds or more of the union respondents felt these should be joint decisions more than half the managers disagreed. Only on two items did a majority of both sets of respondents agree that they should be joint decisions – 'seniority provisions' and 'transfer of workers'. Overall, therefore, whilst there appeared to be substantial union agreement with management's assertion that a range of corporate strategic decisions were a matter for managerial decision making, there was little management agreement with the union's assertion that a broad range of operational decisions should be subject to joint decision making: clearly indicative of a management concern to maintain and protect its managerial prerogative. However, it must be remembered that these attitudes are the product of the US culture and industrial relations system (wherein even with their 'business' orientation trade unions have been more severely weakened during the 1980s than in the UK) and therefore are not necessarily reflective of UK attitudes developed within a different culture and industrial relations system.

Table 8.1 *An appropriate determination of collective bargaining issues*

	Managerial Decision		Joint Decision	
	Management (%)	Union (%)	Management (%)	Union (%)
(a) Where more than 75% of both management and union responses agreed item was managerial decision:				
Management of organisation	100	80		
Products to be manufactured	100	77		
Financial policies	100	82		
Pricing of goods or services	100	91		
Distribution of product	100	91		
Control of plant property	100	75		
Promotion to supervisory	98	91		
Customer relations	94	81		
(b) Where more than 75% of management but less than 75% of union responses felt item was managerial decision:				
Materials and inventories	99	73		
Services to be rendered	97	73		
Property protection	97	65		
(c) Where more than 75% of management responses felt item was managerial decision but more than 50% of union responses felt it was joint decision:				
Business location	100			68
Size of workforce	100			64
Means of manufacture	96			65
Scheduling of operations	95			72
Layout and equipment	93			59
Quality of workmanship	90			76
Discharge of employees	87			50
Selection of employees	86			64
Disciplinary action	82			65
Scheduling of shifts	77			77
(d) Where more than 50% of both management and union responses agreed item was joint decision:				
Seniority provisions			80	91
Transfer of workers			52	74
(e) Where more than 50% of union responses but less than 50% of management responses felt item was joint decision:				
Contracted work			34	91
Job content			32	91
Safety and health			30	86
Assignment of work			31	83
Promotion non-supervisor			49	65

Source: Derived from M. M. Perline and D. J. Poynter, 'Union and management perceptions of managerial prerogative: some insight into the future of co-operative bargaining in the USA', *British Journal of Industrial Relations*, vol. 28, no. 2, July 1990, Table 1, p. 185.

Management styles

Purcell defines **management style** as 'the existence of a distinctive set of guiding principles, written or otherwise, which set parameters to and signposts for management action in the way employees are treated and particular events handled' [19]. It is important to recognise that 'management' style is not necessarily synonymous with 'organisational' style. Whilst there is little doubt about the significance or importance of managerial style in determining the organisation's style of industrial relations, nevertheless, as Purcell points out, 'an important analytical distinction must be drawn ... between classifications of the outcome of the interaction of management and labour and the attitudes, beliefs or frames of reference of the parties, most notably management, in determining the style that they wish to pursue' [20]. Poole took a similar approach in recognising that the development of managerial styles and strategies in industrial relations both influence the industrial relations system and are influenced by it. Therefore, **'management intended style'** should be seen as one input into the organisation's industrial relations system from which 'organisational style' is the output.

Purcell suggests that **management style in industrial relations can be related to two dimensions – individualism and collectivism** (see Figure 8.2). he defines the **individualism dimension** as 'the extent to which personnel policies are focused on the rights and capabilities of individual workers' [21] and in particular 'the extent to which the firm gives credence to the feelings and sentiments of each employee and seeks to develop and encourage each employee's capacity and role at work' [22]. He identifies three stages along this dimension:

1. **Commodity status (labour control)** – the employee is regarded as an individual unit of production to be hired and fired in the light of operational requirements (reliance on external labour market) and therefore has low job security; the managerial focus is on direct overt control of the employee (negative discipline sanction) and the achievement of surplus value (profit).
2. **Paternalism** – the employee is regarded as a natural subordinate deferential role whose freedom is limited by 'well meant' regulation, and management accept a degree of 'social responsibility' to provide benevolent welfare care for *their* employees.
3. **Resource status (employee development)** – the employee is regarded as a potential resource to be developed and nurtured (reliance more on internal labour market and implies the existence of careful selection, training and development programmes, career development strategies, good reward package but linked to individual performance and appraisal, etc.); the managerial focus is on communication and employee involvement to secure commitment.

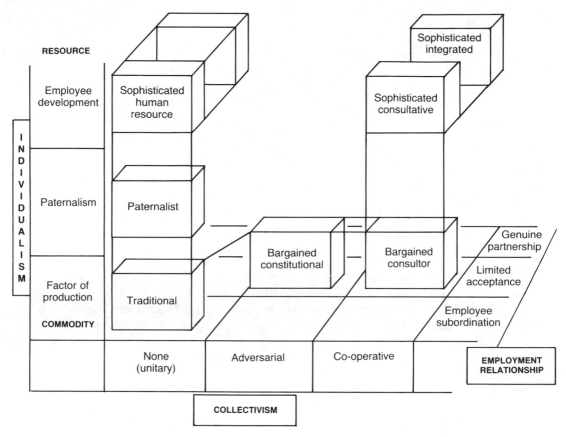

Figure 8.2 *Typology of management styles*
Derived from: J. Purcell, 'Mapping management styles in employee relations',
Journal of Management Studies, September 1987, p. 541

The **collectivism dimension** is defined as 'the extent to which management policy is directed towards inhibiting or encouraging the development
of collective representation by employees and allowing employees a collective voice in management decision-making' [23]. This dimension, Purcell
argues, is reflected in two ways; first, the existence of democratic structures
through which employee interests may be expressed and pursued (this may
range from simple union recognition, through an increasing range of
consultative and bargaining arrangements and agreements, to full employee
participation – including workers directors); secondly, the degree to which
management accepts or opposes, and thereby gives legitimacy to, the
collective processes. Again, he identifies three stages along this dimension:

1. **Unitary** – management overtly or covertly opposes collective
    relationships.

2. **Adversarial** – the managerial focus is on stability, control and institutionalisation of conflict; containment of collective relationships to limited and clearly identified areas of operational decision making; reluctance to concede or compromise even within these areas of bargaining.

3. **Co-operative** – the managerial focus is on 'constructive' relationship beyond simple bargaining of terms and conditions of employment; greater incorporation of employees and their representatives into organisational structures and discussions including aspects of strategic management; greater openness and preparedness to modify plans/decisions in light of those discussions.

Purcell argues that the interrelationship between individualism and collectivism within management style is complex and not, as might be expected, a simple conflict between the two (i.e. that increased emphasis on individualism must automatically imply a reduction in collectivism). He believes that there is no intrinsic reason why the development of an HRM individualistic approach must inevitably imply a move away from collectivism and that it is possible to integrate both 'employee development' and 'co-operative collectivism'. Developments in Britain during the 1980s such as (a) the development of the Human Resource Management concept incorporating greater attention to selection, training, labour flexibility, individualised reward system, etc. and (b) management interest in non-union organisation, derecognition and reduced status for the union and shop stewards may be seen as strategies aimed towards greater individualism. Equally, management strategies directed towards the decentralisation of collective bargaining, creating a stronger link between organisational performance or flexibility and improvements in terms and conditions of employment and the development of Single Union Agreements (which may include an employee council and the so-called no-strike pendulum arbitration clause) could be regarded as moves towards reduced adversarial and increased co-operative collectivism.

However, the **apparent values which underlie the definition of the two axes** in Purcell's model are open to question. On the **Individualism axis** Purcell only refers to management giving 'credence to the feelings and sentiments of each employee' (i.e. to what degree do management *think* about or *believe* they should meet the individual needs of employees). There is no inclusion of the extent to which management accepts the employee's 'right' (even as an individual employee) to express views or, more importantly, seek to modify or influence management policies or decisions. In all three degrees it appears that it is management rather than the employee who identifies which employee needs or wants are to be satisfied – 'We know what is best for you'. The higher order degrees may be more 'employee centred' in respect of the material well-being and 'technical' development of the employee but appear to involve little advancement in terms of employee participation in and influence on management decisions. Indeed, it could be argued that the investment or employee resource development approach is simply the seduction of employees to management goals through responsible autonomy (i.e. management values and objectives become an integrated element within the employee's role). Marchington and Parker [24] argue that it is important to recognise on the Individualism axis that all employers will seek to control labour costs and therefore it is a constant throughout the dimension and not just a feature of the Commodity Status end as implied in Purcell's model. They suggest that the development orientation at the higher levels of this dimension is indicative only of management's 'investment orientation' towards labour which arises from an increasing management concern about the organisation's competitive position, product quality and/or customer satisfaction and therefore, by implication, is the result of economic and technological factors rather than a statement of management value choice.

In defining the **Collectivism axis**, Purcell refers to the *'right'* of employees to have a say in *those* aspects of management decision making which concern them, uses the term 'constructive', (in inverted commas) to signify an apparently important aspect of the Co-operative relationship and refers to the incorporation of employee organisations into the 'organisational fabric'. This begs a number of questions – On whose terms and values? Who defines what is, or what is not, 'constructive'? Does 'constructive' mean behaviour which is reasonable only in management's eyes and that situations should be evaluated and reacted to from a management perspective and with management values? Similarly, Marchington and Parker argue that to see the creation or continuation of relations with unions as evidence of management *commitment* to 'collectivism' is wide of the mark and that the definition should be replaced with management attitudes and behaviour towards trade unions in the workplace and the degree to which a 'partnership orientation' is pursued.

Both axes could be interpreted as a spectrum of management intention from 'coercion' to 'seduction' of employees to management perspectives and values (one as an individual employee and the other through suborning the employees' organisation). This would suggest that management is only prepared to accept challenge by employees in an adversarial mode with limited collective joint regulation – and certainly little influence in the strategic areas of managerial decision making. It could be, of course, that this is the reality of management's 'intended' style; that it simply reflects management's inherent desire to manage with the minimum challenge to its authority and decisions and this will be modified in the organisation's industrial relations style in the light of any employee reaction and power. If the model is to accommodate an intended 'partnership' management style which integrates 'employee development' individualism with *independent* collectivism, it is useful to add a third dimension – **management's attitude towards the underlying employment relationship**. This may range from 'employee subordination' where the maintenance of managerial prerogative is pre-eminent, through a 'limited acceptance' of the right of the employee to decide jointly with management on a range of largely operational decisions, to 'genuine partnership' where all organisational decisions are open to employee participation and influence.

It is possible to locate the earlier Purcell and Sisson's [25] typology of management styles within this amended model:

1. **Traditional** – the employee is regarded as a factor of production to be employed and discarded as necessary and whose cost to management should be minimised (low pay and little sense of job security) and the subordinate position of the individual in the employment relationship is regarded as part of the 'natural order' and any attempt to collectivise the relationship is resisted. It is very clearly based on a belief in management's right to manage and is associated closely with authoritarian management, open hostility towards trade unions (including refusal to recognise or negotiate with them) and reliance on legal rights and protection to support their interests and actions.

2. **Sophisticated Human Resource** – although this style derives from a unitary perspective and may be associated with an absence of, or even refusal to recognise, trade unions, nevertheless it differs from the traditionalist style of management. Management, by adopting positive personnel policies on recruitment, pay, welfare, consultation, etc., seeks to create an organisational climate which ensures 'that individual aspirations are mostly satisfied, that collective action is seen as unnecessary and inappropriate' [26]. The employee is regarded as a flexible organisational resource to be developed and rewarded in the light of his/her abilities or attributes and emphasises communication and involvement to develop employee loyalty and commitment to the organisation with the intention of making collectivism and trade unions both unnecessary and unattractive. Thus management seeks to establish a direct relationship with its employees, without the intervention of trade unions, and its intention in so doing may range from 'sophisticated' employee subordination through to genuine partnership in decision making.

3. **Sophisticated Modern (bargained)** – this style of management recognises that managerial prerogative is diminished by the existence of trade union power. It seeks to regulate the situation by establishing joint institutions and procedures to minimise and institutionalise conflict (whilst maximising the notion of common interest through joint consultation) and concedes limited acceptance of the employee's right to and role in decision making. Purcell and Sisson subdivide this group between:

   (a) **Constitutionalist** – where the basic value structure of management is similar to that of the traditionalist and the importance of managerial control is emphasised in order to minimise union influence or constraints. The relationship is restricted to conflictual 'terms and conditions of employment' and 'the limits on collective bargaining are clearly codified in the collective agreement' [27].

(b) **Consultor** – where the interdependent relationship is formalised primarily with interest groups represented through trade unions but 'every effort is made to minimise the amount of collective bargaining especially of a "conflictual" or "distributive" kind' and 'great emphasis is placed on "cooperative" or "integrative" bargaining; "problems" have to be solved rather than "disputes" settled' [28].

Two further categories may be added:

4. **Sophisticated Consultative** – during the 1980s many organisations, to a lesser or greater degree, have sought to shift from 'constitutional' to 'consultor' on the collectivism axis (thereby reducing any union constraint on their decision making) whilst developing elements of 'employee development' along the individualism axis (thus increasing the employee's understanding of management's position and commitment to the well-being of the organisation). Such developments have been intended to strengthen management's scope and ability to improve the organisation's performance, flexibility, competitiveness, quality, etc. In so doing, management has retained, if not strengthened, its managerial prerogative and afforded only a limited role for employees (either individually or collectively) to influence its decision making.

5. **Sophisticated Integrated** – this combines the existence of a genuine equal collective based partnership with the development of individualism in terms of enhancing the individual's potential contribution to the organisation, rewarding individuals on the basis of their attributes or abilities and, above all, meeting the individual's personal needs for satisfying work, a sense of commitment and identification with the organisation, etc. The primary difference between this style and the 'sophisticated consultative' is the acceptance by all, but primarily management, of the abandonment of notions of 'managerial prerogative' and acceptance of the right of employees, through a variety of collective and individual forms, to participate with management in decision making. Through accepting an equal collective partnership, all parties (the individual and union as well as management) can be considered as having an equal responsibility to create and maintain an organisation which is efficient, responsive, adaptive, productive and profitable.

Most organisations do not fit neatly within one or other of these 'ideal' types. Purcell and Sisson identified the **Standard Modern** as the predominant 'style' of industrial relations management: essentially pragmatic and reactive in character, the approach adopted or the emphasis placed on industrial relations considerations at any particular point in time varying dependent on the values and attitudes of the managers involved and the nature and extent of the pressures they perceive being exerted on them. However, it may be argued that some organisations are hybrids seeking to combine elements of different styles or are in transition from one style to another but lack the 'distinctive set of guiding principles' which Purcell argues is essential for there to be a management 'style'. The extent to which an organisation fits within any of the categories depends on the extent to which management (in particular senior management) is committed to a particular and defined long-term industrial relations policy, philosophy or 'style'.

The industrial relations system

The development of managerial styles and strategies in industrial relations both influence and are influenced by the industrial relations system. This is very evident in respect of the **relative power relationship** in industrial relations. Any management style or strategy must, if it is to be realistic, take account of management's existing relative power position within the industrial relations system whilst at the same time seeking to improve it. Any change in the relative power position between management and trade unions is likely to provoke a modification of management style and strategy. This was seen clearly during the 1980s with economic conditions and government limitations on trade union power affording the opportunity for management to adopt tougher styles and strategies. Marsh found that the companies he surveyed thought they had, during the 1970s, become 'less autocratic and paternalistic and more participative and consultative . . . more "formal" and more "negotiating" in their approaches to employee relations' [29]. However, Purcell and Sisson believe that it is amongst the Standard Moderns that management style is most volatile and where arguments in favour of strategies aimed at achieving long-term stability and co-operation based on a pluralistic perspective became increasingly difficult to maintain in the face of the economic climate of the 1980s which emphasised short-term improvements in productivity and profitability. The change in attitude amongst these organisations between the 1960s and the 1980s is not, in their opinion, 'simply a matter of "macho" managements taking advantage of large-scale unemployment and a government which is hostile to trade unions to settle old scores', but rather that 'the case for tough policies seems increasingly unanswerable as short-term benefits in productivity improvements and union acquiescence become widely reported. The shift towards unitary policies based more on coercion than cooperation is thus largely unchallenged . . . The unions lack the power and the members the will to mount a major campaign against policies which are portrayed as "common sense" and the "economic facts of life"' [30].

It is possible to argue that the absence of effective employee pressure in the 1980s gave management an increased opportunity to exercise choice. For the majority, it may be possible to regard the changes as environmentally determined and, consequently, just as likely to change again in the future if or when economic circumstances and trade union power change. However, some appear to have deliberately chosen a more traditionalist style of management and others have chosen a more sophisticated style. Such management changes will themselves influence the attitudes and actions of employees and trade unions. Certainly, Clegg has suggested from his international comparison of trade unionism that 'trade unions are more likely to accept the methods which Marx prescribed for them, where employers play the part assigned to them in his doctrine of the class struggle' [31].

It is also quite clear that **organisational and managerial structures** have an important influence on managerial styles and strategies in industrial relations. The hierarchical character of management's organisational structure, with strategic authority vested in the most senior positions, means that it is the values, attitudes and perceptions of **directors and senior management** which will predominate in the determination of style and strategy. In the 1970s Winkler [32] found that directors, and by implication senior managers, had little direct contact with either employees or their representatives and usually became involved in industrial relations matters only when an issue had reached the stage of a problem or even crisis for lower levels of management. This was confirmed by Marsh who found 'boards are often content to endorse decisions made elsewhere and only become directly involved where the situation is judged to have become serious enough to merit such attention' [33]. Consequently, they tended to perceive employees and trade unions as a 'problem' or 'cost' – to many directors 'the strike or negotiation was an outside event, beyond their control or participation, roughly analogous to a revolution in a country which supplied their raw material' [34]. They often relied on their past experiences, either on the shop floor or as managers, to analyse current situations and determine strategies; experiences which were selective and inaccurate and, more importantly, gained within a different economic, social and organisational environment. It is significant, perhaps, that during the 1980s it is these senior managers, with their strategic concern for the competitive performance of the organisation, who have been the major impetus for changing the style of industrial relations management, developing HRM strategies and linking these changes directly with the achievement of business objectives.

The organisation's industrial relations activities are also influenced by the **role and attitudes of both operational line management and industrial relations functional specialists** and there may be divergences both between these groups and between them and senior management:

1. Operational management may, when trade union power is strong, seek to create and maintain bargained relationships in order to reduce

operational uncertainties and secure their 'managerial authority'. Batstone *et al.* [35] observed that managers in the 1970s frequently sought to support 'strong' shop stewards who not only represented but also led and controlled their membership. This desire for a 'bargained' managerial security at the operational level may, of course, run counter to the expressed managerial policy at the strategic level to reduce trade union power. The development of a stronger organisational performance culture during the 1980s (including devolution of authority, responsibility and accountability and the creation of cost/profit centres or mini organisations at the operational level) has tended to draw operational management more towards the business outlook of senior management.

2. The objectives of line management and functional specialist may differ. Line management may judge industrial relations objectives and strategies by their effect on the organisation's operation and managerial authority. The functional specialist is also concerned with 'equity', 'justice', 'fairness' and 'satisfaction' for the employees.

The balance between these approaches within the organisation's decision making will depend on the relative status and authority accorded to the two groups within the management structure. The recent adoption of HRM concepts may have an important effect in this context. On the one hand, it has widened the role for 'functional specialists' in a number of less formalised areas such as communication, consultation, participation and organisational development, and, at the same time, brought them into the mainstream of achieving business objectives. On the other hand, it has placed increased emphasis on the 'personnel management' role of all managers – in particular operational line management – and as a consequence is likely to enhance their status and authority in organisational decision making on industrial relations matters.

Finally, the **institutional structure of industrial relations** is closely interrelated with management strategies in industrial relations. Clegg observed that because 'collective bargaining has its regulatory effect by restricting and controlling managerial decisions . . . it has its best chance of being effective when it operates at the points where managerial decisions are taken' [36]. At the same time Purcell and Sisson point out that management is able to 'use the levels at which collective bargaining takes place to control the activities of trade unions' [37]:

1. Bargaining within a **multi-employer framework** through employers' associations may minimise the role of trade unions and shop stewards at the organisational level. The policy of both management and shop stewards is directed primarily externally towards influencing their representatives at the national level.

2. Bargaining at the **corporate level** affords management the opportunity not only to standardise terms and conditions of employment across different sites and thereby avoid competitive comparisons but, in so doing, also to strengthen the role of union full-time officials *vis-à-vis* shop stewards and to absorb and weaken potential militancy at any one particular site.

3. Bargaining at the **organisational level**, whilst strengthening the role of shop stewards, offers management perhaps the greatest opportunity to retain control of operational decisions and to minimise wage costs through productivity improvements by demanding that each organisation justify itself financially. It also has the effect of not affording 'the trade union any role in the determination of broad company policy' and 'leaves divisional and corporate management free to develop policy unbothered with the need to justify their decisions to trade unions, let alone bargain over them' [38].

8.3 Management strategies

Accommodation and institutionalisation

Management's apparent strategy up until the 1960s has been characterised as a continuation of its previous pre-war strategy: namely, a reliance on employers' associations and national agreements. However, below the surface of this formal system there grew up, in much of industry, an array of informal and fragmented organisational 'bargaining' and practices. The Donovan Commission Report (1968) concluded that Britain had two systems of industrial relations: the formal system embodied in official institutions which had as its keystone the industry-wide collective agreement and the informal system at the organisational level which was conducted on a piecemeal basis and lacked any comprehensive and well-ordered strategies or agreements. The prevailing philosophy of the Report towards reform was 'that collective bargaining is the best method of conducting industrial relations' and that there was wide scope for 'extending both the subject matter of collective bargaining and the number of workers covered by collective agreements' [39]. Their central recommendation was to support the development of 'effective and orderly collective bargaining' and the 'extension of collective bargaining' at the organisational level. The problem was compounded, from a management perspective, by the trade union power at both national and organisational level engendered by a strong economy, full employment and a supportive Labour Government (1964–70). Purcell and Sisson believe that, for management 'the overriding need was to gain control of industrial relations in the workplace' [40] and, in Storey's terms, 'the challenge from below met a challenge from above' [41].

Purcell and Sisson have identified three **lines of reform** by which management sought to regain control during the 1960s and 1970s:

1. **Institutionalise and formalise the organisational level industrial relations system** through the establishment of jointly agreed institutions and procedures – in particular trade union recognition and the role of shop stewards; collective bargaining arrangements; and procedures relating to grievances, disputes, discipline, etc. This had the effect of regularising and legitimising the authority and status of both management and trade unions.
2. **Reforming wage and salary structures** to regain control of wage costs – including removing the process of pay determination from the immediate 'point of production' management; establishing wage and salary systems based on formal work study and job evaluation; and linking pay and production through various forms of productivity bargaining. These arrangements were intended to remove anomalies and leap-frogging wage claims and promote greater order and consistency.
3. **Emphasise and revitalise communication and joint consultation** as a means of promoting the notions of co-operation and problem solving between management and employees.

These strategies were closely associated with the development of the Bargained Constitutionalist and Bargained Consultor styles of management (both involving the acceptance of trade unions as an integral part of managing the human aspect of the business). At the national level, this was also a period of a corporatist ideology with attempted Government regulation of the wage element of collective bargaining through incomes policy and debates about formal employee participation in organisational strategic decision making (Bullock Committee on Industrial Democracy (1977)).

However, Purcell and Sisson believe that management currently sees its main problem as being one of flexibility – 'if the fault with unfettered sectional bargaining was its lack of control and excessive flexibility, reformed bargaining and pay structures can be seen to be unduly inflexible' [42]. Consequently, the 1980s have seen a change in management strategy intended not only to reduce the apparent constraint of formalised joint regulation codified in collective agreements but also to reassert its prerogative to manage the business.

Direct challenge

In the early 1980s a combination of rapid economic recession, rising unemployment, and increasing international competition together with a newly elected Conservative government committed to reducing trade union power through legislative controls and enhancing market individualism dramatically altered the balance of power between management and unions both nationally and at the organisational level. This provided the opportunity for management to adopt what has been termed 'macho management techniques' which included:

1. A greater preparedness on the part of management to 'stand firm' in the face of employee or union opposition and less preparedness to compromise in negotiations (including, perhaps, less inclination to use conciliation or arbitration to settle disputes).
2. More emphasis on direct links with employees (including appealing directly to employees over the heads of shop stewards and full-time officials in the form of ballots and even, in some cases, the withdrawal of union recognition).
3. An increased preparedness to use rights established by legislation (including the dismissal or threatened dismissal of strikers and obtaining injunctions and damages against unions).

These strategies are closely associated with the shift towards a Traditional style of management and in some organisations (notably, News International at Wapping and the NCB) they resulted in major, long-running confrontations as management sought to impose major organisational, technological and/or production changes involving large-scale rationalisation and redundancies. However, most organisations, whilst becoming firmer in their dealings with trade unions, have sought to do so without such open confrontation but rather have relied on emphasising communication, consultation and employee involvement and the introduction of work changes and productivity improvements without the financial incentives associated with much of the productivity bargaining of the 1960s and 1970s. Edwards noted that, far from 'macho-management' being the prevailing trend in British industrial relations, 'a more subtle process seems to have been taking place in which firms have certainly been trying to change working practices but in which cooperation and involvement have been seen as important' [43].

Human resource management

The term 'human resource management', which has become increasingly used in Britain during the 1980s, has been applied to a diverse range of management strategies and, indeed, sometimes used simply as a more modern, and therefore more acceptable, term for personnel, employee or industrial relations (i.e. 'old wine in a new bottle'). However, the importance of the 'new wine' aspect of HRM lies in its association with **a strategic, integrated and highly distinctive managerial approach to the management of people.**

The development of HRM strategies in Britain during the mid to late 1980s has clearly been **a response to a combination of external and internal pressures**. A significant change in the overall business environment, primarily related to an increasingly competitive national and international 'market-place', has produced a consequent need for organisations not just to become more productive but also to become more conscious of technology, quality, design and customer service/satisfaction. At the same time, many organisations have instigated internal changes: company mergers, changes in top management, major redundancies, decentralisation of 'people management' activities to line management and attempts to establish a clearer performance related organisation culture (directed towards change, product quality and/or customer satisfaction). Hendry *et al.* argue that these changes 'created needs for new operating structures and systems, and new skills, knowledge and capability from staff' [44]. Therefore, in their view, the focus of HRM has been on the organisation's 'ability to take, and implement, a strategic view of the whole range of personnel practices in relation to business activity as a whole' [45] in order to meet an identified business and skill performance gap and achieve technical change and product market development. Similarly, Armstrong sets out one organisation's implementation of HRM strategies in terms of the three P's: 'People – improving quality, developing potential; Performance – increasing the accountability of managers for results, relating pay more specifically to performance, increasing commitment by better communications and more involvement; Productivity – analysing the use of human resources throughout the organisation so that planned growth is achieved with lower costs per unit of output' [46].

Guest [47] suggests that there are four components to **a distinctive HRM strategy model** (see Figure 8.3):

1. An integrated package of HRM policy goals or outcomes comprising:
    (a) strategic and coherent integration of HRM into both strategic organisational planning and the everyday activities of line managers;
    (b) securing the commitment of employees to the goal of high organisational performance;
    (c) an adaptive, receptive and flexible organisational structure through 'job design' based on the principles of enriching the individual's work, establishing autonomous workgroup arrangements and creating a 'multi-skilled' workforce; and
    (d) high-quality employees and management as well as high-quality production (goods and services).

2. The implementation of a range of specific 'Personnel' policies/practices (job design, selection, appraisal, development, reward, communication etc.) directed specifically towards supporting the achievement of the overall HRM policy goals;

3. An 'ideological cement' of a strong organisational culture, support from

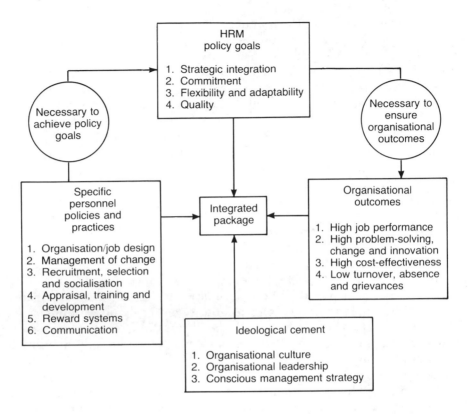

Figure 8.3 *A model of Human Resource Management*
Derived from: D. Guest, 'Personnel and HRM: can you tell the difference?'
Personnel Management, January 1989, Figure 2, p. 49

the organisation's leaders and a conscious management strategy that
organisational success requires the effective utilisation of human
resources;

4. The desired organisational outcomes which provide the criteria by which
    to judge the success of HRM (increased organisational ability to
    innovate and respond to change, greater cost effectiveness, improved
    employee job performance, etc.).

It is clear that the creation of a **corporate culture** is a fundamental part
of the HRM approach. Armstrong describes 'corporate culture' as encompassing 'the company's goals and dominant ideologies ... expressed in
company *values* – what is good for the organisation and what should or

should not happen; organisational *climate* – the working atmosphere of the organisation as perceived and experienced by its members; and management *style* – the way in which managers behave and exercise authority' [48]. However, writers differ in respect of the kind of culture that is required to underpin HRM – particularly in relation to the individualism and collectivism axes of Purcell's model. Guest believes that 'the values underpinning . . . HRM are predominantly individualist and unitarist' [49] and, consequently, **challenge collectivism and the role of trade unions** in the process of managing people within the organisation: industrial relations is no longer perceived, by management, as a central activity. Potential elements within the HRM strategy which accord with this view may range from shifting the emphasis of the collective relationship away from negotiation and agreement and towards consultation; bypassing the shop steward role by establishing or strengthening direct lines of communication and involvement with employees; or more 'macho' elements such as threatening derecognition if a union resists changes in work practices, etc. The whole thrust of such strategic HRM is not, as has been argued for in the past, one of an upward direction of introducing and strengthening the 'people' factor in top-level management decision making but rather a downward direction of ensuring that the 'human resource' (people) conform to the business needs of the organisation. Fowler has described this approach to HRM as 'the complete identification of employees with the aims and values of the business – employee involvement, but on the company's terms' and questions whether it is 'genuinely concerned with creating a new, equal partnership between employer and employed, or . . . offering a covert form of employee manipulation dressed up as mutuality?' [50]. These strategies represent a shift towards a Sophisticated Human Resource style of management (an increased investment orientated individualism coupled with decreased collectivism).

However, other writers believe that the adoption of HRM strategies do not necessarily imply abandoning collectivism but rather a **shift from an adversarial to co-operative style of collectivism**. Armstrong, for example, believes that although integration 'in the sense of getting members of the organisation working together with a sense of common purpose' is one of the fundamental principles underlying HRM, nevertheless 'this must take account of the fact that all organisations are pluralist societies in which people have differing interests and concerns which they may well feel need to be defended collectively' [51]. Similarly, Miller argues that in a 'mature' business (i.e. one which already has established collective bargaining structures and relationships) the achievement of the strategic element of HRM probably requires changes to improve organisational performance and efficiency to be agreed 'through negotiation with a representative body of employees' [52]. The inclusion and maintenance of collectivism within HRM strategies therefore implies a shift towards a Sophisticated Consultative style of management.

'Japanisation'

The so-called Japanisation of organisational industrial relations has received considerable publicity in Britain during the 1980s and, for some, represents an ideal to be pursued. Ackroyd *et al.* argue that this 'Japanisation' can come about in three different ways:

1. 'Direct' through the introduction of Japanese firms into the British economy and industrial relations system (but 'Japanese subsidiaries are not major employers of UK labour' [53]).
2. 'Mediated' by British organisations copying Japanese policies and practices to a greater or lesser extent (but 'such initiatives . . . are likely to be mediated by the orientation of British management and therefore less straightforward in their effects' [54]).
3. 'Permeated' through the development of the British system to emulate Japanese structures and practices (but 'the evidence . . . is very slight' [55]).

Oliver and Wilkinson [56] have observed that 'Japanisation' strategies are based on an integration between personnel and industrial relations practices and new manufacturing methods and working practices – with the former supporting the latter. Certainly this is most often linked in people's minds with the introduction of Single Union Agreements which have been portrayed as a package which seeks to introduce a totally new and integrated approach to organisational industrial relations; the main ingredients being:

1. a single union within the organisation;
2. single status and common terms and conditions of employment for all staff;
3. an employee council or advisory board coupled with open communication and employee involvement;
4. job flexibility coupled with just-in-time production systems and an emphasis on quality;
5. no-strike clause linked to pendulum arbitration to resolve any disputes without recourse to industrial action.

The precise number of such agreements is not known although it has been estimated that there could be between 50 and 200 [57]. In addition, not all agreements contain all the above elements.

Finally, it is important to recognise that the 'Japanese style of management' may not be all what it appears and certainly has to be related to its own specific national culture. Certainly, Briggs believes that the public images of Japanese management, where 'workers are seen as secure in their jobs, protected by the paternalistic attitudes of their employers; management and shop floor workers dress in similar style, and both make valuable contributions to the running of the company; the workers strive for the same goals as the management, having adopted the values of the company wholesale; and contentment reigns – apparent from the workers' dedication and their reluctance to take industrial action', are 'misguided utopian illusions' [58]. She found from an examination of Japanese management in Japan that only the large firms, and, therefore, a minority of employees have lifetime employment; employees 'conform' because of labour control systems rather than are committed; they 'endure' the work situation rather than are happy with it; and there is a subtle but very distinct hierarchy status relationship. She concludes that 'in human terms it is acceptable to the Japanese because it is consistent with their own cultural values, but the cost to the workforce in terms of quality of working life is dear' [59]. Therefore, the introduction of 'Japanisation' into British industrial relations is likely to present a clash between two very different cultures and requires modification if it is to succeed.

8.4 Employers' associations

An employers' association may be defined as **any organisation whose membership is composed of employers and whose purposes include the regulation of relations between employers and their employees or trade unions**. It is important to distinguish employers' associations from purely trade associations which exclude labour affairs and confine themselves to trade matters such as marketing, pricing, technology, etc. However, the majority of employers' associations combine employer and trade functions and, therefore, are concerned with both production and employment matters. Indeed, of the major employers' associations, only the Engineering Employers' Federation is not also a trade association principally because 'engineering' encompasses a wide range of distinct sub-industries with different trading situations and needs. It is also important to recognise that employers' associations are **second degree groupings** (i.e. associations of corporate bodies rather than individuals) and therefore their existence reinforces, rather than creates, the collective bargaining ability and power of the organisations which are its members.

Development

The development of employers' associations is closely related to the development of trade unionism and collective bargaining. Whilst there is evidence of transient local combinations of employers from the early nineteenth century, it was not until the 1890s that more permanent organisations were established – largely as a reaction to the increasing membership and stability of trade unions. Their primary objective was to

protect management's prerogative and resist the development of trade unionism – in some cases by providing financial support to members resisting a union claim and faced with either a strike or lockout. Thus, there was a clear inducement to join an employers' association; the organisation which was not a member could not call on any support if it was needed.

By the end of World War I, employers' associations had become **institutions of collective bargaining** seeking, on behalf of their members, to regulate terms and conditions of employment on a district or national basis through negotiated agreements with trade unions. Such an arrangement meant that individual organisations could collectively negotiate one agreement which would apply to all member organisations rather than being picked off one-by-one: complete organisation (i.e. ensuring that as many employers as possible were members of the employers' association) became important. The non-federated organisation presented a constant potential threat to both other employers and trade unions by paying lower wages and therefore being able to undercut prices. Trade unions saw an expansion of employers' association membership not as a threat to themselves but as a means to extend the coverage of collective agreements and establish a common rate throughout the industry.

The more recent emphasis on **organisational level bargaining**, brought about, first, by full employment in the 1960s and the desire amongst many managements to undertake productivity bargaining which linked pay increases to work changes, has reduced the regulatory effect of national agreements in much of the private sector. As part of this process of change, a number of organisations felt it necessary to leave their employers' association in order to have greater freedom to determine their own strategies. They were supported by their trade unions because it was seen as a way of increasing their members' wages. The pace of this development has accentuated during the 1980s in so far as management has sought to decentralise collective bargaining (away from, or reducing the role of, multi-employer national agreements) in order to better link the negotiation of terms and conditions of employment with the profitability, productivity and working arrangement needs of the organisation as part of its strategy to improve competitiveness and flexibility. This development focused attention on the employers' associations' role in co-ordinating management strategies and bargaining at the organisational level.

Structure and organisation

The number of employers' associations has declined from some 1,350 in 1968 to 293 in 1989. Most of this decline has been due to the demise of small local associations and the amalgamation of others within larger national associations – however, two major associations became redundant in the iron and steel industry (1967) and shipbuilding (1977) when nationalisation created a single employer situation. The size of employers' associations, in terms of the number of members, ranges from 125,000 in the case of the National Farmers Union to only 65 in the case of the British Paper and Board Industry Federation (see Table 8.2). In terms of their **coverage**, Brown [60] found in 1978 that 75 per cent of manufacturing establishments were members of an employers' association (although this is probably an overstatement because some respondents included membership of a trade association), whilst Daniel and Millward [61] found in 1980 that only 56 per cent of manufacturing establishments were members of an employers' association and less than 20 per cent in distribution and professional or miscellaneous service industries. Employers' associations are also to be found in the public sector (e.g. the Association of County Councils and Association of District Councils).

The **structure of employers' associations** is as varied as that of trade unions. However, it is possible to identify four main structural categories:

1. **National federations based on geographic associations** – for example, the Engineering Employers' Federation with an indirect membership of some organisations through its seventeen local associations.
2. **Single national associations** covering a whole industry – for example the Chemical Industries Association with just over 160 organisations in direct membership.
3. **Specialised associations** which represent a distinct segment of an industry – for example, within the printing industry there is not only the British Printing Industries Federation (periodicals and general printing) but also the Newspaper Society (provincial newspapers) and the Publishers' Association (book publishing). Significantly, the employers' association in the national newspaper segment of the industry (Newspaper Publishers' Association) was disbanded together with multi-employer bargaining in the 1980s at the time of the introduction of new computer based technology requiring significant changes in working practices.
4. **Local associations** representing gographically restricted industrial interests – for example, the West of England Wool Textile employers' association.

The variations in current structure can be related to the historical development of industrial relations within the particular industry (Engineering Employers Federation), the number and relative size of the organisations within an industry (Chemical Industries Association) or the distinctively different interests and situations which exist within subsegments of the industry (associations in the printing industry). Nevertheless, the one uniform factor in their development was the employers' acceptance that an industry basis, whatever its form, provided the main focus of their common interest and representational needs. However, whilst such a situation can

Table 8.2 *Major employers' associations*

	Membership			Finances (1989)		
	1979	1989	Change (%)	Gross Income 000s	Total Funds 000s	Total Assets 000s
1. Engineering Employers Federation	5,883	3,761	−36	7,129	21,658	25,072
2. National Farmers Union	125,856	109,838	−13	11,869	11,279	16,834
3. Building Employers Confederation	10,146	9,249	−9	6,324	14,997	17,331
4. Federation of Master Builders	20,328	21,400	5	1,749	4,891	5,924
5. Electrical Contractors Association	2,193	2,406	10	1,653	11,442	29,414
6. Heating & Ventilating Contractors Association	1,185	1,277	8	1,260	461	1,004
7. Federation of Civil Engineering Contractors	518	358	−31	1,594	851	1,425
8. British Printing Industries Federation	3,178	2,911	−8	2,726	979	2,766
9. Publishers Association	257	198	−23	1,176	113	565
10. Newspaper Society	293	240	−18	2,473	969	2,276
11. National Federation of Retail Newsagents	28,367	31,703	12	2,691	1,986	3,582
12. Road Haulage Association	15,045	11,381	−24	1,324	3,450	4,467
13. Freight Transport Association	15,890	13,638	−14	1,592	3,053	6,332
14. Motor Agents Association	(1981) 15,444	13,754	−11	2,775	1,144	6,106
15. British Paper & Board Industry Federation	109	65	−40	981	1,270	1,834
16. Chemical Industries Association	339	160	−53	3,235	205	1,696
17. British Jewellery & Giftwear Federation	2,035	1,945	−4	256	1,138	1,755
Total for all employers associations	293,103	341,261	16	79,811	101,011	168,201
Number of employers associations	340	293	−14			

Source: Annual Report of the Certification Officer, 1980 and 1990.

serve the interests of single industry organisations (whether small or large, single or multi-site) it can present problems for multi-industry organisations. Sisson points out that the increased emphasis on decentralised organisational bargaining, rather than multi-employer industry level bargaining, has led some to contemplate 'a restructuring of employers' organisations based on the CBI and a number of multi-industry regional organisations with internal committees to represent particular industries or sectors; these committees, in turn, might carry out the bargaining agency functions of the existing national employers' organisations' [62]. However, such a change would require not only a major restructure of employers' associations but also a major redirection in the role of the CBI.

It is important to recognise that there is a potential conflict for all organisations between the requirement to accept and abide by policy decisions of the association and the more basic principle that an organisation, when it becomes a member of the association, does not relinquish any of its rights or responsibilities to determine its own affairs and to act in its best interests. It is this conflict which has found expression in the desire of some organisations not to be bound by the decisions and agreements made by the association and to be free to pursue their own strategies in industrial relations at the organisational level. This led some employers' associations to establish a category of **non-conforming member** in order to ensure that such organisations could remain members of the association and so maintain the association's strength and influence both within the industry and outside. Thus, employers' associations appear to require less from their membership in terms of 'collective solidarity' than trade unions. Certainly, if large organisations opt out of their employers' association completely then, coupled with the fact that few small organisations are members of an employers' association because they are non-unionised or cannot afford the subscription, the employers' association can easily become unrepresentative of the industry as a whole.

The **internal organisation** of employers' associations normally vests ultimate authority in a general meeting of its members. However, in practice, the primary responsibility for policy and decision making rests with a general council or executive committee (elected by the membership) and a number of specialist committees which may include co-opted members with particular expertise or interests to represent. These committees usually comprise directors or senior managers and, wherever possible, seek to arrive at decisions on a consensus rather than voting basis so as to avoid splits or factionalism within the membership. Certainly, in view of the likely differences in industrial relations thinking and strategy between larger and smaller organisations and the fact that the voting arrangements in most employers' associations (like that of the TUC) relate size of organisation to value of vote cast, any significant reliance on voting could easily foster a perception of large organisation domination. Nevertheless, the larger organisations do tend to dominate in the membership of the various committees. However, as a consequence of the consensus approach, the policies and decisions of an employers' association are likely to be more 'reactionary' in nature because they have to be founded on the lowest common denominator which will unite the membership. Only a small proportion of associations have a substantial number of full-time staff (many of the smaller associations being run by firms of accountants or solicitors or member organisations). However, this apparent lack of resources, as compared with trade unions, understates the real position.

1. Employers' associations do not maintain funds to support industrial action or provide friendly society benefits.
2. Much of the association's industrial relations resources and expertise lies in the members of its committees and the management of the organisations it represents.

Functions

The primary function of an employers' association is to support and promote the commercial objectives of its members. Its major activities fall into four categories:

1. The direct negotiation of collective agreements with trade unions.
2. Assisting its members in the resolution of disputes.
3. Providing general help and advice to its members on industrial relations matters.
4. Representing its members' views and interests to government and other agencies.

The relative importance attached to each of these activities, in particular the collective bargaining role, will depend on the perceived homogeneity and common interest amongst the members.

The significance of the employers' association's **collective bargaining** role may be assessed in terms of the extent to which the national agreement, negotiated by the employers' association, determines the actual wages and conditions of employees at the organisational level. In this context, it is possible to identify three main categories of agreement.

- *Minimum agreements*. This is probably the largest group and comprises agreements which simply establish national minima above which association members are free to negotiate their own rates or 'company additions' at the organisational level. Apart from these minimum wage rates, other national level terms and conditions of employment are often confined to premiums for overtime and shift working and the length of the working week and holidays. The national agreement is important both in determining a base below which no employee may fall and in creating a climate of expectation that any organisational increase will not be less than that agreed at the national level.

- *Comprehensive agreements*. These establish standard rates of pay and other conditions which are to be applied by members at the organisational level and therefore the employers' association plays a more important direct collective bargaining role. Such an arrangement exists in electrical contracting and amongst local authorities.

- *Partial agreements*. These establish rates of pay which, although not standard, provide the basis for the actual rates of pay at the organisational level. Such agreements may be found in the footwear and printing industries where the agreements made by the employers' association, at either national or district level, establish not only minimum rates but also additional standard piecework prices (footwear) or supplements for specific tasks (printing) which may be applied at the organisational level. At the same time, the employers' association's agreement is likely to contain relatively detailed coverage of other terms and conditions of employment.

So far as management is concerned negotiations should centre on the ability of the organisation to fund a pay increase and, in particular, the linking of pay increases to improvements in productivity. Such individual organisational factors cannot be taken into account adequately within the framework of a multi-employer collective agreement negotiated by an employers' association and as a consequence, Sisson argues, 'most managements are already non-conforming members of their employers' organisation in practice if not in name' [63] through 'topping up' national agreements. This development, and its effect on the collective bargaining role of employers' associations. was recognised in 1968 when the Donovan Commission concluded that 'in the past most employers' associations have seen their central task as the protection of their members by insisting as far as possible on common rules for regulating the terms on which labour was to be employed ... In future they must find their main purpose in the promotion of their members' interests by assisting them to develop orderly and efficient systems of industrial relations within their undertakings and by confining common rules to the areas where they can be applied without hindering this development' [64]. The continued process during the 1980s of organisations withdrawing from national multi-employer bargaining has further emphasised the employers' association role of providing information, advice and support to members conducting their own negotiations rather than negotiating on their behalf.

In their role of **providing advisory/consultancy services** for their members in the conduct of their own industrial relations at the organisational level, employers' associations provide a range of immediate and specialist advice on such issues as recruitment, education and training, work study and job evaluation as well as the more normal industrial relations issues of union recognition, collective bargaining, dismissals, redundancy, etc. The importance of these services to the member organisations is borne out by Brown's survey (1978) which found that 57 per cent of the manufacturing establishments surveyed had sought assistance from the employers' association on labour law matters and 50 per cent on local pay levels [65]. Daniel and Millward confirmed that 'larger establishments were very much more likely to have consulted their association' and 'it is clearly not the case that employers' associations are most frequently used by smaller establishments which do not have the resources to provide their own specialist services' [66]. The greatest utilisation appears to be amongst the large member organisations, particularly where there is a senior industrial relations specialist to maintain liaison with the employers' association. Certainly, Sisson believes that 'employers' organisations probably exert more influence on workplace industrial relations through the performance of these functions than they did through multi-employer bargaining' [67].

Employers' associations may also **assist their members to resolve disputes** by negotiating and operating on their behalf a disputes procedure with recognised unions. Originally the procedure was intended to allow 'the whole power of the associated employers to be deployed on behalf of a member should that be necessary' [68] – a dispute in one organisation could become a dispute in all by the employers' association instigating a lock-out throughout its member organisations. However, the role of the procedure changed with the growth of trade union power and organisational level bargaining. It has become primarily a forum for the conciliation or arbitration of disputes which arise from the interpretation of national agreements or organisational bargaining, and which have not been resolved within the organisation's own internal grievance/disputes procedure. Within this framework, Munns suggested the role of the employers' association is 'to seek the reconciliation of opposing views bearing in mind the interests of the employers generally' [69].

Clearly, such a role presents a conflict for the employers' association between, on the one hand, representing the interests of its individual member organisation and negotiating on its behalf and, on the other hand, seeking to conciliate between its member and the trade unions with whom it is in dispute. Despite this, Brown found that at the end of the 1970s approximately half of the manufacturing establishments surveyed had used a disputes procedure provided by their employers' association during the previous two years and that 24 per cent of the establishments reported an increased usage of such procedures – only the larger establishments appeared to have decreased their usage. In Brown's view this reflected 'both increasing industrial relations activity at smaller establishments and the development of better internal procedures at the larger ones' [70].

Finally, employers' associations, like trade unions, undertake a **representational role** on behalf of their members. Unlike trade unions, however, employers' associations do not have formal direct links with any particular political party. Nevertheless, member organisations may make financial contributions to the Conservative Party and both employers' associations and their members may support other bodies (e.g. Aims of Industry) which seek the maintenance of free enterprise and a reduction in trade union power. Employers' associations seek to project the individual and collective interests of their members to trade unions, government and the general public primarily through publicity campaigns and direct lobbying. In addition, they also present evidence to governmental inquiries and provide the employers' representatives on a range of bodies such as industrial tribunals, ACAS and the NEDC.

The Confederation of British Industry

The Confederation of British Industry (CBI) was formed in 1965 as a merger between the British Employers' Confederation (established in 1919 and primarily concerned with labour affairs), the Federation of British Industries (established in 1916 and primarily concerned with trade and commercial matters) and the National Association of British Manufacturers (primarily concerned with small manufacturing organisations). The merger arose from a perceived need on the part of management to have a single focal point to represent their interests to government at a time of increased emphasis on economic planning and to act as a counterweight to the growing influence of the TUC. However, it is important to recognise that the CBI is not the only representative of employer/management interests (e.g. Institute of Personnel Management and Institute of Directors). Indeed, there is a sense in which the Institute of Directors may be seen as representing 'employers' whilst the CBI and IPM are representing 'organisational management'; and some would argue that the Institute of Directors, which is more representative of smaller companies than the CBI, has exerted a greater influence than the CBI on government policy and legislation during the 1980s.

The **membership** of the CBI includes individual organisations as well as employers' and trade associations. It has some 4,500 individual organisations in direct membership plus 200 associations indirectly representing a further 300,000 companies: these companies have a combined employment of some ten million people. Most importantly, the creation of the CBI has resulted in an expansion of membership, beyond that of the former BEC, into retailing, the commercial sectors of banking and insurance and, above all, public corporations. However, at the time of its creation, a number of employers' associations expressed concern about allowing direct organisational membership of the CBI. For example, the Engineering Employers' Federation felt that 'if companies paid subscriptions to the new body ... they might not also wish to pay to their employers' organisation, particularly if they could exercise influence through the labour committee' and 'considered it unsatisfactory that the largest federation should have only one vote on the 'unwieldy' 400-member council' [71]. Nevertheless, the inclusion of such a provision in the constitution of the CBI has meant that large organisations who are not members of their relevant employers' association are able to play an active role within the CBI. This arrangement does not appear to have weakened the role of employers' associations.

The **objectives** of the CBI are primarily as follows:

1. To formulate and influence policies in respect of industrial, economic, fiscal, commercial, labour, social, legal and technical issues.
2. To provide a focal point for those seeking the views of British industry.
3. To develop the contribution of British industry in the creation of wealth within a free enterprise market situation.

These objectives reflect the combined employer and trade functions of the CBI.

In seeking to meet these objectives, Grant and Marsh argue, 'the CBI must not only be concerned with giving its members an opportunity to voice their opinions; it must also ensure that these opinions are aggregated into a policy which is well informed as well as representative of industrial opinion' [72]. The **organisational arrangements** within the CBI appear to emphasise 'managerial expertise' rather than 'representativeness and democracy'. The ultimate governing and decision making body is the **Council** which meets every month and comprises 400 representatives from each of the CBI's main categories of membership. The function of this Council is to provide guidance to the CBI's various officers and standing committees and to approve any policy proposals made by them. However, effective power and decision making rests with the CBI's **two major officials**, the President (elected on a part-time basis) and the Director General (appointed on a full-time basis), and various **Standing Committees**. The most important of these is the President's Committee, whose function is to advise the President on matters of major policy and to review the CBI's position and strategy. The members of these standing committees are appointed by the President and the Director General. At the local level the CBI has thirteen **Regional Councils** which co-ordinate CBI activities within the region, act as a communication channel between the membership and the CBI centrally and provide a sounding board for proposed policies. In 1977 the CBI introduced its first **National Conference** open to attendance by any member and intended to provide a wider public forum to discuss issues of concern and project the employers' interests. However, unlike the TUC's Annual Congress, it is not the prime governmental body within the CBI and may only make recommendations to the Council. Its primary function is to provide publicity for employers' views.

8.5 Summary propositions

- Management is a discrete group, separate from the owner (shareholder); it is also an amalgam of subgroups with differing interests and responsibilities in industrial relations.
- Management strategies in industrial relations are the result of constrained 'rational' choice, but are always aimed at maintaining managerial security within the organisation's decision making processes.
- Management style is the result of an interaction between management's desire to maintain its prerogative and promote individualism and its preparedness to accept collectivism and management by consent.
- The employers' association's main task is to represent and co-ordinate its members' activities at the organisational level.

Further reading

- M. Poole and R. Mansfield (eds)., *Managerial Roles in Industrial Relations*, Gower, 1980.
  K. Thurley and S. Wood (eds)., *Industrial Relations and Management Strategy*, CUP, 1983.
  J. Storey, *Managerial Prerogative and the Question of Control*, Routledge & Kegan Paul, 1983.
  These books present a range of thinking relating to management and industrial relations; who they are, what factors appear to influence 'strategy' and the nature and importance of managerial prerogative.
- K. Hawkins, *The Management of Industrial Relations*, Penguin, 1978. A readable exposition of the pressures facing management in industrial relations.
- M. Marchington and P. Parker, *Changing Patterns of Employee Relations*, Harvester Wheatsheaf, 1990. A very useful discussion of management styles and strategies during the 1980s based on four case studies.
- E. Wigham, *The Power to Manage: A history of the Engineering Employers' Federation*, Macmillan, 1973. A readable account of the development and work of one of the largest employers' associations.

References

1. H. Koontz and C. O'Donnell, *Essentials of Management*, McGraw-Hill, 1974.
2. Commision on Industrial Relations, Report No. 34, *The Role of Management in Industrial Relations*, HMSO, 1973, p. 3.
3. R. Mansfield, 'The management task' in M. Poole and R. Mansfield (eds), *Managerial Roles in Industrial Relations*, Gower, 1980, p. 10.
4. R. Mansfield, 'Who are the managers?' in M. Poole and R. Mansfield (eds), *op. cit.*, pp. 12–20.
5. D. Simpson, 'The industrial relations of managers' in M. Poole and R. Mansfield (eds), *op. cit.*, p. 104.
6. S. R. Timperley, 'Organisation strategies and industrial relations', *Industrial Relations Journal*, vol. 11, no. 5, 1980, pp. 38–45; J. Purcell, 'The management of industrial relations in the modern corporation: agenda for research', *British Journal of Industrial Relations*, vol. XXI, 1983, pp. 1–16.
7. A. Fox, *Beyond Contract: Power, work and trust relations*, Faber, 1974, p. 239.
8. M. Poole, 'Management strategies and industrial relations' in M. Poole and R. Mansfield (eds), *op. cit.*, pp. 38–49.
9. *ibid.*, p. 40.
10. *ibid.*, p. 44.
11. *ibid.*, p. 42.
12. K. Wilson, 'Social responsibility: a management perspective' in M. Poole and R. Mansfield (eds), *op. cit.*, p. 60.

13. J. Storey, *Managerial Prerogative and the Question of Control*, Routledge & Kegan Paul, 1983, p. 102.
14. W. E. J. McCarthy and N. D. Ellis, *Management by Agreement*, Hutchinson, 1973, p. 94.
15. H. F. Gospel, 'An approach to a theory of the firm in industrial relations', *British Journal of Industrial Relations*, vol. XI, 1973, p. 218.
16. *ibid.*
17. *ibid.*, p. 219.
18. M. M. Perline and D. J. Poynter, 'Union and management perceptions of managerial prerogative', *British Journal of Industrial Relations*, vol. 28, no. 2, July 1990, p. 179.
19. J. Purcell, 'Mapping management styles in employee relations', *Journal of Management Studies*, vol. 24, no. 5, 1987, p. 535.
20. *ibid.*, p. 534.
21. *ibid.*, p. 533.
22. *ibid.*, p. 534.
23. *ibid.*, p. 533.
24. M. Marchington and P. Parker, *Changing Patterns of Employee Relations*, Harvester Wheatsheaf, 1990.
25. J. Purcell and K. Sisson, 'Strategies and practice in the management of industrial relations' in G. S. Bain (ed.), *Industrial Relations in Britain*, Blackwell, 1983, pp. 112–18.
26. *ibid.*, p. 114.
27. *ibid.*, p. 115.
28. *ibid.*
29. A. Marsh, *Employee Relations Policy and Decision Making: A survey of manufacturing companies carried out for the CBI*, Gower, 1982, p. 203.
30. J. Purcell and K. Sisson, *op. cit.*, p. 117.
31. H. Clegg, *Trade Unionism under Collective Bargaining*, Blackwell, 1976, p. 108.
32. J. T. Winkler, 'The ghost at the bargaining table: directors and industrial relations', *British Journal of Industrial Relations*, vol. XII, no. 2, 1974.
33. A. Marsh, *op. cit.*, p. 103.
34. J. T. Winkler, *op. cit.*, p. 196.
35. E. Batstone, I. Boraston and S. Frenkel, *Shop Stewards in Action*, Blackwell, 1977.
36. H. Clegg, *op. cit.*, p. 10.
37. J. Purcell and K. Sisson, *op. cit.*, p. 109.
38. *ibid.*, p. 110.
39. *Report of the Royal Commission on Trade Unions and Employers' Associations 1965–1968* (Donovan Commission), HMSO, 1968, p. 50.
40. J. Purcell and K. Sisson, *op. cit.*, p. 102.
41. J. Storey, *op. cit.*, p. 184.
42. J. Purcell and K. Sisson, *op. cit.*, p. 107.
43. P. Edwards, 'Myth of the macho manager', *Personnel Management*, April 1985, p. 35.
44. C. Hendry *et al.*, 'Changing patterns of human resource management', *Personnel Management*, November 1988, p. 38.
45. *ibid.*, p. 41.
46. M. Armstrong, 'Human resource management: a case of the emperor's new clothes?', *Personnel Management*, August 1987, p. 35.
47. D. Guest, 'Personnel and HRM: can you tell the difference?', *Personnel Management*, January 1989.

48. M. Armstrong, *op. cit.*, p. 33.
49. D. Guest, *op. cit.*, p. 50.
50. A. Fowler, 'When chief executives discover HRM', *Personnel Management*, January 1987.
51. M. Armstrong, *op. cit.*, p. 33.
52. P. Miller, 'Strategic HRM: what is it and what it isn't', *Personnel Management*, February 1989, p. 51.
53. S. Ackroyd *et al.*, 'The Japanisation of British Industry?' *Industrial Relations Journal*, vol. 19, no. 1, 1988, p. 16.
54. *ibid.*, p. 17.
55. *ibid.*, p. 20.
56. N. Oliver and B. Wilkinson, 'Japanese manufacturing techniques and personnel and industrial relations practice in Britain: evidence and implications', *British Journal of Industrial Relations*, vol. 27, no. 2, 1989.
57. 'Single union deals' *IRS Employment Trends*, no. 442, June 1989.
58. P. Briggs, 'The Japanese at work: illusions of the ideal', *Industrial Relations Journal*, vol. 19, no. 1, 1988, p. 24.
59. *ibid.*, p. 28.
60. W. Brown (ed.), *The Changing Contours of British Industrial Relations*, Blackwell, 1981, Table 2.6, p. 18.
61. W. W. Daniel and N. Millward, *Workplace Industrial Relations in Britain*, Heinemann (PSI/SSRC), 1983, Table V.12, p. 121.
62. K. Sisson, 'Employers' organisations' in G. S. Bain (ed), *op. cit.*, p. 134.
63. *ibid.*, p. 132.
64. *Report of the Royal Commission on Trade Unions and Employers' Associations* (Donovan Commission), HMSO, 1968, p. 198.
65. W. Brown (ed.), *op. cit.*, p. 22.
66. W. W. Daniel and N. Millward, *op. cit.*, pp. 122–3.
67. K. Sisson, *op. cit.*, p. 133.
68. Commission on Industrial Relations, Study 1, *Employers' Organisations and Industrial Relations*, HMSO, 1972, p. 28.
69. V. G. Munns, 'The functions and organisation of employers' associations in selected industries' in *Royal Commission Research Paper No. 7*, HMSO, 1967, p. 9.
70. W. Brown (ed), *op. cit.*, p. 20.
71. E. Wigham, *The Power to Manage: A history of the Engineering Employers' Federation*, Macmillan, 1973, p. 216.
72. W. Grant and D. Marsh, *The Confederation of British Industry*, Hodder & Stoughton, 1977, p. 87.

Chapter 9

The government

9.1 Definition

The state may be defined as the **politically based and controlled institutions of government and regulation within an organised society.** In Britain this includes the monarchy, Parliament, government, civil service, judiciary, police and armed services. Although it may be argued that Parliament is the ultimate political governing body within a democratic society, it is the elected **government** of the day which is the most active and important element within the state: it determines the direction, policies and actions of the state machinery. Crouch argues that its importance, so far as industrial relations is concerned, stems from the fact that it 'is the only actor in the situation which can change the rules of the system' [1] by virtue of its law making role. However, Lewis notes that, because of the pluralistic nature of the state and the potential transient existence of any government, 'different organs of the state may pursue different strategies' [2]. Nowhere in industrial relations has this been seen more clearly than in the relationship between the government's law making role and the judiciary's interpretive role.

9.2 The role of government

It is often suggested that both trade unions and employers, but particularly trade unions, are opposed to government or legal intervention in the regulation of industrial relations and that the government, irrespective of its political persuasion, has supported this **principle of voluntarism in industrial relations.** Thus, in 1960 Kahn-Freund was able to say that there is 'no major country in the world in which the law has played a less significant role in the shaping of [industrial relations] than in Great Britain' [3]. However, certainly during the 1970s and 1980s, the government has constantly intervened in regulating both the individual and collective employment relationship.

It would be accurate to say that:

1. Much of the government's legislation prior to the 1970s represented a series of *ad hoc* responses rather than a planned strategy of legal intervention into industrial relations.
2. Trade unions and employers are not opposed to legislation *per se* – certainly not when it is perceived to support their interests.

Therefore, the primary issue in respect of the government's role in industrial relations is not whether it should intervene but rather what degree of intervention, in what areas and for what objective.

Objectives of government

Crouch argues that, like management's objective at the organisational level, the **government's prime overall objective is economic** in character . . .; namely, 'to maintain and enhance the stability and productivity of the British economy' through the pursuit of 'four not easily compatible goals; full employment, price stability, a favourable balance of payments and protection of the exchange rate' [4]. Consequently, its management of, and strategies within, the industrial relations system can be seen as primarily intended to support the achievement of its economic objectives. However, to regard the government's objectives and strategies in industrial relations as purely the result of economic influences disregards the influence of the **more fundamental social objectives** which provide the basis for political differentiation and consequently differential governmental action. The manner in which governments balance their various economic objectives and approach industrial relations matters is conditioned by their view of the nature of the society they wish to create or, at least, encourage: individualistic or corporatist.

It is also important to recognise that the **representative position of the government**, and therefore the basis for its policies and legislation, may be viewed from three quite different assumptions:

1. Some may regard the government as the expression of an inherently distinct **national interest** which, in the area of industrial relations, occupies a neutral position between the conflicting interests of employers and management on the one hand and employees and trade unions on the other. From this standpoint, Farnham and Pimlott argue, the intervention of the government in industrial relations is justified 'either to protect the interests of individuals in their employment when no other means are available, or to uphold the interests of the nation as a whole when these appear to be threatened by particular industrial pressure groups' [5]. However, 'national interest' is an abstract concept

which cannot be determined or assessed in any realistic way. It is whatever the government, mass media or anyone else perceives it to be and, indeed, may often be used by the government or others as an apparently self-evident and acceptable justification for what are in reality ideologically based policies and decisions. The divisions within society over most major governmental policies and decisions suggest an absence of any consensus as to what constitutes the national interest.

2. Some may view the government's policies and legislation as no more than the expression of a **sectional interest** within society which coalesces and expresses itself in a political party and which predominates by virtue of having been legitimised by the electorate. Certainly Lewis argues that 'legal policy cannot be divorced from the interests and ideology of the law makers and from the wider political and industrial conflict' [6]. It is the ideological base of the political party which provides the foundation for a government's legislation and other policies. This view of the government's position appears to be confirmed by the close ideological affinity which exists between, on the one hand, the Labour Party and the trade union movement and, on the other, the Conservative Party and management.

3. From a Marxist perspective, the government may be seen as little more than 'democratic icing' on the top of a political system which, irrespective of the political party in power, inherently supports the **maintenance of the capitalist interest.** Hyman, for example, argues that the possibility of any radical government initiative in economic policy or industrial relations is restricted by 'policy constraints which stem necessarily from the capitalist context of political life' [7] and which lead inevitably to a governmental preoccupation with the need to maintain 'economic stability', 'the confidence of industry' and to 'curb excessive wage increases'. Furthermore, much of the public and political debate on policy options is constrained by 'a notion of "national interest" which is closely bound up with the interests of employers; and a conception of labour organisation, objectives and action (in so far as these conflict with employer interests) as necessarily sectional and probably selfish, irresponsible, disruptive and subversive' [8]. He also points out that an **apparent policy of non-intervention** in economic and industrial relations matters 'did not mean state neutrality; in withdrawing from an active economic role, the state endorsed the propriety and legitimacy of economic relations in which unequal power prevailed . . . non-intervention of the state was non-intervention *in favour* of capital' [9]. From this standpoint, it is the capitalist economic system which, by inhibiting the ability of Labour governments to represent properly the 'non-capital' sectional interests within society, has created the semblance of a governmental consensus of the 'national interest' in respect of economic and industrial relations matters for most of the post-war period.

Liberalism and corporatism

Both Crouch [10] and Strinati [11] have put forward **an analytical framework of governmental relationship to industrial relations** which identifies four alternative forms of industrial relations dependent on the interrelationship between the nature of the dominant political ideology and the relative power and autonomy of trade unions. On this basis, British industrial relations has developed through distinct stages (see Figure 9.1): from 'market individualism' of the nineteenth century based on a dominant liberalist ideology and weak trade unions; through 'collective liberalism' or 'voluntarism' as the dominant liberalist ideology sought to accommodate subordinate ideologies represented by the increasing power and autonomy of trade unionism; to a form of 'bargained corporatism', particularly in the late 1960s and 1970s, resulting from the adoption of a more corporatist dominant ideology as a basis for accommodating trade union power. Since 1979 the dominant political ideology has shifted towards a neo-liberalist/*laissez-faire* basis and trade union power has been weakened through economic factors. Consequently, it may be argued, the basis of industrial relations has shifted towards either 'collective liberalism' or 'market individualism'.

Market individualism is characterised by a rationality derived from the concept of a market system which balances competitive interests and which

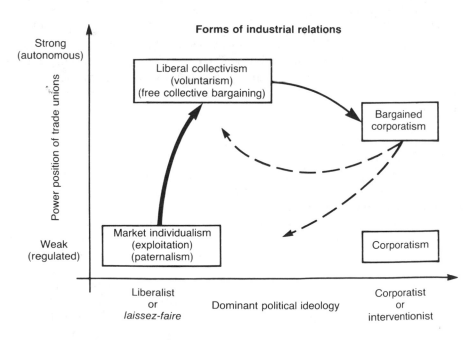

Figure 9.1 *Governmental approaches to industrial relations*

legitimises both the notion of property rights and the notion of an objective basis to income inequalities. Labour is simply a commodity which only has a value in so far as it is bought and sold. Although the role of government is largely passive, Crouch argues it is also 'highly coercive in so far as the law firmly upholds property rights against the countervailing power of subordinates' [12]. However, as he points out [13] 'market individualism' is an inherently imperfect model because:

1. The employment contract is usually between an individual and an organisation, not two individuals.
2. The contract is not simply an economic exchange but one in which the individual is subordinated to the authority and control of the organisation.
3. The individual's dependence on capital for his/her livelihood is not reciprocated by capital's dependence on him/her (a single unit of its labour commodity).

Thus, labour is weak, unorganised and subordinate to the employer through the indirect control of the 'market system' and the relationship between them is, at best, paternalism or, at worst, exploitation. The basic imperfection in the model has been further compounded by the organisation of labour into trade unions as a necessary element in their seeking to redress this imbalance. Consequently, the dominant liberalist ideology has to accommodate the subordinate ideology of collectivism.

The result of such an accommodation can be seen in the **liberal collectivism** form of industrial relations which has dominated much of British industrial relations and which is closely bound up with the concepts of 'pluralism' and 'voluntarism'. Within this framework, Crouch argues, 'the identity of dominant and subordinate interests remains distinct, and a separation of political, economic and ideological dimensions continues to exist' but 'authority usually comes to accept a strategy of indulgence as a means of absorbing subordinate pressure' [14]. The indulgency accommodation is characterised by an acceptance of autonomous trade unions which represent, bargain and reconcile conflicting interests with management through the collective bargaining process. However, by the same process, the dominant interests of management are protected through the delineation of agreed rights and the maintenance of a boundary between issues for collective bargaining and issues for determination by managerial prerogative. The government's role is primarily one of aiding the reconciliation of dominant and subordinate interests and thus 'action to enhance subordinates' rights will exist alongside the limited coercive measures which ensure the perpetuation of domination' [15]. It is not incompatible for government, through its legislative role, to support the extension of both individual and collective employee rights whilst at the same time constraining collective employee power (i.e. as expressed through the activities of trade unions) under the guise of maintaining a 'balance of power' between the parties in their operation of the industrial relations system. Indeed, such apparent impartial actions reinforce the image of the government acting in the 'national interest'.

Crouch [16] argues that the development of liberal collectivism in the post-war period was supported by two important factors:

1. The existence of full employment for a significant part of the period precluded a direct confrontation between dominant and subordinate interests within society.
2. The incorporation of elements of a more interventionist political ideology within the accommodation strategy.

There was an increasing need, irrespective of the political party in power, for more governmental 'management' of the economy if the twin objectives of economic policy (full employment and price stability) were to be achieved. This produced an apparent movement towards a more **bargained corporatism** form of industrial relations. This is characterised by trade unions agreeing to restrain their pursuit of their members' sectional interests as part of a strategy to further the 'national interest' but in return they expect concessions from the government. Thus, 'the government interposes itself between the unions and their normal bargaining partner, the employer, but in so doing becomes itself their bargaining partner; and the government is able to offer several things which cannot be achieved in bargaining . . . such as social policy reforms, workers' rights, changes in economic and fiscal policy' [17]. Tripartite discussions on economic and social issues, in particular incomes policy, formed an integral element of both Conservative and Labour Governments' strategies during the 1960s/1970s. However, the strategy was most evident under Labour Governments where the inherent party ideology favours such a governmental policy.

Since 1979 there appears to have been a significant shift in the dominant political ideology away from corporatism and toward **neo-liberalism/laissez-faire**. The ideological basis of the fundamentalists within the Conservative Party is the removal, or at least significant reduction, of direct governmental economic planning and a reliance on 'free market forces', monetarism and acceptance of high unemployment as a means of maintaining international economic competitiveness and stability. However, whether or not these policies herald a return to 'market individualism' or only a return to 'liberal collectivism' depends on the extent to which:

1. The trade union movement is able to maintain an effective presence in major segments of the British economy despite economic forces tending to reduce their membership and its resolve to take action to support their interests.
2. Management is prepared to take advantage of the change in the dominant

political ideology and further enhance the movement by rejecting the principles which underlie a liberal collectivist form of industrial relations.

The European Community

There is little doubt that Due *et al.* are right when they state that 'the growing political and economic importance of the EC and its institutions are likely to emerge as a new and highly significant factor, exerting substantial influence on the labour market's industrial relations' and that, in particular, 'the interesting feature of EC co-operation is the emergence of quite new actors in industrial relations, such as the EC Commission and the European Parliament – actors whose roles are essentially supra-national' [18]. At a fundamental level there is, currently, a **conflict of political ideology** between the UK Conservative Government and its EC partners. The 'social democratic' ideology of most European countries (based on a more corporatist social partnership between government, capital and labour) is reflected in the direction of EC developments and is at variance with the more 'liberalist/ *laissez-faire*' ideology of the UK Government. Given that the UK *is* part of the EC and a part of its continuing economic and political development and integration, then it may be argued that the Crouch model (Figure 9.1) should be modified to allow for two levels of political ideology – UK and the EC. The question as to which will dominate and have most influence on the development of UK industrial relations will depend on:

1. The degree of political integration within the EC and, in particular, which issues become matters for Community decisions (possibly based on majority decision making) and which remain national decisions.
2. The intended extent of harmonisation of employment matters and the method by which it is to be achieved.

The primary vehicle for achieving developments in the employment area is the **European Social Charter** which Due *et al.* describe as 'a sort of "constitution" for the European labour market' [19]. The objective of the European Commission, in proposing such a Charter, is to ensure that the organisational benefits gained from the 'single market' after 1992 are shared with employees. It aims not only to introduce employment standards but also enhance the rights of employees (whether through unions or not) to be involved in organisational decision making by providing for, amongst other things:

1. All employment should be fairly remunerated and ensure decent rates of pay.

2. An overall improvement in employees' conditions and more harmonisation of working time, flexibility, non-standard employment practices, redundancies, etc.
3. The right of unions to organise, be recognised, negotiate and to undertake industrial action.
4. Employees' rights to information, consultation and participation should be developed.

A number of draft **Directives**, by which the Charter is given effect, are already being considered. For example:

1. A directive on regulating **atypical forms of employment** (covering part-timers, fixed-term contract employees, etc., which management utilise as a 'flexible' resource) to ensure not only that such employees enjoy comparable treatment in respect to terms and conditions of employment but also that the 'social costs' (in respect of national insurance contributions, etc.) are comparable to those of full-time permanent employees (albeit on a pro rata basis).
2. A directive on **working time** which would establish minimum holiday entitlements, a maximum working day and maximum 48-hour working week, minimum breaks between work periods, the notion that Sunday should (in principle) be a 'day of rest', etc.

Currently, the UK Government is resisting these developments because it believes they will inhibit the flexibility and competitiveness of UK and European industry in world markets and because these are matters which should be determined in the light of organisational needs and circumstances rather than uniformly applied by centralised legislation and regulation. Thus, it is resisting the suggestion that the employment area should become a matter for majority voting within the EC governmental arrangements but should remain a matter for unanimous voting – thereby giving the UK the power to veto such developments.

Perhaps more significantly, in terms of the **relationship for managing the industrial relations system**, is the proposal that UNICE (Union of Industrial and Employers' Confederations of Europe) and ETUC (European Trade Union Confederation) not only should play a more significant role in drafting EC employment legislation but also could obviate the need for legislation by concluding their own agreements. This would be an extension of the 'dialogue between social partners' which is prevalent throughout most of Europe [20] but would be counter to the strategy adopted by the UK government during the 1980s to move away from 'tripartitism', and the development of such a role at the European level must inevitably strengthen the demand for a similar role at the national level.

Position of the judiciary and police

The **judiciary is largely autonomous** of the government. Although Strinati [21] argues that this autonomy arises from the judiciary having a 'mediatory role' in social relations, many others cite the apparent hostility of the judiciary towards the interests of employees and trade unionism as evidence of its autonomy being supportive of the dominant ideology within society. It is important to understand that the judiciary occupies a **dual role** within the state system:

1. It interprets and applies statute law legitimised by Parliament.
2. It determines the common law (legal regulation of those areas not covered by statute).

There is little doubt that the common law approach to both individual and collective labour matters is based firmly on a liberal individualistic ideology. This in turn influences the judiciary's interpretation of statute law. Strinati describes the past **conflict between the judiciary and the government** in terms of 'preserving the implications of laissez faire versus the provision of legal recognition of the functions of trade unionism' [22]. This can clearly be seen in the expression of statutory rights for trade unions as 'privileges' or 'immunities' which exempt them from the application of *laissez-faire* legal doctrines. Consequently, Crouch argues, wherever the courts are faced with a situation 'where the scope of the legal immunity is unclear, the judiciary, as guardian of the liberal tradition of Common Law, is likely to revert to a logic of reasoning hostile to combinations' [23].

Any notion of judicial impartiality is further weakened by the **nature of judges and the judgmental process**. The socio-economic and ideological background of judges, and the legal profession from which they come, are more compatible with those of the dominant managerial ideology within society than with those of the subordinate ideology of collectivism and trade unionism. Lord Justice Scrutton [24], as long ago as 1920, recognised the difficulty in industrial relations matters of understanding and relating to ideas and perceptions which were in essence alien to his own. At the same time, the judgmental process requires that the judiciary decide between the rights of contestants in any particular case rather than mediate a compromise. Consequently, Wedderburn argues, 'a court that intervenes in an industrial conflict cannot be "neutral"; it will take one side or the other' [25] and, generally, in so doing add the weight of 'legal right' to management's side.

The creation of **Industrial Tribunals**, with their intended emphasis on a more practical and impartial approach through the inclusion of two 'lay assessors' (one employer and one trade union) was seen by some as a significant move towards overcoming the defects, for labour, of the traditional legal system. However, this has not been the case. Bootham and

Denham [26] found, from an examination of Industrial Tribunal cases covering unfair dismissal connected with trade union membership, that not only do the decisions appear to be very supportive of the managerial prerogative but also the system itself still individualises the contractual relationship even where the issue has its roots in the collective act of seeking to organise and secure union recognition. Furthermore, despite the introduction of this form of special 'labour court', jurisdiction in respect of issues relating to the more important matter of employer and trade union rights in the conduct of industrial disputes remains with the traditional High Court.

Although the formal role of the **police** in industrial relations is restricted to criminal actions which may arise in the course of picketing, there have been a number of newspaper reports of the use of the police apparatus (involving the Special Branch and possible telephone tapping) for surveillance of union 'militants' and during major disputes [27]. However, Kahn *et al.* believe that 'police forces do not ... maintain any regular, systematic intelligence-gathering operation about industrial disputes' [28].

As far as **picketing** is concerned, the function of the police is to maintain 'peace' and 'public order'. In carrying out this function the police have to protect both the rights of those picketing, which the law defines as peacefully communicating and persuading, and the rights of non-strikers and employers to continue working. However, the reality of the purpose of picketing, namely to stop the supply of labour and materials to an establishment, means that these rights are incompatible. Thus, because the law recognises only a limited right of picketing and not the reality, police action to constrain picketing within the law will invariably be perceived as anti-union and supportive of management.

The police role in picketing has been particularly dramatised at times of mass picketing where the numbers of pickets and police involved, and the associated tension, confrontation and sometimes violence, have brought the issue firmly into the area of 'law and order'. Strikers and trade unions are equated to 'disorder', whilst management, non-strikers, police and government are equated to 'upholding the law'. Kahn *et al.* point out that in the past there has been a 'cultural resonance' and even 'empathy' between strikers and police who have generally come from the same community. Certainly, the NCB/NUM dispute in 1984 demonstrated that there is little 'cultural resonance' or 'empathy' where police are drawn in from outside areas in large numbers to confront mass picketing – rather the reverse, an exacerbation of tension and possible violence. Writing before that dispute, Kahn *et al.* noted that the 'line between industrial disputes and threats to public order may become increasingly blurred' and 'if cooperation between government and unions ... is replaced by overt conflict between them, policing industrial disputes will take on further political connotations' [29]. The police role, which is normally confined to the site of the picketing, was significantly extended during that dispute when police both stopped striking miners from leaving Kent and Yorkshire to picket in Nottinghamshire and ejected visiting pickets from private houses under the threat of arrest on the grounds of 'reasonable suspicion' that they would 'breach the peace'.

9.3 Government intervention and strategies

The Labour Government's strategy during the late 1970s, based on a corporatist ideology, was to support trade unionism and collective bargaining, promote the use of conciliation and arbitration processes to resolve disputes, regulate incomes, promote employee participation and enhance employee protection during and at the end of the contract period. In marked contrast, the Conservative Government's strategy during the 1980s, based on a liberalist/*laissez-faire* ideology, has been to redress the perceived power imbalance in favour of trade unions and allow management to re-exert its prerogative, promote 'responsible' trade unionism and protect individual members against union 'tyranny' and promote employment opportunities and labour flexibility through deregulating employment. These strategies are implemented through various methods of influencing or intervening in the industrial relations system: principally as an employer, law maker, 'umpire' and regulator.

Employer

A substantial proportion of the national workforce is employed in the **public sector**: civil servants, prisons, NHS, local authorities (including education, police and fire services), mining, etc. Consequently, the policies and actions of the government in this area are likely to have a significant impact on the industrial relations system as a whole. However, the privatisation of major industries, services and employers during the 1980s (such as British Telecom, gas, electricity, water), the 'opting out' arrangements introduced for schools, colleges and hospitals allowing them to manage their own affairs (including setting terms and conditions of employment) and the requirement for local authorities and the NHS to introduce competitive tendering for many of their services have all contributed to a decrease in the government's role as an employer and a consequent decrease in its ability to control or influence the industrial relations within these sectors.

At the same time, the government's concept of what constitutes being a **'good public sector employer'** has changed. Winchester suggests that the general **ethos of industrial relations within the public sector**, during the early part of the post-war period, was one of 'stability . . . based on implicit understanding that as long as government and senior management discharged their responsibility to be "good" employers, then employees and their union representatives would accept a reciprocal obligation to avoid industrial conflict' [30]. However, this did not mean that disputes and strikes never took place, particularly in the more industrially based public corporations. The concept of 'good' employer can be seen in a number of elements which, in the past, have underpinned industrial relations in the public sector:

1. The government accepted, and even encouraged, unionisation and the establishment of formal collective bargaining machinery within the public sector. Nevertheless, a distinction was generally maintained between the negotiation of terms and conditions of employment at the national level and joint consultation on other issues at the organisational level.
2. Collective bargaining, particularly within the central government and local authorities segments of the public sector, relied on 'comparisons' with the private sector for determining appropriate pay levels rather than the government's 'ability to pay' or 'productivity'. However, these latter issues formed an important part of negotiations within the public corporation segment.
3. 'Independent' pay review bodies and inquiries were used, together with normal arbitration, as important adjuncts to bipartite negotiations in order to resolve differences without the need for industrial action.

It is also important to recognise that much of the public sector displayed **managerial characteristics** which are very different to those in the private sector. The centralised nature of its policy and decision making, although facilitating governmental liaison and control, tended to relegate 'managers' to primarily an administrative role. Management had to implement the tasks allocated to it rather than determine them for itself. At the same time, the ideology projected for and within the public sector of their responsibility for providing a 'public service' to the community has often been associated with an internal unitary ideology in respect of organisational relationships. The employees' commitment to the objectives and activities of the service tended to be taken for granted. The distinctive position of the public sector was further accentuated by the relative absence or difficulty of applying and reconciling market criteria, such as price, competition and profitability, alongside social need and benefit criteria.

Winchester suggests that by the 1980s the public sector had become to be seen as 'the major source of instability in British industrial relations' [31] – at least by the government and management in the private sector. Thomson and Beaumont [32] attribute this shift in perception to three economic factors:

1. Pay increases within the public sector, particularly amongst manual groups such as miners and local authority workers, were perceived to be

setting the level for the 'annual wage round' and therefore significantly contributing to general wage inflation.

2. There was an increasing belief in the need to reduce the growth of public sector expenditure in order to redirect resources to the private sector as a necessary precursor of economic growth.

3. These factors resulted in a tighter application of incomes policy within the public sector and a consequent increase in industrial conflict.

To these may be added a fourth factor; namely, the disputes generated within the public sector as a result of these economic factors included emotive disputes (NHS, dustmen, firemen, etc.) as well as less emotive ones (miners, electrical workers, etc.), but all of them seriously affected the public.

The government's employer role has changed significantly since 1980. Whilst maintaining a stance that 'employers' within the public sector (the public corporations and local authorities) are free in their conduct of wage negotiations, nevertheless the government as the 'paymaster' has imposed strict financial and cash limits. At the same time, the government has severely weakened the 'comparison' basis of pay determination by abolishing the Comparability Commission (set up by the Labour Government in 1979), removing the right of trade unions to refer disputes to arbitration unilaterally (i.e. without the agreement of the employer representatives), and retaining the right to ignore the findings of pay review bodies. Consequently, pay bargaining in the public sector has moved firmly into the areas of 'labour market forces', 'ability to pay' and 'productivity'. The issue has been projected, by the government, as one of pay versus jobs: i.e. pay increases above the cash limits can only be compensated for by a reduction in the number of employees. At the same time, the government has sought to segment and decentralise public sector collective bargaining arrangements by, for example, establishing distinct executive agencies within the 'civil service' and encouraging schools, colleges and hospitals to 'opt out' of the local authority system and giving these separately managed units the freedom to establish their own terms and conditions of employment.

Overall the concept of a 'good public sector employer' has shifted from one based on setting an example of supportive employment and welfare practices to one of following the lead of the private sector by adopting their competitive, flexible, performance related ideas in its own employment practices [33].

Legislator

Kahn-Freund has argued that 'the principal purpose of labour law ... is to regulate, to support, and to restrain the power of management and the power of organised labour' [34]. The government's activities in this respect may be subdivided into three main areas.

Legislation on individual legal rights

Much of the legislation in this area is the product of the late 1960s and 1970s (consolidated in the Employment Protection (Consolidation) Act (1978)): the issue of contract of employment notices, minimum periods of notice, unfair dismissal, redundancy, guaranteed payments for lay-off or medical suspension, maternity leave and payments, time off for public duties, etc. In addition, there was other important legislation in the areas of equal pay, health and safety at work, sex discrimination and race relations.

Whilst this legislation can in no way be described as providing an 'employees charter' based on the principles of the 'right to work' and 'right to job security', nevertheless it has established a range of basic legal rights which **apply to all employees** irrespective of whether or not they are members of a trade union or covered by a collective agreement. However, the introduction of these statutory obligations on the employer has not changed the common law basis of the contract of employment. The employee remains obligated to provide honest and faithful service, to do nothing harmful to the employer's interests and to obey all reasonable instructions; whilst the employer is obligated only to pay wages and to take reasonable care to ensure the employee's safety. Thus, wherever the legislation delimits the right not in absolutes but in terms of 'reasonable' (as, for example, in the rights relating to time off for union activities or unfair dismissal), 'reasonableness' has to be judged in the context of the contract of employment.

It may be argued that the creation of these statutory obligations has come about as the **result of, rather than replacement for, trade unions and collective bargaining.** They may be seen as legal recognition and confirmation of benefits which already had been achieved by trade unions in a significant number of organisations through collective bargaining and, in effect, a transfer of such benefits to other less well-organised or non-unionised groups and organisations. At the same time, the establishment of this legal 'floor of rights' has provided a spring board from which well-organised trade unions have sought further improvements through collective bargaining. This legislation has also been an integral factor in strengthening the trade union role at the organisational level and in the greater formalisation of industrial relations. Management has had to review its procedures and methods, generally in conjunction with trade union representatives, to ensure that its policies and practices conform to the requirements of the legislation. However, the development of such legislation can also weaken the position of trade unions in that:

1. Employees may perceive less need to join a trade union for protection.
2. It conditionally 'legitimises' management actions such as dismissal and redundancy and implies that trade union resistance to such lawful management action is unreasonable.

The 1980s have seen little further development of individual employment rights (indeed, the government removed the limitations on the hours of work of women in the Sex Discrimination Act (1986)); rather the government has concentrated on establishing rights for the individual in their relationship with a trade union. However, as noted earlier, individual employment rights may return via the implementation of the EC Social Charter.

An important part of the government's intervention in this area was the establishment of specialised **Industrial Tribunals** intended to provide an easily accessible, quick, inexpensive and relatively informal forum in which employees could seek legal redress for any infringement of these statutory rights. The Tribunals, which are regionally based, comprise a chairman with legal experience and two lay assessors drawn from panels of practitioners nominated by the TUC and CBI respectively. Despite the potential division between the two lay assessors the vast majority of Tribunal decisions are arrived at on a unanimous basis. It is intended that an aggrieved employee should not be inhibited from pursuing his/her case; hence, the relative informality of the proceedings, the intention that each side (employee and management) should present their own case and that costs will only be awarded against the losing side if the Tribunal consider the employee's claim or management's defence has been frivolous or vexatious. However, the system has become increasingly legalistic with approximately one-third of employees and half the employers being represented by solicitors or barristers. In this respect the employee is more hampered than the employer by the inability to obtain legal aid to pursue cases before an Industrial Tribunal.

However, many employers believe that it is too easy for an employee to make an unfounded claim in order to express a grievance in public or in anticipation that the employer will offer an out-of-court payment to avoid the inconvenience of a Tribunal hearing, and in so doing, cause the employer to expend considerable time and effort in preparing to defend the case. This can be mitigated, to a certain extent, in two ways:

1. There is a facility for conciliation through ACAS prior to any formal Tribunal hearing.
2. The employer may request a pre-hearing by the Tribunal to determine whether there are sufficient grounds to justify the case proceeding to a full hearing. This pre-hearing cannot stop the employee from exercising his/her right to a full hearing, although if he/she does proceed the Tribunal may be more disposed towards awarding costs if the case is found in favour of the employer.

The Industrial Tribunals are supplemented by the **Employment Appeals Tribunal** whose composition is similar to that of the Industrial Tribunals and which acts as the appellate body for their decisions. The EAT also deals with such matters as appeals against the decision of the Certification Officer in respect of the granting of a certificate of independence or the political activities of trade unions. Despite the creation of this system of specialised 'labour courts' it is important to remember, as Hepple points out, that they are not a form of industrial arbitration but a 'court substitute' 'with the function of adjudicating disputes by the application of legal rules' [35]. Inevitably their growth has had the effect of overlaying the management of industrial relations with decisions based on legalism and legal values.

Legislation on collective rights

In this area of its legislative role the government **determines the power and status of the participants** in the industrial relations system. Until the 1970s governmental intervention, based on a liberal collectivism approach, was primarily one of providing immunities for trade unions from the application of the *laissez-faire* doctrine by the courts. The voluntarist nature of industrial relations was upheld by the absence of any positive legal support for trade unions seeking to organise and obtain recognition from management and by the refusal to regard collective agreements made between trade unions and management as legally binding and enforceable arrangements. Having safeguarded the industrial position of trade unions through the provision of legal immunities, the government did not seek to directly control the exercise of industrial power.

However, Lewis points out that since 1970 'successive governments representing different interests and ideologies have turned the legal framework of industrial relations into a political football' [36]. In 1971 the Conservative Government, through the **Industrial Relations Act**, attempted a comprehensive reform of collective labour law which, still within a basically corporatist ideology, sought to balance some positive gains for trade unions (such as a statutory recognition procedure and rights to disclosure of information) and the individual employee (unfair dismissal) against greater regulation of trade unions' activities (particularly the closed shop and industrial action). However, most of these provisions proved unworkable at the time because the majority of trade unions openly resisted the legislation by refusing to register and the majority of employers appeared to decline to exercise the rights they were given under the legislation. Nevertheless, the period of the Industrial Relations Act did show that the creation of such statutory obligations in the area of collective rights could also create situations where individuals, by exercising their legal rights, could upset the collective system of regulation.

The basis of collective labour law was changed by the Labour Government during 1974–76 through the **Trade Union and Labour Relations Act (1974)** and the **Employment Protection Act (1975)**, which, together, repealed much of the Industrial Relations Act (but keeping the unfair dismissal legislation) and provided trade unions with legislative support in areas such as obtaining recognition, the granting of paid time-off work to undertake trade union duties, the disclosure of information for the purposes of collective bargaining and consultation prior to redundancies.

The legislation strengthened the collective bargaining role of trade unions and was complimented by the government's strengthening of the policy of involving unions in tripartite discussions over economic and social issues and incomes policy.

However, the Conservative Party felt that these measures tilted the balance of power in industrial relations in favour of trade unions and, in particular, in favour of shop stewards and unofficial groups at the organisation level. Consequently, the Conservative Government has, since 1980, sought to restrict the power of trade unions and strengthen the position of management through the **Employment Acts (1980 and 1982)**, the **Trade Union Act (1984)** and the **Employment Acts (1988 and 1990)**. This legislation involves three main elements:

1. It seeks to restrict the power of trade unions to undertake industrial action by:
    (a) making secondary industrial action and picketing unlawful;
    (b) narrowing the definition of a trade dispute for which trade unions may claim immunity for their actions;
    (c) restricting immunity only to the breach of contracts of employment;
    (d) making trade unions financially liable for unlawful acts carried out by its officers or members;
    (e) strengthening the employer's right to dismiss strikers; and
    (f) reducing the level of supplementary benefit which may be paid to strikers.

2. It establishes what Lewis refers to as 'rights to disorganise' by:
    (a) removing the statutory recognition procedure contained in the Employment Protection Act;
    (b) codifying the right not to belong to a trade union firmly alongside the right to belong; and
    (c) protecting the position of non-unionists by making the closed shop inoperable, including significantly enhanced compensation for an unfair dismissal and trade union liability if it pressures for such a dismissal.

3. It seeks to intervene in the internal affairs of trade unions to ensure greater democracy by:
    (a) protecting the individual from unreasonable exclusion or expulsion from a trade union;
    (b) requiring that the union's NEC and General Secretary be directly elected by the membership through a secret ballot;
    (c) restricting trade union political activities;
    (d) requiring the use of secret ballots in respect of strike action; and
    (e) establishing a Commissioner for the Rights of Trade Union Members to assist individuals taking legal action against their union.

Despite the fact that these legislative restrictions were resisted by trade unions in the early part of the 1980s and were closely associated with a number of major disputes where, through employer action to enforce these new rights, unions were fined for contempt of court and had their funds sequestrated, nevertheless it appears that trade unions have now resigned themselves to having to work within this legal regulation. Certainly, it would appear that the Labour Party does not intend, if returned to power, to repeal all this legislation but rather may introduce a more positive 'right to strike' (which would reduce the employers' ability to dismiss strikers) and introduce legislation which would strengthen the unions' collective bargaining role and right to be involved in organisational decision making.

Legislation establishing collective bargaining machinery

The government's role in this area originated in the Trade Boards Act (1909) which came about because of a concern regarding the low level of wages in the 'sweated trades'. The criteria for the establishment of Trade Boards was subsequently amended to the absence of adequate machinery for the regulation of wages (Trade Boards Act (1918)), and later their title was changed to Wages Councils. In 1988 there were twenty-four **Wages Councils** plus two Agricultural Wages Boards covering a total of 2.5 million employees. The bulk of these employees are in four industries: retail, catering, clothing and agriculture. These industries are characterised by a high proportion of small and scattered organisations, a high proportion of female and part-time labour and a low level of unionisation.

Wages Councils are **tripartite bodies** composed of representatives from trade unions and employers plus independent members whose role is to conciliate between the two sides or, if necessary, to vote with one or other side in order to finalise an 'agreement'. The agreement is expressed in the form of a wages regulation Order which is legally enforceable on the organisations covered by the Wages Council. Enforcement is undertaken by the **Wages Inspectorate.** However, as Pond [37] identified, there has been concern about its effectiveness – between 1971 and 1981 the proportion of employers found to be underpaying increased from 15 per cent to 41 per cent and in 1981 there were only eight prosecutions amongst the 12,000 establishments where infringements of Wages Councils' orders were discovered. Yet between 1979 and 1981 the number of inspectors was reduced by a third to 119.

The **function of Wages Councils** may be viewed from three different but not mutually exclusive standpoints:

1. As a means of **dealing with the problem of low pay.** Bayliss argued in 1962 that Wages Councils had been overtaken by the advent of full employment under which 'the main protection which workers have against being compelled to accept socially "unreasonable" pay has been

the state of the labour market itself' and that 'if statutory wage regulation were abolished overnight only a small proportion of those who are . . . provided with legal minimum wages and conditions would find themselves receiving unreasonably low wages' [38]. However, this does not appear to be the reality in the 1980s. They remain the lowest paid industries and certainly there is no evidence to suggest that wage levels in these industries would be higher without Wages Councils – rather the reverse. Therefore, it seems that Wages Councils still have an important role in maintaining wage levels in these industries.

2.   As a **precursor and aid to the development of voluntary collective bargaining arrangements.** It has been argued that by providing this initial statutory support to collective bargaining the government allows trade unions to demonstrate their ability to represent and bargain on behalf of the employees in the industry and, in so doing, are able to develop their organisation to a sufficient level to be able to maintain voluntary collective bargaining arrangements. This view is reflected within the Employment Protection Act (1975) which allowed the Secretary of State, after an investigation by ACAS, to convert a Wages Council into a Statutory Joint Industrial Council which does not include the independent members. However, none have been converted into SJICs. Indeed, ACAS reported [39] that the lack of progress in developing collective bargaining necessitated the retention of Wages Councils and that there might be scope for their extension into other areas of low pay. Thus, Wages Councils do not appear to have provided a half-way house towards voluntary collective bargaining.

3.   As the **use of state power to maintain collective bargaining** in circumstances where the economic and industrial relations situation precludes it being maintained on a voluntary basis. Bayliss suggested that they may be 'regarded as ambulances which pick up those who are too weak to survive without help' [40]. Their importance lies in the provision of governmental support for the extension of the process of joint regulation, if only in respect of basic wages and conditions, into areas where trade unions are unable to achieve a sufficient power base to demand and maintain it themselves.

Although, as Gabriel and Palmer note, trade unions have in the past 'been decidedly ambivalent about the wages council system, fearing that it kept wages depressed and weakened union organisation' [41], there are others who see them as 'interfering with market forces by keeping wages, prices and unemployment artificially high' [42]. Certainly, the **Government's approach to the reform of Wages Councils** in 1986 [43] was based on a belief that their existence hindered the expansion of employment in these service industries by:

1.   Restricting the offer and acceptance of jobs at wages which might be

acceptable. Evidence that a high proportion of employees in these industries are female and/or part-time and that 30 per cent of employees are paid the statutory minimum rate was cited to substantiate the claim that pay rates are higher than necessary to recruit and retain staff. Furthermore, it was argued that the wage level set by Wages Councils had important repercussions in bolstering up the whole wage structure in Britain.

2. Pricing, in particular, young people out of possible jobs.
3. Creating a bureaucratic administrative burden for both the government (in monitoring and enforcing the Orders) and the small companies which comprise the majority of employers in these industries.

This thinking was in line with the government's earlier abolition of other statutory-based wage determination machinery (Schedule 11 of the Employ-ment Protection Act (1975) and the House of Commons Fair Wages Resolution).

However, some employers feared that the complete abolition of Wages Councils could 'leave the way open for the introduction of a national minimum wage under another government' [44]. It was perhaps this, together with a genuine concern about the problem of low pay, which led bodies such as the Institute of Personnel Management [45] to recommend the retention of Wages Councils with legally enforceable awards but with the independent members adopting a more mediator/arbitrator role within the negotiating process – leading possibly to their transformation into SJICs.

Under the **Wages Act (1986)** the scope of Wages Councils was restricted by excluding those under 21 years of age (approximately half a million), and limiting their regulation to setting only a basic minimum hourly rate and overtime entitlement and no other terms and conditions of employment. Furthermore, the Act withdrew the power of the Secretary of State to establish any further Wages Councils. Consequently, Wages Councils now only provide the barest of protection or the minimum in collective bargaining.

Regulator

The government is always concerned about the level of incomes as part of its role in managing the economy. However, it is important to distinguish between a passive regulatory role exercised through the government's fiscal and monetary policies (incomes management) and a more active role in directly regulating the results of collective bargaining (incomes policy). It is quite clear that this latter active role formed an important element of the government's intervention in industrial relations during the 1960s and 1970s (see Table 9.1). Towers defines an incomes policy as 'a package of measures, applied simultaneously or sequentially, which seek to intervene directly in

Table 9.1 *Incomes policies in the 1960s and 1970s*

Year	Pay policy	Institutions
Conservative		
1961	Pay pause	
1962	2–2½% guiding light	National Incomes Commission (1962–4)
Labour		Tripartite Declaration of Intent
1965 (Apr)	3–3½% norm (exceptions for productivity, low-pay, to attract manpower and to restore serious erosion of comparability)	National Board for Prices and Incomes (1965–70)
		'Early Warning System' for critical wage increases (Nov. 1965)
1966 (July)	Six-months freeze Six-months severe restraint	
1968 (Apr)	3½% ceiling (exceptions for productivity and major revisions of pay structures)	
1969 (Dec)	2½–4½% norm	
Conservative		
1970	N–1% (applied to pay settlements in the public sector)	
1972 (Nov)	Stage 1 – Six-months freeze	
1973 (Apr)	Stage 2 – £1 + 4% (max £250 p.a.)	
1973 (Nov)	Stage 3 – £2.25 a week or 7% (max £350 p.a.; threshold agreements 40p per week for each per cent increase in RPI above 6%)	Pay Board (1973–4) Price Commission (1973–4)
Labour		
1974	Wage increases in line with RPI	Social Contract
1975 (July)	Phase I – £6 per week for those earning less than £8,500 p.a.	
1976 (Aug)	Phase II – 5% (min £2.50 per week and max £4 per week)	
1977 (July)	10% maximum (exception for productivity agreements)	
1978 (July)	5% maximum (exceptions for productivity agreements and special cases)	
1979		Standing Commission on Pay Comparability (for public sector) (1979–80)

the processes of income determination and the working of labour markets for the purposes of moderating the rate of price inflation, and which also seeks to contribute towards greater equality in the distribution of pay and improvements in labour market efficiency' [46].

. The whole emphasis of the government's strategy during the 1980s has been to avoid any form of 'incomes policy' whilst vigorously following a policy of 'incomes management'. However, the issue of an 'incomes policy' has returned to the debating agenda in the late 1980s not least because of the possibility of a return of a Labour Government and, irrespective of a change of government, the increasing possibility of more harmonisation of employment arrangements through closer European ties. Two issues have received considerable discussion:

1. **National Minimum Wage**. In the late 1980s the Labour Party accepted the idea of some form of National Minimum Wage (to be set through tripartite negotiations between government, union and employers). As Blackburn points out the establishment of such a national minimum wage 'is not necessarily a very revolutionary reform' but would simply 'bring Britain's low pay strategy into line with other western European countries' where such schemes 'are not designed to promote equality, but merely to relieve the worst extremes of poverty' [47] (i.e. are 'safety nets') and appear to have had little impact on either employment levels or income distribution. Indeed, he notes that some observers see these minima as 'molehill levels' and that the real problem of low pay can only be tackled by having some form of 'maximum income limits' as well as 'minimum wages'.

2. **Central Forum**. The 1990 TUC Congress endorsed the proposal put forward by some trade unions [48] to co-ordinate the timing of major collective bargaining arrangements with the government's annual Economic Review, a 'public discussion' between government, CBI and TUC on the UK's economic prospects (a similar arrangement to that which exists in Germany and Japan) and the setting of the national minimum wage. However, the trade unions have been at pains to emphasise that this would not be an 'incomes policy' nor would it involve statutory pay restraint.

It is, therefore, useful to examine the UK's experience with incomes policies during the 1960s and 1970s. However, it must be recognised that the nature of incomes policy during that period was short term, negative and economic in character, generally involving a temporary restriction on the level of pay increases as an aid to achieving a reduction in inflation, price stability and international competitiveness. If an incomes policy is to be successful over a long term it must, in some way, seek to address the issue of social fairness in pay levels – which the current proposals appear to be attempting.

Davies identified several key issues which arose in all incomes policies and which affected its acceptability:

• *Criteria to be used as the norm for pay increases.* Davies argues that the criteria 'must make some sort of economic sense; they must be simple enough to be easily understood; and . . . they must also be flexible enough to encompass broadly accepted notions of fairness' [49]. The economic basis for most of the norms was either the expected growth in the 'national product' or, more usually, the existing or anticipated rage of inflation. Thus, most incomes policies sought to restrict pay increases to a level lower than the rate of inflation and, where they lasted longer than one year, to do so on a progressively restrictive basis. The notable exception to this pattern was 1972–73 which also introduced the 'threshold' principle which in fact aggravated the inflation rate because its introduction coincided with a sharp increase in the Retail Price index as a result of an increase in world oil and commodity prices.

The criteria which were most frequently used were either a percentage or a flat rate increase. The percentage basis maintains existing differentials whilst the flat rate basis goes some way to favouring the lower-paid employees by giving them a greater relative increase. The limited redistribution effect of incomes policy was further aided by those policies which, although primarily based on a percentage increase, set out minimum and maximum allowable increases. Nevertheless, on the whole the application of **incomes policy did little to change the existing pattern of wage differentials.** Although the incomes policy 'norm' was intended to be a maximum, it invariably represented the minimum which employees expected to receive. Consequently, all employees tended to have the same increase under incomes policy. As Towers points out 'incomes policy, of itself, however ambitious or sincere in its intentions to achieve a fairer distribution of burdens and rewards, can do very little; it requires the support of complementary and effective policies of redistributive justice' [50].

• *Exceptions to the norm.* Davies points out that 'the range of exceptions must . . . be broad enough to allow for some flexibility and the correction of anomalies, but not so broad as to undermine totally the goal of . . . restraining income growth' [51]. Exceptions encompassed both special emotive groups (nurses, police, firemen, etc.) and strong bargaining groups who might have otherwise openly challenged the incomes policy by seeking to secure higher wage increases through direct action (miners). The major governmental concern in this strategy was that, having made a concession for one group based on a certain principle, other groups might then claim that the same principle applied to them. However, the principal exception allowed under most incomes policies was for improvements in productivity. Clearly, providing for such an exception is in line with the very objective of incomes policy (enhancing the performance of industry) and it may be argued that it encouraged a shift in bargaining towards 'ability to pay' and 'productivity' criteria. However, it also created a major loophole by which trade unions and employers colluded in negotiating increases above the norm under the pretext of productivity improvements. Despite any requirement that such agreements be self-financing, their success depended on the ability of the government adequately to supervise the operation of the incomes policy.

● *Control and enforcement*. Clearly, as Davies argues, the most effective policy is likely to be 'a voluntary one based upon the active support of those affected' and 'largely administered by the parties themselves' [52]. He believes that only the Social Contract (1975–9) came close to this pattern; in most incomes policies control was exercised by the government through some institution established for that purpose. In seeking to maintain control over wage bargaining the government was faced with a number of problems:

1. The decentralised character of the British industrial relations system mitigates against control. Effective control ideally requires the existence of strong centralised trade unions, employers and collective bargaining; without this it is difficult for the controlling institution to be aware of or cope with the very large number of negotiations at the organisation level. Hence most incomes policies placed emphasis on centralised public sector negotiations under the direct or indirect control of the government itself and very visible to the private sector.
2. Incomes policy can only attempt to control the wage rates negotiated between trade unions and employers and not the actual earnings of employees resulting from overtime, bonus payments, etc.
3. It is difficult to establish effective sanctions against those who break the incomes policy: indeed, who should be sanctioned – the employer for giving such an increase, the employees for obtaining it or both? Thus, most incomes policies were 'enforced' through argument and persuasion rather than coercive sanctions.

● *Co-operation*. It must be recognised that the effectiveness of an incomes policy depends on the co-operation of both employers and trade unions. Indeed, in the private sector the government has to rely on the employer for much of the policing of incomes policy. Trade unions are somewhat hesitant about becoming involved in the operation of an incomes policy because it may undermine their credibility with their membership. To co-operate with an incomes policy requires them to restrain their collective bargaining activities and in so doing allow the government to determine the pay increase for their membership. This may lead to a rift between the membership and their officers and an undermining of the collective regulatory system. Their support is likely to be dependent on the preparedness of government to include them in economic and social planning – a social contract.

Conciliator

Government support for the processes of conciliation and arbitration has existed since the Conciliation Act (1886) and Industrial Courts Act (1919). This has played an important part in the government's policy of seeking to **maintain industrial peace** within the industrial relations system by encouraging trade unions and management, wherever possible, to utilise these facilities, rather than industrial action, to resolve their disputes. However, during the 1960s and 1970s the government also sought to use arbitration as a means of **influencing the outcome of negotiations** by indirectly enlisting the conciliator or arbitrator as an agent for the maintenance of the government's incomes policy. However, during the 1980s, the government's view of arbitration has changed from it being seen as an independent third-party intervention to assist the two sides to find a compromise solution to their dispute to one of it being an unreasonable restriction on management's freedom and responsibility to make the right decision in the best interests of maintaining the profitability and competitiveness of the business. (See Chapter 16 Conciliation and Arbitration.)

9.4 Summary propositions

- The government's primary objective in intervening in the management of the industrial relations system is to maintain the stability and productivity of the economy.
- The nature of the government's approach to industrial relations is dependent on the type of dominant political ideology (liberal or corporatist) and the relative power/autonomy of trade unions.

Further reading

- D. Strinati, *Capitalism, the State and Industrial Relations*, Croom Helm, 1982. This book examines the relationship between class structure, class conflict and state power and puts forward a sociological explanation of some of the determinants of state intervention in industrial relations.
- C. Crouch, *The Politics of Industrial Relations*, Fontana, 1982. This book is a very readable examination of the development of government intervention in industrial relations throughout the post-war period.
- G. S. Bain (ed.), *Industrial Relations in Britain*, Blackwell, 1983. Part V (The State and its Agencies) examines the role of law, both collective and individual, and incomes policy; Chapters 7 and 8 in Part III examine industrial relations in the public sector and the problem of Wages Councils and low pay.

References

1. C. Crouch, *The Politics of Industrial Relations* (2nd edn), Fontana, 1982, p. 146.
2. R. Lewis, 'Collective labour law', in G. S. Bain (ed.), *Industrial Relations in Britain*, Blackwell, 1983, p. 361.
3. O. Kahn-Freund, 'Legal framework', in A. Flanders and H. A. Clegg (eds), *The System of Industrial Relations in Great Britain*, Blackwell, 1960, p. 44.
4. C. Crouch, *op. cit.*, p. 141 and pp. 147–8.
5. D. Farnham and J. Pimlott, *Understanding Industrial Relations* (2nd edn), Cassell, 1983, p. 185.
6. R. Lewis, *op. cit.*
7. R. Hyman, *Industrial Relations: A Marxist introduction*, Macmillan, 1975, p. 125.
8. *ibid.*, p. 145.
9. *ibid.*, p. 132.
10. C. Crouch, *op. cit.*; C. Crouch, *Class Conflict and the Industrial Relations Crisis*, Heinemann, 1977.
11. D. Strinati, *Capitalism, the State and Industrial Relations*, Croom Helm, 1982.
12. C. Crouch (1977), *op. cit.*, p. 28.
13. C. Crouch (1982), *op. cit.*, p. 143.
14. C. Crouch (1977), *op. cit.*, p. 30.
15. *ibid.*, p. 31.
16. C. Crouch (1982), *op. cit.*, p. 146.
17. *ibid.*, p. 213.
18. J. Due, J. S. Madsen and C. S. Jenson, 'The social dimension: convergence or diversification of IR in the Single European Market?', *Industrial Relations Journal*, vol. 22, no. 2, 1991, p. 88.
19. *ibid.* p. 93.
20. 'Bipartite/tripartite consultation: an international survey', *European Industrial Relations Review*, June 1988, pp. 22–8.
21. D. Strinati, *op. cit.*, p. 41.
22. *ibid.*, p. 42.
23. C. Crouch (1982), *op. cit.*, p. 159.
24. Quoted in K. W. Wedderburn, *The Worker and the Law* (2nd edn), Penguin, 1971, p. 26. ©K. W. Wedderburn, 1965, 1971.
25. K. W. Wedderburn, *op. cit.*, p. 25.
26. F. Boothman and D. Denham, 'Industrial tribunals: is there an ideological background?', *Industrial Relations Journal*, vol. 12, no. 3, 1981, pp. 6–14.
27. *The Guardian*, 19 April 1984.
28. P. Kahn *et al.*, *Picketing: Industrial disputes, tactics and the law*, Routledge & Kegan Paul, 1983, p. 86.
29. *ibid.*, pp. 211–12.
30. D. Winchester, 'Industrial relations in the public sector', in G. S. Bain (ed.), *op. cit.*, p. 176.
31. *ibid.*, p. 153.
32. A. W. J. Thomson and P. B. Beaumont, *Public Sector Bargaining: A study of relative gain*, Saxon House, 1978.
33. S. Freeman and G. Morris, 'The state as employer: setting a new example', *Personnel Management*, August 1989, pp. 25–9.

34. O. Kahn-Freund, *Labour and the Law*, (3rd edn), Stevens, 1983, p. 4.
35. B. Hepple 'Individual labour law' in G. S. Bain (ed.), *op. cit.*, p. 143.
36. R. Lewis, *op. cit.*, p. 392.
37. C. Pond, 'The low paid' in G. S. Bain (ed.), *op. cit.*
38. F. J. Bayliss, *British Wages Councils*, Blackwell, 1962, p. 74.
39. ACAS, *Annual Report 1980*, HMSO.
40. F. J. Bayliss, *op. cit.*, p. 145.
41. C. Gabriel and S. Palmer, 'Wages councils: reformation or dissolution?', *Personnel Management*, February 1984, p. 29.
42. *ibid.*, p. 26.
43. 'Wages Councils – striking a balance', *Employment Gazette*, April 1985, p. 136; *European Industrial Relations Review*, May 1985, p. 31.
44. C. Gabriel and S. Palmer, *op. cit.*, p. 29.
45. *The Future of Wages Councils*, IPM, 1982.
46. B. Towers, 'A return to incomes policy?' *Industrial Relations Journal*, vol. 12, no. 2, 1981, p. 9.
47. S. Blackburn, 'The problem of riches: from trade boards to a national minimum wage', *Industrial Relations Journal*, Summer 1988, p. 134.
48. 'A New Agenda: bargaining for prosperity in the 1990s', GMB/UCW, 1990.
49. R. J. Davies, 'Incomes and anti-inflation policy' in G. S. Bain (ed.), *op. cit.*, p. 435.
50. B. Towers, *op. cit.*, p. 15.
51. R. J. Davies, *op. cit.*, p. 438.
52. *ibid.*, p. 439.

PART C

Processes

Chapter 10

Communication and joint consultation

10.1 Definition

In its broadest sense communication may be defined as **the process of conveying information between people** and clearly is an essential and continuous element of industrial relations. It is a central feature of not only the bipartite processes of joint consultation and collective bargaining but also of each party's own internal procedures for determining policies, strategies and decisions. It is carried out on both an intra- and inter-organisational basis as well as an interpersonal basis. The nature, scope and manner of such communications is immensely varied:

1. The 'information' is often a mixture of fact, interpretation, opinion and attitude.
2. The purpose of the communication may be to persuade and influence others as well as to inform them.
3. The information may be imparted informally as a personal communication between individuals or formally as an official communication associated with the individuals' organisational roles.
4. The form of the communication may be oral or in writing, direct to all concerned or indirectly through representatives.
5. The communication may consist of a single, one-way transmission of information or form an integral part of a continuing dialogue.

However, whilst communication is an inherent facet of all aspects of industrial relations, the term is also used in a more **restrictive sense** to refer to **the direct conveying of information from management to union or employees either within, or outside, any arrangement for joint consultation or collective bargaining.** It may, therefore, be viewed as a process in its own right.

Joint consultation has been variously described as 'the discussion between management and workers . . . of matters of joint concern which are not the subject of negotiations with trade unions' [1], 'an exchange of opinion, by means of which the participants may say what they like, but decide nothing, take no executive action' [2], 'a means of communicating prior to decisions being made or explaining the reasons for certain decisions after they have been made' [3] and 'leading to advice to management but leaving free management's right and responsibility to make the final decision' [4]. Any definition of joint consultation, as a process, inevitably differentiates it from negotiation. **Joint consultation** may be defined as a:

> **process wherein management determines the issues on which the views and opinions of its employees are to be sought and retains the discretion to decide the final outcome without subjecting it to joint agreement with employees or their representatives.**

The extent, therefore, to which employees are able to influence the final decision or to have their wishes and interests taken into account is dependent exclusively on the 'goodwill' of the management making the decision. However, it must be recognised that, in practice, the difference between the processes of joint consultation and negotiation is often less tangible than the above definition suggests and the two processes tend to blur into each other.

10.2 Communication

One of the most **popular myths** of industrial relations, heard from both participants and outsiders alike, is to ascribe any failure to resolve problems, and even the existence of such problems in the first place, to 'misunderstandings' or 'inadequate communication' between management, employees and/or unions. Indeed, some might go so far as to suggest that management could demonstrate its concern for employees through more effective communication of its plans and the reasons for its decisions and thereby reduce (if not remove) the need for employees to seek the protection of trade unionism to safeguard their interests. However, the CIR noted that it would be entirely wrong to 'overrate the significance of communications both as a cause of the problems facing managements and employees and as a means of solving problems . . . Communications cannot in themselves remove conflict of interest and values' [5].

Industrial relations problems do not often arise solely because of miscommunication between the participants involved. More often the source of the conflict lies in the differences of objectives, interests, perceptions and attitudes which significantly affect the way in which information and situations are interpreted. Hussey and Marsh certainly believe that 'bargainers are already rational when they select information which strengthens their case and ignore that which does not' [6] and greater disclosure of information will not change this. The act of management communicating its reasons for a particular decision or action will not, by itself, ensure that employees and unions either accept the logic of management's thinking or agree with its solution. Communication between management, employees and unions, on both the interpersonal and interorganisational levels, can provide no more than *a means* for them to identify their differences, develop a better understanding of each other's point of view and seek to accommodate their differing interests within a mutually acceptable solution to their problems. Certainly, Drennan [7] believes that management should understand three basic rules about communication:

1. The reactions of employees to any event will be favourable only if it matches or exceeds their expectations.
2. Where an announcement will fall short of expectations, there are only two alternatives to avoid trouble: improve the content of the announcement until it does match expectations, or take time to reduce expectations to the level of the subsequent announcement.
3. Preparing employees for unwelcome news (i.e. moving expectations in a negative direction) requires time and sensitive handling.

It is important that any organisation should establish an adequate system of internal communications. However, in the industrial relations context, communications has the added dimension of being interorganisational as well as intraorganisational in character. Management and union have **different perceptions of the purpose of communication.** So far as management is concerned, the general purpose of providing information is to increase the employees' and representatives' knowledge and understanding of the organisation's problem and management's position, thereby removing any misconceptions which may previously have existed. The trade unions, however, regard the main purpose of acquiring information as being to strengthen their position in respect of the processes of collective bargaining and joint decision making within the organisation. It is necessary, when considering a systematic approach to communication, to recognise that different information serves different purposes and therefore requires different means for its dissemination.

It is possible to identify four broad categories of information:

1. Information which may be classified as being of **general knowledge** about the organisation – for example, the information often contained within a company newspaper which is intended to keep people in touch with what is happening on both a work and social level and which may help the individual to feel part of the organisation.
2. Information which needs to be regularly communicated in respect of the normal **work situation** – for example, the communications between

manager and subordinates both on an informal person-to-person basis and also, perhaps, through regular formal briefing groups.

3. The communication of **major changes** in either company policy or the work of the organisation which will affect all, or a significant number of, employees – for example, the circulation of special management notices or the holding of special meetings relating to the introduction of new processes, redundancy, etc.

4. The communication of detailed information, often of a quantitative nature, to employee representatives as a feature of the **collective bargaining** process. This may be divulged on either a permanent regular basis or on an *ad hoc* as the issue becomes one for negotiation.

There are three main segments to **the organisation's formal communication network**:

1. There should be a **system of information cascade throughout the managerial hierarchy** in order to ensure that managers are well informed and briefed on the current organisational situation and future developments and, therefore, can maintain a co-ordinated approach to the management of industrial relations within the organisation.

2. There must be, at all levels of the organisation, a **system of communication from management to:**
    (a) **employees** (dissemination of information);
    (b) **representatives** (disclosure of information)
        (In order to cope with situations which may require a major communication throughout the organisation, management should seek to ensure that its system is capable of briefing the management hierarchy and communicating with employees and their representatives on an integrated and speedy basis.)

3. There is the **system of communication amongst employees** – that is, the formal communication between employees, shop stewards and full-time officers. It may be argued that this system is the province of the employees and their union and not, therefore, a matter for management involvement. However, much of its content relates to organisational issues and a significant part of its operation takes place within the workplace. Therefore, management should give careful consideration to what assistance it can, and is prepared to, give to aid the effective operation of this system.

Disclosure of information

The term 'disclosure of information' refers to:

> **the transfer to employee representatives of information generated as an integral part of the managerial function of planning, controlling**

and decision making and traditionally retained within the exclusive possession of management.

Torrington and Chapman believe that it is perhaps unfortunate that the word 'disclosure' immediately 'implies a reluctance on the part of the holder of the information to let anyone else see it' [8]. Moore, on the other hand, believes that it 'correctly acknowledges that unequal access to information prevails, and confirms the notion that such discriminatory access represents a real power resource to a company and its managers in their dealings with trade unions' [9]. Certainly, management has not been noted for its general preparedness to 'open books' to employee representatives except, perhaps, where it has felt that to reveal such information would tactically help to strengthen and substantiate its position in a negotiation. However, Moore also believes that the term 'tends to direct emphasis towards the *provider* of the information, together with considerations (managerial, legal and accounting) which motivate and constrain him' and 'attention is diverted away from the needs and problems of the *user*' who 'may well be an active seeker and acquirer of company information, and not merely a passive and receptive destination for it' [10]. Dickens argues that the apparent unanimity regarding the desirability of disclosure of information owes 'much to the fact that [it] can mean different things to different people and that different expectations are held as to its possible effects' [11].

The potential **relationship between disclosure of information and the nature of collective bargaining** is shown in Figure 10.1. Where unions are at a significant disadvantage to management in their bargaining power relationship and there is little, if any, disclosure of information by management, the result if often one of non-bargaining and the imposition of solutions. Where, despite the existence of unequal bargaining power, management adopts a policy of a high level of disclosure of information to unions, this is likely to result only in trade union frustration and employee alienation as they perceive that they are powerless to affect or influence anything in the light of the information they receive. However, where there is a more equal balance of bargaining power between the parties, then a low disclosure of information by management is likely to result in the predominance of overt collective industrial action by employees and trade unions. In the absence of any information from management to modify their expectations or by which to assess management's case, the belief may easily arise that management is simply being intransigent in its attitude and must therefore be pressured to change its position. Where, on the other hand, there is a high degree of disclosure of information by management it is possible for the parties to adopt a more integrative (joint problem solving) approach to collective bargaining. The more traditional distributive bargaining approach is characterised by the existence of bargaining power on the part of trade unions (but not necessarily equal to that of management) and the disclosure of a limited, and often very selective, range of information.

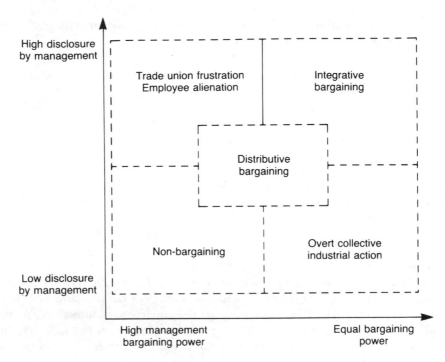

Figure 10.1 *Disclosure of information and collective bargaining*

A number of **arguments against the disclosure of information** have been put forward – principally by managers.

● *Relative power relationship.* It is argued that in the competitive, conflictual environment of the negotiating process, which is at the heart of collective bargaining, the possession of knowledge by one party to the exclusion of the other is an important determinant of relative power relationship. Therefore, any disclosure of such exclusive knowledge may affect the power balance to the detriment of the original information holder – in this case management. Management may feel, particularly in a distributive bargaining situation, that its ability to achieve the best possible result, and one which would otherwise be acceptable to the other party, could be severely hampered if its negotiating limits were more easily identifiable by the union negotiators as a result of management's prior disclosure of operational, financial and other information. Alternatively, particularly in situations of 'bad' business, management may see the disclosure of information as a means of restraining union aspirations and thereby reducing conflict within collective bargaining. Dickens found that 48 per cent of managers surveyed saw disclosure of information leading to 'better' collective bargaining (i.e. 'more "moderate", "responsible" or "realistic" union demands' although 59 per cent saw the major disadvantage being the ' "misinterpretation" or "misuse" of information or the inability of unions to understand it' (i.e. they would not interpret it in the same way as management) [12]. However, once the principle of 'disclosure of information' has been established to meet management's needs in this way it becomes difficult, if not impossible, to move away from this principle when it might be to management's disadvantage to disclose information.

- *Expansion of joint regulation.* The disclosure of managerial information on a formal and regular basis may lead to pressure for the expansion of joint regulation into much wider areas of decision making. Certainly, there would appear to be little real purpose or advantage in disclosing information if its assumptions, logic and implications cannot, at the very least, be questioned and debated by the recipients. However, it is a relatively small step, but a very important one and one which may easily be made, to move from simply discussing the information to questioning the validity of the associated management decision and then seeking to modify it or even bring it under some more permanent mode of joint regulation. To many managers this would represent a substantial and serious erosion of what they currently regard as their managerial prerogative and control within the organisation.

- *Varying degrees of precision of information.* There are varying degrees of precision in the information which management handles and, indeed, it may be argued that one of the attributes of good management is to be able to make decisions in spite of the inadequacies and uncertainties of the information at its disposal. Furthermore, a great deal of management activity is concerned with gathering information, analysing it and planning for a range of contingencies that might or might not happen. Managers, therefore, are reluctant to divulge this information not only because its imprecision may appear to reflect adversely on their capability and credibility as managers but also because an unnecessary amount of time and effort may be spent discussing issues which never materialise, thereby possibly creating difficulties and conflict with their employees and unions where none need have arisen.

- *Confidential information.* The more important, and from the unions' viewpoint most worthwhile, organisational information is often regarded as confidential and restricted to senior management. Whilst there is no evidence to suggest that employee representatives, if provided with this information, are any more likely than management to 'offer it to the highest bidder', nonetheless senior management are reluctant to disseminate it more widely than they believe to be absolutely necessary. They may also consider it improper to disclose information to employee representatives when it has not been made generally available to the majority of managers. From the employee representatives' position, it must also be recognised that access to such information, and in particular the need to maintain its confidentiality, is likely to place a strain on relationships with constituents.

Despite these managerial reservations, there have been several **pressures for greater disclosure of information** both from within the organisation and outside:

1. In the normal course of collective bargaining, management has itself placed greater emphasis on linking pay with productivity, performance and working arrangements, etc., and on adopting a more joint problem solving approach. If industrial relations and collective bargaining are to be related to the 'needs of the business', this not only widens the scope of collective bargaining but also entails **more complexity and sophistication in the conduct of negotiations.** The successful establishment and maintenance of co-operative bargaining requires management to disclose more detailed information regarding the organisation's present and planned operations than would be the case with distributive bargaining.
2. There has been an increasing acceptance amongst management that the maximisation of the organisation's potential and its adaptation to change of any kind can only be achieved successfully if there is **greater employee involvement in the organisation.** However, this requires that employees should have access to more managerial information; without information there can be little, if any, effective involvement or trust between management and employees.
3. The pressure for greater disclosure of information to unions should be seen in the context of a **general pressure within society during the 1970s for more openness** in many aspects of community life – most notably in the political and governmental systems at all levels. This was linked with the belief, amongst many people, that industry and commerce should be more socially responsible and accountable for its decisions and activities. The establishment of a legal requirement for such disclosure of information should, therefore, be viewed as part of this general development as well as an integral element in the development of specific employment protection legislation.

The Employment Protection Act (1975) provided a **legal requirement for the disclosure of information**, on request, to the representatives of independent trade unions for the purpose of collective bargaining. This information has to be both:

1. information without which the trade union representatives would be to a material extent impeded in carrying on such collective bargaining; and
2. information which it would be in accordance with good industrial relations practice to disclose for the purpose of collective bargaining (S. 17(1)).

In addition, the Act places two restrictions on the process of disclosure:

1. **Certain types of information are specifically excluded;** information which:
   (a) would be against the interests of national security to disclose;
   (b) could not be disclosed without contravening a prohibition imposed by or under an enactment;
   (c) has been communicated to the employer in confidence;
   (d) relates specifically to an individual unless he/she has consented to its being disclosed;
   (e) would cause substantial injury to the employer's undertaking by its disclosure for reasons other than its effect on collective bargaining;
   (f) has been obtained by the employer for the purpose of bringing, prosecuting or defending any legal proceedings (S. 18(1)).

2. Even when the information is regarded as being appropriate to collective bargaining and not of a precluded nature there are **safeguards for the employer in respect of the manner of disclosure**; management cannot be required to:
   (a) produce, allow inspection of, or copy any document; or
   (b) compile or assemble any information which would involve an amount of work or expenditure out of reasonable proportion to the value of the information in the conduct of collective bargaining (S. 18(2)).

It is important to recognise that:

1. The independent trade union must already be recognised by management before it has any legal right to seek information.
2. The onus is on the trade union representatives to ask for the information they require rather than on management to provide it automatically, and they must also know the manner in which management collects this information.
3. The amount of information that might legally be requested depends on the extent to which issues within the organisation are subject to joint regulation through collective bargaining; management is under no legal obligation to disclose information in respect of those issues which are simply a matter of joint consultation (except redundancy).

The **enforcement procedure** for this piece of legislation has been described by Torrington and Chapman as bizarre [13]. It consists, in essence, of two stages. Initially, the independent trade union may present a complaint to the Central Arbitration Committee that the employer has failed to comply with a request for information. The CAC must then decide whether or not the complaint can be resolved through conciliation by ACAS. If the CAC decides that conciliation is inappropriate, or if after conciliation the matter still has not been resolved, then a formal hearing will be held at which union and management may present their case. If the CAC finds in favour of the union it will make a declaration specifying both the information to be disclosed and a period of time, of not less than one week, in which the employer must disclose the information to the union representatives.

The second stage only comes into operation if the employer fails to comply with the CAC's declaration. In that event, the trade union, in addition to presenting a further complaint regarding the employer's non-compliance and obtaining a declaration in its favour, may also present a formal claim for improvement or change in the employees' terms and conditions of employment. The CAC, acting in its normal arbitration capacity, will then hear both the union and management's case in respect of that claim and make such an award as it feels is appropriate. The content of such an award has legal effect as part of the employees' contract of employment. Although there is no direct compulsion on the employer to disclose information, this procedure is intended to pressure management to disclose the information at least during the CAC arbitration hearing or allow its case, for example against a union claim for a wage increase, to be weakened by default.

The *ACAS Code of Practice* [14] provides guidance as to the range of information which management may be expected to disclose in line with good industrial relations practice. The main areas of information are:

1. **Pay and benefits:** the principles and structure of payment systems (including job evaluation and grading criteria); earnings and hours of work (analysed by workgroup, grade, plant, department, sex, etc.); distribution and make-up of pay; total wage bill; details of fringe benefits and other non-wage labour costs.
2. **Conditions of service:** policies on recruitment, redeployment, redundancy, training, equal opportunity and promotion; appraisal systems; health, safety and welfare.
3. **Manpower:** numbers employed (analysed by grade, department, location, age and sex); labour turnover and absenteeism; overtime and short-time working; manning levels; planned changes in work methods, materials, equipment or organisation; manpower plans; investment plans.
4. **Performance:** data on productivity and efficiency; savings from increased productivity and output; return on capital invested; sales and state of the order book.
5. **Financial:** cost structures; gross and net profits, allocation of profits; sources of earnings; assets and liabilities; details of government financial assistance; transfer prices; loans to parent or subsidiary companies and interest charged.

The Code also suggests that 'cost information on individual products; detailed analysis of proposed investment, marketing or pricing policies; and price quotas or the make-up of tender prices' [15] represent the type of information which, dependent on the circumstances, employers would generally wish to withhold on the grounds that it might cause substantial injury to the organisation.

It may be argued that much of the information referred to in the ACAS Code is already known to trade unions and employee representatives and that, as a consequence, the legislative requirement for the employer to disclose such information is not an important benefit to them. Clearly, for both collective bargaining and employee participation in decision making, the most important information lies in the categories of Performance and Financial. Both the CBI and TUC [16] have suggested that the information relating to mergers and takeovers, expansions and closures, research and development and production plans should be disclosed. However, whilst the TUC felt that full information on these topics was essential to a comprehensive appreciation of an organisation's position, the CBI pointed out that it was in these areas that the issues of confidentiality and effect on the competitiveness of the organisation would place the greatest constraints on disclosure. This difference in approach underlines, perhaps most clearly, that even where a topic has been designated in the ACAS Code as being appropriate for disclosure there is no guarantee that it will be translated into usable specific information.

In their survey of **CAC references relating to disclosure of information** between 1977 and 1981, Hussey and Marsh [17] found that although there had been 151 references, of which 41 resulted in a full hearing, the annual rate of references had declined from 74 in the first sixteen months of its operation to only 18 in 1981. They attributed this decline to a range of possible factors not least the use of detailed information being the antithesis of traditional collective bargaining; its potential 'undermining' effect on union claims or arguments in a worsening economic climate; the possible improvement of disclosure practices at the organisational level; and union disenchantment with the legal process. From their examination of CAC awards they found that the phrase 'materially impeded' had been interpreted in such a way as to restrict the disclosure of information where the CAC considered the union already had sufficient information, where it believed the union could obtain the information from other sources (e.g. its members) or where it believed the information was unnecessary for the issue being negotiated. Significantly, they also found that the CAC, whilst supporting the general principle of a 'free-flow' of information from management to union, nevertheless interpreted 'good industrial relations practice' to include restricting the disclosure of information where it might cause or extend the conflict between the parties. However, as the CAC itself has pointed out, it is important to recognise that whilst 'a positive award may have given the union less than it was asking for, . . . a nil award may disguise the fact that during the informal procedures . . . a considerable release of information took place' [18]. Certainly, another review of CAC awards [19] found that even where an award was made the union often found the information to be of little use in collective bargaining.

The relative influence, or lack of influence, of the legislative provisions is reflected at the organisational level where Daniel and Millward found not only that employee representatives believed they received less information than management believed it gave, but also that when it came to specific requests for information under the Employment Protection Act 20 per cent of manual and 14 per cent of non-manual representatives reported having made a request but only 9 per cent of managers reported having received such a request. Daniel and Millward attribute this latter discrepancy to the possibility that 'the worker representative did not mention his statutory right to the information and the manager might well have not known the request had statutory backing unless he initially refused to provide the information' [20]. Perhaps, as Moore argues [21], a strong union may not need information to substantiate its bargaining position, whilst a weak union may not be able to benefit from greater disclosure of information.

Information agreements

Although few organisations have a formal Information Agreement with their unions, they are, where they exist, concerned primarily with information relating to changes in company policy or operations and information required for collective bargaining. The first stage in the process of developing such an agreement must be a discussion between the parties as to its purpose. Whilst it may not be possible to arrive at a common perception of its purpose, the parties should at least gain a better understanding of each other's differing views. The agreement may then cover the following areas:

1. The items of information to be disclosed – taking account of both what information is already available and what information can reasonably be made available.
2. The level in the organisation or collective bargaining process at which the information is to be disclosed – for example, there is a need for information in the early stages of the grievance procedure as well as in organisational level negotiations over pay and other major issues.
3. In what form, when and to whom the information is to be given – not only information provided on a regular basis but also information which may be required on an *ad hoc* basis and which cannot, therefore, be specified easily in advance.
4. The possible need for clarification of the information once it has been provided.

5. Facilities for the discussion of the information amongst employee representatives and between them, their constituents and full-time officer.

6. A procedure to be utilised if there is a dispute as to whether or not an item of information can, or should, be provided – this will need to take account of the confidentiality aspect and may incorporate a role for ACAS or some other outside body.

Obviously, the wider disclosure of information traditionally retained within the exclusive possession of management raises the issue of the **training needs of the employee representatives;** the recipients of the information must be capable of understanding and using it. However:

1. What should be the **objective of the training?** Training should not be taken to imply indoctrination or ensuring that employee representatives perceive the information in the same way as management, but the provision of the necessary technical knowledge and analytical tools for the employee representatives to be able to examine the information, analyse it and arrive at their own conclusion.

2. Who should accept **responsibility for the training?** As a result of the differences in perspective, interests and objectives between unions and management, trade unions have tended to regard the training of employee representatives as their exclusive responsibility. They are concerned that any training organised by management will seek to inculcate a management perspective of the information and problems. However, like supervisory and management training in industrial relations, it can be argued that both management and trade unions have an equal interest in improving competence and that a joint involvement, not only in the training of employee representatives but in all industrial relations training, is desirable.

Dissemination of information

The emphasis of organisational communication in the 1980s shifted away from 'disclosure' of information to *trade unions* in support of the collective bargaining process and towards 'dissemination' of information to *employees* in order to secure their greater involvement in and identification with the organisation's interests and objectives. This shift has, therefore, been closely associated with the change in underlying concept from employee 'participation' to employee 'involvement' – much of the dissemination of information takes place through forms of employment involvement (e.g. team briefings). This change has often been accompanied by a feeling, particularly amongst unions, that such direct communication from management to employees is an attempt by management to subvert the collective representational role of shop stewards and trade unions and is in conflict with the recognised principles of collective bargaining. Indeed, such an approach of appealing to employees over the heads of their representatives (both shop stewards and full-time officers) has formed an integral element of some organisational strategies aimed at weakening union and shop steward power and influence and strengthening managerial prerogative. Whilst, obviously, management must always retain its right to communicate direct to its employees whenever the need arises, it must also be conscious that in doing so it may affect its relationship with the trade union and its representatives. The two processes of 'dissemination' and 'disclosure' should be regarded as complementary rather than competitive; there is a very **fine line between communicating information and seeking to pre-empt/or pressure the employees' decision** – some might argue that it is legitimate for management to do the former but not the latter.

Hussey and Marsh [22] found that 42 per cent of the organisations surveyed in 1979 provided an annual statement to employees regarding the financial position of the company (the proportion rose to 75+ per cent amongst larger organisations). They believe that the development of this form of dissemination of information may be attributed to a number of factors:

1. The debate regarding 'industrial democracy' and the possibility of legislative compulsion during the 1970s.
2. A belief in some organisations of the 'natural right' of employees, like shareholders, to receive information concerning the organisation for which they work.
3. Demands from employees or their representatives and, in response, the management seeking to correct an 'imbalance' of information within the organisation by 'broadening the understanding of employees of the company's affairs and . . . countering union information with information of its own' [23];
4. A desire in some organisations to present a 'progressive image' which would 'enhance the company in the eyes of the business community' [24].

In examining the **objectives** of such employee reporting they point out that Reeves's [25] distinction between company centred aims and employee centred aims 'has the advantage of identifying, and indeed polarising, immediate management interests on the one hand and the social and moral responsibilities of management on the other' [26]. **Company-centred aims** are based on a desire to reinforce management's influence and control within the organisation through increasing employee involvement and identification with the interests of the organisation, promoting a greater awareness and understanding of management's position, improving productivity and reducing disputes. **Employee-centred aims**, on the other hand, are based on more 'ethical' considerations such as the organisation's 'responsibility' to inform its employees and the desirability of employee representatives having information to support their role in joint consultation and other forms of participation in decision making. Hussey and Marsh found that most managers included 'greater involvement of employees in the affairs of the company'; 'encouraging a sense of responsibility' and 'discharging the proper responsibilities of the company' amongst the objectives of employee reporting whilst only a handful included 'motivating employees towards high productivity' and 'moderating high wage demand' [27]. When compared to Dickens' survey, mentioned earlier, it would appear that management do not see the direct dissemination of general company financial information to employees in the same light as disclosure of information to trade unions within the collective bargaining framework. Such employee reporting would appear not to be intended as a direct threat to the collective bargaining role of trade unions but rather, perhaps, as an indirect conditioning of their members' expectations.

The general picture of **employee attitudes** towards such dissemination of information appears to be 'satisfaction' within a scepticism about the process. Hussey and Marsh found that:

1. Although a substantial majority of the employees in each occupational category felt employee reports were very or quite interesting the proportion declines (perhaps not surprisingly) from the managerial to the unskilled level [28].
2. Significantly more of those aged 50+ believed reports to be very or quite interesting than those aged 16–20 [29];

but

3. A substantial majority of employees agreed with the statement that 'by the time management tells us anything we have heard from other channels' (the 'grapevine') and 'the information the company gives is often biased to show only the managers' side.' Only a minority agreed that 'management is very frank and honest about giving information' [30].

The **Employment Act (1982)** requires companies employing more than 250 employees to include a statement in their annual report:

> 'describing the action that has been taken during the financial year to introduce, maintain, or develop arrangements aimed at –
>   (i) providing employees systematically with information on matters of concern to them as employees;
>   (ii) consulting employees or their representatives on a regular basis so that the views of the employees can be taken into account in making decisions which are likely to affect their interests;

    (iii) encouraging the involvement of employees in the company's performance through an employees' share scheme or by some other means;

    (iv) achieving a common awareness on the part of all employees of the financial and economic factors affecting the performance of the company' (S.1).

However, Marchington and Wilding concluded, from a survey conducted in 1983, that 'in terms of changing actual practice on employee involvement [the law] is likely to be marginal not only because there are no sanctions which can be used against employers who file a nil return but also because most of the larger companies will have no trouble in putting together a catalogue of involvement practices from somewhere within the organisation' [31]. They believe that only if organisations accept the 'spirit and philosophy' of the legislation will they meet the increasing pressure from the EC, through the implementation of the Social Charter, for greater provision of information and consultation with both employees and their representatives.

10.3 Joint consultation

The **development of joint consultation** has been chequered. In the nineteenth and early twentieth century it was almost a natural progression for the employer to discard joint consultation within the organisation when moving to collective bargaining through an employers' association. During both World Wars joint consultation was seen as being complementary to collective bargaining in improving work efficiency for the war effort. After World War II joint consultation tended to decline in importance as trade unions extended the scope of collective bargaining and it became regarded by most trade unionists as a weak substitute for collective bargaining. In the 1960s and 1970s some managements sought to introduce or strengthen staff joint consultation, sometimes alongside the creation of staff associations or 'house unions', as a means of weakening the attraction of white collar unionisation amongst their employees.

    A number of surveys show the relatively widespread **extent of joint consultative arrangements.** Brown [32] found that joint consultative committees (JCCs) existed in 42 per cent of manufacturing establishments (although the proportion was higher in larger establishments); the Daniel and Millward [33] and Millward and Stevens [34] WIRS surveys confirmed a relatively unchanged picture between 1980 and 1984 with 34 per cent of all establishments having consultative committees but noted that the proportion was higher in the public sector; whilst Marsh [35] found a much higher proportion (80 per cent) of establishments having formal joint consultative arrangements. Bassett believes that the apparent stability in consultative arrangements during the recession of the early 1980s, as evidenced by the WIRS surveys, shows that 'while employers are not much minded to scrap their consultative committees, they're not much minded either to introduce them' because, first, 'employers taking a much tougher line in negotiation simply *don't* feel the need to consult with their employees any more' and secondly, 'companies are adopting a whole range of sophisticated techniques to help manage their employees' [36]. However, Marchington [37] identifies two different schools of thought about the development of joint consultation during the 1980s: one which believes that there has been a 'trivialisation and marginalisation' of joint consultation while the other believes there has been a 'revitalisation' intended to challenge the role of trade unions and collective bargaining in the organisation.

Purpose of the process

A means for management to improve efficiency within the organisation

The CBI regards the primary purpose of joint consultation as being 'to enlist the cooperation of all employees in the efficient operation of the company . . . and in the implementation of management's decisions' [38]. Within this 'managerial' approach the content has tended to be confined to specific operational needs and problems; the process has been primarily one of discussing and implementing decisions already made by management; and the criterion for success has been the effect it has on the output of the organisation. Henderson argued that resistance to change within the organisation can only be overcome by 'a continuous process of explanation and discussion – explanation of why the changes are necessary, how they will fit in with long-term objectives, what the benefits and the disadvantages will be; discussion of what the changes will mean to employees, of the problems which will arise and how they can be resolved . . . Consultation must be continuous since change itself is continuous' [39].

The creation of industrial harmony between management and employees

This view is closely related to the unitary perspective of industrial organisations and therefore is, at best, only applicable to a limited range of issues where management and employees have a substantial degree of common interest. As with communication, joint consultation by itself cannot create industrial harmony except in so far as it is clearly evident to the employees that their needs and interests, as expressed through the joint consultative process, have been accommodated within management's decision making. Yet, because the process enshrines the concept of decision making being the sole responsibility of management, there will always be a residual element of suspicion that management listens to its employees and then proceeds to implement its decisions unchanged. Industrial harmony depends on the acceptability of management's decisions and actions not the act of consultation by management.

A means towards industrial democracy within the organisation

It is this aspect which appears to be of most interest to trade unions and employee representatives. However, the nature of the decision making process is such that it cannot realistically be considered part of some process of industrial democracy (i.e. as 'a means of settling democratically the purposes of industrial undertakings' [40]). The essential characteristic of joint consultation is that management retains its prerogative to make unilateral decisions, whilst the notion underpinning industrial democracy is that the decision making process should be subject to some form of partnership between management and employees. These two concepts of decision making are fundamentally incompatible. Indeed, many managers favour joint consultation rather than collective bargaining precisely because it involves less erosion of their prerogative.

Even if there is a greater preparedness on the part of management to allow the operation of JCCs to be subject to increased joint decision making, management will still retain overall control of the process through its ability to determine which issues are to be put into the process and the timing of such consultation within its own internal decision making arrangements. In the absence of any effective influence in these areas employees and their representatives may always argue that management could, and should, have involved them earlier and are likely to be suspicious about the genuineness of any professed management desire to involve them more fully in organisational decision making. Thus, joint consultation can, at best, play only a limited role in developing industrial democracy within the organisation.

A grievance forum

The CBI noted that joint consultation may be used for 'matters of personal concern to employees which are not appropriate for formal negotiations' [41]. It is perhaps surprising, at first glance, that such an activity should form part of joint consultation; it involves a reversal of the normal process of management consulting employee representatives on matters of concern to management to one of employee representatives drawing management's attention to issues which are of concern to employees. In part this may be a reflection of the period when collective bargaining was not as strong or comprehensive as it is today and when the industrial relations system at the organisational level lacked the formality of defined and agreed procedures to cope with collective, as well as individual, grievances. Nevertheless, it does serve a number of useful purposes even within today's industrial relations system:

1. The constraints and atmosphere surrounding joint consultation are likely to be less threatening than those which surround negotiations and the

grievance procedure with their immediate implications of a possible 'failure to agree' and the imposition of sanctions.

2.   It allows employees to raise general complaints or concerns on issues which are either not normally subject to negotiation or are difficult to formulate as a precise grievance capable of resolution through negotiation.

3.   It provides employee representatives with a forum which may be used as an adjunct to the normal negotiating arrangements in which they may raise an issue to sound out management's position as a prelude to and, depending on the response, justification for raising it subsequently in a formal negotiation.

In practice, joint consultation does not serve one purpose to the exclusion of the others but involves a combination of all these elements.

Relationship to collective bargaining

The relationship between joint consultation and collective bargaining is generally conceived as one of differentiation and separation. However, in examining this relationship, it is important to bear in mind that **the process of joint consultation and the institutions of joint consultation are not necessarily coterminous;** (i.e. the process of joint consultation is not the exclusive province of JCCs nor, in practice, are other processes excluded from the operation of JCCs). Whilst the boundary between the institutions of joint consultation and collective bargaining may be relatively clear (by reference to their constitution, composition and subject matter), the boundary between the processes of joint consultation and negotiation is more diffuse. If, in a JCC, management says 'If we make this change to our original decision will it now be acceptable?' and modifies its stance to take account of employee objections, how does this differ to negotiation? The real difference lies, first, in there being no requirement placed on management by the process itself to make such a modification, and secondly, in the result not being expressed as a formal joint agreement which may be regarded as binding and enforceable on management but as a management action or decision which will not be opposed by employees in its execution. Thus, it is often difficult to distinguish, by reference to the behaviour of the participants or the nature of the outcome, whether the process utilised within a JCC is consultation, negotiation or a mixture of the two. Clearly, it is extremely difficult to divorce consultative discussions on work changes and efficiency from discussions of what such changes will mean in terms of the economic benefit to both management and employees.

Comparisons between joint consultation and collective bargaining invariably appear to rest on the **notion that both common interest and conflict are inherent elements of the management/employee relationship**

which need to be handled in different ways. With this in mind, Henderson suggested that 'negotiation is a means of reconciling divergent interests, consultation a means of promoting action where there are no obvious conflicts' [42]. However, McCarthy believed this contains an important and unacceptable paradox: namely, 'that management should only agree to share responsibility on controversial and conflicting subjects ... on non-controversial and common interest issues ... it cannot do more than consult' and 'that agreements are only possible when the two sides are basically opposed; when they are really united there cannot be any question of an agreement' [43]. A more realistic approach is to accept that every aspect of the employment relationship has the potential for conflict. The distinction between joint consultation and collective bargaining is therefore concerned with the formal identification of those aspects of the employment relationship in which this conflict should be legitimised and subject to joint agreement by inclusion within the process of collective bargaining.

Clearly, the balance between joint consultation and collective bargaining changes as employees and trade unions expand the scope of collective bargaining and the basic conflictual nature of the employment relationship becomes more recognised. This led McCarthy to comment, in the 1960s, that JCCs must 'change their character and become essentially negotiating committees ... or they are boycotted by shop stewards ... and fall into disuse' [44], and Hawkins to note, in the late 1970s, that 'the atmosphere of consultation must remain as non-controversial as possible to preserve the fiction that there is no real conflict of interest' [45]. However, because of the ambiguity of the process used within JCCs, it is difficult to identify the extent to which there has been any change, if at all, in their character. Certainly, McCarthy's view appears to be challenged by recent surveys of workplace industrial relations. Daniel and Millward found that the existence of JCCs is closely allied to the existence of union recognition and collective bargaining [46] and both they and Brown found that employee representatives on approximately half of the JCCs were selected via the union or its members. This led Brown to comment that the 'degree of recognition afforded to shop stewards is unlikely to be threatened by the introduction of consultation' [47].

Singleton noted that the difficulty in determining the precise relationship between joint consultation and collective bargaining arises 'not in recognising that there are two processes but in trying to draw a sharp line between them emphasised through different institutional arrangements' [48]. Nowhere is this more evident than on the question of who should be the **employee representatives.** In a situation where joint consultation is perceived as being an entirely separate process and institution from collective bargaining (one which is concerned primarily with management consulting its employee), then there is a strong argument that employee representatives need not be related directly to any trade union role and any employee, whether a union member or not, may both participate in the election of employee representatives and offer him/herself as a candidate for election. Employee representatives in the collective bargaining process and institution are, however, drawn exclusively from the ranks of trade union members and are there to represent both their members and their union as an organisation. Therefore, if joint consultation and collective bargaining are seen as overlapping processes and institutions often dealing with the same matters but at different stages, then it is necessary to ensure at least a degree of commonality on the employees' side of the two institutions. Without some formal confirmation of the union's role within the consultative institution there is always the danger that management might use, or be perceived by the union and employees to use, joint consultation as a method of avoiding having to negotiate with the union. However, whilst their presence in both institutions may mean a constant pressure for the transfer of items from the consultative institution to the collective bargaining institution, it should also ensure a more co-ordinated and coherent transfer when the need does arise.

The separation of joint consultation from collective bargaining is also often attempted by simply excluding from its **subject matter** any item which normally is a subject of negotiation. Inevitably this means that if the scope of collective bargaining expands, which has been the case in the past, then the scope of joint consultation must reduce. The result can be the creation of what may be termed the 'car park, canteen and toilet syndrome'. In other words, JCCs, which were intended to provide an avenue for management to consult its employees, become relegated to the role of a minor grievance forum and a communication vehicle for management to disclose general information about the state of the organisation. However, Daniel and Millward found that both managers and employee representatives regarded production, employment and pay issues as the most important items discussed within JCCs and that 'very few consultative committees discussed nothing of substance' [49]. This suggests a significant revival of joint consultation during the 1970s.

Models of joint consultation

Joint consultation may be regarded as:

1. a means either to defer the growth and recognition of trade unions or to restrict the range of collective bargaining;
2. a development phase between initial trade union recognition and full negotiating rights; or
3. a process which may continue alongside, and complementary to, the collective bargaining process.

Marchington and Armstrong [50] argue that the belief that, during the 1980s, there has been overall either a 'revitalisation' or 'marginalisation' of joint consultation is too simplistic. The realities of the way joint consultation is operated suggests four different models:

1. **The non-union model.** Here the main objective of the JCC is to avoid employee dissatisfaction from arising (and the need for union representation) and creating a closer identification with the organisation by informing employee representatives of the organisation's position (as seen by management) and persuading them that management's decisions are 'right'. However, as Marchington points out, the establishment of such an employee forum 'may eventually lead to an increasing awareness of ambiguities and contradictions, and perhaps its ultimate demise' [51] – it may become the means by which employees identify and develop interests distinct from management's and provide the basis for the future development of unionism and collective bargaining.

2. **The marginal model.** In this model, joint consultation consists of relatively trivial items presented in a bland way with the JCC having little role in decision making or even making recommendations. Marchington and Armstrong believe that this marginalisation of joint consultation arises because 'employers feel less need to consult with employees in any meaningful way since management control is enhanced in a recession' [52]. However, as Marchington points out, it may be difficult to actually abandon joint consultation because of the 'considerable symbolic value attached to the consultative committee, and its continuation is taken as a measure of management commitment to the workforce' [53] but, at the same time, the marginalisation of joint consultation reduces any need to abandon it. This model may be associated with either strong collective bargaining because trade unionism is strong or equally a weakening of collective bargaining where management has the power advantage.

3. **The competitive model.** This involves the 'revitalisation' of joint consultation with more emphasis on high-level information and discussion of the organisation's current and future situation combined with the development of various direct forms of employee involvement (team briefings, etc.). Through this, Marchington argues, 'militant expressions of trade unionism can be constrained by a more knowledgeable workforce' and the JCC can be used 'to persuade stewards to adopt a more moderate and supportive perspective towards the company' [54]. Management will seek to keep consultation and collective bargaining distinct from each other whilst enhancing the content of consultation.

4. **The adjunct model.** In this model, sometimes referred to as the 'advanced' form of consultation, informing, consulting and negotiating are integrally linked together in the process of handling industrial relations within the organisation; although it may still, perhaps, retain some distinction between negotiating focusing on distributive issues/

approaches whilst consultation focuses on more integrative issues/approaches. Marchington believes that joint consultation is 'seen to be a key part of the representative institutions . . . to play a part in company issues and to help lubricate relations in a more informal and less highly charged atmosphere than that of annual negotiations or dispute resolution' [55].

Organisational arrangement of joint consultation

Whilst the process of joint consultation may be applied without any formal institutional structure, there are a number of **advantages in establishing formal joint consultative machinery:**

1. It may help to overcome the organisational complexity of many enterprises which tends to hinder the operation of informal means of consultation – particularly between employees and senior management.
2. It should facilitate the processing of issues which are of general application and which otherwise would have to be handled by each manager individually with his/her subordinates – a procedure which would be time consuming, cumbersome and, most importantly, subject to possible variation in its treatment.
3. Through regular meetings and the publication of minutes it ensures that joint consultation is accorded a proper place in the organisational system and confirms management's commitment and responsibility to consultation with its employees.

The establishment of such formal structures is perhaps most necessary within organisations which do not have trade unions or where trade unionism is weak; but even then, Henderson points out, management should be aware of the potential 'limitations of a committee in which employee representatives do not have the independence and authority of responsible trade union backing' [56]. The same caution is also applicable where, even though there is strong trade unionism and collective bargaining within the organisation, management seeks to maintain a clear separation of the two processes, institutions and subject matter and insists on employee representatives for the joint consultative machinery being drawn from the ranks of all employees irrespective of their union membership.

The first stage in establishing or developing joint consultative machinery is to determine its **aim, function and level of operation.** In doing this, it is important to have regard not only to the size and organisational arrangement of the enterprise but also the nature of collective bargaining (see Figure 10.2). In this latter respect the organisation may adopt either of two broad approaches. It can, because of a perceived limited range of issues which do not involve negotiation, combine the two processes within the negotiating

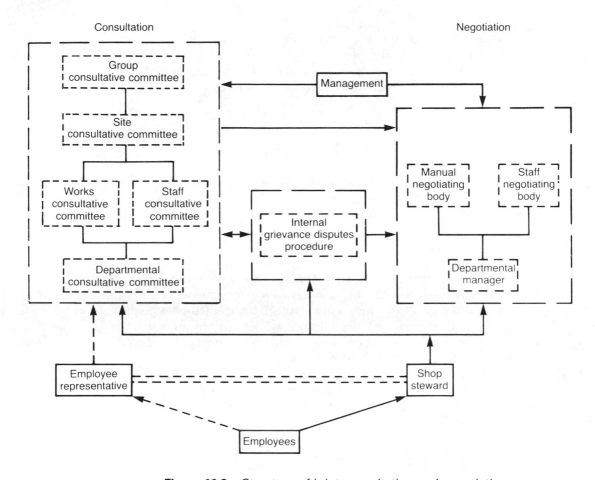

Consultation   Negotiation

Figure 10.2 *Structure of joint consultation and negotiation*

machinery. Alternatively, it can maintain separate institutions of joint consultation and negotiation and, at the same time, expand the scope of employee involvement through the joint consultative machinery without the need to formally conceded that these issues are subject to joint determination.

Assuming that there are two sets of machinery, then the **terms of reference** of the JCC need to be specified by a combination of defining its subject matter and the nature of its authority. The **subject matter** may be identified in terms of:

1. excluding from its deliberation anything which is subject to negotiation (by which is generally meant terms and conditions of employment but

which may in fact include a much wider range of issues which are normally discussed and agreed between management and union representatives at both the organisational and departmental levels);

2. setting out a positive list of the items which are to be regarded as matters for joint consultation (for example, production plans, quality and elimination of waste); or

3. predefining nothing and simply deciding on an *ad hoc* basis whether and when an issue should be dealt with more properly in the collective bargaining machinery. (This can, of course, only be used where shop stewards are formally represented within the JCC and able to ensure that there is no management abuse of this privilege.)

The **level of authority** vested in the JCCs may be either purely advisory to management's decision making or it may have, in effect, a delegated authority from management to make decisions. In this latter situation, any decision made by the committee may be considered binding on management and therefore the process utilised within its working is likely to be much closer to negotiation than consultation.

The **organisation** of JCCs tends to reflect the hierarchy of the enterprise with committees at departmental to group level. Quite often the differentiation between manual and non-manual employees seen within the negotiating machinery is also reflected within the consultative machinery. The effective strength of joint consultation lies, in the first place, at the bottom of this pyramid where employees are involved in areas of decision making with which they are familiar, can make a contribution and which have perhaps the greatest impact on their working lives. Nevertheless, the higher levels of committee are also important in that they provide an opportunity for the discussion of broader strategic and policy issues and the establishment of a framework for the operation of the departmental committees.

The work of all these committees is usually conducted on a fairly **formal basis**. The chair is normally, at the departmental level, the department manager and, at the site level, a senior manager or the personnel manager. In some organisations the role rotates on a yearly basis between a management representative and an employee representative elected by the committee members. Formal minutes of the committee's meetings are published and should set out both the items which have been discussed and any action which has been recommended. These minutes also serve as a means of reporting the activities of one committee to another. It is neither necessary nor usual (unless the committee has a decision making role) for there to be equal numbers of management and employee representatives because management has an implied right of veto. It is quite usual for management to co-opt additional management representatives as and when their specialist contribution is required.

Finally, it should be remembered that formal joint consultation is an **indirect method of employee participation** in management decision making.

There is a need, particularly on the employee side but also on the management side, to ensure that there are adequate links between the representatives who are discussing the issues within the committee and the people they are there to represent. The agenda must be known in advance so that, on the employee side, the representatives may discuss the issues with, and obtain the views of, the employees who will not be present at the meeting. At the same time management has the same need to discuss the issues, particularly with supervisory management, in order to present a corporate view on the matters to be discussed. After the committee meeting there is then a need to reverse the process and report back details of the discussion and any outcome that has resulted. It is only in this way that joint consultation can be meaningful to the mass of employees as well as to the few who are members of such committees.

10.4 Summary propositions

- Improved communications between management and employees/unions will not, of itself, solve problems; it can only provide a means for them to gain a better understanding of each other.
- 'Disclosure of information' to trade unions in support of collective bargaining has been complemented, but in some organisations replaced, by 'dissemination of information' to employees as part of a process of seeking greater employee identification with and commitment to the interests of the organisation.
- The institutions of joint consultation and collective bargaining do not automatically differentiate the processes of 'consultation' and 'negotiation'.

Further reading

- R. Hussey and A. Marsh, *Disclosure of Information and Employee Reporting*, Gower, 1983. A very useful survey of both disclosure of information to trade unions and dissemination of information to employees.
- 'Disclosure of Information', *CIR Report 31*, HMSO, 1972.
  'Communications and Collective Bargaining', *CIR Report 39*, HMSO, 1973.
  'Disclosure of information to trade unions for collective bargaining purposes', *ACAS Code of Practice 2*, HMSO, 1977.
  These pamphlets provide a useful discussion of the problems involved in disclosing information to trade unions and employees.

- J. Henderson, 'The case for joint consultation', *Industrial Society*, 1970.
  J. Henderson, 'A practical guide to joint consultation', *Industrial Society*, 1970.
  These pamphlets examine both the issues involved in joint consultation and the practical steps that are needed for its successful operation.

References

1. 'Written evidence of the Ministry of Labour', *Royal Commission on Trade Unions and Employers' Associations* HMSO, 1965, p. 23.
2. H. A. Clegg and T. E. Chester, 'Joint consultation' in A. Flanders and H. A. Clegg (eds), *The System of Industrial Relations in Great Britain*, Blackwell, 1960, p. 325.
3. D. Torrington and J. Chapman, *Personnel Management* (2nd edn), Prentice Hall, 1983, p. 448.
4. N. Sear, 'Relationships at factory level' in B. C. Roberts (ed.), *Industrial Relations: Contemporary problems and persepctives*, Methuen, 1962, p. 163.
5. 'Communications and Collective Bargaining', *CIR Report 39*, HMSO, 1973, p. 2.
6. R. Hussey and A. Marsh, *Disclosure of Information and Employee Reporting*, Gower, 1982, p. 41.
7. D. Drennan, 'How to make the bad news less bad and the good news great', *Personnel Management*, August 1988, pp. 40–3.
8. D. Torrington and J. Chapman, *op. cit.*, p. 436.
9. R. Moore, 'Information to unions: use or abuse?', *Personnel Management*, May 1980, p. 34.
10. *ibid.*
11. L. Dickens, 'What are companies disclosing for the 1980s?' *Personnel Management*, April 1980, p. 28.
12. *ibid.*, pp. 29–30.
13. D. Torrington and J. Chapman, *op. cit.*, p. 442.
14. 'Disclosure of Information to Trade Unions for the Purpose of Collective Bargaining', *ACAS Code of Practice 2*, HMSO, 1977, pp. 3–4.
15. *ibid.*
16. *The Provision of Information to Employees: Guidelines for action*, CBI, 1975; *Industrial Democracy*, TUC, 1975.
17. R. Hussey and A. Marsh, *op. cit.*, pp. 17–33.
18. Central Arbitration Committee, *Annual Report 1979*.
19. 'CAC disclosure of information awards', *Industrial Relations Review and Report*, January 1980.
20. W. W. Daniel and N. Millward, *Workplace Industrial Relations in Britain*, Heinemann (PSI/SSRC), 1983, p. 152.
21. R. Moore, *op. cit.*, p. 37.
22. R. Hussey and A. Marsh, *op. cit.*, pp. 53–66.
23. *ibid.*, p. 60.
24. *ibid.*
25. T. K. Reeves, 'Information disclosure in employee relations', *Employee Relations*, vol. 2, no. 3, 1980.

26. R. Hussey and A. Marsh, *op. cit.*, p. 62.
27. *ibid.*, Table 7.2, p. 62.
28. *ibid.*, Table 12.2, p. 117.
29. *ibid.*, Table 12.3, p. 117.
30. *ibid.*, Table 10.4, p. 90.
31. M. Marchington and P. Wilding, 'Employee involvement inaction?' *Personnel Management*, December 1983, p. 35.
32. W. Brown (ed.), *The Changing Contours of British Industrial Relations*, Blackwell, 1981, Table 4.9(b), p. 78.
33. W. W. Daniel and N. Millward, *op. cit.*, Table VI.2, p. 130.
34. N. Millward and M. Stevens, *British Workplace Industrial Relations 1980–1984*, Gower, 1986, Table 6.1, p. 139.
35. A. Marsh, *Employee Relations Policy and Decision Making: A survey of manufacturing companies carried out for the CBI*, Gower, 1982, Table 5.5, p. 134.
36. P. Bassett, 'Consultation and the right to manage 1980–1984', *British Journal of Industrial Relations*, vol. 25, no. 2, 1987, pp. 283–6.
37. M. Marchington, 'A review and critique of research on developments in joint consultation', *British Journal of Industrial Relations*, vol. 25, no. 3, 1987, pp. 339–52.
38. *Communication and Consultation*, CBI, 1966.
39. J. Henderson, *The Case for Joint Consultation*, Industrial Society, 1970, p. 12.
40. H. A. Clegg and T. E. Chester, *op. cit.*, p. 324.
41. *Communications and Consultation*, CBI, 1966.
42. J. Henderson, *A Practical Guide to Joint Consultation*, Industrial Society, 1970, p. 4.
43. W. E. J. McCarthy, 'The Role of Shop Stewards in British Industrial Relations', Research Paper 1, *Royal Commission on Trade Unions and Employers' Associations*, HMSO, 1966, p. 36.
44. *ibid.*
45. K. Hawkins, *A Handbook of Industrial Relations Practice*, Kogan Page, 1979, p. 40.
46. W. W. Daniel and N. Millward, *op. cit.*, Table VI.4, p. 135 and Table VI.5, p. 136.
47. W. Brown, *op. cit.*, p. 178.
48. N. Singleton, 'Industrial Relations Procedures', *Department of Employment, Manpower Paper 14*, HMSO, 1975, p. 11.
49. W. W. Daniel and N. Millward, *op. cit.*, p. 139.
50. M. Marchington and R. Armstrong, 'The nature of the new joint consultation', *Industrial Relations Journal*, vol. 17, no. 2, 1986, pp. 158–70.
51. M. Marchington, 'The four faces of employee consultation', *Personnel Management*, May 1988, p. 45.
52. M. Marchington and R. Armstrong, *op. cit.*, p. 160.
53. M. Marchington *op. cit.*, p. 47.
54. *ibid.*, p. 46.
55. *ibid.*, p. 47.
56. J. Henderson, *A Practical Guide to Joint Consultation*, *op. cit.*, p. 4.

Chapter 11

Collective bargaining

11.1 Definition

Collective bargaining, which Flanders argued 'could more appropriately be called joint regulation' [1], has been described by Dubin as 'the great social invention that has institutionalized industrial conflict' [2] and by the Donovan Commission as 'a right which is or should be the prerogative of every worker in a democratic society' [3]. It may be defined as a:

> **method of determining terms and conditions of employment which utilises the process of negotiation and agreement between representatives of management and employees.**

Certainly it occupies a central position in British industrial relations. Despite the changing economic circumstances and decreased union membership and power during the 1980s, collective bargaining is still important for a high proportion of both manual and non-manual employees in all sectors (see Table 11.1). However, the apparent increase between 1980 and 1984 in the proportion of all establishments reporting collective bargaining as being the basis for the most recent pay increase (Table 11.1(b)) is misleading and resulted from structural changes in the economy and the consequent change in the relative proportions of manufacturing and public sector establishments within the survey (collective bargaining is much more prevalent in the public sector than in the private sector). More significantly, within private manufacturing, whilst the proportion of establishments reporting collective bargaining as being the basis of the most recent pay increase decreased from 65 per cent to 55 per cent for manual workers and remained at about a quarter for non-manual employees, the proportion of employees covered by collective bargaining remained high at nearly 80 per cent of manual employees and 60 per cent of non-manual employees. This is because collective bargaining is more likely to be a feature of larger rather than smaller establishments; indeed, in 1984 over 80 per cent of establishments in

Table 11.1   *The extent of collective bargaining*

(a) Proportion of employees affected by collective bargaining

	Manual		Non-manual	
	Male (%)	Female (%)	Male (%)	Female (%)
Manufacturing	79	72	45	48
Non-manufacturing (including public sector)	77	68	65	70

Source: ACAS, *Industrial Relations Handbook*, HMSO, 1980 (Appendix 1).

(b) Collective bargaining basis of most recent pay increase

	Manual		Non-manual	
	1980 (%)	1984 (%)	1980 (%)	1984 (%)
Proportion of all establishments	55	62	47	54
Private manufacturing:				
Proportion of establishments	65	55	27	26
Proportion of employees	84	79	63	59
Private services:				
Proportion of establishments	34	38	28	30
Proportion of employees	53	53	37	40

Source: N. Millward and M. Stevens, *British Workplace Industrial Relations 1980–1984*, Gower, 1986 (Tables 9.1, 9.3, 9.4, 9.9 and 9.10).

private manufacturing with more than 100 manual employees (or over 200 in the case of non-manual employees) reported that pay for these groups was determined by collective bargaining in one form or another [4]. The figures also, perhaps surprisingly, show a significant role for collective bargaining in private service industries with the pay of over a half of manual employees and 40 per cent of non-manual employees being determined by collective bargaining.

11.2 The nature of collective bargaining

The essential characteristic of collective bargaining, the Donovan Commission noted, is that 'employees do not negotiate individually, and on their own behalf, but do so collectively through representatives' [5]. Clearly, therefore, collective bargaining can exist and function only if:

1. the employees themselves are prepared to identify a commonality of purpose, organise and act in concert; and
2. management is prepared to recognise their organisation and accept a change in the employment relationship which removes, or at least constrains, its ability to deal with employees on an individual basis.

The collective bargaining process provides a **formal channel through which the differing interests of management and employees may be resolved on a collective basis.**

The legislative framework

The law, in respect of the **individual contract of employment**, is based primarily on nineteenth century *laissez-faire* concepts and, Aikin and Reid argue, makes two fundamental assumptions about the nature of the contract of employment:

1. that it 'has been arrived at by two parties of equal bargaining strength'; and
2. that it is 'intended to bind only those two individuals' [6].

However, these assumptions are questionable for the majority of employees.

The contract of employment is not a simple personal contract between two individuals but is a contract between an individual and a corporate entity which has its own legal existence independent of the managers who are, at any point in time, its current controllers. An individual employee cannot, by any criteria, be regarded as having equal bargaining power to that of the employing organisation. Indeed, this imbalance is reflected in the asymmetric nature of the rights and obligations of the two parties established under the common law [7]. The variable terms of the contract of employment (that is, the terms specifically detailed in the contract which are in addition to any unwritten but universal terms implied by the common law) are not arrived at by agreement between the individual employee and his/her 'employer'. In practice, they are simply transferred into the contract of employment from a collective agreement which has been negotiated and agreed between representatives of management and union and which is intended to be applied to all employees who come within the designated group. Certainly, Wedderburn argues that 'the ordinary worker scarcely recognizes his individual contract of employment . . . but he will frequently be sharply aware of an agreement between his union and the employer' [8].

Nevertheless, there has been a shift during the 1980s towards the development of individual contracts, particularly amongst managers and some professional/technical groups, involving appraisal and performance rewards as integral parts of this individualisation process.

Despite its role as a central activity of the industrial relations system, collective bargaining is perhaps most noted for its **lack of legal regulation**. In Britain, unlike the USA and other countries, there is no legal requirement on the employer either to recognise a trade union for collective bargaining purposes or, having recognised a trade union, to 'bargain in good faith'. Nor, apart from a short period under the Industrial Relations Act (1971–1974), have collective agreements been regarded as contracts capable of legal enforcement between the signatory parties – the employer and union. The legal position of collective agreements was clearly set out in 1969: 'The fact that the agreements prima facie deal with commercial relationships is outweighed by the other considerations, by the wording of the agreements, by the nature of the agreements, and by the climate of opinion ... Agreements such as these, composed largely of optimistic aspirations, presenting grave practical problems of enforcement and reached against a background of opinion adverse to enforceability, are ... not contracts in the legal sense and are not enforceable at law ... they remain in the realm of undertakings binding in honour' [9].

Even during the brief incursion of the Industrial Relations Act in the early 1970s, when there was a statutory presumption that collective agreements were legally enforceable contracts, employers were prepared to acquiesce to union demands for the inclusion of a specific clause within the collective agreement stating that it was not to be regarded as a legally enforceable contract. It is only, therefore, through the express or implied incorporation of the collective agreement into the individual contract of employment that there is any legal basis for enforcing the terms of a collective agreement. It is this lack of external legal regulation, in respect of collective bargaining and the collective agreement, which has given rise to the notion of **voluntary collective bargaining**.

However, the issue of **whether or not collective agreements should be legally enforceable** is still relevant in the overall context of the legal framework surrounding industrial relations [10]. There appear to be four main **advantages** claimed for the legal enforcement of collective agreements:

1. Collective agreements would have to become both more comprehensive and more precise in defining the rights and obligations of each party if their meaning and intent is to be capable of legal interpretation should the need arise.
2. It would put pressure on union officials, as representatives of one of the signatory parties, to use their best endeavours to ensure that their members complied with the terms of the agreement – particularly the 'no strike' clause contained within the Grievance/Dispute procedure. This, it

is anticipated, would reduce the incidence of unconstitutional or unofficial strikes.

3. It would allow management to manage the organisation secure in the knowledge that once an agreement had been concluded, for example on the introduction of new work methods, its terms would be adhered to.

4. It would induce a long-term attitudinal change in industrial relations which could result in employees benefiting by increased wages and greater job security.

Whilst it is difficult, if not impossible, to prove or disprove the last claimed advantage, there is little doubt that a number of **problems** exist in respect of the others.

● *What constitutes a collective agreement?* It would appear, from the first claimed advantage, that all collective agreements are assumed to be formal written documents whereas in practice, as Wedderburn points out, the term 'can refer to anything from a resolution of a JIC down through district or company agreements to "practice" arranged on the shop floor' [11]. Whilst undoubtedly the process of collective bargaining has become more formalised at the organisation level, nevertheless many arrangements (agreements) are still made between managers and shop stewards in respect of operational situations at the departmental or workgroup level. It would be extremely difficult and time consuming to ensure that all these arrangements are written down in sufficient detail to allow for legal interpretation and, therefore, would tend to remain outside the scope of the law. This would result in a two tier system of collective agreements.

● *What is the purpose of establishing the collective agreement itself as a legal contract directly enforceable between the signatory parties (union(s) and management or Employers' Association)?* The terms of a collective agreement are indirectly enforceable between management and employee through their incorporation into the individual contract of employment. Since it is management which most often argues in favour of the legal enforceability of collective agreements, it would appear that its primary purpose is to make trade unions, as organisations, liable to a legal penalty (injunction and/or damages) if they seek officially to act contrary to the terms of the collective agreement or do not disassociate themselves from such unofficial actions by their members. However, collective bargaining is a dynamic process – many terms of a collective agreement need to be interpreted, clarified or redefined as circumstances change or a new situation is encountered which was unforseen at the time the collective agreement was negotiated. In such situations a legal requirement to maintain the existing term would inhibit the trade union's ability to renegotiate and/or require the courts to determine whether or not the situation had changed sufficiently to make the existing term inapplicable. Inherent in the notion of legal enforceability of collective agreements is the need to determine the boundary between maintaining an existing term and redefining the term (negotiation).

● *What effect will it have on strike activity?* Drawing on the American experience, it has been recognised that 'legally enforceable collective agreements do not necessarily mean that fewer days are lost because of strikes, but strikes tend to be concentrated in the period of renegotiation of the agreement' [12]. The legal enforcement of collective agreements may, at best, do little more than encourage more prolonged disputes.

The functions of collective bargaining

The term 'collective bargaining' was originally used by the Webbs [13] to identify **one method whereby trade unions could maintain and improve their members' terms and conditions of employment.** Their analytical framework, derived from observation of trade union activity in the late nineteenth century, viewed trade unions primarily as a form of labour cartel which sought to redress the imbalance in the labour market indirectly by restricting employee competition for work through control of the number of entrants (apprentices) and directly by regulating the price of labour. From their observations they identified three major categories of trade union activity:

1. **mutual insurance** (the provision of friendly society benefits in the event of sickness, unemployment, industrial action, etc.);
2. **collective bargaining** (the negotiation of terms and conditions of employment direct with employers on behalf of their members); and
3. **legal enactment** (the lobbying for legislation supportive to their members' interests).

At a minimal level mutual insurance could, even without any acceptance of collective bargaining by the employer, provide trade union members with a limited capacity to withstand impositions or pressures from the employer. However, the real power of trade unionism lay in replacing individual bargaining by collective bargaining. Through collective bargaining employees could achieve better terms because the employer could not take advantage of the individual's differing personal circumstances and needs. Nevertheless, collective bargaining was to be viewed only as a transient phenomenon. As trade union membership and power increased, and the working classes achieved a more influential position within society, so the emphasis would shift from mutual insurance through collective bargaining to a system of statutory regulation. Ultimately, the employees' terms and conditions of employment would depend not on their variable industrial power to force satisfactory terms from an employer but on a wider and more uniform social, political and legal acceptance and enforcement of these rights on their behalf.

More modern writers, however, have concentrated on collective bargaining as a **process of interaction between management and union.** Flanders, in his critique of the Webbs [14], argued that the use of the word 'bargaining' was misleading and that collective bargaining should more properly be regarded as a **method of job regulation, distinguished from others by the joint authorship of the rules it produced.** His objections to the Webbs' view, which in turn have been criticised by Fox [15], centred on two interrelated areas.

1. The collective bargaining process is neither equivalent nor an alternative to individual bargaining. In Flanders' view, an inherent element in the process of bargaining is its culmination in some act of exchange – in this case an exchange between work on the part of the employee and wages on the part of the employer. Collective bargaining, however, does not involve the actual sale or hire of labour as an active part of the process; this still remains a matter for determination on an individual basis between the employer and the potential employee. Whilst Fox has criticised this differentiation of individual and collective bargaining on the grounds that 'individual bargaining' also need not result in an exchange if the proposed terms are considered to be unsatisfactory by either party, this does not detract from Flanders' central argument that the collective agreement is 'a body of rules intended to regulate . . . the terms of employment contracts', that 'collective bargaining is itself essentially a rule-making process' and, therefore, it is 'more correct to refer to collective bargaining as regulating, rather than replacing, individual bargaining' [16]. Despite its regular renegotiation, the collective agreement has a permanent existence within the organisational system independent of the individuals who are its employees and any potential employee is, in practice, unable to vary its terms in respect of his/her individual contract of employment.

2. The process of negotiation in collective bargaining cannot, Flanders argued, be equated to any process of labour market bargaining at an individual level. Negotiation is, in reality, a pressure group activity and the resultant collective agreements are, therefore, 'compromise settlements of power conflicts' [17]. In this context, the strike should not be regarded as the collective equivalent of the individual's refusal to accept employment, or resignation from employment, when the terms of employment are not satisfactory. At the individual level it is assumed that if an employee is not satisfied he/she will seek work elsewhere on a permanent basis, whilst at the collective level it is assumed that the strike is only 'a temporary refusal to work in accordance with the prevailing employment contracts . . . combined with the firm intent, at least on the part of the great majority of workers involved, of not terminating their

contracts' [18]. However, Fox believed that the process of individual bargaining also utilised power in the determination of the terms of the contract but that the extent of the power disparity between the parties was obviously much greater than in collective bargaining and almost exclusively in favour of the employer. It was this obvious power disparity which precluded any expectation on the part of the employee that an improved offer from the employer could be secured and led the dissatisfied employee to seek alternative work – it was the only realistic avenue open to relieve dissatisfaction.

Clearly, as Harbinson noted, the important difference between individual and collective bargaining lies in the fact that the latter 'is strictly a relationship between organisations' [19] and therefore an indirect regulation of the relationship between management and employee. It may, as both Fox and Flanders agree, be viewed as a political process encompassing more than just economic issues and may be contrasted with other rule making processes which have different sources of authority: **unilateral regulation** (by management, employees or union) and **state regulation** (by legislation or government policy).

Chamberlain and Kuhn have suggested that collective bargaining serves a number of distinct functions; each emphasising a different concept of the process and a different stage in its development:

1. A **market or economic function** wherein it 'determines on what terms labour will continue to be supplied to a company by its present employees or will be supplied in the future by newly hired workers' [20]. In this context the collective agreement may be regarded as a formal contract and the grievance procedure as a non-legal means for ensuring the employer's compliance with its terms. The process is primarily concerned with determining the substantive terms on which people are to be employed.

2. A **governmental function** in which collective bargaining may be regarded as principally a political process based 'on the mutual dependency of the parties and . . . the power of each to "veto" the acts of the other' [21]. The bargaining relationship may, using a political analogy, be viewed as a continuing 'constitution' in which the collective agreement is a body of law, determined by the management/union negotiators as the legislature, and executive authority is vested in management who must exercise it in accordance with the terms of the constitution. The grievance procedure is available both as a judicial process, to deal with any differences in respect of interpretation and application of the law or the exercise of executive authority, and as a supplementary legislative process, to agree on issues not covered by the collective agreement. The content of collective bargaining is concerned as much with procedural issues and the distribution of power and authority as it is with substantive issues and the distribution of money.

3. A **decision making function** which 'allows workers, through their union representatives, to participate in the determination of the policies which guide and rule their working lives' [22]. The collective agreement is, in effect, a formal memorandum of the decisions that have been reached and is a limitation on management's freedom and discretion to act unilaterally. The grievance procedure forms an integral part of the joint decision making process and the distinction between matters of right and matters of interest is blurred. The concept of mutuality, which underlies this view of collective bargaining, recognises that 'authority over men requires consent' and 'involves defining areas of joint concern within which decisions must be sought by agreement' [23]. The extent to which collective bargaining may function in this more organic and flexible manner is largely dependent on:
   (a) the desire of the employees and their unions to be involved in such decision making;
   (b) the degree to which they have power, if necessary, to force the employer to accept such joint decision making; and
   (c) the degree to which management is willing to accept the requirement that its decisions must be subject to agreement with employees before they may be implemented.

These differing views of collective bargaining are not mutually exclusive and most negotiations contain elements of all three. Whilst the broad function of collective bargaining is to establish, in respect of both substantive and procedural terms, a **common rule** for a defined group of employees on a jointly agreed basis, it must also allow for **diversity and variation** if it is to cope with the uniqueness of each industrial relations situation.

The collective bargaining relationship

Whilst conflict of interest between management and employees forms an inherent part of their relationship and provides the input into the collective bargaining process, the collective bargaining relationship itself is founded on their **mutual dependence**. Both parties need to reach an agreement or solution to their differences. The freedom not to reach an agreement can only exist if both parties have a viable alternative. If only one party has such an alternative then the other, because of its necessity to reach an agreement, has no bargaining strength and must therefore settle on whatever terms are offered. It has been argued that, in modern industrialised societies, neither management nor employees have such viable alternatives – employees, as a collective body, are unable or not prepared to relinquish their employment and seek other work, and the employer cannot quickly and easily replace a part of his workforce. However, the perception of the degree of mutual dependence may vary; for example, management's perception of its dependence on its existing workforce may decrease at times of high unemployment. Nevertheless, the initial intention of both management and employees at the commencement of any negotiation is to reach a satisfactory resolution of their differences and maintain their employment relationship.

It is this absolute requirement to achieve some form of agreement in order to maintain the employment relationship and the organisation's operations which led Chamberlain and Kuhn to use the term **conjunctive bargaining** to refer to situations where 'the parties agree to terms as a result of mutual coercion and arrive at a truce only because they are indispensable to each other' [24]. The use, or threatened use, of coercion is a dominant feature of such bargaining and the terms of the resultant agreement are dependent on the relative bargaining power of the two parties. The relationship between the parties is such that the minimum co-operation needed to reach, and maintain, the agreement is generally regarded also as the maximum desired co-operation.

Collective bargaining cannot proceed beyond this level, to what Chamberlain and Kuhn referred to as **co-operative bargaining**, unless both parties accept that 'neither will gain additional advantages unless the other gains too' [25]. The dominant feature of this collective bargaining approach is the willingness of the parties to make concessions in order to achieve objectives which would not otherwise have been possible. This does not imply that the two parties are pursuing a single common interest but that their different interests are more capable of achievement if each is prepared to allow the other to move towards its objective. For example, productivity bargaining allows management to improve productivity and efficiency and employees to obtain higher pay and possibly greater job security. These two approaches **equate to the distributive and integrative bargaining models** put forward by Walton and McKersie [26]. Distributive bargaining reflects a basic conflict between the parties over the division of some limited resource (e.g. pay and profits) and may be equated to a fixed-sum game wherein one side's gain is the other side's loss. Integrative bargaining reflects a greater commonality of perception and acceptance of the issue to be resolved and results in a problem solving approach or varying-sum game wherein the parties, by co-operation, can increase the value of the resource to be distributed between them.

It would appear, on the surface, that conjunctive bargaining should be abandoned in favour of co-operative bargaining. However, the **transition from conjunctive bargaining to co-operative bargaining involves perceived dangers** for both sides:

1. It requires management to be willing to extend the scope of collective bargaining into areas where trade unions and employees wish to have influence but where management may be reluctant to give up its prerogative.
2. Equally, it requires trade unions to enter into joint agreements with

management in areas where they have previously preferred to reserve their right to challenge management after the decision has been made.

3. It can lead to an increasing divorcement between employees and their representatives if trade union negotiators are perceived as apologists for, and an adjunct of, management.

4. Perhaps least likely, it can result in a diminution of the trade union function within the organisation as management becomes more aware of, and sympathetic to, the employees' interests.

5. Perhaps most importantly, it may be argued that co-operative bargaining cannot be maintained on a permanent basis because eventually it will become perceived as conjunctive bargaining. The principle of co-operation will itself become an expected feature of all negotiations and the minimum basis on which one, or both, of the parties will be prepared to conclude an agreement. It may even reach the stage where coercion, the primary ingredient of conjunctive bargaining, is used in order to secure 'co-operation'.

It is therefore better to view the two approaches as being complementary aspects of any negotiation rather than as two distinct forms – one desirable and the other undesirable.

However, the desirability of a more co-operative approach to the bargaining relationship and an expansion of its joint decision making function has been forcibly argued by McCarthy and Ellis [27]. In their view, management in every organisation is continually faced by two challenges:

1. the challenge from within the organisation derived from increased employee expectations in both monetary and managerial terms; and

2. the challenge from outside the organisation derived from a variety of factors but principally market competition and the need for technological change.

Management should not, in their opinion, respond to the latter by attempting to suppress the former through an authoritarian style of management. Rather they should pursue a policy of **management by agreement** where decision making authority would be 'shared with workers through an extension of the area of joint regulation' and 'unions would have the right to seek to influence management policy in *any* area' [28]. The principal effect of adopting this approach would be to 'change the emphasis of bargaining from recriminations over the past to planning for the future' [29]. The content of collective bargaining would, through the development of what they term **predictive bargaining**, shift from claims, disputes and grievances arising from the actions or non-actions of either party (but principally management) to future problems which are likely to affect the employment relationship and which, if not previously catered for, could be the source of formal disputes between them.

Whilst such a joint problem solving approach is conducive to the development of a co-operative bargaining relationship, McCarthy and Ellis also clearly accept that it will not automatically result in an absence of conjunctive bargaining and its associated use of coercive power. They recognise that there are **limitations to the concept** of management by agreement and that 'the right of ultimate recourse to unilateral action on the part of either party is derived from a frank admission that there are major and at times irreconcilable differences between management and workers'. Consequently 'workers must have the right, in the end, to determine how far they are prepared to modify their demands as a result of taking into account what are essentially management problems' and 'similar rights must also be permitted to management' [30]. However, they believe that the atmosphere created by a changed relationship between the parties could induce a greater acceptance of the use of external conciliation or mediation to resolve their differences rather than resorting to the use of industrial power.

It is clear from these views of the bargaining relationship that it is to be regarded, even in its most co-operative form, as a **bipartite process** which, Flanders noted, makes no 'provision for bringing to light and safeguarding the public interest in the results of collective bargaining' [31]. The primacy of management and employees reaching any agreement which they believe to be to their joint benefit is implied in the acceptance of the voluntary nature of the collective bargaining process. The **public interest**, which is in practice indefinable, has to be assumed to be demonstrated through government policy or legislation. However, government intrusion into the direct collective bargaining process between management and union, for example to influence or legally regulate the level of pay increases, acts as an external constraint on the two negotiating parties rather than as an active participation of a third party in the negotiating process. In most negotiations the notion of public interest forms a subjective element of the negotiating arguments and not a distinct and separate interest which has to be reconciled with the other two before an agreement may be reached. If a wage agreement in one organisation or industry, which is acceptable to the parties concerned, is likely to result in 'excessive' comparability claims elsewhere, it has to be resisted by the managements within the other organisations and industries and not by a self-imposed restriction on the part of the initial negotiators for the good of others. The involvement of the public interest in the collective bargaining process, on a continuing basis, would require a fundamental change in the nature of the process.

However, within the **public sector** the bipartite nature of the collective bargaining process is, to varying degrees, distorted by the special role occupied by government. Whilst in the civil service the government is itself the management, and therefore nominally the bipartite nature of collective bargaining is maintained, nevertheless the objectives and strategy of the 'management' in its conduct of negotiations are significantly influenced by what the 'management' believe is appropriate in the wider public interest –

the government, as an employer, must set an example which will influence and be followed by others. In other parts of the public sector the government may be regarded primarily as a third party, able to inject the public interest through its participation in the management determination of its negotiating strategy or through its role as paymaster. The public interest, as defined through government policy, is a continual ingredient in public sector collective bargaining.

11.3 The institutions of collective bargaining

Perhaps one of the most noticeable features of the British system of industrial relations is that there is **no single uniform structure of collective bargaining** – rather, it is characterised by its variety [32]. This variety arises from differences in respect of four aspects of the collective bargaining structure [33]:

1. Collective bargaining may be **conducted at different levels** within the industrial relations system ranging from the national or industry level, through the regional or district level to the organisational level. It is quite common for the employee's terms and conditions of employment to contain elements from more than one collective agreement. An industry level agreement may provide only a framework, specifying minimum substantive terms or leaving certain terms to be determined locally, and therefore will be supplemented by agreements made at the organisational level.
2. There is **variation in the coverage of the bargaining units** (the group of employees to be covered by a particular collective agreement). In one organisation or industry all manual workers may be covered by the same collective agreement whilst in another organisation or industry different categories of manual workers may have their own separate agreements.
3. The **form of collective bargaining may vary** from a very formal approach involving precise and comprehensive written agreements to a more informal approach relying on unwritten understandings.
4. The **scope of collective bargaining** may be restricted to the main substantive terms of wages, hours, etc., or expanded to encompass a wide range of procedural and managerial issues.

National multi-employer bargaining

The term **national or industry agreement** generally refers to a multi-employer agreement which covers employees of a given description within a specified industry or sub-industry. It is important to remember that no industry has a single national agreement covering all employees: the collective bargaining institutions, and the resultant collective agreements, are generally segmented on a sub-industry and/or occupational basis. Although national agreements are intended to cover only those organisations within the industry that are members of the Employers' Association which has negotiated the agreement, nevertheless many organisations which are not members of the Association also apply the terms of the agreement as an alternative to negotiating their own collective agreements. However, the non-federated organisation, and its employees, do not have access to any disputes procedures which have been negotiated between the Employers' Association and the trade unions for resolving differences relating to the interpretation and application of the national agreement.

It is possible to identify three main categories of multi-employer collective bargaining institutions: **statutory, formal voluntary** and *ad hoc*.

Statutory machinery

Wages Councils were established in situations where trade unions were too weak to secure collective bargaining on a voluntary basis. Although it was originally intended that they should provide only a temporary protection within which trade unionism could develop and eventually establish voluntary collective bargaining arrangements, in practice, they became a permanent form of collective bargaining institution. They **differ from other forms of collective bargaining arrangements** in certain important respects:

1. They can be established, varied or abolished by the Secretary of State for Employment.
2. The Secretary of State not only nominates which trade unions and Employers' Associations are to be represented on the Wages Council but also appoints three independent representatives (one to act as chair) whose role is to help the two sides to reach an agreement or, failing this, to vote with one side or the other in order to reach a conclusion to the negotiation.
3. Before they are finalised any proposed agreements have to be circulated to all employers and displayed in the workplace for a period of time during which objections may be lodged with the Council.
4. The final agreement is promulgated as a statutory Wages Council Order with which *all* employers in the industry are legally obliged to comply;
5. If the employer does not comply with the terms of a Wages Council Order, the employee(s) may complain to the Wages Inspectorate who have the power, ultimately, to prosecute.

It is important to remember that the statutory element within this form of collective bargaining relates only to the establishment and maintenance of the collective bargaining machinery and the enforcement of its terms and conditions of employment. The determination of the terms of any agreement remain principally a matter for direct negotiation between the two parties concerned but always bearing in mind the existence of the three independent members. However, there has been a reduction in this statutory support for collective bargaining in that under the **Wages Act (1986)** the scope of Wages Councils has been restricted by excluding those under twenty-one years of age and limiting their regulation to setting only a basic minimum hourly rate and overtime entitlement and no other terms and conditions of employment. At the same time, the power of the Secretary of State to establish new Wages Councils was removed. Consequently, Wages Councils now only provide the barest of protection or the minimum in collective bargaining.

Formal voluntary machinery

This term may be applied to those institutional arrangements (in industries such as chemicals, civil engineering, local government, gas and electricity) which have been established on a voluntary basis between trade unions and employers and which involve a high degree of formality in their operation, **often based on a written constitution** detailing their function, membership, voting arrangements, etc. The degree of formality associated with this type of arrangement, in some cases extending to a permanent and separate secretariat to maintain it, can create an impression that it is almost independent of the employers and trade unions which negotiate within it. Although it is possible to identify a common base for this form of institutional arrangement (Whitley Committee (1916)), there is, at the same time, a marked variation between industries not only in the precise method of operation but even in the titles of the institutions – Joint Industrial Council (JIC), National Joint Industrial Council (NJIC), National Joint Council or Committee (NJC).

Ad hoc *machinery*

In many industries (like engineering, printing and textiles) which had established collective bargaining machinery prior to the Whitley Committee (1916), the collective bargaining arrangements did not have the high degree of formality associated with JIC's, NJCs, etc. In these industries multi-employer **collective bargaining was conducted simply through the medium of a meeting** between the various trade unions and Employers' Associations as and when necessary.

It may be argued that the **purpose of industry-level bargaining is twofold:**

1. From the **trade union point of view** it ensures that a common rule is applied across as wide an area as possible and even outside those federated organisations which are obliged to follow the national agreement. In the wages sphere it reinforces the concept of a 'rate for the job' based on the inherent nature of the job rather than the financial or productivity position of a particular organisation or its geographical

locality. It equalises the union's bargaining strength across organisations and establishes a minimum which may be enhanced, but not reduced, at the organisational level where the union has sufficient strength or the organisation's financial or productivity position warrants such enhancement.

2. From the **management point of view** it allows organisations to present a collective response to trade union pressure. In so far as its terms are applied unaltered at the organisational level, it stabilises the wage costs for all organisations at a uniform level and prevents 'unfair' competition between organisations based on differing wage levels. However, the wage rate set at the national level in many private manufacturing industries tends to be that which can be afforded by the least productive and profitable organisations within the industry.

It is important to distinguish between **three potential roles for industry-level bargaining** in respect of pay bargaining:

1. It may **determine actual rates** to be paid – as in the public sector.
2. It may **act as a floor**. Elliott describes this situation as one where 'when national wage rates rise all workers who currently enjoy rates in excess of the nationally agreed rate have their rates adjusted upwards either to re-establish some fixed relationship with the nationally agreed rate or because the change in the national rate provides the agreed signal for a change in workplace rates' [34].
3. It may **act as a safety net**. Elliott points out that in this situation the industry level 'provides only some agreed minimum below which nobody will be allowed to fall' [35] and therefore any increase in the national rate will only affect those who were marginally above the old national rate but are now below the new national rate.

Organisational single-employer bargaining

The term 'organisational bargaining' may be used to cover a variety of different levels and forms of collective bargaining:

1. **Company- or group-level bargaining** where all employees of a given type within the organisation, irrespective of their place of work, are covered by a single bargaining arrangement. In non-federated organisations this may take the form of a comprehensive agreement whilst in federated organisations it is more likely to involve the enhancement of nationally agreed terms and the determination of terms not covered by the national agreement.
2. **Plant or site bargaining** in multi-site organisations. This level of bargaining is particularly important in those organisations which are multi-industry as well as multi-site and therefore the nature of the work

and processes involved will vary between the sites and require different terms and conditions of employment. At the same time each site may, on an individual basis, be either federated or non-federated to the appropriate Employers' Association for that industry and therefore the agreements reached at this level may be either comprehensive or an enhancement of the nationally agreed terms.

3. **Departmental or workshop bargaining** relating to such issues as bonus or other PBR schemes and work arrangements. This level of bargaining may often take place within the operation of the organisation's grievance/disputes procedure.

It is important to recognise that organisational bargaining is not confined to one or other level but may take place at a combination of levels. For example, in addition to any industry-level bargaining, there may be bargaining at the company level (pensions and other common issues), the site level (enhancement of nationally agreed terms) and the departmental level (the employees' actual working arrangements). The same may also apply where there is no industry-level bargaining or the organisation is non-federated at either the company or site level.

Organisational bargaining has two important advantages:

1. It encourages management to develop a more positive approach to industrial relations within its organisation – particularly in respect of wage bargaining. Industry-level bargaining tends to weaken management's control of its wage costs in that the determination of wage rates and other substantive terms is outside its direct control and may even be inappropriate to its circumstances. Management, by bargaining at the organisational level, is better able to link wages with changes in work methods and increased productivity. At the same time, its wage bargaining may be conducted within a comprehensive and organisationally related framework of industrial relations policies.

2. Both management and employee representatives become responsible for, and committed to, the agreement they reach. The terms of the collective agreements are no longer decided for them by people outside the organisation and over whom they have little direct control or even influence, but are decided by themselves in the light of their own needs and aspirations.

However, **organisational-level bargaining may also present certain problems:**

1. In the area of pay bargaining, it may provide greater scope for 'comparability inflation'. The granting of a pay increase in one organisation, because of changes in work methods or improved profitability, can easily give rise to expectations that similar increases

will be given in the future or in other organisations where there is not the same willingness or opportunity for such productivity/profitability based pay increases. It provides the opportunity for the development of a 'key bargaining' strategy on the part of trade unions; that is, selecting one organisation which can afford the pay increase and then seeking to achieve the same level of pay settlement in other organisations.

2. Without a coherent policy and co-ordination of the various bargaining arrangements within the organisation, it is easy for organisational bargaining to become fragmented and degenerate into a series of 'catching up' or 'leap frogging' claims. The existence of too many small bargaining units, each with its own separate agreement and bargaining date, can lead to constant comparability claims between the various groups. This situation is accentuated, and co-ordination made more difficult, in those organisations where there is a variety of unions representing distinct groups of employees.

3. Because of the multiplicity of negotiations and agreements, organisational bargaining is less susceptible than industry bargaining to external verification and regulation during any period of incomes policy.

Decentralisation of collective bargaining

Some degree of organisational single-employer bargaining is inevitable. Much of the non-substantive aspects of collective bargaining (i.e. those related to 'job' as opposed to 'pay' regulation) have always been, and need to be, conducted at the immediate workplace or point of production rather than at the national level. At the same time, national multi-employer agreements need to be interpreted and applied at the workplace level. **Decentralisation of collective bargaining is not a new phenomenon** – in 1968 the Donovan Commission identified the existence of a 'two tier' arrangement of collective bargaining in much of the manufacturing sector in which the informality and fragmentation of organisational level bargaining undermined the supposed regulatory effect of industry level bargaining. This arose largely from the inability and inappropriateness of formal multi-employer industry agreements to regulate the increasing range of issues which were becoming subject to collective bargaining. Perhaps most importantly, changes in working methods and improvements in productivity could not, given the diversity of organisational requirements, be regulated effectively from the national level. The subsequent reform of collective bargaining in much of the private sector, based on greater formalisation of bargaining at the organisational level, was part of a conscious management strategy aimed at regaining managerial control and, it has been argued, further reduced the role of industry level multi-employer bargaining and national agreements. The central issue in respect of decentralisation of collective bargaining relates to what is the most appropriate level for the 'determination of pay and other terms and conditions of employment' (substantive terms).

It is important to understand, as Deaton and Beaumont point out, that there are **two distinct dimensions to decentralisation**: 'the move away from multi-employer to single-employer structures, and secondly, within the single employer category, the decision to bargain at either the company or plant level' [36]. However, decentralisation need not be an 'either/or' situation in that the 'two tier' arrangement has applied, and continues to apply, in many situations with companies 'topping-up' national terms and conditions to a lesser or greater extent (i.e. negotiating some terms and conditions at the organisational level) (see Figure 11.1). The degree of 'top-up' depends to a large extent on whether the national agreement is a comprehensive agreement setting out the full range of terms and conditions in detail (intended to be applied relatively unchanged at the workplace) or is a minimal agreement which only sets out a few basic terms and conditions leaving significant areas not covered in the national bargaining to be bargained at the organisational level. The 'top-up' can, of course, be bargained at either a corporate or site level within the single employer. Furthermore, within single employer bargaining (outside any national agreement) corporate and site level bargaining can co-exist with some terms being uniform across the organisation (e.g. pensions) while others vary between different sites of the organisation. Therefore, it is perhaps more useful to regard 'centralisation' and 'decentralisation' 'as constituting the two ends of a spectrum encompassing greater or lesser degrees of centralisation rather than mutually exclusive alternatives' [37].

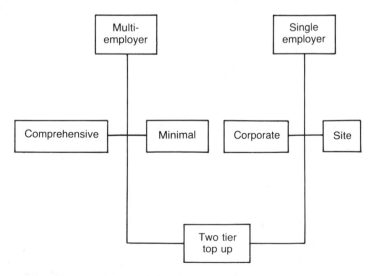

Figure 11.1 *Structure of collective bargaining*

Brown's [38], Daniel and Millward's [39] and Millward and Stevens' [40] surveys provide some, albeit conflicting, information regarding the **relative importance of the various levels of bargaining** for pay determination in the late 1970s and early part of the 1980s (see Table 11.2). Brown's 1977/8 survey of manufacturing industries showed that in 36 per cent of establishments multi-employer bargaining represented the 'most important' level for manual workers' wages and only 18 per cent of establishments for non-manual employees' wages, whilst single-employer bargaining at corporate or establishment level was considered 'most important' in over half of the establishments for both manual and non-manual workers' wages. Millward and Steven's comparison of the 1980 and 1984 surveys shows that where collective bargaining was the basis of the most recent pay increase some 40 per cent of establishments in manufacturing and 54 per cent of establishments in private service industries still regarded multi-employer bargaining as the most important level for manual workers. However, this level is clearly less important for determining the pay of non-manual workers in manufacturing, although, perhaps surprisingly, was regarded as the most important level for non-manual employees in some 36 per cent of establishments in the private service industries. In contrast, Brown and Terry [41] concluded that single-employer bargaining was most important for 75 per cent of manual workers in manufacturing industries.

Brown's survey showed that, in the late 1970s, there were **significant differences between industries**. Whilst single-employer bargaining at corporate or establishment level was 'most important' for both manual and non-manual employees in the Chemical and Engineering industries (despite

Table 11.2 *The most important level of bargaining influencing most recent pay increases (% of establishments)*

| | Manufacturing | | | Manufacturing | | | | Services | | | |
| | 1977/78 | | | Manual | | Non-manual | | Manual | | Non-manual | |
	Manual (%)	Non-manual (%)		1980 (%)	1984 (%)	1980 (%)	1984 (%)	1980 (%)	1984 (%)	1980 (%)	1984 (%)
Industry	33	17	National/regional	41	40	18	19	57	54	43	36
Regional	3	1									
Corporate	11	15	Company/division	15	20	29	36	28	33	36	52
Establishment	42	40	Plant/establishment	41	38	49	42	9	11	7	11
Other	1	2	Other	1	1	3	2	3	3	10	–
No bargaining	10	25	No bargaining*	35	45	73	74	10	12	10	15

Note: *Basis of most recent pay increase.

Sources: 1977/78: W. Brown (ed.), *The Changing Contours of British Industrial Relations*, Blackwell, 1981 (Table 2.1, p. 8 and Table 2.3, p. 12); 1980/84: N. Millward and M. Stevens, *British Workplace Industrial Relations 1980–1984*, Gower, 1986 (Table 9.6, p. 232 and Table 9.12, p. 238).

both industries having national multi-employer agreements), multi-employer bargaining at industry level was 'most important' for manual workers and 'significant' for non-manual employees in industries such as Food, Drink & Tobacco; Textiles; and Clothing & Footwear [42]. In addition, he found that the importance of multi-employer industry level bargaining in manufacturing varied in relation to the **size of the establishment** – the industry level was considered to be 'most important' in those with 50–99 employees but only 'marginally important' in those with more than 1,000 employees [43]. Deaton and Beaumont's analysis [44] found that:

1. Multi-employer bargaining was associated with a high regional concentration of organisations (i.e. operating within a similar labour market), high union density within the industry and multi-unionism.
2. Single-employer bargaining was associated with larger establishments, multi-site organisations, foreign ownership, organisations operating within non-competitive product markets and the existence of specialist industrial relations managers at a senior level.

Significantly, high labour costs as a proportion of total costs, the existence of payment-by-results systems and the existence of powerful workgroups (represented by their degree of skill, knowledge or experience) did not appear to correlate with either structure of bargaining; although the former might be expected to induce multi-employer bargaining to avoid wage competition and the latter two might be expected to induce single-employer bargaining.

Clearly, the **effect of industry bargaining on actual wage and earnings** levels will depend on which role it is fulfilling. Brown and Terry argued that in much of the private sector the national agreement provided little more than a 'safety net' and that in reality 'increases in . . . nationally negotiated rates appear to be the result of belated and increasingly unsuccessful attempts to raise the rates into a more realistic relationship with actual standard earnings' [45]. In other words, industry-level wage rates followed, and were responsive to, organisational-level bargaining rather than vice versa. However, Elliott found, in comparing national basic wage rates to standard weekly earnings between 1968 and 1978, that whilst the national basic rate declined as a percentage of weekly earnings in industries such as Shipbuilding, Motor Vehicle Retail and Repair and the Co-operative Societies (which suggests an increasing importance of organisational bargaining), it increased in Engineering, Electrical Contracting, Printing and Building. He concluded that 'nationally negotiated rates may continue to play an important role in the wage determination process throughout substantial areas of manufacturing' [46]. The increasing importance of the national rate may have been indicative of the worsening financial position of many organisations, a tougher management stand on wage increases and a weakening of the trade unions' ability to enhance national rates through organisational bargaining (more employees were coming closer to the 'safety net' role of the national rate rather than it providing a 'floor' to be built on).

The **evidence of the 1980s** shows, as Purcell points out, that 'multi-employer bargaining, conducted by employers' associations, is declining in importance in many industries' and 'single employer bargaining is being restructured, often to the level of the establishment or the business division' [47]. He cites three main factors inducing these changes:

1. The devolution, as an integral part of corporate strategy and business policy, of more authority and responsibility to managers of distinct profit centres or business within the organisation. Thus, he argues, 'the driving force for change comes not from the application of strategic thinking in industrial relations but from shifts in business policy' and 'the need . . . to make the structures of industrial relations fit the corporate need of profit centre and business unit decentralisation' [48].
2. The continuing and increasing need to be able to take account of local circumstances and link pay with productivity or performance to secure greater organisational flexibility.
3. The economic, political and legal environment of the 1980s has not only provided the impetus and opportunity for management to initiate changes in bargaining structures but has also weakened any trade union resistance.

Certainly, the 1980s has seen a significant number of national multi-employer bargaining arrangements being abandoned or their influence decreased. One survey [49] identified sixteen private sector multi-employer bargaining arrangements which were abandoned between 1986–9 (covering some 700,000 employees) and a further ten (covering 170,000 employees) where the influence of the national agreement was reduced – to this must be added the subsequent abolition of national multi-employer bargaining in the water industry and, largest of all, the engineering industry in 1989. A number of reasons can be identified for these developments:

1. Management's desire to **reform working practices**, particularly in relation to the introduction of new technology: for example, in national newspapers and independent television (where there were only a relatively small number of employers facing a competitive situation).
2. The **withdrawal of major organisations** in the industry from the national bargaining arrangements in order to conduct their own pay bargaining: for example, National Westminster Bank in the banking sector; Tesco and other major supermarket groups in the Multiple Food trade; Sealink, Cunard and P & O in shipping.
3. **Disputes and failures to reach agreement** at national level: for example, in the engineering industry, although pay had been negotiated on a two tier system for many years the national agreement on the working week,

holidays, etc., was generally implemented throughout the industry and it was the unions' campaign for a shorter working week and the subsequent dispute which led to the ending of national bargaining on pay and all conditions. As Pickard notes, 'the sticking point was the employers' insistence that . . . any national deal should be in the form of an enabling agreement, committing member companies to reduce hours only if they could negotiate productivity savings to pay for the change . . . it was exacerbated unintentionally by the union decision, when talks broke down, to take local, rather than national, industrial action . . . the unions were negotiating settlements at some of the targeted companies of precisely the type the employers had envisaged in trying to secure a national enabling agreement: a cut in the working week to 37 hours, with productivity clauses which lowered the cost to the company' [50].

4. **Privatisation:** for example, the water industry and the de-regulation of bus/coach transport.

However, it would be wrong to regard the movement as all one way – i.e. towards the abandonment of multi-employer bargaining. It is significant that in three cases (licensed clubs, lace finishing, and flax and hemp) new national multi-employer bargaining arrangements have been established following the restriction of the scope of the Wages Councils by the Wages Act (1986) in order 'to restore the influence of joint regulation' [51]. Similarly, in multiple food retailing a new multi-employer bargaining arrangement covering smaller firms was established following the withdrawal of the big supermarket groups. It would seem that multi-employer bargaining may still be more attractive than single employer bargaining for the smaller unionised organisation. Certainly, Pickard notes that 75 per cent of the EEF's members have fewer than 100 employees and 'expects that smaller companies will now need its help more than ever' [52]; however, whether this will be as a national negotiator remains to be seen.

Booth suggested, in analysing collective bargaining structure in the early 1980s, that 'the distinction between industry-level and organisation-level bargaining is largely irrelevant' [53] in respect of **pay determination in the public sector** because they were either single-employer industries or the national agreements were comprehensive and automatically applied at the employer organisation level. However, this is no longer so true. The government [54] has indicated that it believes national pay bargaining in both the public as well as the private sector is outdated, inflationary and creates unemployment and, consequently, should be replaced with local pay determination which relies less on a comparability model and more on the performance of the organisation and local labour market conditions. As Fatchett points out, 'for a Government committed to the belief in the supremacy of the free market, national level collective bargaining is regarded as an inefficient interference with the operation of markets' [55]. Certainly, the government's programme of privatisation and management reforms in the

remaining parts of the public sector have sought to encourage the decentralisation of collective bargaining through the establishment of distinct
executive agencies in the Civil Service, hospital trusts in the NHS, direct
grant maintained schools (all of which have the right to determine their own
terms and conditions of employment) and by encouraging local authorities
to 'opt out' of national agreements, etc. At the same time it has sought,
within national agreements, to encourage the development of a more 'two
tier' structure through the introduction of an element of locally negotiated
pay to be related either to individual performance or to the recruitment
and/or retention of staff with skills which are in short supply.

The greater emphasis on **single-employer bargaining structure** has
presented a major problem for multi-site organisations; namely, whether to
**centralise bargaining at the corporate level or decentralise it at the site
level.** In their surveys, Daniel and Millward noted that 'the larger the
number of people employed on site, the greater was the importance attached
to plant bargaining' and 'the larger the number of people employed by the
enterprise, the greater was the importance attached to company or corporate
bargaining' [56], whilst Brown suggested that the choice between site and
corporate level was 'strongly affected by the heterogeneity of a company's
products and by the history of its evolution by merger, takeover, or internal
growth' [57]. Deaton and Beaumont [58] concluded from their analysis that
corporate bargaining was associated with establishment size and the existence
of industrial relations specialists, whilst site bargaining was associated with
high labour costs as a proportion of total costs.

Ogden [59] notes that whilst the **choice of organisational bargaining
structure is primarily a management decision**, it can result as much from a
'defensive response' to trade union pressure as an 'offensive initiative' by
management. He suggests that management may seek corporate bargaining
as a response to its inability to constrain the bargaining effects of powerful
workgroups at the site level or the union's use of inter-site comparisons. The
development of corporate bargaining offers management a means of restricting the scope of site bargaining. However, he points out that such a move
may involve a cost to management. Corporate bargaining is not conducive to
productivity bargaining and detailed work changes which need to be
determined and negotiated at the point of production. Equally, unions may
themselves welcome corporate bargaining as an opportunity to extend the
scope of collective bargaining into areas of strategic corporate decision
making – this could not be achieved so easily if bargaining was confined to
the site level.

Kinnie argues strongly that, whilst accepting that management has three
alternative organisational bargaining structures (centralised, decentralised or
a 'half-way house'), management should reject the latter alternative. In
examining examples of centralised and decentralised bargaining structures he
notes that 'the structures of management and bargaining are closely matched,

producing a consistent pattern of control' [60]. In the centralised organisation, the existence of an integrated production pattern and central control of finance and production matters meant that centralised bargaining facilitated the regulation of union inter-site comparisons. In the decentralised organisation, diversified production and markets coupled with inter-site competition for investment resources from the centre accentuated the divisions between the sites and allowed management, in the absence of any effective inter-site co-ordination, to justify decentralised bargaining and eliminate inter-site union comparisons. However, in organisations which had adopted a half-way house structure (centralised control of finance but decentralised collective bargaining) management and bargaining structures were inconsistent and led to union representatives questioning the autonomy and authority of site management, perceiving central guidelines to site management as interference with local autonomy and an attempt to impose central control and concentrating on inter-site comparisons as sites on lower wages sought to achieve the levels of the other sites and they, in turn, sought to maintain their differential.

However, it is perhaps inevitable that most multi-site organisations will adopt a form of half-way house structure if only because, as McCarthy *et al*. point out, 'the successful operation of plant agreements ... appears to necessitate a central coordinating function for company industrial relations activities to ensure that so far as possible management actions are consistent between different groups and at different times' [61]. Certainly, Kinnie suggests that decentralisation of management and bargaining structures 'do not necessarily lead to an increase in decision-making discretion for establishment managers' [62], whilst Purcell [63] believes that management can 'have the best of both worlds' by corporate co-ordination and control of 'decentralised' bargaining through budgetary control mechanisms and monitoring personnel activities of individual sites, units, etc. Indeed, he refers to one survey [64] which found that two-thirds of companies with decentralised bargaining had a corporate policy on pay settlements, issued pay guidelines or held consultations between site and higher-level management before the start of negotiations. The effect of this may be to create a **two tier system within the organisation** similar to that identified by the Donovan Commission in the 1960s in respect of the relationship between industry and organisational bargaining and subject to similar tensions and conflicts.

11.4 The content of collective bargaining

The content of collective bargaining may, for convenience, be divided into three areas – substantive, procedural and working arrangements.

Substantive rules

In this section the term substantive is used to refer exclusively to those terms of employment, such as wages, hours, holidays, etc., which can be converted into monetary terms; normally, however, the term would also encompass agreed working arrangements. The negotiation of these terms of employment is often regarded as the primary purpose of both trade unions and collective bargaining. The most important element within this area is the regulation of **rates of pay** including such items as overtime rates and when they should be applied; minimum earnings levels for PBR schemes; the level of guaranteed payment when work is not available for the employee; and allowances for special working conditions such as shift working or working in abnormal conditions. Generally these items are renegotiated annually in the light of any change in the cost of living, comparisons with the level of wages in other occupations and organisations, and the productivity and profitability of the organisation or industry.

Whilst increases in pay tend to be gradual and on an annual basis, the reduction in the **hours of work** has been more erratic. Before 1914 many industries worked a 72-hour, 6-day week and it was not until after World War I that the 8-hour day (48-hour, 6-day week) was generally achieved. This reduced to a 44-hour, 5½-day week after World War II and eventually reached a 40-hour, 5-day week in the mid-1960s. During the 1980s there has been further pressure and some success, particularly amongst manual workers, for a reduction in the normal working week (to a 37/35-hour, 4 or 4½-day week), partly as a response to the high level of unemployment and partly to bring them into line with the norm for most non-manual employees. However, although the pressure for shortening the working week may be couched in terms of creating more leisure or job opportunities, the reduction of basic working hours in the past has not usually resulted in fewer hours being worked but a transfer of those hours from payment at normal time rate to payment at overtime rate thereby enhancing the employees' earnings. A real reduction in the actual hours worked would require either the employees to accept a reduction in their level of earnings or the employer to agree to a substantial increase in basic wage rates in order to maintain the employees' existing level of total earnings.

At the same time as reducing hours of work, there has also been an increase in the length of **paid annual holidays**. However, this development has been a phenomenon primarily of the post-war period. It was not until 1928 that a government inquiry recommended that employees should receive a minimum of one week's paid holiday and even this was not generally achieved until the end of World War II. By the latter part of the 1970s this had become four weeks. Payment for holidays is normally made at normal basic pay or, in the case of employees under PBR schemes, average earnings. However, in Europe many employees receive extra payment for the period of their holidays – in some cases double payment. This may be regarded as simply deferred wage payments given to employees at a time when they are likely to incur extra expenses or it may be regarded as a recognition of the need for employees to make full use of their holiday if they are to remain effective as employees for the remainder of the year.

In recent years there has also been a trend towards the inclusion of **fringe benefits**, such as pension, sick payments and even the provision of cheap loans and private medical facilities, within the scope of collective bargaining. A major impetus for the provision of such benefits was provided by the restrictions placed on the level of pay increases during periods of incomes policy in the 1970s. Both employers and trade unions looked to alternative, and less obvious, methods of rewarding employees – particularly non-manual employees. However, it should be recognised that where such fringe benefits become the subject of negotiation and collective agreement they can no longer be regarded as optional items for which employees should be grateful but standard terms to which they have a right.

Finally, it is important to remember that improvements in the substantive terms of employment have, in Britain, been achieved by trade unions through the process of direct bargaining with employers rather than, as in some other countries, through statutory regulation of minimum terms.

Procedural rules

If substantive rules can be viewed as the result of collective bargaining in respect of economic issues, then procedural rules should be viewed as the outcome of negotiations over the exercise of managerial authority and decision making.

The joint determination of procedures at the organisational level establishes a **regulatory framework** for resolving the primary conflict between management's desire for control of its labour and the employees' desire for protection against arbitrary management decisions and actions. These rules introduce a degree of certainty into the organisational relationship between management, employees and trade unions by defining how various issues are to be handled and the expected roles of the various parties. The decision to recognise a trade union, and therefore enter into negotiations with it in respect of the determination of substantive terms of employment, is clearly the first and most important step in management's acceptance of a constraint on their authority within the organisation: what issues are to be subject to joint regulation. Beyond this initial point it is possible to establish joint procedures in respect of virtually any aspect of management decision making. The extent to which this will happen will depend largely on the willingness of management to accept a sharing of responsibility for decision making within the organisation. Where unions are recognised it is usual for there to be joint procedures in respect of grievances, discipline, redundancy, job evaluation, use of work study, etc.

Perhaps the most important aspect of the procedural relationship between management and trade union relates to what is often referred to as **status quo**. The concept underlying status quo is that management should not implement any change in working arrangements or terms and conditions of employment until it has been negotiated and agreed with the unions concerned or the disputes procedure has been exhausted. Whilst this may be regarded as a serious restriction on management's freedom to implement such changes as it believes are necessary for the well-being of the organisation, it may also be viewed as a protection against the unknown for the employees concerned. Certainly, many managers would argue that the existence of a status quo provision allows trade unions and employees to delay negotiations in order to put greater pressure on management in the hope of securing a greater concession for agreeing to the change. However, the reverse is equally true if there is no status quo clause: management is more able to resist making concessions once the change has been implemented and is being worked by the employees.

Procedural rules, because they are concerned with the regulation of decision making and the participation of employees and their representatives in the affairs of the organisation, may be considered to be of more importance than substantive, economic rules. They share power and authority rather than money.

Working arrangements

The detailing of working arrangements within collective agreements is **associated primarily with the development of organisational level bargaining**. Where collective bargaining has sought to relate pay and productivity it has become necessary to define the work changes which are to be made in return for the wage increase. It is quite common to find productivity agreements containing provisions relating to such issues as manning levels, inter-job flexibility, time flexibility, use of contractors, etc. The definition of working arrangements is also important in the context of 'new technology' agreements covering the introduction of new work operations within the organisation.

However, it is important to realise that, whilst the general aim of productivity or new technology agreements is to improve work flexibility, **the fact that working arrangements are codified within a collective agreement may itself create** inflexibility. It provides an accepted definition of what is, and therefore what is not, part of the employee's job and may be used by employees as the justification for not carrying out other work which may be required of them by management. The joint determination of working arrangements is not confined exclusively to the negotiation of formal collective agreements but may also form a part of the operation of other systems within the organisation – for example, the involvement of trade unions in the joint operation of a job evaluation system implies their involvement in jointly agreeing the job description on which the evaluation is to be carried out.

11.5 Summary propositions

- The process of collective bargaining is concerned with regulating both economic and managerial relationships.
- Collective bargaining is a voluntary, bipartite process; its character is determined by management's and employees' perception of the nature of their mutual interdependence.
- Bargaining structure is dynamic and varies between different industries and organisations; however, the emphasis of collective bargaining regulation regulation has shifted away from multi-employer industry-level bargaining to the organisational level in order to respond more effectively to variations in organisational situations and needs.

Further reading

- F. Blackaby (ed.), *The Future of Pay Bargaining*, Heinemann, 1980. This book contains a series of contributions relating to the structure, problems and reform of pay bargaining.
- N. W. Chamberlain and J. W. Kuhn, *Collective Bargaining*, McGraw-Hill, 1965. Chapters 5 and 17 are useful in providing an examination of the collective bargaining process – particularly conjunctive and co-operative bargaining.
- ACAS, *Industrial Relations Handbook*, HMSO, 1980. Part B of this book sets out the collective bargaining arrangements for each industry.

References

1. A. Flanders, *Industrial Relations: What is wrong with the system?*, IPM, 1965, p. 21.
2. R. Dubin, 'Constructive aspects of industrial conflict' in A. Kornhauser, R. Dubin and A. M. Ross (eds), *Industrial Conflict*, McGraw-Hill, 1954, p. 44.
3. Report of *Royal Commission on Trade Unions and Employers' Associations* (Donovan Commission), HMSO, 1968, p. 54.
4. N. Millward and M. Stevens, *British Workplace Industrial Relations 1980–1984*, Gower, 1986 (Tables 9.3 & 9.4).
5. *Royal Commission on Trade Unions and Employers' Associations*, op.cit., p. 8.

6. O. Aikin and J. Reid, *Employment, Welfare and Safety at Work*, Penguin, 1971, pp. 19–20. Reprinted by permission of Penguin Books Ltd. ©Olga Aikin and Judith Reid, 1971.
7. R. Hyman, *Industrial Relations: A Marxist introduction*, Macmillan, 1975, p. 24.
8. K. W. Wedderburn, *The Worker and the Law*, Penguin, 1971, p. 160. © K. W. Wedderburn, 1965, 1971.
9. *Fords v. T&GWU and AUEW* (1969).
10. Green Paper on *Trade Union Immunities*, HMSO, 1981.
11. K. W. Wedderburn, *op. cit.*, p. 163.
12. *Trade Union Immunities*, *op. cit.*, p. 55.
13. S. and B. Webb, *Industrial Democracy*, Longman, 1902.
14. A. Flanders, 'Collective bargaining: a theoretical analysis', *British Journal of Industrial Relations*, vol. VI, 1968, pp. 1–26.
15. A. Fox, 'Collective bargaining: Flanders and the Webbs', *British Journal of Industrial Relations*, vol. XIII, 1975, pp. 151–74.
16. A. Flanders (1968), *op. cit.*, pp. 4–6.
17. *ibid.*
18. *ibid.*, p. 7.
19. F. H. Harbison, 'Collective bargaining and American capitalism' in A. Kornhauser *et al.* (eds), *op.cit.*, p. 270.
20. N. W. Chamberlain and J. W. Kuhn, *Collective Bargaining*, McGraw-Hill, 1965, p. 113.
21. *ibid.*, p. 121.
22. *ibid.*, p. 130.
23. *ibid.*, p. 135.
24. *ibid.*, p. 428.
25. *ibid.*, p. 429.
26. R. E. Walton and R. B. McKersie, *A Behavioral Theory of Labor Negotiations*, McGraw-Hill, 1965.
27. W. E. J. McCarthy and N. D. Ellis, *Management by Agreement*, Hutchinson, 1973.
28. *ibid*, pp. 96–7.
29. *ibid*, p. 102.
30. *ibid.*, p. 108.
31. A. Flanders, *Collective Bargaining: Prescription for change*, Faber & Faber, 1967, p. 19.
32. ACAS, *Industrial Relations Handbook*, HMSO, 1980, Appendix 1.
33. W. E. J. McCarthy, P. A. L. Parker, W. R. Hawes, and A. L. Lumb, 'The Reform of Collective Bargaining at Plant and Company Level', *Department of Employment, Manpower Paper No. 5*, HMSO, 1971.
34. R. F. Elliott, 'Some further observations on the importance of national wage agreements', *British Journal of Industrial Relations*, vol. XIX, 1981, p. 370.
35. *ibid*
36. D. R. Deaton and P. B. Beaumont, 'The determinants of bargaining structure: some large scale survey evidence for Britain', *British Journal of Industrial Relations*, vol. XVIII, 1980, p. 201.
37. 'Pay bargaining: to centralise or decentralise?', *Industrial Relations Review and Report*, No. 397, August 1987, p. 13.
38. W. Brown (ed.), *The Changing Contours of British Industrial Relations*, Blackwell, 1981, pp. 5–19.

39. W. W. Daniel and N. Millward, *Workplace Industrial Relations in Britain*, Heinemann (PSI/SSRC), 1983, pp. 117–213.
40. N. Millward and M. Stevens, *op. cit.*
41. W. Brown and M. Terry, 'The changing nature of national wage agreements', *Scottish Journal of Political Economy*, vol. 25, no. 2, 1978, pp. 119–33.
42. W. Brown (ed.), *op. cit.*, Tables 2.1 and 2.3.
43. *ibid.*, Tables 2.2 and 2.4.
44. D. R. Deaton and P. B. Beaumont, *op. cit.*, p. 210.
45. W. Brown and M. Terry, *op. cit.*, p. 125.
46. R. F. Elliott. *op.cit*, p. 375.
47. J. Purcell, 'How to manage decentralised bargaining', *Personnel Management*, May 1989, p. 53.
48. *ibid.*
49. 'Developments in multi-employer bargaining: 1', *IRS Employment Trends 440*, May 1989.
50. J. Pickard, 'Engineering tools up for local bargaining', *Personnel Management*, March 1990, pp. 41–2.
51. *IRS Employment Trends 440, op. cit.*, p. 8.
52. J. Pickard, *op.cit.*, p. 55.
53. A. L. Booth, 'The bargaining structure of British establishments', *British Journal of Industrial Relations*', vol. 27, no. 2, 1989, p. 226.
54. Employment for the 1990s, HMSO, 1989.
55. D. Fatchett, 'Workplace bargaining in hospitals and schools: threat or opportunity for the unions?', *Industrial Relations Journal*, vol. 20, no. 4, 1989, p. 255.
56. W. W. Daniel and N. Millward, *op. cit.*, p. 189.
57. W. Brown (ed.), *op.cit.*, p. 13.
58. D. R. Deaton and P. B. Beaumont, *op. cit.*, p. 212.
59. S. G. Ogden, 'Bargaining structure and the control of industrial relations', *British Journal of Industrial Relations*, vol. XX, no. 2, 1982.
60. Dr Kinnie, 'Local versus centralised bargaining: the dangers of a "halfway house"', *Personnel Management*, January 1982, p. 33.
61. W. E. J. McCarthy *et al.*, *op. cit.*, p. 70.
62. N. Kinnie, 'The decentralisation of industrial relations? – recent research considered', *Personnel Review*, vol. 19, no. 3, 1990, p. 33.
63. J. Purcell, *op.cit.*, p. 55.
64. P. Marginson *et al.*, *Beyond the Workplace: Managing industrial relations in the multi-establishment enterprise*, Blackwell, 1988.

Chapter 12

Employee participation and involvement

12.1 Definition

The notion of **employee participation** is not new. It has existed, in one form or another, and been debated since the late nineteenth century. However, it is a term which does not have a universally accepted meaning and, indeed, is capable of three distinctly different interpretations.

● *A socio-political concept or philosophy of industrial organisation.* This concept may more often and more appropriately be termed 'workers control' or 'industrial democracy'. This approach focuses attention on changing the existing balance of industrial power and creating a system which, Hyman argues, involves 'the determination by the whole labour force of the nature, methods and indeed purpose of production' [1]. Its central objective is the establishment of employee self-management within an organisation whose ownership is vested in either the employees or the state and whose managerial function is exercised ultimately through a group, elected by the employees themselves, which has the authority over all decisions of the organisation including the allocation of 'profits' between extra wages and re-investment [2]. The achievement of such employee participation, certainly on a widespread basis, would require a significant, if not complete, change in the economic and authority relationships not only within organisations but also society.

● *A generic term to encompass all processes and institutions of employee influence within the organisation.* Thus, Walker argued that 'employee participation' exists whenever 'those at the bottom of the enterprise hierarchy take part in the authority and managerial functions of the enterprise' [3] and Farnham and Pimlott included all those 'social or institutional devices by which subordinate employees, either individually or collectively, become involved in one or more aspects of organisational decision making' [4]. On this basis, employee participation began with the inception of trade unions and includes the entire spectrum of management/employee relationships from simple information-giving by management, through joint consultation, collective bargaining and other institutionalised forms of joint regulation, to workers control.

- *A discrete term to denote a nebulous but distinct evolutionary development of the traditional joint regulatory processes.* This development seeks to promote greater employee influence within the existing organisational system. It is important, with this approach, to differentiate 'employee participation' from the other joint regulatory processes. This can be achieved in two ways:

1. For any process to be termed participative there must be more than just the receipt of information on the part of employees or their representatives; there must be some capacity for them to influence decisions at least by changing them after they have been made or, preferably, by jointly determining them with management in the first place. Consequently, 'real' participation can be distinguished from 'pseudo' participation, such as management information-giving and possibly joint consultation, by emphasising Patemen's requirement for both sides to have 'equal power to determine the outcome of decisions' [5].
2. Most importantly, Wall and Lischeron differentiate 'employee participation' from the long-standing process of collective bargaining by emphasising 'the involvement of [employees] in the decision making processes which traditionally have been the responsibility and prerogative of [management]' [6]. Elliott believes that such an evolutionary development requires that 'the unions should be shouldering new responsibilities in what should involve at least a lessening, though probably not a rejection, of the adversary system, and managements should be sharing some of their decision-making powers' [7].

Focusing on this third approach, employee participation may be defined as a:

philosophy or style of organisational management which recognises both the need and right of employees, individually or collectively, to be involved with management in areas of the organisation's decision making beyond that normally covered by collective bargaining.

The very nature of the process means that it is directed towards the joint determination and solution of a wide range of problems at all levels of the organisation rather than the more narrow distributive 'wage/work collective bargain' concept of management/employee relations. As Brannen points out, employee participation is concerned with 'the control of workers, in the sense both of control by them and control exerted on them within the system of production' [8] whilst the IPM note that it is 'designed to provide employees with the opportunity to influence and, where appropriate, take part in decision-making on matters which affect them' [9].

However, during the 1980s there has been a change in direction and emphasis (closely associated with the Human Resource Management concept) which is indicated by the adoption of the term employee 'involvement' rather than 'participation'. **Employee involvement** has been variously described as 'the means used to harness the talents and co-operation of the workforce in the common interests they share with management' [10], 'any activity which helps to release the full potential of people at work' [11] and 'a range of processes designed to engage the support, understanding, optimum contribution of all employees in an organisation and their commitment to its objectives' [12]. It may, therefore, be defined as

> **measures introduced by management intended to optimise the utilisation of labour and at the same time secure the employee's identification with the aims and needs of the organisation.**

It is clear that whilst 'involvement' is intended to enhance the support and commitment of employees to the objectives and values of the organisation (as determined by management), participation is designed to provide the employees with the opportunity to influence and take part in organisational decision making.

12.2 Approaches to participation and involvement ≡

Pressures for participation

There have been three main pressures for the development and extension of employee participation – social, industrial and political.

The 1960s and early 1970s was a period of significant **social development** centred around the culmination of the movement away from post-war austerity and the 'coming of age', in terms of working and voting, of the first generations whose formative years had been ones of relative peace rather than war. The period can be characterised as one of:

1. economic prosperity with stable and secure employment (including periods of labour scarcity);
2. increased knowledge and awareness derived from education and the mass media; and

3. greater preparedness to question established values, attitudes and institutions.

Most importantly, it produced a change in attitudes towards formally constituted authority in many spheres of society (family, schools and universities, the church, political parties and even government and the state) and a focusing of attention on the concept of 'government by consent'. The period saw the demise of the 'deferential society' and the rise of the 'democratic imperative', that is, 'those who will be substantially affected by decisions made by social and political institutions must be involved in the making of those decisions' [13].

In the **industrial sphere** these developments resulted in **increased aspirations amongst employees** – not only in terms of material rewards (wages) but also the management of the organisation (authority). At the same time, the increased size and complexity of industrial organisations contributed to the **alienation of employees** from their work. At one extreme of the organisation industrial power and major decision making was concentrated in the hands of a limited number of senior managers (usually remote from the mass of the organisation's employees), whilst at the other extreme the emphasis on the division and specialisation of labour in order to improve efficiency and productivity tended to reduce employee identification with both the end product of the organisation and the organisation itself. This led to attention shifting away from the purely legal and economic aspects of the contractual relationship between employer and employee and towards the psychological and sociological aspects of the relationship between the individual and his/her work situation. There was a greater acceptance of the notion that industrial organisations have both an economic function (the provision of goods or services in the most efficient way) and a social function (the provision of a satisfactory and meaningful work environment for the people who produce those goods or services).

At a more practical level the period since the early 1960s has also been one of **technological, industrial and economic change.** Change, at the organisational level, can be carried out more smoothly, quickly and effectively with the active and full participation of the employees concerned than if management makes the decision alone and then seeks to implement it against the negative reaction of employees. The process of involving employees in decisions which affect their working lives can result, through the contribution of the employees' knowledge and experience, in a direct improvement in working practices and operations and, through the process of joint analysis and solution of organisational problems, in a more committed workforce. It is this pressure for organisational change in order to become more efficient and competitive at a time of weakened trade union power and influence which has been foremost in the shift towards employee 'involvement' rather than 'participation' practices during the 1980s.

These social and industrial pressures have been reflected and reinforced in the **political sphere** where the debate has centred on two main issues:

1. The apparent contradiction between the notional democratic basis of society outside the organisation and the absence of meaningful employee participation within the organisation.
2. The need to obtain understanding, co-operation and consent in industrial and economic change.

Although **all major political parties have become committed to the principle of increased employee participation,** Labour and Conservative governments have displayed significant differences in respect of not only the favoured form of participation but also the means to be employed in securing its adoption.

● *Labour Government policy.* Labour Government policy has favoured direct legislative intervention to obtain the adoption of more formalised and representative forms of employee participation including worker directors: (for example, the appointment of worker directors as part of the reorganisation of the British Steel Corporation (1967) and Post Office (1977), the Bullock Committee of Inquiry on Industrial Democracy (1975) and the subsequent White Paper (1978) advocating the establishment of Joint Representation Committees which, in organisations of over 2,000 employees, could instigate a ballot of the employees to secure one-third employee representation on the board).

● *Conservative Government policy.* On the other hand, Conservative Government policy has reflected management's view of 'involvement' rather than 'participation' and has sought to rely on a process of voluntary evolution at the organisational level for its implementation. The Employment Act (1982) simply requires companies with more than 250 employees to report, as part of their normal Annual Report, on their arrangements for providing information to employees, consulting regularly with employees or their representatives, encouraging the involvement of employees through share ownership and other financial schemes, and achieving a common awareness on the part of employees of the financial and economic factors affecting the performance of the organisation. However, it would appear that many personnel managers and directors disagree with the government's policy, arguing that some form of legislation is inevitable and that employers should be obliged to disclose information and financial performance to all employees [14].

The political pressure within the UK has, in part, resulted from the experience of the European Community. The principal influence has been the existence, since 1972, of an EC draft Directive which, if implemented, would require companies to establish employee participation. This could take the form of worker directors (elected or co-opted to a supervisory board within a two tier board structure or elected within a one tier structure), a works council or other system established by collective bargaining. However, any alternative system of participation established by collective bargaining would have to be equivalent in effect – access to information supplied to members of the board, the right to request special reports and undertake investigations and the right to be consulted on major decisions such as the closure, transfer or extension of the organisation's activities. In addition, all employee representatives within the system would have to be elected by proportional representation through a secret ballot of the employees.

Certainly, Dickson's survey [15] of management and shop steward perceptions of the reasons for introducing participation reflects these factors. He was able to classify their responses into four categories:

1. **Moral** – ideological belief in the right of employees to participate in decisions which affect them.
2. **Power** – 'pragmatic recognition' of the employees' collective power within the organisation.
3. **Union** – direct union activity which 'pushed' management towards greater participation.
4. **Political** – pressure from the political system for organisations to adopt more participative management arrangements.

Significantly, he found that shop stewards placed much less emphasis than management on power and union pressures. This suggests that shop stewards do not see the introduction of participation as resulting from the existence of strong unionism or perhaps their response is indicative of a perception that participation and trade unionism are distinctly separate.

Forms of participation or involvement

The traditional functional view of industrial organisations contrasts the managerial role of directing and co-ordinating the activities of the organisation (through the functions of planning, organising, motivating and controlling) with the employees' role of being recruited and trained to perform certain defined tasks (the function of doing). Walker believes that employee participation 'bridges the gap' between these functional roles by establishing forms of interaction through which 'workers', while remaining in workers' positions, may take part (directly or through representatives) in certain functions defined as 'managerial' [16]. Clearly, there are a variety of ways, not least through joint consultation and collective bargaining, whereby this interaction may take place and may be differentiated by reference to three constituent elements (see Figure 12.1):

1. **Method or extent – direct forms** allow employees to be personally and actively involved in the decision making process; **indirect forms** restrict the mass of employees to a relatively passive role and rely on employee representatives to carry out the active role of discussing and deliberating with management on their behalf.
2. **Level within the organisational hierarchy** – the process can, of course, take place at any level from that of the employee's immediate superior to the board level.
3. **Objective or scope** – the managerial functions and decisions which provide the content of the participatory processes may be **task centred** (concerned primarily with the structure and performance of the operational work situation) or **power centred** (concerned with the more fundamental managerial authority and decisions which determine the framework or environment within which operational decisions have to be made).

With this approach it is possible to contrast **two different, but complementary, strategies.**

• *Direct forms of involvement.* Direct forms, such as the development of formal and regular briefing groups or consultative meetings between the employees and their supervisor (more open style of management) and/or the creation of new participative work organisation arrangements (work re-design), focus attention on the individual employee or work group and the immediate operational situation (task centred). This strategy may be referred to as **descending participation** in so far as management invariably initiates the development for its own purposes (participation is offered) and, as part of the change, may transfer authority and responsibility from itself to the employees for a limited range of work related decisions (e.g. methods of working, allocation of tasks, maintenance of quality, etc.). However, the content of the process is confined largely to the implementation phase of operational decisions already made by management. This approach is intended to directly motivate the individual employee, increase job satisfaction and enhance sense of identification with the aims, objectives and decisions of the organisation (all of which have been determined by management).

• *Indirect forms of participation.* Indirect forms, such as widening the content of collective bargaining, the creation of Works Councils and the appointment of worker directors, focus attention on the exercise of the managerial prerogative and the balance of power between management and employees in the organisation's decision making process (power centred).

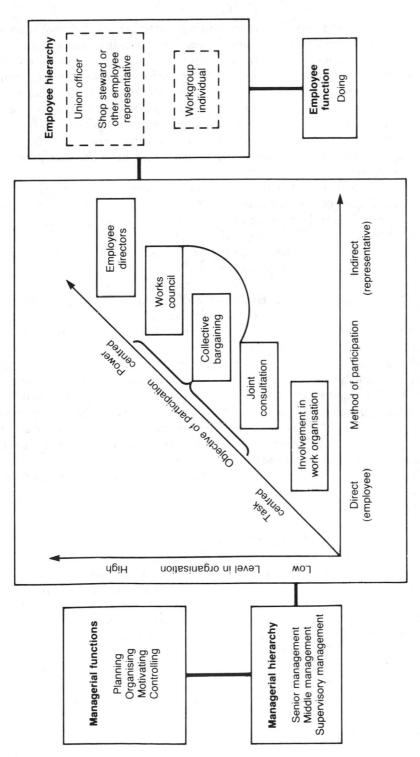

Figure 12.1   *Forms of employee participation*

This strategy can be referred to as **ascending participation** because it seeks to protect the interests of the employees by extending their collective influence into a wider range of decisions at the higher levels of the organisation and because, in relation to the extension of collective bargaining and the appointment of worker directors, the initiative for the development may come from the employees and their unions (participation is demanded). Thus, it is primarily concerned with extending employee influence, through the process of negotiation and joint regulation, into the areas of policy and major organisational planning which previously have been the sole prerogative of management.

There is a further, and perhaps overriding, element to be considered – namely, the **degree of participation** (i.e. the extent to which employees or their representatives influence decisions). The existence of 'participation' as opposed to 'involvement' must depend ultimately on how far employees are able, or are allowed, to influence management thinking and contribute to the determination of decisions. Irrespective of the form, the process of interaction used may range, in practice, from only management information giving, through consultation and negotiation to committed joint decision making. Clearly participation does not exist simply because an organisation adopts the forms of participation – whether of the direct, descending kind or indirect, ascending kind. Participation is primarily a philosophy, not a particular institutional form. Therefore, employee participation can take place at any time and in any institution so long as management is prepared fully to involve employees or their representatives and share with them the responsibility for decision making. This factor is particularly important when seeking to judge whether or not the operation of existing institutions of joint consultation or collective bargaining are part of the organisation's evolution towards greater employee participation.

Finally, mention must be made of **financial forms of participation**. These may be grouped into two types – both of which are direct individual forms:

1. **Supplementary financial participation schemes**. Such schemes involve payments to employees based on the organisation's performance (measured in terms of its profits, value added, level of production or sales) and are supplementary in the sense that they are additional to the employee's normal remuneration. The payments, which are often paid once or twice a year, may be constant between employees (each receives the same amount) or may vary depending on such factors as the individual's length of service and level of normal remuneration (senior employees and those with longer service receive the most). Such schemes should not, therefore, be confused with direct productivity payments made to employees as a result of a collective agreement or bonus schemes. Bell has suggested that there are two main reasons for the introduction of such schemes:

(a) it is inherently right that employees should receive a share of the profits, added value, etc., that they have helped to create; and

(b) that unlike bonus schemes, which directly motivate the individual to increase production, they provide an 'incentive to the workforce as a whole to cooperate with management in improving performance' [17].

2. **Share ownership schemes**. These distribute the employees' portion of the profits, etc., in the form of shares either directly to each individual employee or indirectly into a trust which holds the shares on behalf of all employees. It is argued that such schemes enhance the employees' sense of identity with the organisation and perhaps change their attitude because they become part-owners of the business. However, Bell points out that under most schemes the 'employee will become a shareholder not because he wants to but because the company wants it' [18] and most employees dispose of their shares as soon as they are able under the terms of the scheme. Certainly, from the management's point of view, share ownership schemes have the advantage that payment in newly issued shares, as opposed to cash under a supplementary financial scheme, does not affect the organisation's current expenditure or cash flow – it merely dilutes the existing shareholders' equity (the same profits will have to be distributed over a larger number of shares).

However, it must be remembered that financial participation merely shares money, not power, authority or decision making within the organisation, and is, Marchington argues, 'on its own and without any associated joint regulation of management decision making, a very dilute form of industrial democracy' [19].

Management and union perceptions of employee participation/involvement

There appears to be little disagreement between management and trade unions that participation is a good thing – in principle. However, there are quite significant differences in respect of its intended objective, the means to be adopted and the organisational environment within which it is to be implemented.

The **management view** appears to be based on a **perception of consensus**. The BIM assume that there is 'a community of interest between employer and employee in furthering the long term prospects of the enterprise' and consequently the primary purpose of increased employee participation is to 'achieve a greater commitment of all employees to the definition and attainment of the objectives of the enterprise' [20]. A similar view is put forward by the IPM. Buckingham argues that 'the differences between the two sides of industry are dwarfed by our overriding national need to compete successfully with the rest of the world' [21]. This is then reflected in his statement of the principles underlying the IPM's approach to employee participation; for example,

1. 'employee participation and involvement plans and strategies should take as their starting point the high degree of common interest and mutual interdependence which must exist in any successful organisation'; and
2. 'the fundamental emphasis of any participation and involvement programme should be on increasing the profitability and success of the organisation . . . and increasing the sense of common purpose and motivating employees to maximise their contribution by endeavouring to gain their understanding of, and commitment and contribution to, the organisation's success' [22].

Through the adoption of such a strategy, which acknowledges and utilises the employees' aspirations to be more involved, management believes it will improve the technical quality of decisions, increase the acceptability of those decisions, encourage employee identification with the success of the organisation and improve job satisfaction. The emphasis of management's approach is, therefore, one of improving organisational harmony, efficiency and productivity (employee 'involvement').

The **trade union view** of employee participation, on the other hand, appears to be founded on the assumption that the enterprise is a **pluralistic organisation**, with sectional and competing interests, which has to be formally regulated on a joint basis. They emphasise, therefore, participation as a means of sharing power and providing employees with greater influence in the organisation's decision making through the enhancement and strengthening of existing representational systems, particularly collective bargaining, and, possibly, the introduction of worker directors. Certainly, many writers challenge the managerial notion of organisational consensus as a basis for developing employee participation. Marchington believes that the high degree of common interest or mutual interdependence assumed by the IPM 'may not be present in all that many organisations' [23] and Ramsay argues that 'participation schemes are subject to an ongoing context of conflicting interests between management and labour' and therefore 'management proposals are an exercise in pseudo-democracy insofar as they attempt to impose an instrumental and integrative framework' [24]. Indeed, ACAS points out that the TUC and many trade unions are 'cautious of forms of participation which seem to bypass established management–union arrangements' [25].

These differences in perception can be seen in the findings of a number of surveys – particularly in respect of direct v. indirect forms of participation.

1. Warner [26] found that management's perception of the degree of employee influence on decision making remained relatively constant as between direct and indirect forms of participation (their mean rating was between 'little' and 'moderate'). However, shop stewards' perceptions of employee influence through direct forms of participation was, with the exception of 'protection of work environment', lower than that of management (in only one of the other six decision areas was their mean rating higher than 'little'). Significantly, they rated employee influence through indirect participation higher than management (in four of the seven decision areas their rating of employee influence was between 'moderate' and 'much').

2. Dickson found that whilst 'shop stewards were suspicious of direct participation unaccompanied by indirect participation' because it 'might be an attempt by managers to gain greater productivity from employees without a commensurate increase in employee benefits', managers 'favoured the introduction of direct participation prior to indirect participation in the hope that some of the perceived positive effects could be transferred to indirect participation' [27].

3. Bartlett, auditing the perceived 'potential value' and 'success' of various categories of participation in four companies, found little disagreement between managers and subordinates regarding the potential value of forms of 'codetermination' (Joint Safety Committees and Management by Objectives) or forms of 'negotiation' (collective bargaining over strategic plans and terms and conditions, productivity bargaining and joint job evaluation committees) but increasing discrepancy in respect of 'consultation' and 'reporting' forms of participation. In auditing the perceived success of the various forms he found that 'the only method that both groups rate as highly successful in practice is that in which their interests most clearly coincide – the joint safety committee', whilst 'conversely maximum disagreement emerges over collective bargaining over company strategic plans' [28].

4. In this latter area of decision making Wilson et al. found that out of 150 strategic decisions surveyed only 29 (19 per cent) involved trade unions. Their analysis of these cases shows that in only three of the nineteen private sector organisations, as opposed to nine out of the ten public sector organisations, did the management rate the union influence as 'quite a lot' or higher. However, they note that even in these cases the union is 'wholly reactive to managerially defined topics' and 'if the unions are in any degree negative towards the decision, their influence achieves little or nothing' [29].

5. Poole believes that industrial efficiency is the main objective of management with regard to both 'involvement' and 'participation', since it may enable the skills and abilities of workers to be effectively tapped, reduce employees' resistance to technological change, raise the level of worker satisfaction leading to a more contented workforce and is a

means for improving industrial relations. He argues that 'the higher the level of decision-making the less likely it has been for workers to have any major influence on the outcomes of events, and the more vigorously managerial "prerogatives" have been defended' [30]. In his view, 'the bulk of schemes for employee participation initiated by management have been restricted in terms of the scope, level and range of issues involved' [31] and while many of these schemes 'may have had important effects in so far as industrial "efficiency" is concerned, it is doubtful whether they imply any significant erosion of managerial "prerogatives"' [32].

6. Neumann identifies a number of constraints on workers' propensity to participate; these include personal apathy, mistrust of management motives, deeply held values and beliefs and fear caused by lack of knowledge and confidence [33].

Implementation of participation/involvement

In seeking to achieve greater employee 'participation' or 'involvement' it is important to recognise that although the initiative for implementation lies primarily with management there are likely to be **diverse expectations** regarding both its purpose and form. Marchington believes there is an inherent danger that management 'may assume that *their* definitions and *their* solutions are acceptable to the different interest groups' [34]. Whilst management may, initially, seek to limit the process to the provision of information, consultation and/or the establishment of direct forms of involvement, nevertheless 'what managements appear to regard as the maximum acceptable to them ... the stewards seem to regard as the minimum basis upon which to build up their influence over a wider range of issues and with more joint decision making' [35].

The **first stage** in any implementation process should involve, therefore, discussions (without preconceptions of the outcome) between management, employees and unions in order to identify and, if possible, reconcile these differing expectations. The ultimate objective should be to develop an agreed and accepted approach – without this, one or other of the parties may soon become disillusioned and withdraw from, or actively obstruct, the implementation and operation of the process. Indeed, Williams believes that 'a clear philosophical or thinking base for participation which has been talked through in the company is more important than any formal structure which may ultimately emerge' [36].

Perhaps the most important prerequisite is **management commitment**. Commitment to the ideal must not only exist in a formal statement of corporate philosophy and principles but be seen to be applied in the decisions that managers make. This requires management to modify its belief that it alone, because of its professional/technical expertise and access to the relevant information, has the ability to make objective decisions based on 'the good of the organisation' or that employees and their representatives are incapable of assimilating and understanding the full range of information and issues and are likely to seek 'partisan' solutions or decisions. All those involved in the participative process (employees, stewards and managers alike) will require both training in the interpersonal skills necessary to manage the new situation effectively and sufficient time to develop those skills and adjust to their new roles.

The introduction of participative arrangements and institutions does not produce instant changes in attitudes or behaviour – only gradual evolution. It is an organic process and, once started, builds up its own momentum. Participation or involvement at one level or on one issue is likely to lead to an expectation and demand for its adoption at other levels and on other issues. It is difficult, if not impossible, for management to call a halt at any particular point and, in effect, say 'employees may participate so far, but no further'. McCarthy and Ellis believe that management should accept from the start that 'within a system of management by agreement there would no longer exist any area of management decision-taking where management itself could claim an absolute and unilateral right to resist union influence in any form' [37].

The development of greater employee participation or involvement is an **organisational strategy** and not something to be left to the discretion of individual managers. No manager can, realistically, be allowed to opt out or subvert the process by giving insufficient information or time to allow for effective participation. However, it is important to recognise that supervisors and junior management in particular may feel that they have the most to lose through the implementation of employee participation. They may perceive their authority and decision making being transferred to employees through direct participation and being bypassed through indirect participation involving stewards or employee representatives meeting and discussing issues with senior management. This can be overcome to a large extent by ensuring that 'employee participation' is not confined to just 'workers' but also encompasses all levels of management itself. Indeed, it can be argued that participation should start with management itself – with supervisory, junior and middle management being more involved in higher managerial decision making. Enhancement of their role in this direction could compensate for any downwards loss.

The most frequent argument against the adoption of greater employee 'participation' is that there is not always sufficient **time for participation** to take place before a decision has to be made. Clearly, the involvement of employees is always likely to increase the time span of making decisions – although in the long run it may be quicker because the decision is more acceptable. However, when time constraints do arise, which is perhaps less often than management imagines, management may have to make the decision without the full involvement of the employees. This does not, of itself, negate the principle of moving towards greater employee participation.

Such exceptions may be accepted more easily by employees and their representatives if they are generally involved in decision making than if they are generally excluded. The overall process of 'participation' can improve management's credibility (in terms of its capacity to arrive at the 'right' decision) in the eyes of its employees and their representatives.

One of the most difficult aspects of implementing 'participation' is to **reconcile greater employee participation with the established role of collective bargaining**. Although Bell believes that the development of employee participation on the basis of an extension of collective bargaining 'would increase the range of issues on which there could be confrontation' [38], ACAS has suggested that the 'willingness to compromise . . . perhaps gives to collective bargaining an effectiveness as a form of employee participation which is absent from other forms where neither party feels committed to reach agreement' [39]. Certainly, as Hawkins points out, collective bargaining is 'based on the assumption that the right to make policy and initiate changes lies with management and that the role of the employees' organization is to react to management proposals and if necessary modify them through negotiation' [40]. As a consequence 'the role which shop stewards and trade union officials tend to find most congenial is that of reacting to initiatives from management' [41] and therefore they may be unprepared for, or wary of, any involvement in processes or institutions which appear to compromise their role and make them party to management decisions. For many trade unionists their very independence, and that of their trade union, depends on their right and ability to oppose management and therefore any form of employee participation which seeks to reduce their opposition also reduces their independence. However, this may be less of a problem if the organisation's style of industrial relations is a 'sophisticated bargained consultor' with its emphasis on problem solving, co-operative bargaining relationship and the blurring of the distinction between negotiation and consultation, rather than a 'constitutionalist' with its conjunctive bargaining relationship which seeks to maintain a clear distinction between negotiation and managerial prerogative to decide.

The content of collective bargaining has been widened, in many organisations, to include discussions of issues not directly related to the determination of terms and conditions of employment. Clearly, therefore, where employee participation is to be implemented in forms additional to the normal collective bargaining arrangements it is necessary to define the boundary between the two processes/institutions. The BIM has implied that the boundary of collective bargaining can be delineated by reference to the legal definition of the subject matter of a trade dispute [42]. It has also suggested that management should develop a formal **Participation Agreement** covering:

1. The objectives of the participative system and the principles underlying it.
2. The range of subjects appropriate to the participative system.

3. The structure and constitution of any participative institutions (e.g. participation committees or councils) which are established.
4. The terms of reference, method of selection and period of tenure of employee directors if such appointments are agreed, and their relationship to employee representatives on the participation committees or councils.
5. Confidentiality of information where appropriate.
6. Method of selection of employee representatives.
7. The role of managers and how their interests as employees are to be represented.
8. The facilities of employee representatives to carry out their role and particularly reporting back to their constituents.
9. Training of managers and employee representatives in participative practices [43].

However, any delineation between employee participation and collective bargaining must, in practice, be flexible and reflect the complementary, rather than competitive, nature of the two processes. Issues which arise in one may have implications which require consideration and decisions within the other.

Finally, it is important to remember that, within unionised organisations, the introduction of employee participation is likely itself to be the subject of discussion between management and unions. Management will, because employee participation concentrates on individuals as 'employees' rather than 'trade union members', seek to ensure that the interests of **non-unionised individuals and groups** are taken into account in the operation of the participatory processes as well as those of unionised individuals and groups. This has the potential for creating conflict between management and trade unions who may well view the full involvement of non-unionised employees on equal terms as a management attempt to weaken their role and power within the organisation. Certainly, whilst some trade union leaders have been prepared to consider the concept of employee 'involvement' and its practical application, the trade union movement in general is suspicious of a development which appears to be an attempt to undermine trade union organisation. For example, the TGWU has set out guidelines for its negotiators on the introduction of employee 'involvement' or 'participation' arrangements [44]:

1. All aspects of employee involvement or participation should be subject to negotiation by the union.
2. Employee representatives should be chosen in line with the union representative machinery.
3. Working groups should be accompanied by the presence of a shop steward.
4. In no case should schemes be allowed to undermine union structures or collective bargaining.

12.3 Involvement in work organisation

A survey in 1988 by the Department of Employment [45] in respect of what action was being undertaken by companies to promote employee 'involvement' shows that 42 per cent of the practices referred to in the company reports related to some form of **direct communication or meetings with employees** (e.g. company magazines or newsletters; employee reports; circulars; noticeboards; line management communication/meetings (both formal and informal); briefing groups; quality circles, etc.). Significantly, most of these practices relate primarily to communicating to employees rather than involving employees.

Many organisations have sought to introduce **'team briefings'** as a means of securing employee involvement and commitment to the organisation. These arrangements generally involve a cascade approach to communicating information from the top to the bottom of the organisation and regular direct meetings between a group of employees and their immediate supervisor or manager during which information relating to the organisation as a whole, as well as immediate work group information, can be communicated and discussed. It provides, through the discussion element, an opportunity for two-way communication and some employee influence on management decision making. It may also marginalise the role of the union because it allows management an opportunity to explain its problems and solutions and gain employee acceptance and commitment as well as, as Marchington points out, providing line management with 'a regular mechanism via which to pick up concerns and grievances at the earliest opportunity' [46]. However, the increased use of 'peripheral' employees (e.g. part-timers, those on short-term contracts, etc.) may mitigate against the effectiveness of team briefings. Marchington notes that in one retail organisation employees, even when they were paid for attending such meetings outside their normal times, 'had other commitments outside of working hours, whilst others were unwilling to come in on their day off' [47].

The increased emphasis placed on the concept of a socio-technical system and **job redesign** has come about through a concern both to improve the quality of working life and to adapt organisations and working arrangements to significant market and technological changes. It has been recognised that previous approaches to work organisation based on 'scientific management' principles (rationalisation, specialisation and centralisation) have not always secured the expected improvements in productivity and often have resulted in frustration and alienation amongst employees.

In approaching the issue of job redesign it is important to recognise its **dynamic qualities**:

1. White suggests that 'fairly massive change is likely to be the norm rather than exceptional' and therefore the development of participative forms of work organisation should be seen as 'a procedure not for dealing with a

unique situation but starting a process of planning, implementation and appraisal which is open ended' [48].

2. Its introduction will produce a constant challenge to and change in management's role; not least because 'the very process of involving employees and the generation of new ideas is bound to modify the original plans' (management's) and 'the genuine participation of employees develops their potential for initiative, and the capacity to exercise discretion and control over their own work' (creates desire for more participation) [49].

3. Its real significance is as an integral part of an overall strategy of developing employee participation. Bell believes that 'without direct participation, giving the individual a greater personal satisfaction in his own job, participation at other levels is unlikely to be successful, and will have little meaning for most employees' [50]; conversely employee involvement cannot be isolated or confined solely at this level or in this form.

The development of participative work organisation may be viewed both as a **means** (a process of management through which organisational/ operational changes may be more easily achieved) and as an **end** in its own right (that individuals gain 'some control over how their work is done, how it is developed and organised, and changes that are made to it' [51]). However, it may be argued that such an approach to developing 'responsible autonomy' is, in reality, little more than expanding or enhancing the employee's job or work situation so that it appears to allow the employee some degree of 'self-control' (but only in areas and in a direction which supports the achievement of management objectives and increases organisational effectiveness and efficiency) and requires employees to adopt and pursue management ideals and values as an integral part of their working situation.

The individual's work needs

Much of today's approach to participative forms of work organisation owes its origins to the ideas of people such as Maslow, Herzberg and McGregor. Maslow [52] argued, as long ago as the 1940s, that people have a hierarchy of needs ranging from the basic physiological need for food, clothing and shelter to higher self-esteem and self-actualisation needs to use and develop their skills and ability, and that once the lower order needs were satisfied they ceased to be a motivator. Herzberg [53] identified that those aspects of a person's job which had the greatest potential for providing satisfaction arose from the job's content in terms of personal achievement, recognition, responsibility and growth. McGregor [54] argued that management viewed its employees from a Theory X basis (that people are essentially lazy and disinterested, must be directed and controlled and are only motivated to work by monetary incentives), whereas in reality a Theory Y perspective may be more appropriate (that people wish to obtain satisfaction and achievement from their work and therefore are capable of assuming responsibility and generating self-motivation and self-control).

More recent research and experience has demonstrated that employee motivation and satisfaction is dependent on a complex interrelationship of economic, social and psychological factors and is not necessarily constant either between individuals or over time for the same individual. Perhaps more importantly, the work done in the area of job design has challenged existing concepts in so far as technology is regarded as a variable which often can be changed or modified to meet the social needs of the employees and organisation. Thus, it is possible to identify a range of **beneficial characteristics of work** which can enhance the individual's level of job satisfaction and motivation. These have been set out by the Department of Employment Work Research Unit as follows [55]:

1. Tasks should, as far as possible:
    (a) form a coherent job;
    (b) make a significant and visible contribution;
    (c) provide variety of method;
    (d) allow feedback on performance;
    (e) entail the use of discretion in carrying out the work; and
    (f) carry attributable responsibility for outcomes and particularly control of work.

2. Tasks should not, as far as possible:
    (a) be paced (that is, require completion in a time determined not by the worker but the machine or system);
    (b) be short cycle; or
    (c) create social deprivation (that is, put those who prefer to be isolated in a crowd or isolate those who prefer social activity).

3. Jobs and work organisation should:
    (a) provide opportunity for learning;
    (b) lead to some future desired by the job holders;
    (c) enable people to contribute to decisions affecting their jobs and the goals of the organisation;
    (d) ensure that the goals and other people's expectations are clear;
    (e) provide a degree of challenge; and
    (f) provide training and information adequate to perform at acceptable levels.

Bailey argues that as far as the individual is concerned 'specialization takes place in organizations both on a horizontal plane in terms of specialization of tasks at the same level, and vertically in terms of specialized functions and decisions' [56]. Thus, it is possible to improve job satisfaction by **restructuring the individual's job** in three different ways:

1. **Job rotation** allows the individual to achieve a degree of variety of work by rotating between different, but generally related, tasks on the horizontal plane.
2. **Job enlargement** can create more complete and satisfying jobs by combining previously separate, specialised tasks on the horizontal plane within one single job.
3. **Job enrichment** can increase the individual's responsibility by devolving, on the vertical plane, additional functions such as record keeping, quality control, etc., previously carried out by management.

All of these forms of restructuring allow the individual a greater degree of control over his/her work situation, although it is only the latter which provides for involvement in areas of decision making which have been traditionally the prerogative of management. However, as Hawkins points out, it would be wrong to assume that 'desire for intrinsic satisfaction with, or "self-actualisation" in, the job is an overriding priority of most workers for most of the time' [57]. Most employees are also concerned with their extrinsic rewards (money) and may well expect an improvement in the level of these extrinsic rewards as an integral and justified part of any proposal to restructure their work and increase their job flexibility or responsibility.

The workgroup

Much of the thinking and developments in the area of work redesign has centred on organisational changes which involve an enhancement of the status of the work group. Bailey has suggested that 'the degree of autonomy and facility for self-organisation' inherent in group working provides the employees with 'the opportunity to influence and exercise leadership' through 'delegating complete task responsibility to the group' [58]. It is in the area of **delegation of authority to the workgroup** that work redesign has, perhaps, the most to offer in respect of increasing employee participation in decision making. Most importantly, it may encompass employee involvement in the setting of goals, objectives or targets to be achieved by the group and employee determination of the division and allocation of tasks and responsibilities between individuals.

The development and enhancement of the workgroup has serious implications for the **role of management** – particularly the first line supervisor. Certainly, Bailey believes that for many managers 'the idea of autonomous groups has all sorts of connotations of loss of control, threat to their position and authority and anarchy on the shop floor' [59]. However, it would be wrong to assume that the delegation of authority to workgroups involves an abandonment of leadership or direction. Bell suggests that the critical question to be decided is 'whether the leader should come from within the group itself and remain part of it, a peer among peers, or should he be appointed from outside, a manager with the managed?' [60]. In this context, he argues that the continuation of an emphasis on external managerial supervision will result in the process of decision making becoming 'one of consultation or at most joint decision making, not delegated authority' [61]. If the status of the work group is to be enhanced to its full potential for employee participation the supervision role must change from one of directing and controlling the work of individuals to one of co-ordinating and providing a resource, when required, to aid workgroups in achieving their agreed tasks and goals.

The role of the union

Trade union resistance to the introduction of participative forms of work organisation may stem from a number of factors:

1. Management's apparent emphasis on the intrinsic rewards of increased job satisfaction resulting from such changes may be seen as an attempt to play down the importance of extrinsic rewards.
2. Trade unions may regard management's primary intention in introducing such work changes as being the improvement of productivity and costs rather than increasing the participation of employees in decision making and, as such, may conflict with trade union objectives such as maintaining existing levels of employment.
3. The proposed work and organisational changes may involve the breaking down of traditional demarcation lines between groups of workers – particularly between maintenance and production workers.
4. The development of 'direct' forms of participation may be regarded as an attempt to undermine the existing representative arrangements with a consequent diminution in the role of trade union and shop steward.

Consequently, Bailey argues that trade unions may be suspicious and perceive the possible introduction of participative forms of work organisations as 'no more than a subtle way of exploiting the worker to achieve greater production without rewarding him for his efforts' [62].

In approaching this issue, trade unions may adopt either of **two strategies**:

1. avoid discussing any changes until such time as management is able to present its proposals formally for negotiation in respect of the consequent changes in terms and conditions of employment (including pay); or

2. accept involvement from the very beginning in the planning and development of the new system in order to directly influence the nature of the changes.

Whilst the introduction of participative systems, if they are to have any real meaning, should be themselves developed and introduced through a fully participative process, nevertheless it must be recognised that trade unions are wary of any involvement in the early stages of decision making which may result, or be argued by management to result, in the union being committed to a particular course of action and unable to challenge it subsequently. The objective of the trade union, when dealing with the introduction of participative forms of work organisation, must be to improve the opportunities for its members to directly participate in decision making without weakening their representative role and influence in other facets of the organisation.

The adoption of participative forms of work organisation, in particular those based on the devolution of authority to the work group, has the capacity both to enhance and to detract from the **shop steward's role**. It can reduce the shop steward's role of representing work-related problems to supervision (these now become a matter for internal group resolution) and allow the steward to concentrate on a more positive role within the wider representational systems within the organisation. Like the supervisor, the relationship with members over work-related issues becomes one of being a resource to which they may turn in order to aid the group in resolving its problems. However, it can provide a means of direct communication and decision making between employees and management, without recourse to the shop steward, which may reduce the shop steward's authority with both management and members.

12.4 Worker directors and Works Councils

Most other European countries have a legal requirement for the establishment of Works Councils and employee representation at board level (worker directors). However, so far as **Works Councils** are concerned it is important to remember that in most cases it comprises only or primarily employee representatives and as such 'provides a forum in which employee representatives can be consulted and informed' [63]. It is principally a consultative body of employee, as opposed to union, representatives which runs in parallel to the union/management negotiation of terms and conditions of employment. Although there may be a legal requirement for management to consult with the Works Council on major issues such as rationalisation and redundancy, nevertheless they appear to lack any real decision making power and, generally, have been established in the absence of strong uionism and collective bargaining at the organisational level – unlike the UK. Consequently, it may be argued that in the UK the functions of the Works Council have been carried out by shop stewards through the expansion of the scope of collective bargaining to cover more than just the determination of terms and conditions of employment. However, some companies (such as Cadbury-Schweppes and Bulmers) have established Employee Councils covering the whole organisation as the pinnacle of their communication and consultation arrangements.

The European Commission has adopted a draft Directive for the establishment of **European Works Councils** (EWC), at the request of employees or their representatives, in organisations with more than 1,000 employees and at least two establishments of more than 100 employees in different member states [64]. The EWC would include at least one representative from each country in which the organisation has an establishment, would meet at least once a year and would be provided with information on the organisation's economic and financial situation; investment, production and sales position and plans; and its employment situation. In addition, it would have the right to be consulted on any management proposal which could have serious consequences for employees. This initiative is a response to the inability of national laws and arrangements to deal adequately with transnational organisations whose decisions in one country may well affect employees in another and the consequent possibility of unequal treatment of employees in different countries. Clearly, the establishment of a EWC in an organisation which has British establishments could lead to the establishment of similar bodies at the site and/or company level within Britain – if such consultative committees or councils do not already exist.

Not only is **employee representation on the board (worker directors)** widely established by law in many European countries [65] but there has been a European Commission draft Directive since the early 1970s (revised in 1988) which proposes worker directors as one, but not the only, model for employee participation in organisations with more than 1,000 employees. However, few organisations in Britain have introduced worker directors – the most notable examples have been the British Steel Corporation (1967) and the Post Office (1977).

It is evident that management and trade unions have **differing perceptions of the worker directors' role:**

1. **Management** tends to regard the worker director primarily in terms of establishing a 'coalition' between employees and management. Worker directors can, by contributing their views and experience, improve the quality of board room discussions and decisions; secure greater employee commitment to the decisions made at the board level; and reduce conflict by making employees more aware of the problems and constraints which face management. Hawkins suggests that the

assumption underlying the European experience of worker directors is that the 'presence of workers on company boards will encourage a climate of mutual confidence and cooperation throughout the enterprise' [66].

2. **Trade unions** are split in their view of the relevance and importance of worker directors. Some take the view that the introduction of worker directors would detract from their role as a countervailing power to management and inhibit their ability to challenge management decisions. Other trade unions, and the TUC, take the view that they should seek to establish joint control at all levels of the organisation where decisions are made which affect employees and that 'in the absence of board-level representation, trade unionists find it very difficult to influence . . . key decisions' [67]. The function of worker directors is to do more than simply give their views to management – it is to represent and jointly make decisions on behalf of the employees.

Clearly, these differences in perception are reflected in differences of view regarding the relationship of the worker director to management, trade unions and the collective bargaining system.

The board of directors and management

A crucial part of the debate on worker directors has centred on the power and functions of the board on which employees would be represented. Two main alternatives have been discussed – **retaining the existing single (unitary) board or creating a new supervisory board as part of a two tier board structure** (as in Germany). In essence the debate is about whether the worker director should be an integral part of the normal management of the organisation or concerned only with broad policy issues and the general overseeing of management.

The main argument in favour of adopting the **supervisory, two tier board structure** is that it would reduce the risk of confrontation because the worker directors would be involved only in less contentious long-term policy issues rather than immediate strategies and decisions. This view was clearly supported by the Minority Report of the Bullock Committee of Inquiry on Industrial Democracy. The employer members, who produced the Minority Report, argued that the existing unitary board was 'in effect the apex of a Company's management team' and therefore they were 'completely opposed to the introduction into existing Boards of representatives of special interests . . . which might provoke a confrontation or extend the scope of collective bargaining into top level management decision-making' [68]. They felt that the supervisory board 'should not involve itself with the detailed decision-making of existing Boards of Directors, not even with the determining policy; but should be primarily concerned with the quality of the management of the company and its capacity to run the company profitably and competitively' [69]. This view was also evident in the BSC experiment where the worker directors were appointed only to the lower divisional boards, whose responsibility was simply to advise the divisional managing director, rather than to the main board which was the only body which had authority to make major policy decisions.

However, the Main Report of the Bullock Committee favoured the retention of the existing **unitary, single tier structure**. In their opinion the creation of a two tier structure could confuse, rather than clarify, the process of management and responsibility for decision making within the organisation and lead to conflict between the two levels in respect of the nature and extent of their functions. They felt that the debate between the two approaches was somewhat academic in that 'many United Kingdom companies have developed a de facto two tier system, delegating responsibility for the formulation and implementation of policy from the main board perhaps to a management committee' [70].

Most importantly, they argued that a two tier structure could negate the very thing that the introduction of worker directors was intended to achieve; namely, employee participation in organisational decision making. In their view, the establishment of a two tier board system 'would, in its desire to preserve the freedom of management, so delimit the powers of the [supervisory] board on which employees are represented that employee participation in decision-making would be very restricted' [71]. Certainly, Costello's examination of the Irish experience of worker directors in seven state enterprises suggests that the exclusion of worker directors from the more operational management decision making may make their role impotent. He found that because the board's responsibilities were confined to the establishment of broad corporate objectives 'this precluded worker directors from raising many of the issues which were of concern to the employees who had elected them. Most of these issues were seen to fall within management's responsibility and attempts to raise them in the boardroom were invariably ruled out of order' [72].

It is important to recognise that the introduction of worker directors, even on the existing unitary board, is unlikely to affect significantly the **power and decision making of senior management**. Certainly, the Main Report of the Bullock Committee accepted that 'senior management will continue to be relied upon for detailed advice on the formulation of corporate policy and for the implementation of board decisions, and at the top level will act, as now, as an informal or formal management committee' [73]. Brannen *et al.* found that in the BSC experiment formal and informal meetings of management and full-time directors were more significant in organisational decision making than formal board meetings [74]. Furthermore, Batstone *et al.* found that in the Post Office the worker directors 'did not act as a caucus, and therefore did not exploit to the full the power which they formally possess', the 'consumer representative generally favoured management policies' and 'the union nominees themselves tended to accept the notion of the full-timers as *primi inter pares*' [75]. The ability of worker directors to exert an effective influence on management decision making is likely to be inhibited by:

1. The infrequency of formal board meetings.
2. Their exclusion from other directorial and senior management meetings.
3. The predominant role of the board being the formal endorsement of proposals or decisions offered by senior management.
4. Their reliance, in the absence of any alternative source, on these same senior management for information and advice on which to base their decisions or challenges to the proposals laid before them.

At the same time worker directors will be expected by the other directors and senior management to respect the confidentiality of much of the information they receive and to adopt an 'objective' (i.e. management) view of the issues under consideration. Consequently, the worker director is always in danger of becoming, or being seen as, part of management – the role as a 'director' dominates over the role as an 'employee'.

So far as the **legal responsibilities of worker directors** are concerned, the TUC argued in their evidence to the Bullock Committee that company law equated 'interests of the company' with 'interests of the shareholders' and therefore worker directors should have an analogous rather than identical legal responsibility to that of the shareholder directors and should be accountable to the employees. However, the Bullock Committee felt that the creation of differential legal responsibilities could negate the notion of collective responsibility for board decisions and, in effect, create two boards within the one. Even though proposals for the introduction of worker directors have not been implemented, company law has been amended to require *all* directors to have regard to the interests of both shareholders and employees.

Another crucial area of debate has centred on whether they should be in **a minority on the board or have parity with shareholder directors** – in the BSC experiment the worker directors were in a minority, whilst in the Post Office there was equal representation. Even in Germany, where parity of representation was legislated for in 1976, the chairman of the board (elected by the shareholders) has the casting vote in board decisions. The Bullock Committee reported from their visits to Sweden and Germany that it had been suggested that minority representation 'has given employees a valuable insight into the process of development and determination of company policy at the top level and access to management information' which 'has been useful to employees and their trade unions in discussions and negotiations with management at other levels of the enterprise' [76]. It has been argued that even a minority representation allows employees to influence management decision making, thereby ensuring that management gives more attention to their interests, and has the additional advantage of ensuring that worker directors do not have to accept collective responsibility for any board decisions with which they disagree. However, it also allows shareholder directors to maintain their control of the whole framework of policy and decision making and to determine the extent to which they will allow employees' views and interests actually to influence their decisions. The TUC is very clear that without parity of representation worker directors have no effective share in decision making; so far as they are concerned, equality of responsibility requires equality of representation.

The Bullock Committee Main Report was in no doubt that minority representation restricted the potential effectiveness of employee participation and therefore recommended a parity basis of representation but on a **2X + Y formula** (2X denotes equal numbers of shareholder and worker directors and Y denotes co-opted independent members). The addition of the independent members would, it was hoped, not only bring in expertise from outside the organisation but also ensure the retention of consensus as the norm for board room decision making. However, Mr Nicholas Wilson argued in a note of dissent from the Main Report [77] that the introduction of this third group of directors could, in practice, increase the likelihood of polarisation and negotiation within the board room with the independents being required to act in some form of arbitration role which would result in imposed decisions which did not have the full support of the board.

Trade unions and collective bargaining

The third crucial area of debate on worker directors has involved their **method of selection**. The point at issue is whether they are to act essentially in an individual reporting capacity or in a representative capacity on behalf of the employees as a group. In both the BSC and Post Office the worker directors were not elected but appointed by the Chairman from a list of trade union nominees and were, as Brannen *et al.* point out, regarded as 'experts in their own right ... people who could bring to the board the authentic view of the average man on the shop floor' [78]. There are two main alternatives in the selection procedure – linked to some form of works council consultative system or linked to the established trade union based collective bargaining arrangements (see Figure 12.2).

The selection of worker directors through the trade union machinery has been criticised largely because it is seen as a strengthening of the role of the trade union within the organisation at the expense of the rights and interests of non-union employees. Consequently, some have advocated the adoption and utilisation of a **works council consultative structure** as the basis for the selection and reporting back of worker directors because it can encompass all employees irrespective of whether or not they are union members. This

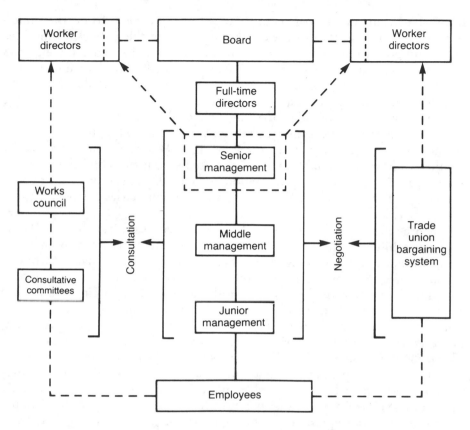

Figure 12.2   *Channels of representation*

approach underpinned the proposals in the Bullock Committee Minority Report that:

1. worker directors could be nominated by either an independent recognised trade union or ten employees;
2. a candidate must have been a member of a consultative committee for at least three years; and
3. an election would only be valid if there were not less than three candidates for each office and not less than 60 per cent of the electorate voted.

The Bullock Committee Main Report rejected this approach largely because 'any attempt to bypass this structure would be seen as an attack on trade unions and collective bargaining' [79]. Indeed, Elliot noted that in the BSC worker directors were in reality a 'third channel' 'divorced not only from the main union bargaining procedure but also from the union consultative process' [80]. It is clear that the view of the Bullock Committee was strongly influenced by government support for encouraging and strengthening the role of trade unions and collective bargaining. The reduction, during the 1980s, in government support for trade unions and employer attempts to revitalise joint consultation are likely to encourage management to resist the idea of a single channel of representation based on trade unions. However, it must be recognised that the strengthening of joint consultation by linking worker directors to a Works Council may easily conflict with existing established and accepted systems of collective bargaining based on trade union representation and, therefore, can only be effective if there is a clear and accepted delineation of the boundaries between the two sets of machinery.

Those who support the **single channel of representation via the trade union machinery**, where such machinery exists and is accepted by management for collective bargaining, argue that its use will ensure that the work of worker directors complements rather than conflicts with the collective bargaining arrangements by supporting the extension of employee influence at other higher levels of management within the organisation. At the same time it provides a ready-made mechanism for representing the employees' interests and ensuring the worker director's accountability to the employees. The Bullock Committee identified that 'such machinery would provide the expertise and independent strength necessary to support employee representatives and to enable them to play an effective role in decision-making on the board' [81]. It proposed that the introduction of worker directors should be triggered by a request from one or more independent recognised trade unions which would have to be supported, through a ballot, by a majority of the employees voting providing that those in favour represented at least a third of the organisation's employees. Following a successful ballot all independent recognised unions would be eligible for membership of a Joint Representation Committee (JRC) which would have responsibility initially to determine how the employee representatives should be selected and on a continuing basis to provide the necessary support for the worker directors and act as the interface between them and the collective bargaining process. The Bullock proposals did not envisage that individual worker directors would be subject to direct election by the employees.

Clearly, the introduction of worker directors presents potential **role problems for the shop stewards** who are likely to provide the majority of such board members. Marchington and Armstrong's survey found that the two main problems anticipated by shop stewards, should they become a worker director, were 'role conflict' and 'loss of contact with membership/ development of élites'. Certainly, shop steward involvement in board level management decisions can undermine their position as employee representatives and compromise their traditional oppositional role within collective bargaining. Marchington and Armstrong found that 'fears were expressed by stewards about the difficulty of balancing reconciling interests, particularly when they have been exposed to management reasoning and become incorporated into management thinking' [82]. However, other stewards felt that they should take advantage of any opportunity to obtain information from management, influence their decisions and represent their members; and, as Marchington and Armstrong point out, shop stewards are already exposed to potential role conflict within normal collective bargaining – particularly productivity bargaining. The elevation of a small group of shop stewards to the board room may easily create a divorced élite which becomes unrepresentative of employees and members. Marchington and Armstrong suggest that the extent to which this may happen will depend, at least in part, on the 'type' of steward ('popularist' or 'leader' – with the latter most likely to become divorced and élitist) but that it can be mitigated by both management and trade unions ensuring that there is an adequate institutional framework to ensure a continued interchange between worker directors, other shop stewards and employees/members.

Some people have expressed concern regarding the **position of non-unionists** under the single channel arrangement – in particular, managers and other professional groups of employees. The Bullock Committee rejected any notion of reserving one worker director's seat for this group and, clearly, if any such provision were to be made it could provide, or at least create the impression of providing, management with an in-built majority on the board. The alternative, as suggested by the Bullock Committee, would be for any distinct group which is not represented by an existing independent recognised union within the organisation to establish their own staff or employee organisation which, providing it achieved a certificate of independence, could seek inclusion on the JRC.

Although the Bullock Committee did not recommend any specific qualification regarding **eligibility to become a worker director**, most employers have argued strongly that they should be an employee of the organisation (the Minority Report suggested a minimum of ten years service). However, the Bullock Committee did not preclude the possibility that, as in Germany, a union full-time officer who was not an employee of the organisation might appropriately be selected as a worker director. Certainly they did not feel that a worker director who was a shop steward or branch official should be required to relinquish his/her trade union office – as had been the case in the early days of the BSC experiment. In their opinion the retention of the union position aided the integration of the worker director role with the collective bargaining process and facilitated the maintenance of links with other employees. In addition, they did not feel it necessary to formally preclude worker directors from any discussions at board level associated with collective bargaining, although they pointed out that the shareholder directors with support from the co-opted members were likely to ensure that any management strategy in respect of a negotiation would not be discussed by the board.

Legislation or evolution

There are major differences between trade unions and management on the role of law in promoting worker directors. The TUC has favoured a legal compulsion on organisations to adopt worker directors on a parity basis. It is felt that this is the only way in which management can be pressurised to accept worker directors. However, it may be argued that the need to adopt a compulsory approach is founded as much on the apparent lack of interest displayed by most employees in such a development. Employers, on the other hand, favour a more flexible approach which would allow management and trade unions in each organisation to develop the form of participation most suited to their needs and circumstances. The CBI proposed in its evidence to the Bullock Committee that the role of legislation should be restricted to requiring organisations to conclude a Participation Agreement which might include provision of employee representation at the board level, in a variety of different possible ways, but would also cover representative structures at other levels in the organisation.

The Labour Government White Paper on Industrial Democracy (1978), produced in response to the Bullock Committee Report, was a compromise between these two views. Whilst recognising that employees should have a statutory right of representation at the board level, the government felt that it would be wrong to compel, through legislation, the adoption of any particular form. They proposed that, as far as possible, management and trade unions should be free to negotiate and agree whatever form of representation was considered most suitable for them.

12.5 Summary propositions

- Employee participation is a philosophy of organisational management, not a particular institutional form, and therefore its successful implementation and operation depend primarily on management's acceptance of the philosophy.
- Management favours task centred, direct forms of 'involvement' centred on the individual employee; trade unions favour power-centred, indirect forms of 'participation' based on the established representational role of trade unions in collective bargaining.
- The most effective structure of employee participation within an organisation is one which combines direct employee involvement in decisions relating to their immediate work situation with indirect participation at the board level on major organisational decisions, whilst not undermining the representational role of established trade unions.

Further reading

- J. Elliot, *Conflict or Cooperation: The growth of industrial democracy*, (2nd edn), Kogan Page, 1984. Parts II and III examine both the trade union and management attitudes towards employee participation.
- D. Guest and K. Knight, *Putting Participation into Practice*, Gower, 1979. A very useful examination of the implementation of participation at various levels.
- J. Bailey, *Job Design and Work Organisation*. Prentice Hall, 1983. A comprehensive study of participative forms of work organisation.
- *Bullock Committee of Inquiry on Industrial Democracy*, HMSO, 1977. An important text on worker directors.
- M. Poole, *Towards a New Democracy: Workers' participation in industry*, Routledge and Kegan Paul, 1986. A very useful examination of a range of issues and factors affecting employee participation.

References

1. R. Hyman, *Industrial Relations: A Marxist introduction*, Macmillan, 1975, p. 180.
2. International Labour Office, 'Participation of Workers in Decisions within Undertakings', *Labour–Management Relations Series*, No. 33, 1969, pp 30–42.
3. K. F. Walker, 'Workers' participation in management: concepts and reality' in B. Barrett, E. Rhodes and J. Beishen (eds), *Industrial Relations and the Wider Society*, Open University, 1975, p. 436.
4. D. Farnham and J. Pimlott, *Understanding Industrial Relations* (2nd edn), Cassell, 1983, p. 421.
5. C. Pateman, *Participation and Democratic Theory*, CUP, 1970, p. 67.
6. T. D. Wall and J. A. Lischeron, *Worker Participation*, McGraw-Hill, 1977, p. 36.
7. J. Elliot, *Conflict or Cooperation: the growth of industrial democracy* (2nd edn), Kogan Page, 1984, pp. 124–5.
8. P. Brannen, *Authority and Participation in Industry*, Batsford, 1985, p. 31.
9. *IPM Code of Professional Conduct and Codes of Practice*, 1990. p. 26.
10. D. Farnham and J. Pimlott, *Understanding Industrial Relations* (4th edn), 1990, p. 82.
11. Involvement and Participation Association, *Industrial Participation*, autumn 1989, p. 2.
12. *IPM Code of Professional Conduct and Codes of Practice*, op. cit.
13. Commission of the European Communities, 'Employee Participation and Company Structure', *Bulletin of the European Communities*, Supplement 8/75, p. 9.
14. 'Personnel directors at odds with Government policy on participation', *Personnel Management*, December 1990, p. 5; P. Crofts, 'IPM comes out in favour of new statutory right to information', *Personnel Management Plus*, November 1990, p. 1.
15. J. Dickson, 'The relation of direct and indirect participation', *Industrial Relations Journal*, vol. 12, no. 4, 1981, pp. 27–35.
16. K. F. Walker, op. cit., p. 435.

17. D. W. Bell, *Industrial Participation*, Pitman, 1979, p. 139.
18. *ibid*.
19. M. Marchington, *Managing Industrial Relations*, McGraw-Hill, 1982, p. 151.
20. BIM, *Employee Participation: The way ahead*, 1977, p. 1.
21. G. Buckingham, 'Participation in practice: the emerging consensus and what to do about it', *Personnel Management*, October 1980, p. 38.
22. *ibid*.
23. M. Marchington, 'Employee participation – consensus or confusion?', *Personnel Management*, April 1981, p. 38.
24. H. Ramsay, 'Phantom participation: patterns of power and conflict', *Industrial Relations Journal*, vol. 11, no. 3, 1980, p. 47.
25. ACAS, *Employee Participation – A Look at the Current Scene*, undated, p. 4.
26. M. Warner, 'Workplace participation and employee influence: a study of managers and shop stewards', *Industrial Relations Journal*, vol. 13, no. 4, 1982, Tables 3 and 4, p. 20.
27. J. Dickson, *op. cit.*, p. 32.
28. B. Bartlett, 'Auditing to progress participation', *Personnel Management*, February 1982, pp. 34–5.
29. D. C. Wilson *et al.*, 'The limits of trade union power in organisational decision making', *British Journal of Industrial Relations*, vol. XX, 1982, p. 333.
30. M. Poole, *Towards a New Industrial Democracy: Workers participation in industry*, Routledge & Kegan Paul, 1986, p. 17.
31. *ibid.*, p. 44.
32. *ibid.*, pp. 47–8.
33. J. Neumann, 'Why people don't participate when given the chance', *Industrial Participation*, spring, 1989.
34. M. Marchington (1982), *op. cit.*, p. 155.
35. *ibid.*, p. 154.
36. D. Williams, 'Multi-level participation at Cadbury Schweppes' in D. Guest and K. Knight, *Putting Participation into Practice*, Gower Press, 1979, p. 193.
37. W. E. J. McCarthy and N. D. Ellis, *Management by Agreement*, Hutchinson, 1973, p. 96.
38. D. W. Bell, *op. cit.*, p. 221.
39. ACAS, *op. cit.*, p. 8.
40. K. Hawkins, *The Management of Industrial Relations*, Penguin, 1978, p. 134.
41. *ibid.*, p. 130.
42. BIM, *op. cit.*, p. 2.
43. *ibid.*, p. 3.
44. 'Employee involvement and the trade unions', *IRS Employment Trends*, no. 459, March 1990, p. 3.
45. 'Employee involvement', *Employment Gazette*, October 1988.
46. M. Marchington, 'Employee involvement schemes', *BIM Employment Bulletin & IR Digest*, March 1989, p. 2.
47. *ibid*.
48. G. C. White, 'Technological Change and Employment, *DE Work Research Unit, Occasional Paper 22*, July 1982, p. 11.
49. DE Work Research Unit, *Meeting the Challenge of Change: Guidelines*, June 1982, pp. 11–12.
50. D. W. Bell, *op. cit.*, p. 5.

51. O. Tynan, 'Improving the Quality of Working Life in the 1980s', *DE Work Research Unit, Occasional Paper 16*, November, 1980, p. 4.
52. A. M. Maslow, 'A Theory of Human Motivation', *Psychological Review*, vol. 50, 1943.
53. F. Herzberg, *Work and the Nature of Man*, World Publishing Co., 1966.
54. D. McGregor, *Human Side of Enterprise*, McGraw-Hill, 1960.
55. O. Tynan, *op. cit.*, p. 3.
56. J. Bailey, *Job Design and Work Organization*, Prentice Hall, 1983, p. 77.
57. K. Hawkins, *op. cit.*, p. 121.
58. J. Bailey, *op. cit.*, p. 79.
59. *ibid.*, p. 106.
60. D. W. Bell, *op. cit.*, p. 209.
61. *ibid.*
62. J. Bailey, *op. cit.*, p. 177.
63. 'Works councils: the door opens', *Labour Research*, April 1991.
64. 'Draft directive on European Works Councils', *European Industrial Relations Review*, no. 206, March 1991.
65. 'Survey of board-level employee representation', *European Industrial Relations Review*, no. 205, February 1991.
66. K. Hawkins, *op. cit.*, p. 137.
67. TUC, *Industrial Democracy*, 1977, p. 45.
68. *Report of the Committee of Inquiry on Industrial Democracy* (Bullock Committee), HMSO, 1977, p. 176.
69. *ibid.*, p. 178.
70. *ibid.*, p. 72.
71. *ibid.*, p. 77.
72. M. Costello, 'Ireland's experiment with worker directors', *Personnel Management*, October 1983, p. 57.
73. *Bullock Committee Report*, *op. cit.*, p. 79.
74. P. Brannen, E. Batstone, D. Fatchett and P. White, *The Worker Directors*, Hutchinson, 1976.
75. E. Batstone, A. Ferner and M. Terry, *Unions on the Board*, Blackwell, 1983, p. 165.
76. *Bullock Committee Report*, *op. cit.*, p. 93.
77. *ibid.*, pp. 163–6.
78. P. Brannen *et al.*, *op. cit.*, p. 138.
79. *Bullock Committee Report*, *op. cit.*, pp. 110–11.
80. J. Elliott, *op. cit.*, p. 172.
81. *Bullock Committee Report*, *op. cit.*, p. 111.
82. M. Marchington and R. Armstrong, 'Employee participation: problems for the shop steward', *Industrial Relations Journal*, vol. 12, no. 1, 1981, p. 50.

Chapter 13
Industrial action

13.1 Definition

The use, or threat, of industrial action is perhaps the most controversial issue in industrial relations. Those who emphasise the potentially harmful consequences of a system which accepts and even encourages the use of such power argue, like Hutt, that it 'is an intolerable abuse of economic freedom . . . a type of warfare under which privileged groups can gain at the expense of the unprivileged' and embodies the unacceptable principle that 'power to disrupt may be properly relied upon by those who are in a position to organize disruption (to secure whatever objectives they believe are good, or for their own advantage)' [1]. Those who emphasise the critical role played by the display of power in influencing both the management/employee relationship and the outcome of any specific negotiation argue, like Grunfeld, that 'it is only the ultimate power of trade union officials and their rank and file members to disrupt production, services or the conduct of an enterprise by the withdrawal of labour which prevents even the most enlightened managerial regime from becoming mere paternalism' [2] or, like Kornhauser *et al.*, that 'collective bargaining would have little meaning were it not for the possibility of a strike, with attendant losses on both sides, since there would be little pressure on the parties to modify their positions and reach agreements' [3].

Whilst the strike is the most obvious and frequently discussed form of industrial action, it is important to recognise that:

1. it is only one of a range of activities which may be classified as 'industrial action'; and
2. 'industrial action' is not the exclusive province of employees/unions but may also be instigated by management.

The term 'industrial action' may be applied to:

> **any temporary suspension of normal working arrangements which is initiated unilaterally by either employees (whether through their union or not) or management with the objective of exerting pressure within the collective bargaining relationship.**

Therefore, the potential for industrial action is a constant, integral but generally quiescent element in the negotiating process and its use confirms the relative bargaining advantage between the parties and acts as an inducement to make concessions which will lead to an acceptable solution.

13.2 Function and forms of industrial action

The conflict of interest which is inherent in industrial organisations is usually expressed and resolved through negotiation within established procedures and institutions of collective bargaining without recourse to industrial action by either party. The existence of a conflict of interest should not, therefore, be seen as synonymous with the use of overt collective industrial action. In examining the role of industrial action within the industrial relations system it is necessary to consider not only its function in the conduct of the collective bargaining relationship and the various forms it might take but also the factors which may influence its use (see Figure 13.1).

Function of industrial action

Conflict within social structures, such as the industrial relations system, may be viewed from **three perspectives**:

1. The expression of conflicting ideas and interests represents a **direct challenge to the internal order and stability of the social system**. It is feared that, without such order and stability, the social system may degenerate into a state of anarchy and lawlessness. Therefore, it is the expression of conflict which is perceived as being the problem to be controlled or even removed.
2. Conflict is a **necessary prelude to the development of a new social order**. A social system can only move from one state of order to another if the existing status quo is overtly challenged and defeated. Therefore, it is the status quo which is perceived as the issue to be resolved.
3. The open expression of conflict is an **important element in the maintenance of stability within the social system**. It provides the means for identifying and balancing different interests within a dynamic and constantly developing social system.

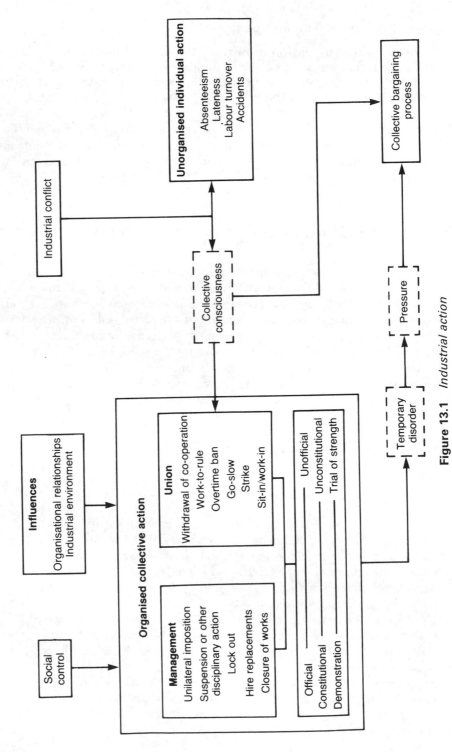

Figure 13.1 *Industrial action*

This latter functional perspective underlies the **institutionalisation of conflict** within industrial relations. The growth of organised labour, and its consequent recognition by both employers and the state through the development of collective bargaining arrangements, resulted in trade unions becoming an accepted part of 'the establishment' at both organisational and national levels. Thus, Dubin argued that trade unions and management became 'joint managers of discontent' within an industrial relations system which had 'self-limiting boundaries that distinguish permissible from subversive industrial disorder' [4], whilst Clarke regarded the strike as 'the price paid for industrial self-regulation of conditions of employment' and the means to 'bring into the open, and serve to dispel, long-festering grievances, or achieve socially and/or economically desirable improvements' [5]. Jackson argues that the development of, and reliance on, the process of collective bargaining has itself diminished any fundamental challenge to the status quo on the part of employees 'by persuading them to accept, ultimately, the need for compromise, and by leading them to believe that gains can be made within the confines of the present system' [6].

However, it is important to distinguish between **communal and non-communal conflict** [7]. It is only the former, where despite conflict there remains a basic community of interest between the parties concerned, which can be regarded as having a functional role in maintaining the stability of the industrial relations system. Where there is no apparent underlying community of interest (non-communal conflict) it will be difficult to achieve compromise between the parties within the normal operation of the system. Whilst the survival of the firm may provide a basis of common interest for most employees, union and managers in most situations, nevertheless Hyman believes that 'not all conflicts are capable of containment and absorption by the social structures which give rise to them' and that 'unless and until the basic structure of industry and society is radically recast . . . the institutionalisation of industrial conflict will of necessity remain partial and precarious' [8].

It is perhaps inevitable that industrial action should be **perceived as exclusively an employee or union phenomenon**. Its use is often an expression of dissatisfaction not just with the content of a negotiation but also with the adequacy of argument and verbal persuasion to resolve the issue. In this latter respect, management has little cause to express dissatisfaction with the negotiating process because of the underlying nature of the collective bargaining relationship. Where employees or union are seeking to change the existing arrangements, management can, if it wishes to maintain the status quo, adopt a passive approach by simply saying 'no' within the negotiations and thereby place the onus on employees or union to take the initiative and responsibility for utilising direct industrial action in pursuance of their claim. Equally, where management initiates the change it can, if the employees or union refuse to accept its proposals, adopt a strategy of imposing the new arrangements unilaterally and thereby, again, place the onus on the employees or union to take direct industrial action as a means of resisting the change. In both cases management's strategy would not be regarded, by most people, as 'industrial action' but simply the legitimate exercise of managerial prerogative; whereas any employee or union reaction will almost certainly be perceived as industrial action. Yet, in reality, management's initial strategy also represents the use of power to influence the collective bargaining relationship and therefore, as Hyman points out, 'the act of striking is merely one point in a chain of events' [9].

A strike or any other form of industrial action is often **perceived as an irrational act**. Hyman [10] suggests that, apart from those who reject the basic principle of conflict in organisations, such a view is founded on two main beliefs:

1.   That **any conflict of interest can, and should, be resolved within the recognised procedures and institutions** of the industrial relations system including reference to arbitration as an alternative to the use of industrial action. This view presumes that there is a logical and objective solution to a problem and ignores the role played by perceived relative power in determining the outcome of any negotiation. Certainly, it may be argued that both parties should be capable of assessing their relative positions in the initial determination of their bargaining limits. However, this **ignores**:
     (a) the difficulty of identifying and assessing power;
     (b) the fact that it may have to be demonstrated periodically in order for it to be assessable; and
     (c) the need within a negotiation for both parties to be able to demonstrate the importance they attach to an issue and their resolve to stand firm.

2.   That the **costs to employees of undertaking industrial action far exceeds any gain that may result from its use**. Certainly Gennard's research [11] shows that strikes, although not necessarily other forms of industrial action, can involve the employees in significant financial loss, and possible hardship, with only minimal relief through strike benefit from their union or Social Security payments for their dependants. However:
     (a) the initial expectation of most strikers is that their dispute will be of a short duration and therefore potential financial loss is unlikely to be a significant factor in deciding to strike but may become more important in a 'return to work' decision as the strike lengthens;
     (b) the assessment by either party of their position at the beginning or during a strike cannot be judged purely in economic terms or as a single, isolated incident. Its significance lies as much in the fact that it represents the expression of a resistance point and an unwillingness to compromise and, as such, conditions the future management/employee relationship.

Hyman, however, suggests that industrial action can also be regarded as a **rational social action**: 'a calculative attempt to obtain alterations in the work situation or the employment relationship' [12]. Whilst the ultimate function of industrial action is to support and strengthen the process of establishing new and more favourable terms under which the employment relationship may continue, its immediate purpose is to create **temporary industrial disorder** within the existing employment relationship. All forms of industrial action, whether they seek to stop or merely interrupt the production processes, are in Dubin's view 'weapons for maximising industrial disorder' [13] within one or both of the economic and authority relationships of the organisation. The pressure created by such actions stems from not only the economic consequences for the organisation but also management's general concern to maintain an ordered labour environment within which to plan and execute its operational decisions. It is important to realise that the disorder is intended to be only temporary – it is an intervention strategy within the negotiating interaction. As such, it is an integral and necessary element of the industrial relations system and its use is not necessarily indicative of some breakdown in the regulatory system as a whole but merely a recognition that the 'logic' of argument and verbal persuasion is inadequate for resolving the conflicting interests which are present on that issue at that point in time.

Forms of industrial action

It is useful to start by distinguishing between **unorganised individual forms of action** (such as absenteeism, turnover) and **organised collective forms of action** (such as strikes, work to rule, go slow). Whilst both categories of behaviour express discontent, their difference lies primarily in the intention behind them. Hyman argues that with 'unorganised conflict workers typically respond to the oppressive situation in the only way open to them as *individuals*: by withdrawing from the source of the discontent', whilst 'organised conflict . . . is far more likely to form part of a conscious strategy to change the situation which is identified as the source of the discontent' [14].

However, it is not clear whether these different categories of expressing discontent are **interchangeable and alternative**. There is some evidence from Knowles' early study [15] to suggest that there is an inverse relationship between the two patterns of behaviour (i.e. where the level of organised collective action is high the level of unorganised individual action is low), from which it is possible to infer that in weakly organised groups, or groups which have little industrial power, conflict may be manifest through unorganised individual action. Conversely, there is evidence from Bean [16], Kelly and Nicholson [17] and Edwards [18] to suggest that the two behaviour patterns are complementary (i.e. groups displaying high levels of organised collective action are also likely to display high levels of unorganised individual action). Nevertheless, it is important to recognise, as Turner *et al.* pointed out, that 'if the collective expressions of specific discontent are suppressed or inhibited in some forceful way, they may find an outlet in a more dispersed and individual fashion' [19]. This is particularly important in relation to increased legal restrictions on collective industrial action.

Clearly, the conversion of discontent into organised collective action requires the **existence or creation of a collective consciousness** amongst the employees if there is to be the necessary solidarity to commence and sustain the action. Batstone *et al.* suggest that the 'mobilisation of strike action', and by implication the mobilisation of any collective action, should be seen as 'a social process involving systems of influence and power' [20]. The mobilisation of the collective consciousness requires dissemination of information, consultation and eventually 'negotiation and agreement' amongst the employees involved and the outcome of this process is determined primarily by the quality of the leadership's (shop stewards and/or full-time officers) network of influence amongst the membership. Batstone *et al.* believe that the mobilisation of the collective consciousness requires a balance to be struck between the union's requirement for unionateness amongst its membership and the membership's instrumental requirements of the union. Thus, they argue that it is only through 'political notions such as fairness and justice . . . that workers can easily justify challenging the status quo' but that these 'notions of conflict and union principles . . . must be related to the experience and perceptions of the workers concerned' [21]. At the same time, the leadership must balance the creating of a collective consciousness with the need to maintain direction and control of its expression within the negotiating process.

Employee discontent may be expressed through a **variety of organised collective action**:

1. **Withdrawal of co-operation**: withdrawal of representatives from joint institutions, particularly those associated with consultation and productivity; excessive use of the formal procedures; strict interpretation of any status quo provision; absence of flexibility on the part of employees and their representatives in the resolution of work problems.
2. **Work to rule**: strictly interpreting the duties specified in the contract of employment, collective agreement, job description or other rules (e.g. safety procedures) and requiring precise instructions from management regarding the execution of work.
3. **Overtime ban**: collective refusal to work outside normal contractual hours of work, thereby affecting the rate of production.
4. **Go slow**: working without enthusiasm and at a lower level of performance/output than normal.
5. **Strike**: temporary withdrawal of labour and stoppage of work.
6. **Work-in/sit-in**: occupying the workplace and, possibly, continuing to

work but denying management access to or control of the output thus 'demonstrating that the plant is a viable concern' or 'preventing the transfer of plant and machinery to other factories' [22]. Thomas argued that 'occupation demonstrates publicly in a most vivid manner that management is no longer in control' [23].

The strike is often depicted as the ultimate and most favoured form of collective action in that, by stopping work and leaving the workplace, the employees clearly demonstrate both the importance of the issue in dispute and their solidarity. Certainly it is easier for the union to ensure that there is collective solidarity (all members are complying with the required action) in a strike than in other forms of industrial action. Other forms (except the work-in or sit-in) may be seen as preliminary action intended to develop collective consciousness and to be abandoned in favour of strike action if they do not achieve the required concession from management. Alternatively, they may be regarded as of equal importance, or even preferred, to strike action because:

1. They involve the employees and union in less financial loss than a strike whilst still exerting a significant cost on the management in terms of lost production (although, a ban on overtime may, in practice, be beneficial to management by reducing its labour costs).
2. They may not be perceived as breach of contract on the employees' part, but simply the carrying out of those duties which they are contractually obliged to do. Certainly, if management takes disciplinary action in such situations it is likely to reinforce the employees' collective consciousness and solidarity.

There appears to have been a significant change in the **relative incidence of strike action compared with other forms of industrial action**. Flanders noted that during the 1960s there was an 'increasing use of "cut price" industrial action such as overtime bans, working to rule and going slow' [24]. Hyman [25] attributes this to, first, the increasing affluence of employees and an associated increase in their financial commitments which reduced their willingness to lose pay through strike action and, secondly and most importantly, the effectiveness of these other forms of industrial action in securing concessions from management. However, the more recent survey findings of Brown [26], Daniel and Millward [27] and Millward and Stevens [28] suggest a relative decline during the 1970s and 1980s in the use of these other forms of industrial action due to management being 'more prepared to hold out against limited actions when they are operating at a low level of capacity (and thus when overtime bans and the like are relatively painless) than when they want to maximise production' [29].

These surveys provide an interesting insight into the **relative import- ance of the alternative forms of industrial action:**

1. Approximately half of the industrial action reported, for both manual and non-manual employees, was action other than strike action.
2. The overtime ban was the most frequently used form of alternative action for both groups.
3. The work to rule accounted for a larger proportion of the industrial action amongst non-manual employees than amongst manual employees. This may result from not only their preference for a 'constitutional' form of industrial action but also their greater facility to utilise a formal job description as the legitimate source for defining the limits of their work requirement.

At the same time Kelly and Nicholson identified 'a significant positive correlation between minor stoppages and other actions' [30], whilst Edwards noted 'a tendency for the following combinations to be used: short and long strikes; strikes and overtime bans; and overtime bans and working to rule' [31]. This appears to confirm the view that the various forms of organised collective industrial action may form a package of weapons which are both complementary and alternatives.

Industrial action may also be categorised by reference to other factors.

Official and unofficial

In the past, as Turner *et al.* noted, the term **official** was primarily intended to designate, within the union organisation, that it would financially support its members and that 'except in comparatively rare cases where a union has specifically declared itself against a particular stoppage . . ., the term "unofficial" has little meaning' [32]. 'Official' also had the effect of designating the existence of a dispute to other trade unionists and thereby enlisted their support by, for example, not crossing picket lines. In its strictest sense, the term **unofficial** could be applied to industrial action which was not authorised or approved by the appropriate person or body within the union's rules and this could, of course, vary between unions dependent on their constitution. It is this constitutional variation which led Turner *et al.* to comment that 'it is not at all unusual for a strike to be official for some of the workers involved and unofficial for others' or 'under some union constitutions, where the power to authorize strikes is shared between local and national bodies . . . that a dispute may be declared, even for the same group of workers, official and unofficial at the same time' [33].

It is unfortunate that the term unofficial has often been used loosely to refer to any industrial action initiated by employees or shop stewards rather than by the full-time officer or NEC of the union and to imply that the action is, by definition, also irresponsible and should be subject to greater control from the centre. It may be argued that the development and strengthening of collective bargaining at the organisational level, primarily in the hands of shop stewards, required that control of industrial power should be vested and exercised at that level. Yet, in most unions the formal organisational authority for sanctioning the use of industrial action remained at a higher level remote from the negotiations.

Consequently, there was a range of situations between 'official' and 'unofficial' which could be classified as **'quasi-official' industrial action**:

1. Industrial action which was supported by the union but not formally approved because:
   (a) the union hierarchy felt it would be impolitic to be seen supporting such action; or
   (b) there was insufficient time, before the industrial action was over, for it to be considered by the appropriate authority within the union; or
   (c) the union did not wish to pay strike benefit to its members (this was only applicable in those unions which had a strike fund/benefit).
2. Industrial action unofficially encouraged by the full-time officer in order to strengthen the union's negotiating position by using it as evidence of the members' deep concern over the issue under negotiation.
3. Industrial action initiated by shop stewards as an integral part of their collective bargaining role (a role recognised by both management and union).

The term 'unofficial' (i.e. not part of the union's negotiating strategy), therefore, only really applied to:

1. Industrial action initiated by shop stewards to express their dissatisfaction with the course of negotiations being conducted by the full-time officer and which was, perhaps, directed as much against their union as against their employer.
2. Industrial action initiated by members without the support or approval of their shop stewards (the 'unofficial-unofficial' action).

Nevertheless, the distinction between 'official' and 'quasi-official' or 'unofficial' was important in respect of the potential role of the union in the conduct of negotiations:

1. In many situations of unofficial or quasi-official action the union, particularly the full-time officer, was able to adopt, or be invited by management to adopt, a 'quasi-conciliation' role between management and the shop stewards or employees undertaking the industrial action. Whilst management would usually insist that the full-time officer exert his/her authority as the formal representative of the union and secure a return to normal working before any further negotiations took place, this may have involved prior informal acceptance by management that there were areas in which they were prepared to negotiate and through which a satisfactory conclusion was possible.

2. The union is endorsing and supporting the members' demands by making a strike official. Therefore, by not making the action official the union was not tied to those demands and could adopt, what was to the union hierarchy, a more realistic approach to the negotiations.

However, the legislative changes introduced during the 1980s have sought to make trade unions legally accountable for the actions of its officers and committees and the distinction between 'official' and non-official industrial action has become important in respect of giving management greater freedom to dismiss employees involved in unofficial industrial action (Employment Act, 1990).

Constitutional and unconstitutional

Unconstitutional action, whether official or not, is initiated in contravention of a clause in most grievance/disputes procedures stating that industrial action, by either party, should not be undertaken until all the stages of the procedure have been exhausted. This clause, in effect, defines the circumstances in which industrial power may legitimately be exercised. It is often argued that unconstitutional action is unacceptable because it breaches the jointly agreed and established procedures for resolving differences between management and employees; acceptance of the use of unconstitutional action may be tantamount to repudiation of the regulatory framework itself. However, such reasoning is only valid if both the procedure is adequate and management does not abuse its inherent bargaining advantage by delaying negotiations within the procedure.

The **importance of the distinction** between constitutional and unconstitutional action, like that between official and unofficial action, lies not so much in one being necessarily 'right' and the other 'wrong' but in their differing effect on the bargaining relationship. The use of constitutional action is a previously accepted part of that relationship, whilst the use of unconstitutional action is, from the management's point of view, a distortion of the relationship which has to be removed before negotiations can continue. It is important to remember that, whilst the majority of unconstitutional action is also likely to be unofficial, the two concepts are not synonymous.

A number of the so-called new style agreements based on single union recognition have included a **specific 'no-strike' clause** (i.e. an undertaking by the union that, in return for referring any dispute to binding arbitration, it will not instigate industrial action). This is distinct from simply agreeing to use the process of binding arbitration to resolve any outstanding disputes – that is, establishing an arrangement which will substantially reduce, if not remove, the need to undertake industrial action. Certainly, as Hillage points out, many trade unions are 'deeply suspicious of agreements limiting what they see as a fundamental right to withdraw labour' [34] and, as Hall notes, the TUC's guidelines on no-strike clauses recommends that unions should 'not make recognition agreements which remove the right to take industrial action . . . this is not meant to deter unions from agreeing to procedures for arbitration' [35]. The significance of the 'no-strike' clause has been increased by the introduction, in the Employment Act 1990, of the provision allowing management to be able to selectively dismiss employees undertaking unofficial industrial action without them being able to claim unfair dismissal. A union will not be able to make industrial action official if it has accepted a 'no-strike' clause and therefore any action by its members or employees will automatically be 'unofficial' and they will be vulnerable to selective dismissal.

In many European countries it is normal for there to be a requirement not to undertake industrial action **during the period of the collective agreement**. However, such requirements 'are generally *relative* insofar as they only relate to the provisions of an existing agreement' [36] and therefore unions are free to undertake industrial action on any matter not covered by a collective agreement (for example, management proposals for work changes, rationalisation, etc.), if there is no agreement, procedural or otherwise, covering these eventualities.

Demonstrative action and trials of strength

The principal intention of **demonstrative action** is to highlight the importance employees attach to the issue in dispute or to express their dissatisfaction with the progress of a negotiation. It is particularly appropriate in what are often termed 'perishable disputes' – those situations where dissatisfaction needs to be displayed immediately while the issue is fresh or where 'power' exists only at that point in time. Delay in the use of industrial action until the recognised procedure is exhausted may allow management to implement their decision and thereby make it more difficult for the employees to secure a favourable decision (for example, the dismissal of an employee or redundancies). In the past such action has been generally unconstitutional, unofficial and of short duration. However, the requirement for unions formally to ballot members before undertaking industrial action (Trade Union Act, 1984), as opposed to having a 'show of hands' at a meeting, has reduced, if not negated, the union's or members' ability to undertake immediate demonstrative action. **Trials of strength**, on the other hand, involve a more protracted use of industrial action as an integral element of the negotiating process and with the intention of confirming or modifying the perceived relative bargaining advantage between the parties. It is, therefore, likely to be constitutional, official and of longer duration.

Management's use of industrial action

Whilst this may be less obvious than that of employees and generally seen as an indirect response to actions initiated by employees, management does have at its disposal a number of actions which may be regarded as involving the unilateral use of industrial power:

1. Management has the ability, and it might be argued the right, to **impose unilaterally** new working arrangements or terms of employment. It is possible to include in this category such actions as withdrawing the facility to work overtime and thereby enhance earnings, the speeding up of work or implementing changes in work standards/job content without the agreement of the employees or union.

2. Management may, where employees refuse to accept a change or as a response to a work to rule, overtime ban or go slow, exert pressure by utilising their managerial authority to take **disciplinary action**.

3. Management may **dispense with the services of employees** either on a **temporary basis** (lock out) or on a **permanent basis** (dismissing employees, seeking to hire replacement). Whilst the lock out and hire of replacements was relatively common in the early days of trade unionism, it has become much rarer today. However, the increased freedom given to management under the Employment Acts (1980, 1982 and 1990) to dismiss strikers has led to a greater preparedness on the part of some management (e.g. British Rail in 1985) to dismiss striking employees as a prelude to re-engaging a chastened workforce, excluding militants or hiring replacements, or even as part of reducing its workforce. The extent to which such actions are successful will depend, in particular, on the unions' ability to mobilise support for dismissed strikers or ensure that insufficient people come forward from the ranks of the unemployed to act as an alternative workforce. At times of high unemployment trade union power in these areas is weakened.

4. Management may utilise its ultimate sanction of **closing or threatening to close the organisation**. The use of this sanction, because of its implied permanency, may be considered a much more powerful sanction than the employees' temporary stoppage of work through strike action. However, it may be argued that such action is only of limited use to management. It is only credible, and therefore effective in exerting pressure on employees and union, where either the organisation's continued economic viability is clearly in question or the organisation is multi-site (or even multinational) and has the capacity to recoup lost production by expanding output elsewhere. Such action by management is most likely to be associated with redundancies or a major work change and may provoke retaliatory action on the part of employees in the form of a work-in or sit-in.

Britain's strike pattern

There are **three indices of strike activity**:

1. **Number of stoppages** – this makes no distinction between strikes and lockouts; however, certainly in the post-war period, the number of lockouts has been very small.

2. **Number of workers involved** – this includes both those directly and indirectly involved (laid off or on short time) at the establishment where the stoppage occurs but excludes workers indirectly involved at other establishments; it tends to overstate the number of strikers but, perhaps more importantly, understate the number of people not working as a consequence of the strike action.

3. **Number of working days lost** – this is the number of workers involved multiplied by the length of the stoppage and, when expressed as a figure per 1,000 employees, is the most commonly used index for comparison purposes.

However, the statistics **measure the extent rather than the effect** of strike activity:

1. The Donovan Commission argued that Britain's high incidence of short unofficial/unconstitutional strikes during the 1960s had a disproportionate effect on production by undermining management's confidence and initiative to make changes within the organisation. Turner [37], on the other hand, argued that the effect of these strikes was confined largely to the organisation within which they occurred and it is the longer strikes which have the greatest effects on production because, after a certain period, they will indirectly affect the working of other organisations not involved in the original dispute.

2. The use of the phrase 'working days lost' can be misleading; it implies that the time lost could, and would, have been used productively and profitably. However, the loss of production time is not always necessarily proportional to the loss of output or profits. For example, the 1971 postal strike, although disruptive to the general public and other organisations, was beneficial to the GPO because it curtailed the unprofitable letter and parcel services whilst increasing demand for the profitable telecommunications service.

3. It is extremely difficult to 'cost' the effects of any strike action. Certainly, Fisher believed that 'counting up costs in the manner so generally adopted is of a very dubious value' and that 'he who cries hurt loudest may be he who has most to gain' [38].

An examination of **Britain's strike figures** shows a number of trends (see Appendix 2 and Figures 13.2–13.6).

1. **Number of stoppages** – before World War II there were only four years in which the number of stoppages exceeded 1,000. After 1941 there was a steady increase in the number of stoppages, and between 1955 and 1979 the number was consistently above 2,000 with a peak of 3,906 in 1970. From 1980 there has been a steady and significant decline to 630 in 1990.

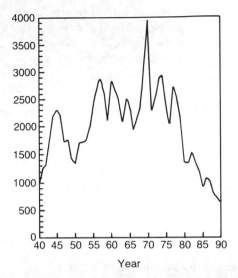

Figure 13.2   *Number of stoppages, 1940–90*

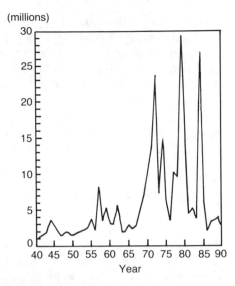

Figure 13.3   *Working days lost, 1940–90*

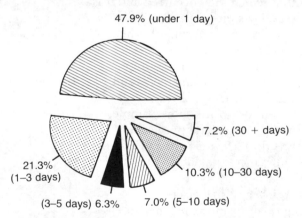

Figure 13.4   *Stoppages (by duration), 1990*

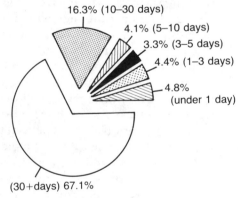

Figure 13.5   *Working days lost (by duration of stoppage), 1990*

2.   **Number of working days lost** – in the period 1950–67 the number of working days lost averaged 3.2 million, with a range of 1.4 to 8.7 million, and in only three years did it exceed 5 million. In marked contrast the period 1968–80 had an annual average of 11.7 million working days lost, with a range of 4.7 to 29.5 million, and in only two years was it below 5.0 million. After 1980 it fell to below 5 million, apart from 1984 and 1985 as a result of the NUM strike. However, as Figure 13.6 shows, if major stoppages involving more than 0.5 million working days are discounted the level of working days lost through other

(millions)

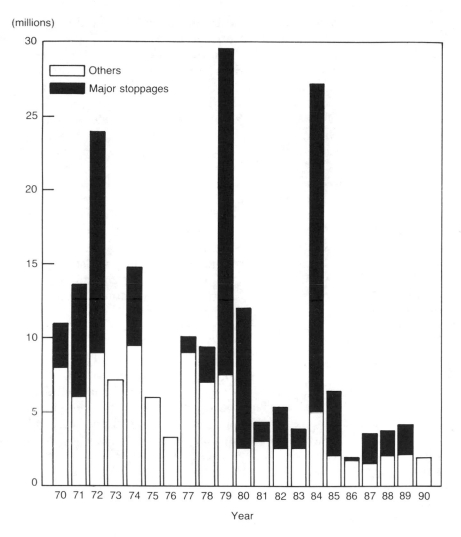

Figure 13.6 *Working days lost through major stoppages (0.5 million days plus), 1970–90*

disputes was below 10 million working days throughout the 1970s. Indeed, in many years a substantial proportion of the total working days lost were accounted for by a single national dispute [39]:

1971 – postal workers (46%)   1972 – miners (45%)
1974 – miners (38%)   1979 – engineering (54%)
1980 – steel (74%)   1984 – miners (83%)
1985 – miners (63%)   1987 – telecommunications (41%)
1989 – local government (49%)

It is important to note that the decentralisation of collective bargaining has the effect of turning a union campaign (as, for example, the engineering unions' campaign for a shorter working week during 1989 and 1990) into a series of small strikes rather than one big one.

3. **Duration of strikes** – whilst in the early 1960s over three-quarters of strikes lasted less than three days, by the late 1970s the proportion had dropped to less than half but in 1990 had risen again to 69 per cent. However, although strikes lasting less than three days account for a significant proportion of the number of strikes, they account for only a small proportion of the working days lost. For example, in 1990 the 69 per cent of strikes lasting less than three days accounted for only 9 per cent of the working days lost, whilst the 17.5 per cent of strikes lasting more than ten days accounted for 83 per cent of the working days lost.

4. **Unofficial strikes** – the official figures relating to unofficial strikes do not recognise the existence of quasi-official strikes. The statistics do, nevertheless, show significant variations. For example, whilst 90 per cent of all strikes being unofficial remained relatively constant during the period 1971–80, the percentage of working days lost through unofficial strikes fluctuated. In 1971/1972 and again in 1979/1980 official strikes accounted for over 75 per cent of the working days lost, but during the intervening period they accounted for less than 50 per cent and in four of the six years as little as 15–25 per cent of the working days lost. The years 1971/1972 and 1979/1980 were associated with major confrontations between unions and government over the introduction of industrial relations legislation and/or incomes policy. It is, therefore, to be expected that these years would produce the highest percentage of working days lost through official strikes. The official statistics ceased to distinguish between official and unofficial strikes in 1981.

5. **Causes of strikes** – Knowles [40] divided the causes of strikes into three main groups: basic issues (wages and hours of work), solidarity issues (recognition, closed shop, inter-union disputes) and frictional issues (working arrangements, discipline, redundancy, etc.). In 1990, 40 per cent of strikes related to basic issues of wages and hours, and accounted for some 80 per cent of the working days lost. Strikes relating to solidarity issues accounted for only some 3 per cent of strikes and strikes concerned with frictional issues the remaining 58 per cent of strikes but only 15 per cent of working days lost. However, within this latter group redundancy appears to have remained low as a cause of strikes (6 per cent) despite the increased scale of redundancies during the late 1970s and 1980s [41], and discipline and dismissals still account for 13 per cent of strikes despite the introduction of Unfair Dismissal legislation in 1971.

6. **Industrial variation** – strike activity is not evenly spread across all industries or organisations. Since the late 1960s strike activity has spread from manual workers in the traditionally strike-prone industries

(mining, manufacturing, transport) and become a significant feature in other industries (in particular the public sector) and amongst non-manual employees. As Edwards identified, in comparing the 1980 and 1984 workplace industrial relations surveys, 'the proportion of private manufacturing plants reporting any strikes fell from 22 per cent to 10 per cent, while in vehicle manufacturing the collapse of strike action was even more dramatic (from 67 per cent of plants affected to 23 per cent)' but that 'this was balanced by sharp increases in public administration and education' [42].

Influences on industrial action

All too often the general level of industrial action or its use in a particular situation is seen simply in terms of an **agitator/communications explanation**. Industrial action is attributed either to the presence of agitators on the union side, who encourage the expression of conflict for their own power aggrandisement or as part of a deliberate design for social, economic and political revolution, or to the fact that management's intentions have not been effectively communicated to employees and that if they had, or as soon as they are, the conflict will cease. Whilst undoubtedly the existence of these factors does contribute to, or occasionally cause, the use of industrial action, nevertheless Hyman argues that such an approach is too simplistic and assumes that 'industrial peace is the norm and conflict pathological' [43].

Before examining some structural factors which may influence the extent of industrial action it is important to note the conclusions reached by Edwards:

1. He argues not only that 'the strike-proneness of industries or plants cannot be seen as the result of the operation of a few distinct "independent variables"' but also that the 'structural influences have highly changeable effects' [44] between different levels of the industrial relations system (national and organisational) and over time.
2. He believes that because some 75 per cent of the variance in strike activity at the organisational level cannot be correlated with structural variables it 'depends on the day-to-day decisions of managers, shop stewards and others' and 'it is no good blaming a "poor" strike record on [structural variables] . . . the greater part of the responsibility lies in the handling of industrial relations' [45].

Certainly, Lane and Roberts' **social action approach** to examining a strike at Pilkingtons in 1970 [46], and the more recent NCB/NUM dispute in 1984/1985 [47], show that no strike can be explained purely in terms of 'structural' factors but that these must be related to the motives, attitudes and perceptions of the participants. Therefore, there is no single or simple causal explanation for the extent or distribution of industrial action, rather than structural factors interact with the aspirations of the participants to produce decisions.

Economic environment

It is frequently argued that aggregate strike activity can be correlated with the **business cycle of expansion and recession**. However, there is an apparent contradiction in the relationship. Hunter argues that the general expectation is of 'strike frequency falling in recession and rising in boom periods' [48] as the union's relative bargaining power is weakened or enhanced by economic conditions. Edwards, on the other hand, points out that 'workers may have more reason to strike in a recession that in a boom if they have to defend themselves against an employer's attack, and, in a boom, employers may be willing to grant workers' demands without a strike' [49]. This apparent contradiction may be reconciled if strike frequency (number of strikes) is related to strike duration (length of strike). The evidence suggests that although strike frequency may increase during periods of economic boom, most strikes are of short duration. Equally, although strike frequency may reduce during periods of recession, any strike activity undertaken may be more severe (longer duration) as the pressure from employees/unions produced by declining living standards is met by increased management resistance resulting from declining profits of the organisation. During the 1960s and 1970s there was a widespread belief that Britain was more strike-prone than other countries – particularly its industrial competitors such as Sweden, Germany and Japan. However, it is important to realise that all countries (with the exception of Japan) experienced an increase in strike activity between the mid-1960s to mid-1970s. Indeed, Screpanti argues that there have been three major international strike waves occurring in 1869–75, 1910–20 and 1968–74 which correlate with the upper turning point (boom to recession) of the long-term economic cycle of the western capitalist economic system which comprises 20–30 years of rapid economic growth followed by an equally long period of stagnation and recession during which strike activity is severely reduced as a result of the effect on 'levels of employment, wage rate and other elements of workers' welfare and self-confidence' [50]. However, within this cycle there may be peaks and troughs of strike activity in individual countries which are the result of country-specific economic, social and political factors as well as particular factors which may affect individual industries or organisations.

The relationship between **unemployment and strike activity** operates at two levels:

1. At the **micro level** of specific disputes or negotiations management may seek to link low profits, spare capacity and high unemployment directly with the threat of redundancy if employees/unions do not moderate

their stance – thus weakening the employees' resolve to utilise industrial action.

2. At the **macro level** – it may be argued that as the economy changes from expansion or stability to recession there is likely to be a maintenance, or even increase, in the frequency and duration of strike activity as employees and unions seek, in the light of their experience in the previous period of boom when they were strong, to utilise strike action to protect themselves from a decline in their living standards. Only after the recession conditions have existed for some time, and therefore affect the perceptions of the participants, will unemployment exert any general influence on strike propensity and lead to a decline in strike activity.

It is important to recognise that even where the macro-economic environment is unfavourable to employees/unions, the micro-economic environment of the organisation may remain favourable. For example, the expanding market and profitability of the newly 'privatised' Jaguar cars in 1984 may explain management's preparedness to increase their wage offer in response to a strike threat, whereas Austin Rover responded to a similar situation by invoking legal sanctions against the unions to stop the strike action.

However, the effect of the economic environment on strike activity in Britain during the 1970s was complicated by **greater government intervention** over this period. Although the reduction in strike activity during 1975/1976 may be linked to the development of the Social Contract between government and the TUC, Davies [51] suggests that the operation of incomes policy generally had little effect on the level of strike activity, whereas strike activity tended to increase at the point of return to 'normal' collective bargaining as unions sought to make up for any losses sustained during the period of restraint. Certainly, government action to control wages within the public sector (whether through formal incomes policy or not) has, to a large extent, been responsible for the increase in propensity for industrial action amongst groups such as civil servants, nurses, firemen, teachers, etc., as well as the more traditional groups such as miners.

Industrial/organisational environment
Kerr and Siegel argued, from an examination of the **inter-industry propensity to strike** in eleven countries during the inter-war period, that an industry's relative strike propensity depended on:

1. The **employees' industrial location relative to society** – industries will be strike prone where 'the workers form a relatively homogeneous group which is usually isolated from the general community and which is capable of cohesion' and comparatively strike free where 'workers are individually integrated into the larger society, are members of trade groups which are coerced by government or the market to avoid strikes, or are so individually isolated that strike action is impossible' [52].

2. The **nature of the work and people employed** – where the work is 'physically difficult and unpleasant, unskilled or semiskilled, and casual or seasonal, and fosters an independent spirit . . . it will draw tough, inconstant, combative and virile workers, and they will be inclined to strike', whereas where the work is 'physically easy and performed in pleasant surroundings, skilled and responsible, steady, and subject to set rules and close supervision, it will attract women or the more submissive type of man who will abhor strikes' [53].

Certainly, those industries such as coal mining, docks, iron and steel and shipbuilding which traditionally have been relatively strike prone display many of the above characteristics. Nevertheless, it does not explain either the increased use of strike action in other industries or, more importantly, the wide variation in strike activity between establishments within the same industry.

Subsequently, Kerr [54] postulated a number of **organisationally related factors** which may affect strike propensity:

1. **Size of organisation** – large organisations, with higher levels of unionisation, greater emphasis on formalised relationships, and greater divorcement of employees from both management and union officials, tend to be more strike prone than small organisations.
2. **Production pattern** – organisations with seasonal or intermittent production patterns or subject to frequent production changes or crises are more likely to be strike prone.
3. **Rate of technological development** – organisations experiencing rapid technological changes in their methods of production, thereby creating stress in the organisation, tend to be more strike prone.
4. **Nature of the work** – assembly-line type of work, with its associated 'de-skilling' of work, close supervision, boredom and frustration, tends to produce greater employee dissatisfaction than other work systems.
5. **Cost factors** – organisations which are loss making or only marginally cost effective are, because of management's emphasis on cost savings, more likely to be strike prone.
6. **Market factors** – organisations operating in price sensitive markets, which preclude or create difficulties for passing on higher costs, tend to be more strike prone.

Smith *et al.*'s inter-industry analysis of strikes in Britain during the period 1966–73 [55] found that higher than average strike activity appeared to be associated with high earnings levels in the industry, labour costs representing a high proportion of total costs, a high proportion of large establishments in the industry and a low proportion of female employees. Edwards' analysis of strike proneness at the organisational level [56] suggests that whilst size is a significant factor, the nature of the work system and technology do not appear to correlate with strike proneness. Nevertheless, because technology and work patterns are not constant for all groups within an organisation, this does not mean that such factors are not important for particular groups of workers. Thus, Kerr's factors may exert a structural influence which induces strike activity in a given situation but do not provide a general causal explanation for variations in strike propensity between industries or organisations. Indeed, Kerr recognised that they 'do not necessarily predetermine the nature of a collective bargaining relationship' but rather they establish the limits within which 'the parties normally are free to create a bad relationship or a good one' [57].

Industrial relations environment

Kerr also identified a number of factors in the **management/union bargaining relationship** which could influence the propensity to strike:

1. If the union has to fight for recognition from a reluctant and hostile management, the resultant relationship is more likely to be characterised by aggression, a reluctance to co-operate and the overt use of power. Once the relationship and procedures have become established the union has less need to rely on its 'industrial muscle' to maintain its position and acceptance by management.
2. The existence of factionalism or insecurity within or between unions may lead to increased aggression from a union's leadership as it seeks to demonstrate both its ability and preparedness to protect the interests of its members. It is often said that shop stewards and elected union officials become more aggressive bargainers in the period prior to their re-election than they are after their position has been reconfirmed by winning the election. Kerr notes that it is ironic that 'situations which further local democracy and autonomy seem to work against peace' [58].
3. An organisation is more likely to be strike prone if it is a 'lone bargainer', isolated from the employer solidarity provided by an employers' association, and/or if it is a 'pattern setter' in respect of terms and conditions of employment in the area or industry.

At the macro level, the Donovan Commission attributed the rise in strike activity during the early 1960s (excluding coal mining) to the breakdown in the regulatory role of the 'formal' industry level bargaining and its replacement by **fragmented bargaining** at the organisational level in response to the enhanced power of trade unions. Certainly, strike prone industries such as coal mining, docks and car manufacture have in the past been characterised by strong trade unionism, fragmented bargaining and fluctuating earnings. Thus, it was anticipated that greater formalisation and centralisation of organisational bargaining would reduce the incidence of strike activity. The experience of both the coal mining industry and British Leyland seems to confirm this. The reduction in the number of strikes in mining during the early 1960s was associated with a shift of bargaining from the pit to national level. British Leyland's policy of industrial relations reform in 1979/1980 based on a reduction in the number of bargaining units and more centralised bargaining was also associated with a decline in strike activity. However, other factors such as the economic circumstances and management style were also significant influences.

It is often argued that strike proneness may be influenced by the **strength of trade union organisation** – indicated by union density and the existence of shop stewards. However, whilst these indicators may provide some evidence of collective consciousness amongst the employees, they do not, in themselves, provide an indication of the employees' preparedness to strike. High union density in the public sector has not been associated with high strike proneness – indeed, quite the reverse for most groups. The centralised/national bargaining throughout much of the public sector acts as an influence against high strike frequency.

The incidence of strike activity may be associated with **formalisation** of the industrial relations system at the organisational level. Turner *et al.* concluded that the 'formalisation of company bargaining procedures and of shop stewards' status to be a factor encouraging labour conflict' [59]. However, it is difficult to isolate this factor from the influence of organisational size since they also found formalisation, standardisation and the provision of shop steward facilities to be related to organisational size. Creigh and Makeham [60] also sought to relate strike activity to bargaining arrangements. They concluded from their analysis that strike activity correlated both with the proportion of workers paid on PBR schemes, the proportion of workers receiving overtime payments and labour costs as a proportion of total costs (indicators of relative bargaining frequency) and with plant size and organisational concentration within the industry (indicators of relative remoteness of contact between management and employees).

Social control

The propensity to strike will, obviously, be affected by the **attitude of society towards the use of industrial action**. The ambivalent attitude displayed by society on this issue has been summed up by Frayn: 'public opinion . . . unquestioningly concedes the right of men in a free society to withdraw their labour. It just draws the line at strikes' [61]. At the individual level one's own strike may be seen as legitimate whilst the other person's strike is often regarded as unreasonable and unnecessary. Strikes which affect or threaten to affect the daily life of 'the man in the street', through the immediate absence of goods or services, may be regarded as less reasonable than those which appear to affect only the employer through lost production. Wolfson [62] contrasted the essentially private interest of management, union and employees in the issue and result of a dispute with the public interest in the means used to resolve the dispute.

However, it is important to realise that the **public interest is not a**

single, homogeneous entity. Society's attitude towards industrial action, and therefore its influence on the propensity to strike, can vary at different levels within society. At the **immediate level of the striker** it can act to either reinforce or undermine the cohesiveness of strike action. The normally close community relationship displayed in the mining industry, which in the past has provided community support based on an acceptance of the legitimacy and necessity for industrial action, was seriously divided in the 1984/1985 dispute between working and non-working miners. In contrast, electricity workers, who have a similar if not greater industrial power to that of miners, tend to be dispersed within a wider multi-interest community and therefore are subject to undermining pressures from friends and neighbours when their industrial action leads to 'blackouts' and inconvenience within the community.

At the wider level, the 'public interest' is often perceived as being expressed by government and the mass media. The **mass media** tend to emphasise the harm and losses generated by the use of industrial action. During the Ambulance work-to-rule in 1989 the mass media dramatised the effect on patients in terms of possible deaths (despite the fact that emergency services were being maintained). Such coverage not only exerts pressure on strikers to return to work but also acts as a socialisation process implying that all industrial action is in some way morally reprehensible and to be discouraged.

Government translates the 'public interest' into **formal social control** through the creation or modification of the legal framework surrounding industrial action. Since 1980 the Conservative Government has sought to strengthen this formal social control through **legislation** which not only narrows the area of lawful industrial action but also makes it easier for management to take legal action against trade unions which act unlawfully. It is important to recognise that defining something as unlawful implies that it is morally 'wrong' and thereby forms part of the general socialisation process.

In addition the government has reduced what many believe is a **state subsidy of strike activity** – namely, the payment of Supplementary Benefit to the striker's dependants. Gennard [63] argues that this state subsidy theory is based on a belief that the availability of Supplementary Benefit:

1. increases the employee's preparedness to strike or continue a strike by mitigating his/her potential financial loss;
2. reduces the union's responsibility to provide financial support to its members and thereby removes any incentive for it to moderate its claim or seek a settlement; and
3. reduces the employer's resistance.

However, his research shows that the availability of Supplementary Benefit has little influence on the decision to strike or continue a strike, whilst

Durcan and McCarthy [64] have shown that despite Supplementary Benefit payments most households lose some 60 per cent of their disposable income during a strike. Nevertheless, as Gennard points out, many believe that state support should be confined to those 'who, through no fault of their own, are unable rather than unwilling to help themselves' and 'strikers are in a condition of need through their own voluntary actions' [65]. Consequently, the Conservative Government amended the Supplementary Benefit provisions so that in addition to only receiving benefits for dependents and not him/herself, the striker is assumed to receive strike pay from the union (irrespective of whether he/she does or not) and this is deducted from his/her entitlement.

13.3 The legal framework

In Britain, unlike other European countries, there is **no positive right to strike**. At common law a strike is both a breach of the individual's contract of employment and a collective restraint of trade; but, because it can be regarded as socially necessary, industrial action has been given a degree of protection by statute law (**immunity from a claim for damages**). Thus, trade unions are not, and never have been, outside the law, but rather it is the law which has delineated the extent of their freedom to act. The Conservative Government's Green Paper on Trade Union Immunities (1981) recognised that these immunities 'do not abolish the offences and wrongs against which they provide protection. Rather they remove liability in the circumstances of a trade dispute' and 'if they were repealed altogether, then trade unions and individuals would be at risk of legal action every time they organised a strike' [66]. However, during the 1980s the Conservative Government has, in stages, significantly reduced the boundary of lawful industrial action (see Figure 13.7). Clearly, the twin concepts of 'a trade dispute' and 'trade union immunities' are central to this change in the legal status of industrial action.

Trade dispute

The immunities which individuals or trade unions enjoy are confined to actions undertaken in contemplation or furtherance of a trade dispute. The original **definition** of a trade dispute was contained in S.5(3) of the Trade Disputes Act (1906):

> any dispute between employers and workmen, or between workmen and workmen, which is connected with the employment or non-employment, or the terms of employment, or with the conditions of labour, of any person.

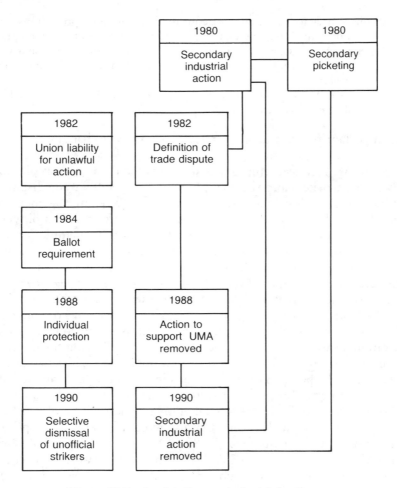

Figure 13.7 *Legislation on industrial action*

However, the definition has been changed during the 1970s/1980s and is now:

A dispute between workers and their employer which relates wholly or mainly to one or more of the following–
- (i) terms and conditions of employment or the physical conditions in which any workers are required to work;
- (ii) engagement or non-engagement, or termination or suspension of employment or the duties of employment, of one or more workers;
- (iii) allocation of work or the duties of employment as between workers or groups of workers;
- (iv) matters of discipline;
- (v) the membership or non-membership of a trade union on the part of workers;
- (vi) facilities for officials of trade unions;

(vii)   machinery for negotiation or consultation, and other procedures, relating to any of the foregoing matters, including the recognition by employers or employers' associations of the right of a trade union to represent workers in any such negotiation or consultation or in the carrying out of such procedures.
[S.29(1) Trade Union and Labour Relations Act, 1974 as amended by S.18(1) Employment Act, 1982]

Three important points emerge in respect of the 1982 changes.

1.   The **phrase 'between employers and workmen' has been replaced by 'between workers and their employer'**. As a result a trade dispute exists only if there is a direct and specific dispute between management and employees. It removes any dispute between workers and employers other than their own or between a trade union and an employer where the workforce itself has no dispute with management. Consequently, trade unions and their members do not have immunity when undertaking industrial action in furtherance of a general policy; for example, the International Transport Workers' Federation 'blacking' of certain ships as part of its general campaign against flags of convenience [67] or the POEU's instruction to its members not to connect Mercury Communications to British Telecom's system following the government decision to privatise BT and end its monopoly [68]. This change could also affect the position of trade unions in respect of 'political strikes' in response to government legislation or policy in that the dispute is not directly and specifically between employees and their employer but with the government. Furthermore, because worker is defined as a person 'employed by that employer' (S.18(6) 1982 Act), the House of Lords held that a dispute regarding allocation of work between workers is limited to employees or groups employed by the same employer and does not encompass the 'farming out' of work to contractors – this is a business decision [69].

2.   The **phrase 'between workmen and workmen' has been deleted**. This change has the effect of removing immunity from any dispute between groups of workers or trade unions where the employer is not involved. However, this does not mean that all inter-union disputes are outside the definition of a trade dispute and therefore have no protection of immunity. Indeed, the government recognised that 'in most cases, disputes between workers or trade unions automatically involve the employer of the workers concerned' [70]. Disputes over such issues as work demarcation or union representation for particular groups of workers invariably involve the employer both in the causation and resolution of the dispute. Therefore, this change appears to be largely cosmetic and is likely to affect only a very small number of disputes.

3.   The **phrase 'is connected with' has been replaced by 'relates wholly or mainly to'**. The effect of this change is to require that the predominant

purpose of the trade dispute is industrial and to ensure that immunity does not apply to actions which are intended primarily to further the wider fraternalistic or political aspects of trade unionism. Instead of claiming that there was some, albeit slight, connection between their actions and one of the items listed, trade unions have to show that it is the major element in pursuing their action. Whilst this provides for legal action against trade unions and their members on the grounds that their intention is 'political' rather than 'industrial', it requires the courts not only to separate the differing elements present in many disputes but also to determine criteria for assessing the relative importance of the various elements before deciding which predominates: a matter largely of subjective perception rather than objective fact.

Finally, a trade dispute exists even though it relates to **matters occurring outside Britain** so long as the employees undertaking the industrial action in Britain are likely to be affected, in respect of one of the items listed, by the outcome of the dispute outside Britain. During the period of the Trade Union and Labour Relations (Amendment) Act (1976) the qualifying statement was removed so that employees in Britain had immunity if they undertook industrial action in support of any employees anywhere in the world. The effect of the qualifying statement is to restrict immunity to those situations where the British employees have a direct interest in the dispute abroad. This applies primarily to the employees of multi-national companies whose ability to switch production and investment between countries and pay variable terms and conditions of employment may affect the position of British workers.

Clearly, the objective of recent Conservative legislation has been to narrow the definition of a trade dispute and thereby exclude from immunity any industrial action which is not directed primarily towards the industrial situation or the employer/employee relationship.

Trade union immunities

The basic immunities for both trade unions and their members in respect of **civil liability** in tort (damages) was established by the Trade Disputes Act (1906). This gave trade union members protection against civil liability for conspiracy and gave organisers of industrial action protection against liability for inducing another person to breach a contract of employment (subject, in both cases, to their actions being 'in contemplation or furtherance of a trade dispute'). It also gave trade unions virtually complete immunity from actions in tort for all acts committed by its members or officials irrespective of whether or not they were carried out in contemplation or furtherance of a trade dispute.

A major area of civil liability was highlighted during the 1960s – the **tort**

of intimidation. In 1964 the House of Lords [71] held that the 1906 Act provided protection for the act of inducing a breach of contract of employment (calling a strike) but not threatening such a breach (threatening to go on strike). They argued that such a threat amounted to intimidation and therefore trade union officials and members could be liable for unlawful conspiracy to intimidate. This decision created a virtually untenable situation in which calling a strike was lawful but threatening to call a strike was unlawful. The situation was immediately rectified by the Trade Disputes Act (1965) which specifically provided that threatening to breach a contract of employment could not be actionable in tort.

However, the 1906 Act provided no immunity for members or trade union officials to directly induce a **breach of commercial contract**. Yet, any inducement of employees to breach their contract of employment through sympathetic or secondary action was intended to induce indirectly a breach of commercial contract through the employer's inability to maintain supplies to the primary organisation in dispute. The general thinking of the courts [72] appeared to be that whilst inducement to breach a contract of employment was protected by the 1906 Act, nevertheless the use of an unlawful act (breach of contract of employment) as a means to induce a breach of commercial contract rendered the whole process unlawful and therefore not protected by the civil immunities of the 1906 Act. This uncertainty was only finally resolved by the Trade Union and Labour Relations (Amendment) Act (1976) which formally extended immunity to cover inducement to breach any contract and not just contracts of employment.

In the view of the Conservative Government the 1974/1976 legislation 'licensed all industrial action even if it were directed against those far removed from the original dispute' [73]. The extent of the immunities was highlighted in 1979 when the House of Lords [74] reversed a Court Appeal decision and held that the immunities provided protection to any industrial action so long as the people carrying out the action genuinely believed that it might further a trade dispute. The Court of Appeal had argued that industrial action which was either too remote from the original dispute to be considered as action 'in contemplation or furtherance of a trade dispute' or was incapable of furthering a trade dispute could not be construed as being protected by the immunities. Consequently, **secondary industrial action** (i.e. sympathetic or supportive industrial action by employees at organisations not involved in the primary dispute) was one of the first areas to be tackled by the Conservative Government. S.17 of the Employment Act 1980 limited the extent of lawful secondary action where:

1. the purpose of the secondary action was to prevent or disrupt the supply of goods or services between a customer or supplier and the employer involved in the primary dispute;

or

2. the purpose of the secondary action was to prevent or disrupt the supply
    of goods or services between a customer or supplier of the employer
    involved in the primary dispute and an associated employer of the
    employer involved in the primary dispute, where such a supply of goods
    or services was in substitution for the original supply;

and

3. in both cases, the action was likely to achieve the purpose of preventing
    or disrupting the supply of goods or services.

The intention was to reduce the likelihood of industrial action spreading to
organisations which had no connection with or influence over the primary
dispute, or at least provide legal redress for breach of commercial contract to
organisations so affected. However, much of the sympathetic or secondary
action has, in the past, been confined to the direct customer/supplier
situation and this remained lawful; but, in the case of blacking, only
providing it sought to disrupt the supply to the primary dispute and not
other customers as well.

Under S.4 of the Employment Act 1990 immunity for calling, threatening to call or otherwise organise secondary action has been removed
completely. As a result, any industrial action taken by employees (who are
not party to the primary dispute) whether to exert industrial pressure by
interrupting production or services or simply to show support or solidarity
for other workers in dispute is unlawful. This would apply as much to one
group of employees seeking to support another group of employees within
the same organisation as it does to employees of a different organisation. It is
important to note that the trend in some organisations during the 1980s to
'break up' the organisation into a series of distinct legal entities with separate
bargaining arrangements for each, as part of their strategy of devolution and
decentralisation, makes the potential impact of removing immunity from
secondary industrial action more serious. The practical effect of the
legislative change is to further segment and isolate trade unionists and make
it impossible, lawfully, for them to express their fraternalism one with
another.

Trade union immunity has been further restricted as part of the
Government's legislative strategy to make the operation of **Union Membership Agreements** (closed shop) unlawful. Having provided, under the
Employment Acts (1980 and 1982), protection for individuals by making it
unfair to dismiss an employee for not being a member of a trade union if
they genuinely objected, the UMA was not sufficiently supported in a ballot
or there had been no ballot, S.10 of the Employment Act 1988 removed the
trade union's power to enforce a UMA by removing immunity from any

action intended to pressure an employer to dismiss (post-entry) or not employ (pre-entry) a person who is not a member of a union.

At the same time as removing immunities from certain types of industrial action, the legislation has clearly established **trade union liability for unlawful actions**. Section 15 of the Employment Act 1982 removed the wider organisational immunity afforded to trade unions and brought their immunities into line with that afforded to individuals (immunity only for acts carried out 'in contemplation and/or furtherance of a trade dispute'). It also provided that **trade unions can be held liable for any unlawful act which is authorised or endorsed by a responsible person within the union** (i.e. its Executive Committee, President, General Secretary or any employed official, committee or other person). However, the union is absolved from liability if the official or committee, in authorising or endorsing industrial action, exceeds their authority as specified in the union's rules and their action is repudiated by the Executive Committee, President or General Secretary of the union. To provide an effective **defence**, such repudiation:

1. must be carried out as soon as is reasonably practicable;
2. must be notified in writing to the person or committee which authorised or endorsed the action; and
3. the Executive Committee, President or General Secretary must not subsequently behave in a manner which could be construed as being inconsistent with their repudiation of the action.

However, the court accepted that the AUEW was not liable as an organisation when its members, in conjunction with other groups of employees, followed the recommendation of a joint negotiating committee to strike but against the expressed advice of its union official [75]. Whilst the intention was to induce trade union leaders to exert greater control over their members and use their best endeavours to ensure that they acted lawfully, the effect could be quite the reverse. The membership, as had been the case with injunctions in the past, could ignore their union's instruction simply because they knew that the law was compelling the leadership to act in order to protect the union from any claim for damages or fines for contempt. As a result, the influence of the union's formal leadership over both its members and the resolution of the dispute could be weakened.

The government has removed this 'loophole' (i.e. the union not being responsible for the actions of shop stewards because they are not 'employees' of the union): S.6 of the Employment Act 1990 extends the union's liability to 'any officer elected or appointed in accordance with the rules of the union to be a representative of its members' or 'any committee comprising a group of people constituted in accordance with the rules of the union'. Furthermore, to absolve itself from any liability for an unlawful act the union must, in addition to the requirements placed on it by the 1982 Act, take reasonable steps to provide individual written notice of its repudiation to all members involved in the action and their employers and the written notice must contain a statement informing the members that the union will give no support to unofficial industrial action and that if they are dismissed they will have no right to claim unfair dismissal.

In addition to seeking an **injunction** (against either individuals or a trade union) to stop the continuation of any unlawful act, the employer may claim **damages**. However, S.16 of the Employment Act 1982 limited the level of damages that may be awarded against a trade union dependent on its size:

Up to 4,999 members	£10,000
5,000–24,999 members	£50,000
25,000–99,999 members	£100,000
100,000 or more members	£250,000

Such damages may not be enforced against the political or provident funds of a trade union. Whilst at first sight the maximum level of damages appears relatively small, it must be realised that they apply to each individual legal action brought against a trade union and not each individual dispute. Therefore, if a trade union instigates unlawful secondary action at a number of organisations in support of a single dispute it could face a number of actions for damages – each involving the maximum level of compensation. The members of the Newspaper Publishers' Association collectively sued the NGA for some £3 million in respect of its secondary action in support of the 'Stockport Messenger' dispute. In addition, as was seen repeatedly in 1983/1984, trade unions can also face unlimited fines for contempt of court when they fail to abide by injunctions awarded by the court and high administrative costs of sequestration when they refuse to pay such fines. The combined effect of these measures could be a return to the pre-1906 situation where a trade union, even one of the 'giants', could be bankrupt as a result of a small number of disputes or even one major dispute.

As part of the government's strategy to make the union leadership more accountable to the membership, S.10 of the Trade Union Act 1984 has **removed immunity from industrial action which is not supported by a ballot**. To retain immunity the ballot must be:

1. by individual secret voting;
2. the ballot paper must indicate that the proposed industrial action is in breach of contract;
3. a majority of those voting must be in favour of industrial action; and
4. the union's authorisation and instigation of industrial action must take place within four weeks of the ballot;

to which S.7 of the Employment Act 1990 has added:

5. the ballot must specify which official(s) has authority to call the industrial action.

The Donovan Commission argued in 1968, in response to similar proposals, that they were founded on 'a belief that workers are likely to be less militant than their leaders and that, given the opportunity of such a ballot, they would often be likely to vote against strike action' [76]. Certainly it reflects a distrust of a 'show of hands' at a mass meeting where individuals may feel pressured into 'going along with their fellows'. The requirement to include a reference to 'breach of contract' in the ballot paper suggests a hope that it will weaken the individual's inclination to use industrial action. Certainly, the government believes that the reduction in strikes in 1985 can be attributed to the legal requirement to ballot members; despite the fact that the majority of ballots have resulted in a vote in favour of strike action.

However, perhaps most importantly, the requirement that the action be authorised within four weeks of the ballot may seriously affect the negotiating relationship. It may change the balance between threatening industrial action and actually carrying it out in favour of the latter. Management's perception of any threat will depend on there having been a ballot to demonstrate its veracity, but once the ballot has been held the union must invoke the action within four weeks if it is to retain its immunity. It may be argued that this will either enhance the threat pressure on management and force a concession more easily or threats will be eradicated completely from the negotiating process. At the same time, the use of a formal ballot to instigate industrial action may lengthen the action if the union negotiators insist on a further ballot to stop the action rather than recommending an immediate return to work after a successful conclusion to the negotiation.

Furthermore, the strength which it may be argued a union can draw from a positive majority vote of its members in favour of industrial action has been to some extent undermined by the **protection of the individual** afforded under the subsequent Employment Act 1988. Section 1 of the Act gives the individual union member the right to seek, through the courts, to restrain the union from continuing with industrial action if the individual member believes the ballot was not a 'properly conducted secret ballot'. More importantly, however, S.3 of the Act specifies that it will be 'unjustifiable discipline' for a union to expel, discipline or otherwise discriminate against a member who does not take part in industrial action – even when it is official, lawful and has been supported by a majority of the membership in a ballot. This strikes at the very heart of both the fraternalist solidarity expected by unions and the democratic principal of majority rule/decision making [77].

Picketing

Whilst the act of striking provides the initial withdrawal of labour from the employer, the act of picketing seeks:

1. to persuade other employees to join or otherwise support the strike;
2. to withhold supplies or alternative labour from the employer; and/or
3. to ensure that the strikers do not return to work before the dispute is settled.

However, the law only recognises the purpose of picketing as being to peacefully obtain or communicate information or peacefully persuade any person to work or not work. Under the 1906 Act it was lawful for one or more persons, in contemplation of furtherance of a trade dispute, to attend at or near any place (other than a person's place of residence) for the purpose of picketing. Thus, the only real restrictions on picketing were that it should be peaceful and that it should not take place outside a person's home. However, during the 1970s a minority of situations became associated with 'mass picketing' (involving hundreds, and in some cases thousands, of people and sometimes involving violence against those who sought to cross the picket line) and 'flying pickets' (groups of strikers going or being sent to picket organisations in an attempt to spread the strike or secure the blacking of goods). Despite the infrequency of such occurrences the Conservative Government felt that the right to picket should be restricted.

Consequently, S.16(1) of the Employment Act 1980 provided that it is **only lawful for a person to attend at or near his/her own place of work** or, in the case of union officials, at or near the place of work of a member whom they are accompanying and whom they represent. Thus, the law has introduced a distinction between primary and secondary picketing similar to that made in respect of industrial action: primary picketing (at one's own place of work) is lawful but secondary picketing (at a place other than one's own place of work) is unlawful. Furthermore, the phrase 'his own place of work' restricts the employee to the actual site, depot, etc. where he/she normally works and therefore it would be unlawful secondary picketing to picket even another site of the organisation or its head office. At the same time the Code of Practice on picketing [78] has sought to reduce the size of pickets by advising that in normal circumstances there should not be need for more than six people at any one entrance. Although the Code is not itself directly enforceable, any contravention of its guidance may be taken into account by a court in hearing a claim in respect of unlawful picketing [79]. The fact that seeking, through picketing, to persuade employees of other employers not to deliver goods is tantamount to inducing a person to breach their own contract of employment (secondary industrial action) has been recognised in the Employment Act 1990 and pickets undertaking such activity still retain immunity even though the general immunity for secondary industrial action was removed.

Picketing is perhaps the one remaining area where the **criminal law** intrudes into the conduct of industrial relations. In so far as picketing is conducted outside the employer's premises in a public place then the conduct of the individuals on the picket line is subject to action by the police and criminal law in respect of 'obstruction of the highway', 'breach of the peace', 'abusive behaviour' or even 'assault'. In the past, the police have exercised discretion in carrying out their duties and generally have sought not to exacerbate a situation by arresting pickets. However, the 1984 NCB/NUM dispute once again focused attention on the role of the police and the 'law and order' issue. The widespread mass picketing, mass policing and increasing violence highlighted the inherent incompatibility of the practical intention of picketing, the legal rights relating to picketing and the rights of others to continue or return to work. The use of large numbers of police to ensure that handfuls of working miners got past pickets and the large number of pickets arrested led, as Kahn *et al.* [80] predicted, to the loss of any 'cultural resonance' or 'empathy' between strikers and police and its replacement by a perception, at least amongst the strikers, of the police undertaking a 'political' or 'partisan' role in supporting management and the government and weakening the strike [81].

The criminalisation of industrial action, particularly picketing, is likely to increase as a result of the Conservative Government's most recent proposals. They have proposed, as part of a new Public Order Act, to give police the power to limit the number of pickets or move them from the path of workers and, perhaps most importantly, to introduce a new offence of disorderly conduct and to tighten up the law relating to riot – both of which could be applied to picketing (particularly mass picketing). Indeed, during the 1984/1985 mining dispute a large number of pickets were charged by the police with riot offences although subsequently found 'not guilty' by the courts.

Dismissal of strikers

Whilst one or two judges have attempted to suggest that a strike should be regarded as a unilateral suspension of the contract of employment, the traditional basis of the **common law** has maintained it to be a breach of the contract of employment sufficient to justify the employee's dismissal. A lawful withdrawal of labour can only be achieved if the employees give notice equivalent to that required to terminate their contract – that is, resign.

This basic common law principle was carried through into the **Unfair Dismissal legislation** in 1971. However, the principle was mitigated by the basic intention of the legislation to ensure that all dismissals were treated in an equitable manner. The legislation provided that **for the dismissal of a striker to be fair, management could not be selective** but had to dismiss all employees who had gone on strike or none and, if it wanted subsequently to offer re-employment, it must re-engage all strikers or none. However, a court decision in 1978 highlighted that, as the wording of the law stood, equity had to be demonstrated amongst the group which had taken part in the industrial action and therefore if only one of the original strikers had returned to work then the employer could not fairly dismiss those who remained on strike. At the same time it was argued that because there was no time limit set for judging equity in respect of the re-engagement of strikers management could be guilty of an unfair dismissal if it offered re-engagement to some, but not all, dismissed strikers even though it did so months or even possibly years after the dispute was over.

Section 9 of the **Employment Act (1982)** clarified and strengthened the provisions relating to the dismissal of strikers:

1. By delineating the group of employees within which equity must be judged as being the group on strike at the time of the individual's dismissal. Although the Bill proposed that the employer should be able to dismiss strikers only after they had received a written warning of their impending dismissal at least five days before it was to become effective, this was not carried through into the Act. Therefore, an **employer may fairly dismiss strikers at any time and without warning providing all of them are dismissed.**
2. **By introducing a time limit of three months after which a dismissed striker may be re-engaged** without the employer becoming liable for a claim for unfair dismissal because other strikers who were dismissed at the same time have not been re-engaged.

Furthermore, management has been given **complete freedom to dismiss unofficial strikers** by the Employment Act 1990. Section 9 of the Act removes any right for an employee to take a claim before an Industrial Tribunal if he/she is undertaking official industrial action at the time of the dismissal. The only limitation placed on management by the legislation is that if the union repudiates the industrial action, irrespective of whether or not the union has informed the individual members of the repudiation, then the employee is not deemed to be undertaking official industrial action until a full working day later. In addition, trade union immunity has been removed for calling, threatening to call or organising industrial action in support of anyone dismissed while taking part in unofficial industrial action. The consequence is that management may selectively dismiss amongst those employees engaged in unofficial industrial action (shop stewards, 'ring-leaders', 'troublemakers' – or for any other reason!).

This is perhaps the **most fundamental part of the law relating to industrial action.** As the law stands, employees have no right whatsoever to strike; irrespective of the cause of the strike or whether it is official or unofficial, constitutional or unconstitutional, the employer can dismiss strikers at any time. Thus, the effectiveness of any strike is dependent, at least in part, on the 'goodwill' of the management (the opposition). If the strike is effective in bringing pressure to bear on management they can seek to remove the pressure by threatening to dismiss those on strike and in a climate of high unemployment the threatened loss of a job may be a powerful deterrent. Certainly, the dismissal of strikers by British Rail in 1985 appeared to be a significant factor in the subsequent 'no' vote on industrial action by NUR guards and British Rail's unilateral introduction of one man operated trains. The dismissed men were, the union argued, hostages for the union's agreement to this change in working practices.

The establishment of immunities from claims for damages for trade unions and their members, when acting in contemplation or furtherance of a trade dispute, would appear to be of questionable value whilst the employees who undertake such lawful action risk being dismissed. There appears, therefore, to be a need to consider the establishment of a positive right for the individual to undertake industrial action without fear of losing his/her job; at least in respect of official and constitutional strikes. It is this aspect of legislation which, in most European countries, gives the basis of the 'right to strike' – a lawful strike (if not all strikes) is regarded as a suspension not breach of the contract of employment and therefore does not give rise to any right to dismiss [82].

Other possible measures

Two other measures have been suggested, and tried, to restrict the incidence or effect of strike action.

● *Restriction of the right to strike amongst certain groups of essential workers*. In this context 'essential' refers to the workers' position within the general community rather than within any individual organisation and is generally felt to include such groups as gas, electricity, water and sewerage, health services, dustmen, etc. It is argued that a strike by these employees exerts pressure on their employer only through the effect it has on a wide range of other employers and/or the general public and that such disruption of the general community is acceptable. Differential treatment of such employees existed within the Conspiracy and Protection of Property Act (1875) in that gas, water and later electricity employees were liable to criminal prosecution if, by breaching their contract of employment, they deprived inhabitants of their supply of gas, water or electricity (repealed only in 1971).

The issue of restricting the right of such groups to strike has come to the fore again as a consequence of a number of strikes in these essential services during the late 1970s and 1980s. However, any move in this direction must consider the following points:

1. The power to disrupt the community has, in the main, been exercised with restraint and essential services or supplies have usually been maintained by the strikers themselves during the dispute. The removal of the 'right to strike' may itself provoke strong resististance.

2. It would be difficult to establish accepted criteria for determining which groups of employees should be covered by this restriction. Indeed, it can be argued that because of the interdependent nature of industry there are many groups whose strike action can seriously affect all or a wide section of the community (e.g. oil delivery drivers).
3. The complete removal of the 'right to strike' from such groups would need to be accompanied by the introduction of some acceptable system of arbitration if the employees are not to be left powerless in relation to their employer and the determination of their terms and conditions of employment. It may be argued that the introduction of such an acceptable system of arbitration would itself make the use of industrial action by employees unnecessary.

● *A cooling off period.* The use of a cooling off period before the implementation of a strike in certain situations. Such a provision was contained in the Industrial Relations Act (1971), based on the working of the Taft Hartley Act in the USA, and allowed the government to apply to the court for an order delaying strike action for up to 60 days in those situations where it felt that the strike would seriously affect the national economy, national security or public order or would endanger life. It provided an opportunity for the government to intervene in a major dispute by requiring the parties to reconsider their respective position. However, whilst the purpose of a cooling off period is to provide an opportunity for further negotiations, the time can equally be used to 'hot up' the dispute as both sides play 'brinkmanship' in delaying concessions during the designated period or make their preparations for the strike which might ensue.

Enforcement of the law

Although it is government, through Parliament, which establishes the limits of trade union rights to undertake industrial action, it is **management which has to enforce** these limits. The nature of the civil law is such that it is the aggrieved party, not the state, which has to take action to protect its legal rights. In the past it had been argued that management was reluctant to take legal action against either the trade unions with which it had to deal or its employees and that the use of law was incompatible with its primary objective to resolve the dispute and secure its production. Reliance on, and frequent use of the law, it was argued was likely to sour rather than improve industrial relations within the organisation.

However, the period since 1980 has seen an **apparent increased preparedness by some managements to resort to the law** as part of their strategy for handling industrial disputes. Clearly this development can be related not only to changes in the law, particularly the removal of trade union organisational immunity, but also the general development of a 'tougher' management approach to industrial relations in the 1980s. Younson's survey [83] of some twenty cases between September 1980 and April 1984 provides an interesting insight into this development:

1. 9 cases related to picketing (7 secondary picketing and 2 'nuisance' or 'intimidatory' picketing), 6 related to 'blacking' and only 3 related to secondary industrial action;
2. in 18 cases the court awarded an injunction and in only 1 case did the court hold that the trade union had acted lawfully;
3. contempt fines were awarded in 4 cases (most notably, £675,000 levied against the NGA in the 'Stockport Messenger' dispute).

Younson concluded that the 'cases have not generally been initiated by employers involved in the "primary" dispute' [84]. However, this was before the introduction of the ballot requirement of the 1984 Act.

A later survey by Evans [85] covering the period May 1984 to April 1987 found a substantial increase in the number of injunctions. Of the 80 cases surveyed:

1. 11 cases related to picketing, 16 to secondary industrial action and 47 to pre-strike ballots;
2. in 65 cases the injunction was sought by the direct employer or ex-employer and 12 by third-party customers of suppliers;
3. 59 cases involved large employers (i.e. more than 500 employees);
4. in 67 cases the injunction was sought against the union, as an organisation, rather than members, shop stewards or individual union officers and involved 26 different unions with 6 being involved in 5 or more cases, which led Evans to comment that 'the availability of injunctions and damages against unions and the loss of immunities for union funds have clearly proven attractive to employers' [86];
5. injunctions were secured in 73 cases: leading to the union's immediate withdrawal of the industrial action in 31 cases, the initiation of contempt proceedings in 9 cases and a claim for damages in only 3;
6. 29 cases were in Printing, 18 in Shipping/Transport and, significantly, 14 in the Public Services: the latter, Evans attributes to their obvious high-profile, immediate effect on the public creating political pressures to respond and 'the introduction of "commercialism" into managerial strategies and culture which has in turn undermined traditional trust and bargaining relations with unions' [87].

The **trade union response** to this plethora of court actions by employers had been initially to ignore court decisions, contempt of court fines and sequestration even to the extent, as in the NUM case, of moving their funds outside the UK. However, it became clear that prolonged resistance of this kind could easily result in a substantial loss of funds and an almost permanent state of union funds being tied up under the control of sequestrators. In this context, the News International and miners' disputes of the mid-1980s and their associated court cases may have acted as a watershed in determining the trade union movement's response to this legislative change. If they are to protect their funds, which are already threatened by declining membership, the unions have to adopt a stance of disassociating the formal union organisation from unlawful industrial action.

13.4 Summary propositions

- Industrial action is primarily an institutionalised means for employees and unions to exert power within the collective bargaining relationship through the temporary introduction of disorder into the economic and authority relationships of the organisation.
- Organised collective industrial action requires the development of a collective consciousness amongst the employees concerned.
- There is no simple or single causal explanation for variations in the extent of strike activity over time, between industries or between organisations; rather various structural influences interact with the aspirations of the participants.
- The legal framework of 'immunities' provides a formal social control over the use of industrial action and since 1980 this control has been significantly tightened.

Further reading

- R. Hyman, *Strikes* (4th edn), Macmillan, 1989. An extremely readable and comprehensive examination of strikes and industrial conflict from a sociological perspective.
- E. Batstone, I. Boraston and S. Frenkel, *The Social Organization of Strikes*, Blackwell, 1978. This study examines the social processes involved in the mobilisation of strike action within an organisation.
- P. Kahn *et al.*, *Picketing: Industrial disputes, tactics and the law*, Routledge & Kegan Paul, 1983. This examines the effect of the Employment Act (1980) on the conduct of industrial disputes.
- Government Green Papers, prepared as a prelude to the various Acts, raise many of the issues relating to the law surrounding industrial action and trade union immunities.

References

1. W. H. Hutt, *The Strike Threat System*, Arlington House, 1973, pp. 282–3.
2. C. Grunfeld, *Modern Trade Union Law*, Sweet & Maxwell, 1966, p. 367.
3. A. Kornhauser, R. Dubin and A. M. Ross (eds), *Industrial Conflict*, McGraw-Hill, 1954, p. 12.
4. R. Dubin, 'Constructive aspects of industrial conflict', in A. Kornhauser *et al.*, *ibid.*, p. 45.
5. R. O. Clarke, 'Labour–management disputes: a perspective', *British Journal of Industrial Relations*, vol. XVIII, 1980, p. 23.
6. M. P. Jackson, *Industrial Relations* (2nd edn), Croom Helm, 1982, p. 185.
7. L. A. Cosser, *The Functions of Social Conflict*, Routledge & Kegan Paul, 1956.
8. R. Hyman, *Strikes* (3rd edn), Fontana, 1984, pp. 108–9.
9. *ibid.*, p. 111
10. *ibid.*, p. 110–44.
11. J. Gennard and R. J. Lasko, 'The individual and the strike', *British Journal of Industrial Relations*, vol. XIII, no. 3, 1975; J. Gennard, 'The effects of strike activity on households', *British Journal of Industrial Relations*, vol. XIX, 1981, pp. 327–44; J. Gennard, 'The financial costs and returns of strikes', *British Journal of Industrial Relations*, vol. XX, 1982, pp. 247–56.
12. R. Hyman, *op. cit.*, p. 136.
13. R. Dubin, *op. cit.*, p. 44.
14. R. Hyman, *op. cit.*, p. 56.
15. K. G. J. Knowles, *Strikes*, Oxford University Press, 1962.
16. R. Bean, 'The relationship between strikes and 'unorganised' conflict in manufcturing industry', *British Journal of Industrial Relations*, vol. XIII, 1975, pp. 98–101.
17. J. Kelly and N. Nicholson, 'Strikes and other forms of industrial action', *Industrial Relations Journal*, vol. 11, no. 5, 1980, pp. 20–31.
18. P. K. Edwards, 'Strikes and unorganised conflict; some further considerations', *British Journal of Industrial Relations*, vol. XVII, no. 1, 1979.
19. H. A. Turner, G. Clack and G. Roberts, *Labour Relations in the Motor Industry*, Allen & Unwin, 1967, p. 190.
20. E. Batstone, I. Boraston and S. Frenkel, *The Social Organization of Strikes*, Blackwell, 1978, p. 1.
21. *ibid.*, pp. 218–19.
22. *Sit-ins and Work-ins*, Institute of Personnel Management, 1976, p. 2.
23. C. Thomas, 'Strategy for a sit-in', *Personnel Management*, January 1976, p. 33.
24. A. Flanders, *Management and Unions*, Faber, 1970, p. 112.
25. R. Hyman, *op. cit.*, pp. 58–9.
26. W. Brown (ed.), *The Changing Contours of British Industrial Relations*, Blackwell, 1981, p. 83.
27. W. W. Daniel and N. Millward, *Workplace Industrial Relations in Britain*, Heinemann (PSI/SSRC), 1983, p. 215.
28. N. Millward and M. Stevens, *British Workplace Industrial Relations 1980–1984*, Gower, 1986, p. 264.
29. W. Brown (ed.), *op. cit.*, p. 85.
30. J. Kelly and N. Nicholson, *op. cit.*, p. 26.

31. P. K. Edwards, 'The strike-proneness of British manufacturing establishments', *British Journal of Industrial Relations*, vol. XIX, 1981, p. 137.
32. H. A. Turner *et al.*, *op. cit.*, p. 57.
33. *ibid.*, p. 223.
34. J. Hillage, 'No Strike Deals – Can they really work?', *Manpower Policy and Practice 1*, autumn 1985, p. 15.
35. M. Hall, 'An uncertain future for the unions,' *Personnel Management*, September 1988, p. 35.
36. 'The Regulation of Industrial conflict in Europe', *European Industrial Relations Review*, report no. 2, 1989, p. 2.
37. H. A. Turner, *Is Britain Really Strike Prone?*, CUP, 1969.
38. M. Fisher, *Measurement of Labour Disputes and their Economic Effects*, OECD, 1973, p. 184.
39. D. Bird, 'Industrial stoppages in 1990', *Employment Gazette*, July 1991, p. 380.
40. K. G. J. Knowles, *op. cit.*
41. P. J. White, 'The management of redundancy', *Industrial Relations Journal*, vol. 14, no. 1, 1983, p. 36.
42. P. Edwards, 'Industrial action 1980–1984', *British Journal of Industrial Relations*, vol. 25, no. 2, 1987, p. 287.
43. R. Hyman, *op. cit.*, p. 63.
44. P. K. Edwards, 'The pattern of collective industrial action' in G. S. Bain (ed.), *Industrial Relations in Britain*, Blackwell, 1983, p. 228.
45. P. K. Edwards (1981), *op. cit.*, p. 146.
46. T. Lane and K. Roberts, *Strike at Pilkingtons*, Fontana, 1971.
47. 'Industrial relations in the coal industry', *Employee Relations*, vol. 9, no. 2, 1987, pp. 9–15.
48. L. Hunter, 'Dispute trends and the shape of strikes to come', *Personnel Management*, October 1980, p. 48.
49. P. K. Edwards (1983), *op. cit.*, p. 215.
50. E. Screpanti, 'Long cycles in strike activity: an empirical investigation', *British Journal of Industrial Relations*, vol. 25, no. 1, 1987, p. 110.
51. R. J. Davies, 'Economic activity, incomes policy and strikes: a quantitative analysis', *British Journal of Industrial Relations*, vol. XVII, 1979, pp. 205–23.
52. C. Kerr and A. Siegel, 'The inter-industry propensity to strike – an international comparison' in A. Kornhauser *et al.*, *op. cit.*, p. 195.
53. *ibid.*
54. C. Kerr, 'Industrial peace and the collective bargaining environment' in G. S. Golden and V. D. Parker (eds), *Causes of Industrial Peace under Collective Bargaining*, Harper & Row, 1955.
55. C. T. B. Smith, R. Clifton, P. Makeham, S. W. Creigh and R. V. Burn, 'Strikes in Britain', *Department of Employment (Manpower Paper No. 15)*, HMSO, 1978.
56. P. K. Edwards (1981) and (1983), *op. cit.*
57. C. Kerr, *op. cit.*, p. 10.
58. *ibid.*, p. 19.
59. H. A. Turner, G. Roberts and D. Roberts, *Management Characteristics and Labour Conflict*, CUP, 1977, p. 72.
60. S. Creigh and P. Makeham, 'Variations in strike activity within UK manufacturing industry,' *Industrial Relations Journal*, vol. 11, no. 5, 1980, pp. 32–7.

61. M. Frayn, 'A perfect strike' in R. Blackburn and A. Cockburn (eds), *The Incompatibles*, Penguin, 1967, p. 160.
62. T. Wolfson, 'Social control of industrial conflict' in A. Kornhauser *et al.*, *op. cit.*
63. J. Gennard, *Financing Strikers*, Macmillan, 1977, pp. 123–4.
64. J. W. Durcan and W. E. J. McCarthy, 'The state subsidy theory of strikes: an examination of statistical data for the period 1956–70', *British Journal of Industrial Relations*, vol. XII, no. 1, 1974.
65. J. Gennard (1977), *op. cit.*, p. 137.
66. *Trade Union Immunities*, HMSO, 1981, p. 24.
67. *ibid.*
68. *Mercury Communications* v. *POEU* (1983).
69. *Dimbleby & Sons* v. *NUJ* (1984).
70. *Trade Union Immunities*, *op. cit.*, p. 52.
71. *Rookes* v. *Barnard* (1964).
72. *Thomson* v. *Deakin* (1952); *Stratford* v. *Lindley* (1965).
73. *Trade Union Immunities*, *op. cit.*, p. 22.
74. *Express Newspapers* v. *MacShane* (1979).
75. *Austin Rover* v. *T&GWU, AUEW and others* (1984).
76. Report of *Royal Commission on Trade Unions and Employers' Associations* (Donovan Commission), HMSO, 1968, p. 114.
77. J. Gennard, M. Steele and K. Miller, 'Trends and developments in industrial relations and industrial relations law: trade union discipline and non-strikers', *Industrial Relations Journal*, vol. 20, no. 1, 1989, pp. 5–15.
78. *Code of Practice, Picketing*, HMSO, 1980.
79. *Thomas and others* v. *NUM (South Wales)* (1985).
80. P. Kahn *et al.*, *Picketing: Industrial Disputes, Tactics and the Law*, Routledge & Kegan Paul, 1983.
81. P. Wallington, 'Industrial relations, the police and public order – some lessons of the miners' strike', *Employee Relations*, vol. 10, no. 1, 1988, pp. 3–12.
82. 'The regulation of industrial conflict in Europe', *op. cit.*
83. F. Younson, 'Who's been using the law in industrial disputes?', *Personnel Management*, June 1984.
84. *ibid.*, p. 32.
85. S. Evans, 'The use of injunctions in industrial disputes May 1984–April 1987', *British Journal of Industrial Relations*, vol. 25, no. 3, 1987, pp. 419–35.
86. *ibid.*, p. 420.
87. *ibid.*, p. 425.

Chapter 14

Conciliation and arbitration

14.1 Definition

Conciliation and arbitration are intended primarily as adjuncts to the collective bargaining process. The establishment of formal systems and institutions of conciliation and arbitration within the industrial relations system reflects the fact that 'most systems of labour relations . . . presuppose the possibility of disagreement and disputes' [1] between the parties involved. They are available where the parties to a negotiation fail to determine a solution on their own, that is, when they have reached an impasse with no further prospect of movement by either side and, generally, with no further levels of joint negotiating machinery to which the issue may be referred. Therefore, they should be viewed principally as **intervention strategies which utilise the involvement of an independent third party in the conduct of the collective bargaining process**. The intervention may be initiated by the parties themselves (unilaterally or jointly) or by the state, through its delegated agency, as the representative of external interests.

However, the two strategies of conciliation and arbitration are fundamentally different in their method of operation and, in particular, in the relationship between the 'third party' and the other two parties (see Figure 14.1):

1. **Conciliation** may be defined as:

   > a strategy wherein the 'third party' supports the direct bipartite negotiating process by assisting the parties to identify the case and extent of their differences, to establish alternative solutions and their various implications and to develop and agree a mutually acceptable settlement.

   The responsibility for making decisions and reaching a solution still remains a joint one between management and union – as it would if there was no intervention. The conciliator acts as a medium for the

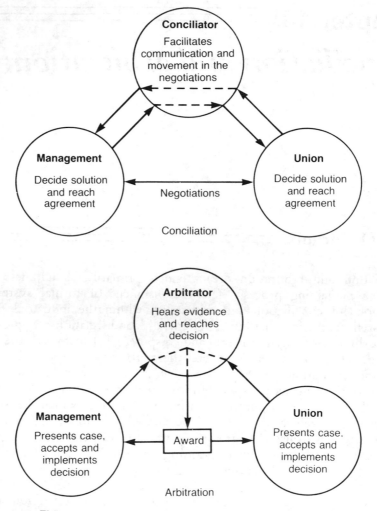

Figure 14.1   *Conciliation and arbitration processes*

continuation of the dialogue. Wood describes it as 'a catalyst, aiming to lead the parties to an agreement without himself interfering in the actual decision making' [2], whilst Goodman and Krislov point out that the conciliator 'has no authority to compel . . . nor to impose a settlement' [3].

2. **Arbitration**, on the other hand, may be defined as:

> **a strategy wherein direct negotiation between management and union is replaced with a process of adjudication which involves the third party in making a decision (award) between the two conflicting positions.**

The arbitrator 'is empowered to take a decision which disposes of the dispute' [4] and, therefore, is not required to seek a direct reconciliation between the two parties; as Wood notes, 'the parties lose their power over the settlement entirely' [5]. It is the arbitrator's decision, rather than a joint decision of the two parties, which determines the settlement and he/she may accept one or other of the positions put to him/her or, as is perhaps more often the case, determine a point somewhere between the two positions.

Margerison and Leary have suggested that conciliation (and, by implication, arbitration) is little more than 'short term crisis intervention to aid the resolution of a dispute' [6] and that there is a third, and perhaps more useful, intervention strategy which may be adopted – mediation. However, the term **mediation** is itself often used in two quite different ways:

1. In the **short-term** resolution of a particular dispute, it may be defined as a process in which the third party is 'more active in assisting the parties . . . going so far as to submit his own proposals for settlement' [7]. As such, it is simply a subgrouping within conciliation, differentiated only on the basis of the degree of initiative taken by the third party, because it is still a fundamental requirement of the process that the outcome should be determined and agreed by the parties themselves.
2. Mediation may be viewed as a **long-term** intervention strategy, and therefore qualitatively different to either of the normal processes of conciliation or arbitration, which Margerison and Leary believe is concerned 'not only to resolve existing conflict, but to plan for the prevention of similar conflict' and involves 'help with the implementation of decisions at both the interpersonal and organisational levels' [8]. In this respect it is a form of organisational development intervention requiring the third party to act as a continuing consultant to both parties with the objective of permanently improving their relationship.

14.2 The nature of conciliation and arbitration

The precise nature and role of conciliation and arbitration within the industrial relations system depend primarily on two factors:

1. The perceived relationship of these processes to the 'normal' bipartite process of direct negotiations between management and union (including the possible use of industrial action).
2. Whether these processes are to be used by the parties on a voluntary or compulsory basis.

Relationship to the collective bargaining process

It is perhaps inevitable that conciliation and arbitration are contrasted, as processes, with the direct bipartite process of management/union negotiations or, as intervention strategies into the negotiating process, with the parties own use of industrial action. However, it is important not to lose sight of the fact that they are an **integral part of the total collective bargaining system** and not simply some form of external appendage to the system (see Figure 14.2). This is most evident in the case of conciliation. The process of direct negotiation is continued with its reliance on achieving compromise between the parties and the necessity for the parties themselves to determine and agree the final settlement – but in a different form and under a different title. Although arbitration involves a significantly different and less direct process, it is nevertheless generally preceded by some form of direct negotiation between the parties during which they have sought, through offers and compromise, to resolve their differences and the parties will continue to seek to influence, although not directly determine, the final outcome through the presentation and argument of their case to the arbitrator.

Conciliation and arbitration may often be used simply to bridge the final gap between the parties or solve outstanding issues within an otherwise successful negotiation. Therefore, the use of these intervention strategies, like the use of industrial action by the parties themselves, cannot be regarded as automatic evidence of the failure or breakdown of collective bargaining because they are themselves part of that system. Their use is indicative only of an inability of the direct negotiation process, in a specific set of circumstances, to resolve the differences between the parties and the desire of the parties to pursue alternative strategies to secure a settlement. Certainly, Goodman and Krislov found that 66 per cent of the trade union officers and 81 per cent of the managers surveyed did not feel that the use of conciliation should be regarded as an indication of an immature approach to industrial relations [9].

The merits of third-party intervention strategies of conciliation and arbitration, as compared with the participants' own intervention strategy of industrial action, may be viewed from three different perspectives:

1. From an **ends perspective** (which emphasises the inherent requirement for the collective bargaining system to achieve a resolution to disputes) they may be viewed as parallel, equal and alternative strategies – each available in the event of a breakdown in negotiations and each capable of securing a settlement and the continuation of the contractual relationship.
2. From a **quality of means perspective** (which places emphasis on the achievement of a settlement through processes based on a joint and

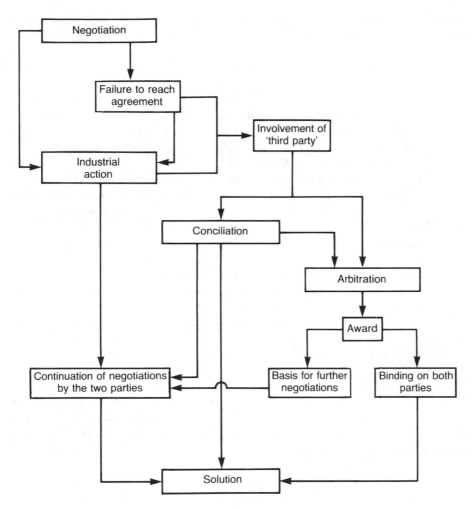

Figure 14.2 *Relationship of conciliation and arbitration to collective bargaining*

direct agreement and regulation) arbitration may be regarded as
subordinate and inferior to either conciliation or the participants' own
use of industrial power to resolve their differences.
3. From an **effect of means perspective** (which places greatest emphasis on
the maintenance of industrial peace and the avoidance of disruption
within the industrial relations system) the intervention strategies of
conciliation and arbitration may be perceived as preferable and superior
strategies to the use of industrial action.

The attitude, in Britain, towards the role of conciliation and arbitration reflects elements of both these last two perspectives. The **primacy of voluntary and direct negotiations** is reflected in a number of ways:

1. There is a general belief amongst all the parties that conciliation or arbitration should not be used until the normal, jointly agreed negotiating and disputes procedures in the organisation or industry have been exhausted. However, Kessler notes that the existence of unofficial and unconstitutional strikes has led, in practice, 'to some undermining of this rule, otherwise conciliators would have stood on the touchlines while serious disputes took place' [10].
2. Where third-party intervention is invoked there is a clear preference amongst management and unions for conciliation rather than arbitration and there is no automatic resort to arbitration if conciliation fails.
3. Whilst in the majority of cases where arbitration does take place it is invoked by a joint request from the two parties, either side may be reluctant or even refuse to accept, formally and in advance, to be bound by the outcome of the award. Thus, arbitration may be used not to provide the final settlement but rather to provide a fresh basis for further bipartite negotiations.
4. Conciliation may be invoked to circumvent an impasse in the negotiating process created by the use of industrial action and thereby allow the negotiations to continue albeit in a slightly different form.

Clearly, it can be important for the continuation of negotiations and the securement of a settlement that these third-party intervention strategies are available. Goodman and Krislov [11] found that both managers and trade union officers felt that conciliation could play a **positive role in supporting the negotiating process**:

1. It can provide an avenue for the maintenance of the negotiating dialogue at a time when it would otherwise break down. Indeed, there may be occasions, such as outright refusal by either side to negotiate on a particular issue, where conciliation provides perhaps the only possible means for establishing or maintaining contact between the parties.
2. The introduction of a third party, who must be informed of the issues and viewpoints involved in the dispute, requires both parties to set out their position in a reasoned and orderly manner. The act of having to prepare a 'statement of case' for the conciliator or arbitrator may itself provoke a re-examination of the situation and movement in position by either or both parties.
3. The conciliator or arbitrator, because he/she is independent and has not been involved in the development of the dispute, is able to approach the issues with a fresh and unprejudiced mind. He/she is able, having identified the common ground as well as the points of difference between the parties, to indicate approaches which may not have been seen by the parties to the dispute.

4. The use of conciliation or arbitration may allow the proposal of a solution which has been precluded by the mandates within which either or both of the negotiators have been required to negotiate by their principals. Thus, the 'blame' for a solution outside the original mandate can be shifted from the negotiator to the third party. It would appear, however, that this role for conciliation and arbitration is generally perceived as being confined to the 'other side' – Goodman and Krislov found that only some 17 per cent of trade union officers and 22 per cent of managers felt that conciliation 'had helped *them* to withdraw from a difficult position' [12].

Whilst conciliation or arbitration may be necessary to ensure the maintenance of the collective bargaining relationship, it is important to realise that their use, particularly on a frequent basis, **may distort the relative bargaining power** between the parties concerned. Machinery for conciliation and arbitration, within an industrial relations system which retains the primacy of the right to strike, is offering 'employers and workers the choice of seeking a settlement of disputes between them through such procedures or by a trial of strength' [13]. Conciliation and arbitration do not replace industrial action but complement it: industrial action remains part of the process of exerting pressure for change in decisions (it may be threatened or used during negotiations before an impasse is identified or it may be used if the results of conciliation or arbitration are unacceptable). In this context the use of conciliation or arbitration can be regarded as no more than a voluntary postponement of industrial action rather than precluding its use. Alternatively, Loewenberg *et al.* argue that 'arbitration, if effective, neutralizes bargaining power' [14] in that the issue is decided by argument before an independent assessor rather than by industrial muscle. However, as Hyman points out, this ignores the fact that 'the power relationship of the parties – shaped ultimately by an assessment of the damage that each can inflict in open conflict – provides the background to any resort to arbitration' [15]. In practice the conciliator or arbitrator seeks to secure a settlement which is not only 'right' in relation to the facts of the case as presented, but also acceptable to the two parties in terms of their assessment of the likely gains/costs associated with the use of industrial action.

It is significant that **both management and trade unions may perceive the intervention of conciliation or arbitration to be a weakening of their bargaining power**. From the management perspective, whilst a specific union request for conciliation or arbitration may be perceived as indicative of the union's lack of bargaining power (i.e. its membership is not prepared to resort to the use of industrial action), the use of either strategy may be seen as potentially detrimental to management's bargaining position and, in particular, its decision making authority and responsibility. Decisions which can have a profound effect on the operation and success of the organisation now involve an 'outsider' who has no long-term commitment or responsibility to the organisation. Goodman and Krislov point out that, despite having reached the limits of their concessions in direct negotiations, management often feels that its last offer is regarded during conciliation or arbitration as an 'irreducible minimum above which a compromise would be made' [16]. It believes that trade unions can, through conciliation or arbitration, obtain a settlement which is beyond the level warranted by their case and/or beyond the limit to which management is able or prepared to go. As a result, management may, if it believes conciliation or arbitration to be likely, either keep offers in reserve for this phase (thereby reducing the prospects of a solution through direct negotiations and so creating a self-fulfilling prophecy) or make informal 'without prejudice' offers during the negotiation which may be withdrawn in the event that the issue does go to conciliation or arbitration [17]. In response to this latter strategy, the union must decide whether the possible gains from conciliation or arbitration are likely to be substantial and certain enough to justify rejecting, and therefore losing, the last offer on the table.

From the trade union perspective the processes of conciliation and arbitration may be seen as potentially supportive of management's bargaining power in that their use involves a restriction on the union's capacity to mobilise its industrial power and exert the maximum pressure on management. Management's pursuit of conciliation or arbitration may be perceived by unions as little more than a strategy to weaken, or at best postpone, their use of industrial power and thereby secure a more favourable settlement for management. Consequently, rather than relinquish or postpone the use of industrial action, the union or its members may regard it as both legitimate and necessary for there to be a demonstration of industrial power and employee feeling to accompany or precede the intervention of conciliation or arbitration. The use of industrial action in such circumstances is intended to influence the conciliator or arbitrator as much as, if not more than, management.

Goodman and Krislov point out that there appears to be a fairly widespread belief amongst managers and trade union officials that 'the stronger party in a dispute would not permit conciliation' [18]. This suggests not only that the participants regard any call for conciliation or arbitration as a sign of weakness but also that conciliation or arbitration can and will take place only in those situations where the relative bargaining power between the parties is reasonably evenly balanced. However, a suggestion of 'going' to conciliation or arbitration may, at one level, be no more than a strategy within the negotiating process to induce further concessions and a settlement, and as such may be initiated by either party irrespective of their relative bargaining advantage. A 'real' demand for conciliation or arbitration, on the other hand, is likely to arise where the initiating party believes its case to be strong, on logic or equity grounds, but it lacks the necessary industrial power to achieve an acceptable settlement. The demand for conciliation or arbitration is, in effect, a challenge to the stronger party to forgo its bargaining advantage and allow an opportunity for the weaker party to achieve a better settlement than would have been obtained through a continuation of direct negotiations.

An examination of **government policy towards conciliation and arbitration** reveals three distinct features.

- *To maintain industrial peace.* Ever since the late nineteenth century conciliation and arbitration have played an important role in the government's policy of seeking to maintain industrial peace within the industrial relations system. The government has sought to minimise the use of industrial action not only be establishing and maintaining the facilities for conciliation and arbitration (at public expense) but also by encouraging management and unions to avail themselves for these facilities. In addition, the government has had the facility to take a more direct role by itself initiating the processes of conciliation or arbitration in those disputes which it considers to be serious because of their effect on the economy or the community. The ultimate success of conciliation or arbitration in this area depends on their being perceived by management and unions as, in some way, more fair and equitable processes for the resolving of differences than the use of industrial power.

- *To influence the operation of the industrial relations system.* Governments have sought to use the availability of conciliation and arbitration as a way of influencing the operation of the industrial relations system. Evidence of this can be seen in a number of different areas. For example, most governments have tried to weaken unofficial or unconstitutional strikes by resisting the use of conciliation or arbitration until the normal recognised negotiating procedures have been exhausted (i.e. there has been a return to work by the employees and the issue has been restored to the normal procedures). Governments have also sought to use conciliation or arbitration to extend collective bargaining by specifically legislating for its use in certain situations where an employer is resisting the trade union (e.g. the trade union recognition procedure under the Industrial Relations Act, 1971, and the disclosure of information procedure within the Employment Protection Act, 1975). During the 1980s the government changed the balance of bargaining power within the public sector by restricting the unions' access to arbitration (e.g. teachers and the civil service). The right to invoke arbitration unilaterally has been withdrawn and replaced by the requirement for a joint request. This has significantly reduced trade union power and increased management's power. Arbitration can only take place if both parties agree and, as already pointed out, the stronger party may well resist the intervention of conciliation or arbitration.

- *To influence the outcome of negotiations.* Some governments have sought to use the processes of conciliation and arbitration to directly influence the outcome of negotiations – particularly wage negotiations. They have sought, in some cases by exhortation and in others by direct instruction, to enlist the conciliator or arbitrator as an agent for the implementation of their incomes policy. Clearly, such an approach has immense implications for the continued acceptability of conciliation and arbitration to management and unions. Whilst it might appear that management would welcome support from conciliators or arbitrators in keeping down wage increases, nevertheless the long-term acceptability of conciliation and arbitration depends on their impartiality and their freedom from external influence or control. Many would agree with McCarthy and Ellis that governmental 'policies designed to influence income movements and incomes criteria must be separated from those policies designed to reform collective bargaining and contain industrial conflict; both in their day-to-day application and in their form of organisation' [19]. Government attempts in this area led, in the early 1970s, to increasing criticism of the Department of Employment's conciliation service – to such an extent that the CBI and TUC jointly established their own independent conciliation panel. It was this indication of management and union joint concern regarding the official institution for conciliation which was largely responsible for the creation of ACAS, in 1974, as an autonomous body outside governmental control.

The relationship between direct negotiations and the processes of conciliation and arbitration is complex, varied and dynamic. However, there appear to be **two fundamental and inherent dilemmas** in that relationship:

1. All parties in the industrial relations system would agree that there is a clear need for conciliation and arbitration to be readily available in order to provide channels for the resolution of differences which cannot be settled in the negotiating dialogue. Nevertheless, excessive reliance on these processes may well undermine the process of direct negotiations in that one or both parties become reluctant to make concessions in the negotiating dialogue for fear of prejudicing their position, and the final outcome, should conciliation or arbitration be used. In particular, arbitration is generally perceived as involving some element of 'splitting the difference' between the two sides and therefore, if the parties believe there is a high probability of the issue going to arbitration, there is little incentive for either side to move towards the centre by making concessions in the negotiating dialogue.

2. The government's desire to maintain industrial peace (i.e. minimise the use of industrial action) appears to be in conflict with its desire to contain or influence the level of wage increases. It is unrealistic to seek to encourage management and unions to maintain industrial peace and settle their differences through conciliation and/or arbitration when their differences, certainly on wage matters, stem from government incomes policy – particularly if the discretion of the conciliator or arbitrator is restricted by the same government policy. The most probable result in this situation is, as has been demonstrated in the past, more concerted

and prolonged industrial action as trade union industrial power is directed not at achieving concessions from management but towards changing government policy.

Voluntary or compulsory

The term **voluntary** generally implies that management and union have complete discretion to make, or not make, such *ad hoc* or permanent arrangements as they consider necessary and appropriate for resolving any impasse that may arise during their negotiations. The facilities established and maintained by the state at public expense are available should the parties wish to make use of them rather than establish their own individual arrangements. The term **compulsory**, on the other hand, implies a removal of management's and union's freedom to determine their own affairs and involves the imposition, through legislation, of an external requirement that their disputes must, if they cannot be resolved through the direct negotiating dialogue, be referred to conciliation/arbitration machinery. Such an approach is generally associated with a legal restriction on the employees' right to strike and may be applied to all employees or only those in certain specified industries or situations.

However, it is important to recognise that any system of conciliation or arbitration need not be wholly voluntary or compulsory but **may contain elements of both approaches**. The voluntary or compulsory nature of the processes can apply at any or all of three distinct phases of their operation – the establishment of the institutions, the use of processes and the implementation of the outcome (see Figure 14.3). Compulsion by the government, therefore, need not encompass all three phases but may be directed towards only one of them. For example, the government may apply compulsion in the implementation of any outcome from conciliation or arbitration whilst leaving the parties free to decide, in the first place, whether to make use of these processes; or it may establish a compulsory requirement that these intervention processes be used in certain or all disputes whilst leaving the issue of whether the outcome is implemented to the discretion and agreement of management and union. Equally, within an essentially voluntary approach, management and union may determine whether to establish machinery and what form it will take and then, as part of their joint agreement, accept a self-imposed compulsion in its use and the implementation of its outcome (a form of 'voluntarily compulsory' system).

The British experience of conciliation and arbitration has been characterised by its voluntary nature. Only during two important, but abnormal, periods (1915–18 and 1940–51) has Britain sought to graft a comprehensive system of compulsory arbitration onto its normal collective bargaining arrangements. Even then, however, Britain's approach to compulsory arbitration was based on government support for **unilateral arbitration**.

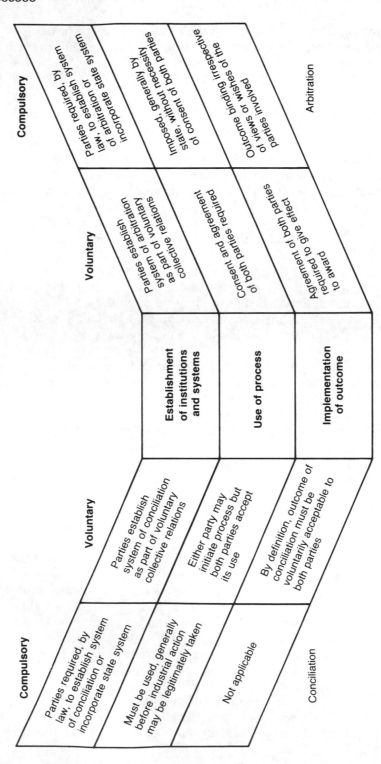

Figure 14.3 *Typology of conciliation and arbitration*

Hepple points out that, rather than impose arbitration against the wishes of both parties, the underlying principle of the British system was that 'at the request of either party to a dispute, the matter could be referred by the appropriate government minister for arbitration without the consent of the other party' [20] and the resulting arbitration award was legally binding. More recently, compulsory arbitration has had a limited role to play in respect of specific issues such as trade union recognition (Industrial Relations Act, 1971) and disclosure of information (Employment Protection Act, 1975). This largely voluntary approach is in marked contrast to other countries, such as the USA and Australia, who have maintained differing but more permanent systems of compulsory arbitration. It is therefore useful to examine the reasons for the adoption of compulsory arbitration and some of the issues associated with its operation.

In both Britain and the USA the **pressure to introduce compulsory arbitration** resulted from the existence of a state of war and the emphasis placed on the need to minimise any loss of production resulting from strikes and to regulate wage levels at a time of inflationary pressures within the economy. It was, therefore, the product of special external pressures and a temporary measure to be removed once, or soon after, the emergency was over. The pressure in Australia, however, came much earlier (1890s) as the trade unions sought, through extensive and often bitter industrial conflict, to extend collective bargaining into the key industry of sheep-rearing [21]. It was the product of an internal crisis within the country's industrial relations system and was regarded as a 'bold social experiment' intended to restructure the collective bargaining arrangements and promote greater justice and equality in wage determination.

In Australia the system has become an integral and dominant part of the collective bargaining arrangements. Walker [22] points out that approximately 90 per cent of all employees, public and private sectors alike, are covered by awards or agreements made under the system and the subject matter includes not only wages and conditions of employment but also issues such as jurisdictional disputes between unions, approval of union rules and the enforcement of union membership agreements. However, the system does not replace management/union negotiations; rather, such negotiations are carried out within the procedures of statutory tribunals and the framework of their awards. Awards may result from agreements reached, with or without the aid of conciliation, during the arbitration proceedings, or the tribunal may register voluntary agreements and thereby 'confirm and give effect to the result of . . . negotiations' [23]. In practice, therefore, the system involves 'an intertwining of negotiation, agreement-making and arbitration' [24].

Loewenberg [25] points out that in the USA, after the comprehensive approach of World War II (during which some 20,000 disputes were handled in five years), the emphasis of compulsory arbitration shifted towards the maintenance of essential services. In 1947 (following a high level of strike activity in the previous year) a number of states sought to establish legislation to restrict strikes and provide for compulsory arbitration in a range of essential services such as electricity, gas, water, fuel, etc. However, these industries were in the private sector and became the subject of a series of successful legal challenges based on the Taft-Hartley Act (1947) which applied to all employees other than government employees and which permitted strikes – consequently 'most of these laws have atrophied with inactivity' [26]. In the public sector it was not until the 1960s that Federal and State government employees were permitted to organise and bargain on a collective basis. However, many state legislatures were, at the same time, anxious to maintain a restriction on the employee's right to strike – particularly those employees involved in public safety – and consequently provided for compulsory arbitration in respect of specific groups such as police, firemen, prison guards or, more generally in some States, any essential service or where there was a danger to public health or safety. Thus, effective compulsory arbitration only applies to a very limited range of government employees and, perhaps more importantly, was introduced at a time of trade union recognition and when collective bargaining was still in its initial stages of development.

Hepple [27] believes that the most significant feature of the British experience of compulsory, or unilateral, arbitration is not so much that it was superimposed, as a wartime emergency, on an already relatively well-established system of voluntary collective bargaining, but rather that the participants, in particular trade unions, supported its continuation after the end of that emergency. Hepple argues that the unions' willingness to support the system derived from three main factors:

1. There was an 'almost total absence of enforcement of the penal sanctions against stoppages' [28] – even during the war.
2. The system was useful to trade unions in situations where they were weakly organised or where the strike weapon was ineffective.
3. In situations where the unions were well organised or had industrial power the processes of arbitration and negotiation/industrial action could be used in tandem.

Although the right to seek unilateral arbitration continued after 1951, the use of industrial action was no longer prohibited. The removal of sanctions, however ineffective or little used, increased employers' concern that the system was too one-sided. At the same time the government became concerned about the inflationary effect of arbitration awards. Consequently, the legal right to invoke unilateral arbitration was abandoned in 1959. All that remained was S.8 of the Terms and Conditions of Employment Act, 1959 (later incorporated within Schedule 11 of the Employment Protection Act, 1975 but rescinded by the Employment Act, 1980). The provision allowed trade unions to use the process of unilateral arbitration against an employer whose terms and conditions of employment were less favourable than the established or recognised ones in that industry. It supported trade union efforts in seeking to secure 'common rules' across an industry or trade.

Experience of the operation of compulsory arbitration in its different forms highlights four main issues.

- *Is it to be unilateral or compulsory arbitration?* Under the former the initiative to invoke the process, and thereby secure statutory support for the implementation of any award, is at the discretion of one or other of the negotiating parties; under the latter it is the government which prescribes the circumstances in which arbitration must take place. Whilst in theory, under unilateral arbitration, both management and unions have an equal right and opportunity to make use of the process, in practice it will be perceived by most employers as being biased in favour of the trade union. It is perhaps unfortunate that the inherent nature of the process is such that it is more suited to deal with quantifiable disputes concerning wages, hours, etc. (which are generally trade union initiated) than it is to deal with disputes over changes in working arrangements and practices (which are important to and initiated by management). At the same time, managements often argue that whilst they invariably comply with any arbitration award, whether or not they like its terms, trade unions have greater freedom to ignore the findings of an unacceptable award and seek to improve on it by direct pressure on the employer. However, as Walker points out, compulsory arbitration is more likely to remove from the negotiating parties their 'responsibility for reaching agreement, and for the terms of agreement' and encourages them 'to stand firm and emphasises points of difference rather than common ground' [29].

- *The extent to which industrial action should, and can, be prohibited.* Concern about the level and effect of strike activity has been the principal reason behind the introduction of compulsory arbitration – Loewenberg *et al.* argue 'arbitration becomes a *quid pro quo* for denying the right to strike' [30]. However, experience of the operation of compulsory arbitration, in Britain during wartime and in Australia, demonstrates that it has not led to a reduction in strike activity. Indeed, Australia's strike record with compulsory arbitration is significantly worse than Britain's experience without it! Loewenberg *et al.* believe the fundamental dilemma is that 'unwillingness to prosecute recognized violations serves to encourage further violations' and 'token prosecutions promote resistance' [31]. It would seem, therefore, that a reduction in strike activity relies on imposing sanctions against all and every breach of the prohibition. Yet realistically, compliance on a wide scale cannot be imposed by state force (certainly not without provoking resentment and possible confrontation between government and trade unions) but has to be voluntarily accepted by the parties – in particular trade unions.

McCarthy argues that it is somewhat ironic that access to unilateral arbitration may be most important for those 'many groups who are unable to use industrial action' [32] – groups with a low level of unionisation; groups where the use of the strike weapon lacks support because of social considerations; or groups where the strike weapon is ineffective, in the short term, in exerting pressure on the employer. Many white collar and/or public sector employees fall into the latter two categories.

● *Assuming that compulsory arbitration is not applied to all employees in all situations, which industries and/or situations should be covered by the system?* Discussion in Britain has centred on the special position of 'essential services'. However, given the complex and interrelated nature of modern economies, it can be argued that many industries could fall within the definition of essential services. Thus, it is likely to include a much wider range of industries than simply fire, police and health services: for example, coal mining, electricity, gas, petroleum production and distribution, all forms of transport, agriculture, and significant parts of government and local authority services. Furthermore, if an industry is designated as essential, and therefore subject to compulsory arbitration, is the process to be applied in all disputes irrespective of the number of employees involved, the actual effect of any possible strike or even whether the issue is really suitable for resolution through arbitration? The alternative, as practised in some states in the USA, is to leave the government or courts to determine, on an *ad hoc* basis, which disputes are serious enough to be subjected to an arbitration award. Such an approach is less likely to undermine the voluntary collective bargaining process.

● *Whether or not the public interest should be taken into account in the determination of arbitration awards.* In the USA, state interest in the outcome of arbitration has been achieved by specifying, within the legislation establishing the arbitration system, the criteria on which arbitrators should base their decision, whilst in Australia the government is able to present its case direct to the arbitrator as a third interested party to the dispute. Clearly, the direct or indirect involvement of the government in the determination of the outcome of the arbitration process shifts the focus of the process away from the simple resolution of a dispute between management and unions and towards the promotion of public policy on wages and other issues. Consequently, the system may become less attractive to management and unions alike.

Pendulum arbitration

In pendulum arbitration (alternatively referred to as 'straight choice', 'final (or last) offer' or 'flip-flop' arbitration) **the role of the arbitrator is**

restricted to choosing between the final positions of the two parties, unlike conventional or 'open' arbitration where the arbitrator can exercise judgement as to what is fair and equitable in the circumstances and propose a 'compromise' award. It has received considerable attention since the mid-1980s when it first came to prominence in the UK as part of the 'new style' Single Union Agreements. However, by no means all of these agreements include provision for pendulum arbitration; one survey in 1989 showed that only 24 out of 52 such agreements (46 per cent) contained a pendulum arbitration clause [33]. Equally, a number of writers [34] have noted that pendulum arbitration is not necessarily a new innovation in British industrial relations; it was used by the Coal Industry Conciliation Boards at the turn of the century and, similarly, the independent members on Wages Councils have, since the inception of the Trade Boards in 1908, provided a form of 'pendulum' through having to vote with one or other side if the unions and employers are unable to reach a satisfactory jointly agreed solution. ACAS have noted that 'approximately 25 per cent of references to arbitration are disputes of right . . . and require the arbitrator to make a straight choice between one position or the other' [35]. Furthermore, Brown's [36] survey of arbitration awards between 1942 and 1985 found that 31 per cent of cases dealing with annual pay claims had been of a straight choice type, that arbitrators had not always made a 'compromise' award in the other cases even though they had had this option and that where a 'compromise' award was made it was rarely pitched half-way between the union's claim and management's offer but rather a larger proportion came closer to the management's position than that of the union.

The concept of pendulum arbitration **originated in the USA** where, like ACAS noted in relation to the UK, the 'pendulum' nature of grievance arbitration in *'matters of right'* had been a well-established part of the process of contract interpretation. However, the development of pendulum arbitration in the USA in *'matters of interest'* was closely associated with the extension of collective bargaining rights to public sector employees in the 1950s and 1960s; some of whom were, at the same time, legally restricted in their right to strike. If groups of 'essential' employees were to forgo or be denied the right to strike then it was felt necessary to have some form of compulsory third-party intervention to resolve disputes; but conventional or 'open' arbitration was perceived to have two potential drawbacks: the 'chilling' effect (a reluctance of either or both sides to move to their real final position because of a perceived need to keep something in hand if the issue went to arbitration and the arbitrator 'split down the middle') and, stemming from this, the 'narcotic' effect (the reliance on third-party arbitration to resolve disputes becoming habit forming).

The essential issue, therefore, was **to make compulsory arbitration compatible with encouraging the parties to 'negotiate in good faith'**. Stevens [37] argued that the role of industrial action within collective bargaining is to introduce a 'cost' to either or both sides if a settlement is not

achieved through the negotiation process. Therefore, if the use of industrial
action is to be precluded, it is necessary to introduce a similar 'cost' element
within the arbitration process which would induce full movement during
negotiations and so overcome the 'chilling' and 'narcotic' effects. He argued
that the introduction of a 'win/lose' situation in the arbitration process
would introduce such a 'cost' element: if either side did not adopt a
reasonable final negotiating position then the arbitrator would be likely to
find in favour of the other party (i.e. there would be a consequent loss). On
the face of it, this contradicts the central philosophy of negotiation based on
the achievement of a mutually acceptable compromise. Certainly, Kessler
argues that 'for one side to defeat totally the other is not a basis for
continuing stable and orderly relations ... the essence of collective
bargaining is compromise and flexibility' [38] and Yeandle and Clarke have
noted that in one organisation 'the option of pendulum arbitration was
consciously rejected ... since it was felt likely to promote a potentially
divisive approach which would not be compatible with the overall personnel
philosophy' [39].

However, pendulum arbitration only introduces a 'winner take all'
situation if it is used and arguably it is the threat of this which induces the
two parties to bargain more reasonably to find their own mutually
acceptable solution. As Singh has noted, pendulum arbitration is primarily 'a
final deterrent – instead of industrial action – to ensure that the parties
genuinely engage in realistic collective bargaining ... are induced to make
reasonable offers' and its success 'could be judged by the number of times it
is not used' [40]. If the potential resort to pendulum arbitration does act as a
deterrent and increase reasonableness in the preceding negotiations, then the
win/lose element it introduces into the collective bargaining process is likely
to be small and, arguably, no more of a threat to the integrity of the
collective bargaining process than the potential use of power through
industrial action to force a change in position on one or other party. In what
are, after all, subjective issues it could be argued that it is better to lose
through argument in front of an independent third party who will be
exercising some degree of fairness and equity in their judgement than be
coerced to concede through force.

Although there has been some discussion [41] in Britain about following
the USA example and introducing pendulum arbitration alongside restricting
the right to strike amongst essential public sector employees, the government
has, during the 1980s, moved in the opposite direction and sought to
maintain its prerogative to determine public sector pay by revoking the right
of a number of public sector groups to 'unilateral arbitration' and refusing
to use arbitration in some major disputes (e.g. ambulance dispute in
1989/90). Pendulum arbitration in Britain has been adopted primarily in the
private sector as part of the 'new style' agreements aimed at reforming
organisational industrial relations. Experience of such pendulum arbitration
has highlighted a **number of issues:**

Recession proof

As Bassett notes, it has been argued by some union supporters that pendulum arbitration is 'recession-proof' in that 'the decision is not based on purely economic factors, but on the soundness of the argument presented' and 'the case that seems most just should carry the day, no matter how industrially weak in traditional union muscle terms the employees might be' [42]. However, in a dispute of interest regarding an annual pay increase the arbitrator, in effect, has to choose between the arguments used by management and union to justify and substantiate their case (not just simply the actual figures being offered and claimed) and these arguments may centre on very different concepts of 'equity': for example, a management case based on 'ability to pay' (internal organisation factors) and a union case based on 'cost of living' or 'comparability' (external factors). Whilst under conventional or 'open' arbitration the arbitrator is absolved from having to make an apparent choice between the 'rightness' of either set of arguments, within pendulum arbitration the award can appear to approve one or other of these bases for determining pay increases. Therefore, the extent to which pendulum arbitration is 'recession proof' is questionable; in periods of recession or financial constraints the arbitrator may well feel that the management's argument based on 'ability to pay' is the more reasonable and the deterrent effect argued for pendulum arbitration may well lead the union to drop its claim to come closer to the management's offer in order to demonstrate its reasonableness to the arbitrator.

Lack of flexibility and fairness

The theory of pendulum arbitration assumes that one or both of the positions put to the arbitrator will be equitable – the deterrent effect assumes both sides will have negotiated in good faith to their final positions and any inequitable aspects will, therefore, have been ironed out. However, this may not always be the case and, as Kessler points out, 'if the two parties do not converge in bargaining, the arbitrator could be left in a very difficult position' [43] and may be required to choose between two positions, neither of which he/she regards as totally reasonable. Lewis notes that this can be overcome, albeit only on a selective basis, by the use of 'obiter dicta' within the award and that 'the formulation of a preferred compromise by the arbitrator, even while making a pendulum award, can assist industrial relations in the longer term' [44]. Such an approach accords with the notion that at least part of the role of the 'third party' is to bring some independent scrutiny and fresh ideas to bear in trying to find a solution to a dispute.

Difficulty in defining the final claim/offer

Clearly, under pendulum arbitration the arbitrator needs to know the final positions of the two parties between which he/she has to decide. However, as Singh points out, this is not always as easy as it seems: 'is it at the point of the breakdown in negotiations or at the point of submitting the reference to the arbitrator or some other point?' [45]. This raises the issue of whether the parties are entitled to change their position between the final stage of the negotiation and putting their case to the arbitrator. Arguably, such a shift, presumably to present a more reasonable case to the arbitrator, is tantamount to the 'chilling' effect (holding something back for the arbitration award); certainly, the management at Sanyo, faced with a revised union position immediately prior to the arbitration hearing, believed that 'the integrity of pendulum arbitration entirely depends upon both parties declaring their final position for consideration at the final negotiating discussions. ... The concept behind pendulum arbitration is to make negotiators carefully consider the content and direction of their final negotiating position in the knowledge that, without agreement, these positions would be tested by arbitration. ... Changes made at the arbitration stage are not in keeping with the concept behind the pendulum arbitration process' [46]. Yet, to disallow such movement right up to the last minute appears to be contrary to the flexibility advocated within dispute resolution. The position at Sanyo was further complicated because the parties differed in their interpretation of the term 'mediation' prior to arbitration: the management felt it was to be simply a clarification of the two side's final positions whilst the union envisaged that it 'would involve a full-blown attempt by the parties to arrive at a settlement with the assistance of a mediator' [47].

Difficulty in handling multi-issue disputes

In a complex multi-issue dispute the arbitrator, under simple pendulum arbitration, would be required to choose between the 'total packages' put forward by the two parties without taking account of the merits of the parties' positions on each individual issue. Consequently, it could be argued that it would be preferable to require the arbitrator to exercise his/her pendulum choice on each item rather than on the package as a whole. Certainly, ACAS felt that 'where several issues are under discussion at the same time, it may be unhelpful for an arbitrator to be compelled to endorse the full position of one side or the other if long-term stability and equity are the aim' [48]. However, Kessler points out that the adoption of 'issue by issue' arbitration would mean 'moving away from the concept of pendulum arbitration to a situation where the arbitrator is in effect producing his or her own package' [49]. It is important to recognise that if the preceding negotiations have been conducted on a reasonable basis (which is likely to have involved trading off between the various items of the package before the two sides reach their final positions) then, if the arbitrator starts to mix up the two packages by choosing bits from each, this may well take the final award package beyond the intended final positions of one or both parties. This may result in the parties deciding, in future, to hold back a bit in their negotiations for such an eventuality; thereby, reintroducing the 'chilling' effect into their negotiations.

One state in the USA (Iowa) has sought to overcome some of these problems by adopting a **'tri-offer' approach** involving mediation, fact-finding by an independent third party and finally issue by issue pendulum arbitration. If the dispute does go to the final stage of arbitration, the arbitrator may select either the union, management or fact-finders recommendation as the award for each issue. Certainly, the inclusion of a requirement for mediation prior to arbitration allows third-party intervention to facilitate the two parties resolving their own problem before being called on to adjudicate between the two positions and the inclusion of a fact-finding 'inquiry' type process allows flexibility for the third-party to introduce new ideas and possible solutions for consideration by the two parties. Research in the USA [50] has shown that over a five-year period, 70 per cent of all cases presented at fact-finding were found to have been settled without going to pendulum arbitration and when a dispute did go to arbitration the arbitrator often confirmed the fact-finder's recommendations. However, it may be argued that the introduction of a third independent set of proposals (the fact-finder's), which may differ to those of either the union or management, means that there is little practical difference between this approach to 'pendulum' arbitration and the more traditional 'open' arbitration.

14.3 Institutions of conciliation and arbitration

Conciliation and arbitration, on both a voluntary and statutory basis, have a long history in British industrial relations. Legislation can be traced back to the Statute of Apprentices (1562) and during the nineteenth century there were attempts to legislate for conciliation and arbitration in both specific industries, such as the Cotton Arbitration Act, 1800 (which dealt with some 1,500 cases in three years), and on a more general basis, such as the Arbitration Act, 1824 [51].

The framework of modern state support for conciliation and arbitration was established at the turn of the century:

1. **Conciliation Act (1896)** gave the Minister general powers to investigate the cause and circumstances of any dispute and to appoint a conciliator (on an application from either party) or an arbitrator (on a joint application from both parties).
2. **Industrial Courts Acts (1919)** established a permanent arbitration body (tripartite in character involving employer and union nominees as well as independent persons) to which the Minister could refer a dispute provided that both parties consented to arbitration, and that any arrangements for conciliation or arbitration within the industry had been exhausted.

This body was called the Industrial Court but was retitled the Industrial Arbitration Committee in 1971 and then the **Central Arbitration Committee** (CAC) in 1975. CAC arbitration panels, comprising an independent chairman and two 'side' members drawn from employer and trade union panels, normally sit in public and receive both written and oral evidence from the parties concerned. The CAC inherited a unilateral arbitration function under the Fair Wages Resolution of the House of Commons (this required organisations in receipt of government contracts to provide terms and conditions of employment comparable to those usually applied within the industry). Its unilateral arbitration role was expanded to cover pay structures or collective agreements which were discriminatory (Equal Pay Act (1970)) and union recognition claims, disclosure of information to trade unions and Schedule 11 claims that an employer was not observing recognised or general terms and conditions of employment (Employment Protection Act (1975)). However, the Employment Act (1980) repealed the statutory union recognition procedure and Schedule 11 and, in 1983, the Conservative Government abolished the Fair Wages Resolution. Consequently, the CAC's role is now confined to voluntary arbitration and unilateral arbitration in respect of equal pay claims and disclosure of information claims.

The 1919 Act also gave the minister power to set up *ad hoc* **Courts of Inquiry**. These have been used on a limited number of occasions when a particular dispute has involved matters of major importance affecting the public interest. Their function is to investigate a dispute and then report and make recommendations to the minister who, in turn, is required to present the report to Parliament. A Court of Inquiry, Sharp argued, differs from the operation of the CAC in that its objective is 'not so much to settle the case by direct contact with the parties as to elucidate the facts for the benefit of the parties and public' [52] and 'serves a need where an airing of issues in the glare of deep publicity is a useful safety valve in an intractible dispute of general importance' [53]. In so doing, of course, its report has often provided the basis for a resolution of the dispute.

During the period of operation of this legislation the responsibility for conciliation and arbitration rested with the government. Nevertheless, the conciliation service of the Department of Employment achieved a high degree of respect and acceptance from both management and unions. However, by the early 1970s the independence of the service was under great pressure from two directions. First, many people began to perceive, within a government administered conciliation and arbitration service, a conflict between its role in resolving disputes and the maintenance of the government's incomes policy. Secondly, with the advent of the Industrial Relations Act (1971) the industrial relations system became subject to greater legislative regulation involving new bodies such as the National Industrial Relations Court and the Commission on Industrial Relations (CIR) and new roles for the conciliation and arbitration service. Consequently, as Farnham and Pimlott note, in the early 1970s 'the long-established voluntary system of state conciliation and arbitration almost ceased to exist' and 'a body of opinion emerged . . . which called for the establishment of a conciliation and arbitration service independent of government control and civil service influence' [54]. This led, in 1974, to the establishment of the Advisory, Conciliation and Arbitration Service (ACAS).

Advisory, Conciliation and Arbitration Service

The establishment of ACAS brought together, in one organisation, a range of industrial relations services which had previously been the responsibility of the Department of Employment and the CIR. Its **organisation** comprises a Council, headquarters staff and eight regional offices employing, in 1990, 574 staff (including the CAC and Certification Office). The **Council** consists of a full-time chairman and nine part-time members – three nominated by the CBI, three by the TUC and three 'independents'. Although all the Council members are appointed by the Secretary of State, ACAS's **independence** derives from it not being 'subject to directions of any kind from any Minister . . . as to the manner in which it is to exercise any of its functions' (Para 11(1), Schedule 1, Employment Protection Act (1975)). Certainly it has been government policy not to seek to interfere in its activities or decisions [55]. Jim Mortimer, former Chairman of ACAS, notes that under the Labour Government ACAS 'decided that [it] should not act as the interpreter, monitor and, least of all, as enforcement agent for the incomes policy' and under the Conservative Government it 'decided not to be involved in drawing up the codes of practice on picketing and the closed shop' [56] because in both situations it could be seen as instrumental in carrying out government policy. Whilst the Council, as a whole, is responsible for determining general policy and any important point of principle arising from its work, the individual Council members also play an active part in the day-to-day work of ACAS – for example, conciliating in major disputes or leading major inquiries. However, it is through the **regional offices**, which handle most of the conciliation and advisory work, that ACAS is 'readily accessible to all parts of the country and arrangements can be made to handle cases wherever they arise' [57].

The work of ACAS may be divided into five main areas of activity.

Collective conciliation
ACAS is available to provide collective conciliation at the request of either or both parties involved in a dispute or may offer to conciliate on its own initiative. It maintains the tradition of not seeking to conciliate where existing organisational or industry procedures have not been exhausted or where one party is opposed to the intervention of conciliation. It is important to note that the number of requests for collective conciliation has

not only risen substantially since the creation of ACAS but has remained, since 1975, consistently above the number of stoppages in Britain.

Throughout most of the 1980s the number of collective conciliation and arbitration cases declined in line with the decline in the number of stoppages, but since 1988 there appears to have been a slight increase in their use whilst the number of stoppages continued to decline (see Figure 14.4). ACAS believes that this confirms their acceptability as a conciliator and their ability to help secure a settlement before industrial action takes place; indeed, in over 80 per cent of collective conciliation cases there is no industrial action.

An analysis of the issues and sources of requests for collective conciliation (see Table 14.1) shows that pay and conditions of employment have been the most frequent issue (50–60 per cent), whilst trade union recognition, the second largest group, has declined from 21 per cent in 1975 to 14 per cent in 1990. This latter decline is probably attributable to a general decline in new instances of trade union recognition since the peak in the early 1970s and the demise of the statutory recognition procedure and its eventual removal by the Employment Act, 1980. Significantly, the proportion of cases relating to Dismissal and Discipline or Redundancy has increased from 15 per cent in 1975 to 23 per cent in 1990. It is also important to note that the proportion of requests for collective conciliation coming solely from the trade union side has declined from 56 per cent in 1975 to 32

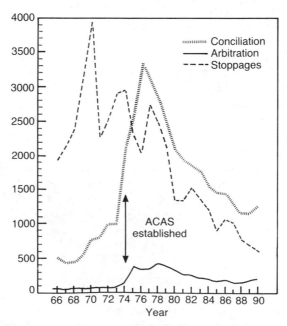

Figure 14.4 *Stoppages of work, collective conciliation and arbitration, 1966–90*
Sources: ACAS, *Annual Report 1982*, pp. 20, 30 (for period 1966–82); ACAS, *Annual Reports 1984–90*

Table 14.1 *Analysis of issues and sources of requests for collective conciliation*

| | Source of request | | | | | | | | | | | | | | | | | | | |
| | Union | | | | Employer | | | | Joint | | | | ACAS | | | | Total | | | |
Issues	1975	1978	1984	1990	1975	1978	1984	1990	1975	1978	1984	1990	1975	1978	1984	1990	1975	1978	1984	1990
1. Pay and conditions of employment	574	835	230	111	197	348	100	49	339	389	483	383	38	80	41	27	1,148 57%	1,652 61%	854 59%	570 50%
2. Trade union recognition	334	363	179	133	43	43	22	9	37	45	16	15	2	–	4	2	416 21%	451 17%	221 15%	159 14%
3. Demarcation/change in work practices	6	7	2	10	13	11	2	10	3	8	4	44	2	–	–	3	24 1%	26 1%	8 1%	67 6%
4. Other trade union matters	20	77	19	20	15	18	3	5	12	31	19	20	2	4	–	5	49 2%	130 5%	41 3%	50 4%
5. Redundancy	56	56	28	42	22	14	11	9	21	20	26	48	3	1	6	10	102 5%	91 3%	71 5%	109 10%
6. Dismissal and discipline	109	98	44	39	38	47	28	18	51	71	108	87	10	2	3	3	208 10%	218 8%	183 13%	147 13%
7. Others	30	71	28	8	14	23	3	4	23	43	35	23	3	1	4	3	70 3%	138 5%	70 5%	38 3%
Total (%)	1,129 56%	1,507 56%	530 37%	363 32%	342 17%	504 19%	170 12%	104 9%	486 24%	607 22%	691 48%	620 54%	60 3%	88 5%	58 4%	53 5%	2,017	2,706	1,448	1,140

Source: ACAS, *Annual Reports*.

per cent in 1990 whilst joint requests increased not only in proportional terms from 22 per cent in 1978 to 54 per cent in 1990 but also in absolute terms at a time when the total number of requests for collective conciliation more than halved. This probably reflects the increasing introduction of conciliation as a stage in jointly agreed disputes procedures. ACAS-initiated conciliation, on the other hand, has remained a constant but very small proportion of the total. However, this does not include those situations where ACAS conciliators have 'run alongside' a dispute by maintaining informal contact with the parties concerned – this occurred in 260 cases during 1990. Finally, the vast majority of collective conciliation is conducted at the regional office level and only some 103 disputes, generally of an industry wide nature, were dealt with at the headquarters level during 1990.

Arbitration

ACAS officials do not, themselves, arbitrate. To do so would be detrimental to the confidentiality and impartiality of their conciliation role. It would seriously affect the relationship between the conciliator and the two parties in dispute if they felt that the same people or organisation might be called upon to decide the issue by arbitration. However, ACAS does make provision, if both parties wish, for the appointment of a single arbitrator or board of arbitration or the referral of the dispute to the CAC. ACAS also has responsibility for maintaining the CAC and certain industry arrangements for arbitration in the public sector – for example, the Post Office, Police and Railway Tribunals. In addition, ACAS can, as an alternative to formal arbitration, set up a committee of inquiry to investigate the facts and underlying causes of a dispute. However, this is infrequently used – for example, in 1982 one such committee was set up to look into a dispute between ASLEF and British Rail.

It is important to note that, like collective conciliation, the number of requests for arbitration rose quite steeply after the creation of ACAS although since 1978 the number steadily declined in line with the decline in the number of stoppages and requests for collective conciliation. The decline is not the result of dissatisfaction with arbitration but rather, as with the other two indices, a reflection of the worsening economic situation and the associated increase in management power in collective bargaining. Of the 196 arbitration cases handled in 1990, 171 (86 per cent) were dealt with by a single arbitrator, 8 by a board of arbitration, 10 by a single mediator, only 1 by a committee of inquiry and 6 by the Police and Railway Tribunals; none were referred to the CAC [58]. The number of arbitrations relating to pay and conditions of employment certainly declined significantly between the 1970s and 1980s in absolute terms (see Table 14.2). However, 'grading' (disputes about job evaluation, grading, etc.) which accounted for 77 arbitrations (39 per cent) in 1990 was only introduced as a distinct category in 1989 and, in earlier years, these disputes would have been included in the more general 'pay and conditions' category; when the two groups are added

Table 14.2 *Analysis of issues for collective arbitration and mediation*

Issues	1975	1978	1984	1990
1. Pay and conditions of employment	242	360	134	53
	79%	86%	66%	27%
2. Grading	n/a	n/a	n/a	77
				39%
3. Dismissal and discipline	46	39	63	52
	15%	9%	31%	27%
4. Trade union recognition	3	–	–	n/a[*]
5. Demarcation	4	9	–	n/a[*]
6. Other trade union matters	4	4	–	n/a[*]
7. Redundancy	1	1	–	n/a[*]
8. Others	6	8	5	14
Total	306	421	202	196

Note: [*]n/a indicates issue no longer designated as a distinct category.
Source: ACAS, *Annual Reports*.

together for 1990 they still account for 68 per cent of all arbitrations. Nevertheless, ACAS attributed the increase in arbitration cases in 1990 (from a 1989 figure of 169) primarily to a growth in 'grading' cases and they certainly far exceed the 10 per cent of arbitrations which relate to 'annual pay' issues [59]. The number of arbitrations relating to 'dismissal and discipline' has remained fairly constant in absolute terms but risen to around 30 per cent of the total. Perhaps the most significant feature is not just the fact that issues such as 'trade union recognition', 'demarcation', 'other trade union matters' and 'redundancy' provided so few arbitration cases in the past (this perhaps confirms the inappropriateness of arbitration as a means of resolving many disputes or a preference for the use of conciliation), but rather that they are no longer designated as specific categories in the ACAS statistics (perhaps reflecting the change in industrial relations climate and perceived diminuation in the role of unions in the 1980s).

Individual conciliation

ACAS has an important role to perform in relation to legislation on individual rights. Under this legislation ACAS has a duty, after the individual has made a complaint to an Industrial Tribunal, to seek a conciliated settlement if either party requests it or if ACAS considers there is a reasonable prospect of success; to this end ACAS receives copies of all originating applicants (IT1) and respondent replies received by the Industrial Tribunals. In addition, the individual can take a claim to ACAS that action has been taken in respect of which a complaint *could* be made to a Tribunal. These are generally referred to as 'non-IT1 cases' and in 1990 13,672 (25 per cent) of the cases received by ACAS came into this category – in 1984 the number was only 6,693 (16 per cent) but had risen to a high of 17,724 (36 per cent) in 1989. In reviewing this situation ACAS noted that 'almost all of these cases were in the unfair dismissal jurisdiction and virtually all were brought to the Service's attention by employers rather than employees' [60]. The review confirmed a problem which ACAS had identified in 1984 when they criticised some managements for seeking, through ACAS conciliation, 'our assistance in "rubber stamping" agreements already made to "ease out" employees specifically in order to prevent any subsequent claim being determined by a tribunal' [61] by virtue of S. 140(2), Employment Protection (Consolidation) Act (1978) – an agreement reached during ACAS conciliation debars an employee from making a claim to the Industrial Tribunal. The principal role of the conciliation officer is to offer assistance to the parties involved to help them establish the facts and clarify their views and to seek, where possible, a conciliated settlement – in ACAS's view this should not 'in any way affect or limit the rights of individuals to pursue complaints to industrial tribunals' [62] nor 'seek to persuade complainants to withdraw' [63].

In 1990 ACAS received a total of 52,000 individual conciliation cases (see Table 14.3). The increase of just under 10,000 since 1984 is largely accounted for by the advent of cases under the Wages Act, 1986 relating to non-payment of wages due, wages in lieu of notice, etc. By far the largest area of individual conciliation remains Unfair Dismissal; although this area has declined as a proportion of the total from 88 per cent to 75 per cent, because of the increased total number of cases resulting from the Wages Act, it still accounts for some 35,000 cases each year. The apparent improvement in the 'settlement' rate for Unfair Dismissal cases should, however, be qualified by reference to the IT1/non-IT1 division between cases: of the 22,500 cases 'settled' in 1990 some 13,500 were non-IT1 cases and, therefore,

Table 14.3 *Individual conciliation cases, 1984 and 1990*

	Unfair Dismissal		All Discrimination		Wages Act		Other		Total	
	1984	1990	1984	1990	1984	1990	1984	1990	1984	1990
Received	37,006	37,568	1,410	3,516	n/a	8,114	4,307	2,877	42,723	52,071
Settled	17,238	22,516	249	791	n/a	2,261	1,252	873	18,739 45%	26,441 56%
Withdrawn	7,909	6,333	382	1,115	n/a	2,445	1,756	856	10,047 24%	10,749 23%
To tribunal	11,039	6,376	453	845	n/a	2,013	962	796	12,454 30%	10,030 21%
Completed (% of total)	36,186 88%	35,225 75%	1,084 3%	2,751 6%	n/a	6,719 14%	3,970	2,525 10%	41,240 5%	47,220

Source: ACAS, *Annual Reports.*

only some 8,000 Tribunal claims were successfully conciliated by ACAS; whereas in 1984 out of 17,000 'settled' cases only 6,500 were non-IT1 cases and, therefore, 10,500 Tribunal claims were settled by conciliation via ACAS. However, there is little doubt that the number of cases going to the Tribunal has significantly decreased; this is perhaps to be expected now that the basic legislation is nearly twenty years old and its provisions should be known by most management (although, it would appear, not so much amongst the managers of small firms!). It is significant that claims in respect of 'discrimination' have almost trebled between 1984–90 although a third of such claims were withdrawn in 1990. Overall, ACAS appears to have a large measure of success in its individual conciliation role with approximately 50 per cent of cases being settled without recourse to an Industrial Tribunal.

Advisory

ACAS is committed 'to help management and unions to create constructive relationships in which change can take place smoothly and differences be resolved before they become disputes' [64]. In this respect its role as an advice centre is of crucial importance and is available to any individual or organisation on any aspect of industrial relations or personnel management. Its work in this area ranges from a simple telephone enquiry, through a visit to the individual or organisation, to more protracted projects, surveys or training within organisations. During 1990 ACAS officers dealt with over 400,000 enquiries and were involved in nearly 7,000 advisory meetings and 964 surveys, projects, training or other in-depth assistance. Approximately 45 per cent of this advisory work was concerned with individual employment rights and 20 per cent was concerned with pay and reward systems. The remaining 35 per cent was spread between handling change and the effective use of people; communication, consultation and involvement; and collective bargaining arrangements. Just over 50 per cent of this work was done in organisations employing less than 200 employees. In addition ACAS has produced three Codes of Practice on Discipline, Disclosure of Information and Time-off for Trade Union Duties. The recommendations contained in these Codes may be taken into account in hearings before Industrial Tribunals.

Inquiries

This aspect of ACAS's work has been inherited from the CIR and involves conducting longer-term investigations into matters of general concern in industrial relations or the industrial relations of particular organisations or industries. These inquiries may arise from ACAS's involvement in collective conciliation or from an advisory visit or project. In carrying out this work, as in its advisory and collective conciliation work, ACAS has been anxious to encourage and support the use of joint working parties of management and unions as a means of securing an improvement in industrial relations [65].

Voluntary conciliation/arbitration procedures

Perhaps the most common form of third-party conciliation or arbitration is that contained within the disputes procedures negotiated between employers and trade unions. In 1981 Brown [66] found that over half of the establishments surveyed had made use of such an external disputes procedure operated by their Employers' Association during the previous two years. However, 37 per cent of the establishments surveyed had made provision for the involvement of some other third party, such as ACAS, for disputes which arose in connection with pay and conditions of employment. The inclusion of such a provision within a procedure was more likely to occur where trade union density within the organisation was high; was more prevalent amongst foreign-owned companies than British companies; and more common in those organisations which undertook wage bargaining on their own than those which bargained through an Employers' Association. Twenty-seven per cent of the establishments which had procedures for such third-party intervention had made use of it during the previous two years whilst only 4 per cent of establishments which did not have such a provision had resorted to conciliation or arbitration.

Millward and Stevens' 1984 survey found that whereas 79 per cent of establishments had provision for third-party intervention within pay procedures only 17 per cent had used it in the previous year [67]. Perhaps most interestingly they found that the proportion of establishments specifying ACAS as the 'person or organisation' for such third-party intervention decreased from 35 per cent in 1980 and 27 per cent in 1984 and the proportion specifying Employers' Association had decreased from 10 per cent to 8 per cent. However, the proportion of establishments specifying the 'third-party' intervention as 'higher-level management' had almost doubled from 27 per cent to 51 per cent and the proportion specifying 'union official' had increased from 7 per cent to 24 per cent. This perhaps reflects the decentralisation of responsibility for collective bargaining to the establishment level in many organisations and apparently therefore the corporate level management and national level union officials being the 'third-party' intervention.

In drawing up a clause or agreement on arbitration it is important that the parties should give consideration to the following issues:

1. **Scope of arbitration**. It is often argued, and indeed is the practice in the USA, that disputes of right (i.e. the interpretation and application of an existing agreement) are more suited to arbitration than disputes of interest (i.e. the determination of new terms and conditions of employment). However, the majority of agreements in Britain do not specifically exclude disputes of interest from the possibility of arbitration. At the organisational level it may be appropriate to specifically exclude from arbitration any issue which is determined by national agreements.

2. **Method of referral**. There are three methods of referral:
   (a) unilateral, where either party has the right to invoke arbitration without the consent of the other party;
   (b) joint, where both parties have to agree to refer the matter to arbitration;
   (c) automatic, where the issue goes to arbitration if it remains unresolved after a certain stage in the negotiating or disputes procedure. This latter method is, in effect, a joint referral because it involves a prior joint acceptance of the use of arbitration for unresolved differences. The majority of agreements in Britain provide for a joint or automatic method of referral. However, it is important to ensure that any referral is preceded by conciliation.

3. **Arbitration body**. The agreement should specify how the arbitration is to be conducted – by a single arbitrator or a board of arbitration; on a permanent or *ad hoc* basis. The majority of arbitration in Britain is conducted by a single arbitrator who must, of course, be acceptable to both parties. Where a board of arbitration is used it is quite common for the employer and trade union to select one member each and either jointly, or through ACAS, agree on an independent chairman. Clearly, whether or not the arbitrator is to be permanent will depend largely on the extent to which the parties believe that such services will be needed.

4. **Standing of the arbitration award**. The parties must agree, either when drawing up the procedure or prior to each arbitration, whether the arbitration award is to be binding on them. The alternative is to accept that the award will be used only as a basis for further negotiation between the parties. Normally, arbitrators do not give, and are not asked to give, the reasons for their decision because this is more likely to provoke further argument and disagreement between the parties.

14.4 Summary propositions

- Conciliation and arbitration provide channels through which management and unions may, if they wish, seek to resolve their differences by introducing a third party; the availability or use of such processes does not automatically mean an avoidance or reduction in the use of industrial action.
- Conciliation is supportive of the joint regulatory collective bargaining process, whilst arbitration, on any extensive scale, undermines that process.
- The 'winner take all' concept underlying pendulum arbitration is incompatible with the principles of compromise and flexibility underlying the negotiation process and organisational experience in the

UK suggests that it requires modification to bring it closer to conventional 'open' arbitration.

Further reading

- ILO, *Conciliation and Arbitration Procedures in Labour Disputes*, 1980. This provides an extensive comparative study of both conciliation and arbitration, in particular, the government's role.
- J. J. Loewenberg, W. J. Gershenfeld, H. J. Glassbeek, B. A. Hepple and K. F. Walker, *Compulsory Arbitration*, Lexington Books, 1976. Examines the experience of compulsory arbitration in five countries (including Britain, Australia and the USA). Chapters 6 and 7 provide a very useful comparison and analysis.
- ACAS, *Annual Reports*. Particularly useful are 1975 (detailing the establishment of ACAS), 1978 (Chapter 10 – Approach to Individual Conciliation), 1981 (Chapter 6 – Joint Working Parties), 1990 (up-to-date detailing of variety of ACAS work).

References

1. ILO, *Conciliation and Arbitration Procedures in Labour Disputes*, 1980, p.v.
2. Professor Sir J. Wood, 'The case for arbitration', *Personnel Managment*, October 1980, p. 52.
3. J. F. B. Goodman and J. Krislov, 'Conciliation in industrial disputes in Great Britain: a survey of the attitudes of the parties', *British Journal of Industrial Relations*, November 1974, p. 327.
4. ILO, *op. cit.*, p. 15.
5. Professor Sir J. Wood, *op. cit.*
6. C. Margerison and M. Leary, *Managing Industrial Conflict: The Mediator's Role*, MCB Books, 1975, p. 3.
7. ILO, *op. cit.*, p. 15.
8. C. Margerison and M. Leary, *op. cit.*, p. 3.
9. J. F. B. Goodman and J. Krislov, *op. cit.*, p. 336.
10. S. Kessler, 'The prevention and settlement of collective labour disputes in the UK', *Industrial Relations Journal*, vol. 11, no. 1, 1980, p. 17.
11. J. F. B. Goodman and J. Krislov, *op. cit.*, pp. 341–8.
12. *ibid.*, p. 340.
13. ILO, *op. cit.*, p. 31.
14. J. J. Loewenberg, W. J. Gershenfeld, H. J. Glasbeek, B. A. Hepple and K. F. Walker, *Compulsory Arbitration*, Lexington Books, 1976, p. 210.
15. R. Hyman, *Strikes* (3rd edn), Fontana, 1984, p. 114.
16. J. F. B. Goodman and J. Krislov, *op. cit.*, p. 347.
17. W. E. J. McCarthy and N. D. Ellis, *Management by Agreement*, Hutchinson, 1973, p. 125.

18. J. F. B. Goodman and J. Krislov, *op. cit.*, p. 349.
19. W. E. J. McCarthy and N. D. Ellis, *op. cit.*, p. 124.
20. B. Hepple, 'Compulsory arbitration in Britain' in J. J. Loewenberg *et al.*, *op. cit.*, p. 88.
21. K. F. Walker, 'Compulsory arbitration in Australia' in J. J. Loewenberg *et al.*, *op. cit.*, pp. 2–3.
22. *ibid.*
23. *ibid.*, p. 23.
24. *ibid.*, p. 25.
25. J. J. Loewenberg, 'Compulsory Arbitration in the United States' in J. J. Loewenberg *et al.*, *op. cit.*
26. *ibid.*, p. 148.
27. B. A. Hepple, *op. cit.*
28. *ibid.*, p. 86.
29. K. F. Walker, *Industrial Relations in Australia*, Harvard University Press, 1956, p. 365.
30. J. J. Loewenberg *et al.*, *op. cit.*, p. 185.
31. *ibid.*, p. 198.
32. W. E. J. McCarthy, 'Three Studies in Collective Bargaining', *Research Paper No. 8, Royal Commission on Trade Unions and Employers' Association*, HMSO, 1968, p. 42.
33. 'Single union deals', *IRS Employment Trends*, no. 442, June 1989.
34. Sir J. Wood, 'Last offer arbitration', *British Journal of Industrial Relations*, vol. XX, no. 3, 1985, pp. 414–24; J. G. Treble, 'How new is final offer arbitration?', *Industrial Relations*, vol. 25, no. 1, 1986; A. Brown, 'Research findings show that criticisms of the arbitration process are mostly without foundation', *Personnel Management*, May 1990, p. 2.
35. ACAS, *Annual Report 1984*, p. 39.
36. A. Brown, *op. cit.*
37. C. Stevens, 'Is compulsory arbitration compatible with bargaining?', *Industrial Relations*, vol. 5, no. 2, 1966.
38. S. Kessler, 'The swings and roundabouts of pendulum arbitration', *Personnel Management*, December 1987, pp. 40, 42.
39. D. Yeandle and J. Clark, 'Growing a compatible IR setup', *Personnel Management*, July 1989.
40. R. Singh, 'Final offer arbitration in theory and practice', *Industrial Relations Journal*, winter 1986, pp. 329–30.
41. Institute of Directors, *Settling Disputes Peacefully*, 1984.
42. P. Bassett, *Strike Free: New industrial relations in Britain*, Macmillan, 1987, p. 116.
43. S. Kessler, *op. cit.*, p. 40.
44. R. Lewis, 'Strike-free deals and pendulum arbitration', *British Journal of Industrial Relations*, vol. 28, no. 1, 1990, p. 49.
45. R. Singh, *op. cit.*, p. 334.
46. Sanyo management quoted in S. Kessler, *op. cit.*, p. 41.
47. *ibid.*
48. ACAS, *Annual Report 1987*, p. 22.
49. S. Kessler, *op. cit.*, p. 40.
50. D. G. Gallaher and M. D. Chaubey, 'Impasse behaviour and tri-offer arbitration in Iowa', *Industrial Relations*, vol. 21, no. 2, 1982, pp. 129–47; R. Hoh, 'The effectiveness of mediation in public sector mediation systems: the Iowa experience', *The Arbitrator's Journal*, vol. 39, no. 2, 1984, pp. 20–40.

51. See I. G. Sharp, *Industrial Conciliation and Arbitration in Great Britain*, Allen & Unwin, 1950 for discussion of voluntary and statutory arbitration in nineteenth and early twentieth centuries.
52. *ibid.*, p. 362.
53. Professor Sir J. Wood, *op. cit.*, pp. 52–3.
54. D. Farnham and J. Pimlott, *Understanding Industrial Relations* (2nd edn), Cassell, 1983, p. 196.
55. ACAS, *Annual Report 1975*, Appendix B, p. 42.
56. J. Mortimer, 'ACAS in a changing climate: a force for good I R?', *Personnel Management*, February 1981, p. 24.
57. ACAS, *Annual Report 1975*, p. 6.
58. ACAS, *Annual Report 1990*, Table 6, p. 54.
59. *ibid.*, Figure 3.1, p. 22.
60. *ibid.*, p. 26.
61. ACAS, *Annual Report 1984*, p. 63.
62. ACAS, *Annual Report 1990*, p. 28.
63. ACAS, *Annual Report 1978*, p. 79.
64. ACAS, *Annual Report 1975*, p. 18.
65. ACAS, *Annual Report 1981*, Chapter 6.
66. W. Brown, *The Changing Contours of British Industrial Relations*, Blackwell, 1981, pp. 47–50.
67. N. Millward and M. Stevens, *British Workplace Industrial Relations 1980–84*, Gower, 1986, Table 7.6, p. 181.

PART D

Practices

Chapter 15

Policies, procedures and practices

15.1 Definition

A **policy** may be defined as **a statement of objectives and the strategy for their achievement.** It is useful to distinguish between a **company industrial relations policy**, which expresses the organisation's overall philosophy or style towards its employees and its conduct of industrial relations affairs, and **specific policies** (such as one dealing with sickness and absence) which set out the objectives and approach to be adopted by management when confronted with the specified issue. Whilst any policy may, and it can be argued should, be expressed through the medium of a formal written document, it is important to remember that the absence of such a document does not necessarily imply the absence of a policy but only that its content has to be deduced solely from the actions and practices of management. Indeed, Gill and Concannon suggest that many managers 'interpreted "managerial industrial relations policy" as simply the way in which they handled their industrial relations problems' [1] and Hawkins argues that 'in reality a formal policy statement will often seek to articulate and justify well-established attitudes and operating methods' [2].

A **procedure** may be defined as **an operational mechanism which details and regulates the manner in which a specified issue is to be handled.** It provides the means for the implementation of a policy and the achievement of the objectives contained within it. Where such procedures are determined by negotiation between management and unions and involve employee or union representatives in their operation, they also represent an important part of the system of joint regulation by providing a body of rules which defines the extent and manner in which both management and trade union power is to be exercised within the organisation.

Where a trade union is recognised procedures generally are the subject matter for joint agreement; however, even in situations of strong unionisation, the extent of jointly agreed industrial relations policies is significantly more restricted. Each side retains its right to determine, and then to seek to

453

implement, its own policies and approaches on many industrial relations issues. This reflects the relative ease with which management and unions are able to reconcile their differences in respect of operational details of a procedure, whilst an agreement on the content and approach of a policy, particularly the company industrial relations policy, requires a more fundamental reconciliation of differing attitudes, beliefs and philosophies. Nevertheless, the two aspects are interrelated in that the procedures to be adopted in handling industrial relations situations are themselves an expression of an underlying philosophy regarding the nature of the relationship between management, employees and union.

A **practice** may be defined as **a set of decisions or actions which are made in response to a given problem or situation.** Where such decisions or actions are made within the framework of an existing formal policy they may be regarded as a process of policy interpretation and application. Certainly, it should always be remembered that, by itself, a policy is of little value. It is the application of the policy through the practices of management which provides positive evidence of not only the precise meaning and effect of the policy but also, and more importantly, management's intention both to implement and be constrained by that policy. However, it is this process of policy interpretation and application which is, at the same time, a significant part of the 'custom and practice' within the organisation. It places constraints on the range of options available in future decision making by creating an expectation that the same response will apply to similar situations in the future. Indeed, in the absence of any formally expressed policy such decisions and actions assume increased importance not only by providing the sole evidence of a policy but also by easily becoming regarded as the policy itself – a policy of simply implementing 'custom and practice'.

15.2 Development of policies, procedures and practices

It was not until the late 1960s that concern for the development of formal industrial relations policies and procedures at the organisational level achieved prominence. The CIR pointed out that for many organisations 'the main industrial relations policy decision had been to join their employers' association and observe the agreements on basic terms and conditions which it negotiates with relevant trade unions' [3] thus causing, in the opinion of Cuthbert, 'many companies to neglect to put their own systems in order and to neglect development of a Company Industrial Relations Policy, and, within this framework, comprehensive company bargaining arrangements' [4]. Certainly, the growth of informal, and often fragmented, bargaining at the organisational level led the Donovan Commission to observe that 'at present boards can leave industry-wide agreements to their employers' association, and the task of dealing with workers within those agreements to their subordinate managers' [5]. In their view this did not provide a sound basis for the development of effective industrial relations. They recommended that management, particularly boards of directors, should review industrial relations with the objective of developing formal substantive and procedural agreements of factory and company levels. They sought to encourage management to accept greater responsibility for a 'positive' response to their internal industrial relations problems rather than their more traditional response of joining an employers' association and relying on 'external' industry agreements and decisions to regulate their industrial relations.

It is a significant measure of the changes which have taken place in British industrial relations since the 1960s that in 1980 Marsh found that a substantial proportion of establishments had 'become more formal, either institutionally, procedurally or in relation to the setting down of rules' [6]. Since the early 1980s, however, management policy has shifted towards less formality and collectivism and greater organisational flexibility and individualism. This shift in management style and policy has been the product of a strategic review by management of its industrial relations style, objectives and the effectiveness of the industrial relations system to meet external pressures and constraints (in particular its economic environment) and, not least, to support and integrate more closely with its business objectives.

It is within the framework of seeking to create and maintain a positive and integrated managerial response to industrial relations at the organisational level that the process of developing policies and procedures has to be considered (see Figure 15.1). The process may involve a major **comprehensive** review across the entire spectrum of employee relations matters or be **confined** to a single specific aspect. However, regardless of the extent, the impetus to develop new policies and procedures, or redefine existing ones, is generated by some **pressure for change** being exerted on the organisation's industrial relations system:

1. Pressure may come from within the organisation's industrial relations system itself; for example: the advent, growth, decline or change in the pattern of trade unionism; a belief amongst the management that all or some of the existing policies and procedures are inadequate to cope with current or future industrial relations problems; or simply a change in the managerial 'style' of the organisation.
2. Pressure may be external to the organisation's industrial relations system but still generated from within the organisation itself; for example a change in the organisation's economic, technological or operational needs.
3. Pressure for change may come from outside the organisation; for example, the advent of new employment legislation or fresh

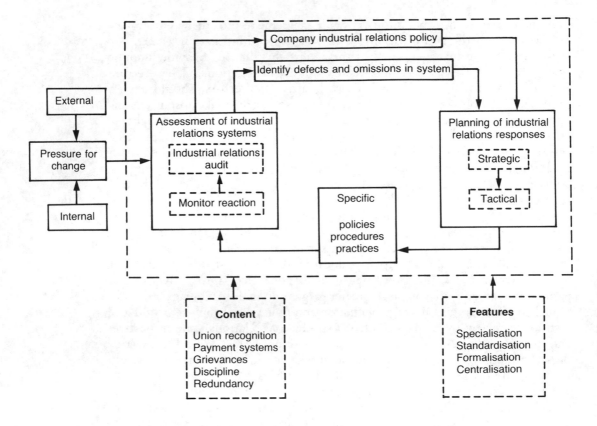

Figure 15.1   *Process for developing policies, procedures and practices*

interpretations of existing legislation, changes in government policies or general developments in the field of industrial relations.

Industrial relations audit

An industrial relations audit is simply **a systematic examination and evaluation of part or all of the organisation's industrial relations system** with the objective of assessing its effectiveness both in resolving industrial relations problems and in aiding management in the achievement of its objectives. Certainly, Jennings *et al.* [7] believe that an industrial relations audit or analysis, including an assessment of the effectiveness of current policies, procedures and institutions, is an essential element in the satisfactory identification of management's industrial relations training needs.

An audit, therefore, should not be regarded solely as a special occurrence undertaken periodically but also as part of management's continual monitoring of the operation of the organisation's industrial relations system. In this latter form, the audit is clearly a matter for the management of the organisation; particularly the industrial relations specialist in those organisations which have such a role. However, if the audit is to be carried out as a major exercise encompassing a review of the whole industrial relations system then consideration has to be given to whether it is preferable to use an 'outsider' (e.g. a management consultant). The use of an outsider does not, in any way, imply an abrogation of responsibility by management but may be preferred either because the organisation's management have neither the time nor expertise to devote to such an exercise or because the outsider is, by being independent of management, in a better position to make an objective assessment of the system. In this situation it is important to ensure that the management works closely with the outsider because not only must their needs be identified but they must also, ultimately, take responsibility for any decisions which may follow from the audit.

The extent to which **trade unions and their representatives** should be involved in this audit phase, whether it is carried out by management or an outsider, will depend largely on whether management wishes to encourage the development of joint regulation of the industrial relations system beyond the operational level of procedures and practices and into the policy determination level.

The precise **content** of an industrial relations audit will, of course, vary according to which aspects of the industrial relations system are to be examined. Nevertheless, the information sought within any audit may be conveniently classified under three headings.

- *Quantifiable information.* For example, the number and extent of disputes or strikes (expression of overt and organised conflict) or the level of absenteeism and turnover (indication of the degree of hidden, individual conflict). However, the audit is concerned not only with the simple numerical quantity of these items, expressed in terms of the working days lost, lost production or the cost of recruitment, but also with some qualitative assessment of the manner in which these issues have been handled. The existence of disputes, occasional strikes or absenteeism within an organisation does not, by itself, establish that the industrial relations system is deficient. Such a judgement may only be made after an assessment of the causes and, perhaps most importantly, whether or not they could have been avoided or better handled. In addition, information may be gathered relating to the use made of procedures, particularly the grievance and disciplinary procedures (how often they are used, what issues are raised, at what level in the procedure are problems resolved and is it the 'correct' level).

- *Assessment of the appropriateness of the processes and institutions.* This will involve considering not only the formal arrangements of procedures, communications, negotiating and consultative institutions but also the way in which they operate: the range of topics covered, how the processes are differentiated, and the way in which the arrangements at the various levels of the organisation are integrated. Also, the audit should examine **managerial responsibilities** for the handling of industrial relations; whether the role of the management representatives in these procedures and institutions is adequately defined and whether the various levels of management are aware of, and trained for, their responsibilities.

● *Ascertain the attitudes of the participants* – towards both the general state of industrial relations within the organisation and any specific problem areas. Such information may be obtained by the use of a formal attitude survey (possibly carried out by an outsider), or through the normal processes of management communication/consultation. Information gathered during this part of an audit may also provide useful information relating to the effectiveness of the organisation's formal and informal communications network.

Two points must be borne in mind:

1. Information must be gathered in respect of not only the formal expressions of how the system or its parts should operate but also how it operates in practice.
2. The information obtained during the audit is only the prelude to an **evaluation** of the effectiveness of the system.

Therefore, it is important that management should establish clear criteria by which to judge whether the policies, procedures, institutions and practices are 'bad', 'satisfactory' or 'good'. They may be judged against external criteria such as legislative provisions or Codes of Practice and comparisons may be made with other similar organisations in respect of the wording and operation of policies and procedures, wage and earnings levels, strikes, absenteeism, etc. Perhaps most importantly they must be evaluated in terms of supporting the achievement of business objectives.

Company industrial relations policy

Marsh suggests that 'the style in which a company approaches its employee relations activities is related to policy and to its philosophy of management' [8]. A clearly defined Company Policy is fundamental to the development and maintenance of an orderly approach to industrial relations within the organisation. Its primary **purpose** is to provide a clear statement of the organisation's employee relations objectives. This, the CIR argued, 'promotes consistency in management and enables all employees and their representatives to know where they stand in relation to the company's intentions and objectives' and 'encourages the orderly and equitable conduct of industrial relations by enabling management to plan ahead, to anticipate events, and to secure and retain an initiative in changing situations' [9].

In the first instance, the policy should be regarded as a **management statement for the guidance of managers.** In all organisations the individual manager's responsibility for handling industrial relations and resolving employee problems has to be balanced against the organisation's requirement for a measure of corporate consistency in its treatment of all its employees. Without a statement of corporate intent and objectives individual managers have no common point of reference as to the expectations placed on their role in handling industrial relations. Furthermore, there is often more than one solution to an industrial relations problem that will, in the short term, satisfy the needs of management, but only one which will *best* meet the long-term strategy. The Company Policy provides the framework within which individual managers may make decisions not on an expediency basis in isolation from other decisions but as an integral part of a more consistent and positive organisational approach. Hawkins argues that an **effective** Company Policy is one which 'provides managers who are responsible for the conduct of industrial relations with a framework of general principles which they regard as helpful and within which they are able to act decisively on day-to-day problems' [10]. In the absence of such a policy framework, consistent decision making may perhaps be achieved only by centralised decision making.

It is also important, as Neal pointed out, not to lose sight of the fact that 'industrial relations is an integral element in business management, not something set apart' [11]. Certainly, the CIR argued that the Company Industrial Relations Policy should be integrated with, and supportive of, the **organisation's corporate business strategy** and 'reflect the interaction of industrial relations with policies in other areas, such as production, marketing or finance' [12]. The integration of this policy with those in other functional areas may only be achieved effectively through senior management as a group, preferably at the board level, accepting responsibility for authorising the industrial relations policy and ensuring that it is implemented by all managers. The acceptance of such responsibilities is a demonstration of senior management's commitment to the policy.

However, the policy should be formulated with the **involvement of the line management and supervision** who will be required to interpret and apply it within their day-to-day operational decisions. Certainly, Hawkins believes that the policy requires to be 'based on some kind of interdepartmental consensus if it is to mean anything in practice' [13]. It is an expression of a corporate managerial perception of, at a general level, the nature of the industrial organisation and the role of the industrial relations system within it and, at a more specific level, the extent to which it wishes trade unions, shop stewards and employees, through the process of collective bargaining, consultation and use of procedures, to participate directly or indirectly in the organisation's decision making. The involvement of line management should not be confined simply to ensuring that they understand, implement and communicate the policy after it has been formulated by senior management but should include the opportunity for them to influence the content of the policy. Indeed, such a process of consultation and participation during the formulation stage provides a useful mechanism for creating a better understanding between senior management and lower levels of the management hierarchy, or between line management and industrial relations specialists, and assists in generating a greater commitment to the final policy amongst all levels of management.

The extent to which **employee or union representatives** should be involved in discussions about, or even the determination of the Company Policy is, as with the industrial relations audit, dependent on whether management regards it as solely an expression of management objectives for the guidance of management. Certainly if, in the content of the policy, management expresses a desire to increase employee participation in the organisation's decision making then it would appear that a good point at which to start demonstrating such commitment is in the determination of the content of the industrial relations policy itself. However, it must be recognised that the formulation of an acceptable 'joint' industrial relations policy is a lengthy process requiring the recognition, acceptance and then reconciliation of differing attitudes, beliefs and philosophies. If such differences are either ignored, or simply papered over, the resultant policy statement is likely to be ambiguous and lead to mutual recriminations and claims of breach of faith. Indeed, it may be argued that a jointly agreed industrial relations policy can only evolve over a period of several years and that, initially, it requires management to clarify and develop its own industrial relations policy through an analysis, from its perspective, of the organisation's industrial relations problems and a determination of the objectives it wishes to pursue. However, regardless of whether employee or union representatives are involved in the formulation of the policy, there is a need for the policy to be **communicated to all employees** so that they are aware of, and able to assess, management's intention.

If the Company Policy is to achieve its purpose of expressing management's corporate intentions and promoting orderly, consistent industrial relations within the organisation, it is advantageous that it should be set out in a **formal written document:**

1. The discipline and precision required in producing such a document itself helps management to clarify its thoughts and intentions.
2. A written document ensures that all managers, supervisors, union representatives and employees receive the same information. This allows managers and supervisors to develop consistent industrial relations decisions and, in discussions with union representatives and employees, to identify areas of agreement or difference in their approach.

3. A written policy may be easier to change in the light of changed circumstances than one based solely on less tangible custom and practice.

However, it must be recognised that the industrial relations policy, in seeking to promote greater **consistency** in management decision making may also appear to reduce management's **flexibility** in decision making. The extent to which this is likely to happen depends primarily on the degree of formality and precision of not only the Company Policy but also the other specific policies and procedures utilised by management. Hawkins suggests that many managers would argue that the flexibility which is desirable in industrial relations and which 'allows managements to consider each grievance or claim on its merits . . . also requires informality' [14]. However, a policy is not an instruction manual and cannot, therefore, be so all-embracing that it provides the automatic solution to any situation. It is the very complexity and uniqueness of each industrial relations situation which ensures that even when policies and procedures are well defined there is still a need, in seeking to resolve any particular problem, for individual managerial discretion in the implementation of the policy.

The intention of a written policy is not to describe some idealistic state of Utopia to be realised in the distant future but to specify realistic and achievable objectives which, by influencing the attitudes and behaviour of the participants, may be achieved in the medium term. Hawkins argues that the creation of a policy statement whose content 'may be so bland as to be meaningless' [15] fails to provide either a positive framework for influencing behaviour and decision making or a basis from which to assess the implementation of the policy. Thus, the policy content should be both specific and easily understood.

The precise **content** and wording of a Company Policy will depend on a variety of factors: the technological and economic situation of the organisation; the attitudes, objectives and style which management wishes to pursue within the organisation's industrial relations system, and whether the policy document is perceived as being simply a statement of management's broad approach to industrial relations or as a more detailed exposition of the direction managers should adopt in their industrial relations decision making. In drawing up its policy, management should ensure:

1. that it provides a sound basis for establishing managerial initiative throughout the industrial relations system (it should be a **proactive** rather than reactive document); and
2. that it does not conflict with the law.

The issues which can be considered for inclusion in the policy may be conveniently grouped under five headings:

1. **Managerial principles** relating, for example, to management's right to manage its business and make operational decisions; its intention not to

negotiate under duress or to make concessions without a corresponding gesture from trade unions; and its right to communicate directly with its employees on any matter.

2. **The relationship between management and employees** including the recognition of the value of employees as an asset of the organisation; their right to represent grievances to management and to join trade unions who may act on their behalf; the basis on which trade unions are to be recognised for collective bargaining and representing their members' interests; and management's desire to develop a climate of mutual acceptance, trust and co-operation within the organisation.

3. **The determination of terms and conditions of employment** through, where appropriate, recognised institutions of joint consultation and/or collective bargaining, and the intention to be bound, and to expect employees and trade unions also to be bound, by agreements reached within any recognised collective bargaining machinery; the achievement of stable, or reducing, costs through increased productivity; the maintenance of a fair and equitable payment system which rewards both the value of the job to the organisation and the performance of the individual.

4. **The approach to employment** to be adopted in ensuring that the organisation has an adequate level of trained and experienced workforce for its needs consistent with maintaining security of employment for the individual employees (recruitment, training, motivation, promotion and termination of employees).

5. **The role of procedures** in resolving problems speedily and in a mutually acceptable manner; in contributing to employee participation and joint decision making; and the extent to which third-party processes of conciliation and arbitration may be used.

Marsh found a **variety of policies and philosophies** amongst the organisations he surveyed although few were expressed in written documents. The statements of philosophy included [16]:

1. To maintain good employee and industrial relations through good communications, procedures and agreements with trade unions.

2. To encourage a participative, open environment.

3. Ultimately sound industrial relations depends upon strong and purposeful line management working within proper controls, procedures and disciplines. Without pursuing a policy of confrontation, the company recognises its responsibility to initiate and implement change, to exercise and, where necessary, to regain control of the management function.

4. To maintain the identity of interest between the company and its employees. To provide for equality of opportunity, for the development of individual ability, and for constructive relations with the recognised trade unions.

5. To ensure that the necessary human resources are available, trained, utilised and motivated so as to fulfil the company's long- and short-term requirements.

6. To provide fair rewards for a fair day's work; reasonable working conditions and terms of service; work that satisfies the individual's needs for involvement and the full use of abilities and skills; and opportunities for advancement and self-realisation. This policy should lead to the employment of the minimum number of people commensurate with the efficient running of the business.

7. To respect, understand and develop the need for harmonious industrial relations through communication, participation and joint consultation.

8. Know all employees – don't let trouble makers start – get rid of them at any price – never a strike – virtually no industrial action. (An organisation of under 200 employees.)

It is interesting to note that of the 69 statements quoted by Marsh only five referred to trade unions; one of which included the encouragement of trade union membership. The emphasis of most organisational philosophies on industrial relations appears to centre on the direct relationship between management and its employees.

Planning of industrial relations responses

It is only within the framework of an identifiable Company Policy and knowledge of the current state of industrial relations within the organisation gained from an 'audit' that management may, realistically, plan for the future. Such planning involves the **conversion of policy intentions into specific actions or outcomes to be achieved within broadly defined time periods.** Thus, it is often useful to regard the strategic plan as operating in the long term and the tactical as operating in the short term.

As in other facets of business management, **strategic planning** in industrial relations involves identifying the pressures on, and consequent changes required in, the organisation's industrial relations system over a specified period. In preparing such a plan management must take into account not only other organisational strategic plans (investment, product and market situation, technology) but also potential changes in the external economic and social environment. It is, of course, more difficult to assess the precise strength, speed and direction of such external pressures over which management has no direct control. Indeed, part of the resultant strategic industrial relations plan may involve management trying to weaken those pressures which are felt to be undesirable by campaigning, both within the organisation and in the public forum, against their acceptance. At the same time trade unions and employees may be campaigning for their adoption.

In preparing the strategic plan management needs to identify the **most**

likely trends and probable alternatives that may arise during the period under consideration and evaluate their possible implications for both the content and organisation of the industrial relations system. Obviously, such assessments are subject to a degree of error and therefore the predictions within the strategic plan need to be re-evaluated periodically. It may be argued that it is only by practice and constant refinement that management can improve the quality of its judgement and long-term planning in such a subjective area as industrial relations. Furthermore, the process of determining the plan may be more important than the plan itself. Discussions within management, necessary for the successful determination and evaluation of the strategic plan, provide a focus for managerial thought and create the opportunity to lay the foundations for innovation and a proactive approach to industrial relations within the organisation.

Tactical planning is primarily concerned with the specific objectives to be realised within the industrial relations system in the short term – possibly the forthcoming year or 18 months (the precise length depending very much on the sequence and timing of wage negotiations within the organisation). The tactical plan, in addition to **defining the objectives**, should **assign a relative importance** to them (very often one may not be achievable without the prior achievement of another) and **identify the manner of their achievement and by whom.** Some objectives are capable of achievement only by the senior management/industrial relations specialist, whilst others must be sought more diffusely through the co-ordination of the actions of individual managers in the normal course of their management. The objectives should be couched in terms of the minimum which is acceptable and the maximum which is desirable. Management must also, in drawing up the plan, give consideration to the objectives which employees and trade unions might also be wishing to achieve. In assessing the importance of any individual objective, management must assess the cost it is prepared to accept in order to achieve it – the cost may be considered and expressed in terms of what management is prepared to 'trade off' in exchange during negotiations or in terms of what degree of pressure, perhaps in the form of industrial action, it is prepared to withstand.

Strategic and tactical planning are, of course, interrelated in that the latter is the final refined version of the initial phase of the former. Such a formal framework of planning facilitates not only a consistent and orderly management initiative in industrial relations but also the examination of, and response to, any employee or union claim. However, to be effective the planning must, first, ensure that there is co-ordination between the distinct industrial relations subsystems covering different groups of employees (if they are separate). For example, the introduction of a work reorganisation for manual employees is likely to have major implications for the staff who supervise them and this must be planned for. Secondly, all managers must be aware of both the strategic and tactical plans – certainly, as the very minimum, in so far as they relate to their particular role. In this way they are then able to ensure that their industrial relations decisions do not conflict with, and preferably help to further, the overall objectives the organisation is seeking.

All that has been considered above in respect of the desirability for management:

1. to be proactive rather than reactive;
2. to determine what *it* needs from the industrial relations system to achieve its business objectives; and
3. to pursue an integrated approach to the development of an 'overall' Company Policy which reflects its desired style of employee management and a strategic and tactical plan to implement industrial relations change,

has been written about, discussed and, in some of the more progressive organisations, practised since the early 1970s. It could be argued that all that writing and discussion has, in part, contributed to the more proactive approach adopted by management more generally during the 1980s. Perhaps it simply required the spur of competition, recession and heightened concern for organisational performance to emphasise the need to put it into practice. However, whilst much of the consideration of style, strategy and policy in the late 1960s and 1970s was within a 'corporatist' (collective) environment and therefore emphasised the management/union relationship, its implementation in the 1980s within an 'individualist' environment has emphasised the management/employee relationship.

Specific policies, procedures and practices

The final stage of the process involves the implementation of policy, procedural changes and management decisions designed to meet the identified needs of the organisation. It is this part of the process which is most likely to be subject to joint regulation with trade unions through collective bargaining. Therefore, it may be regarded as the **formal interface** between, at an organisational level, management and union and, at a more individual level, managers and employees. At both levels it is the decisions and practices implemented through policies and procedures which determine the nature of the management/employee relationship, provide the clearest evidence of management's intentions, and by which management is judged as an employer.

Whilst the management process of policy and decision making is important in determining the employees' substantive terms and conditions of employment, including the content of their work and how it is to be carried out, it is the procedural outcomes which prescribe the manner in which these decisions are to be implemented. **Jointly agreed procedures limit the exercise of managerial authority and establish a regulatory framework** within which the conflict between management's desire for control of the labour environment and employees' desire for protection against arbitrary management action will be handled. It is through the roles ascribed to shop stewards, full-time officers and the various levels of management in the operation of these procedures that their overall roles and responsibilities for the conduct of industrial relations within the organisation are given effect. Procedures define the accepted standards of organisational behaviour for both management and union representatives and should remove, or at least reduce, any uncertainty they may otherwise have as to how they should set about resolving issues between them. Without procedures the parties to an issue have not only to determine the content of a solution but also to decide the method whereby they are to proceed in seeking to establish the solution. The **process of joint determination of specific procedures is as valuable and important to the development of a stable industrial relations system as the resultant procedures.** The discussion required in drawing up a procedure, and defining the roles, rights and responsibilities of both parties at all levels of its operation, provides an opportunity for both sides to gain a better understanding of their respective positions and attitudes. Thus, it is again important that the people within the organisation who will be required to operate the procedure, particularly supervisory management and shop stewards, should be involved in its determination – if only in commenting on any proposals before they are finally agreed between management and union. The joint agreement of procedures may also involve a limited joint agreement of policy through the inclusion of a 'statement of intent' as the preamble to the procedural mechanism.

When drafting these procedures, it is important that they should be clear and concise: it is vitally important that everybody is able to understand the intention and requirements of all aspects of the procedure. Although it is virtually impossible to draft a procedure which will, from the very outset, cope with any eventuality which may arise, nevertheless the principle to be applied in the operation of any procedure is that **once it is agreed and implemented it should be followed.** If, in particular circumstances, it is subsequently found that the procedural mechanism is inadequate, management and union must then jointly consider whether the situation should be treated as an exceptional occurrence for which a special 'one-off' procedural arrangement is suitable and acceptable, or whether, if the situation is likely to occur again, the formal procedure itself should be amended. Thus, procedures should be regarded as dynamic arrangements which may require to be revised or modified in the light of both their operational effectiveness and changed circumstances within which they are expected to operate rather than 'inhibit change by becoming sacrosanct' [17].

Gill and Concannon [18] have suggested that **organisational differences**

in the content and range of policies and procedures, and the managerial process which develops them, can be attributed to four factors:

1. The authority relationship between line management and specialist staff for the conduct of industrial relations (specialisation).
2. The extent to which consistency in decision making and action is being sought (standardisation).
3. The codification of policies, procedures and practices in formal written documents (formalisation).
4. The degree to which the organisation has autonomy in its industrial relations decision making (centralisation).

Certainly, most organisations, whether unionised or not, are likely to have policies and procedures in respect of individual employee grievances, discipline and safety. The existence and recognition of trade unions within the organisation will generate further policies and procedures in respect of negotiating and payment systems, disputes, the shop steward's role, and the management of work changes (including the introduction of new technology, the transfer, redeployment and retraining of employees, and redundancy).

15.3 The management of industrial relations decisions

Flanders suggested from his study of the Fawley productivity agreement in the early 1960s that 'there is more room and more need for internal managerial debate in resolving labour relations problems than in dealing with technical questions, if only because the reactions of people are not so easily assessed as the working of machines' and that 'labour relations are being formed, for good or ill, by the whole of management, at all levels and in all departments, whether its members are conscious of this or not' [19]. Whilst there is little doubt that the second statement is true, there is great scope for debate about the validity of the first statement, particularly in the context of complex and rapidly developing technology. In Brown's 1978 survey of manufacturing establishments only 24 per cent of respondents felt that personnel or industrial relations considerations were important in decisions relating to fixed capital investment and only 40 per cent felt they were important in major changes in production methods [20]. However, there appears to have been a greater awareness during the 1980s that industrial relations must support the achievement of the business objectives and that major business developments such as the introduction of new technology, flexible working practices and quality management can only be achieved successfully if proper consideration is given to the industrial relations implications.

The management of industrial relations involves different **groups of managers** with differential involvement in industrial relations decision making (see Figure 15.2). Both Brown's and Daniel and Millward's [21] surveys found industrial relations specialism to be a feature of medium to large organisations. Indeed, the latter commented that, particularly but not exclusively amongst establishments employing less that two hundred employees, 'personnel work is chiefly carried out by people who are not formally employed as personnel specialists' [22]. Furthermore, they found that specialist representation at the board level was most likely where company level bargaining was more important than establishment level [23]. Marsh's survey in 1980 showed that the designation of a board member with responsibility for employee relations had accelerated since 1965 and particularly during the 1970s [24].

[For the remainder of this section the term 'industrial relations specialist' applies, in the absence of a specific industrial relations or personnel specialist within the organisation, to any other manager who has formal organisation-wide responsibility for industrial relations matters.]

In the past it could reasonably be argued that at the **strategic level** of policy making, planning and the determination of unit wide issues it was the industrial relations specialist who had primary responsibility for analysing and assessing any industrial relations situation and then presenting alternative strategies and recommendations for discussion by, and ultimate approval of, the senior management group. Departmental management may have been involved in this process either by the industrial relations specialist when examining the situation or by the senior management when arriving at a final decision or both. At the **operational level** the responsibility for making decisions relating to grievances, discipline, work changes and the interpretation of collective agreements and policies rested with the immediate supervisory management and their superiors (departmental management) in consultation with the industrial relations specialist.

It is evident, in this model, that **the industrial relations specialist and departmental management have a key role as the link between strategic and operational decisions.** They are able, by being involved in both levels of decision making, to facilitate the translation of policies into day-to-day practice and to recognise when an operational decision is in fact a strategic one because of its implications for the organisation. In the absence of such an overlap *within* their roles the linkage between the two levels of decision making can only be achieved by a process of formal communication *between* roles thereby creating an additional barrier to the smooth and effective transference of decision making from one level to the other. In those situations where the departmental management is excluded from the strategic level of industrial relations decision making, and therefore the primary responsibility for providing the linkage between the two levels falls on the

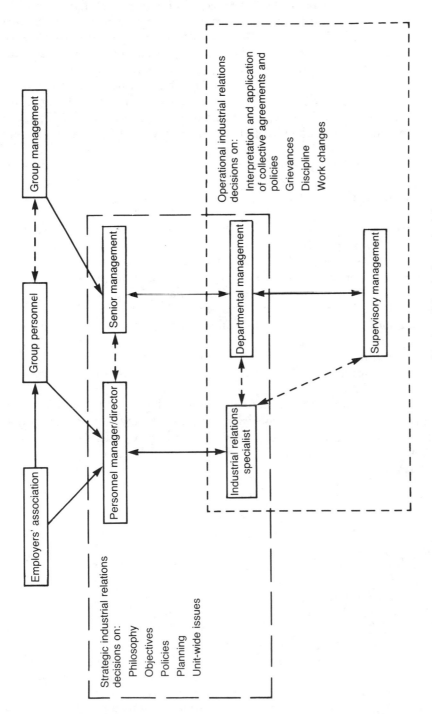

Figure 15.2 *Management of industrial relations decisions*

industrial relations specialist role, the potential organisational divide between line management and specialist may easily become a reality. A similar situation could arise within the 1980s strategy to reorganise responsibility for industrial relations management by, at one level, decentralising and incorporating it into the line manager's general responsibility (particularly as an integral part of a general development of managerial authority and responsibility to product, cost or budget centres), whilst at the top level reconstituting the corporate industrial relations specialist as primarily a policy maker or 'consultant' role. This is likely to reduce the interaction between the various levels.

Line versus staff

Managers have always subscribed to the view that 'to the extent that they inevitably deal with people or "personnel" it might be said that all managers are personnel managers' [25]. Certainly, Marsh found that 'very few companies thought of an employee relations function as relieving line management of all its employee responsibilities' [26]. Even in the 1950s Myers and Turnball [27] identified a spectrum of relationships ranging from line management having total responsibility for all personnel affairs, through Personnel having a delegated responsibility to advise and service, to Personnel having a delegated, or usurping through the default of line management, responsibility for decision making in certain areas of personnel or industrial relations.

However, it may be argued that the debate as to whether the personnel/industrial relations specialists should be advisory or executive, whilst perhaps useful in analytical terms, is to a large extent illusory. As the CIR noted, the reality in most organisations is that 'ultimately, management's responsibility for industrial relations is collective' [28]. If the specialist's formal role is only 'advisory', line management cannot afford, because of the complexity and importance of industrial relations matters to the organisation as a whole, to consistently ignore its advice. Equally, if the specialist's formal role is 'executive' it cannot ignore the views and operational needs of line management and impose decisions if they are to be successfully implemented – it must also gain the commitment of the line management. In either situation it is, in reality, the **quality and effectiveness of their industrial relations advice or decisions,** not their formal role, which determines the degree of influence the industrial relations specialist may have within the decision making process. The CIR pointed out that the specialist's importance in the decision making process rests on the fact that 'he is in a position to make an overall study of the company needs, consult and involve the people who will be concerned . . . produce proposals, and finally secure agreement to them' [29]. In most organisations the specialist and the line management develop, over time, a working relationship in respect of the division of responsibility for decision making on industrial relations matters. This relationship is likely to vary even between different managers within the same organisation as a result of their varying interest and competence in the area of industrial relations.

However, the perception of the **specialist's organisational role** may be important in determining the relationship between line management and industrial relations specialist. Is it an integral part of the management team seeking to implement managerial objectives or as some form of special intermediary between 'management' and 'employees'? Certainly the industrial relations specialist is, where the organisation is unionised, required to maintain close contact with unions and shop stewards, to develop an understanding of their position on industrial relations issues which arise and to explain, and if necessary argue, their position to other members of management. It is this aspect of the role which may lead line management to perceive the specialist as aligning with what they may regard as the unreasonable demands of the union and undermining management attempts to control the work situation. Nevertheless, this part of the role is essential if all the 'facts' of a given situation are to be available to management before it makes a decision and if the implications of any decision are to be fully understood. In this respect the specialist may be regarded as the organisation's 'conscience' on industrial relations matters ensuring that employee views and needs are fully heard in arriving at decisions. However, in other aspects of the role (developing industrial relations policies and strategies and implementing decisions) the specialist is clearly part of the corporate management and as such committed to the achievement of managerial objectives. It is interesting to note that most of the 28 per cent of companies surveyed by Marsh in 1980 which perceived the employee relations function as 'performing an "intermediary" or "honest broker" role between company and employees . . . were expressing theory rather than practice, since they themselves had no personnel staff' [30].

Multi-site organisations

One characteristic of the post-war period has been the development of not only **multi-plant organisations** (i.e. organisations having more than one location or site) but also **multi-product/industry organisations** (organisations whose operations encompass, generally at different locations, significantly differing products and technologies). The management patterns of such organisations are varied. In one the group level may act as no more than a holding company or banker for the group with each operating company maintaining complete autonomy for its decisions; in another, the group may be broken down into product divisions with divisional management having the primary responsibility for co-ordinating the activities of a number of locations/operating units within the division; in others, co-ordination, or even control, may be exercised from the group level. In addition, the relationship of one individual unit to another may vary from direct competitors to integral parts of the group's overall operations.

The concern for an integrated approach to industrial relations is perhaps greatest where the different locations are not only similar in respect of their product and technology but also interdependent in the overall production process. The CIR argued that 'the desire to delegate authority to ensure that local management are able to take into account industrial relations needs such as local productivity deals and local labour market conditions was . . . balanced by an objective of avoiding the creation of precedents at one location which would prove awkward if raised by employees elsewhere' [31]. Marsh [32] found that in multi-plant organisations, although divisions were invariably 'wholly' or 'partly' independent, only 6 per cent of plants were 'wholly' independent and the majority (58 per cent) were only 'partly' independent, that is, subject to periodic advice and direction or only certain actions could be taken without company approval. Certainly, Kinnie suggests that decentralisation of management and bargaining structures 'do not necessarily lead to an increase in decision-making discretion for establishment managers' [33], whilst Purcell [34] believes that management can 'have the best of both worlds' by corporate co-ordination and control of 'decentralised' bargaining through budgetary control mechanisms and monitoring personnel activities of individual sites, units, etc. Indeed, he refers to one survey [35] which found that two-thirds of companies with decentralised bargaining had a corporate policy on pay settlements, issued pay guidelines or held consultations between site and higher level management before the start of negotiations.

In multi-plant organisations the specialist's **function at the location level has two different, and potentially conflicting roles:**

1. A functional responsibility to the group-level management for ensuring that the activities at the location level conform to any group policies and strategies.
2. An operational responsibility to the location management for implementing industrial relations policies, strategies and decisions which are supportive of their operational needs.

Thus, it acts as a two-way link – explaining to the location management the need for conformity with group policy and explaining to group management the desirability, in certain situations, of their location adopting a differential approach. Which takes precedence is a matter for the collective judgement of location and group management. However, it is vital, if such conflicting interests are to be avoided in the first place or satisfactorily resolved when they do arise that the location management is involved in the determination of the group policies and strategies on industrial relations affairs so that its views and particular needs may be taken into account.

An organisation that is a member of an **Employers' Association** generally accepts the principle that it will abide by the policies, decisions and agreements reached by that association. In most situations these have to encompass a wide range of organisations which are in membership, and therefore there is often scope for the individual organisation, when implementing them, to interpret and adapt them to their own needs and circumstances. Indeed, there is a general expectation that they will do so; but nevertheless, there may be situations where the policy, decision or agreement is in direct conflict with the needs of the organisation. The management must then decide whether to implement it, leave the Employers' Association or negotiate an alternative directly with the unions to apply exclusively to their organisation. The situation becomes more complex when one location of a multi-plant organisation is a member of an Employers' Association whilst the other locations are not. It may lead to the situation where (as happened to one organisation) a location rejected, as part of its annual plant negotiations, a union demand for an extra week's holiday because it was contrary to group policy. A few weeks later the Employers' Association, of which the location was a member, made such a concession and so the location was obliged to apply it irrespective of the wishes of its group management, thereby creating the very precedent the group were seeking to avoid. The situation is even more complicated where, as Marsh found, 'membership of up to six associations was not unknown' [36] among multi-plant organisations.

15.4 Summary propositions

- To achieve an orderly and consistent industrial relations system management needs to adopt an integrated approach to policy development, planning and decision making.
- The development of a policy and planning framework acceptable to both management and union is a lengthy process requiring the mutual recognition, acceptance and reconciliation of differing attitudes and beliefs.
- Decision making within management on industrial relations matters is not the sole province of either industrial relations specialist or line management but a collective responsibility requiring the involvement and commitment of both.

Further reading

- A. Marsh, *Employee Relations Policy and Decision Making: A survey of manufacturing companies carried out for the CBI*, Gower, 1982.

Chapters 3, 4, 8 and 9 provide useful information in respect of the management of industrial relations and policy making.

- K. Hawkins, *The Management of Industrial Relations*, Penguin, 1978. This examines the pressures for change in the industrial relations system during the late 1960s and 1970s and their implications for management. Chapter 6 is concerned with the role of policies.
- M. Marchington and P. Parker, *Changing Patterns of Employee Relations*, Harvester Wheatsheaf, 1990. A useful examination of the management of industrial relations in the 1980s drawing on four extensive case studies.
- N. H. Cuthbert and K. H. Hawkins, *Company Industrial Relations Policies*, Longman, 1973. Chapters 1–3 are particularly useful in respect of the development and content of a company industrial relations policy.
- 'The Role of Management in Industrial Relations', *CIR Report 34*, HMSO, 1973. This examines the roles of the various management groups in the formulation and implementation of industrial relations policies and decisions.
- 'Industrial Relations in Multi-plant Undertakings', *CIR Report 85*, HMSO, 1974. This examines the issues for both management and union organisation in the conduct of industrial relations within multi-plant organisations.

References

1. C. G. Gill and H. M. G. Concannon, 'Developing an explanatory framework for industrial relations policy within the firm', *Industrial Relations Journal*, vol. 7, no. 4, 1976/1977, p. 15.
2. K. Hawkins, *A Handbook of Industrial Relations Practice*, Kogan Page, 1979, p. 229.
3. 'The Role of Management in Industrial Relations', *CIR Report 34*, HMSO, 1973, p. 5.
4. N. H. Cuthbert, 'Industrial relations and the development of company policies' in N. H. Cuthbert and K. H. Hawkins (eds), *Company Industrial Relations Policies*, Longman, 1973, p. 16.
5. Report of *Royal Commission on Trade Unions and Employers' Associations* (Donovan Commission), HMSO, 1968, p. 41.
6. A. Marsh, *Employee Relations Policy and Decision Making: A Survey of Manufacturing Companies Carried Out for the CBI*, Gower, 1982, p. 187.
7. C. Jennings, W. E. J. McCarthy and R. Undy, *Managers and Industrial Relations: The identification of training needs*, Oxford Centre for Management Studies/ Manpower Services Commission, 1983. (This is a working manual of questionnaires which may be used in carrying out an industrial relations audit.)
8. A. Marsh, *op. cit.*, p. 201.
9. *CIR Report 34*, *op. cit.*, p. 6.
10. K. Hawkins, *The Management of Industrial Relations*, Penguin, 1978, p. 190.

11. L. F. Neal, 'Management responsibility' in D. P. Torrington (ed.), *Handbook of Industrial Relations*, Gower, 1972, p. 112.
12. *CIR Report 34*, *op. cit.*, p. 4.
13. K. Hawkins (1979), *op. cit.*, p. 229.
14. K. Hawkins (1978), *op. cit.*, p. 188.
15. *ibid.*, p. 192.
16. A. Marsh, *op. cit.*, Appendix 3, pp. 238–42.
17. D. Torrington and J. Chapman, *Personnel Management* (2nd edn), Prentice Hall, 1983, p. 165.
18. C. G. Gill and H. M. G. Concannon, *op. cit.*
19. A. Flanders, *The Fawley Productivity Agreements*, Faber & Faber, 1964, pp. 38–40.
20. W. Brown (ed.), *The Changing Contours of British Industrial Relations*, Blackwell, 1981, Table 3.1, p. 28.
21. W. W. Daniel and N. Millward, *Workplace Industrial Relations in Britain*, Heinemann (PSI/SSRC), 1983, Table V.1, p. 106 and Table V.13, p. 122.
22. *ibid.*, p. 105.
23. *ibid.*, Table V.15, p. 125.
24. A. Marsh, *op. cit.*, Table 3.2c, p. 68 and Table 3.02c, p. 79.
25. *CIR Report 34*, *op. cit.*, p. 19.
26. A. Marsh, *op. cit.*, p. 49.
27. C. A. Myers and J. G. Turnball, 'Line and staff in industrial relations', *Harvard Business Review*, vol. 34, no. 4, 1956, pp. 114–15.
28. *CIR Report 34*, *op. cit.*, p. 26.
29. *CIR Report 34*, *op. cit.*, p. 12.
30. A. Marsh, *op. cit.*, p. 49.
31. 'Industrial Relations in Multi-plant Undertakings', *CIR Report 85*, HMSO, 1974, p. 16.
32. A. Marsh, *op. cit.*, Table 9.02, p. 225.
33. N. Kinnie, 'The decentralisation of industrial relations? – recent research considered', *Personnel Review*, vol. 19, no. 3, 1990, p. 33.
34. J. Purcell, *op. cit.*, p. 55.
35. P. Marginson *et. al.*, *Beyond the Workplace: Managing industrial relations in the multi-establishment enterprise*, Blackwell, 1988.
36. A. Marsh, *op. cit.*, p. 12.

Chapter 16
Union recognition

16.1 Definition

Trade union recognition may be defined as:

the process by which management formally accepts one or more trade unions as the representative(s) of all, or a group, of its employees for the purpose of jointly determining terms and conditions of employment on a collective basis.

It is perhaps the most important stage in the development of an organisation's industrial relations system. It confers legitimacy on the trade union's role of representing and protecting its members' interests at the workplace. Torrington and Chapman argue it symbolises 'an irrevocable movement away from unilateral decision making by the management' [1], whilst Singleton sees it as a 'renunciation of sole management authority in respect of the matters covered in the recognition agreement' [2]. Similarly, Towers argues, in the context of the recent debate about derecognition, that 'trade union rights to oppose, to bargain, to organise – even to exist – are at stake should a derecognition movement prosper' [3].

16.2 Recognition in context

The focus of the union recognition issue has shifted between the 1970s and 1980s. At the core of this shift is the issue of whose interests should predominate in determining the shape of recognition and, through that, collective bargaining. During the 1970s, the emphasis was on developing a codified and coherent approach to the recognition process at the organisational level to support the development of collective representation and bargaining with, if necessary, statutory support for unions encountering management resistance to granting recognition. The initial recognition of a union was regarded as a starting point for a continuing process of enhancement as the relationship between management and the union(s) developed with subsequent extensions of the scope of collective bargaining and involvement of the union/employees in joint decision making with management. However, the emphasis during the 1980s has been on management strategies aimed at redefining or even removing recognition, simplifying or rationalising bargaining arrangements and reducing the impact of collective bargaining to support the achievement of greater organisational performance and flexibility. However, at the same time, trade unions have sought new areas in which to recruit and seek recognition to replace those lost through the decrease in the manufacturing sector.

Extent of trade union recognition

It is important to recognise that the term **'non-unionism'** may be used to refer to two different types of situation:

1. Type A: where an organisation has a policy not to recognise unions for any employees or for particular groups of employees (such as managers) and, therefore, it is a distinct aim or element of management's employee relations strategy to avoid any collective relationship (i.e. non-unionism results from management decision).
2. Type B: where union membership within the organisation or group of employees is low or non-existent and, therefore, unions are not recognised because of the absence of employee pressure for representation (i.e. non-unionism results from the employees' decision not to join unions).

Bassett [4] notes that **union recognition and non-unionism can often exist side by side** within an organisation. Thus, it has been quite common for manual employees to be represented by unions whilst non-manual employees are non-unionised; for one or more plants within an organisation to recognise unions while other plants are non-unionised; or even, on an international level, for an organisation like IBM (which is generally regarded as a non-union organisation) to be highly unionised in some countries but not in others. What is not clear is whether such variations within organisations result from differential management policies (through devolved managerial responsibility for industrial relations) or differences in employee attitudes towards trade unionism. Certainly, **changes in the structure and pattern of employment** during the 1980s have increased the existence of Type B non-unionism through decreases in male employment, the manufacturing sector, manual work and large organisations and increases in female and/or part-time employment, the private service sector, non-manual work and smaller organisations. These latter employment growth sectors are also the very sectors which traditionally have been more difficult for trade unions to organise and, therefore, trade unions have not been able to convert this employment growth into any substantial growth in union membership and recognition. At the same time, the growth of 'greenfield site' developments (such as new business parks, out-of-town retail and distribution centres, etc.) present management with an opportunity to establish new approaches to employee relations (including Type A non-unionism) particularly if it does not involve the transfer of staff from existing, possibly unionised, sites. Therefore, whilst the decline in UK trade union membership and density from its peak in 1979 indicates an increase in Type B non-unionism, any trend towards more Type A non-unionism is more difficult to identify. However, it may be argued that in so far as employees do not join unions, management does not need to adopt a formal policy of non-unionism.

The **pattern of trade union recognition** varies both between manual and non-manual employees and between the different sectors of the UK economy; however, it still remains quite high despite the pressure on trade unions from the economic recession, government policy and management strategies during the 1980s (see Table 16.1). Millward and Stevens' survey [5] shows that in 1984 virtually all establishments in the Public Sector recognised unions for both manual and non-manual employees; just over half of the establishments in Private Manufacturing industries recognised unions for manual employees, although only a quarter recognised unions for non-manual employees; and approximately one third of establishments in Private Service industries recognised unions for manual and non-manual employees. Clearly, recognition depends on the existence of union membership within the organisation and, as the figures show, recognition is much higher when expressed as a percentage of the establishments with union members – even the lowest being 75 per cent (Private Manufacturing with non-manual union members).

Millward and Stevens argue that the **apparent decline in union recognition** between 1980 and 1984 amongst manual employees in Private Manufacturing (the percentage of establishments recognising unions dropped from 65 per cent to 55 per cent whilst the proportion of establishments with manual union members which recognised unions remained at 85 per cent 'appears to be predominantly a structural change arising from the disproportionate rate of closure of large manufacturing plants' [6], which generally had high union membership and recognised unions, rather than from any sustained management campaign in manufacturing industries to withdraw from union recognition. Their survey [7] also identified a number of other significant features of the pattern of recognition in the Private Sector between 1980 and 1984:

1. **Foreign owned establishments**, contrary to what might have been expected, showed a small increase in the proportion recognising unions (so far as manual employees were concerned this was because more of

Table 16.1 *Trade union recognition, 1980 and 1984*

	All establishments		Private manufacture		Private service		Public sector	
	1980 (%)	1984 (%)	1980 (%)	1984 (%)	1980 (%)	1984 (%)	1980 (%)	1984 (%)
Manual employees:								
% of establishments with 'some union members'	64	68	76	66	42	47	88	95
Union recognition:								
% of establishments	55	62	65	55	33	38	76	91
% of establishments with manual union members	86	91	85	85	80	81	92	99
Non-manual employees:								
% of establishments with 'some union members'	55	58	36	34	34	35	98	100
Union recognition:								
% of establishments	47	54	27	26	28	30	91	98
% of establishments with manual union members	87	92	74	75	82	85	93	99

Note: Not all the increase in recognition amongst manual employees in the public sector should be regarded as real but may result from a measurement error between the two surveys. Any error in this group carries over into the overall figure for all establishments.
Source: N. Millward and M. Stevens, *British Workplace Industrial Relations 1980–1984*, Gower, 1986 (Tables 3.1 and 3.5).

these establishments had manual union members in 1984 than in 1980, whilst for non-manual employees it appeared to be because they were more prepared to recognise unions where membership existed).

2. Establishments that were **head offices of a group** were more likely to recognise unions for their non-manual employees in 1984 than 1980.
3. Establishments with more than 10 per cent of their manual employees belonging to **ethnic minorities** were less likely to recognise unions in 1984 due to a lower proportion of such establishments having union members within the organisation.
4. Establishments that utilised **marginal or peripheral workers** (freelance workers, home workers, agency temps, short-term contracts, etc.) were much less likely to recognise unions for non-manual employees despite being just as likely to have union members within their workforce.

Thus, trade union recognition appears to have weathered the pressures of the early 1980s and, overall, remains largely intact. However, there has been, at the same time, some simplification or rationalisation of recognition and bargaining arrangements and even some derecognition.

Union derecognition in the 1980s

Claydon believes that the recent debate about derecognition is 'essentially over whether fundamental change or underlying stability has been the main characteristic of British industrial relations during the 1980s' [8]. He defines derecognition as 'a decision to withdraw from collective bargaining in favour of other arrangements for regulating employment relations' [9]. This does not include situations where, as part of a management strategy to simplify or rationalise recognition and collective bargaining arrangements, one or more unions lose negotiating rights in favour of another union (most notably the introduction of a Single Union Agreement). Claydon provides a useful framework for examining derecognition by reference to both the **breadth and depth of derecognition**:

1. **Breadth** – the proportion of the organisation's workforce affected by derecognition:
    (a) **general:** derecognition of union(s) for all employees throughout the organisation or discrete business unit;
    (b) **grade-specific:** derecognition of union(s) for a specific grade or class of employees across the whole organisation or business unit;
    (c) **plant-specific:** derecognition of union(s) at one plant or unit whilst union(s) remain recognised elsewhere in the organisation.

2. **Depth** – the extent to which union(s) retains elements of a collective representational relationship with management:
    (a) **partial:** union(s) retain some negotiating rights over non-pay issues and may be consulted over pay;
    (b) **derecognition as bargaining agent:** union(s) retain(s) right to be consulted on collective issues and to represent members on individual matters;
    (c) **collective derecognition:** union(s) only retain(s) right to represent members on individual issues;
    (d) **complete derecognition:** union(s) only able to provide members with minimum legal advice and services (e.g. injury at work, unfair dismissal, etc.) and management may or may not discourage union membership;
    (e) **deunionisation:** union(s) has (have) no rights or facilities and union membership is discouraged.

Formal union derecognition has, according to ACAS, 'remained rare' [10] and appears to have been only a **very limited feature of the private sector** (despite the very emotive Government action at GCHQ in 1984). Nearly half of the 56 cases of derecognition identified by Claydon took place in two industries (shipping, and newspaper and book publishing); each of which experienced a long, bitter and well-publicised derecognition dispute (News

International and P&O/NUS) which set the trend for other organisations in those industries. By far the biggest group of the 39 cases he examined in more depth involved the withdrawal of all collective union rights on a 'grade specific' basis for some or all non-manual employees which 'indicates that often collective bargaining has not been rejected completely' but rather 'derecognition may have been a reversal of a pragmatic decision to recognise white collar workers in earlier years' [11]. Perhaps most significantly, in only a small number of cases did management refer to poor industrial relations or previous disputes as a reason for derecognition, but in 14 cases there was a change in either the ownership or senior management of the organisation which led to a significant change in attitude towards unions and collective bargaining.

A number of **internal organisational factors appear to be important influences on the process of derecognition:**

1. Changes in **management** within the organisation can lead to a change in industrial relations strategy and a direct challenge to the union's former position.
2. The **union's** ability to withstand any management challenge or questioning of recognition will be reduced if:
   (a) there is a low density of unionisation within the organisation or group of employees affected by the derecognition which allows management to question the representative nature of the union (e.g. significantly below 50 per cent density);
   (b) if the employee group affected has only a 'marginal' interest in the collective bargaining process (such as senior or middle managers or professional groups);
   (c) if there is limited membership support for the union (i.e. the employees within the affected group display a high degree of individualism as a result of their work situation; e.g. researchers, journalists, etc.);
   (d) if the link between the workplace and any national bargaining arrangement is weak (i.e. decentralisation of collective bargaining – particularly the removal of any multi-employer national agreement – isolates the employees at the organisation level and reduces the availability of wider union support to resist attempts to derecognise).

These union characteristics are particularly relevant to non-manual employees in the private sector or groups where there are significant proportions of female and/or part-time employees (e.g. retail) and this has implications in respect of union attempts to strengthen their membership and recognition in these potential employment growth areas. It may also act as an example to be applied eventually to manual workers within the organisation. At the same time, continued decentralisation of collective bargaining is likely to weakening any relationship between the workplace and national level and make trade unions more vulnerable to the possibility of derecognition.

Derecognition does not appear to have been a universal or even common element of management strategies to respond to competitive pressures or a shift in the general balance of power between management and union. The evidence, Claydon notes, suggests that most unionised organisations have responded to these pressures and achieved change, flexibility, and improved performance 'by imposing or negotiating change through existing bargaining machinery rather than rejecting it . . . derecognition is probably an extreme reflection of a much wider shift in the frontier of control *within* collective bargaining rather than a sign of a systematic movement for its rejection' [12]. In his view, derecognition will 'remain limited, if more common than in the past' and 'be piecemeal and possibly temporary' [13]. Similarly, Towers suggests that whilst 'there is currently no major movement towards derecognition . . . what was once extremely rare is now becoming more commonplace and, in some sectors, derecognition initiatives seem to be becoming almost fashionable' [14]. However, derecognition has serious implications for those affected not least, as Townley [15] points out, because it is only *recognised* unions which have legal rights to time off for union activities, disclosure of information and consultation over such matters as redundancy, the transfer of the business, health and safety, and pensions.

At the same time, it is important to recognise that the 1980s was not a period of all one-way traffic for unions. **Union gains in recognition** must be put alongside this limited and piecemeal development in derecognition. Some evidence of union recognition gains can be seen from the work of ACAS. Throughout the 1980s they have been involved in some 150 cases each year of collective conciliation over recognition issues (14 per cent of their total collective conciliation cases) although this has only resulted in recognition gains in a limited number of cases and for a relatively small number of employees: for example, a third of cases covering 5,000 employees in 1986 [16] and a quarter of cases covering 2,800 employees in 1987 [17].

Legal intervention

Traditionally, British trade unions have sought to secure **recognition through direct representation to management** based on their own efforts and ability to recruit sufficient members in the workplace to be able to demonstrate, if necessary by industrial action, the desire of the employees to be represented by a trade union. However, during the 1970s (under the Industrial Relations Act (1971) and the Employment Protection Act (1975)) a **statutory procedure** existed which could be invoked by trade unions as an alternative to industrial action when management was not prepared to grant recognition voluntarily. Although the existence of this statutory procedure provided additional pressure on an employer who was reluctant to grant recognition, it was not, as Hawkins notes, intended 'that recourse to the statutory machinery would or should become the standard method of resolving recognition disputes' [18]; the procedure was intended to be used only as a last resort. During 1976–9, ACAS handled 2,066 recognition cases under its voluntary conciliation machinery and 1,168 under the statutory procedure – granting some form of recognition in 1,524 cases covering approximately 133,000 employees [19].

The inadequacy of the statutory procedure to deal with an employer who was determined not to grant recognition was clearly demonstrated in the Grunwick case (1977) where, despite Lord Denning's statement that 'this statute makes great powers available to trade unions ... they can bring immense pressure on an employer who does not wish to recognise a trade union' [20], Torrington and Chapman note that 'the management not only refused union recognition, but also dismissed all of a substantial number of employees who took strike action, refused to cooperate with an ACAS ballot of employees' opinion, refused to accept the recommendation and ... despite every form of persuasion, including mass picketing and union attempts at blacking supplies, ... remained firm in refusing to recognise and in the end the state agencies were as powerless as the trade union movement' [21]. Since its repeal in 1980, ACAS's work in this area has declined substantially.

Despite the demise of the statutory recognition procedure, trade union members, and potential members, are afforded a degree of **legal protection** against actions by the employer designed to discourage trade union membership or activity:

1. It is **unfair to dismiss** an employee because he/she is, or intends to become, a member of a trade union or takes part, or intends to take part, in its activities at an appropriate time (S.58, Employment Protection (Consolidation) Act, 1978), attracting a special damages award. But it is not unfair to dismiss the employee for going on strike to secure recognition.

2. The employee is also protected against **action short of dismissal** taken by the employer to prevent, deter or penalise him/her for being or seeking to become a member of an independent trade union or taking part in its activities (S.23, Employment Protection (Consolidation) Act, 1978). However, without an agreement or the consent of the employer, 'appropriate time' is confined to outside the employee's normal working hours; thus, a trade union member seeking to recruit other employees into the union during working time, without prior consent of the employer, has little legal protection from either disciplinary action or even dismissal.

3. Once the union is recognised by the employer, shop stewards have the right to **time off from work without loss of pay** to carry out those duties which relate to the organisation's industrial relations; and any trade union member has the right to time off, but not necessarily with

pay, to participate in the wider activities of the trade union not directly related to the organisation's industrial relations (e.g. delegate to national conference).

16.3 The recognition process

The recognition claim

Prior to any union claim for recognition, it is desirable that management should already have a **policy relating to trade unionism and trade union recognition.** In developing such a policy, management should consider whether it wishes to:

1. maintain a neutral stance (by simply accepting the employees' right to join a trade union if they so desire);
2. discourage the growth of trade unionism;
3. openly encourage the development of trade union membership and recognition within the organisation; or
4. require recognition to be granted only on an exclusive, single-union basis.

Then, when faced with a claim for recognition, management may refer the union to its policy as a statement of its position and the principles on which recognition will be granted.

The **initial reaction of management to a claim for recognition,** particularly in non-unionised organisations may be one of the following.

1. The assumption that the claim for recognition emanates from, and is inspired by, some **agency external to the organisation**. The claim may be seen as an expression of the desire of the union to enhance its power by increasing its membership and field of activity rather than an expression, on the part of the employees, of their desire to be represented by a trade union. However, the fact that recognition is an interorganisational arrangement between the company and the union, rather than an intraorganisational arrangement between the management and its employees does not mean that the members themselves have not been involved in the union's decision to seek recognition; often it is the union members themselves who make the initial approach to their full-time officer.
2. The assumption that some action, or lack of action, on their part is the immediate cause of the request for recognition. Whilst it is often true that a specific occurrence within the organisation, such as redundancy, a major work change or a low pay increase, may cause **dissatisfaction**

amongst employees and provide the impetus for increased trade union membership and a claim for recognition, it would be wrong for management to assume that identifying the cause and removing it will automatically result in a lessening of trade union interest or a withdrawal of the recognition claim. Equally, the immediate establishment by management of consultative committees or other forms of employee involvement as an alternative to trade union recognition may be regarded as manipulative and confirm the desire to achieve trade union representation.

3. The demand that the **union justify its claim** to represent sufficient employees to warrant recognition by supplying details of the number and extent of its membership within the organisation. The desire of management to acquire such information before it makes a decision ignores the fundamental point that it is not the level of union membership at the time the recognition claim is presented which should be the prime justification for the recognition of a trade union but the potential number of employees who wish the union to represent them in joint determination of their terms and conditions of employment.

It is only through a logical approach to determining trade union recognition and collective bargaining arrangements at the workplace that the worst features of multi-unionism and inter-union disputes may be avoided. Before responding to a claim for recognition it is important that management should determine its own objectives and strategy. It must consider what is the most appropriate 'bargaining unit', whether the union seeking recognition is an appropriate 'bargaining agent' and what 'degree of recognition' it is prepared to concede (see Figure 16.1). These are equally applicable to resolving claims for an extension of existing recognition and bargaining arrangements or dealing with competing claims for recognition as they are to determining an initial recognition claim. It is only after determining the answers to these three interrelated issues that management is in a position to discuss with the union the precise terms under which recognition may be granted.

The bargaining unit

The bargaining unit is the **base on which the organisation's subsequent collective bargaining institutions and agreements are built.** In determining the extent of a bargaining unit it is necessary to bear in mind that it will comprise a group, or groups, of employees who may ultimately 'be covered by jointly negotiated terms and conditions of employment; . . . on whose behalf a union or unions can be expected to raise individual and collective grievances; . . . among whom a union can be expected to carry out its recruitment and organisational maintenance activities including the appoint-

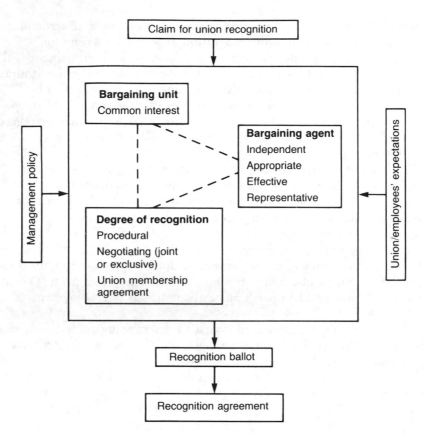

Figure 16.1 *Trade union recognition process*

ment . . . of shop stewards; . . . who will be covered by joint procedural arrangements' [22]. The precise boundaries of the bargaining units should, if there is to be more than one, be defined in such a way as to limit the number of units within the organisation, so as to facilitate orderly industrial relations and reduce the likelihood of fragmented and competitive bargaining arrangements, whilst at the same time ensuring that each bargaining unit has its own internal homogeneity based on the common interest of the employees within it.

The CIR identified a number of factors which might be used to establish the degree of **common interest** amongst employees and therefore the boundary of a bargaining unit:

- *Characteristics of the workgroup.*
1. Job skills and content – the existence of common job techniques, responsibilities or skills; involvement in similar production or provision of services; working in close proximity.

2. Payment systems – criteria or level of pay determination within the organisation.
3. Other conditions of employment – similarities or differences in hours of work, holidays, sick pay and retirement provisions or other fringe benefits as well as physical working conditions.
4. Training, qualifications and experience – similar requirements for apparently different work groups.

● *Trade union membership and collective bargaining arrangements.*
1. Trade union membership – the existence of common trade union membership amongst different groups.
2. Attitude towards collective bargaining – the existence of support for the principle of collective representation is essential for a viable bargaining unit.
3. Employee preference of association – the desire of different work groups to be related.
4. Existing collective bargaining arrangements – either within the organisation or elsewhere in the industry.

● *Management structure and authority.*
1. Recruitment, promotion and transfer of employees – the pattern of these activities may link or differentiate workgroups.
2. Geographical location – the existence of geographically scattered and diverse workgroups may mitigate against a single unit to cover all dependent on size and precise nature of work.
3. Management structure – autonomous operating units are likely to justify separate bargaining units.
4. Unilaterally operated management procedures – the existence and extent of consultative committees, grievance, disciplinary or other personnel procedures.

In seeking to apply these factors, it is the **combination and interrelationship** which determines the extent and nature of the homogeneity. The precise limits of the bargaining unit (the jobs to be included) may be determined on one or a combination of organisational, geographical, vertical or horizontal criteria. For example, in recognition issues relating to white collar employees the vertical boundary, in respect of how far the bargaining unit should extend into managerial and executive grades, is often of considerable concern to management. Before attempting to draw the precise boundaries of a bargaining unit, it is often useful to identify **core groups** of employees whose basis of common interest is clearly identifiable and distinguishable, and then seek to incorporate other, less fundamentally related groups around them.

The bargaining unit has recently become the focus of attention in two ways:

1. The process of centralising or decentralising collective bargaining within multi-site organisations has necessitated not only a technical redefinition of the boundaries of the bargaining unit(s) but also a more fundamental reassessment of the importance attached to the various common interest factors – often in favour of organisational economic/budgetary factors.
2. The development of Single Table Bargaining or Single Union Agreements.

The bargaining agent

In considering the nature of the proposed bargaining 'agent' management should satisfy itself that the union seeking recognition is independent, appropriate and representative. Whilst management can only be certain of the **representative** nature of the union after the final ballot phase of the recognition process, when employees are aware of precisely what they are being required to decide, it should, nevertheless, at this stage seek to assure itself that the union has a sufficient level of support, amongst the employees likely to comprise the bargaining unit, to justify further discussion. So far as **independence** is concerned, obviously, if the union seeking recognition has a certificate of independence there can be little doubt regarding its independence. However, if the proposed bargaining agent is an internal staff association, comprised solely of the company's own employees, it is important that management, in the interests of orderly and effective industrial relations, ensures that the association is not dependent on management. This is not to say that management should automatically refuse to recognise such associations (although their recognition may present future problems in respect of either claims by other unions for recognition for the same group of employees or the creation of joint bargaining arrangements involving TUC affiliated unions). However, management must ensure that it is in no way involved in the formation or running of such associations:

1. It should not make any financial or other provision to the association which it does not, or is not prepared to, make available to other trade unions.
2. It should not seek to influence the policy or activities of the association, particularly through senior management membership of the association.
3. It should seek to encourage the association to employ its own independent officials.

In seeking to determine **appropriateness**, management should be satisfied that the union is capable of taking into membership all employees who are likely to comprise the bargaining unit. Where this is not the case, management has a number of alternatives available:

1. refuse to proceed with the claim for recognition on the grounds that the union is inappropriate;
2. restrict the level of recognition to exclude the actual negotiation of terms and conditions of employment, otherwise one group of employees is likely to receive different wages and conditions to other closely related groups;
3. consider opening discussions with a trade union which is capable of taking all the employees into membership; or
4. discuss with the claimant union the possibility of proceeding on the basis of a joint recognition involving one or more additional unions.

Appropriateness, in management's eyes, may also relate to the union's perceived attitude towards establishing and maintaining a co-operative approach to industrial relations (particularly in respect of such issues as labour flexibility, strategies to enhance employee involvement and commitment to the organisation, etc.).

The degree of recognition

It is possible to identify **two distinct levels of recognition** which may be granted to a trade union.

- *Procedural recognition*. The union's right is restricted simply to representing its members, either individually or collectively, in grievance or disciplinary matters. Thus, the union has no involvement in the initial determination of terms and conditions of employment nor is it accepted as the representative of the entire bargaining unit, but it may make representations to management when its members have a complaint regarding the application of managerially determined terms and conditions or when management's actions are considered to be unfair or unreasonable. This level of recognition may be suitable if the union seeking recognition is either an inappropriate union for the whole bargaining unit and no progress can be made to secure the inclusion of other unions in the recognition process, or, as a result of the final ballot, the union is unable to achieve the necessary level of support to justify the granting of full negotiating rights.

- *Negotiating recognition*. This is the level which the recognition process is intended ultimately to achieve. The union participates fully and equally with management in the joint determination of the terms and conditions of employment which will apply to all employees in the bargaining unit. The exact range of issues over which bargaining is to be conducted is a matter for agreement between the management and claimant union – before the issue of trade union recognition is put to the final ballot of employees concerned. Whilst initially the range of issues may be restricted to the wages and conditions elements of the employment contract, over time the range may be extended through the development of joint procedures to include a wider range of topics and issues.

The ballot

In their guidance to employers on the use of ballots in union recognition the CIR emphasised that 'where the issues are not clear cut, the ballot is likely to produce a blurred and indecisive result which is at best likely to be a waste of time and effort and at worst may harm industrial relations by raising expectations which remain unfulfilled' [23]. Thus, in **preparation for the ballot,** it is imperative that any problems relating to the proposed bargaining unit, bargaining agent or level of recognition should be resolved in discussions between management and the claimant union. This will determine what question is to be put to which employees. In addition, management and union need to agree the precise wording of the ballot question(s), the conduct and administration of the ballot and how the results of the ballot are to be implemented. Immediately prior to the ballot management and union, ideally jointly, should circulate information regarding their views on recognition and any possible consequential collective bargaining arrangements to all employees involved. This may be supported by meetings, preferably in work time, between employees and both management and union (separately or jointly) to answer questions or discuss any of the issues raised in the written documents. The objective is to ensure that the employees are fully informed of the issues involved in recognition and the importance of their decision.

Neither the law, the CIR nor ACAS have been prepared to define a precise threshold **level of support** which the union should achieve in a ballot in order to be granted recognition. It is, therefore, the joint responsibility of management and union to agree a figure which will represent the target level of support. However, there is a tendency amongst some management to argue that this figure should be at least a majority, and in some cases a substantial majority of 66 per cent or 75 per cent, of the actual number of employees in the bargaining unit. This, it is argued, will demonstrate that the union has the support of a majority of the people it is seeking to represent. Nevertheless, the implication of this approach is that any non-vote represents, in effect, a vote against recognition. Therefore, it is perhaps more realistic and fair to base the target on a percentage of the votes cast, thus ensuring that abstentions count neither for nor against recognition and the result will be determined by those interested enough to vote. However, whether the percentage should be a simple majority of the votes cast (50 per cent + 1) or some other lower or higher figure is a matter for discussion and agreement between the parties. Certainly, both the CIR and ACAS have recommended recognition where the support for the union was less than 50 per cent, partly because it is clear that the degree of support, including trade union membership, normally increases once the union is recognised and able to demonstrate its ability to represent the interests of the members of the bargaining unit.

The recognition agreement

The **objective** of the recognition agreement is to establish the foundation on which future stable and long-term collective bargaining arrangements will be built. However, because the recognition of a union involves fundamental changes in attitudes, relationships and systems of handling industrial relations matters, the production of such an agreement is often time consuming and may involve considerable differences between the parties over matters of 'principle'. It is important to remember that this will be the first occasion on which management and union will have negotiated formally with each other and therefore the conduct of these negotiations, like the handling of the recognition process before it, will be significant in setting the climate for future negotiations and the long-term relationship between management and the union.

The precise content of the agreement will depend on the level of recognition to be granted to the union and the outcome of the negotiations between management and union. The agreement should, assuming that it is for full negotiating rights, cover three main areas:

Rights of management and union
Management will invariably insist that their right to manage the affairs of the organisation in the most efficient, productive and profitable manner is stated clearly in the recognition agreement and accepted by the union. Although the union's formal right to negotiate and reach agreement with management is thus generally confined to matters relating directly to terms and conditions of employment, management's 'absolute' right to manage the affairs of the organisation is often mitigated by an undertaking to inform or consult with the union when it proposes to make certain changes in the organisation or working arrangements of the employees which the union represents. In addition, management may wish, within the recognition agreement, to express its right to select, promote and reward employees on their individual merit and to determine the exact nature of the duties and responsibilities of any job. The recognition agreement should also express management's acceptance of the trade union's right to represent its members' interests. Furthermore, the agreement may, if appropriate, express management's encouragement of employees to become members of the union and actively

participate in its affairs and its agreement to provide reasonable opportunities and facilities for the representatives of the recognised union to recruit new employees. The union may request a **check-off agreement** whereby the employees' union contributions are deducted from their wages by the employer and paid direct to the union. This not only saves the union time and effort in collecting contributions but also ensures that members do not inadvertently fall into arrears and thereby cease to be members. However, if management enters into such an agreement it should:

1. advise employees that it is their personal decision whether or not they have their contributions deducted in this way;
2. obtain their written authorisation;
3. advise them that in any period during which they do not receive pay it will be their responsibility to make arrangements to maintain their contributions.

Scope and institutions of collective bargaining

The recognition agreement should identify those issues which will be subject to formal joint negotiation (such as wages and allowances, hours of work, holidays, fringe benefits, etc.) and, where appropriate, the relationship of organisational bargaining to any multi-employer national agreements. It will also be necessary for management and union to decide whether or not they wish to distinguish these issues from those which will be subject only to consultation by the establishment of separate, distinct machinery for the two processes. The establishment of separate machinery not only confirms *joint* responsibility for negotiated matters and *management* responsibility for decisions in respect of consultative matters but also, Singleton argues, allows within the consultative machinery for a 'fuller interchange of views over a wider range of subjects if it is clear at the outset that the discussion is free from any element of bargaining' [24]. The recognition agreement should also specify the disputes procedure to be applied in the event of a failure to agree being reached during negotiations and state the intention of both management and union to abide by and implement agreements reached in negotiations and that, in the event of a failure to agree, neither will undertake industrial action until the disputes procedure has been exhausted.

Shop steward's role and facilities

It is vital that the recognition agreement should detail the method by which an employee is to become formally recognised as a shop steward, how he/she should carry out the role and what facilities should be afforded. All too often management assume that they have no right to involve themselves in the **selection and accreditation** of shop stewards and that this is entirely a matter for the employees and union to decide. Whilst it is true that management should not seek to determine or even influence which employees are selected as shop stewards, nevertheless, they may jointly agree with the union certain basic rules. These may include that individuals must satisfy certain basic **qualifications** relating to length of service as an employee and member of the union before they are entitled to stand for election as a shop steward; that shop stewards will **hold the position for a defined period** after which they must stand for re-election; that once elected shop stewards will receive **formal credentials, signed by both union and management,** confirming their appointments and even that their credentials, and therefore recognition as a shop steward, may be revoked in the event of them committing gross misconduct as an employee.

Stewards remain active working members of their workgroup, plant or department and therefore must seek permission from their immediate supervisor whenever they wish to leave their place of work to conduct union business. It must be made clear that such permission will not be unreasonably withheld, but may be refused if their absence would be detrimental to the safety or operational needs of the organisation. The Code of Practice states that shop stewards should not lose pay when undertaking such duties as 'collective bargaining with the appropriate level of management; informing constituents about negotiations or consultations with management; meetings with other lay officials or with full-time union officers; . . . interviews with and on behalf of constituents on grievance and disciplinary matters; . . . appearing on behalf of constituents before an outside official body' [25]. Finally, both the agreement and credentials should include statements that shops stewards should use the appropriate procedures when representing their members, use their best endeavours to ensure that members abide by any agreement made between the union and management and, where appropriate, that they are not entitled to represent members outside their constituency.

The management should also agree with the union an **appropriate number of shop stewards** for the bargaining unit and the **defined constituencies** within which they will carry out their role (taking into account any particular circumstances such as the needs of part-time employees or shift workers). So far as is reasonably practicable, shop stewards should be provided with sufficient **facilities** to adequately carry out their role. Perhaps most importantly, and as a minimum, they should have access to a room in which to interview individual members to discuss problems; a room in which to meet collectively as shop stewards and to meet their full-time officer; and access to a telephone and notice boards [26].

16.4 Forms of recognition

The 1980s have seen the development of interest in Single Table Bargaining and Single Union Agreements as means of both rationalising union recognition and fostering a more co-operative and flexible industrial relationship, whilst the Union Membership Agreement (closed shop) has been made inoperable by legislation.

Single table bargaining

The existence of more than one bargaining unit in an organisation has been closely associated in most people's minds with the issue and problems of multi-unionism. However, it is important to remember that:

1. Where more than one union has recruited and represented the employees *within* a bargaining unit they have generally established some form of joint negotiating arrangement to undertake collective bargaining for that bargaining unit.
2. The fact that there is only one union within an organisation has not automatically meant only one bargaining unit.
3. The apparent fragmentation of collective bargaining represented by multiple bargaining units disguises management's role and success in co-ordinating the outcomes of these different negotiations.

The distinction between manual and non-manual groups, in particular, has remained strong within organisations and has been closely associated with differences in their status and terms and conditions of employment and, therefore, different bargaining units. Table 16.2 shows that a high proportion of establishments which recognise unions have only one bargaining unit for either manual or non-manual employees and a significant proportion recognise only one union within these bargaining units. The term 'single table bargaining' (STB) refers to the situation where **a single bargaining unit is established with one negotiation covering both manual and non-manual employees whilst still recognising more than one union** – in contrast to a Single Union Agreement which involves not only a single bargaining unit but also a single union. However, most STB arrangements still exclude managers above a defined level and, therefore, rarely cover *all* employees within the organisation.

It is important to recognise, according to Marginson and Sisson, that such a unification of bargaining arrangements is 'underpinned by a common pay and grading system for both manual and non-manual workers' and 'it is usual for all staff, whether manual or non-manual, to receive an annual salary paid monthly and to have the same hours, holidays, and pension and sick-pay entitlements' [27]. Clearly, therefore, any move towards rationalisation of bargaining units into single table bargaining encompassing both manual and non-manual employees is **closely inter-related with the development of single status and harmonisation** in terms and conditions of employment. Marginson and Sisson found that only a handful of organisations, principally in the private sector, have introduced STB during the 1980s

Table 16.2 *Trade union recognition and bargaining units, 1980 and 1984 (% of establishments with recognised unions)*

	All establishments		Private manufacture		Private service		Public sector	
	1980 (%)	1984 (%)	1980 (%)	1984 (%)	1980 (%)	1984 (%)	1980 (%)	1984 (%)
Manual employees:								
Only 1 recognised union	65	65	63	58	86	80	55	62
Only 1 bargaining unit	77	82	76	72	90	88	70	83
Non-manual employees:								
Only 1 recognised union	43	39	65	69	68	63	28	25
Only 1 bargaining unit	57	61	66	77	74	70	48	55

Source: N. Millward and M. Stevens, *British Workplace Industrial Relations 1980–1984*, Gower, 1986 (Tables 3.7 and 3.8).

and, from these organisational experiences, identified three **main reasons for management wishing to move to single table bargaining**:

1. To make the bargaining process more efficient and remove potential sources of conflict within the organisation.
2. To instigate changes in working practices – particularly those associated with demarcation and labour flexibility.
3. To help achieve single status or harmonisation (either as a matter of philosophy/policy or as a more pragmatic aspect of achieving changes in working practices).

In their view the pressure to remove the distinction between manual and non-manual employees, thereby increasing the possibility and even need for single table bargaining, will continue as a consequence of:

1. The impact of both UK and European legislation on
    (a) the harmonisation of non-pay aspects of conditions of employment; and
    (b) 'equal pay for work of equal value' requiring a single, integrated and coherent pay and grading system within organisations.
2. Technological developments blurring the traditional boundaries between manual and non-manual work.
3. The increasing management emphasis on securing employee involvement and commitment amongst all employees.
4. The continuing union amalgamation trend, perhaps inevitably, not only reducing the number of unions in organisations but also increasing the likelihood of manual and non-manual employees being members of the same union.

For their part, trade unions have been prepared to consider such a rationalisation of bargaining arrangements particularly if it is perceived as the only alternative to a single union arrangement (involving union competition for 'sole' recognition and consequent loss of recognition for some unions) or even, perhaps, non-unionism. Indeed, faced with the need to strengthen their position as bargaining has been decentralised, the unions have, in some cases [28], been the instigator of the move towards STB.

It may be argued that the creation of a single body at the organisation level within which to conduct employee relations allows the **development of a 'broader strategic perspective'** beyond the simple negotiation of pay and conditions. Certainly the terms of reference for the STB body are generally couched in broad terms such as 'all matters affecting employees at work' and therefore also provide 'employers with a forum to inform and consult union representatives on company plans and performance' [29] (i.e. potential integration of the processes of negotiation and consultation). Consequently, the development of STB may aid unions in extending their participation and influence into a wider range of organisational issues through more information and involvement in discussions relating to business policy and strategic issues. However, some organisations still appear to wish to differentiate the two processes of negotiation and consultation by either having different meetings or changing the people involved.

With multiple bargaining units, the unions are able to represent the distinct interests of the employees within each separate bargaining unit, leaving management, through co-ordinating its responses to the various negotiations, to ensure that consistency is maintained within the organisation as a whole. However, as with any form of joint union negotiating arrangement, **single table bargaining requires the unions to reconcile the differing and, possibly, competing interests of their various memberships** in order to present a united front to management. It involves, therefore, a transfer of 'responsibility for reconciling the different interests within a workforce from management to unions' [30]. Thus, the way in which **representation amongst the various unions on the STB body** is to be determined or allocated may become important. Clearly, if representation is allocated pro rata to the unions' membership within the organisation then the union with the largest membership is likely to dominate and the interests of smaller groups of employees may be submerged or lost. Conversely, if all the unions have equal representation irrespective of the level of their membership it may be perceived as giving undue weight, in terms of decision making, to the smaller unions. An IRS survey [31] shows a variety of practices have been adopted: some STB arrangements have simply opted for one or other of these approaches, while others have established a 'checks and balances' arrangement such as having a Joint Negotiating Committee with equal union representation but accountable to a Joint Negotiations Advisory Committee whose composition is pro rata to the union's membership level.

Certainly, Marginson and Sisson believe that 'the key significance of single-table bargaining is not that it replaces existing arrangements but that it adds a "top" tier where matters affecting all employees . . . can be discussed' and that 'failure to maintain levels of negotiation which are specific to particular groups, and which take place below the single bargaining table, can lead to frustration' [32]. Single table bargaining should not be seen as simply a process of abolishing existing separate bargaining arrangements and replacing it with one, all encompassing body. It may involve a tiered approach, with the STB body acting as the forum for negotiation, consultation and discussion of issues affecting all employees and setting general parameters for any negotiations to be conducted in relation to specific groups of employees, with this lower level negotiation being conducted as a 'sub-committee' and, therefore, accountable to the STB body.

Single union agreements

A 'single union agreement' (SUA) is a situation in which **management formally grants one union sole and exclusive recognition rights within the organisation.** This is significantly different to 'single unionism' within separate bargaining units or its evolutionary development through a process of either union amalgamation or the withering away of membership amongst other unions which had been recognised. A SUA is a formal declaration by management that part of its industrial relations strategy is (a) to have only one bargaining unit and (b) to recognise only one union within the organisation. However, the development of SUAs during the 1980s is about more than just rationalisation of recognition and bargaining arrangements – recognition is only one element of a **package of strategic industrial relations developments.** Indeed, Bassett describes them as a 'radical industrial relations package' which 'hold out . . . the prospect of stable, consensual industrial relations, and so stable company performance, allowing companies to concentrate on production, not on *ad hoc* solutions to keep it going' [33], while Gennard notes that employer interest in SUAs lies in their perceived advantage in 'providing a greater opportunity . . . to secure a more flexible, cooperative and less conflict-prone workforce' and as 'a necessary pre-condition for the development of a managerial philosophy embodying teamwork, quality consciousness and flexibility' [34].

Despite the focus which has been given to the development of SUAs during the 1980s (not least because of the publicity given to the 'no-strike' element and the friction, if not hostility, between unions over SUAs), their **introduction appears to have been limited.** One survey in 1989 [35] identified some 50 single union agreements and although initially SUAs were regarded as a feature of foreign owned, particularly Japanese, electronics companies setting up on a 'greenfield site' (where management wished to introduce a new philosophy of industrial relations), their introduction has extended into a much wider range of industries and situations; similarly, whilst their introduction was primarily associated with the EETPU (and indeed was the reason for its expulsion from the TUC), now most of the major unions have concluded SUAs. Certainly, as ACAS has pointed out, so far as new recognition is concerned 'where recognition was achieved single union arrangements almost always proved the way forward' [36] and therefore SUAs may become a more prominent feature of UK industrial relations as the most likely future management response to recognition claims.

The **SUA package** may include a number of elements in addition to 'exclusive recognition':

1. **Labour flexibility:** removal of traditional job boundaries and introduction of functional flexibility, requiring employees to transfer between jobs and/or undertake whatever task is required and within their capabilities based on increased training.
2. **Single status:** the harmonisation of terms and conditions of employment is necessary not only to support the achievement of labour flexibility but also 'to secure co-operative attitudes and some degree of common purpose and commitment from the workforce' [37]. However, as Bassett points out 'the Japanese in particular are highly status-conscious, and clearly regard *single* status as unthinkable', they 'prefer to describe their initiatives as "common terms and conditions" ' [38].
3. **Employee participation:** most SUAs provide for the establishment of some form of company Advisory Board or Council which discusses and aims to reach decisions on a consensus basis on a wide range of employee related issues (including terms and conditions of employment). However, the employee representatives on this body are 'employee' not 'union' representatives and it is only if this Advisory Board is unable to reach a consensus that the union is involved in direct negotiations with management and then, if necessary, arbitration. Thus, whilst Bassett is able to argue that 'the strong moral force of decisions reached in this way certainly predisposes the company to accept them', nevertheless he recognises that 'the unions have only a tangential impact on a structure such as this' [39].
4. **Pendulum arbitration/'no strike' provision:** most SUAs seek to remove the *need for* resort to industrial action by providing for the automatic use of arbitration to resolve such disputes. However, it is the inclusion of an additional 'no strike' clause in some SUAs (by which the union *forgoes in advance the use of* industrial action) which is regarded by some as an abandonment of a fundamental trade union principle – the right to withdraw labour.

The fact that trade unions have accepted such SUAs may be as much a reflection of their weakened position during the 1980s and their desire to secure or maintain membership as it is of any real change in industrial relations philosophy. There is little doubt that, in some cases, trade unions have accepted the inevitability of a SUA as an alternative to no union at all. However, as Gennard identifies [40] the proposed introduction of a SUA may **heighten the competition and introduce conflict between unions** by affecting traditional patterns of recruitment or representation, particularly where:

1. other unions already have membership or negotiating rights within the establishment which will be lost;
2. other unions are represented and/or have negotiating rights at other establishments of the organisation and therefore might reasonably expect a similar pattern in any new establishment;
3. another union has been recruiting and seeking recognition from the employer but has not been selected for 'sole recognition'.

Perhaps the most important concern, however, relates to the **'beauty contest' approach** which may be adopted in granting sole recognition and the implications this has for the management/union/employee relationship. An example of this approach is:

> 'the company outlined in some detail its proposed personnel philosophy and policies . . . each union was asked whether it wished to be considered for single recognition on these broad terms. . . . The prize . . . was the creation of new jobs and new union recruits in an area of very high unemployment.' The management 'held meetings with full-time officers of each union, at which the latter made detailed and in some cases highly professional presentations – including the use of videos – on their approach to employee and industrial relations. . . . As a result, two unions were shortlisted for further, more detailed discussions . . . [a union] was ultimately selected because it was felt it had the approach to relations between managers and employees and between companies and unions which was most compatible with the personnel philosophy and policies for the new unit' [41].

This shows clearly how the 'beauty contest' approach to granting sole recognition may be little different to management determining which agency should have its advertising contract. It becomes virtually a commercial contract between management and a 'labour agent', decided on the basis of which agent will meet *management's* requirement, and the continuation of the contract is dependent on the agent maintaining management support – perhaps the ultimate in management sponsorship! It is the antithesis of the traditional process of recognition which requires the union first to secure the backing of the employees by recruiting them as members before seeking the right to represent them (i.e. it is the employees who 'contract' with the union, it is *their* organisation and it is their support which is essential for the continued existence of the union within the organisation). Indeed, where the SUA is being concluded for a 'greenfield site' even before employees have been recruited, the employees will have no opportunity to express their views regarding which union they want. Although the IRS survey [42] found that two-thirds of the SUAs had union membership levels of over 70 per cent, a small minority had less than 25 per cent.

The **TUC has sought to regulate the introduction of SUAs** through a Code of Practice to supplement the general Bridlington Principles relating to 'poaching' of members. Under the Code, a union contemplating a SUA should notify the TUC who may then suggest that the union discusses the matter with other possibly interested or affected unions. In addition, unions entering into a SUA should not agree to a 'no strike' clause but this does not preclude accepting a term requiring automatic arbitration of any dispute. Perhaps, most significantly, the TUC has accepted a relaxation of the principle in respect of a union seeking to organise where another union is recognised but has only a small number of members which, as Gennard notes, could be 'significant for unions in the context of the reputedly low level of membership . . . from the single-union agreements' [43]. However, another union can only challenge the 'recognised' union if management is prepared to review its stance and accept that union recognition should be determined primarily by the wishes of the employees rather than the needs of management.

Union membership agreement

The **closed shop** was defined by McCarthy in 1964 as a situation 'in which employees come to realise that a particular job is only to be obtained and retained if they become and remain members of one of a specified number of trade unions' [44]. This reflects the relative informality of most such arrangements at that time. More recently, through the advent of legislation and greater formality, the term **Union Membership Agreement (UMA)** became more common: an agreement which 'has the effect of requiring the terms and conditions of every member of a specified class of employee to include a condition that he must be or become a member of the union(s) who are parties to the agreement' (S.30, Trade Union and Labour Relations Act (1974)).

Torrington and Chapman argue that such an arrangement may be regarded as the next 'logical step beyond recognition in establishing the union as the mode of communication with, and representation of, employees' [45]. However, it is important to recognise that there are **various types of closed shop** based on the point at which they operate in the recruitment/selection process:

1. The **post-entry** closed shop which requires an employee to join the designated union (or one of them if there is more than one designated union) within a specified period after commencing work.

2. The **pre-entry** closed shop which requires that a potential employee already be a member of the designated union(s) before being offered employment.
3. The **hiring hall arrangement,** not very prevalent in Britain, where potential employees are sought via the union office which selects, from amongst its members seeking work, those whom it will forward to the management for their consideration.

It is difficult to assess the precise **extent** of the closed shop. In 1964 McCarthy estimated that 3¾ million employees (36 per cent of trade unionists) were covered by a closed shop arrangement, of which ¾ million were in a pre-entry type of closed shop. Gennard *et al.* [46] estimated that in 1978/1979, 5.2 million employees (40 per cent of trade unionists) were covered by a closed shop, of which 1.1 million were white collar employees, and confirmed that the number covered by a pre-entry closed shop remained at about ¾ million. Certainly, in 1984 ACAS reported both a decline in the coverage of existing UMAs, primarily as a result of declining employment in the older production industries, and a slowing down in the introduction of new UMAs [47]. Figures for 1989 suggest that some 2.6 million employees (25 per cent of trade unionists) were still covered by some form of closed shop with, perhaps surprisingly, 1.3 million being in a pre-entry closed shop [48]. Metcalf argues that this 'spectacular decline . . . has been caused by the interaction of economic forces, by employers rethinking their industrial relations and by changes in the law' [49].

The closed shop is perhaps the one aspect of industrial relations on which everybody has firm, and often emotive, opinions. As Hanson *et al.* point out 'those who dislike the closed shop in principle may prefer to use the term "compulsory unionism", emphasising the coercive element of the closed shop, while those who see it as a perfectly reasonable way of enabling trade unions to achieve some degree of organisational strength may prefer to talk about "union security" ' [50].

In addition to any argument that the closed shop restricts management's ability to recruit and select whom it wishes, the major **arguments against** closed shop arrangements in general centre on its effect on the individual employee and the power it gives to trade unions:

1. The requirement that an employee should have to join a trade union in order to obtain or maintain employment is regarded as an **infringement of some basic right of individual liberty.** This was certainly reflected in the government's Green Paper (1981) which concluded that the principle 'that people should be required to join a trade union as a condition of getting or holding a job runs contrary to the general traditions of personal liberty in this country' [51]. However, this argument seems to ignore the fact that an employee's individual liberty is already 'infringed' by the contract of employment. The terms of that contract include working under the control

of the employer, accepting management's instructions and giving 'honest and faithful' service. The requirement to join a trade union, certainly for new employees, may be argued to be no more than a further term of the contract of employment which they must consider, as with other terms, when they decide whether to accept the offer of employment. The central issue would appear to be whether, within a modern industrial society, the employee's obligations to management should still be regarded as fundamentally distinct from any obligation to the union or fellow employees or whether they are both equal parts of a package of requirements which it is reasonable to expect the employee to accept in return for his wages.

2. The **use of coercion to secure membership is regarded as contrary to the principle of voluntary association** which is presumed to underlie trade unionism. Trade unions should confine their activities to securing 100 per cent trade union membership through persuasion and a positive demonstration of their advantages. However, this argument appears to ignore the fact that 'control' and 'coercion' are as much a part of a trade union's organisation and government as 'representation' and 'responsiveness'. The fraternalistic nature of trade unionism requires that individual members may need, and if necessary be pressured, to subordinate their immediate personal interests and goals in preference to the objectives and needs of the total membership or the union as an organisation. The principle of the use of coercion is not contrary to the principles of trade unionism – the issue is whether such coercion should be confined to the internal management of its members once they have been recruited by voluntary means or whether it may be utilised externally to obtain members in the same way that it is used externally against management in collective bargaining.

3. The closed shop **increases trade union power in collective bargaining** by making any instruction for industrial action 100 per cent effective. However, it may be counter-argued that such power is no more, and some would argue less, than the power of management to lock out employees or even close the organisation permanently. More importantly, such power may, in reality, be illusory. More than one shop steward or union officer has claimed that it is better, and just as powerful, to have 60–70 per cent committed trade unionists than it is to have 100 per cent nominal members which includes a significant minority who may not, at heart, be in sympathy with trade union ideals. The extent to which trade union power is increased by the existence of a closed shop will, in practice, depend on the nature of the membership, the product and technology of the organisation and the position of the union's membership within the production or service process.

4. It is argued, from the point of view of internal union government, that the closed shop **allows the union the opportunity to take its membership for granted.** Once management has agreed to the establishment of a closed shop the union's recruitment task is accomplished virtually for ever unless it is subject to periodic reapproval. Certainly, Allen believed that compulsory unionism could 'remove the one check on the authority of trade union

leaders which operates automatically and which ensures that the democratic mechanism in trade unionism is used to the best advantage' [52] – namely, to leave the union. However, if a large enough group of employees became dissatisfied and resigned from their union, management is unlikely to implement the terms of the closed shop by dismissing them; rather they are likely to seek a reconciliation between the union and its dissident members or terminate the agreement.

5. There is the implication that **employees may lose their job if they openly disagree with union policy or alienate its officials.** However, for such a situation to arise the employee must first be expelled from the union. It is rare, and certainly against 'natural justice', for a member to be expelled simply because he/she has voiced dissatisfaction with union policy or officials, or sought to persuade others through the proper union channels. However, expulsion may result if the dispute with the union is conducted in an unconstitutional and disruptive manner. The most likely situation in which a member will be expelled is when he/she continues to work in defiance of a union instruction to strike. (During the 1984 NCB/NUM dispute a number of 'working areas' sought and obtained court injunctions to stop the NUM from taking such disciplinary action against them.)

The **arguments in favour** of the closed shop are based, Hanson *et al.* argue, on a belief in 'the social utility of strong labour unions' [53]. Similarly, McCarthy suggested coercion and restriction of individual 'liberty' are utilised 'to assist in the maintenance and improvement of the unions' powers of job regulation, and in order to make possible greater opportunities for group protection and advancement' [54]. He argued that the demand for a closed shop represented an 'additional readiness' by union members to take action against non-unionists arising from difficulties in organising the labour force (membership function), difficulties in controlling the labour force (discipline function) and/or the desire to control alternative labour (entry control function). Thus, it may be regarded as an **instrument for trade union security** which management is forced to accept by the threat or actual use of strike action.

However, Dunn, in seeking to explain the growth of the closed shop during the 1970s in new industries and occupations, suggested three possible explanations:

1. Although its spread 'can be linked with growing union militancy in an increasingly hostile environment', it also 'has been associated with a managerial search for order and stability under the same conditions' [55].
2. The establishment of a closed shop was, in fact, relatively inconsequential for both union and management; it was the 'final piece of the jigsaw' of which 'the crucial pieces . . . are union recognition, the acknowledgement by management that stewards should have formal status and take responsibility for negotiations over wages and

conditions, the conclusion of a comprehensive domestic agreement' [56]. He cites, as possible evidence for this, the fact that management had not sought to use the negotiation of a closed shop as an opportunity to deal with multi-unionism and that unions appeared to have been ready not to coerce existing non-unionists to join.

3. The establishment of a closed shop 'has become a kind of ritual through which workers express good trade union principles' and 'a symbol of those principles rather than an instrument to solve certain practical problems of organisation and discipline' [57].

He concluded that all three explanations may be reconciled within a framework of 'mature industrial relations' in which the closed shop becomes 'the joint property of management and unions, its growth stimulated by values shared by trade union officials and industrial relations managers concerning order and conformity to which shop floor and individual values should be subjugated' [58].

The closed shop **confirms the position of the union**, provides it with a greater sense of organisational security and alleviates any perceived need on its part to act aggressively in its dealings with management in order to recruit and maintain its membership. The increased **union control and authority**, achieved as a result of the closed shop, may be exercised to ensure that the membership observe the terms of any agreement made on their behalf with management. Furthermore, management is able to dispense with any special procedural or consultative arrangements for non-unionists within the bargaining unit, thus confirming the union(s) as the primary channel, together with the normal line management system, for communication and representation between management and employees.

At the same time, the establishment of a closed shop removes, what is often referred to as, the **free rider:** an employee who is not a member of the union, and therefore does not contribute to it, but nevertheless receives the improvements in wages and conditions negotiated by the union. The alternative, which would be unacceptable to both union and members for fear of creating a pool of cheap non-union labour, would be to restrict wage increases and other improvements exclusively to union members. It is this group of employees who may become the focus of attention at times of industrial action – particularly if they, with or without management encouragement, seek to continue working or avoid the financial hardship being experienced by the union members.

The legal provisions of the 1980s differ in one fundamental respect from the earlier attempt at legislative regulation under the Industrial Relations Act (1971). The earlier legislation sought to **directly regulate** what were then termed 'agency shops' or 'approved closed shops' by establishing a statutory procedure (similar to that for recognition) which could be invoked by unions when an employer refused to grant a closed shop voluntarily. This procedure specified not only the level of approval required in a ballot of employees before such a closed shop would be granted (a simple majority of those eligible to vote or two-thirds of those voting) but also that an existing closed shop could be challenged if 20 per cent of the employees signified such a desire. The 1980s legislation has sought **indirectly to regulate** the closed shop; initially by specifying the conditions under which it will be deemed to be unfair to dismiss an employee for not being a member of a trade union. The apparent need for such legislation was highlighted by three British Rail employees who, having been dismissed in 1976 following the introduction of a UMA, eventually obtained a ruling from the European Court of Human Rights that their dismissal had been contrary to the European Convention on Human Rights.

The legislation has been introduced in several stages:

1. Initially, under the **Employment Acts (1980 and 1982)**, the government sought to regulate the operation of UMAs and provide protection for those who did not wish to be a member of a trade union by making it an unfair dismissal if the employer dismissed an employee for not being a member of a trade union if:

    (a) the employee genuinely objected on grounds of conscience or other deeply held personal conviction to being a member of any trade union whatsoever or of a particular trade union (S.7(2) 1980 Act);

    (b) the employee had been among those employees who belong to the class to which the union membership agreement related since before the agreement and had not at any time while the agreement had that effect been a member of a trade union in accordance with the agreement (S.7(2) 1980 Act);

    (c) the union membership agreement had not been approved by an employee ballot during the previous five years in which either not less than 80 per cent of those entitled to vote or not less than 85 per cent of those who voted were in favour (S.3 1982 Act).

    At the same time:

    (d) trade unions could be 'joined' in any dismissal proceedings if they sought to induce such an unfair dismissal by threatening or organising industrial action (S.7 1982 Act) and the individual was given protection against being unreasonably denied admission or expelled from a union (S.4(2) 1980 Act);

    (e) the level of compensation that could be awarded for such unfair dismissals was increased substantially above that for 'normal' unfair dismissals;

    (f) the accompanying Code of Practice encouraged an 'anti-UMA' approach by employers by stating that 'employers are under no obligation to agree to the introduction or continuation of a closed shop, notwithstanding that it has been endorsed in a ballot of employees' [59] and that the legally specified minimum level of support for the approval of a UMA 'does not prevent an employer from deciding that the required majority should be higher . . . or that there must be minimum percentage turnout' [60]. ACAS declined to be involved in drawing up this Code of Practice on the grounds that it would impair its impartiality.

2. The Government then, under the **Employment Act (1988):**
    (a) made the 'post-entry' UMA unenforceable by repealing the earlier constraints and replacing it with an automatic and blanket presumption of unfairness to dismiss an employee for non-membership of a trade union (S.11 1988 Act);
    (b) reduced the trade union's power to enforce a UMA by removing immunity from any action intended to pressure an employer to dismiss (post-entry) or not employ (pre-entry) a person who is not a member of a union (S.10 1988 Act).

3. Finally, under the **Employment Act (1990)**, the government has made the pre-entry closed shop inoperable by making it unlawful to refuse employment on the grounds that the person is not a member of a union or is unwilling to become a member of a union (S.1 1990 Act). (This is the effect of the wider non-discrimination in recruitment in respect of both membership or non-membership of a union set out in S.1.)

16.5 Summary propositions

- Trade union recognition is not a single event but a dynamic process.
- A logical and consistent approach by management in responding to claims for union recognition at the workplace provides the basis for avoiding multi-unionism and disorderly collective bargaining arrangements.
- The Recognition Agreement may be distinguished from other agreements affecting the employer/employee relationship in that it defines the character and extent of the interorganisational relationship between the company and union.
- The 1980s have seen a shift in the emphasis of recognition from supporting collectivism and union power (through the Union Membership Agreement) to supporting organisational co-operation and flexibility (through Single Table Bargaining and Single Union Agreements).

Further reading

- C. Hanson, S. Jackson and D. Miller, *The Closed Shop*, Gower, 1982. This provides a useful comparison of the extent, operation and legislative environment of the closed shop in Britain, the USA and Germany.

- B. Towers, *A Handbook of Industrial Relations Practice*, Kogan Page, 1989. Deals with the practicalities of coming to terms with trade union recognition.
- P. Bassett, *Strike Free: New industrial relations in Britain*, Macmillan, 1987. This provides a useful examination of both the background and nature of Single Union Agreements.

References

1. D. Torrington and J. Chapman, *Personnel Management* (2nd edn), Prentice Hall, 1983, p. 153.
2. N. Singleton, Industrial Relations Procedures, *DE Manpower Paper 14*, HMSO, 1975, p. 5.
3. B. Towers, 'Trends and developments in industrial relations: derecognising trade unions: implications and consequences', *Industrial Relations Journal*, vol. 19, no. 3, 1988, p. 184.
4. P. Bassett, 'Non-unionism's growing ranks', *Personnel Management*, March 1988, pp. 44–7.
5. N. Millward and M. Stevens, *British Workplace Industrial Relations 1980–1984*, Gower, 1986, pp. 50–95.
6. *ibid.*, p. 64.
7. *ibid.*, p. 65.
8. T. Claydon, 'Union derecognition in Britain in the 1980s', *British Journal of Industrial Relations*, vol. 27, no. 2, 1989.
9. *ibid.*
10. ACAS, *Annual Report 1990*, p. 11–12.
11. T. Claydon, *op. cit.*
12. *ibid.*
13. *ibid.*
14. B. Towers, *op. cit.*, p. 184.
15. B. Townley, 'Union recognition: a comparative analysis of the pros and cons of a legal procedure', *British Journal of Industrial Relations*, vol. 25, no. 2, 1987, pp. 177–99.
16. ACAS, *Annual Report 1986*, p. 26.
17. ACAS, *Annual Report 1987*, p. 20.
18. K. Hawkins, *A Handbook of Industrial Relations Practice*, Kogan Page, 1979, p. 51.
19. R. Price and G. S. Bain, 'Union growth in Britain: retrospect and prospect', *British Journal of Industrial Relations*, vol. XXI, no. 1, 1983.
20. Quoted in K. Hawkins, *op. cit.*, p. 52.
21. D. Torrington and J. Chapman, *op. cit.*, p. 156.
22. CIR, *Trade Union Recognition: CIR Experience*, HMSO, 1974, p. 3.
23. CIR, *Ballots and Union Recognition: A guide for employers*, HMSO, 1974, p. 8.
24. N. Singleton, *op. cit.*, p. 11.
25. ACAS, 'Time Off for Trade Union Duties and Activities', *Code of Practice* 3, p. 4.
26. 'Union Facilities', *IDS Study No. 482*, May 1991.

27. P. Marginson and K. Sisson, 'Single table talk', *Personnel Management*, May 1990, p. 46.
28. 'Single-table bargaining – a survey', *IRS Employment Trends*, no. 463, May 1990, pp. 5–11.
29. *ibid.*, p. 10.
30. *ibid.*, p. 5.
31. *ibid.*, p. 9.
32. P. Marginson and K. Sisson, *op. cit.*, pp. 49, 48.
33. P. Bassett, *Strike Free: new industrial relations in Britain*, Macmillan, 1987, p. 90.
34. J. Gennard, 'Motives for and incidence of seeking Single-union Agreements' in B. Towers (ed.), *Handbook of Industrial Relations Practice*, Kogan Page, 1989, p. 248.
35. 'Single union deals', *IRS Employment Trends*, no. 442, June 1989, pp. 5–11.
36. ACAS, *Annual Report 1986*.
37. P. Bassett, *op. cit.*, p. 101.
38. *ibid.,*, p. 100.
39. *ibid.*, pp. 102–3, 105.
40. J. Gennard, *op. cit.*
41. C. Yeandle and J. Clark, 'Growing a compatible IR set-up', *Personnel Management*, July 1989, pp. 37–8.
42. *IRS Employment Trends*, no. 442, *op. cit.*
43. J. Gennard, *op. cit.*, p. 258.
44. W. E. J. McCarthy, *The Closed Shop in Britain*, Blackwell, 1964.
45. D. Torrington and J. Chapman, *op. cit.*, p. 157.
46. J. Gennard, S. Dunn and M. Wright, 'The extent of closed shop arrangements in British industry', *Department of Employment Gazette*, January 1980, pp. 16–22.
47. ACAS, *Annual Report 1984*, p. 10.
48. M. Stevens, N. Millward and D. Smart, 'Trade union membership and the closed shop in 1989', *Employment Gazette*, November 1989, pp. 615–23.
49. D. Metcalf, 'Can the closed shop ban open new doors for unions?', *Personnel Management*, September 1989, p. 33.
50. C. Hanson *et al.*, *The Closed Shop*, Gower, 1982, pp. 8–9.
51. *Trade Union Immunities*, HMSO, 1981, p. 66.
52. V. L. Allen, *Power in Trade Unions*, Longman, 1954, p. 59.
53. C. Hanson *et al.*, *op. cit.*, p. 9.
54. W. E. J. McCarthy, *op. cit.*, p. 260.
55. S. Dunn, 'The growth of the post-entry closed shop in Britain since the 1960s: some theoretical considerations', *British Journal of Industrial Relations*, vol. XIX, no. 3, 1981, p. 281.
56. *ibid.*, p. 283.
57. *ibid.*, p. 289.
58. *ibid.*, p. 293.
59. Department of Employment, *Code of Practice – Closed Shop Agreements and Arrangements*, HMSO, 1983, p. 11.
60. *ibid.*, p. 17.

Chapter 17

Negotiation

17.1 Definition

Unfortunately, and confusingly, the terms 'collective bargaining' and 'negotiation' often appear to be used synonymously. It is perhaps more useful to regard negotiations as part of collective bargaining. The term 'collective bargaining' emphasises the structural/institutional arrangements of industrial relations and encompasses the parties, goals, environments, and content as well as the processes utilised in resolving the conflict of interest between management and employees. The process of negotiating has been described by Walton and McKersie as 'the deliberate interaction of two or more complex social units which are attempting to define or redefine the terms of their interdependence' [1]; by Gottschalk as 'an occasion where one or more representatives of two or more parties interact in an explicit attempt to reach a jointly acceptable position on one or more divisive issues' [2]; by Brown as 'an intentional activity carried out between representatives whose role is legitimized by those whom they represent' [3]. The term 'negotiation' is applied specifically to:

> **the inter-personal process used by representatives or management and employees/union, within the various institutional arrangements of collective bargaining, in order to resolve their differences and reach agreement.**

The essential characteristics of a negotiation are:

1. it is an explicit and deliberate event;
2. it is conducted by representatives on behalf of their principals;
3. the process is intended to reconcile differences between the parties involved; and
4. the outcome is dependent, at least in part, on the perceived relative power relationship between the participants.

It is important to recognise, however, first that the process of negotiation takes place both within the management and employee/union groupings as well as between them and, secondly, that it is just as likely to occur between an individual shop steward and supervisory management at the department/section level in the context of handling grievances and discipline as it is to be utilised by senior management, personnel specialists and union full-time officers at the organisational level in the context of the annual wage agreement or other major issues.

17.2 The negotiator

The negotiator, whether as an individual or as part of a negotiating team, is carrying out a task on behalf of an interest group. It is only by interacting with negotiators representing other interest groups that a reconciliation of the groups' differing interests can be achieved. A negotiator must, through the process of negotiation, seek to become as aware of the goals, aspirations and strategies of the other interest groups as his/her own.

The psychological basis of negotiation

It may be argued that the **relative real power advantage** between management and employees is a more important determinant of the final outcome of any negotiations than the skills and abilities of the individual negotiators [4]. Indeed, some would say that, because management's ability to withhold employment permanently by closing the organisation is seen as a far more powerful sanction than the employees' limited ability to withold their labour only on a temporary basis, management has an inherent power advantage in all negotiations and is able to determine both the issues and limits of any negotiation. Negotiations may be regarded as merely a facade of marginal issues and gains. However, if the underlying assumption (that management is prepared at all times and for any reason to close its organisation permanently) is untrue then the real power balance between the two parties must be regarded as being both more balanced, and at the same time more variable from one negotiation to another, with both management and employees being prepared to accept the short-term, temporary closure of the organisation as a means of exerting pressure on each other.

Torrington and Chapman note that whilst the 'power of the two parties may not actually be equal . . . they are both willing to behave as if it is' [5]. However, this apparent 'power equalisation' within the negotiation process will only exist if there is the desire, on both sides, to take account of the needs of the opposing interest group and seek an agreement which is mutually acceptable. It is the **perceived relative bargaining advantage** which is important in conditioning both the behaviour of the negotiators and the outcome of their negotiations. This may be expressed in the following way:

A. Management's perceived bargaining advantage $= \dfrac{\text{Their perception of costs to union/employees of not agreeing to management's offer}}{\text{Their perception of costs to union/employees of agreeing to management's offer}}$

Union/employees' perceived bargaining advantage $= \dfrac{\text{Their perception of costs to management of not agreeing to union's claim}}{\text{Their perception of costs to management of agreeing to union's claim}}$

B. Perceived relative bargaining power $= \dfrac{\text{Management's perceived bargaining advantage}}{\text{Union/employees' perceived bargaining advantage}}$

Thus, bargaining advantage is expressed in terms of each side's perception of the relative costs to the other side of agreeing or not agreeing (A above). For example, management will perceive itself to have a bargaining advantage if it believes the costs, to the union and employees, of not agreeing to its offer outweigh the costs of agreeing. Generally these costs are difficult to quantify. In addition to assessing the potential financial cost to union and employees of undertaking industrial action to secure an improved offer, management must also 'cost' such items as the failure of the union negotiators to meet their members' expectations and their desire to maintain credibility with their members. It is possible, on this basis, for both sides to enter a negotiation with a perceived bargaining advantage over the other. These initial perceptions of bargaining advantage, and therefore the perceived relative bargaining power (B above), will be refined during the course of the negotiations as more information regarding the objectives and strategies of both parties becomes available.

Magenau and Pruitt [6] put forward **a model of negotiating behaviour** based on three variables: the motivation of the negotiator to maintain a demand (MD) or to reach an agreement (MA) and the level of trust between the negotiators (see Figure 17.1). They argue that the strength of the motivation to maintain a demand is determined by the perception of relative bargaining power and the level of aspiration underlying the demand, whilst the strength of the motivation to reach an agreement is determined by the perceived value of the agreement and the urgency with which it is sought. It is the balance between these two motivations, related to the level of trust between the negotiators, which produces different negotiating behaviour. Thus, even where there is high trust, if the motivation to maintain a demand significantly exceeds the motivation to reach an agreement (MD > MA) the likely outcome is the adoption of distributive bargaining behaviour based on

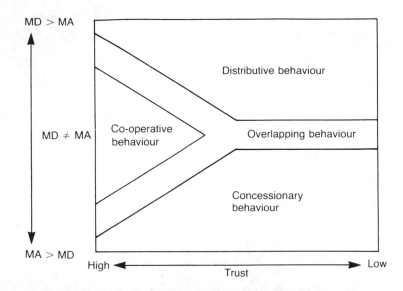

Figure 17.1 *A model of negotiating behaviour*
Source: J. M. Magenan and D. G. Pruitt, 'The social psychology of bargaining', in G. M. Stephenson and C. J. Brotherton (eds), *Industrial Relations: A social psychological approach*, John Wiley, 1979, p. 204

coercion of the other party. If, on the other hand, the motivation to reach an agreement significantly exceeds the motivation to maintain the demand (MA > MD) the behaviour pattern adopted is likely to be concessionary. However, it is in the middle area, where motivation to maintain the demand and motivation to reach an agreement are approximately equal, that 'neither distributive behaviour nor simple concession-making seems appropriate, and the bargainer takes coordinative initiatives to the extent that he trusts the other' [7]. Most negotiations take place in, or move towards, this centre area and are medium trust relationships. Consequently it is not unusual to find all three types of behaviour being displayed within a single negotiation.

The existence of a desire on the part of both parties to reach a mutually satisfactory conclusion to their negotiations does not preclude the **threat, or use, of industrial sanctions** by either party. Indeed, Hawkins argues that 'the ability of each side to apply sanctions is a fundamental aspect of their bargaining power' [8], as is, therefore, the accompanying feeling of duress it may create in the other side. The use of threats during negotiations, whether implicit or explicit, may be regarded as part of the necessary flow of information between negotiators in order to arrive at a common view of their relative bargaining advantage. If the threat is unsuccessful in achieving this common view, because the recipient implicitly rejects its validity or strength, the party making the threat must then decide whether to demonstrate its validity and strength by carrying out the threat. The perceived relative bargaining advantage will then be confirmed or modified by whether or not the sanction is imposed and, if it is, the effect it has. The use of threats and their implementation are intended as a demonstration and confirmation by one party that their perception of the relative bargaining advantage is correct, and also to produce a changed perception in the other party and therefore a settlement more favourable to themselves. They are not, generally, used as an attempt to impose one party's initial position on the other.

The successful conclusion of a negotiation is largely dependent on the negotiators' assessment or judgement of the other party's position and intention. This will be derived from the negotiators' **perception of what is said and how it is said.** In this context it is important to remember that perception is reality and therefore, as Warr points out, 'habits, expectations, attitudes and prejudices . . . affect what we see and the conclusions we draw' [9]. Not only will negotiators for different interest groups interpret data and arguments in different ways during the course of the negotiations but different members of the same negotiating team may interpret the course and outcome of the negotiations differently dependent on their perceptions, recall and emphasis. Furthermore, negotiations involve an interpersonal process between the negotiators which overlays the interorganisational aspect inherent in their representational role. Certainly Warr emphasises that the perception of the negotiators comprises a mixture of 'emotional, feeling reactions with conclusions drawn from factual information' [10]. The manner of the negotiators and their personal relationships, therefore, may be as influential as facts and arguments in determining the outcome of a negotiation.

All negotiations involve some degree of **pressure or stress for the negotiators.** Such pressures may arise not only from the difficulties inherent in seeking to identify how a compromise may be achieved but also from such additional pressures as extremely long or complex negotiating sessions, the imposition of 'unreasonable' time constraints within which a settlement has to be reached, the perceived high cost of a 'wrong' decision, perceived 'unreasonable' demands being exerted on the negotiator by either his/her principals or the other negotiator, or even a desire on the part of the negotiator to be seen to 'succeed'. Warr believes that on such 'occasions when balanced, complex judgement is required, psychologically we close up under tension and fall back on simpler all-or-nothing reactions' [11]. The hardening of attitudes and positions resulting from such pressures are counter to the flexibility generally required from negotiators in order to establish areas of compromise. If negotiators perceive themselves to be under such pressure it is likely to be communicated to the other negotiator by subjecting them in turn to demands which may begin to be perceived as being 'unreasonable' and may result in a 'take it or leave it' conclusion to the negotiation.

Warr argues that in order to achieve a mutually satisfactory compromise negotiators must 'persuade, cajole and coerce each other to move their positions closer together' [12]. Most negotiators, whilst recognising the **necessity of making concessions** by moving away from their initial position, are nevertheless often hesitant to make such moves and may even regard them as tantamount to a loss on their part. This perception of concessions equating to loss may arise in two ways:

1. Once a concession is offered it cannot easily be withdrawn and therefore tactically it represents a reduction in the bargaining zone and limits the negotiator's scope for any further concessions on that issue.
2. It may be regarded as conveying a loss of image and prestige in the eyes of the other negotiator who may be encouraged to stand firm in anticipation of further concessions to come.

This latter loss may be felt most when the negotiator has maintained a position for some time during the negotiations, has developed a range of arguments to substantiate that position and has resisted any suggestions from the other negotiator that the stance should be modified. To overcome the apparent losses engendered by making concessions the negotiator may seek to make the concession offer conditional upon a successful conclusion being reached on all issues within the negotiations, or conditional upon an 'equal' concession coming from the other party on the same or another issue, or may minimise the extent of the concession, and therefore minimise any potential loss, and regard it as the prelude to a process of mutual concessions wherein more significant concessions (losses) may be made but only on a reciprocated basis.

Task of the negotiator

Negotiators are acting, in a representative capacity, as the link between principals who themselves never meet. The **objective of the negotiator** is, therefore, to reach an agreement which is mutually acceptable not only to the negotiators involved but also to the principals they represent and which, in the light of the circumstances prevailing at the time, secures the maximum possible advantage to their interest group.

The **elements of the negotiator's task** may be set out as follows:

1. To provide advice to his/her principals on, and subsequently prepare, the initial bargaining objectives and strategy for the interest group.
2. To arrange and conduct negotiating meetings.
3. To state, explain and defend the interest group's case.
4. To listen to, investigate and seek to understand the other party's case.

5. To assess, within the predefined strategy and in the light of information gained during the negotiation, when to adjust or confirm positions and/or when to exert pressure on the other party's negotiator to modify positions.
6. To inform, advise and consult with his/her principals on the progress of the negotiations and, if necessary, revise the objectives and strategy of the interest group.
7. To seek to influence the other party's negotiator, and through this the other party's principals, to modify their position.
8. To maintain an effective and continuing personal relationship with the other party's negotiator.

Kniveron has classified the **skills required by a negotiator**, in seeking to carry out these tasks, under three headings [13]:

1. **Social interpersonal skills.** These allow the negotiator to recognise, interpret and utilise both the verbal and non-verbal communications which are an essential part of any negotiation. The negotiator must pay close attention not only to what is said but also to the manner in which it is said, and equally to what is not said. It is these 'clues' which aid the negotiator to interpret and assess the attitudes and strength of feeling of the other party and, from this, make judgements as to what is, and is not, important within the context of that negotiation. Facial expressions, the words and phrases used and, if the negotiation comprises more than one person on each side, who says what all provide important information for determining real, as opposed to stated, positions and for indicating areas of possible concession and compromise.
2. **Information handling skills.** The negotiator must be fully conversant with the issues under negotiation and the context within which they are to be negotiated. In the initial preparation phase, the negotiator must decide what information will be required, how it is to be presented and within what framework of argument and justification. During the negotiating encounter the negotiator must have sufficient knowledge and flexibility in its use to be able to respond readily to points or counterarguments raised by the other party.
3. **Discretionary judgement skills.** The negotiator must, as the representative of an interest group, make judgements regarding the implementation of the predetermined strategy and in particular determining when and how changes in arguments and position should take place. Kniveron argues that ultimately it is the negotiator's responsibility 'to assess all aspects of the information content and social skills experience, and estimate whether the solution is the best that could be reached in the circumstances, and to assess whether it will be acceptable to the parties represented' [14].

The negotiating 'team'

The concept of negotiation being a team, rather than individual, activity may be applied at **two levels:**

1. The activities of the negotiator result from a **system of interaction between negotiator and principals** (see Figure 17.2). At this level, the 'team' includes roles which, whilst they are not direct participants in the negotiating encounter, nevertheless establish the boundaries of the negotiation and the negotiator's authority and ultimately approve and control the negotiating activities.
2. Many negotiating encounters involve **more than one representative on each side** and therefore the actions of each member of the negotiating team need to be carried out within defined roles and co-ordinated within the overall bargaining strategy.

Relations between negotiator and principals

Walton and McKersie note that the negotiator occupies a key role which 'makes decisions about strategy and tactics and ... exercises influence regarding the objectives pursued but ... ultimately must account to his principals' [15]. Ultimately the **principals** controlling all negotiations, and negotiators, within the organisation are the union members and senior management. At the organisational level, whilst the management negotiating team generally is directly accountable to its principals (senior management), the union negotiating team may only be indirectly responsible to its principals (union members) through a Joint Shop Stewards Committee. At the departmental level the reverse is often the case with the shop steward being directly accountable to the members and the supervisor or manager only being responsible to senior management through a superior.

Walton and McKersie, in their study of the bargaining process, used the phrase **intra-organisational bargaining** to describe the relationship between negotiator and principals. This relationship involves reconciling not only differing views within the interest group (factional conflict) but also differences between the negotiator and the interest group (role boundary conflict).

Factional conflict arises because of the heterogeneous nature of both the management and union/employees groups on whose behalf the negotiation is conducted. There may be differences not only over the **objectives** to be pursued and the **priorities** to be attached to them but also over the **means** to be adopted to achieve them. Whilst this form of intra-organisational bargaining is perhaps most clearly evident within the union/employees interest group, particularly within a Joint Shop Stewards Committee where each shop steward represents a potentially different interest subgroup and to whom the union negotiating team is accountable for the final agreement that

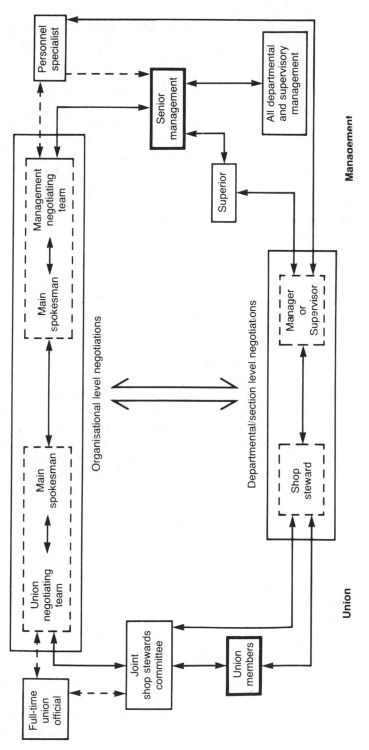

Figure 17.2 *Negotiating relationships*

is reached, it is also an integral part of the development of a corporate bargaining strategy on the management side. In wage bargaining factional conflict may involve issues such as whether the same pay increase should be applied to all grades rather than certain grades, such as skilled workers, receiving a higher increase; whether a pay increase should be pursued at the expense, if necessary, of a reduction in the length of the working week; whether a pay increase should be linked to improvements in productivity; whether industrial action should be undertaken or resisted in order to secure what is perceived to be a reasonable level of settlement. Negotiators cannot isolate themselves from this area of conflict because they are bound 'to prefer (or see a necessity for) a position which differs from that of some elements' [16] of the interest group they represent.

Walton and McKersie argue that **role boundary conflict** arises primarily because the 'negotiators for the two parties have a relationship with each other not shared or valued by their respective principals' [17] and that, as a consequence, the negotiator may conflict with his/her principals when he/she 'cannot, or prefers not to, ignore the demands and expectations of his opponent' [18]. Negotiators therefore experience role conflict because they are unable to satisfy the other negotiator's expectations of their role whilst at the same time satisfying the expectations of their own principals. In essence, negotiators may be confronted by a difference between the expectations of their principals and what they believe, in the light of their past knowledge and experience of the other party and their assessment of the current negotiation, to be realistically obtainable within a mutually acceptable solution. Walton and McKersie divide the principals' expectations of the negotiator between **substantive expectations** relating to the issues and content of the negotiation and **behavioural expectations** concerned with the attitude and approach to be adopted by the negotiator during the course of the negotiation and suggest that the negotiator may respond to the perceived role conflict by conforming to, ignoring or seeking to modify either or both of these sets of expectations (see Figure 17.3).

They argue that certain **response strategies** are not available to the negotiator:

1. Any strategy involving modifying the principals' behavioural expectations of the negotiator is not feasible in the short time scale of most negotiations.
2. A strategy involving conformity with the principals' substantive expectations will not allow the necessary latitude to the negotiator to resolve the inter-organisational conflict with the other interest group's negotiator.
3. A strategy which involves ignoring both the principals' substantive and behavioural expectations may lead to the negotiator's complete loss of credibility and possible rejection and replacement by another negotiator.

Response to
principals' substantive expectations

		Modify	Ignore	Conform
Response to principals' behavioural expectations	**Modify**	Not feasible	Not feasible	Not feasible and not acceptable
	Ignore	Direct pressure for change from the negotiator	Negotiator likely to be rejected by principals	Not acceptable
	Conform	Indirect pressure for change from negotiation process	Change sought after negotiation complete	Not acceptable

Figure 17.3 *Negotiator's response to role conflict*
Source: R. E. Walton and R. B. McKersie, *A Behavioral Theory of Labor Negotiations*, McGraw-Hill, 1965, p. 304)

Thus, the negotiator has, in effect, only three viable alternatives:

1. Ignore the principals' behavioural expectations which are an integral support to their substantive expectations and directly confront them in order to argue for a modification and reduction in their substantive expectations to a level which the negotiator believes will allow a mutually acceptable solution to be reached in the inter-organisational negotiations.
2. Continue to give the appearance of conforming to the principals' behavioural expectations and allow the indirect pressure of the apparent intransigence of the other interest group to change the principals' substantive expectations of what is achievable.
3. Ignore the principals' substantive expectations during the negotiation and, after its conclusion, minimise the apparent losses sustained in the principals' substantive expectations by justifying the settlement on the grounds that it was the best that could be achieved in the circumstances.

It is on the basis that 'the negotiator usually gains a realistic view of the situation considerably in advance' [19] of the principals, that Walton and McKersie maintain that the **purpose of intra-organisational bargaining** is to bring 'the expectations of principals into alignment with those of the chief negotiator' [20]. The formal **mandate** within which negotiators are required to carry out their task, and which therefore defines their degree of autonomy by identifying when they should refer matters back to the principals for further consideration, is the result of such intra-organisational bargaining.

Team negotiations

It may be argued that the varied nature of both the task and skill of the negotiator is made easier if there is more than one representative present at the negotiating encounter. It affords the opportunity for **role and skill specialisation**, particularly between information handling/analysis skills and social/presentation skills. It is possible to identify a number of distinct roles which may be undertaken by different members of the team:

1. Negotiator – main spokesperson and controller of the team.
2. Recorder – notes what is said and the reactions of the opposing team.
3. Analyst – prepares information, considers strengths and weaknesses in both cases, examines implications and effects of concessions.
4. Specialist – provides detailed knowledge and experience of the issue under negotiation.

It is important that each member of the negotiation team is aware both of their own role and that of the other members right from the preparation stage. For example, the recorder and analyst roles generally play little part in the actual interchange within the negotiation encounter but supply information for use by the negotiator role.

Whilst the involvement of more than one person may strengthen the negotiations, it is also a potential source of weakness. The existence of differing personalities and perceptions within the negotiating team may increase the opportunity for the opposition to identify, and then utilise, any factional conflict which exists. It is vital, therefore, that **control** is exercised by the negotiator role over all members of the team to ensure that the roles are supportive of one another and combine to present an integrated corporate stance. The individual members of the team must only enter the formal and informal interchanges within the negotiating encounter with the prior knowledge and consent of the co-ordinating negotiator role. Any disagreements within the team should not be expressed in the presence of the opposition but reserved for debate during any adjournment.

17.3 The negotiating encounter

The negotiating encounter usually involves a number of distinct phases – preparation, opening the encounter, the negotiating dialogue, and termination (see Figure 17.4). However, in small negotiations, particularly at the departmental level, the divisions are often less clear, whilst in some other negotiations the timing of Phases I and II may not be the same for both parties. For example, the side taking the initiative in seeking the negotiation (A) may undertake its preparation, state its case and have its position clarified by the other side (B) before B is able to undertake its own

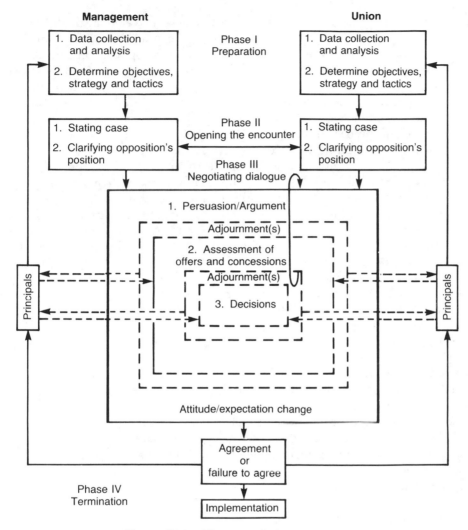

Figure 17.4 *The negotiating encounter*

preparation, state its own case on the issue involved and have its position clarified by A.

Phase I – Preparation

Preparation is invariably the key to successful negotiating. It allows negotiators to develop a clear understanding of their task and increases their confidence in their ability to carry it out. Few negotiations are either concerned with single, simple issues or unconnected with other issues within the organisation. Preparation must take into account the **wider context of**

environmental constraints and pressures which surround both the orga-nisation and the parties involved as well as the issue itself. In addition, consideration must be given to what is likely to be the **opposition's position**, and justifying arguments, and what will be their reaction to any planned arguments and offers to be made during the course of the encounter – Torrington points out that 'negotiators have to prepare counter-attack as well as attack, defence as well as initiative' [21].

Part of the preparation may involve **agreeing an agenda** between the two parties. The meeting to agree an agenda may be the only formal link between the parties during this phase of the encounter. It provides an opportunity, although not the only opportunity, for each party to gauge informally the other's position on the various issues prior to the formal opening of the encounter. Each party may well have different perceptions of the strategic or relative importance of the various issues and, therefore, determining the **sequence in which issues are to be considered** may itself be the first area of negotiation between the parties. Obviously any 'technical' linkage between issues may predetermine the sequence (one issue cannot be considered until the outcome of another is known). Outside this particular constraint, Torrington argues, 'both sides may welcome a sequence of topics which starts with something easy on which they can quickly agree' [22] thereby establishing the right atmosphere for the rest of the meeting. However, others argue that it is better to start with those items over which there is likely to be the most difficulty and on which a 'satisfactory conclusion' to the whole negotiation is dependent. The ability to hold out the prospect of concessions on the 'easier' issues may be more useful in aiding an agreement on the difficult issues than referring back to them, once they have already been made, as evidence of 'good faith'.

The negotiator and principals, as well as gathering and analysing such quantitative and qualitative data as is available or considered necessary, must also determine their **bargaining limits** on the issues to be negotiated. These limits comprise the **target they wish to achieve** and the **resistance point beyond which they are not prepared to make any further concessions**. Figures 17.5 and 17.6 set out management and union bargaining limits in respect of a number of issues which might well form the basis for an annual wage negotiation.

It can be seen (1A in Figure 17.5) that on the issue of a general pay increase management's bargaining limits range from a target of 4 per cent (based perhaps on the financial state of the company) to a limit of 7 per cent (based perhaps on their assessment of the going rate of settlements) whilst the union's bargaining limits range from a target of 12 per cent (based perhaps on the increase in the cost of living) to a limit of 6 per cent (based perhaps on their assessment of the minimum their members will accept). This would give an overall **bargaining zone** of between 4 and 12 per cent and a **likely settlement zone** of between 6 and 7 per cent – thus an agreement is possible.

However, suppose management wishes to make changes to improve productivity (2 in Figure 17.5). Whilst management would like, as a target, to secure an unconditional acceptance of these work changes, it is prepared to increase its general pay offer by either up to a further 2 per cent in return simply for a commitment from the union to enter into further productivity discussions or up to a further 8 per cent if the union will accept the proposed changes now. The union, on the other hand, wants a further 8 per cent above its general pay claim if it is to agree now to the proposed changes, although it is prepared to accept 6 per cent. However, it is not prepared to accept less than an additional 3 per cent for a commitment to enter into separate productivity discussions. These bargaining limits can be transposed on top of the bargaining limits for the general pay increase. It can be seen (1B in Figure 17.5) that there is now no overlap in the bargaining limits in respect of separate productivity discussions because the 1 per cent gap in respect of the 'value' of a commitment to productivity discussions erodes the 1 per cent overlap in respect of an 'acceptable' general pay increase. Consequently, agreement on this basis is likely to be very difficult. If, however, the productivity changes are negotiated now (1C in Figure 17.5) it would appear to create a larger likely settlement zone because the 2 per cent overlap generated by the differences in respect of the 'value' of the work changes is added to the 1 per cent overlap in respect of an 'acceptable' general pay increase.

On the other issues (Figure 17.6) there are no overlaps between the bargaining limits. This is not unusual; particularly on those items where change is not easily expressed in small degrees. On the issues of shift premiums, overtime rates and the working week it would appear that a settlement is to be found only at the limits of both parties. However, on the issue of an increase in holidays there is a clear gap between the bargaining limits of the two parties. Whilst both sides are prepared to settle for an increase of two days, management is only prepared to accept this as an alternative to a shorter working week. Consequently, the relative ease with which these issues may be settled will depend on the conduct of the pay/productivity negotiations and whether management or the union prevails in respect of the reduction in the working week and increased annual holiday being regarded as alternatives.

Once the bargaining limits have been determined, it is then necessary to prepare the **information and arguments to be used** during the encounter. Whilst Torrington argues that 'only the simplest details can be attempted, and that these need projection for maximum impact and penetration' [23] during Phase II of the encounter, nevertheless these main points and arguments need to be supported by more detailed information and subsidiary arguments during Phase III. It is important to remember, when preparing this package of information and argument, that it will need to justify not only the initial case being put forward on each issue but also each successive 'fall back' position as concessions are made and there is movement

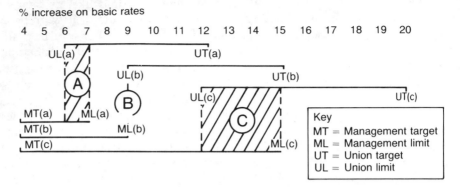

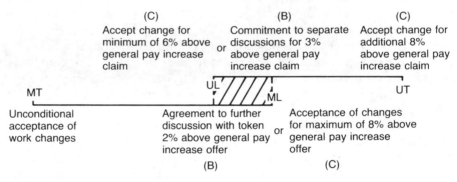

Figure 17.5 *Negotiating limits (general pay increase and productivity improvements)*

away from the target point and towards a settlement or the limit point. Each position should be capable of being sustained by some apparent 'logical' information and argument. This, perhaps, is the crucial difference between negotiations and simple bargaining.

Phase II – Opening the encounter

This phase of the negotiation is often referred to as 'the dialogue of the deaf' or 'challenge and defiance' because, as Torrington notes, 'the negotiators appear to be ignoring the arguments presented by the others and concentrating their whole efforts on the presentation and consolidation of their own case' [24]. However, for both parties, the real **objective** of this phase is to reveal only the broad outline of its own position whilst gathering as much information as possible concerning the opposition's case (to confirm or

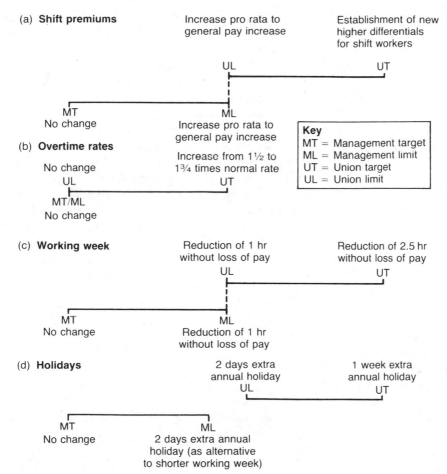

Figure 17.6 *Negotiating limits (items additional to general pay increase)*

modify prior conceptions regarding the opposition's bargaining limits). This phase is generally characterised by a higher degree of **formality** than the subsequent phase of the encounter in that each side initially seeks to confine itself to presenting a previously prepared statement of their position. Each side is, nevertheless, listening very carefully to the opposition's case, noting the opposition's reaction to its own case and preparing to seek 'clarification' of the other's position.

The issue of **who should open the encounter** is generally determined by which party is seeking the negotiation. Thus, in a negotiation relating to a wage increase it is the union which normally opens by stating its justification for an increase and the level of increase it expects, whilst management will open the encounter if it is seeking the agreement of the union to work changes, redundancy, etc. It may be argued that whichever side opens the encounter, whilst it has the initiative to set the tone and boundaries of the negotiation, is also at an initial disadvantage in respect of gathering information because it is first to start disclosing its position. Therefore, the negotiator must decide the **nature of the initial opening statement**. The negotiator may adopt either a stance of only stating the problem and then requesting the opposition to reply by setting out what they intend to do about it or go further and also set out the desired solution and then invite a response from the opposition. The negotiator must decide how specific the opening statement is to be and how much information it is to contain.

Although both parties realise that this opening phase is only the prelude to a real dialogue and compromise, the opening statements will tend to emphasise the justice of their respective target positions and the impossibility, or at least the difficulty, of making any concessions. Therefore, in order to obtain additional information, it is necessary for each negotiator to persuade the opposing negotiator to expand their formal opening statement. This may be achieved by using such **tactics** as expressing disbelief that the opposition really means what it is saying, apparently misunderstanding the opposition's position or by direct questions and requests for further clarification. These are all designed to get the opposition to restate its position using different words which may, as a result, convey more information regarding their attitude to the issues under negotiation.

It is important to remember that the **style and tone** adopted by the negotiators during this opening phase will set the scene for the subsequent dialogue in Phase III. If either negotiator adopts, or is perceived to adopt, an unduly aggressive attitude it may prejudice the movements, based on concessions and compromise, necessary in the next phase. The keynote throughout the opening phase should, therefore, be 'firm and clear' but not 'belligerent'.

Phase III – The negotiating dialogue

This phase is often referred to as 'thrust and parry' because, as Hawkins notes, each side is seeking 'to develop its own case and undermine the arguments put forward by the other' [25]. The movement from Phase II to Phase III of the encounter may occur either as a conscious decision of both negotiators, possibly involving an adjournment to consider the information gained during the opening phase, or as a more instinctive movement generated by the process of clarifying each other's position during the opening phase. The more formal the negotiating situation, the more likely it is to be the former.

The **objective** of the negotiator during this phase should be to use information, arguments and counterarguments in such a way that:

1. the perceptions and attitudes of the opposing negotiator are modified (thereby reducing expectations); and

2. a mutually acceptable agreement is secured which involves the greatest possible movement in the opponent's position for the least necessary movement in his/her own position.

This phase of the encounter is perhaps more **characterised by a problem solving orientation** – the problem to be resolved being the identification of a point of mutual acceptability. Both parties generally accept the need to move away from their target points and towards the likely area of settlement, if one exists, or the identification that no settlement is likely within the existing bargaining limits of the two sides. This phase therefore involves a less formalised, more flowing approach to the negotiations with much greater interplay between the negotiators and the generation of ideas, suggestions, offers and counteroffers. It consists of a cycle of activity moving from persuasion to offers and concessions which results, if acceptable, in a decision or, if unacceptable, a return to the persuasion stage and further offers and concessions. The negotiators may, where there is more than one item to be dealt with and there is a 'perceived' impasse on one of them, agree to put it aside for further consideration at a later stage in the dialogue and concentrate their attention on an alternative item.

This phase is also characterised by the development of a **more interpersonal, and less representative, role relationship between the negotiators** even, as previously noted, to the extent that the expectations of their respective principals may be perceived, individually or jointly, as an impediment to their achieving a solution. Where the negotiators are part of a negotiating team they may, particularly when the negotiation continues over a number of meetings, make use of 'off-the-record' **informal meetings** to explore their respective positions and possible reactions to offers that might subsequently be made in the formal meeting. The danger of this approach is that it may easily be regarded as 'behind the scenes collusion' by the other members of the negotiating teams and therefore treated with a degree of suspicion.

Another feature of this phase is the relative frequent use made of **adjournments**. At the **tactical** level, an adjournment may be required because a negotiator wants 'time out' to consider the arguments/offers put by the other party, or for the opposition to consider arguments/offers and reconsider their position, or, if part of a negotiating team, because the opposition has succeeded in dividing the team and the negotiator needs an opportunity to re-establish control. At the **strategic** level, the negotiator may require an adjournment in order to confer with principals and, in the light of the progress of the negotiations, seek to modify their expectations and thereby revise the mandate and bargaining limits. Whoever calls for an adjournment should ensure that it is not perceived as a sign of weakness or hesitancy by leaving the opposition with something to think about during the period of the adjournment.

A number of **tactics** may be employed in order to secure some movement in the opposition's position. These may be divided between those of a negative (aggressive) character and those of a more positive (conciliatory) nature:

1. **Negative.** A negotiator may direct questions at those amongst the opposition's team who appear the weakest, least experienced or most conciliatory in an attempt to split the opposition and create factional conflict within their team; challenge the competence or representativeness of the opposing negotiator; threaten to withdraw any concessions already made or even withdraw from the negotiations completely unless the opposition adopts a more 'realistic' attitude or position; impose a deadline by which the opposition must agree; and imply or threaten that there will be serious consequences for the opposition if no agreement is reached. All of these are intended to put pressure on the opposition.

2. **Positive.** The negotiator may highlight the weaknesses in the opposition's information and arguments, in particular those aspects of the issue which they either are not aware of, have failed to give due weight to or wish to ignore, whilst at the same time emphasising his/her areas of strength; pre-empt movement from the other side by, as it were, reading the opposition's mind and suggesting a concession they might make without significantly damaging their position; offer a 'quid pro quo' by linking hypothetical concessions – preferably a smaller concession from him/her than the one he/she expects the opposition to make in response; refer to the nature and extent of concessions and agreements already made by both parties. These tactics are intended to emphasise the mutuality of the negotiation and are based on the inherent desire of both parties to make concessions and compromises in order to reach a satisfactory agreement.

It must be remembered that both parties should benefit from the negotiation and the negotiators need to be seen to be representing and protecting their principals' interests. Thus, it may become necessary for one negotiator to offer the opposition face-saving reasons for why they have been unable to secure a settlement within their bargaining limits.

Phase IV – Termination

The termination phase is just as important to a successful negotiation as either the preparation or encounter phases. During the final stage of the negotiating dialogue, once an overall agreement is in sight, it is very easy for the negotiator to experience a psychological uplift at the apparent success of the negotiations and to suffer a lapse of concentration. It is at this point that a negotiator may, without fully realising it, commit him/herself to a course of action which may have been resisted earlier in the negotiation or even agree to something new, perhaps of only a relatively minor nature, which is 'thrown in' by the opposition at the last moment without sufficiently considering its implications. Therefore, the negotiator should not regard the dialogue phase as completed until all issues have been satisfactorily resolved and both negotiators agree there are no further issues to be considered.

The **objective** of the termination phase is to ensure that the two negotiators have a common perception of the content and terms of their agreement. This may be achieved by reiterating the decisions reached and putting them in a **formal written agreement** to be signed by the two negotiators. Indeed, the attempt to put the agreement into writing may highlight differences in perception with regard to the outcome of the negotiation and may require further 'refining' negotiation to establish the precise terms of the written agreement. However, the negotiators may not be in a position to sign the written agreement until it has been formally approved by their principals. Perhaps all too often the less formal negotiation conducted at the departmental/section level between shop stewards and supervisors or managers suffers because its outcomes are not codified in written agreements and are therefore liable to differential interpretation by the two sides.

During this termination phase neither negotiator should exhibit **undue signs of elation** with the result; this will only suggest to the opposition that in some way they have been unsuccessful in the negotiation, that there was more that they could have achieved, or that they have missed some important implication of the agreement they have concluded. This may lead to a desire on their part to seek immediately to reopen the dialogue and reconsider the concessions they have made or to resist the implementation of the agreement. The mutual acceptability of any agreement rests, to a large extent, on the personal trust between the negotiators concerned that neither has tried to deliberately 'hoodwink' the other. Indeed, if a negotiator believes that the opposition has missed some important point which, when it becomes known, may jeopardise the successful implementation of the agreement, he/she must give serious consideration to drawing the matter to the opposition's attention.

Both parties should ensure that the negotiations are followed by, preferably, a **joint communication** of its terms to all their principals, both members and management. The agreement reached is for their use and therefore they should be aware of its details.

Finally, perhaps the most difficult termination arises when there is an evident **failure to agree** between the two parties. Negotiators must be prepared to recognise when they have exhausted all possibilities of concession and compromise and that further negotiation on the issue is more likely to lead to entrenched and antagonistic attitudes than a resolution of the problem. In such situations the termination involves identifying the negotiators' respective final positions and therefore the exact extent of their disagreement. The negotiators are, in effect, defining the issue which must be presented to their principals for further examination and possible renegotiation at a higher level involving fresh negotiators.

Conventions of negotiation

It is generally important to observe certain conventions in conducting negotiations.

1. **Role of negotiator** – Each negotiator has the right and authority to state and argue his/her side's case and reach an agreement on their behalf. Thus, subject to 2 below, the negotiator has the authority to commit his/her principals and neither negotiator should seek to appeal over the head of the opposing negotiator and undertake 'negotiations' direct with their principals. However, management does not, generally, accept that this restricts their right to communicate direct with their employees to inform them of the details of their final offer when it has been rejected.

2. **Approval of principals** – The negotiator may, if necessary, make an agreement conditional upon its acceptance by his/her principals. On the management side, this will arise when the negotiator has, on his/her own authority, gone beyond the bargaining limits established as part of the mandate, which is only likely to happen if the negotiator feels that the principals will accept his/her judgement in this matter. On the union side, shop stewards and full-time officers are, because of their elective accountability to the membership, likely more often to want to refer any settlement to their members for approval before formally agreeing it with management. This does not mean, however, that they do not have the confidence of their membership or that the membership is likely to reject the solution they have negotiated. Rather it is an acknowledgement of the fact that they are the servants of the membership and cannot impose solutions on them.

3. **Setting for the negotiation** – Generally it is management which provides the room, etc. to be used during the negotiation and whilst it may be possible to create an environment which puts the union representatives at a disadvantage, for example facing a window or sitting in low chairs, this is not conducive to establishing an atmosphere of mutual trust between the two parties. Therefore, management should, as far as possible, ensure that the union negotiators have the same facilities as themselves and should ensure that coffee, tea, refreshments, etc. are provided as appropriate.

4. **Team negotiation** – If the negotiation is to be conducted by a team it is important to ensure that there is only one main spokesperson and that the two sit opposite each other so that they may communicate directly to each other rather than across other members of the teams.

5. **Personal conduct** – At no time should a negotiator lose his/her temper during the encounter; to do so is to lose the initiative and control of

the negotiation. Neither should he/she indulge in a personal attack on the opposing negotiator; the other negotiator is carrying out a role and the two negotiators are likely to meet again on future occasions.

17.4 Summary propositions

- Negotiation is not simply a 'ritual' but a process which allows the representatives of different interest groups to reach a mutually acceptable settlement of an issue whilst, at the same time, seeking to maximise the advantage to be gained for their interest group.
- A successful negotiator is one who has command of the facts and is able, through argument and persuasion, to encourage movement away from prearranged positions.

Further reading

- G. Atkinson, *The Effective Negotiator*, Quest Research Publications, 1977. A comprehensive examination of the negotiating sequence, strategy and tactics.
- P. Warr, *Psychology and Collective Bargaining*, Hutchinson, 1973. Examines the psychological elements of negotiation drawing on the experience of one particular negotiation.
- R. E. Walton and R. B. McKersie, *A Behavioral Theory of Labor Negotiations*, McGraw-Hill, 1965. A standard work on the strategies and tactics which may occur in various bargaining models.

References

1. R. E. Walton and R. B. McKersie, *A Behavioral Theory of Labor Negotiations*, McGraw-Hill, 1965, p. 3.
2. A. W. Gottschalk, 'The background to the negotiating process' in D. Torrington (ed.), *Code of Personnel Administration*, Gower Press, 1973.
3. W. Brown, *Piecework Bargaining*, Heinemann, 1973, p. 25.
4. A. Flanders, 'Collective bargaining: a theoretical analysis', *British Journal of Industrial Relations*, vol. 6, no. 1, 1968, p. 6.
5. D. Torrington and J. Chapman, *Personnel Management* (2nd edn), Prentice Hall, 1983, p. 187.

6. J. M. Magenau and D. G. Pruitt, 'The social psychology of bargaining' in G. M. Stephenson and C. J. Brotherton (eds), *Industrial Relations: A Social Psychological Approach*, John Wiley, 1979.
7. *ibid.*, p. 205.
8. K. Hawkins, *A Handbook of Industrial Relations Practice*, Kogan Page, 1979, pp. 206–7.
9. P. Warr, *Psychology and Collective Bargaining*, Hutchinson, 1973, p. 5.
10. *ibid.*, p. 8.
11. *ibid.*, p. 10.
12. *ibid.*, p. 30.
13. B. H. Kniveron, 'Industrial negotiating: some training implications', *Industrial Relations Journal*, vol. 5, no. 3, autumn 1974, pp. 27–37.
14. *ibid.*, p. 32.
15. R. E. Walton and R. B. McKersie, *op. cit.*, p. 282.
16. *ibid.*, p. 293.
17. *ibid.*, p. 284.
18. *ibid.*, p. 299.
19. *ibid.*, p. 295.
20. *ibid.*, p. 5.
21. D. Torrington, *Face to Face*, Gower Press, 1972, p. 35.
22. *ibid.*, p. 34.
23. *ibid.*, p. 34.
24. *ibid.*, p. 39.
25. K. Hawkins, *op. cit.*, p. 201.

Chapter 18
Pay and productivity

18.1 Definition

The 'wage–work' exchange is at the heart of both the individual's contract of employment and the collective agreement negotiated between management and union. In this context, pay may be used in a restrictive sense to cover only **direct monetary payments** of basic wage or salary plus any variable additional earnings resulting from allowances, overtime working or output bonuses, or in a wider sense to cover the **total remuneration package** including pension and sickness provisions, welfare and social facilities (such as subsidised canteen) and fringe benefits (such as company cars, cheap loans, etc.). In return for these payments and benefits employees are expected to carry out their allotted role/task efficiently and to the best of their capabilities. Efficiency and productivity are the terms perhaps most often used in respect of labour utilisation within the organisation. In a narrow sense the term **productivity** may be used simply to refer to **output per person employed** (labour productivity). However, the NBPI remarked in the 1960s that 'industry and services use other resources as well as manpower – such as buildings, equipment, raw materials and fuel' [1] and therefore productivity may more usefully be seen in a wider context as the **relationship between the output of the organisation and its overall use of all resources** – not just the labour element. The formal manner in which the wage–work exchange is expressed through the organisation's wage and salary system is perhaps one of the clearest indications of the organisation's basic philosophy, values and attitudes towards its employees.

It is not the intention in this section to examine the operation and problems of different forms of wage/salary systems [2] but rather to examine the principles and perceptions which underlie the choice of system, the appropriateness of a particular pay level and the linking of pay to productivity.

18.2 Pay bargaining

Pay bargaining must be seen in both economic and socio-political contexts. In the former it may be regarded as the determination of the price at which a commodity (labour) will be bought and sold – reminiscent of the old annual hiring of servants and farm labourers. As such, it centres on the individual's desire to maximise income and through this living standards, and management's desire to minimise the organisation's wage costs which are a negative element in the financial balance sheet. In the latter context, it centres on the determination of a 'fair and reasonable' payment for the contribution made by one of the organisation's assets.

Equity in pay

The axiom of 'a fair day's wage for a fair day's work' is often put forward as if there were a universal, absolute and self-evident criterion by which it is possible to judge the merits (or otherwise) of the outcome of pay bargaining. However, notions of what constitutes 'a fair day's wage' and 'a fair day's work', and therefore what is a fair and equitable equation between the two, are matters of **individual perception**, and the criteria by which management, unions and individual employees make such judgements are many and varied (see Figure 18.1). 'Equity' is, therefore, not an absolute but a relative concept requiring comparisons to be drawn with other factors, individuals or situations and, as Jaques noted, often involves 'the nature of differential treatment rather than equal treatment of individuals' [3].

A living wage
Income from employment provides the means for satisfying both economic and social needs. Therefore, a living wage implies something more than simply a 'subsistence wage' which provides only for the basic necessities of food, clothing and shelter. Jaques suggests that there are three distinct types of income expenditure:

1. Constrained expenditure, equating to a subsistence level of income, which is characterised by 'excessive concern over each item of expenditure' [4].
2. Discriminatory expenditure, wherein the individual's income is sufficient to allow choice in satisfying needs and requirements.
3. Indiscriminate expenditure, equating to the existence of surplus income, which is characterised by 'spur-of-the-moment spending, driven by whims and fancies' [5].

On this basis, the 'living wage' sought by most employees is that which will

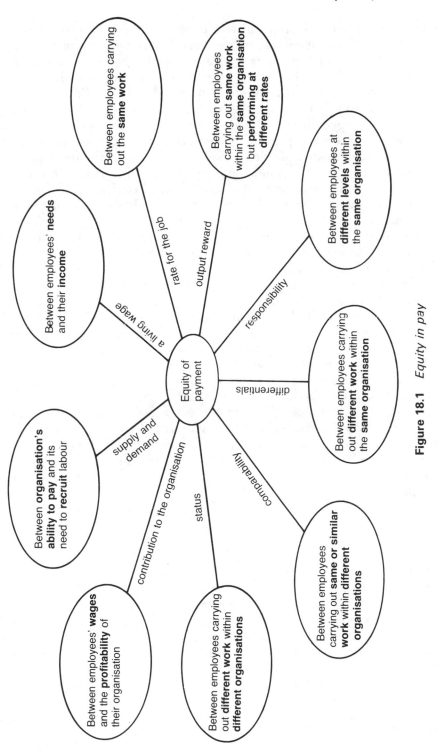

Figure 18.1 *Equity in pay*

be sufficient to meet, in full, their discriminatory expenditure needs plus allowing them to indulge in occasional indiscriminate expenditure.

The actual amount of money required to do this will, of course, be dependent on the particular domestic circumstances of the individual. Where there is **more than one income into the family**, the traditional view has been that the principal income (that of the male) provides for the family's discriminatory expenditure whilst the second (that of the female) is seen as a supplementary income to provide for indiscriminate expenditure. Hence, the common perception that married females undertake employment primarily for social, interpersonal reasons and regard their income as simply 'pin money' and are, therefore, less concerned about an equitable wage or salary. Yet, in many families the female is the major or sole source of income or a combination of the two incomes is necessary in order just to satisfy the family's constrained expenditure needs. Therefore both males and females are likely to display an equal concern in ensuring that the level of their incomes is sufficient, and remains sufficient, to meet living needs.

The amount of money, in absolute terms, required to provide a living wage is dynamic in respect of changes in both the individual's perception of expenditure needs and the cost of meeting these needs. Therefore, the concept of a living wage tends to be perceived and expressed in terms of the individual's **standard of living relative to the rate of inflation and changes in the cost of living**. Pay increases equal to, higher than or lower than the past rate of inflation are generally regarded as maintaining, increasing or reducing the individuals standard of living irrespective of the level of income or pattern of expenditure. Most employees expect management to ensure, through regular pay increases, that their standard of living is not eroded and, if possible, improved. Both management and union negotiators recognise the extreme difficulty of establishing a payment system which differentiates between the varying domestic needs of employees and even question its relevance in pay bargaining. The distribution of income on the basis of need is generally regarded as a matter of social and political, rather than industrial, policy to be achieved through the mechanism of taxation and the provision of social benefits.

Rate for the job

Employees who carry out the same work, or utilise the same skills, should receive the same level of payment irrespective of any actual, or potential, individual variation in either the quantity or quality of their work. It is the type of work performed by the employee, rather than individual attributes or abilities, which should be the prime determinant of pay. This belief underlines the **fraternalistic** characteristic of trade unionism by reinforcing the group identity and loyalty of the employees concerned and emphasising its indivisible nature. In effect, the weaker, less able member of the group is protected, in financial terms, at the expense of the freedom of the stronger, more able member to maximise income potential whether it is derived from physical strength, skill or intellectual ability. Indeed, manual workers are often resistant to any form of **merit payment** system which seeks, generally at management's discretion, to reward individual attributes and which, in their view, suggests favouritism. The concept of applying a single rate for a given job may be extended beyond the boundary of a single organisation through the negotiation and application of national rates.

Output or performance reward

Employees who produce more or better output should receive more pay. An equitable payment system is one which recognises that whilst different employees may have the same intrinsic skills and abilities to perform a particular job, and for which they receive the same basic rate, nevertheless they have differing capacities for effort and performance of that work for which they should receive differential rewards. However, such schemes are not intended simply to reward employees when periodically they exert extra effort in their work but, as their generic title suggests, to motivate employees to work permanently at a higher level of effort and performance than they would otherwise do. The NBPI noted in the late 1960s [6] that for Payment by Results (bonus) schemes to be successful:

1. There must be an effective system of measurement to determine both the datum base of the 'standard' level and the individual's own level in relation to that datum.
2. The pace of work should be primarily employee rather than machine controlled and the employee must be able to identify the extent to which his/her effort makes a direct contribution to pay.
3. The proportion of the individual's pay derived from an incentive scheme should be such that it is large enough to be worth striving for but not so large or fluctuating that failure to achieve the payment will prejudice the employee's ability to budget expenditure. It should not, therefore, be used as an alternative to establishing equitable basic pay rates.

Responsibility

Whilst it is possible for manual and most clerical work to consider equity in terms of the individual's 'physical' output, the contribution made by many other jobs to the overall performance of the organisation can only be assessed in the **less tangible forms of judgement and decision making** (particularly those involving technical, professional, supervisory and managerial work). It is in these fields that the equity principle based on level of responsibility within the organisation is to be found. There appears to be a general acceptance of the view that the individual's pay should correspond in some way to the level of authority and accountability of the job. Whilst it is possible to compare jobs on the basis of their **time span of discretion**, that is the elapsed time before an error of judgement may be identified and rectified [7], the more usual method is by a formal system of **job evaluation** which compares jobs in relation to a number of predetermined factors.

Within job evaluation it is the job, not the person, which is being assessed. However, it is important to recognise that it is not an objective, scientific or impartial method of assessment. Whatever the precise system, it is necessary first to decide what factors are to be included and, most importantly, what weighting is to be given to each of these factors. The relative size of these weightings indicates those job attributes which should be rewarded more than others. It is these weightings which make it difficult to use the same job evaluation scheme for different types of work. A scheme devised primarily for managerial/technical jobs, which places highest weightings on such factors as education, experience and responsibility for people and decisions, would, if applied to manual or clerical work, produce a very low score for most of these jobs. This does not mean that these jobs are worth less but rather that the basis of their worth stems from other factors. They are employed to type, file, assemble, mind a machine, etc., rather than make decisions or take responsibility for others.

Differentials

Different kinds of work within the same organisation should receive different levels of payment because of their respective **value and importance to the achievement of the organisation's objectives.** For example, those involved in the primary function of the organisation, whether it is manufacturing a product or providing a service, may well regard support employees as being less important than themselves. However, the individual's perception of the value of his/her work relative to the work of others in the organisation is often distorted by a lack of detailed knowledge concerning the content of the other work and an exaggerated view of the conditions, constraints and pressures of his/her own. Indeed, very often the jobs with which direct comparisons are most likely to be made are the ones which are perceived as a constraint on the individual's own work and which he/she feels should be done better or done away with. Differential comparisons are likely to be made not only in respect of the level of pay but also in respect of working hours, holidays, pension and other fringe benefits.

Comparability

Comparisons with the level of wages being paid in other organisations implies the existence of a common labour market and that the employer should be prepared to pay the apparent 'going rate' for labour. Indeed, it is perhaps the closest an individual employee may come to identifying the **current market rate** for his/her particular type of labour without actually seeking alternative employment with another organisation. For the employer to offer wages below this rate may be perceived as indicative of a lack of concern for the welfare of employees or a desire to obtain labour at the cheapest price possible by taking advantage of their relative inertia and immobility, whilst for the employee to accept less than this rate may be perceived as almost an admission that he/she is not worthy of a higher rate.

Status

Status may be defined as the **relative value placed on a job or occupation by society** as a whole. A job or occupation is generally considered to be 'underrated' by its incumbents, and possibly outsiders, when the rewards to all employees in that group, irrespective of the organisation which employs them, are perceived to be significantly lower than that warranted by the tasks they have to perform. Status comparison is perhaps the most important concept of equity, and at the same time the most difficult to determine, for those specialist and sometimes unique jobs such as civil servants, police, nurses and teachers. The common factor is that they work for a 'single employer' (the State) and therefore cannot realistically seek the same work at a higher rate of pay with an alternative employer. It is because of their peculiar position that both permanent pay review bodies (doctors, nurses, senior civil servants) and *ad hoc* inquiries have utilised comparisons with 'benchmark jobs' in the private sector as a basis for determining a 'fair' increase. Some have argued for the development of a **National Job Evaluation** system to relate these jobs with other more widely dispersed jobs in society. However, it is the very uniqueness of these jobs, both in relation to each other and in relation to any outside job, which presents serious difficulties for determining the factor weightings which might be applied in any such job evaluation scheme.

Contribution to the organisation

Both management and employees perceive a need for some **equitable relationship between the returns to labour and the returns to capital** – each is an essential part of the overall productive and financial performance of the organisation. However, whilst management may perceive a greater need than employees for the organisation to make sufficient provisions for dividends and reinvestment, employees will wish to ensure that such provisions are not at the expense of recognising their contribution to the achievement of profits. Indeed, even though an increase in profits has not been derived from a direct contribution by labour, but as the result of other factors, it may be argued that labour, as an asset and investment in the business, has a right to receive a share of this improvement in the same way as capital has a right to receive a share when the improvement results from the actions of labour. It is to meet this perceived need for equity that some organisations have introduced **profit sharing, share ownership or other schemes** which seek to distribute the value added by the organisation. However, as with incentive payment schemes, these should not be used to 'top up' unequitable wages and salaries.

Supply and demand

Most managers would argue that the level of wages should not be beyond their ability to pay and does not need to be above a level which allows them to recruit labour of the right type, skill and experience. However, if the level necessary for recruitment is higher than the level justified by the organisation's ability to pay, and management determine their pay level on the basis of the latter, they are likely to experience a movement of employees away from their organisation and difficulties in recruiting new employees to replace them. Equally, if the level justified by the organisation's ability to pay exceeds the level necessary to recruit labour, and management uses the latter to determine its pay level, they are unlikely to have difficulty in recruiting employees and their existing employees are unlikely to leave but there may be feelings of resentment amongst the employees at not receiving what they perceive to be an equitable wage. Thus, management must strike a balance between these two approaches if the organisation is to both retain the commitment of its existing employees and be able to recruit new ones.

Clearly these differing concepts of equity interrelate and, therefore, a successful wage or salary system, or pay negotiation, is one which recognises and seeks to reconcile them. North and Buckingham argued, some 20 years ago, in favour of a 'three tier wage system based upon agreed job worth, performance-based variability, and a share in prosperity element' [8].

Developments during the 1980s

A number of pay related developments have taken place during the 1980s as management has sought to link pay systems to the achievement of business objectives.

Profit related pay (PRP)

In 1987 the government encouraged the introduction of payment schemes in which part of the individual's pay is directly and formally linked to the organisation's profits by allowing income tax relief on half this pay element up to the point where PRP is the lower of 20 per cent of the employee's pay or £3,000. However, the suitability and success of such arrangements has been questioned. Duncan points out that the presumption underlying the government's strategy was that 'the profit-linked element of pay should replace some portion of previously fixed earnings so that 'normal' pay will vary with profitability' [9] but a recent survey concluded that 'contrary to the government's hopes, PRP is not linking pay to profits by replacing a significant part of basic pay but is generally being paid as a bonus on top' [10]. Furthermore, the survey notes that PRP had not made much impact in that by the end of 1990 there were 1,179 schemes covering only some

230,000 employees and that many of them were not new schemes but simply conversions of previous profit sharing arrangements.

The main arguments in favour of introducing such pay arrangements centre on providing the employee with a sense of identification with, and a share of, the success of the business whilst providing management with a 'wage cost buffer' in periods of reduced profitability. However, as Duncan notes, the general applicability of the scheme is reduced by the fact that the legislation (a) specifically excludes employees with less than three years' service, (b) allows management to exclude part-timers who work less than twenty hours a week and (c) excludes the public sector – even those segments which have been re-organised to be self-financing, market orientated or to compete with private sector organisations on an equal basis. At the same time he argues that 'despite the much-vaunted flexibility of the provisions, they promote but one kind of scheme and method of relating pay to performance which is unlikely to be suited to the pay objectives, pay priorities and individual circumstances of a majority of firms' [11]. The effect of the introduction of PRP on the negotiating process is debatable: on the one hand, it may be argued that 'if workers are to have a significant part of their pay linked to profit, it is likely that they would wish to have a greater say in the management decisions which may affect that profit' [12], whilst on the other hand 'as PRP grows, the role of trade unions as pay negotiators will diminish, since an increasing part of pay depends on profits' [13].

Performance related pay

As Fowler points out 'paying more to employees who work well than to those who work less well is a practice as old as employment itself' [14]. However, increased emphasis on 'performance related pay' has been an integral element of the industrial relations strategy of many companies during the 1980s as they have sought to change the culture of the organisation towards a more customer, quality or performance orientation, or, in the case of the public sector, sought to introduce a more commercial or managerial attitude. Nevertheless, the development of 'performance related pay' during the 1980s has been **different to earlier approaches** in three important respects:

1. Previous forms of 'merit rating' were concerned with assessing the employee's personal qualities in respect of commitment, co-operation, initiative and dependability (i.e. inputs into the work situation), whilst 'performance' is concerned with assessing the employee's output.
2. Previous 'output incentive schemes' relied primarily on quantified production output data as the assessment measure, whilst the measurement of 'performance' involves setting individual working objectives (within the context of departmental and organisational

objectives) and may include qualitative assessment of the achievement of both performance targets and personal or self-development goals.

3.   A number of organisations have sought to remove the distinction between an annual pay award (based on general factors such as cost of living changes) and individual performance payments and merge the two to make all salary progression dependent on individual performance. This raises serious questions in respect of the trade union's negotiating role. As the CAC pointed out in a recent decision regarding the trade union's claim for disclosure of information in respect of a performance related pay scheme: 'It is clear to us that the new payment system will severely restrict the role of the trade unions in negotiations. It will not, however, reduce the importance of the task of the trade unions to monitor what is happening to ensure there is fairness. Indeed the downgrading of the negotiating function in its simple sense adds added importance to the more sophisticated monitoring and checking that the individual managers will need from their trade unions to ensure that distortions are not growing unchecked' [15].

However, in Fowler's view it would be misleading to regard this renewed emphasis on 'performance' as implying that other factors are no longer important in that 'if staff are to be recruited and retained, salary levels have to keep up with the market, and market rates are probably the biggest single determinant of the overall scale of annual increases' and therefore perform-ance related pay schemes 'have to provide the majority of staff with at least some pay increase annually, and their operation would be prejudiced by any significant increase in pay or price inflation' [16].

Flexible or cafeteria benefits

A number of organisations [17] have sought to introduce a more flexible approach to the provision of benefits by allowing individual employees to determine, from a menu and within an overall budget, what package of specific benefits they would like to meet their own particular needs and circumstances. The system generally involves a 'core' of 'basic' benefits which all employees receive and a 'ceiling' on the extent to which the employee may add to, or include, a particular benefit. In establishing such an approach it is necessary to consider how frequently the employee may choose to amend his/her package of benefits and how the individual benefits are to be 'valued' (in either absolute or relative terms). However, such an approach does provide trade unions (and management) with the opportunity to divorce the issue of seeking to increase the range and extent of such benefits (based on desirability of the benefit) from the cost of providing them (which has to be offset against wages). The two issues can be determined or negotiated separately.

Arguments used in pay bargaining

The annual wage negotiation may be regarded as a **periodic review of the equity of the wage or salary level**. The various concepts of equity have, therefore, to be translated into specific and quantified claims and offers. In putting forward their various arguments the negotiators must eventually agree on a common 'language' with which to communicate. One of the areas of argument will centre on whether the negotiators are going to talk and negotiate in terms of a **fixed or percentage increase on rates or total earnings**. A fixed increase of £x per week will result in all employees receiving the same monetary increase but will have the effect of closing, in percentage terms, the relative differentials between grades. A percentage increase will have the effect of maintaining the differentials in percentage terms whilst giving different grades varying monetary increases and therefore widening the differentials in monetary terms.

The debate between the use of rates or earnings as the basis for calculating and judging an increase is essentially one between establishing an equitable value for the job (rate) and maintaining the employees existing standard of living (earnings). Often negotiators will confine their primary negotiation to a **benchmark job or grade** from which the increase for other jobs or grades may subsequently be agreed. This job or grade may be the one with the greatest number of employees, the one considered to be the basic job or grade for the particular bargaining unit concerned, or the one most directly comparable with outside groups or organisations.

A further major area of argument relates to the accuracy and relevance of the **statistical and accountancy data** used to support the various positions adopted during the course of negotiation. The fact that information is presented in a numerical form, often from sources independent of either negotiator, does not guarantee that it will be accepted as irrefutable. All information is subjective in that it has to be initially selected, presumably on the basis of its usefulness in supporting an argument, and subsequently interpreted and may therefore be questioned on the basis of the accuracy of its collection, the appropriateness of the calculation or inference drawn from it, as well as its relevance to the matter under negotiation. Furthermore, even if there is joint acceptance of both the concept of equity to be applied and the accuracy of the relevant information, there is still a need to agree the **time scale** over which the relative positions are to be compared. The negotiators must agree the point in the past at which an equitable relationship existed between the comparators under consideration.

Cost of living
Arguments based on changes in the **Retail Price Index** are appeals to the equity of maintaining a 'living wage'. It is the minimum which most employees and unions will consider to be a reasonable increase even in

periods of economic recession. However, the RPI is only representative of 'average' expenditure across a range of households and areas and may not, therefore, provide a true reflection of the effect of inflation on a particular individual's or group's cost of living.

The RPI is concerned with **expenditure after tax and other deductions** from income. Therefore, to apply changes in the RPI to changes in gross wages or salaries is not to compare like with like. A given percentage increase in gross pay will only give the same percentage increase in net pay if the person does not pay tax or superannuation (i.e. there are no deductions to be made); if the person is paying income tax and superannuation, the percentage increase in net pay will be less than the gross pay percentage increase because there is no 'tax free' element in the pay increase. It is because of the individual variability of the relationship between increases in gross and net pay that pay negotiations tend to avoid the issue. Management, in particular, will argue that:

1. it is the gross wage which determines its wage bill and costs; and
2. it is a matter for government to determine the relationship between gross and net pay through its taxation and fiscal policies.

The government sought, in the early 1980s, to refine the RPI by introducing a **Prices and Taxation Index** which more accurately reflected the effect on disposable incomes of changes in the level of taxation. The hope was that when a reduction in taxation resulted in employees retaining more of their gross income this would have the effect of offsetting, at least in part, their demands for wage increases based on rises in the cost of living. This approach was quickly discredited because it tended to show a figure in excess of that calculated by the traditional RPI. In the later 1980s, the government sought to distinguish between 'headline inflation' and 'underlying inflation' with the 'underlying inflation' figure excluding changes in mortgage interest rate and VAT taxation (essential elements of the government's monetarist strategy). Again, this distinction was not accepted by negotiators, particularly on the trade union side, because the elements excluded by the underlying inflation figure are significant contributors to the individual's expenditure and cost of living.

Generally cost of living is negotiated from a **historical viewpoint**, over the period since the previous settlement, rather than in respect of the future. This is largely because the rate of increase in the past is known whilst the future rate is a matter of personal judgement and prediction which may be affected, subsequently, by a wide range of factors. Both unions and management are, perhaps, always concerned that an underestimation or overestimation on their respective parts may not be fully compensated for at the next negotiations and that, even if it is, they will have lost out during the period of the agreement. However, with this historical perspective employees are, in fact, *always* disadvantaged in that the value of their wages is being eroded from the moment it is agreed and will not be restored until the next negotiation.

There appears to have been some resurgence of interest in **long-term agreements** (i.e. agreements lasting two or more years). They had previously been a feature of UK collective bargaining in the early to mid-1960s when, as in the mid-1980s, inflation was relatively low, but higher inflation and the adoption of incomes policies during the 1960s and 1970s enhanced the notion of an 'annual pay round'. It has been estimated that only some 6 to 8 per cent of agreements in the UK are of more than twelve months duration whereas some 65 per cent of agreements in the USA are of three or more years duration [18]. The initiative for long-term agreements has come from management who believe that they can provide a period of relative pay stability and help cost planning and the implementation of major organisational changes. However, it is important to recognise that 'the duration of settlements and the interval between pay increases should not ... be confused. ... while many agreements have been concluded which run for two or three years – so moving away from an "annual round" of negotiations – in relatively few instances have negotiators opted for pay rises at intervals other than 12 months' [19]. Indeed, most of these agreements provide for some form of indexation, threshold or re-opening clause should future inflation or external pay levels exceed the levels expected when the agreement was concluded. Whilst it may be argued that such **threshold clauses (indexation)** removes the need for unnecessary conflict and pseudo-negotiations around the cost of living, and therefore allows negotiators to concentrate on the issue of a 'real' wage increase, in practice most wage negotiations achieve little more than ensuring that wage levels remain in line with inflation and the amount of room left for negotiating 'real' wage increases is very limited. In addition, such automatic increases in pay as a response to an increase in inflation further increases the pressure of inflation at a time when the government is often seeking, through a variety of measures, to reduce it. Finally, the decision to increase pay, both in terms of timing and amount, is outside the direct control or influence of management thereby complicating, or even undermining, efforts at budgetary control within the organisation. However, Dean notes that in 1975 the Australian Arbitration Commission reintroduced an indexation system (which had previously existed between 1921 and 1953) but at a level less than full compensation for changes in the cost of living [20].

Comparability

Arguments derived from the equity concepts of responsibility, differentials, comparability and status may be loosely referred to as comparability arguments because they all centre on the relationship in pay between different groups of employees. Comparisons may be made in respect of both internal and external relativities. Torrington and Hall note that in the case of internal relativities 'the period between settlements can be crucial to perceived relativities' [21] and demonstrate how, with the same absolute pay increase, differences in the settlement dates for two groups can significantly alter the total amount received by each group. Certainly, internal relativities provide the most important basis for 'leap frogging' bargaining as one group seeks to close a differential and the other seeks to restore it. Torrington and Hall also note that importing a new job or skill into an organisation through the introduction of new technology can both upset existing differentials and introduce a new external comparitor [22].

In presenting or countering comparability arguments it is important to:

1. identify the groups with which comparisons are to be made;
2. establish what differences exist, both in terms of their pay and the nature of their work; and
3. assess whether or not differences in pay are justified.

In carrying out the second and third phases, particularly in respect of external relativities, it is important to have regard not only to rates of pay but also to earnings, hours, holidays and other fringe benefits. It is necessary at some stage to **evaluate the worth** of, for example, holidays, index linked pension, or a company car, for it may be argued that in the absence of such benefits an employee should receive a higher level of pay. It is perhaps not surprising, in view of the difficulty of measuring output, the uniqueness of the jobs and employer, the absence of a 'profit motive' and the general lack of industrial strength, that many non-manual employees in the **public sector** rely on comparability as a means of determining their pay. This may be undertaken on a permanent and formalised basis (as was the case with the Civil Service Pay Research Unit) as part of the annual review (as in the case of police, teachers, nurses, fire service and armed services) or on an *ad hoc* basis when it becomes apparent, sometimes as a result of the militancy of the employees concerned, that their level of pay has dropped significantly in relation to other groups.

However, comparability need not always involve reference to other specific groups of employees but may utilise information in respect of the dispersion of wage levels. In particular, reference may be made to the **average for the industry**, the **national average** or the group's changed relative position in the **national pay league** (implying that anything less is unacceptable and a sign of a 'bad' employer) – the latter two comparitors are appeals to status equity.

Going rate of settlement

The argument is often put forward that the employer should offer a pay increase in line with that offered by other employers. It is another form of comparability but, rather than comparing the actual rate of wages paid to different groups, the comparison is made with the **level of settlement achieved in recent negotiations** either in that industry or more generally.

The implication is that there is some kind of norm level of settlement during a given 'pay round'. In reality there is normally a spread of settlements in any given period and therefore it is possible to select those figures which best support the argument to be put forward. However, the use of this argument does avoid the need to identify direct comparator groups of equivalent employees and, at the same time, provides the opportunity for unions to seek to transfer a level of settlement achieved by one group, perhaps because of their industrial power, productivity or other reasons, to other, less fortunately placed groups. The concept of a 'going rate of settlement' seeks to bypass the reasons for variations between different situations and superimpose some form of commonality.

Profitability

The profitability of an organisation is the most usual method of determining the organisation's **ability to pay**. The essential problem in this area is how to **define profits and assess whether the organisation is profitable**. The reference point for determining the amount of profits may be taken at either the pre-tax level, in the same way that wages are negotiated on a pre-tax basis, or at the post-tax level, that is the amount left for the organisation to distribute between labour, shareholder and reinvestment. However, it is not just the absolute level of profits, which may appear excessively large when expressed in £millions or £billions, that establishes the profitability of an organisation but the relationship of that level of profits to assets, sales, return on capital employed, wage costs, etc., on both a current basis and over a period of time. Trends are as important as the current figures. The lack of a 'reasonable' level of profits in the current pay period does not, therefore, signify an inability to pay. It may be possible for the organisation to meet a current wage increase out of reserves provided from previous years of profitability.

However, in the absence of sufficient current profits, or a lack of reserves, management may well argue that an excessively high wage increase will result in **higher costs and prices** with a resultant loss of competitiveness. The exact effect an increase in wages will have on the costs and prices of the organisation will depend primarily on their proportion of total costs – if it is small the effect may be insignificant in respect of the final selling price but at the same time important as a variable cost under management's direct control.

The problem, for employees and unions, in assessing profits and profitability is that their **information** is limited to that supplied by management. Although unions may request further detailed information, the onus is on them to identify fairly precisely what information they require for their purposes. The situation is further complicated in respect of **group companies** through such practices as the consolidation of accounts and the existence of transfer pricing policies, possibly on an international scale. In this situation it is important to establish whether the company or site in negotiation is to be treated as an autonomous, self-financing organisation which must justify its own levels of pay or whether it is to be regarded as part of a group, backed by the combined resources of the whole group and able to draw on the profits or funds of the whole to meet any shortfall in its own ability to pay.

Productivity

Even though the organisation's profitability has not improved, unions may seek to justify a wage increase on the grounds of an improvement in the **overall productivity of the organisation**. It is therefore not necessary, as with direct productivity bargaining, to identify a precise linkage between some change in the utilisation of labour and the change in the level of output. The assumption is simply that if overall productivity has improved then the labour element must have made some contribution and therefore should be suitably rewarded. Whether the contribution has come from using new machinery or simply working harder does not matter and does not have to be proved. The two most common criteria used to establish an improvement in overall productivity are units of output per employee or value of sales per employee. Comparisons between the changes in either or both of these may also be made with the changes in earnings per employee in order to demonstrate that the former have been greater than the latter and thereby justify a pay increase.

These above arguments may, of course, be used singly or together to justify a given wage position. For example, a union may initially claim X per cent increase based on the change in the cost of living plus Y per cent to bring the level of wages into line with other comparable groups plus a further Z per cent because of improvements in the organisation's overall performance. However, it is unlikely that management will be prepared to negotiate these as separate items and so during the course of negotiation these arguments are likely to become integrated into a total package of justification for a settlement not below X per cent and preferably somewhere between X per cent and X + Y + Z per cent.

Daniel's examination of one annual pay round in manufacturing in the 1970s provides an interesting insight into the **varying relevance and use of these arguments** [23]. He found that cost of living and comparability factors were the main considerations for union negotiators in preparing their wage claims and that the organisation's ability to pay ranked very low. On the other hand, management's primary consideration was ability to pay, measured in terms of the potential effect of any wage increase on prices, profits, cash flow or investment, although comparability ranked a close second. Daniel suggests that 'managers either accepted the legitimacy of pay increases being made on grounds separate from the employer's capacity to pay or they had become reconciled to the inevitability of increases being made on such grounds' [24].

He also found that the order of importance of different factors varied.

Overall management placed 'effect on prices', 'avoiding interruptions' and 'effect on cash flow' in the top three positions respectively. However, where the organisation's product demand was rising 'avoiding interruptions' took priority with 'effect on prices' second, but where product demand was falling 'avoiding interruptions' fell to third place. This appears to confirm the effect of the economic environment on the relative bargaining power between management and union. Union negotiators, on the other hand, ranked 'cost of living', 'avoiding redundancies', 'avoiding interruptions' and 'competitive position of organisation' as the top four factors both overall and where the organisation's product demand was falling. However, where product demand was rising the importance of 'avoiding interruptions' rose to second place, 'profits' jumped from sixth to third, 'avoiding redundancies' fell to fourth, and 'competitive position' fell to sixth. It would appear from this that union negotiators place importance on both avoiding redundances and interruptions. Significantly, 'earnings of others' was ranked third only where the organisation's product demand was fluctuating. This suggests that whilst the union's use of 'cost of living' arguments will apply in any situation, 'comparability' only plays a significant role where it is difficult for the unions to identify any positive or negative position within their own organisation.

In respect of the influence each side's arguments has on the other, Daniel found that 52 per cent of management negotiators felt the union's cost of living argument was most persuasive as compared to only 15 per cent in respect of comparability arguments. However, only 29 per cent of union negotiators appeared to find management's ability to pay argument persuasive and 42 per cent responded that no argument had been most persuasive or their claim had been accepted. This latter position was, at least in part, due to 38 per cent of managers giving little or no information to union negotiators in respect of the organisation's financial position. Daniel comments that it is 'a little difficult to see how managers could expect effectively to deploy arguments about the financial position of the establishment in periodic negotiations over rates of pay when they denied union negotiators the basic information on which they could assess such arguments' and concluded that 'while the financial circumstances of plants had influenced management priorities and had influenced the degree of difficulty associated with negotiations, they appeared not to have influenced the level of settlement reached' [25]. It would appear that pay bargaining is more of a socio-political process than an economic one.

18.3 Productivity and work changes

The nature of 'bargaining' over the introduction of new working methods has changed over the period since the early 1960s as a result of changes in the economic and industrial environment. In the 1960s the introduction of new working methods was conducted against a background of demand for both product and labour and therefore the keynote was negotiating a more efficient use of a scarce resource. The background of the early part of the 1980s was one of recession and declining demand for labour and therefore the introduction of new technology focused attention on its effect on employment. At the same time the reduced power of employees and unions resulted in less emphasis on bargaining to introduce change. However, the adoption of the concept of the 'flexible' firm in the later 1980s appears very similar to productivity bargaining in the 1960s – both in its content (flexible working practices) and its means of introduction (through negotiation).

Productivity bargaining

PBR and other incentive bonus schemes emphasise the actual achieved level of output of the individual or group as the basis for the additional productivity payment. McKersie and Hunter defined the essential characteristic of productivity bargaining, which differentiates it from other forms of bargaining or payment systems, as being management and union formally '*negotiating* a package of changes in working method or organisation, *agreeing* on the precise contents of the package, their worth to the parties and the distribution of the cost savings' [26] [my italics]. **Productivity bargaining emphasises formal changes in a series of often interrelated working arrangements which may hinder the efficient utilisation of labour.** It is generally future orientated in that the additional productivity payment to employees is fixed at the time of negotiating the agreement and paid on the employees' acceptance of the new working arrangements without being linked to the achievement of any specified level of extra production. Management, therefore, control the achievement of increased productivity through their implementation and utilisation of the new working arrangements. Stettner has described productivity bargaining as 'bargaining to make change acceptable' [27] and in this context it requires a greater degree of trust and co-operation than conventional wage bargaining.

This form of bargaining, characterised by **major comprehensive agreements** at site level, was particularly associated with **capital intensive industries** (such as the petro-chemical industry). The first major 'classical' productivity agreement negotiated in Britain was at the Esso Refinery, Fawley (1960), and, in the view of Flanders, was 'without precedent or even proximate parallel in the history of collective bargaining in Great Britain' [28]. However, McKersie and Hunter's analysis of productivity agreements negotiated during the early 1960s suggests that they were, in fact, spread relatively widely across different types of industries and that there was no one common factor or single, universal reason for their introduction and development. They noted that from the mid-1960s 'the influence of a prolonged period of strongly administered prices and incomes policy served to generate a virtual explosion of productivity bargaining' [29] and contrasted the 73 agreements made between 1960 and 1966 with the 4,091 agreements made between the beginning of 1967 and the end of 1969. Incomes policy allowed pay increases above the stated norm if it was financed from improvements in productivity. Thus, there was a direct incentive for both management and unions to undertake 'productivity bargaining' to justify a pay increase above the norm at a time when a norm increase would reduce the employees' living standards. However, many of these later so-called productivity agreements were not of the comprehensive type but little more than output related bonus schemes designed and introduced to circumvent the constraints of incomes policy.

Two factors in particular induced management to look more closely at productivity and labour utilisation in the 1960s:

1. **Full employment coupled with expanding demand** meant that increased output had to be met from within the existing level of manpower. Furthermore, full employment enhanced the power of employees and unions to claim, and receive, wage increases at the organisational level significantly above those negotiated at the national level. Thus productivity bargaining offered the opportunity to overhaul, or tighten up, payment systems by removing anomalies and inconsistencies; to reduce and maintain overtime at the minimum necessary level; and to link pay levels with improvements in productivity thereby stabilising wage costs and improving budgetary forecasting. However, it is important to recognise that the influence of full employment and high demand not only were the cause of the concern for productivity but also, through increasing the power of employees and unions, made formal joint bargaining the only realistic solution.

2. The existence of **restrictive demarcation labour practices** which hindered the effective use of labour – particularly skilled labour. The existence of working arrangements over which management felt it had little control resulted, it was argued, not only in lower productivity but also in a general lowering of managerial morale and capacity to innovate. Many managers believed that any change or improvement in working arrangements would be met by employee resistance, and possibly industrial action, because it challenged an established 'custom and practice' and as a consequence became disinclined to even think in terms of change. The effect on the organisational climate of the existence of restrictive practices was identified as early as 1951 when Zweig noted that 'the restrictive spirit harms more than restrictive rules' and that 'every legitimate and commonly agreed practice can become restrictive if the restrictive spirit is infused into it' [30]. Confronting these problems through productivity bargaining was an attempt by management to regain a measure of control. However, management's view of these

practices being restrictive on the achievement on their task has to be balanced against the employees' and unions' view that they provide, in the absence of any other method, a measure of job protection and security. To employees and unions they are 'protective' rather than 'restrictive' practices. Indeed, it was noted that 'restrictive labour practices are often most remarked in industries where there is little security of employment (especially if there has been a history of high unemployment)' [31].

It is possible to identify a number of areas which formed part of productivity agreements.

- *Job flexibility*: widen the potential scope of the employee's work, in order to avoid production delays and the inequity of some employees having too little work whilst others have too much, through:

1. **Horizontal flexibility** where an employee is required to carry out a wider range of tasks within a similar skill level; (for example, intercraft flexibility or an operator being able to operate more than one kind of machine or part of the process).
2. **Vertical flexibility** where an employee is required to undertake work which is normally of a lower grade or level of skill.
3. **Geographical flexibility** where an employee is required to move temporarily in order to cover an absence or excess workload in another work area.

It is important to recognise that the prerequisite for any flexibility, but particularly horizontal flexibility, is that the employees are trained and competent to undertake tasks outside their normal work.

- *Time flexibility*: enable work to be covered, as far as possible, by employees working normal but changed hours and thereby minimise the use of overtime. Perhaps the most significant item of time flexibility related to the compensation for working overtime: many productivity agreements not only reduced the use of overtime but also removed payment for overtime – overtime working being compensated by time off.

- *Manning levels*: reduction in the number of people required arising from other changes in the agreement (particularly job and time flexibility), the identification of specific overmanning practices associated with existing production or service methods, or the introduction of new methods or technology which require less people. However, unions were anxious to secure a guarantee that no immediate or direct redundancies should result from the introduction of such work changes.

- *Payment structures*: emphasis on output, productivity and working arrangements provided an opportunity to introduce work measurement and/or job evaluation, if these were not already in use, as the basis for a more systematic examination of the content and relative worth of different jobs, and to simplify the payment system by reducing the number of pay grades and consolidating previous variable or supplementary payments into the basic rate.

- *Socio-technical improvements*: many productivity agreements incorporated the notion of workgroups – perhaps as the boundary of expected job flexibility (job rotation) or, more importantly, in the context of the devolution of decision making. For example, one arrangement was founded on the principle of group working in which five people covered four jobs (the 25 per cent 'spare' capacity covered annual holidays, relief shifts, training and sickness absence cover as well as 'overtime' time off) and the group had responsibility for determining which member carried out which job for each shift, who should be allowed to have what time off, and who should work overtime or change shift when required. Whilst each of these decisions may be seen as relatively minor in themselves, nevertheless they had previously been made by supervisors and could be a source of conflict. Indeed, it may be argued that it is the culmination of productivity bargaining and the complete opposite of the restrictive spirit referred to earlier.

North and Buckingham argued that productivity bargaining was 'much more than a short-term wage–work bargain or 'buy out' of restrictive practices' because it allowed for 'a radical restructuring of the industrial relations situation' [32]. Productivity bargaining, by its very nature, emphasises a **co-operative rather than conjunctive approach** to the negotiating situation and Hawkins believed that 'the development of a new style of management appears to have been an essential prelude to the initiation of productivity bargaining' [33]. It had the advantages that:

1. employees and their representatives became involved in areas of decision making which had previously been closed; and
2. management, union and employees had the opportunity to obtain a better understanding of each other's position and perceptions.

The underlying need in productivity bargaining is trust between the parties, and this may be enhanced by the **manner in which management initiates the process**. To be successful and co-operative in its orientation, management should not simply put forward *its* solution to *its* problem and then seek to negotiate the union's agreement to it, but rather present its analysis of future operations and indicate its areas of concern. The union should then be invited to join in what is essentially a joint problem solving exercise by contributing the issues which they feel to be of concern. The two views and sets of issues then provide the basic agenda for the subsequent discussions. This issue may be further complicated if there is more than one bargaining unit and the areas of concern relate to issues or work activity at the boundary of different bargaining units (for example, production, maintenance, supervision). Management must first obtain the acceptance of the unions to negotiating jointly before productivity discussions can realistically proceed.

The process of productivity bargaining generally **differentiates between determining the new working arrangements and negotiating new wage levels.** The determination of the **working arrangements** and their operation is perhaps the most time and energy consuming part of productivity bargaining. However, agreement has to be reached on most, if not all, of these before either side can realistically assess the agreement's worth and prepare their negotiating strategy for the wage negotiation. The responsibility for this may be delegated to a small working party drawn from representatives of both sides and the members may, at least for part of the time, be 'seconded' on a full-time basis. Whilst the working party has authority to reach agreement on the working arrangements, this usually involves lengthy discussions and consultation between the members of the working party and their respective principals (intra-organisational bargaining) and, indeed, there may be issues on which the working party is unable to reach agreement and which must therefore be left for negotiation with the wage element. The advantage of using a working party approach is that discussion may be conducted on a freer basis and with less formal negotiating constraint. In addition, its members become the 'experts' on the agreement at the subsequent negotiation and implementation stages.

In the **wage negotiations** it is important that neither side regards the changes in working arrangements as individual items on a 'shopping list' to be negotiated separately but rather as an integrated package for which a single 'price' has to be agreed. However, this is not to say that productivity bargaining must be abandoned in favour of conventional bargaining if it becomes evident during the negotiations that agreement is difficult or impossible on the basis of the wage levels proposed by management. It may be possible to segment the work changes and agree some in the current negotiation and leave others to be negotiated in the future. Whether this strategy will be appropriate depends on the interrelated nature of the work changes and the relative values the two sides put on the various elements (i.e. whether it results in a realistic bargaining zone in the negotiation).

Finally, having negotiated and agreed the productivity agreement, attention must be given to its **implementation**. A period of time between the signing of the agreement and its full implementation is generally necessary in order to establish new administrative procedures, to inform all management and employees of the philosophy and terms of the agreement and to undertake any training of employees in new tasks or jobs they may be required to undertake. Even after the agreement is notionally in full operation it is quite likely that there will be a need to clarify and 'fine tune' some clauses. The 'experts' from the original working party may be called upon to interpret in the light of their knowledge of the earlier discussions on that issue or part of the agreement.

Clearly, productivity bargaining is a major organisational exercise involving not only the development of a comprehensive package of changes in working arrangements and attitudes linked to higher wages and other benefits for employees but also the union's agreement to both the content of the changes and the distribution of the economic benefits.

New technology agreements

It can be argued that industrial change has been a continuous process since the start of the Industrial Revolution and has always involved the elimination of some types of work and the creation of others. However, the nature and rate of that change became significantly different in the 1980s – to the extent that it has been called the **Technical Revolution**. At the same time, this technical revolution has been introduced in an industrial and organisational climate characterised by recession and weakened trade union power. It is the combination of the nature of the change and the environment within which it is introduced that perhaps made the 'new technology agreements' of the 1980s different to 'productivity bargaining'. Productivity bargaining is primarily associated with changing the working practices of *people* (the people continue to carry out the same or similar work but working more flexibly and hence more effectively). The **emphasis of new technology in the 1980s**, on the other hand, is one of introducing new and radically different *technical systems* based principally on automation and computerisation.

The development and introduction of such systems, aimed at improving organisational/product competitiveness, has a double **effect on employment levels** in that, as Manwaring noted, it results 'in goods which are both less labour intensive to produce and use' [34]. However, perhaps the most important impact of new technology lies in its **effect on the nature of work and the relative position of management, employees and unions** for those who continue to be employed within the new systems. Certainly, Benson and Lloyd argued that automation and computerisation introduce 'logic and memory into production, displacing those previously uniquely human qualities' [35]. Manwaring believes that such systems enhance management's potential control of production because 'the bargaining strength of unions, established in relation to present or past technologies . . . derives from the need of employers to use workers in the process of production' [36]. James adopted a similar view when he argued that not only did the introduction of new technology 'transform jobs in ways which make them inherently less amenable to worker control' but also the pace of such change 'threatens the ability of work groups and unions to maintain a degree of control over the jobs affected' [37] through the gradual modification of custom and practice within the organisation. Changes in the character of jobs affect trade unions in two other ways:

1. Job losses and the weakening of employee control appears to be greatest amongst semi-skilled manual groups in manufacturing and clerical/administrative work generally – both important areas in determining the overall level of union density. At the same time, any jobs created by the new technology have been in areas of relatively low unionisation – professional and technical work (particularly in 'high-tech' organisations which have sought as a matter of policy to exclude unionisation).
2. The introduction of new technology may highlight 'demarcation' issues as traditional work boundaries, and even union boundaries, become blurred or eliminated. Certainly, Gennard and Dunn [38] have noted the NGA's efforts to maintain a role for its members in the new computerised direct entry system of printing and the potential impetus such technology has for mergers between unions in the industry.

It is within this context that the **trade unions' response to new technology** must be examined. In 1979 the TUC prepared a report on the introduction of new technology [39] which set out guidelines for union negotiators covering the following points:

1. Full trade union involvement and agreement before new technology is introduced.
2. Inter-union collaboration where appropriate.
3. Access to all relevant information and regular consultation on company plans.
4. Commitment to expand output/services and no redundancies or, if not possible, planned redeployment and/or improved redundancy payments.
5. Training, at full earnings, for those affected by the new technology.
6. Reduce basic working hours and systematic overtime.
7. Avoid disruption to existing pay structures/relativities, maintain or improve income levels, move towards single status (harmonisation).
8. Ensure computer-based information not used for work performance measurement.
9. Maintain stringent standards of health and safety.
10. Establish joint management/union arrangements to monitor and review progress.

Clearly, the trade union response to new technology has been to ensure that its introduction is subject to collective agreement and that its benefits are reflected both in the terms and conditions of the employees and in expanding employment. James [40] identified four **types of agreement** of which only the first has a heavy substantive element closely defining the terms and arrangements under which a single or small number of related changes are to be introduced. They are very similar to the agreements arrived at through productivity bargaining – the only real difference being the type of work change being introduced. The other three categories cover varying degrees of **procedural agreements** which establish the principles and procedures to govern the introduction of new technology on a continuing basis – these may include principles relating to the handling of substantive issues. It is these agreements which James believes should be termed 'New Technology Agreements'.

He argued that the importance of such agreements lies not in their detail but in their guiding principles reflecting a **management/union acceptance of the joint control of work**. Whilst for management the agreement represents 'some degree of freedom from union opposition and probably a measure of union co-operation', for the union and employees it signifies that 'the introduction and ongoing monitoring of the new technology is brought into the area of joint regulation' [41]. However, it would appear to be a somewhat **imbalanced interdependence**. Certainly, Benson and Lloyd concluded from their survey of new technology agreements that 'health and safety is the most strikingly precise of the issues agreed: the others, such as job security, consultation and disclosure, and sharing benefits – are usually either tentative or vague, and all depend heavily on the maintenance of considerable strength and vigilance on the part of the unions' [42]. Indeed, James himself noted that trade unions never or rarely received an assurance from management that no change would be introduced without prior negotiation or agreement or that full information on costs would be made available to them. This casts doubts on whether trade unions have actually achieved any significant measure of joint control of new technology through the negotiation of such agreements.

The union's purpose in seeking full involvement in the introduction of new technology is not just to influence the shape of the new working arrangements, however important this may be, but also to obtain a **share of any economic benefits** for its members. In this context unions have been faced by management resistance to 'paying for change'. Surveys of agreements relating to new technology suggest that trade unions have not been able to secure either a reduction in working hours or direct monetary improvements for their members. As far as increases in wages are concerned, Manwaring noted that 'though unions have often . . . secured agreements that there will be no reduction in earnings and no downgrading for those offered redeployment, they have seldom secured an increase in earnings for operating new technology' [43]. This, at best, represents a somewhat negative achievement. James is less pessimistic in that he believed 'changes in financial rewards subsequent to technical change are frequently dealt with in the normal run of substantive bargaining' although 'the proportion of a pay increase due to the acceptance of technical change may not be specified' [44].

In view of the general paucity of financial information provided to unions by management when either discussing the introduction of new technology or a normal pay bargain, this represents a less than satisfactory process of determining the distribution of the benefits which may result from new technology.

Finally, it may be argued that it has been the reduction in trade union power through recession and their consequent inability to secure substantive negotiations and agreement over the introduction of new technology, rather than any inherent difference in new technology as opposed to productivity changes, which resulted in the primarily procedural nature of many new technology agreements. Certainly, Benson and Lloyd believed that 'the limitation of technology agreements . . . stand alongside the low wage settlements, the abortive industrial actions, the often-hopeless factory occupations and mass redundancies as evidence of trade union weaknesses' [45].

The 'flexible firm'

During the later part of the 1980s, the twin concepts of the 'flexible firm' and 'core/periphery' employees [46] have achieved prominence as possible elements of management's strategy to become more competitive and more responsive to market or customer needs whilst, at the same time, being reluctant to recruit more full-time permanent employees (see Figure 18.2). In addition to seeking pay flexibility through more performance related forms of payment system, management has sought flexibility in three major areas.

• *Numerical flexibility* (i.e. management's ability to increase or decrease its labour quickly in response to organisational requirements). It is useful to distinguish between the following:

1. **A core group of employees** 'with full-time, permanent status . . . central to the longer term future of the organization' [47] who have relative job security and within which management may seek functional, time and pay flexibility.

2. The **peripheral groups of employees** who may provide an employment 'buffer' for the organisation and which may be either:
    (a) full-time employees who have 'skills that are more readily available in the labour market . . . have less access to career opportunities, little investment in their training . . . and tend to be characterized by high labour turnover which makes workforce reductions relatively easy by natural wastage'[48]; or
    (b) employees working under a variety of casual, temporary or part-time contracts to meet short-term labour needs and, consequently,

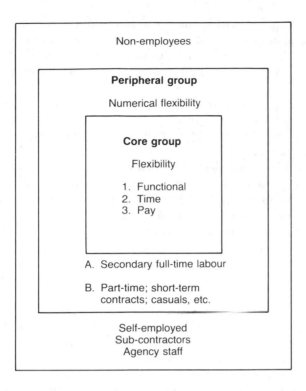

Figure 18.2 *The flexible organisation*

with very little job security or, indeed, job interest; as Towers points out it is this group of employees which trade unions are 'strongly campaigning to recruit . . . into membership and to negotiate rights equal to those of permanent workers' [49].

3. **People who are not direct employees** of the organisation but nevertheless may be considered a part of its 'human resource'. This group may include ex-employees whom the organisation has assisted to become self-employed in the same area of work as when they were employees (possibly as part of a re-organisation and/or redundancy package with a guarantee of a certain level of work for a period of time from their ex-employer) or the contracting out of non-core activities (such as catering). The organisation is no longer constrained by an employer relationship in its dealings with these people.

● *Job, task or functional flexibility* whereby the range of tasks or duties the employee may be required to undertake is broadened (vertically or horizontally) with, consequently, less role specialisation. For many **non-manual employees** this has taken the form not of simply increasing the range of specific tasks identified within their job description (content) but rather by making the description of the role and duties less restrictive and more focused on the responsibilities and performance of the individual (output) – this is particularly so where performance appraisal and/or payments have also been introduced.

So far as **craft/production flexibility** in production is concerned, one IDS survey noted that 'the danger of "multi-skilling" becoming trade-less semi-skilling was a real one' but that there was 'no evidence to suggest that craft identity is being eroded in these agreements' [50]. Rather, the introduction of functional flexibility in this area has led to 'craft' employees acquiring additional closely related skills rather than becoming multi-skilled (i.e. being able to do a complete small job rather than divide its distinct tasks between different trades) and process employees becoming responsible for first-line maintenance. Indeed, Cross has identified that in only some 10 per cent of the organisations he surveyed in 1989 had any significant degree of interchangeability between maintenance and production employees been achieved [51]. Although the purpose of this inter-craft and craft/production flexibility is intended to reduce 'downtime' and maximise the use of capital machinery, management appear to regard the training of craft employees to do process work as 'uneconomic' except for providing a further source for emergency cover. At the same time, it is important to recognise that such flexibility is dependent, at least in part, on the product or technology of the organisation; for example, the safety aspects of dangerous materials or processes in the chemical industry may be a significant limiting factor. Consequently, this type of flexibility may be more appropriate 'in companies operating high-speed, high-volume production lines' [52].

A further aspect of functional flexibility has been the introduction of **teamworking or groupworking** based on the concept that each person in the 'team' is capable of doing most, if not all, tasks. This form of flexibility raises two important issues:

1. **Relationship between the supervisor and the work group**. It is clear, according to one survey, that there are 'sharp differences between companies in what they really mean by teamworking, and in particular over the function of the team leader' [53]. Some organisations regard the 'team leader' as little more than a 'senior operator' (responsible for optimising plant operations and undertaking general administrative duties); others regard it as an 'assistant' to the supervisor (dealing with work allocation, operational problem diagnosis, etc. but not such matters as discipline); while others give it an enhanced role in 'people management' (including, for example, assessing members of the team in relation to performance-related pay increases). Clearly the introduction of teams with their own 'leaders' has repercussions for the role of the supervisor; for example, in one organisation the introduction of

teamworking led to the 'virtual abolition of the supervisor's role, with manufacturing cells operating as "autonomous work groups" under a system of joint union/management supervision' [54].

2. **Team stability.** Teamworking, to be successful, requires the individuals to identify with and be committed to *their* team. Therefore, whilst it may provide for greater functional flexibility as between the members of each team, it may introduce a degree of 'employee' inflexibility or resistance in respect of temporary or permanent moves between teams (particularly if teamworking is associated with any form of group based performance related pay).

● *Time flexibility.* Management has sought to introduce more time flexibility amongst its employees in order to assist in ironing out peaks and troughs in workload. One impetus for seeking increased time flexibility amongst employees has been the introduction of a **shorter working week**. It is significant that as the UK engineering industry has been leading the move towards a 37-hour week for manual employees, the German engineering industry has agreed to move to a 35-hour week by 1995 in two stages; however, this agreement is subject to the following conditions:

1. 'in years in which a reduction in working time coincides with a pay review, the material effects of the reduction in working time are to be taken into consideration . . . hours cut will be offset to some degree against pay increases'; and
2. either side can request review of the hours cut 'in the light of the general economic situation, in particular the employment situation in the industry and developments in working time elsewhere in the EC' [55].

Similarly, UK management has generally insisted that the introduction of a shorter working week should be self-financing. In approaching the issue of time flexibility, whether or not in the context of reducing the basic working week, management has placed increased **emphasis on the productive use of working time** by a variety of different methods [56]:

1. **Eliminating or reducing breaks.** Reducing the length of paid breaks (teabreaks, lunch, etc. – i.e. unproductive parts of the paid basic working week) can achieve a reduction in the basic week without reducing the 'productive' part of the working week. Similarly, removing fixed 'unpaid' breaks and requiring that they be taken as and when operational conditions allow again reduces unproductive time when 'machines' have to stop.
2. **'Bell-to-bell' working.** Being at place of work (and, in 'Japanese style' companies, having the work station prepared and ready to start) at the official start-time rather than clocking-on at the start-time and then

taking time getting to work station and starting-up. However, it is important to recognise, in the context of reducing breaks, washing-up time, etc., that 'given time, they tend to reappear unofficially . . . there is a natural tendency to "unwind" towards the end of the working day' [57].

3. **Flexitime.** This is an arrangement where 'employees may, within prescribed limits, choose their starting and finishing times' [58] (i.e. the basic contracted weekly hours remain unchanged but are averaged out over a longer period, with employees being required to work a fixed core period each day but having flexibility to determine their own starting and finishing times outside that core). The benefit for management is increased control over working time: it allows the workplace to be covered for a longer period of time each day (but probably with less employees outside the core period), reduces the need for paid overtime to meet workload needs, and reduces absenteeism and 'lax time' (i.e. employees taking extra time at lunch breaks or other time off to go shopping, to go to the doctors, etc.). The benefit for the employee is that it may ease travel arrangements and the combining of work and domestic duties.

   However, it may be difficult to apply to those employees who are tied to team/group working, specific shift patterns or production lines or have managerial responsibilities. Consequently, it would appear that 'few flexible hours schemes apply to manual workers' and 'even in the age of single-status agreements, flexitime is still seen mainly as a white-collar benefit' [59]. At the same time, some trade unions 'fear that it may dilute claims for a shorter working week and that it may in fact lead to more employer control over the working lives of staff' [60]. Certainly, flexitime requires some form of time recording and, therefore, for many non-manual employees it has been associated with the introduction of formal time recording systems – some computerised with plastic cards, others using more traditional time clocks.

4. **Annualised hours or flexi-year.** This involves expressing the employee's contractual requirement not in hours per week but hours per year. The objective of introducing such an arrangement is to allow management greater flexibility to tailor the employees' working time to production/output requirements and, in particular, to reduce or eliminate paid overtime to meet normal production needs. However, it is important to recognise that its success, like so many other aspects of flexibility, depends on 'cooperation between employees and management, and amongst employees themselves . . . with systems likely to work better if employees are able to make their own informal rostering arrangements when cover is likely to be required at short notice' [61].

5. **Revised shift patterns.** Reductions in weekly hours and increases in holidays reduce the employees' working time and therefore more 'cover' is required to maintain the same production hours. This has generally

been achieved by new shift patterns (five-team rather than the traditional four-team working); however, the 'extra' team has normally been created from within the existing employees by decreasing staffing levels rather than increasing the number of people employed.

6. **'Pay-back' shifts.** Shifts which are part of the employees' contracted hours but which are not allocated but kept in reserve; therefore, the employee 'owes' the company these hours and can be required to work at short notice to cover absences or peak loads. Whether or not the company will require these hours does not matter – they are available to be used if needed. This concept is not new – certainly, one organisation in the chemical industry introduced a similar arrangement in the early 1970s which gave management the right to a fixed number of unpaid 'abnormal' (overtime) hours per year and the employee the right to an equivalent number of hours time-off whether or not he/she was required to work overtime ('time in anticipation').

So far as the **process for achieving flexibility** is concerned, IDS surveys question the extent to which organisations have adopted a truly integrated approach and believe that 'the so-called "Flexible Firm", employing the whole gamut of flexible working practices, sub-contracting, and short-term contracts is very much a paper concept' [62]. They show that 'for the vast majority of companies flexible working consists of slow change over a number of years' which 'may take the form of an initial "enabling" clause or agreement, which is subsequently built on and enlarged' [63] and that perhaps 'agreements on flexibility are less important than the climate in which change is made' [64]. At the same time, management's strategy in the later 1980s appears to have changed from the 'macho' imposed stance adopted by at least some managements in the early 1980s: for example, Towers argues that 'the current vogue in companies for ways of increasing labour flexibility is reminiscent of the productivity bargaining fashion of the sixties' [65]. This is confirmed by the IDS survey which reported that 'negotiated deals . . . with a trade-off of money for new working practices, remain the norm . . . but where the price is not right, there has been considerable shopfloor resistance even in industries where competitive pressures are intense' and that 'while job-loss remains a feature of flexible working, pledges on job security and "no compulsory redundancy" clauses are becoming an important pre-condition of many deals' [66].

Certainly, there is little doubt that Towers is correct when he states that 'it is now no longer axiomatic to complain that the performance of British workers is inferior to their counterparts in other countries' [67]. Labour productivity in UK organisations has improved quite dramatically during the 1980s as a result of the interrelationship between significant reductions in the numbers employed and the introduction of a range of labour flexibility arrangements.

18.4 Summary propositions

- There is no universal, absolute or self-evident criterion by which to judge equity in pay; rather it is a relative concept derived from comparisons with a range of factors.
- The arguments used in pay bargaining reflect both its economic and socio-political nature.
- Productivity bargaining relies on a co-operative rather than conjunctive approach to bargaining and directly links improvements in terms and conditions of employment with changes in working methods.
- The introduction of new technology at a time of recession weakened the employees' ability to control work and the trade unions' ability to bargain over productivity improvements.
- The emphasis on labour flexibility in the late 1980s appears very similar to productivity bargaining in the 1960s – both in its content (flexible working practices) and its means of introduction (negotiation).

Further reading

- D. Torrington and L. Hall, *Personnel Management: A new approach* Prentice Hall, 1987. Part VI provides a concise summary of various forms of payment system and further reading in this area.
- F. Blackaby (ed.), *The Future of Pay Bargaining*, Heinemann, 1980. A series of papers examining some of the problems and possible solutions in respect of pay bargaining and wage levels.
- R. B. McKersie and L. C. Hunter, *Pay, Productivity and Collective Bargaining*, Macmillan, 1973. This covers the development of productivity bargaining up to the beginning of the 1970s and the content and implementation of productivity agreements.
- I. Benson and J. Lloyd, *New Technology and Industrial Change*, Kogan Page, 1983. This provides a useful examination of the development of technical change and management/union responses.
- C. Curson, *Flexible Patterns at Work*, IPM, 1986. This examines a range of changes which organisations have introduced during the 1980s to enhance work flexibility.

References

1. NBPI, *Report No. 23: Productivity and Pay during the Period of Severe Restraint*, HMSO, 1966, p. 13.
2. D. Torrington and L. Hall, *Personnel Management: A new approach*, Prentice Hall, 1987, Part VI; T. Lupton and A. M. Bowey, *Wages and Salaries*, Penguin, 1974.

3. E. Jaques, *Equitable Payment*, Heinemann Educational Books, 1967, p. 146.
4. *ibid.*, p. 182.
5. *ibid.*, p. 181.
6. NBPI, *Report No. 65: Payment by Results Systems*, HMSO, 1968.
7. E. Jaques, *op. cit.*
8. D. T. B. North and G. L. Buckingham, *Productivity Agreements and Wage Systems*, Gower, 1969, p. 95.
9. C. Duncan, 'Why profit related pay will fail', *Industrial Relations Journal*, vol. 19, no. 3, 1988, p. 186.
10. 'Profit Related Pay', *Incomes Data Services Study 471*, December 1990, p. 1.
11. C. Duncan, *op. cit.*, p. 197.
12. *Incomes Data Services Study 471*, *op. cit.*, p. 3.
13. *ibid.*, p. 5.
14. A. Fowler, 'New directions in performance pay', *Personnel Management*, November 1988, p. 30.
15. CAC decision in respect of British Airways, quoted in *Incomes Data Services Report 570*, June 1990, p. 27.
16. A. Fowler, *op. cit.*, p. 33.
17. 'Flexible Benefits', *Incomes Data Services Study 481*, May 1991.
18. CBI Pay Databank (UK) and Bureau of National Affairs (USA), quoted in 'Long-Term Agreements', *Incomes Data Services Study 450*, January 1990, pp. 3, 10.
19. *ibid.*, p. 1.
20. A. J. H. Dean, 'Roles of governments and institutions in OECD countries' in F. Blackaby (ed.), *The Future of Pay Bargaining*, Heinemann 1980, p. 176.
21. D. Torrington and L. Hall, *op. cit.*, p. 490.
22. *ibid.*, p. 513.
23. W. W. Daniel, 'Influences on the level of wage settlements in manufacturing industry' in F. Blackaby, *op. cit.*
24. *ibid.*, p. 151.
25. *ibid.*, pp. 156, 158.
26. R. B. McKersie and L. C. Hunter, *Pay, Productivity and Collective Bargaining*, Macmillan, 1973, p. 5.
27. N. Stettner, *Productivity Bargaining and Industrial Change*, Pergamon, 1969.
28. A. Flanders, *The Fawley Productivity Agreements*, Faber & Faber, 1964, p. 13.
29. R. B. McKersie and L. C. Hunter, *op. cit.*, p. 24.
30. F. Zweig, *Productivity and Trade Unions*, Blackwell, 1951, p. 19.
31. Royal Commission on Trade Unions and Employers' Associations, *Research Paper No. 4: Productivity Bargaining/Restrictive Labour Practices*, HMSO, 1967, p. 50.
32. D. T. B. North and G. L. Buckingham, *op. cit.*, p. 21.
33. K. Hawkins, 'Productivity bargaining: a reassessment', *Industrial Relations Journal*, spring 1971, p. 20.
34. T. Manwaring, 'The trade union response to new technology', *Industrial Relations Journal*, vol. 12, no. 4, 1981, p. 20.
35. I. Benson and J. Lloyd, *New Technology and Industrial Change*, Kogan Page, 1983, p. 182.
36. T. Manwaring, *op. cit.*, p. 22.
37. B. James, 'The Trade Union Response to New Technology', Internal Papers in Economics (No. 5), Middlesex Polytechnic, 1980, p. 2.
38. J. Gennard and S. Dunn, 'The impact of new technology on the structure and

organisation of craft unions in the printing industry', *British Journal of Industrial Relations*, vol. XXI, no. 3, 1983, pp. 17–32.

39. TUC, *Employment and Technology*, 1979.
40. B. James, *op. cit.*, p. 8.
41. *ibid.*, p. 11.
42. I. Benson and J. Lloyd, *op. cit.*, p. 176.
43. T. Manwaring, *op. cit.*, p. 18.
44. B. James, *op. cit.*, p. 10.
45. I. Benson and J. Lloyd, *op. cit.*, p. 182.
46. J. Atkinson, *Flexible Manning: The way ahead*, Institute of Manpower Studies, 1984.
47. A. Evans and J. Bell, 'Emerging themes in flexible work patterns' in C. Curson (ed.), *Flexible Patterns of Work*, IPM, 1986, p. 11.
48. *ibid.*
49. B. Towers, 'Managing labour flexibility', *Industrial Relations Journal*, vol. 18, no. 2, 1987, p. 83.
50. 'Flexible Working', *Incomes Data Services Study No. 407*, April 1988, pp. 4, 6.
51. Dr. M. Cross, 'Total productive maintenance', paper presented to North East Maintenance Association Conference (1989), quoted in 'Flexibility at Work', *Incomes Data Services Study 454*, March 1990, p. 3.
52. 'Flexibility at Work', *Incomes Data Services Study 454*, March 1990, p. 4.
53. *Incomes Data Services Study 407*, *op. cit.*, p. 7.
54. *Incomes Data Services Study 454*, *op. cit.*, p. 4.
55. 'The Shorter Working Week', *Incomes Data Services Study 461*, July 1990, p. 9.
56. 'Reorganising Working Time', *Incomes Data Services Study 417*, September 1988.
57. *Incomes Data Services Study 461*, *op. cit.*, p. 7.
58. 'Flexitime', *Incomes Data Services Study 477*, March 1991, p. 1.
59. *ibid.*
60. *ibid.*, p. 4.
61. 'Annualised hours 2: manufacturing flexibility', *IRS Employment Trends 489*, June 1991, p. 12.
62. *Incomes Data Services Study No. 407*, *op. cit.*, p. 1.
63. *ibid.*
64. *Incomes Data Services Study 454*, *op. cit.*, p. 5.
65. B. Towers, *op. cit.*, p. 79.
66. *Incomes Data Services Study No. 407*, *op. cit.*, p. 1.
67. B. Towers, *op. cit.*, p. 80.

Chapter 19

Grievances and disputes

19.1 Definition

The terms 'grievance' and 'dispute' are used to denote a range of situations which, whilst they have a common origin in employee dissatisfaction with some aspects of their terms and conditions of employment, are, as Thomson and Murray point out, 'extremely varied in content and significance for the organisation concerned' [1]. This variety stems from a number of factors:

1. The nature of the issue to be resolved includes **matters of right** which are concerned with the 'interpretation and application of existing rules' and **matters of interest** which 'involve differences relating to the determination of new terms and conditions of employment' [2].
2. The dissatisfaction may be confined to an **individual employee** or be experienced collectively by a **group** or even all employees.
3. The manner of presentation to management may range from **informal presentation** to the immediate supervisor by either an individual, a group of employees or the employees' representative, through **formal presentation within the grievance procedure**, to a **trade union claim being initiated within the recognised negotiating process**.

Whilst it is therefore difficult to draw a precise boundary between grievances and disputes, Thomson and Murray argue their essential difference 'lies in the way they are initiated and in the degree of proposed change in the status quo' [3] (see Figure 19.1). It is largely on this basis that Torrington and Chapman differentiate a **complaint**, where 'dissatisfaction is being expressed, but not in a procedural way', from a grievance, where 'the complaint is presented formally and triggers the procedural machinery' and 'carries with it the idea that the complaint has been ignored or unfairly treated, or there is a difference in interpretation of the working rules' [4].

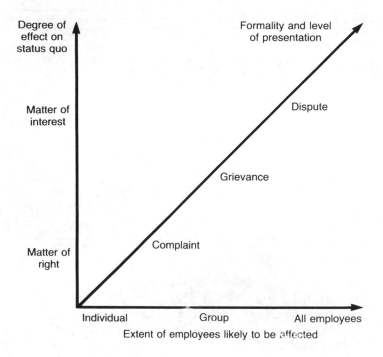

Figure 19.1   *Typology of employee expression of dissatisfaction*

Thus, not all employee complaints result in formal grievances. A **grievance** may perhaps best be defined as:

> **a formal expression of individual or collective employee dissatisfaction primarily, but not exclusively, in respect of the application or non-application of collective agreements, managerial policies and actions or custom and practice.**

Singleton points out that the term 'dispute' is variously applied to grievances 'as soon as a shop steward is involved, when a full-time official of the union is called in' or if it 'is not solved at domestic level and is referred to an external procedure' [5]. In much the same way that a formal grievance may arise if a complaint is not resolved, so a dispute may arise if a trade union claim within the negotiating procedure is not met by management. The use of the term dispute implies, in both situations, that the issue is to be initiated and resolved on an inter-organisation basis between management and the union and may, if necessary, involve the use of industrial action on the union's part if there is a continuing failure to agree. Therefore, a **dispute** may perhaps best be defined as:

a formal expression of collective employee dissatisfaction at the organisational level resulting from either a prior failure to resolve a grievance or a failure to agree on a matter of interest within the negotiating process.

Complaints, grievances and disputes should, therefore, be regarded as overlapping segments of a continuum based primarily on the manner and formality of the presentation of employee dissatisfaction. Whether a specific situation is likely to be regarded as a dispute rather than a grievance depends on the degree of formality of its presentation, the organisational level at which it is initially raised and the extent to which both parties regard the outcome as establishing new terms and conditions of employment.

19.2 The grievance/dispute process

The grievance/dispute process (see Figure 19.2) is concerned with the right of employees to express, and seek to resolve, dissatisfactions they may have in respect of any aspect of their work situation. Consequently, all organisations require some grievance process to resolve this dissatisfaction – irrespective of whether trade unions are recognised or not. It is **complementary, but opposite, to the disciplinary process**: complementary in that they both seek to express and resolve dissatisfaction, but opposite in that the disciplinary process is initiated by management whereas the issues which form the substance of the grievance/dispute process are originated by employees. Thus, it may be argued that, because the process exists primarily for the benefit and protection of employees, its **effectiveness** should be judged by employee (rather than management) satisfaction with its operation.

Relationship to collective bargaining

The grievance/dispute process is complementary to the collective bargaining process in that not only may the misapplication of the terms of any collective agreement form the basis of a grievance or dispute, but also because through the operation of this process employees seek, and are able, to maintain a measure of continuing control over those managerial decisions which affect their work situation. A collective agreement is unable on its own, nor is it intended, to provide the means for joint regulation of the full range and variety of situations encountered in a work situation. The wording of most collective agreements is often imprecise, or even deliberately ambiguous, and

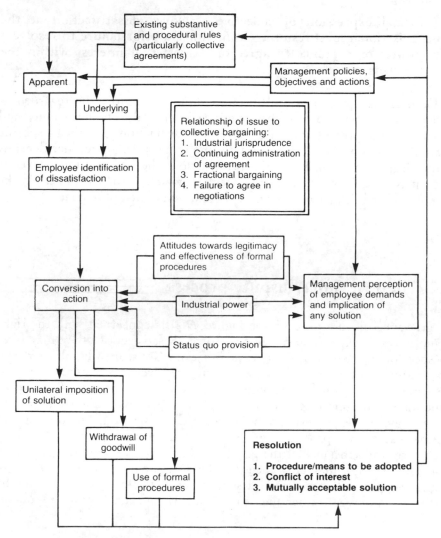

Figure 19.2   *Grievance/dispute process*

involves the use of 'may', 'reasonable', 'where practical', etc. – all of which require clarification as to the precise circumstances in which they will or will not operate. Certainly, Hawkins believes that 'where a grievance procedure either formally or informally includes collective issues within its scope the dividing line between grievance settlement and collective bargaining becomes increasingly blurred' [6].

It is possible to identify four distinct, but overlapping, ways in which the grievance/dispute process is integral to the collective bargaining system.

• *Industrial jurisprudence.* Simply, this means that it may be used by employees or union to ensure that management complies with the terms of any collective agreement to which they are a party. Many employee complaints to their shop steward or supervisor, for example the calculation of their pay, may come under this heading. Indeed the shop steward, through his/her knowledge of the terms of the collective agreements, is very often able to provide an immediate answer to, and resolution of, employee complaints without referring the matter to any member of management. However, it is this function of the process which often leads to the somewhat false assumptions:

1. that the resolution of all grievances or disputes is simply a matter of referring to the appropriate clause in the collective agreement and ensuring that it is being complied with; or
2. that, as Kuhn describes it, 'facts rather than a walkout, reason and argument rather than interrupted production' [7] should determine the outcome.

Beyond this the grievance/dispute process is directly concerned with reaching collective agreements.

• *Continuing administration of collective agreements.* As Kuhn points out, the imprecise wording of most collective agreements means that 'few of its provisions apply automatically or without some person in authority making decisions about the nature of a given situation and the meaning of the agreement' [8]. If employees and union are to maintain the joint regulation established by the initial collective agreement they must continue to negotiate its application with management. Such negotiations, or interpretations and clarifications of the agreement, can only take place when specific situations arise within the workplace to which employees or union believe the collective agreement should apply but management does not, or vice versa. At this level the process goes beyond seeking managerial compliance with the stated terms of the agreement and seeks to jointly agree when and where it should apply. This is achieved by the joint clarification or redefinition of the meaning and intention, if not the wording, of the collective agreement. The results of such negotiations may not be recorded in formal written agreements and become part of the regulatory framework through precedent and 'custom and practice'. This aspect of the process is of increased importance in the early stages of a new agreement when either side may be seeking to extend the scope of its application and the other side seeking to restrict it.

• *Fractional bargaining.* The grievance/dispute process is also utilised to reach agreement on issues not covered by the terms of existing collective agreements. This, as Kuhn notes, 'can arise from any management activity with which the workers become dissatisfied and feel they have the power to negotiate' [9]. The use of the grievance/dispute process to formulate new collective agreements allows employees and union to extend the areas over which they have a measure of joint regulation on an *ad hoc* basis. It provides an opportunity for continuing pressure on, and erosion of, managerial prerogative. In contrast to the main recognised negotiating machinery, which usually results in agreements that are intended to apply to all employees in the 'bargaining unit', the formal effect of agreements reached within the grievance/dispute process is confined to the workgroup immediately affected at that time by management's decision. However, in so far as the agreement is considered by both parties to be satisfactory for the specific situation in which the problem arose, it also creates (through precedent) an expectation on the part of employees and union that its terms may be applied to other groups or in the future should the need arise. Thus, the gains made by one group through the grievance/dispute process may become regarded as terms which should apply to all.

● *Resolution of any failure to agree which arises during negotiations*. It is to this aspect of its function, as a formal part of the main collective bargaining system, that the term 'dispute' is commonly applied. At this level of its operation the process may require both parties to submit their case to some external examination by referring the issue to an industry level disputes procedure, if the organisation is a member of an employers' association, or by the involvement of a third party such as ACAS. Whatever method is used, any resolution becomes part of the final collective agreement in the same way as the other terms on which there was no failure to agree.

Thus, the grievance/dispute process is as much concerned with the determination of rules as it is with their interpretation and application.

Causes and expressions of employee dissatisfaction

The initial stage of the grievance/dispute process involves the employee(s) identifying the cause of their dissatisfaction and the change required to remove it. Most employee dissatisfaction is related either to the manner in which existing terms and conditions of employment are applied to specific situations or to some managerial action or non-action undertaken in pursuance of their policies and objectives. However, the variety of issues, the differing levels at which the process operates and, through this, the various ways in which dissatisfaction may be presented to management, make it difficult to quantify the frequency or relative importance of **different types of issues encountered** within the grievance/dispute process. This is further complicated by many organisations not keeping complete records of the use made of either the grievance or dispute procedures.

Thomson and Murray [10] found that in relation to formal grievances, as opposed to complaints or disputes, two broad types of issues were fairly common amongst the thirty-five plants covered by their survey:

1. **Monetary issues** ranging from simple errors of payment calculation to losses of pay or changes in pay associated with payment by results systems, or appeals on job grading and evaluation.
2. **Work issues** including the allocation of work, the transfer of employees from one type of work to another or the physical conditions under which the work had to be carried out (grievances in respect of the allocation of overtime or time off, such as holidays, were less frequent).

Contrary to popular perception, they found that issues relating to **employee welfare**, such as canteens, car parking and toilets, arose only occasionally or rarely in the plants studied. It is also significant that they found virtually no grievances arose in respect of **major technical changes** because 'conflict would have been resolved at the planning stage and hence not emerge as grievances' [11]. An alternative explanation may well be that such major issues were considered to be negotiated items or disputes, rather than strictly grievances, by the organisations concerned.

It would be very easy to conclude from this list of issues that the cause of grievances and disputes is to be found exclusively in the manner in which management implements its operational decisions. However, whilst this may be an important source of employee dissatisfaction, there are, as Thomson and Murray point out from their examination of the literature relating to industrial conflict [12], other potential causes which it is important to recognise if the grievance/dispute process is to fulfil its function. Indeed, the **apparent concern** regarding an operational decision expressed by employees through the grievance/dispute process may, in reality, be only the symptom of some more fundamental, but less tangible, employee dissatisfaction. It is possible to identify four main areas of **underlying concern** which may influence the operation of the process:

1. Perhaps central to many grievances or disputes is the general **need of most employees to achieve some form of satisfaction from their work situation**. The particular satisfaction being sought will, of course, vary both between employees and within each employee over time. Thus, for some it may be financial reward or status, whilst for others it may be the intrinsic quality of the work they perform. The removal of this satisfaction by management, whether deliberate or inadvertent, may cause the employee to seek redress for the perceived loss through the grievance/dispute process. However, in most situations such loss cannot easily be articulated as a specific grievance and therefore is likely to result in the frustrated employee seeking to receive 'due entitlements' which previously may not have been a matter of concern. A series of

what appear to be minor grievances may be a reflection of a more general dissatisfaction with the work situation which will remain unaltered even after the specific grievances have been resolved. Such a feeling of frustration may also arise where the employee's own position remains unchanged but the position or treatment of others is perceived to have improved – a feeling of relative deprivation. These feelings of frustration are not confined exclusively to individual employees but may be experienced and expressed on a group basis.

2. The **nature of the socio-technical system** may itself result in an increased formal use of the grievance/dispute process by employees. This can arise not only from simple employee dissatisfaction in respect of the nature of their work but also from structural factors associated with the relationship of the employees to their work and management. The system may lead employees to feel they have little direct control over the physical work processes they are required to operate and they may seek to balance this loss by gaining more formal control over the managerial decisions which determine the day-to-day work situation (such as changes in the speed, type and quality of the production) through representations to management within the grievance/dispute process. Alternatively, the system may create a perceived separation between employees and their immediate management resulting in the formal presentation of issues which, in other circumstances, might have been raised as informal complaints. This may also arise where employees perceive the decision making process to be centralised away from their own immediate management.

3. Most work situations are likely to involve some degree of **change and adaptation**. However, employees may, particularly where such changes occur frequently and with little notice, feel uncertain in respect of their own position. The instability created in this way may result in the need for continual reassurance that management is taking account of their anxieties and aspirations during its decision making. This can only effectively be achieved by the employees challenging changes when they occur, or are proposed, and seeking to influence them. In this way employees may satisfy themselves that the change is both necessary and causes the least disruption to them.

4. All industrial relations situations relate, in one form or another, to the exercise of **power and authority**. Management's prerogative to make decisions is always likely to be subjected to challenge from employees and union. Thus, any grievance or dispute which arises within an organisation may be concerned as much with questioning management's right to make the decision unilaterally as it is with modifying the content of that decision. The raising of a formal grievance or dispute implies that the issue is considered, by the employees or union, to be an appropriate matter for negotiation and joint regulation. However, for the area of joint regulation to be extended in this way requires management, for its

part, to respond by being prepared to accept and discuss the issue as a legitimate grievance or dispute.

Where employees identify the cause of their dissatisfaction as being a management responsibility, they must then **determine the manner in which their dissatisfaction is to be expressed**. This may take one of three main forms:

1. A **formal approach to management**, on an individual or collective basis, within the appropriate grievance, disputes or negotiating procedures.
2. Seek to **impose their own solution** by, for example, refusing to carry out the work which has caused the dissatisfaction.
3. If they lack the power to unilaterally impose a solution, **withdraw their goodwill** from the management and the organisation through perhaps increased absenteeism, labour turnover and a reduction in morale.

It is the manner in which the dissatisfaction is expressed to management which determines the procedural processes and institutions to be utilised in the resolution of the problem. Whilst a direct formal approach by employees within either the grievance, disputes or negotiating procedures will require a response from management which may then be considered and negotiated over, the employees' imposition of a solution or adoption of an informal withdrawal pattern is at best likely to result in the dissatisfaction only being considered by management as a possible mitigating factor when it applies the disciplinary process to disaffected employees.

The **conversion of latent employee dissatisfaction into manifest forms of action** is influenced by the extent to which the employees accept the legitimacy and effectiveness of the recognised formal procedures for resolving such issues and the perceived power relationship between the employees and management. The acceptance and continued use of the formal recognised procedures depends not only on the fact that they are the constitutional means for resolving any differences or employee dissatisfaction but also on the degree of employee and union satisfaction with their manner of operation and the solutions reached within them. If employees or union feel that the formal procedures do not provide an adequate means for, or even hinder, the effective representation and protection of their interests, they may seek to express and resolve their dissatisfactions outside these procedures. At the same time, the possession of industrial power by a group of employees not only enhances the group's and individual member's confidence to express dissatisfaction but also strengthens their ability to both ensure that management gives due consideration to their problems and positively influences management's decision in their favour. It may also increase the level of expectation amongst the members of the group as to what can, or should, be achieved if they use, or threaten to use, their industrial power. It is such 'strategic' groups which have the greatest capacity to indulge in 'fractional bargaining' through the formal grievance/dispute process, or, where they feel the formal procedures to be inadequate, to press for their reform, or, if necessary, to impose solutions. However, where employees lack both industrial power and confidence in the effectiveness of the formal procedures they are more likely to express their dissatisfaction through some form of individual or collective withdrawal pattern.

Managerial response

The purpose of the grievance/dispute process is not to create conditions within the organisation whereby grievances and disputes do not exist, but rather to provide a means for their agreed settlement without recourse to industrial action. Thus, the **resolution phase** of the process requires some form of **dialogue between employees and management**. It is at this point, when management is responding in the light of its perception of the nature of the employees' dissatisfaction and assessing the likely implications of any solution for the maintenance of its policies, that a **conflict of interest** between employee aspirations and management objectives may become apparent. Such a conflict of interest may only be resolved through negotiation and therefore any outcome, whether it relates to matters of right or of interest, or concerns a single employee or the whole group, will reinforce or modify the existing pattern of rules. Indeed, the continued use of the process to resolve such conflicts is a constant reaffirmation of those procedural rules.

Management's major concern, apart from seeking to obtain a solution which is compatible with its long-term objectives and strategy, is to ensure the **maintenance of the formal procedures** themselves. Whilst employees and union may sometimes view the use of these procedures as delaying or restricting their ability to exert their industrial power in securing a favourable settlement, management views the continued integrity of such procedures as fundamental to an orderly system of industrial relations within the organisation. This concern for the grievance/dispute process is founded on two main arguments:

1. Because any collective agreement is itself a product of an agreed joint negotiating procedure and made in 'good faith' by both sides, it is reasonable to assume that both will wish to discuss, and if necessary negotiate, any differences between them regarding its further interpretation and application.
2. These procedures provide a constitutional forum within which both sides may argue their case and seek to persuade the other on a more or less equal basis and neither, Marsh pointed out, should 'attempt to

obtain settlements more favourable to itself by unconstitutional action'
[13] involving the use of industrial power as a pressure.

Thus, management is concerned to ensure that in any response it makes
it does not encourage, and indeed actively discourages, the use of **unconstitutional action on the part of employees or union**. Initially management's
position is protected by the inclusion of a specific clause in the grievance and
disputes procedures which precludes industrial action by either employees or
management until all the stages of the procedure have been exhausted.
Normally management will seek to enforce this clause through its refusal to
negotiate 'under duress' – whether actual or only threatened. However,
when faced with unconstitutional industrial action it may be necessary for
management to negotiate with the union in order to secure a return to
normal working. In such situations management may seek to maintain its
position on the integrity of procedures and not negotiating under duress by
distinguishing the negotiation of a 'return to work formula' from the original
issue which caused the industrial action and on which negotiations will
continue only when normal working has been resumed. Nevertheless, the
boundary between the two issues and sets of negotiations is often blurred.
Ironically, this distinction may be made clearer where the industrial action is
also unofficial (i.e. not sanctioned officially by the union) because it is not
the union (with whom management is likely to negotiate the return to work)
which instigated the initial duress. Management's position has been strengthened in this area by legislation requiring the union to more closely
disassociate itself from any unofficial industrial action.

In addition, management will be concerned to ensure that the **stages of
the procedure are applied in their correct sequence**. Perhaps the most
frequent occurrence in this respect is for the shop steward or employee(s) to
ignore the first stage of the grievance procedure, generally the supervisor,
either because they feel he/she has no real authority to make a decision and
will simply refer the matter to the next stage of the procedure or because
they believe they will receive a more favourable answer from a higher
management level. In such situations it is up to that higher level of
management to refuse to deal with the issue until the initial stage of the
procedure has been used.

As Marsh pointed out, it is often argued that the grievance/dispute
procedure should be **legally enforceable** 'principally with the object of
reinforcing the process of keeping procedures intact by providing penalties
against unconstitutional action' [14]. It is felt that this would not only
strengthen management's position against unconstitutional action but would
also be complementary to the legal right which individual employees have to
enforce the substantive terms contained in collective agreements. At the same
time it could strengthen the position of the official union organisation in any
endeavour they may make to persuade their members to abandon such

unconstitutional, and often unofficial, action. However, the appropriateness and effectiveness of **legal enforcement are questionable** on a number of grounds:

1. The variety and subtlety of the forms of duress which employees and union may exert on management are such that some (e.g. 'withdrawal of co-operation') are virtually incapable of legal definition and application.
2. Although most unconstitutional actions in the operation of these procedures are instigated by employees or union, in practice they may result from some less obvious action or indecision on the part of management and, it may therefore be argued, are justified in pressuring management to make good its deficiencies.
3. Given the varied nature of both the grievance/dispute process and the issues it is expected to handle, it would be unreasonable to expect that all grievances or disputes should be resolved without the use of industrial power; in some situations compromise may only be achieved through the demonstration of such power.

Management's response within the formal grievance/dispute process may be further constrained by the existence of a **status quo** provision. Such a provision is aimed at ensuring that, where a grievance or dispute arises from a management decision or action, the situation which existed prior to that decision or action should prevail until such time as either an agreement is reached or the grievance/dispute process is exhausted. Management is, in effect, precluded from making any change until agreement has been reached with the employees or union or their failure to agree has been processed to the final stage of the disputes procedure. Without such a provision management would be able to implement its changes and then negotiate with employees and union afterwards. The existence of such a provision places the pressure for settlement more on management than on union or employees. Unlike wage bargaining, where delay in reaching an agreement is to the advantage of management, any delay in reaching a settlement over work changes is to the advantage of union and employees by allowing them to continue to work a system with which they are satisfied and increasing the pressure on management to make concessions in order to secure their agreement to the proposed change as soon as possible.

Finally, whilst the objective of management, union and employees should be to strive for **mutually acceptable solutions**, this may undermine the achievement of long-term objectives. Many grievances and disputes stem from changes within the organisation which involve a clear difference of interest between management and employees. If the difference is felt to be important enough it may even prejudice the achievement of a solution within the procedural arrangements. Thus, whilst mutually acceptable solutions can only be reached by a compromise of interests and objectives, management must balance this against the need to stand by the objectives it has formulated even in the face of strong employee or union objection. Marsh pointed out that 'there is a sense in which procedure can be too successful … for the effect of procedure is to achieve acceptable compromise and it may be that such compromise is not always in the economic or social interest' [15]. In some situations a solution may only be achieved by one or other of the parties abandoning their objective because the cost of continuing to seek its achievement is too high.

19.3 Handling grievances and disputes

The interrelationship between management's grievance/disputes policy, the procedures and the formal interface between management and employees or union to resolve problems is shown in Figure 19.3.

A grievance/disputes policy

The purpose of a grievance/disputes policy should be to **establish the organisational climate, objectives and manner in which managers (individually or collectively) will be expected to respond to any grievance or**

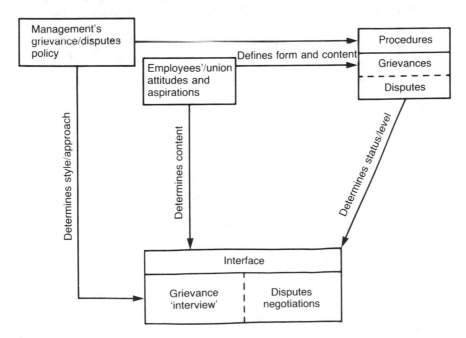

Figure 19.3 *Grievance/dispute policy, procedures and interface*

dispute presented by employees. In so far as the organisation has jointly agreed grievance and disputes procedures, some or all of the objectives contained within management's policy may become translated into jointly agreed objectives as part of the preamble to such procedures. It is within this policy statement that management's concern to maintain the integrity of the procedural arrangements is often most clearly expressed. Thus, the policy may contain statements such as:

1. Management accepts the right of employees, individually or collectively through their recognised union, to present complaints to management.
2. It is in the interests of management, union and employees to establish and maintain formal recognised procedures for dealing with such complaints.
3. Management will endeavour, when reaching decisions, to ensure that situations do not arise which may be the cause of complaint by employees.
4. Any differences which may arise between management and either employees or union should, wherever possible, be resolved quickly and without recourse to the use of industrial action.
5. Management is not prepared to consider or discuss any complaint under duress whether actual or threatened.
6. Wherever there is a difference in respect of a change in existing terms and conditions of employment or working arrangements, status quo will apply until the matter is resolved or the appropriate procedure is exhausted.
7. Management is concerned to ensure that, in responding to any grievance or dispute, it does not create an unacceptable precedent which may subsequently be claimed to apply throughout the organisation.

Grievance and disputes procedure

The grievance and disputes procedure provides the formal mechanism for the identification and resolution of any complaints which employees or their unions may have in respect of their employment or management's actions. All employers are required to inform employees, as part of their contract of employment notice, of both the person to whom they should go initially to seek redress of any grievances relating to their employment and, where applicable, any consequent steps (S.1, Employment Protection Act 1978). Daniel and Millward [16] found that over 95 per cent of establishments with more than 200 employees have an individual grievance procedure – even 70 per cent of establishments employing 25–49 employees had one. However, only amongst establishments employing more than 1,000 employees did the percentage having a procedure to deal with pay and conditions disputes reach 90 per cent. Interestingly, only 68 per cent of establishments recognising trade unions had such a disputes procedure and 26 per cent of organisations with high union density (80–100 per cent) did not have one. The apparent low percentage of establishments in the public sector (at that time) which had such a procedure (58 per cent) reflected 'the prevalence of nationally determined pay scales and of issues arising mainly at the national level' [17].

The precise arrangements of the procedure will, of course, vary between organisations as a result of variations in their organisational structure, the role designated for the personnel specialist (if there is one), whether or not they are unionised, and the structural arrangements for collective bargaining. The situation is further complicated by some organisations having a **single integrated procedure** to encompass all grievances and disputes, whilst others have **separate and distinct procedures** for grievances relating to the interpretation and application of existing collective agreements and management policies and for disputes arising from a trade union claim within the normal negotiating procedure.

The procedure depicted in Figure 19.4 should not, therefore, be regarded as a model which is applicable to all organisations, but rather as an illustration of the operation of one specific procedure which is, perhaps, somewhat atypical in respect of the executive, as opposed to advisory, role undertaken by the industrial relations/personnel specialists within it. Certainly, such an executive role might be regarded as incompatible with the general move during the 1980s to shift more authority and responsibility for the conduct of industrial relations within the organisation to line management. Nevertheless it usefully highlights a number of the issues which need to be considered in both the drawing up and operation of grievance/disputes procedures.

Coverage of the procedure

Certain **issues may be specifically excluded** from the normal grievance procedure because of their special needs. For example, grievances or disputes relating to health and safety matters may require to be referred to the Safety Officer for judgement, whilst complaints regarding the grading of a post may be dealt with through a special appeals procedure involving judgement by a regrading panel. Where issues are excluded in this way, it is important that the preamble to the grievance/disputes procedures should direct the employee to the appropriate procedure for resolving such matters.

The normal grievance/dispute procedure may also be **formally modified to cope with special circumstances**. For example, the procedure depicted in Figure 19.4 was amended to deal with the need to interpret and apply the terms of a new productivity agreement during the initial period following its negotiation. The amendment meant that a grievance could, if it related to the interpretation of that agreement, be referred (between stages 2 and 3 of the normal procedure) to a special joint management/shop steward committee for its 'advice' as to the meaning and intention of the particular clause in the

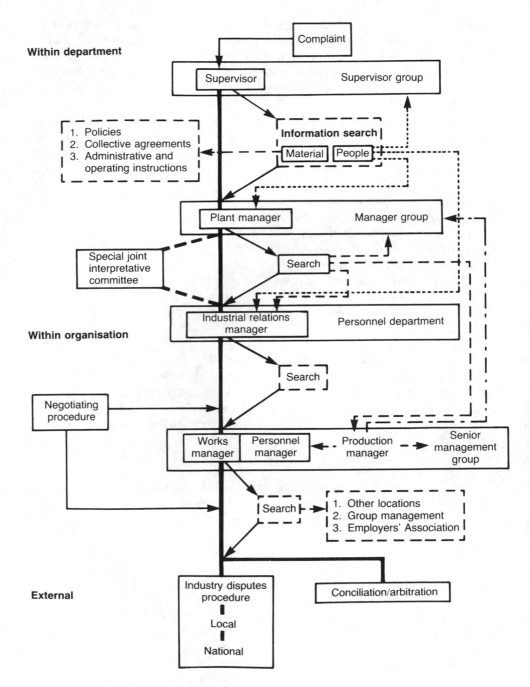

Figure 19.4 *Grievance procedure*

agreement. The importance of this committee lay in its members having been involved in writing and negotiating the original agreement.

Where the procedure is intended to encompass both individual and collective matters, it is important that it should clearly **identify the appropriate stage, or stages, at which collective issues may initially be presented**. Such issues may require to be presented at departmental level, or even higher, depending on the extent of the group presenting the collective grievance.

Stages and system of appeals

The adoption of a staged approach within the grievance/dispute procedure reflects organisational reality – namely, a hierarchy of roles based on **increasing responsibility and authority**. Thomson and Murray note that the purpose of such an approach, in operational terms, is 'to ensure that those with effective authority ... can be reached in an orderly way and also to provide for a review of decisions by a new level of authority at each succeeding stage' [18]. However, it is important to remember that the actual operation of the procedure may be at variance with the latter assumption.

Whilst the **number of stages and levels of management** involved in the grievance/disputes procedure will be largely determined by management's organisational structure, it is necessary to ensure that the operation of the procedure does not become cumbersome and time consuming as a result of there being too many stages. It is essential, therefore, to incorporate only those definable and distinct levels of management authority which can, and should, play an effective role in resolving employee grievances and it may be desirable to exclude certain levels of management from the process.

However, irrespective of the precise number of stages, it is possible to distinguish **three broad levels** at which the procedure operates:

1. **Within a department** the procedure usually allows the departmental manager, who has responsibility for ensuring that the department fulfils its productive targets and complies with the organisation's policies and collective agreements, the opportunity to check, and if necessary correct, the decisions and actions of subordinate line management.
2. **Outside the department but still within the organisation**, the procedure allows more senior management to assess the grievance or dispute within the wider context of the organisation's industrial relations position and strategy and, in particular, assess any implications it may have for other parts of the organisation or the future. At this level, when problems may be regarded as more serious, management may wish to discuss the matter with its Employers' Association and/or the group management and other locations.
3. **External to the organisation:** the procedure may provide for an unresolved grievance or dispute to be subjected to some form of 'third party' scrutiny to judge whether management's decision is 'fair' and, if

applicable, in accordance with the provisions of any national agreement. This may involve the use of conciliation/arbitration or processing the grievance or dispute through a nationally agreed industry disputes procedure (if the organisation is a member of an Employers' Association). Brown [19] found that half of the establishments which had access to such an industry procedure had used it over the previous two years. In 37 per cent of establishments the procedure provided for third-party intervention (such as ACAS) in respect of pay and conditions disputes and 21 per cent in respect of individual grievances. Of those which had such a provision, 21 per cent had used it over the previous two years for pay and conditions disputes and only 5 per cent had used it for individual grievances; but generally the management had been 'very' or 'fairly' satisfied with its use in resolving the dispute.

The internal stages of the procedure involve employees or their representatives presenting their grievance for consideration by management. Thus, for most of the procedure, **management is acting as sole judge** with employees, if satisified, accepting the decision or, if dissatisfied, appealing to a higher level of management. The use of a **joint committee**, comprising both management and union representatives, as the decision making body is usually confined to the external stages of the procedure. Here it acts, in effect, as an arbitration body with the management and union involved in the dispute presenting their case to a committee drawn from organisations and unions not involved in the dispute. Where a joint committee forms part of the internal procedure and is required to reach a decision on the validity or otherwise of a grievance, the issue is unlikely to proceed further unless the committee itself 'fails to agree' on its decision.

It is important to recognise that the **nature of the appeal system** contained within the grievance/dispute procedure means that if at any stage the employee or union receive an answer or decision which is acceptable to them the procedure then ceases. At that point employees or unions are satisfied and no longer have a grievance. There is usually no provision within the procedure, except in respect of external stages, for management to initiate an 'appeal' because it is dissatisfied with a decision reached at a lower level. Therefore, failure to reach a settlement at the lower stages of the procedure may result not just from the unwillingness of the supervisor or manager concerned to make a concession but from a perception that it involves a decision which is outside his/her sphere of responsibility/authority and requires the approval of a more senior manager. It is in this context that Marsh draws a distinction between grievances involving essentially 'appeals to equity' where the procedure is used to decide 'what is fair, and there can be no logical stop to the process', and grievances involving the 'interpretation and application' of collective agreements where 'only the parties at the level at which the agreement was made can logically say how it should be applied or interpreted' [20].

This view of the appeal system, and indeed the formal wording of most grievance procedures, appears to rest on the assumption that each level of management dealing with the grievance is independent in both its decision making role and its relationship to any previous level of the procedure. This assumption is incorrect. In reality the manager at each stage of the procedure is likely to conduct an **information search** before responding to the employees' or union's grievance (see Figure 19.4). Whilst one part of this search involves a 'material search' of relevant documents such as policies, collective agreements or any administrative/operating instructions, the more important part involves conducting a 'people search' amongst others in the organisation who may be able to help. Thus, the supervisor may contact other supervisors who have already dealt with similar problems, or his/her superior to whom the grievance may go if it is unresolved or the industrial relations specialist who has a functional responsibility in this area of management. Similarly, this type of search process is likely to take place at each succeeding stage of the procedure.

This aspect of the operation of the grievance procedure has two important implications:

1. It is not clear what the manager is seeking during a 'people search' – is it simply information, ideas or opinions on which he/she may base a decision or is it some form of decision or agreement amongst the roles as to what is the best course of action which may be implemented? In many situations the latter is more likely and therefore the managerial response within the formal procedure may be regarded as a **corporate decision and response** rather than the decision and response of the individual manager.
2. When a more senior manager is called upon to formally consider a grievance or dispute which has not been resolved at the previous stage he/she is not approaching it as a completely fresh and previously uninvolved level of management. Each will already have been involved, as part of an earlier 'people search', in the determination of the response which has failed to satisfy the employees' or union's grievance. Thus their role is more one of providing the focus and opportunity for the reassessment of the corporate decision that one of passing judgement on the quality and fairness of a lower level manager's decision.

The **role and involvement of supervisors** in the operation of the grievance procedure is of particular importance if grievances are to be resolved as quickly as possible and without the unnecessary use of the higher stages. Most procedures seek to ensure that the employee initially presents the grievance to the immediate supervisor and then, only if it is not resolved, to involve the shop steward as the second stage. In many procedures the individual 'must' do this, in others only 'should', whilst in a few this first step is incorporated into the procedure only as an informal stage. The formal exclusion of the shop steward from the first stage of the procedure may in practice inhibit some employees from presenting their grievances to management.

Concern is frequently expressed that the first stage is **bypassed** by employees and shop stewards because of the supervisor's apparent lack of authority to make the necessary decision. However, this has to be balanced against the equally often expressed perception of many supervisors that they rarely encounter formal grievances from employees. The complaints or queries raised by employees and shop stewards which supervisors answer or resolve as a normal part of their job are often not regarded by them as grievances to which they are responding as Stage 1 of the formal grievance procedure. Nevertheless, as Singleton notes, for many supervisors the 'premature involvement of the union may create in him the feeling that the problem is already outside his sphere of responsibility' [21] and thus induce the supervisor to refer the matter to the next stage of the procedure. It is very important that, whenever a grievance proceeds beyond the supervisor stage, he/she should continue to be involved in the subsequent decision making. If the response made at the supervisor level of the procedure, whether resulting from an individual decision or from a collective managerial decision, is to be changed at a subsequent level, he/she should know why it has been changed and be able to express an opinion on the implications. This will enhance competence in decision making, and the contribution he/she may make to collective decision making.

Formality of the procedure

The inherent desire on the part of both management and employees to exert control over the work situation implies, Thomson and Murray suggest, that joint procedures 'are the best, possibly the only, way of bringing the two separate control systems to terms with each other' [22]. Nevertheless, both sides often still want to retain for themselves, but not necessarily the other side, a degree of informality and flexibility to treat issues on their merits.

Many procedures specify **time limits** within which management has to make a response – ranging from two to five working days at the earlier stages to one to two weeks at the later stages. Whilst this is intended to protect employees and union from undue delay on the part of management in considering a grievance, many managers would argue that it involves a loss of flexibility on their part. The stated time at a particular stage may be insufficient for an adequate consideration of the problem, particularly complex ones, resulting in the issue simply moving to a higher level of the procedure. However, in such special circumstances management may, if it wishes, seek to extend the stated time limits by agreement with the employees or union concerned. It should be remembered that even with time limits it may take three to four weeks before the internal procedure is exhausted.

The desire to have **grievances or disputes presented in a written form** stems from management's concern that without such an arrangement the content of a grievance or dispute is likely to change as it progresses through the various stages of the procedure. This is often regarded by management as a deliberate tactic on the part of shop stewards or the union either to cloud the real issue or to strengthen their case by moving it away from the specific situation which generated the grievance and into arguments based on more general principles. In fact, both union and management perceptions of the character of, and issues involved in, a particular grievance or dispute will inevitably change as it progresses through the procedure. It will be viewed in successively wider organisational and industrial relations contexts. Certainly, any argument that employees 'must' present their grievance in a written form, particularly in respect of the first stage, ignores the general informality of this stage and may well prejudice the position of those employees who either cannot write or have difficulty in expressing themselves in a written medium. However, it is good industrial relations practice for management at all levels of the procedure to keep a formal written record of any meetings or discussions. This will not only help to clarify the nature of the grievance and any points of difference between themselves and the employee or shop steward, but also provide a useful basis for briefing the manager at the next stage of the procedure should the problem remain unresolved. If such records can be agreed with the employee or shop steward involved so much the better.

Finally, the integrity of the formal grievance/disputes procedures can only be maintained if senior managers, having allocated responsibility for dealing with grievances to certain defined levels of management, do not subvert it by offering employees, shop stewards or union officials an **open door policy**. Some senior managers believe that they can demonstrate their goodwill on industrial relations matters and improve trust and understanding within the organisation by allowing employees and/or their representatives free access to them with their problems. Such an approach, like the senior manager or director who deals with employees' grievances while touring the shopfloor, simply encourages the bypassing of the formal procedural arrangements. Managers, whether line or personnel specialist, who are approached by an employee or shop steward with a problem should, even though they could resolve the problem there and then, either refer the employee or shop steward back to the appropriate level of the procedure or discuss and agree the matter with the appropriate supervisor or manager before taking any action. Breaches of procedure by employees and shop stewards cannot be condemned if management itself is aiding and encouraging such breaches.

The formal interface

The formal interface between management and employees or union within the grievance/dispute procedure may take two main forms (see Figure 19.3).

1. The interface for disputes in relation to unresolved grievances or failures to agree arising from union claims is likely to take place within the normal framework of joint management/union negotiations and therefore all the principles of negotiating will apply.
2. At the early stages of the procedure the interface may take place within what is often referred to as a 'grievance interview' and involve a single manager meeting the employee or shop steward. However, it would be wrong to conclude that the **process of negotiating** is not relevant to these meetings: they are an integral part of the collective bargaining system within the organisation and are just as likely to involve the need to achieve a compromise between the parties as any formal negotiation.

Objectives and conduct of the grievance interview

There are three distinct stages to the grievance interview:

1. The manager has to **establish the nature and reasons for the grievance**. In this he/she is largely dependent on the information given by the employee and/or shop steward at the outset of the meeting. However, the manager should be certain that all the relevant information has been obtained and the precise character and extent of the grievance, especially any underlying causes, is understood. Thus, during this stage of the meeting the manager is primarily concerned with listening. Having done this, the manager must then decide whether the matter is within his/her sphere of responsibility. If it is not, it must be agreed with the employee or shop steward that the matter should be referred to the next stage of the procedure and notify the appropriate manager accordingly. If it is, the manager must then decide whether he/she is in a position to make an immediate response or whether time is required to gather more information or consult other members of management. If an adjournment is necessary, the manager should inform the employee or shop steward of the reason for the adjournment and agree a time for a further meeting.
2. The manager, assuming that the grievance is not one which has arisen simply because of the incorrect application of a collective agreement or management policy, has the **responsibility for stating and explaining the organisation's position** on the issue which is the cause of the grievance. He/she must be prepared, in reponse to questions or arguments from the employee or shop steward, to explain and defend the reasons for the response to the grievance in some detail. During this

stage the manager is primarily acting as a spokesperson for management seeking to convince the employee or shop steward of the correctness of management's decision. It is at this point, if the employee or shop steward is not satisfied with the manager's reply to the grievance, that any conflict of interest between management's objectives and the aspirations of employees or union will become apparent.

3.   The third stage of the meeting will be concerned with **identifying alternatives and arriving at a mutually acceptable compromise**. As in any other negotiating situation, the manager cannot successfully undertake this task unless: (i) a target position to aim for and a fall-back position have been identified, and (ii) arguments and strategy for moving towards a compromise have been prepared. The adjournment between stages one and two of the meeting allows the manager to develop and discuss such a strategy with any superior and/or the industrial relations specialist. Indeed, the initial response in the second stage of the meeting may be the manager's opening gambit for what is likely to follow in the third stage.

Preparation for the interview

By the very nature of the grievance/dispute process, in that it is initiated by employee dissatisfaction, there is little that a supervisor or manager can do in preparation for a particular grievance meeting. However, all supervisors and managers should be aware that any action or decision on their part is a potential source of employee dissatisfaction and therefore should always be in a position, if called upon, to explain and justify them. It is principally between the first and second stages of the meeting that management's preparation is undertaken; assessing both the importance of the issue to employees, union and themselves and the likely implications of any possible solution, particularly outside the immediate situation in which the grievance has arisen and for the future. It is on this basis that the strategy for response during the second and third stages of the meeting can be prepared.

Follow-up

Once the grievance or dispute has been settled it is important that both parties are clear as to the precise details of the decision they have reached. It is useful for the outcome of any grievance meeting to be recorded in writing – if only in a letter of confirmation from the supervisor or manager to the employee or shop steward. The supervisor or manager should also ensure that the rest of management, particularly the industrial relations specialist, is informed of the decision. This is essential if industrial relations activities throughout the organisation are to be co-ordinated and integrated. The dissemination of this information to all levels of management should ensure that different solutions are not applied in different parts of the organisation unless the particular circumstances clearly warrant such an approach.

19.4 Summary propositions

- The grievance/dispute process is an integral part of the system of collective bargaining at the organisation level and, as such, is concerned with the determination of rules as well as their interpretation and application.
- The effectiveness of the formal procedures is largely dependent on employee and union acceptance of their integrity and usefulness in resolving their dissatisfaction.
- The managerial response within the grievance procedure is not an independent individual manager's decision but rather a corporate one.
- The process involved in resolving grievances, at all stages of the procedure, is primarily a negotiating one.

Further reading

- A. W. J. Thomson and V. V. Murray, *Grievance Procedures*, Saxon House, 1976. A very useful examination of both the theoretical and practical aspects of grievance procedures.
- J. W. Kuhn, *Bargaining in Grievance Settlement*, Columbia University Press, 1961. Although based on American experience of grievance handling, and some twenty years old, this is nevertheless a useful examination of the relationship of grievance handling and the power of workgroups to the collective bargaining process.

References

1. A. W. J. Thomson and V. V. Murray, *Grievance Procedures*, Saxon House, 1976, p. 18.
2. *Grievance Arbitration: A practical guide*, ILO, 1977, p. 4.
3. A. W. J. Thomson and V. V. Murray, *op. cit.*, p. 18.
4. D. Torrington and J. Chapman, *Personnel Management* (2nd edn), Prentice Hall, 1983, p. 253.
5. N. Singleton, 'Industrial Relations Procedures', *Department of Employment Manpower Paper No. 14*, HMSO, 1975, p. 16.
6. K. Hawkins, *A Handbook of Industrial Relations Practice*, Kogan Page, 1979, p. 141.
7. J. W. Kuhn, *Bargaining in Grievance Settlement*, Columbia University Press, 1961, p. 14.
8. *ibid.*, p. 28.
9. *ibid.*, p. 81.
10. A. W. J. Thomson and V. V. Murray, *op cit.*, pp. 76–83.
11. *ibid.*, p. 79.

12. *ibid.*, pp. 17–50.
13. A. I. Marsh, 'Disputes Procedures in British Industry', Research Paper 2 (Part 1), *Royal Commission on Trade Unions and Employers' Associations*, HMSO, 1966, p. 7.
14. *ibid.*, p. 23.
15. *ibid.*, p. 26.
16. W. W. Daniel and N. Millward, *Workplace Industrial Relations in Britain*, Heinemann (PSI/SSRC), 1983, Table VII.1, p. 160.
17. *ibid.*, p. 162.
18. A. W. J. Thomson and V. V. Murray, *op. cit.*, pp. 139-40.
19. W. Brown (ed.), *The Changing Contours of British Industrial Relations*, Blackwell, 1981, pp. 47–9.
20. A. I. Marsh, *op. cit.*, pp. 5–6.
21. N. Singleton, *op. cit.*, p. 20.
22. A. W. J. Thomson and V. V. Murray, *op. cit.*, p. 128.

Chapter 20
Discipline

20.1 Definition

Formal discipline may be defined as

> **action taken by management against an individual or group who have failed to conform to the rules established by management within the organisation [1].**

Such formal action can often prove to be an emotive and contentious issue, particularly when it results in the ultimate sanction of dismissal. It not only involves subjectives concepts of 'fair' and 'reasonable', 'right' and 'wrong', but also concerns the power, authority and status of management.

However, the maintenance of discipline within the organisation is not achieved simply by a series of isolated occasions of formalised action by management. The formal disciplinary process is only one, but very important, aspect of the much more general managerial function of regulating human behaviour within organisations. This regulation is maintained by a control system based on 'rewards' and 'punishment' (see Figure 20.1). The aim is to ensure that employees conform to the behavioural and performance standards determined by management as being necessary for the achievement of organisational objectives. Management considers compliance with these standards to be the employees' contribution to the wage/work bargain. The **function of the control system** is to reinforce these standards by rewarding compliance and penalising violations. The formal disciplinary process, comprising the disciplinary policy, rules, procedure and their application, can be differentiated from the rest of the control system by reference to the two axes:

1. It is a formalised process; generally codified in written documents and embodying a quasi-judicial sequence of identification of offence, a 'trial' involving submission of evidence by both the prosecution and defence

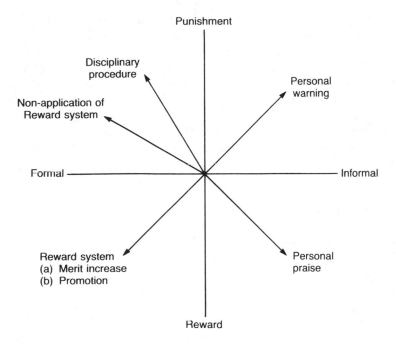

Figure 20.1   *Reward/punishment control system*

and pleas in mitigation, followed by the passing and execution of sentence.

2. It is orientated towards 'punishment' for non-compliance as opposed to reward for compliance.

20.2 The formal disciplinary process

There is an absence of reliable published data relating to the **extent of formal disciplinary action**. In 1967 the Ministry of Labour could only 'guestimate' that between 333,000 and 500,000 employees (1.4 per cent and 2.1 per cent of the total working population) were dismissed each year for misconduct (excluding those dismissed because of sickness, incapacity or unsuitability which they 'guestimated' accounted for a further 1.5 million dismissals per year) [2]. In 1980 Daniel and Millward [3] found that the average annual rate of dismissals amongst the organisations surveyed was 1.1 per cent of employees (equal to 270,000 of the total working population), ranging from 1.8 per cent amongst establishments with less than 100 employees to 0.4 per cent amongst establishments with more than 1,000 employees). Significantly, the number of claims in respect of Unfair Dismissals is only some 30–40,000 per annum.

In view of this difficulty in obtaining accurate data relating to dismissals it is not surprising to find an even greater absence of data relating to formal disciplinary action other than dismissal – warnings, suspensions without pay, demotions, etc. Foxen only states, without amplification, that 'of organisations surveyed it was found that in any one year 4 per cent or less of the employees were involved with action under the heading of "disciplinary" ' [4] (approximately one million employees if applied to the total working population).

A control process

Smith argues that the term control implies 'the possession of authority, the utterance of commands and the operation of restrictions or sanctions to ensure compliance with those commands' [5]. It is management which occupies this position within the formal disciplinary process; an area of employee relations where management still retains its prerogative and few companies have adopted a truly joint approach to the *whole* process. Whilst the procedures for applying the disciplinary rules have become more subject to joint regulation, there has been little, if any, compromise in the determination of the rules. Mellish and Collis-Squires point out that official publications 'seem much "softer" on the question of joint control over the drawing up of substantive rules than they do about the administration of such rules' [6]. They argue that this is almost inevitable given that any legislative incursion into the area of discipline:

1. can only apply to dismissals and therefore has little jurisdiction or concern with the bulk of the formal disciplinary process; and,
2. perceives issues largely in individual terms and separate from the collective bargaining process.

They suggest that if the appropriateness of the disciplinary rules is to be questioned then it can only be done effectively through collective bargaining within the organisation.

Like any other control process within the organisation, the formal disciplinary process **comprises a number of stages** (see Figure 20.2):

1. Definition of desired standards of performance or behaviour; these may be codified in a specific set of disciplinary rules or, more likely, in some form of general works rules or, indeed, may be unwritten and assumed by management to be understood by employees.
2. Assessment of the employee's performance or behaviour against these standards; this assessment is not a formalised, periodic one, as in staff

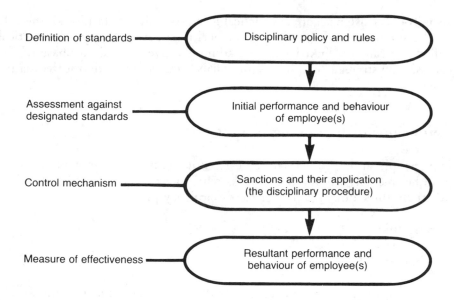

Figure 20.2   *The formal disciplinary process – a control process*

appraisal systems, but takes place only when management believes prima facie that the action of the employee is at variance with the designated standards.

3. The control mechanism itself (the Disciplinary Procedure) to implement corrective action by means of sanctions when the assessed initial performance or behaviour is found to be at variance with the designated standards.

4. Feedback on the effectiveness of the corrective action by assessing whether the resultant performance or behaviour of the employee now conforms to the designated standards.

Thus, the formal disciplinary process has a **legislative phase** (the determination of the rules and the procedure for enforcement), an **administrative or judicial phase** (the application of the control mechanism through the disciplinary procedure), and **interpretative phases** (the assessment by management of initial and resultant performance or behaviour of the employee).

The formal disciplinary process, given its concern with the control of human behaviour, provides a **focus for the conflict** between management's desire for the maximum control of its labour resources and the maintenance of its authority and the employees' desire to establish and maintain as great a degree of protection as possible against arbitrary management action. It may produce conflict, at a strategic level, over the nature of the rule itself and the reason for its existence and, at a tactical level, over the application of the rule and the imposition of sanctions in a specific situation. Whilst this tactical conflict is primarily linked with the administrative or judicial phase of the process, the strategic conflict is primarily concerned with the legislative phase.

A punishment or training process

Many people argue that discipline does not necessarily imply punishment but rather mental or moral training. As with society's penal system, there are potentially three **aims** for the formal disciplinary process:

1. retribution
2. deterrence
3. rehabilitation.

However, apart from general statements that ultimately organisations should aim for a system of 'self-discipline' (a concept that is rarely adequately defined), the debate on the nature of industrial discipline has been confined to a comparison of Negative (punitive) and Positive (corrective) approaches [7].

Beach argues that the **Negative concept** 'encompasses the use of penalties or the threat of penalties to cause people to obey orders and to live up to the rules of the game' and 'achieves only the minimum performance necessary to avoid punishment', whilst the **Positive concept** 'involves the creation of an attitude and an organizational climate wherein employees willingly conform to established rules and regulations' and 'adhere to the desired standards of behaviour because they understand, believe in and support them' [8]. The former implies a retributive/deterrence approach, whilst the latter implies rehabilitation based on an educative socialisation approach. However, both involve bringing pressure to bear on the individual employee or group of employees to comply with the rules and, despite the possible differing managerial intentions, the 'offender' may not perceive a difference in the means employed to achieve compliance – both approaches utilise dismissal as an appropriate managerial response to either a serious non-compliance or a series of minor non-compliances by the individual employee. Indeed Walters and Grusec argue that 'a great deal of … socialisation consists of the suppression or elimination of behaviour', that 'punishment is a tool upon which people have relied extensively to suppress behaviour', and that 'few people would deny that those who deviate from accepted behaviour ought to experience some sort of unpleasant consequence' [9].

Whether or not the sanctions applied within the formal disciplinary process can be classed as 'punishment' requires consideration of the psychological concept of 'punishment'. There are two **general approaches to the definition of punishment**. One concentrates on the **nature of the stimulus** and relies on the notion of unpleasantness and suffering. It defines 'punishment' as consisting of the application of an averse stimulus when the specified behaviour to be eliminated occurs and it is fundamental that the stimulus has the quality of aversion to the recipient. The other approach ignores the notion of unpleasantness or suffering and concentrates on the **function of the stimulus**. Thus, punishment is defined as any stimulus which decreases the likelihood of the particular behaviour being repeated. Furthermore, a distinction can be made between primary and secondary punishment. Walters and Grusec argue that **primary punishment** 'refers to the operation of stimuli that have punishing properties in and of themselves', whilst **secondary punishment** 'designates the operation of stimuli that have taken on punishing properties either by having been paired with primary aversive stimuli or by having been associated with the loss of opportunity to obtain reinforcement' [10].

Several **points of importance for the formal disciplinary process** arise from this:

1. The sanctions of dismissal, suspension without pay, demotion, etc. are, **at best, secondary punishment** – it is the associated loss of pay or status which is the real punishment; verbal or written warnings are not, necessarily, punishment in the sense of being aversive stimuli but are warnings of some future punishment if the behaviour is not corrected. Whilst some employees (such as those whose rewards or career progression is linked to formal performance or appraisal reviews) might not like to receive a formal reprimand because of the possible effect on their career, this does not mean that other employees will place as much emphasis on such **warnings** – particularly those in manual or lower clerical groups for whom there may be little, if any, career prospects. Whether or not any sanction within the formal disciplinary process is punishment depends on the perception of the recipient and not the intention of the instigator.

2. The existence and use of the ultimate sanction of **dismissal** cannot be perceived as rehabilitation but only **retributive or a deterrent to others**. In practice, management are admitting that the differences between the individual's behaviour and the organisation's expectations cannot be reconciled and therefore the only solution is to remove the problem individual from the system. Thus, as Wheeler notes, because 'the nature of the offense generally determines whether corrective discipline or summary discharge is applied' [11], the concept of Positive (corrective) discipline as a rehabilitating process cannot be applied to all actions within the formal disciplinary process, but only, at best, to the less severe offences and sanctions.

3. The fact that the application of a sanction does not lead to the

suppression of the undesired behaviour does not automatically mean that the sanction is not regarded as 'punishment' by the recipient. The **undesired behaviour pattern might be reinforced** by pressures which are stronger than the pressure of the punishment.

4. The development of **'responsible autonomy' forms of management** control over labour, through expanding or enhancing the employee's job responsibilities, decreases the need for management to use *ad hoc* direct formal disciplinary action and replace it with more general and regular performance or appraisal review approaches – a more positive corrective approach.

The disciplinary rules

The actions which warrant formal disciplinary action are commonly categorised between:

1. **gross or serious misconduct** (i.e. offences warranting summary dismissal or at least severe disciplinary action for a single incident); and
2. **minor misconduct** (i.e. offences warranting only a verbal or written warning for a single incident but progressing to more several disciplinary action and eventual dismissal for a persistent offender).

However, Mellish and Collis-Squires point out, such a distinction is only useful in relation to the procedural mechanism and the 'procedures in themselves tell us little about the disciplinary process' [12]. To understand the nature of the process it is necessary to examine the basis of the rules themselves.

The rules enforced through the formal disciplinary process comprise only one part of the norms, both formal and informal, which regulate the relationships within the organisation. Fox [13] and Hill [14] have both identified **two derivations for organisational norms:**

1. The industrial organisation is a microcosm of its external society wherein the individuals who coalesce to form the organisation adhere to common, or dominant, norms and, therefore, carry over these norms and their adherence to them into the industrial setting.
2. The norms of the industrial organisation are not externally derived and common to all members but internally derived and sectionally based with management norms predominating as a result of either socialisation or management power.

It is possible, therefore, to divide the actions within the workplace which may lead to a formal disciplinary response by management into three broad categories:

1. **Actions contrary to some general society norm relating to personal behavior** (fighting, swearing, stealing, drunkenness, etc.). Certainly the work environment constitutes an important grouping where the individual may choose the organisation for which he/she works but has little, if any, choice regarding the people with whom he/she must relate. It is to be expected, therefore, that the organisation's disciplinary rules will reflect those developed within society concerning individual behaviour and relationships; their source and basis of legitimacy is society's code of conduct. However, within the industrial setting, both the individual's group norm and managerial attitude may allow a greater degree of tolerance than the judicial process within society; for example, swearing which might be considered a breach of the peace in the external society may be tolerated within the workplace. Furthermore, it may argued that management includes these rules within the industrial disciplinary process not because they believe that morally they should be the agents for enforcing society's norms in the workplace, but because these acts also have an impact on the achievement of economic/productive objectives by interrupting production and involving loss. However, the inclusion of these offences more easily legitimises the whole disciplinary process.

2. **Actions contrary to specific rules derived from external legislation** (health, safety and hygiene; sexual and racial harassment) whose source and legitimacy are, as Fox notes, 'wholly or partly determined by law emanating from an external political agency' [15]. The failure of an individual or group of employees to comply with these external regulations can result in management being legally liable to either a statutory fine for the breach itself or civil damages for the resulting loss. This perhaps explains the apparent contradiction in management enforcing rules which may hinder the achievement of the organisation's economic/productive objectives, for example, following safety procedures. Negligence may, because of the organisation's liability in respect of customer claims relating to unsatisfactory product quality, be included within this category. The existence and degree of enforcement of these rules are largely determined by the nature of the organisation's product or technology. Hence, Singleton found that 'the technology or function of the organisation may call for special rules' and that 'faulty workmanship is ... likely to be regarded as more serious in a tyre-manufacturing company than in a company making paper bags' [16].

3. **Actions contrary to the managerially determined general work control system** (timekeeping and work performance) **or contrary to the concept of managerial authority and prerogative** (failure to obey instructions and insubordination). These offences are specific to the industrial environment and have few, if any, direct equivalents within the general society's code of conduct. Their source and legitimacy are derived from the legitimacy of management's position within the organisation. The objective

of these rules is to ensure that individual behaviour conforms to managerial expectations: that is, management places limits on the freedom of the individual to undetake actions which might prejudice the achievement of the organisation's economic/productive objectives. The general work control rules are intended to ensure that the specific production processes of the organisation operate smoothly to the required output and standard. The other rules are intended to maintain management's position and authority within the organisation; management cannot manage if its employees are free to disregard its instructions.

Employees' behaviour

The term 'deviant' colloquially implies not only that the behaviour of a particular individual has moved away from some generally accepted norm but that such movement is wrong and should be corrected. It is therefore necessary, when examining industrial discipline, to identify the norms which determine the individual's standards of behaviour and conduct.

A distinction should be drawn between **non-conformist and aberrant behaviour**. In the former the breach of the rule results from the employee's non-acceptance of the legitimacy of the rule; in the latter, although the employee has broken the rule, he/she is not questioning its legitimacy. However, in both cases management will perceive the individual's actions to be a breach of their expectations regarding behaviour/performance and treat the situation as a matter for control through the formal disciplinary process. To the aberrant this will appear fair, providing the punishment is reasonable in relation to the offence, but to the non-conformist it will always appear unreasonable. Most managers, because of their own acceptance of the legitimacy of the rules, will tend to see the non-conformist as, at best, irrational or, at worst, subversive. Consequently, there may be situations where a non-conformist presents the appearance of an aberrant because he/she feels it will be more acceptable and may indeed mitigate the severity of the punishment. However, in the context of the peer group the individual may continue to challenge the rule itself. This distinction was implied in a government report (1973) when it suggested that 'whereas so-called group "indiscipline" normally results from a widespread rejection of a working arrangement or rule and the resolution of any conflict lies in the negotiation of new work standards, individual discipline indicates merely a personal deviation from standards generally accepted by other employees' [17].

An act of individual indiscipline considered actionable by management's norms may, in practice, be derived from the **individual's adherence to some other group norm**. Mellish and Collis-Squires point out that 'the union – or fellow workers – may be a greater disciplining force upon the individual worker than the employer, and the norms they enforce may be significantly at variance with the norms of discipline preferred by the employer' [18]. For example, pilfering in docks and hotels [19] might be so organised that an individual case of disciplinary action by management for theft or fraud would, in reality, be a conflict between workgroup norms and management norms as opposed to a situation of individual aberration.

Consideration also has to be given to whether the formal disciplinary process is concerned only with the 'deviant' behaviour of a small minority. Most managers would say that there are only a small number of 'trouble makers' for whom the application of the formal disciplinary process becomes necessary. This view is reflected in statements that 'most people in an organisation tend to obey most of the rules most of the time' [20], that 'we are considering the occasional transgressor' [21] and that therefore one of the purposes of discipline is 'to prevent indisciplined behaviour by an unruly minority from exercising an undue influence' [22]. However, Benton suggests, when commenting on the pervasive nature of discipline, that 'some employees never complain or become parties to a grievance, but most are subject to some form of discipline when work is spoiled, errors are made, personality clashes arise' [23]. These two, apparently contradictory, views can be reconciled not only by simply differentiating the former to apply to the formal disciplinary process and the latter to discipline in its broad sense of control, but also by reference to the source and legitimacy of the disciplinary rules. On this basis it is possible to argue that:

1. those rules deriving their legitimacy from society's general code of conduct or involving a direct challenge to managerial authority are likely to be contravened by only a small minority of employees because they involve breaches of fundamental socialised norms; but
2. those rules which rely almost exclusively on the managerial perceived need for control over the human part of the production process, for example lateness and poor performance, may well be contravened by a more substantial proportion of the workforce at one time or another because they involve a lesser degree of socialisation on the part of the employee.

Finally, there is clear evidence of the **formal disciplinary process being used in collective issues**. For example, when an employee is warned for refusing to obey a formal instruction to carry out a piece of work, it is possible that it will escalate into a situation where the rest of the group, if similarly instructed, will also refuse to obey. Management may refrain from asking others to do the work but, instead, concentrate on the individual involved as an example (deterrent) to the others. Management may also issue formal warnings, suspension or even dismissals for 'failure to obey legitimate work instructions' as a means of pressuring employees who are undertaking collective action in the form of 'working to rule'. If these sanctions are withdrawn as part of any settlement securing a 'return to normal working' and if management's intention from the start was to withdraw them, they can be seen as an exercise of power within the collective bargaining process. However, if management did not intend to withdraw them or the employees are not sufficiently strong to secure their withdrawal, then they are likely to remain on the individual's record and may be taken into account if the individual is involved in any subsequent disciplinary action.

Managerial reaction

A variety of situations have been identified in which management may be reluctant to use the formal disciplinary process. Boise found that 'second-line supervisors would often not impose penalties on employees for misconduct during peak workloads of the department, and they would hesitate to impose a penalty on an employee when replacements with his particular skills are in short supply' [24]. Maier [25] argued that the supervisor is faced with a *dilemma*: too much use of the formal disciplinary process to enforce compliance with the rules may lose co-operation in meeting production objectives, but if violations are not dealt with through the accepted formal process the supervisor may discriminate between employees and be inconsistent. Therefore, to resolve the dilemma, he/she may turn a blind-eye and ignore the existence of a violation.

It is clear therefore that **not all behaviour which deviates from management's norms and expectations is necessarily subject to sanctions within the formal disciplinary process**. The incidence of deviancy observed within the formal process is only that which management, either individually or as a group, believes requires formalised action because it exceeds some acceptable limit – the tolerance limit. Cuming [26] represents the concept of tolerance by a straight line with the absolute enforcement of the rule at one end and complete non-enforcement at the other, with the point of tolerance being a variable position in between. This spectrum can be modified to identify a series of tolerance points along the continuum: the point at which the contravention of the rule is considered to be a matter for discipline, the point which divides informal from formal disciplinary action, and the points dividing the severity of sanctions to be applied within the formal process.

However, the formal disciplinary process is not applied by managers in a virtual vacuum but within an overall **formalised organisational framework of discipline**. In order to achieve consistency and comply with external constraints such as legislation and trade union pressure, the organisation establishes its own tolerance limits by means of the disciplinary policy and procedure – particularly the classification of offences into those of a major or minor nature. Once the contravention of a rule has been delineated as a major offence then the individual manager, faced with such a contravention, has less freedom to ignore it or treat it other than as a major offence requiring severe formal disciplinary action. The organisational tolerance limits contained in the formal policy and rules restrict the individual manager's degree of tolerance. However, the two tolerance 'limits' are interactive in that the attitudes of managers largely determine the nature of the organisation's tolerance limits which in turn reinforce the individual manager's attitudes.

The **internal control required to ensure consistency** is usually achieved by requiring the individual manager, at least, to consult the personnel specialist or more senior management before taking action. This centralised internal control further restricts the individual manager's discretion. It is possible that the introduction of Unfair Dismissal legislation may have reduced the use of dismissal in favour of the use of lesser sanctions which do not themselves come under the direct scrutiny of the Industrial Tribunals. If such a move has taken place, the effect will have been for the organisation to redefine certain offences/situations as not necessarily warranting summary dismissal, thereby providing the individual manager with greater flexibility to use sanctions short of dismissal. However, even in this situation there will be a degree of centralised control because these situations may be scutinised by an Industrial Tribunal if the employee is subsequently dismissed for a further offence and the previous warning is used as a basis for justifying the eventual dismissal.

20.3 The legal framework

The employer's right to discipline employees is founded on the failure of the employee to fulfil his/her obligations under the terms of the contract of employment. The common law defines the employee's obligations as:

1. To give honest and faithful service.
2. To use reasonable skill and care in work.
3. To obey all reasonable orders.
4. Not to commit misconduct.

However, apart from restricting the employer's ability to take disciplinary action involving loss of pay (such as suspension without pay) unless there is an express or implied right under the contract of employment, the law is mainly concerned with the final stage of the disciplinary process – dismissal. Prior to the Industrial Relations Act (1971) a dismissed employee had only a limited remedy under the common law for a 'wrongful' dismissal and the maximum compensation that could be claimed was an amount equal to the wages the employee would have received during the normal contractual notice period. However, since 1971 the employee has had a statutory right not to be unfairly dismissed and the potential remedies have been expanded to include not only increased compensation but also the possibility of reinstatement or re-engagement. The rest of this section is concerned with the legal framework surrounding such dismissals (Employment Protection (Consolidation) Act (1978) as amended by the Employment Act (1980)).

Coverage of the legislation

The following groups are **excluded:**

1. **Length of service:** originally an employee required 104 weeks continuous service with the employer before being eligible to claim Unfair Dismissal; subsequently this was reduced to 26 weeks but was increased in 1979 to 52 weeks and again in 1986 to 104 weeks. Thus, an employee with less than 104 weeks continuous service is excluded except when the dismissal is for an 'inadmissable reason' (i.e. membership or non-membership of a trade union or participating in its activities) (S.64(3) 1978 Act).
2. **Retirement age:** employees who have reached retirement age are excluded. This exclusion is not applicable if the dismissal is for an 'inadmissable reason' (S.64(1) 1978 Act).
3. **Part-time employees:** employees whose contract of employment is for less than 8 hours per week and those with contracts of employment for between 8 and 16 hours per week, if they have less than five years continuous service, are excluded (Schedule 13(6) 1978 Act).
4. **Fixed term contracts:** an employee working under a fixed term contract of one or more years' duration is excluded if the dismissal results only from the non-renewal of the contract provided the employee has agreed, in writing, to waive rights to make such a claim (S.142(1) 1978 Act amended by S.8(2) 1980 Act).
5. **Employment outside Great Britain:** an employee is excluded if, under the contract of employment, he/she ordinarily works outside Great Britain even though the contract is with a British employer (S.141(2) 1978 Act).
6. **Designated dismissals procedure:** the Secretary of State may, on the joint application of the parties involved and providing the procedure meets certain criteria, 'designate' a dismissal procedure; this has the effect of excluding that group of employees from the normal statutory procedure (S.65 1978 Act). No such procedures have been designated.

Definition of dismissal

The term dismissal applies to any situation where the employer terminates the contract of employment. This may take different forms:

1. **Dismissal with notice** or payment in lieu of notice for disciplinary or other reasons.

2. **Summary dismissal** without notice or payment in lieu of notice (generally for disciplinary reasons resulting from a formal investigation within the disciplinary process).
3. **Instant dismissal** without notice (with or without payment in lieu of notice) for disciplinary reasons but without any formal investigation into the employee's conduct (this is contrary to the rules of natural justice and almost certainly an unfair dismissal).

In all these situations the employee has the right to present a claim to the Industrial Tribunal.

However, in the legal context, the term dismissal also includes **constructive dismissal**. This arises where 'the employee terminates the contract, with or without notice, in circumstances such that he is entitled to terminate it without notice by reason of the employer's conduct' (S.55(2)(c) 1978 Act). It is deemed to be a dismissal where the employee terminates the contract of employment not simply because he/she wishes to take up work elsewhere but because the actions of the employer force him/her to resign. Over the years **two approaches** have been developed on this issue:

1. The first, and perhaps strongest, line has been that for a constructive dismissal to be upheld the employee must show that 'the employer is guilty of conduct which is a significant breach going to the root of the contract of employment, or which shows that the employer no longer intends to be bound by one or more of the essential terms of the contract' [27]. In other words the employee has to show that a single act on the part of the employer was a sufficient breach of the contract to amount to repudiation.
2. The second, more diffuse, line has held that a constructive dismissal could be justified on the basis of a series of minor breaches, none of them individually amounting to repudiation of the contract, providing that taken together they amount to unreasonable action on the part of the employer. It has been held that 'an employer who persistently attempts to vary an employee's conditions of service (whether contractual or not) with a view to getting rid of an employee or varying the employee's terms of service, does act in a manner calculated or likely to destroy the relationship of confidence and trust between employer and employee' [28].

The following examples illustrate the type of circumstances which may constitute constructive dismissal:

1. Reorganisation of the company involving demotion, or loss of status or responsibilities for the employee.
2. Change in the method of determining pay without the agreement of the employee or union.

3. Transfer of an employee to other work without an express or implied term in the contract of employment.
4. Victimisation of the employee by the supervisor.
5. Use of foul language by the employer to the employee.
6. Unfounded accusations of dishonesty.

However, 1 and 3 above have to be considered in the light of a 'justified' dismissal under 'some other substantial reason'.

Reasons for dismissal

As the first step in justifying a dismissal as being 'fair', the employer has to demonstrate that it was for a **specified reason** (S.57 1978 Act) (any other reason is automatically unfair):

1. The capability or qualification of the employee.
2. The conduct of the employee.
3. The employee was redundant.
4. The continued employment of the employee would contravene a statutory duty or restriction.
5. Some other substantial reason such as to justify dismissal.

In addition, the legislation sets out specific criteria for dismissals relating to pregnancy and trade union membership or activity. However, it is the interpretation placed on these statutory provisions by Industrial Tribunals which is most important in relation to the handling of discipline and dismissal in organisations. It is therefore useful to examine briefly certain types of dismissal.

Capability
The two most common reasons for dismissing an employee under this heading are ill health and poor work performance.

To justify dismissal on the grounds of **ill health** the employer must show that:

1. Sickness or ill health was the cause of dismissal.
2. Reasonable efforts were made to ascertain the employee's state of health, including consulting a doctor, and that the employee had been informed that further absence or ill health could result in dismissal.
3. The dismissal was reasonable because of the nature of the employee's work and the effect the absence or ill health had on the organisation and other employees.
4. Reasonable efforts had been made to find suitable alternative work within the organisation bearing in mind the employee's state of health.

It has been suggested that 'in cases of ill health the basic question that has to be determined ... is whether in all the circumstances the employer can be expected to wait any longer and, if so, how much longer' [29]. The answer is a balance between operational efficiency and the success of the undertaking and reasonable job security for employees absent through sickness or other causes beyond their control. The existence of a sick-pay scheme within the organisation does not determine the time an employee is entitled to be absent before dismissal is justified: a dismissal may be fair even before the period of sick-pay has run out if it is evident that the employee will be unable to continue normal work, whilst an automatic dismissal when the period of sick-pay expires may be unfair if the employee is likely to return to normal work in the near future. Even if the absence is due to ill health or injury resulting from the work situation the employer is not required to treat the employee more leniently; one Tribunal went so far as to say that 'the more true it is that illness was occasioned by incidents or attitudes at his place of work, the more reasonable it becomes for the company to reach a decision that they can no longer employ him' [30].

In relation to **pregnancy**, it is an unfair dismissal to dismiss an employee simply because she is pregnant. A dismissal may only be fair if, as a result of being pregnant, the employee is incapable of performing her work or there is a statutory restriction placed on her continued employment once she is pregnant. Even in these circumstances a dismissal might be unfair if suitable alternative work is available and it is not offered to her. In addition, if management refuses to allow the employee to return to work at the end of her statutory maternity leave entitlement, and she has indicated at the appropriate time that she intended to exercise this option, then it will be treated as a dismissal. If management engages a temporary replacement to cover a maternity absence it is entitled to dismiss that replacement when the other employee returns providing the replacement was informed of this when employment commenced.

In dealing with dismissal because of **poor work performance** three aspects need to be considered:

1. Is the employee incapable or inefficient in the performance of the work? The employer only has to demonstrate reasonable grounds for believing the employee to be inefficient and that this is the reason for the dismissal. In judging inefficiency 'management must still require and impose its own standards, at least within certain limits: that is to say, any standard required or imposed must be a reasonable standard' [31].
2. Has the employee been warned previously regarding poor work performance? Normally, failure to give any warning that performance is unsatisfactory, and that continued unsatisfactory performance could lead to dismissal, will result in the dismissal being regarded as unfair. The employee should, therefore, be informed as to the nature of the poor work performance, the acceptable standard that is required and the period of time within which to reach that standard.

3. Has the employer provided the employee with the necessary reasonable support to improve the work performance? The employer should identify the cause of the poor work performance and, if it results from lack of training or other factors within the employer's control, provide the employee with reasonable assistance to overcome these problems.

Conduct

Apart from **unauthorised absence and poor timekeeping**, which generally require a previous warning, most of the offences which come under this heading may justify summary dismissal for one occurrence. However, when dealing with these situations management must carefully examine the circumstances to establish whether they justify dismissal:

1. **Fighting** – the employee should be a willing participant to the fight and not simply defending him/herself against an assault by another employee and if the policy of the organisation is only to dismiss the aggressor management will need to consider what constitutes aggression (is it the first blow or does it include verbal or other forms of non-violent aggression?).
2. **Drinking** – generally the fairness of such a dismissal is based on its effect on the employee's work performance, safety or other aspects of the individual's behaviour such as violence. Management needs to be clear in its mind whether its disciplinary rule relates to the act of drinking or the state of being drunk.
3. **Swearing** – it is important to differentiate between swearing as part of the employee's everyday language and swearing at another person which is intended to be aggressive or abusive. It is also important to take account of tension or bad relationships which might be the cause of the outburst, the past record of the employee and whether the employee is prepared to apologise.
4. **Failure to obey instructions** – to justify dismissal 'disobedience must have the quality of wilfulness' [32] and the instruction must be one that management is entitled to give under the contract of employment. Management must ensure that the employee is aware both that a formal instruction has been given and of the possible consequences which may result from continued refusal. Where the employee genuinely questions the 'legality' of the instruction under the contract of employment, management should be prepared to explain the basis and reason for the instruction.

The most common **criminal act** encountered in the industrial setting is theft from either the employer or fellow employees. However, criminal acts committed by the employee outside the workplace may also justify dismissal. Such situations only arise where the act committed outside the workplace casts reasonable doubt on the suitability of the employee to continue performing the job. In considering dismissal in relation to a criminal act, whether it occurred within the workplace or outside, management should bear in mind the following points:

1. Whether or not the criminal act justifies dismissal depends on its seriousness.
2. The law on Unfair Dismissal and the criminal law are two separate areas of law with different degrees of proof. Therefore, being guilty of a criminal offence does not automatically justify dismissal and, equally, being found not guilty at criminal law does not automatically make a dismissal unfair. The question that has to be answered is does the action of the employee amount to a serious breach of the contract of employment?
3. As a result of (2) management does not have to await the outcome of any criminal proceedings before making a decision to dismiss the employee. However, if management does not wish to take action unless the employee is found guilty, then the employee should not be retained in his/her normal work whilst awaiting the outcome of the criminal proceedings but suspended or moved to work unrelated to the criminal act. The Tribunal may, otherwise, consider any subsequent dismissal to be unfair because management continued to employ the individual in his/her normal work despite knowing that there are doubts regarding the employee's suitability.

'Some other substantial reason'

This is a potential 'catch-all'. However, the most significant line of cases has related to employees refusing to agree to changes in their terms and conditions of employment. Despite the earlier statement that the employer's unilateral change in the contract is potentially a constructive dismissal because it involves a fundamental breach of the contract, nevertheless the employee's refusal to accept such a change may be deemed to constitute 'some other substantial reason' justifying dismissal. Dickens believes that this 'has been so widely interpreted by tribunals as to provide something of an "employers' charter"' [33]. In order for management to substantiate such a defence there must be a proven need for the change and the change must be reasonable in the light of the need; as Aikin points out 'the reasonableness ... is to be considered from the employer's and not from the employee's point of view and is based on his business needs' [34]. The issue which the Tribunal must decide is whether the employer was reasonable in dismissing the employee, not whether the employee was reasonable in refusing the change. Aikin points out that the Tribunal will usually expect the employer to have consulted with employees and/or unions before introducing the change and 'then follow the proper procedure in relation to those who refuse the new terms. They must have the new conditions explained, their own position made clear and given time to come to terms with it. They must understand that they risk dismissal if they cannot comply' [35]

Determination of 'fair' and 'reasonable'

The Tribunal requirement to determine the fairness or otherwise of a dismissal is dependent on whether 'in the circumstances (including the size and adminstrative resources of the employer's undertaking) the employer acted reasonably or unreasonably in treating [the stated reason] as a sufficient reason for dismissing the employee; and that question shall be determined in accordance with equity and the substantial merits of the case' (S.6 1980 Act). Prior to 1980 the employer had 'to satisfy the tribunal that ... he acted reasonably' (S.57(3) 1978 Act). The effect of this change was to neutralise the onus of proof and formlise the requirement that the Tribunal should judge the case not by their standards but those of a 'reasonable employer'. Dickens argues that 'this managerial perspective reduces the applicant's chance of winning a case of unfair dismissal' [36].

In arriving at their decision the Tribunal will take into account a number of factors:

1. was the dismissal for an admissable reason;
2. was the dismissal fair in the sense of equity of treatment between employees (did the employer condone similar behaviour in the past or with other employees);
3. was the dismissal fair in the sense of did the offence or the employee's record justify dismissal as a suitable sanction; and
4. did the employer follow a proper and adequate procedure before arriving at the decision to dismiss.

If the answer is 'yes' on all the above counts then the dismissal will be fair, but if the answer to any one is 'no' then the dismissal *may* be unfair. For example, even though the employee's action might justify dismissal, if the employer has not dealt with it in a proper and adequate procedural manner the resultant dismissal may be judged to be unfair. In such a situation the Tribunal has to determine the seriousness of the employer's procedural error and what effect it has had on the decision to dismiss.

Remedies for an unfair dismissal

The Tribunal has two broad remedies it may apply.

Reinstatement or re-engagement
With reinstatement the employee returns to his/her former position and is treated as if he/she had never been dismissed; re-engagement, on the other hand,

is more flexible in that the job may be with an associated employer or may be comparable or otherwise suitable work. The employer may object to reinstatement or re-engagement on the grounds that it is impracticable. The practicability of either remedy is judged on the basis of not only whether the employer has work for the employee but also the effect the return of the employee might have on the organisation and other employees. In some circumstances the nature of the offence, the attitude of other employees and possible friction between the employee and supervision may make this remedy impracticable. The Tribunal cannot compel an employer to re-employ a dismissed individual but if the employer refuses to abide by an order for reinstatement or re-engagement the Tribunal may award additional compensation of between 13 and 26 weeks' pay.

Lewis argues that 'it was made absolutely clear in the statute that "re-employment" was to be the primary remedy' but that the operation of the system 'still fails to offer job security' [37]. His survey of dismissal cases found that although 72 per cent of applicants initially requested reinstatement or re-engagement this dropped to only 20 per cent by the time of Tribunal hearing. The overwhelming majority of those who changed did so because they perceived there to have been a breakdown in the employment relationship. Thus, it is possible to argue that the failure of the Tribunals to use this remedy has been due to the wishes of the claimants themselves. However, of those that continued to claim 're-employment', only 57 per cent obtained an order from the Tribunal to that effect and in nearly two-thirds of these the employer refused to abide by the order. Of the 43 per cent which were unsuccessful in obtaining an order, half failed because the Tribunal considered it impracticable because of lack of job availability and half failed because the Tribunal felt it would be 'unjust' because of the individual's high contributory fault in the dismissal. Thus, Lewis concluded that 'only a minority of those seeking "re-employment" actually obtained it' [38].

Compensation

The alternative, and most frequent, remedy is the award of monetary compensation for the loss of the employee's job. The compensation is in two parts:

1. **Basic award** – this is equivalent to the amount that the employee would have received if made redundant and is therefore based on age and length of service.
2. **Compensatory award** – this aims to recompense the employee for loss of earnings and benefits as a result of the dismissal. It may include full pay for the contractual notice period if the employee was dismissed without notice or payment in lieu of notice; loss of pay since the dismissal and in the future; and loss of benefits such as pension rights, company car, etc. This compensation is subject to a maximum limit.

The employee is under a **duty to mitigate the loss** by seeking alternative work. If he/she has found alternative work at a lower wage by the time of the hearing the compensatory award will be based on the difference between the two amounts. However, if the Tribunal believe that the employee has not sought work or not been prepared to accept lower paid work they may reduce the award accordingly. In addition, any unemployment benefit the employee has received may be deducted from the compensation and the employee is not entitled to claim unemployment benefit for any period over which future loss of earnings has been calculated. Furthermore, the amount of the compensation may be reduced in respect of the extent to which the Tribunal feels the employee's actions contributed to the dismissal. Thus it is possible for the employee to be judged unfairly dismissed but the level of compensation reduced by as much as 80 per cent. Although the maximum compensation is £14,000 the typical award, because of the relative short service of most complainants, is only some £600.

Procedure

The individual must present a claim for unfair dismissal within three months of the dismissal taking place – although the Tribunal may, in exceptional cases, decide to hear the case 'out of time'. There is facility within the procedure for a **pre-hearing** to assess the merits of the case and its prospects for success. This latter arrangement was introduced in 1980 because of a perceived reluctance of the Tribunals to award cost against 'frivolous' or 'vexatious' claims and so as Capstick notes, 'an applicant who pursued a hopeless case out of ignorance ... or out of a desire simply to see what came out in the wash, was not therefore likely to have to pay his employer's costs even if he lost' [39]. The pre-hearing allows the Tribunal to 'advise' on the prospects of success of either the claimant's or respondent's case and such advice may be taken into account in deciding whether to award costs if the case proceeds and fails. Capstick found that in the first eight months of its operation only 10 out of 932 pre-hearings were at the request of the applicant and the remainder were virtually evenly divided between requests from the respondents and requests from the Tribunal chairman. In 50 per cent of the pre-hearings a warning was given against the applicant but in only seven cases was a warning given against the respondent. Out of 170 cases which went to a full Tribunal hearing, 136 were dismissed, 34 succeeded and in only 10 cases were costs awarded in line with the earlier warning. Similarly Wallace and Clifton found a high percentage of withdrawals following a pre-hearing warning about costs. Perhaps more importantly they found that pre-hearings also delayed the early stages of ACAS conciliation [40].

There is also a facility for **conciliation via ACAS** prior to a Tribunal hearing. In 1990, 40 per cent of unfair dismissal claims were settled by

ACAS conciliation and only 31 per cent went to the Industrial Tribunals [41]. However, Dickens has criticised these conciliated settlements as a cheaper alternative, for the employer, than going to the Tribunal and has argued that 'despite ACAS' statutory duty to pursue settlements on [the basis of re-employment] ACAS officers do not generally attempt to reconcile the parties to the idea of re-establishing the employment relationship ... but merely help arrange the severance terms' [42]. Significantly perhaps, Concannon has identified that re-employment, usually with conditions, was obtained in the majority of the albeit limited number of cases which were referred to **arbitration via ACAS** (i.e. where 'the union had exercised its organisation and power to remove the dismissal decision from being merely a matter of individual rights to one of collective interest' [43]).

This complements Dickens' description of the **typical tribunal applicant** as being 'male, non-union, manual worker dismissed by a small employer in the private services sector' which is 'characterised by small employment units and below average levels of unionisation' and where 'employees in such companies are at a greater risk from dismissal than those employed in large companies' [44]. It would appear that the legislation and Tribunal system only provides a minimal remedy, and little job protection, for non-unionised employees in smaller companies; employees in larger well-unionised companies appear to achieve their protection through their union's representation in the collective bargaining process and dismissal procedure within the organisation.

20.4 Handling discipline and dismissal

The formal disciplinary process at the organisational level comprises three interdependent elements – the disciplinary policy, the disciplinary procedure and the disciplinary interview (see Figure 20.3).

The disciplinary policy

The objective of the disciplinary policy is to **set the organisational climate** within which disciplinary matters will be determined. It is important in providing managers with clear guidelines as to the organisation's expectations of them in their handling of discipline. The policy may be a separate policy document, or incorporated into the preamble of the disciplinary procedure, or as part of an administrative note to managers on how to operate the procedure.

In devising a disciplinary policy, management particularly needs to

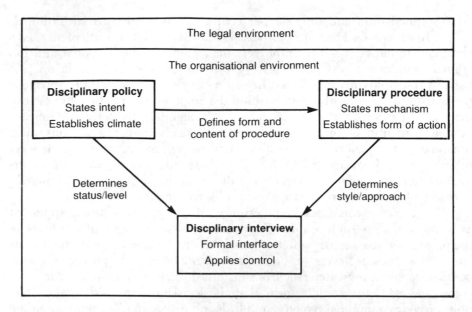

Figure 20.3   *The disciplinary policy, procedure and interview*

consider the objective of the disciplinary process and the role expected of supervisors and managers. The policy may contain statements such as:

1.   It is the employee's responsibility to follow all the Company's rules and working procedures.
2.   Management will, in the first place, seek to correct an employee's poor performance or behaviour through informal counselling by the supervisor.
3.   Management will apply the formal disciplinary process only when informal counselling has been unsuccessful or the actions of the employee are such that informal counselling is inappropriate.
4.   Management accepts that no employee will be formally disciplined without a fair hearing and and opportunity to put his/her case.
5.   Management will seek to act fairly and consistently when administering discipline.

The disciplinary procedure

The purpose of the disciplinary procedure is to provide an **acceptable mechanism within which management may exercise its control over employees** when their performance or behaviour does not reach the required standards. It constrains management's freedom of action by specifying the manner in which such control is to be exercised. The *ACAS Code of Practice* [45] recommends that, irrespective of whether the organisation is large or small, unionised or non-unionised, the procedure should:

1. be a formal, written procedure;
2. indicate to whom it applies and the appropriate employees should be provided with a copy;
3. specify what disciplinary actions may be taken and which level of management has the authority to take such action;
4. ensure that the employee is notified of the complaint, given the opportunity to state his/her case and to be represented either by a union representative or fellow employee;
5. ensure that no disciplinary action is taken without a full investigation and that an employee is not dismissed for a single incident of misconduct unless it is gross misconduct;
6. provide the employee with the right of appeal against any disciplinary sanction.

Whilst it is not possible (because of variations in organisational structure, the role of the personnel specialist, and whether or not the organisation is unionised) to set out a procedure which is applicable to all organisations, most disciplinary procedures are based on the provision of a range of sanctions, increasing in severity, to be applied by progressively more senior levels of management (see Figure 20.4). However, not all disciplinary offences need to be dealt with under the same procedure. Some organisations, because of the particular nature of the offence and the way in which they wish to handle it, have established separate procedures to deal with absence through sickness and poor work performance. If this course is adopted it is imperative that the main disciplinary procedure states that such offences are outside its jurisdiction and which procedure will apply in such situations.

A number of aspects need to be considered in the drawing up and operation of a disciplinary procedure.

The disciplinary rules

Some organisations, in specifying the rules to be enforced through the disciplinary procedure, are content with a general statement referring to a deliberate breach of established regulations or practices, negligence or inefficiency within the individual's control, whilst others specify a long list of offences, and the degree of their breach, divided between gross, serious and minor offences. Obviously, it is not possible to identify every circumstance which might lead to disciplinary action but, nevertheless, it is advisable for the procedure to err towards specificity rather than vagueness. This is particularly true if there is no handbook or works rule book which details the rules with which the employee is expected to comply.

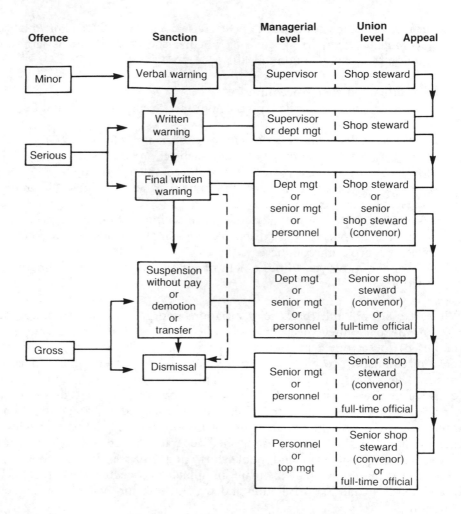

Figure 20.4   *Stages in the disciplinary procedure*

The sanctions
A number of sanctions may be applied under the disciplinary procedure.

● *Verbal warnings.* This is the most frequent and least severe penalty. However, it is necessary to distinguish between informal verbal warnings, which are not part of the formal disciplinary procedure and which are frequently administered by a supervisor or manager as part of the day-to-day control of their subordinates, and formal verbal warnings which form the first stage of the formal disciplinary procedure. These formal verbal warnings are normally recorded in the employee's personnel record and may be taken into account should management need to take further disciplinary action against the employee. It is important that the employee is made aware, at the outset of the interview, that the matter is being treated as the first formal stage of the disciplinary procedure and it may be advisable to emphasise this point by providing the employee with written confirmation of the formal verbal warning.

- *Written warnings.* Any written warning should clearly state the offence for which the employee is being disciplined and, where relevant refer to any previous verbal or written warnings. It should also clearly indicate what future performance or conduct is expected and the likely consequences if there is no improvement. Wherever possible, it is useful to get the employee to sign that he/she has received, and understood, the written warning. Many organisations have two levels of written warnings – a first and final written warning. The danger to be avoided is the employee receiving more than one 'final' written warning. The issuing of two, or even more, 'final' written warnings not only makes dismissal more difficult to justify in the case of that employee but also undermines the value and effect of final written warnings given to other employees. Only in very exceptional situations should a final written warning not be followed by some more severe sanction for a future act of indiscipline.

- *Suspension.* It is important to distinguish between a precautionary suspension with pay pending a disciplinary investigation and a disciplinary suspension without pay as a sanction within the formal disciplinary procedure. Many people argue that a suspension without pay is useful because it involves a loss of money on the part of the employee and without it there is no satisfactory intermediate action between a final written warning and dismissal. However, it must be remembered that any suspension, with or without pay, also affects management and other employees in that the work normally performed by the suspended employee is either not done or has to be done by other employees – perhaps involving the use of overtime. In addition, a suspension without pay, because it is tantamount to the employer breaching the contract of employment by not paying wages, can only be effected if the terms of the contract (either express or implied) allow for it.

- *Transfer or demotion.* These may be used as a sanction in their own right or as an alternative to dismissal. However, whether or not it involves a breach of the contract of employment depends on the narrowness of the employee's job title. Thus it is advisable for management to secure the employee's consent to any transfer or demotion. The application of these sanctions may, in a unionised situation, need to be discussed with the union representative(s) because they involve the removal of one employee and replacement by another.

● *Fines and deductions from pay.* In the nineteenth century it was common for the employer to fine the employee for breaches of the rules, but today this has virtually ceased. The problem has always been that if the amount of the fine was small then it had little effect, but if it was large it could involve the employee in financial hardship and lead to resentment. Initially, the right to fine employees was constrained by the Truck Act (1896) – but this only applied to manual workers. The Wages Act (1986) simplified the legal requirements in respect of fines and extended the scope to include all employees. Consequently, a fine may only be imposed if it is expressly provided for in the employee's contract of employment or the employee indicates agreement in writing. Furthermore, a deduction in respect of retail workers for any cash shortage or stock deficiency is limited to a maximum of 10 per cent of the employee's gross daily wage.

● *Dismissal.* A dismissal should only take place when there is no other alternative available. In this event the employer should ensure that the dismissal is fair and reasonable and in accordance with both the disciplinary procedure and legal framework.

Appropriate level of management

Although the specific levels of management involved in the operation of the disciplinary procedure may vary, the application of formal disciplinary action should always be seen to lie in the hands of line management. The immediate supervisor or manager has responsibility for the day-to-day control of the employee and must therefore play an important part in the formal disciplinary procedure. In spite of the need to at least consult Personnel, and their more direct involvement in the later stages of the procedure, the operation of the procedure should not present the appearance of the employee being 'sent' to Personnel to be disciplined.

Union or other employee representation

Jointly agreed disciplinary procedures generally afford the employee the right to be accompanied by a shop steward at the interview. Thus the employee needs to be advised, in advance, that disciplinary action is being considered and that he/she has the right to be represented and to consult with a shop steward in the preparation of his/her case. The role of the shop steward at the interview is not only to present the employee's case but also to ensure that management conducts the interview in a fair and reasonable manner. At the end of the interview the shop steward should be given a copy of any written warning or confirmation of disciplinary action given to the employee. If the employee has not taken advantage of the opportunity to be represented, perhaps because of the nature of the offence, the shop steward should simply be informed that the employee has been disciplined and was offered the opportunity to be represented but declined. In the case of non-union employees the procedure may specify that the employee can be accompanied by a fellow employee. However, the role of the 'fellow employee' is less clear. Some organisations believe that it is simply to observe and be a witness for the employee at any subsequent appeal as to what happened during the interview; other organisations regard it as a representational role.

Appeals

Provision must be made for the employee to be able to appeal against any disciplinary action; either via the normal grievance procedure or through a special disciplinary appeal mechanism. The procedure should specify a period of time within which the appeal must be lodged and a further period of time within which it must be heard. The appeal should be heard by a level of management not involved in, and more senior to, the initial disciplinary action. Appeals against the more severe disciplinary sanctions may well involve the employee being represented by a full-time official. The management involved in the initial disciplinary action, in addition to being present at the appeal to present their evidence, should be involved with the manager hearing the appeal in determining the decision of the appeal hearing – particularly where a reduction in the original disciplinary sanction is proposed. The subordinate should understand why the initial decision was wrong.

Joint application of discipline

The formal disciplinary process is a managerially determined and operated process and very few organisations have moved beyond the joint agreement of the procedure to the full involvement of unions and employees in the determination of the rules and the administering of the disciplinary sanctions. However, some organisations have involved unions and shop stewards in the appeals mechanism. If the employee has not satisfactorily resolved the appeal with management, a joint body comprising shop stewards and managers will consider the case. Both management and the employee put their case to this body which then delivers its judgement, generally on a unanimous basis. However, in reality, it is not a joint application of discipline but the establishment of a quasi-independent internal tribunal. A similar situation exists in local government with the final appeal stage being to a Committee of the Council where, in effect, management and employee put their respective cases to an independent third party – namely, elected council members.

'Wiping the slate clean'

The procedure should specify that any record of disciplinary action will be removed from the employee's record after a specified time if the employee's conduct is satisfactory over that period. The time intervals may range from three months to two years or more depending on the severity of the sanction imposed – the more severe the sanction the longer it remains on record for consideration should the employee become involved in further disciplinary action. Management has a duty to ensure that the record is removed at the appropriate time and this may be coupled with the employee's right to examine his/her personnel file to ensure that it has been done.

'Totting up' offences

A further, more severe, disciplinary sanction may be applied whenever an employee's behaviour or performance gives rise to a need for disciplinary action. Therefore, to move from one level of sanction to the next does not require the employee to commit a further act of indiscipline of a similar nature. An employee may, taking into account any requirements to 'wipe the slate clean', receive a formal verbal warning for one offence, a written warning for another offence and be suspended without pay, demoted or even dismissed for yet another offence, even though the third offence, on its own, might not justify dismissal.

Disciplinary action against a shop steward

No disciplinary action beyond a verbal warning should be taken against a shop steward, whether as a result of his/her actions as a shop steward or as an employee, before the case has been discussed with the senior steward (convenor) or full-time official. This does not mean that the disciplinary action has to be agreed but simply that the senior steward or full-time official is aware of the circumstances and planned management action.

The disciplinary interview

The disciplinary interview is the most critical phase of the formal disciplinary process. It is **the point at which the formal control mechanism is actually applied** between management and the offending employee. Throughout the interview, the supervisor or manager must remember that, in the absence of a joint disciplinary committee or independent judge, he/she is both the prosecutor (has to present the evidence against the employee) and the judge (has to weigh up the evidence from both sides and make a decision as to whether the employee's actions justify disciplinary action).

The comments below relating to the conduct of the interview apply at all levels of the procedure including appeals hearings. The term 'manager' denotes the person on the management side conducting the interview, whether supervisor, managing director, line manager or personnel specialist.

Objectives of the interview

These are two distinct stages to the disciplinary interview.

• *Establishing the facts of the case*. The manager has to establish the facts of the case from both management's and employee's points of view. A disciplinary interview will, in practice, only take place when management already believes, prima facie, that there has been a breach of the organisation's rules by the employee. Thus, from management's side, the facts are generally established prior to the actual interview either by the collection of data (time-keeping, absence, poor work performance, etc.) or by interviewing witnesses in cases relating to the personal conduct of the employee. However, this information has to be reviewed, at the beginning of the interview with the employee present and having the opportunity to question it – including the cross-examination of any witnesses. The employee must also be afforded the opportunity to present his/her side of the case and, if necessary, call his/her own evidence and witnesses. This first stage is very similar to a grievance interview in that the manager is primarily concerned with listening to and assessing the validity of the evidence presented and ensuring that both sides of the case are heard.

● *Administering the disciplinary sanction*. Having decided that disciplinary action is justified, the manager then has to administer the disciplinary sanction. This stage may follow immediately from the first or there may be a break to allow the manager to consider his/her decision and determine the appropriate course of action. During this stage of the interview the only people who should be present, in addition to the member of management carrying out the interview, are the employee and, where appropriate, the immediate supervisor and shop steward. The purpose of this stage is to ensure that the employee is fully aware of why the disciplinary action is being taken, the nature of the sanction being applied and its effect, and the standard of behaviour or performance expected in the future. The keynote at this stage of the interview is for the employee to be reprimanded but not humiliated.

An inherent danger in the disciplinary interview is that the manager prejudges the situation because he/she has, as part of the preparation for the interview, already investigated management's case and examined the employee's previous record. This can result in the two stages becoming blurred and the manager reprimanding the employee before all the evidence has been heard and considered. The interview should never commence with the manager reprimanding the employee for the alleged offence.

Preparation for the interview

1. The manager has to be satisfied that there is a prima facie case that the employee's performance is inadequate or his/her behaviour has contravened a rule. The manager therefore needs to:

    (a) be certain what rule has been broken;
    (b) determine what evidence there is to substantiate the breach; and
    (c) decide whether or not it is a matter for formal disciplinary action.

2. The manager must be certain of the stage the employee has reached in the disciplinary procedure. It is for this reason that reference needs to be made to the employee's previous record before the interview. The manager must consider:
    (a) what range of penalties are available should the facts of the case be proved; and
    (b) does he/she have the authority, within the procedure, to carry out such penalties.

3. If the employee has, through previous misconduct or because of the seriousness of the offence, reached a stage in the procedure where the manager does not have the authority to administer the likely sanction, the matter must be referred to a higher level of management.

4. If the manager does have the authority to administer the sanction then, so far as the interview itself is concerned, he/she should ensure that:
    (a) the employee is advised that it is a disciplinary interview in order to prepare his/her case and, if necessary, arrange for the attendance of representative and/or witnesses;
    (b) the interview is conducted in a suitable place away from the shopfloor; and
    (c) sufficient time is allowed, free of any interruptions, for an adequate consideration of the case.

Style of the interview

Throughout the interview the manager should keep in mind the twin objectives of the interview – to establish the facts and to administer a disciplinary sanction. Therefore, during the course of the interview the manager should:

1. Present arguments in a clear and concise way.
2. Maintain control of the interview but, at the same time, allow the employee to put his/her case.
3. Concentrate on the facts relating to the performance or behaviour of the employee and not get drawn into personalities.
4. Behave in a calm, rational manner and never get angry or be sarcastic or rude.
5. Make suggestions regarding improvements in the performance or behaviour of the employee and, if possible, encourage the employee to do the same.
6. At the end, summarise the interview and ensure that the employee is aware that he/she has been formally disciplined and has the right to appeal if not satisfied with the decision.

Follow-up

The interview has to be followed up in a number of ways:

1. The employee should receive written confirmation of the disciplinary action. If this is done during or immediately at the end of the disciplinary interview it can appear to the employee that management had already made its decision before the interview.
2. A copy of any such written warning or confirmation should be given to the shop steward and a further copy placed on the employee's personnel file.
3. The manager should inform the appropriate senior management or personnel department, if they were not present at the interview, of the outcome so that they are prepared in the event of a subsequent appeal.
4. The performance or behaviour of the employee requires to be monitored to ensure that an improvement is made and maintained. Should such an improvement materialise the employee should be told that his/her performance or behaviour is now satisfactory.

20.5 Summary propositions

- Whilst the formal disciplinary process is a management orientated control process intended to 'penalise' employees whose performance or behaviour does not meet management's expectations, the disciplinary procedure within its affords an opportunity for employees to limit arbitrary management actions.
- Industrial discipline is as much concerned with the conflict between differing work norms within the organisation as individual breaches of generally accepted norms of personal conduct.
- Unfair dismissal legislation provides little, if any, job security or protection for the employee and, at best, only limited compensation when unfairly dismissed; job security can only be achieved through a strong union presence in the operation of the organisation's disciplinary/dismissal procedure.

Further reading

- Industrial Relations Procedures, *Manpower Paper No. 14*, Department of Employment, HMSO, 1975. Chapter 4 deals with a number of issues to be considered in the operation of the disciplinary procedure.

- *Discipline at Work*, ACAS, 1987. A very useful booklet on managing discipline and dismissal.
- L. Dickens, *et al.*, *Dismissed: A study of unfair dismissal and the industrial tribunal system*, Blackwell, 1985. A very useful discussion of the operation of the Industrial Tribunal system as it relates to unfair dismissal.
- C. J. Carr and P. J. Kay, *Employment Law* (5th edn), M & E Handbooks, 1991. Chapters 10–12 provide an up-to-date outline of the law relating to termination of the contract (including unfair dismissal).

References

1. Hoyt N. Wheeler, 'Punishment theory and industrial discipline', *Industrial Relations*, vol. 15, no. 2, 1976.
2. *Dismissal Procedures*, Ministry of Labour, HMSO, 1967, Appendix 1.
3. W. W. Daniel and N. Millward, *Workplace Industrial Relations in Britain*, Heinemann (PSI/SSRC), 1983, p. 171.
4. T. Foxen, *Effective Discipline*, Industrial Society, 1977.
5. R. Smith, 'Work control and managerial prerogatives in industrial relations', Working Paper, Durham University Business School, May 1978.
6. M. Mellish and N. Collis-Squires, 'Legal and social norms in discipline and dismissal', *Industrial Law Journal*, vol. 5, no. 3, 1976. (Referring to Ministry of Labour Report (1967), Donovan Commission Report (1968), 'In Working Order' (1975) and Industrial Relations Code of Practice (1972). This 'softer' approach can also be seen in the ACAS Code of Practice (1977).
7. See for example, Dale S. Beach, *The Management of People at Work* (2nd edn), Macmillan, 1970; W. F. Dowling and L. R. Sayles, *How Managers Motivate*, McGraw-Hill, 1971; P. Pigors and C. A. Myers, *Personnel Administration* (7th edn), McGraw-Hill, 1973.
8. Dale S. Beach, *op. cit.*
9. G. C. Walters and J. E. Grusec, *Punishment*, W. H. Freeman & Co., 1977.
10. *ibid.*, pp. 31–2.
11. Hoyt N. Wheeler, *op. cit.*
12. M. Mellish and N. Collis-Squires, *op. cit.*
13. A. Fox, *A Sociology of Work in Industry*, Collier Macmillan, 1972.
14. S. Hill, 'Norms groups and power: the sociology of workplace industrial relations', *British Journal of Industrial Relations*, vol. XII, no. 2, 1974.
15. A. Fox, *op. cit.*, p. 29. Reproduced with permission of the publisher.
16. N. Singleton, *Industrial Relations Procedures*, Department of Employment, HMSO, 1975.
17. *In Working Order: A study of industrial discipline*, Department of Employment, HMSO, 1973.
18. M. Mellish and N. Collis-Squires, *op. cit.*
19. G. Mars, 'Hotel pilferage: a case study in occupational theft' in M. Warner (ed.), *The Sociology of the Workplace*, Allen & Unwin, 1973.
20. W. F. Dowling and L. R. Sayles, *op. cit.*

21. T. Foxen, *op. cit.*
22. P. Pigors and C. A. Myers, *op. cit.*
23. L. R. Benton, *Supervision and Management*, McGraw-Hill, 1972.
24. W. B. Boise, 'Supervisors' attitudes towards disciplinary action', *Personnel Administration*, May/June 1965.
25. N. R. F. Maier, 'Discipline in the industrial setting', *Personnel Journal*, vol. 44, April 1965.
26. M. W. Cuming, *The Theory and Practice of Personnel Management*, Heinemann, 1968.
27. *Western Excavations* v. *Sharp*, 1978.
28. *Woods* v. *W. M. Car Services*, 1981.
29. *Spencer* v. *Paragon Wallpapers*, 1976.
30. *McPhee* v. *George H. Wright Ltd*, 1975.
31. *Wood* v. *Heron Fabrics Branch of Courtaulds*, 1974.
32. *Laws* v. *London Chronicle*, 1959.
33. L. Dickens, 'Unfair dismissal law: a decade of disillusion?', *Personnel Management*, February 1982, p. 25.
34. O. Aikin, 'Law at work: a need to reorganise', *Personnel Management*, February 1984, p. 37.
35. *ibid.*,
36. L. Dickens, *op. cit.*, p. 25.
37. P. Lewis, 'An analysis of why legislation has failed to provide employment protection for unfairly dismissed employees', *British Journal of Industrial Relations*, vol. XIX, no. 3, 1981, p. 316.
38. *ibid.*, p. 323.
39. B. Capstick, 'Industrial tribunals: weeding out the "no-hope" cases', *Personnel Management*, August 1981, p. 44.
40. P. Wallace and R. F. Clifton, 'Pre-hearing assessments in unfair dismissal cases', *Employment Gazette*, February 1985, pp. 65–9.
41. *ACAS Annual Report 1990*, Table 11, p. 56.
42. L. Dickens, *op. cit.*, pp. 26–7.
43. H. Concannon, 'Handling dismissal disputes by arbitration', *Industrial Relations Journal*, vol. 11, no. 2, 1980, p. 16.
44. L. Dickens, *op. cit.*, p. 27.
45. 'Disciplinary Practice and Procedure in Employment', *ACAS Code of Practice 1*, HMSO, 1977.

Chapter 21
Redundancy

21.1 Definition

White [1] makes a distinction between 'job redundancy' (where a particular job ceases to exist but the incumbent employees are found alternative work within the organisation) and 'worker redundancy' (where the employees lose their employment). This could be taken to imply that real redundancy only exists in the latter circumstance. Furthermore, some organisations have begun to use the apparently less emotive terms 'deselection' or 'outplacement' for these situations: in these organisations redundancy (or deselection) has become a normal part of operational and labour planning.

However, the term 'redundancy' should be applied to:

any situation where changes in the organisation's economic, operational or technological position results in a reduced labour level; irrespective of whether the reduction is achieved through compulsory dismissals, 'voluntary severance', 'natural wastage' or employee transfers or whether it involves the loss of only a single job or a more significant reduction in part, or all, of the workforce.

The essential qualities of a redundancy situation are that it arises primarily from causes external to the performance and capabilities of the individual employees affected and, most importantly, it involves a potential conflict of interest between management's immediate objectives of maintaining an efficient and profitable organisation and the employees' immediate objectives of protecting their jobs and income. This conflict will arise despite any management arguments that the long-term viability of the organisation is essential if employees are to have any 'job security'. Certainly, there is likely to be as much conflict between management and employees/unions over 'job redundancy' as 'worker redundancy' (e.g. the NCB/NUM dispute in 1984/1985 despite management guarantees of no compulsory 'worker redundancy').

21.2 The organisation, union and individual

Sutherland argues that redundancy has 'assumed a growing importance, most especially so in a political economy apparently dominated by themes such as de-industrialisation and unemployment' [2]. Certainly the number of redundancies increased from under 200,000 per annum in the late 1970s to over 500,000 per annum in the 1980s. Every reduction in an organisation's labour establishment must be viewed not only as possible unemployment for the person who filled it, dependent on how the reduction is achieved, but also a loss of a potential job for those who are already unemployed and for future generations.

Sutherland suggests that there are three perspectives which may be adopted in analysing redundancy:

1. The perspective of the **labour planner** which focuses attention on 'that period of time in the organisation prior to the implementation of a programme involving involuntary quits' [3] and which views redundancy as an element in balancing the organisation's labour requirement.
2. The perspective of the **labour economist** which focuses attention on 'the operation of, and adjustment processes in, the external labour market' [4] and which views redundancy as a means of redistributing labour within the economy.

(Both of these perspectives incorporate a managerial ideology which emphasises the goal of operational efficiency at either the micro or macro level and accepts the legitimacy of redundancy as a means of achieving that efficiency.)

3. The perspective of the **industrial sociologist** which focuses attention on the differing value systems which exist within society and the organisation and which therefore regards the legitimacy of both the goal (operational efficiency) and the means (redundancy) as neither unquestionable nor agreed amongst the participants.

Sutherland further argues that **shifts in government policy towards redundancy** can be explained in terms of changes in the influence of these perspectives. Government policy in the 1960s, as epitomised in the Redundancy Payments Act (1965), was that 'although redundancy may involve the private individual in short run adjustment costs, in the long run the resulting redeployment of labour would prove socially beneficial' [5]. In the 1970s, however, government policy shifted more towards one of 'recognition that the cheapest mode of job creation in the short run was job preservation' [6]. Consequently, government actions, such as the Temporary Employment Subsidy (1975), were directed at avoiding redundancies. The change in policy was closely associated with a change in the level of unemployment. In the

1960s, with an unemployment level of only 1–2 per cent (i.e. full or over-full employment), redundancy could be justified as a means of 'freeing' a scarce resource whilst the individuals who were made redundant were not likely to be unemployed for long. By the mid to late 1970s unemployment was 5 per cent and rising and therefore redundancy could be seen as directly adding to that level and creating a social and political problem for any government which was committed to a policy of maintaining full employment. In the 1980s the focus of attention has shifted back to a labour economics perspective. Redundancy and its associated unemployment is seen as a natural result of wage inflation and a necessary consequence of organisational attempts to create greater operational efficiency and competitiveness in a recession market.

The organisation

Although redundancy may arise from any number of specific reasons, it is possible to identify four main causes:

1. **Structural decline of the industry** within which the organisation is located. For example, an industry may find itself unable to respond to the price competition from similar industries in other countries, thereby losing its traditional markets and having to contract. Britain, as one of the earliest industrialised countries, has been perhaps particularly prone to this form of challenge among its older, and generally less efficient, industries. Alternatively, the industry's product may, through technological development, become out of date – for example, the replacement of traditional natural textiles by man-made fibres or the advent of North Sea gas which no longer necessitated the manufacture of gas from coal. These types of situation are likely to affect all organisations within the industry to a lesser or greater extent but their surplus labour may be able to be absorbed by other expanding industries.

2. **Decrease in the level of economic activity** resulting in declining sales and over capacity. This may take the form of a general recession affecting all industries or it may be confined to a single industry and may, as in the construction industry during the winter period, recur on a cyclical basis. Whether this will result in redundancies in a given organisation depends, to a large extent, on management's assessment of how long this position may last and the financial ability of the organisation to withstand a temporary reduction in sales and output. Equally, a decline in sales and economic activity may be experienced by particular organisations, during either boom or recession, because they are uncompetitive in terms of price or quality. This lack of competitiveness may arise as much from poor management and a lack of

capital investment and 'new technology' as from 'restrictive practices' or high wages on the part of employees.

3. **Introduction of technological change** within the organisation itself, such as new computer-based machinery, which not only results in a requirement for less labour to produce a given level of output but which is also often associated with a change in the level or type of skills required amongst the employees. Thus, some employees may become redundant because they have neither the skills nor the ability or opportunity to acquire the skills needed by the new technology.

4. **Reorganisation of the work situation** to obtain a more efficient use of existing plant and machinery and reduce costs. This is often associated with company mergers and rationalisations or changes in work arrangements.

It is important to recognise that these factors may, in any given situation, **interrelate on a cumulative basis**. For example, a decline in the general level of economic activity in Britain, as a result of inflation and high exchange and/or interest rates, has induced an accelerated structural decline in marginal cost industries through increased foreign competition. In reacting to a structural decline of the industry or a decrease in the level of economic activity, the management of an organisation may seek to maintain its economic viability by reorganising their work methods and/or introducing new technology to cut costs and thereby increase sales. In this situation management's response to the cause of surplus labour may not result in an increase in overall employment security but may, in fact, induce further redundancies.

The structure of industry, as a whole, is dynamic and constantly changing in response to many pressures and therefore it is perhaps inevitable that some redundancies will always be occurring. It is also clearly too simplistic to argue that redundancies are the result of either inefficient management or employees pricing themselves out of jobs through excessive wage increases gained by the industrial power of their trade unionism. Whilst redundancies most often form an integral part of an organisation's attempt to reduce costs and improve its competitive base, they can also arise in dynamic and financially sound organisations through the desire for technological change.

Whenever redundancies are announced in a company there are many who believe that management was both aware of the situation months before and had done little to avoid the situation arising. Certainly, Mumford suggests that 'for the manpower planner, redundancy is generally seen as synonymous with failure' [7]. However, it is rarely management's labour **planning** which has caused the need for redundancy. As Torrington and Chapman point out the labour plan simply 'forecasts demand and supply and then sets up operations to ensure there is a supply to meet the demand' [8] and is dependent for its accuracy and effectiveness on information supplied in respect of projected production patterns. Labour planning can only aid the avoidance of surplus labour if changes in the circumstances which affect the production forecasts are identified early enough. However, effective labour planning can play an important part in minimising the extent and effects of any surplus labour if and when it arises:

1. Accurate labour planning in the past, coupled with close management control of any expansion of staff to meet apparent increases in workloads, should ensure that the organisation is not already carrying an excessive number of employees.
2. Through an analysis of data necessary for the initial determination of the labour plan, such as age and length of service profiles, turnover rates, the skills and experience of employees, etc., management may be able to assess the impact of 'natural wastage' and early retirements on achieving the necessary labour reductions in the required areas over the given period of time.
3. Should it become necessary to reduce the number of employees by other means this information may also be used to assess the implications of adopting various selection criteria.

Finally, it is important to bear in mind that redundancies may also be avoided by the organisation using the **opportunity presented by the existence of surplus labour** to develop new products and activities. There was one notable case, Lucas, where shop stewards, faced by a management decision to reduce the labour force, presented an alternative plan based on diversification into areas and products which they believed to be both economic and socially desirable. It is perhaps unfortunate that most organisations, having at some stage made the decision as to 'what business they were in', feel that a time of high costs, low sales and low profits is not the time to undertake new speculative ventures. Certainly there is a sense in which the lead time required to develop such new ventures is generally too long to be a viable proposition to a management seeking to obtain an immediate, or at least short-term, improvement in their organisation's financial position. Such developments, if they are to take place, have to be considered and agreed before the redundancy becomes apparent, and yet the incentive to think in these terms does not generally arise until the redundancy is a virtual fact.

The trade union

At the **organisational level** trade unions are reluctant to 'agree' to a redundancy, although inevitably they have to 'accept' it. For them, redundancy is a complete negation of the concepts of 'job security' and 'the right to work'. The trade union's **primary objective** is to resist, or at the very least, minimise the extent of any reduction in the organisation's labour force. Indeed, the TUC's guide for negotiators 'is directed mainly towards provisions for avoiding redundancy and keeping workers fully employed' [9]. However, in only a small number of situations has the union's or work-group's resistance to redundancy gone to the extent of a work-in or sit-in, although token strikes to demonstrate the employees' feelings are not uncommon. It is only when redundancy is considered to be unavoidable that the union's **secondary objective** becomes one of seeking to secure the best possible terms for those employees likely to be made redundant.

The main thrust of **union policy**, apart from resisting redundancies or securing the best terms, has centred on seeking to reduce the level of unemployment by increasing job opportunities through shortening the working week and lowering the normal retirement age. A **reduction in the working week** appears to have immense potential for creating job opportunities. However, management have responded to such changes during the 1980s not by increasing the number of employees but by reducing or eliminating paid breaks or by reducing labour levels in order to avoid increasing their per unit costs. At the same time, employees themselves often preclude the translation of a shorter working week into more job opportunities by a reluctance to reduce their actual hours worked and foresake the opportunity to enhance their earnings by working the time at premium overtime rates. In 1983 the TUC reported that 'overtime still stood at an average of around 10 hours per overtime worker per week, even in sectors facing considerable redundancies' and 'there was little indication of hours reductions being tailored explicitly to avoiding redundancy' [10].

The alternative of **reducing the normal retirement age** has encountered resistance from both management and the government. Whilst management is often prepared to utilise voluntary early retirement as part of a redundancy package, generally with some enhancement of the individual's pension entitlement, it is reluctant to accept a permanent and comprehensive reduction in the normal retirement age within the organisation. Any reduction has important implications, at both organisational and national levels, in respect of the funding of pension arrangements. It will require a higher rate of contribution by the individual, organisation and the State over a shorter period to finance the extra payments that will have to be made as a consequence of the individual's longer period of retirement. The House of Commons Select Committee on Social Services (1982) estimated that to reduce the male retirement age to 60, as suggested by the TUC, would cost approximately £2½ billion.

The individual

At the individual level, whilst redundancy may be regarded as an opportunity leading 'in the long run to a more satisfying job, with greater scope for advance' [11], for most employees their initial reaction may be to regard themselves as 'superfluous, no longer needed, obsolescent, useless' [12]. It is important to realise that 'the feeling of self-worth which we derive from work arises because our society decrees that men are expected to work' [13]. The 'Protestant work ethic' regards unemployment as, at best, a cause for sympathy but a necessary fact of economic life or, at worst, a reflection of the individual's inadequacies or simply scrounging.

The individual, in **coming to terms with being redundant**, is likely to pass through four psychological stages:

1. **Shock:** the individual may feel immobilised and lack any sense of purpose or may undertake any activity, however pointless, which keeps him/her occupied. He/she may simply stay at home or seek to 'keep up appearances' by leaving home and returning at normal times and fill in time wandering round, reading in public libraries, etc., and may even not tell family and friends that he/she is redundant.
2. **Defensive retreat:** the individual may underestimate the potential seriousness of the situation; regarding it perhaps as only a temporary situation, under control, which he/she can alleviate by simply applying for a few jobs. He/she may emphasise the positive aspects of being redundant; such as more time with family or an opportunity to do the things around the home which possibly previously he/she lacked either the time or money to do.
3. **Acknowledgement:** this begins 'with a feeling of bitterness and depression, as the positive factors in the situation disappear and the negative aspects come to the fore' [14] and may be associated with the individual exhausting the redundancy compensation or failing to secure new employment as easily as he/she thought.
4. **Adaptation:** through a full realisation and assessment of the situation the individual can proceed to seek either employment or other constructive activities which maintain a purpose and status in life.

21.3 Legal framework

The legal framework surrounding redundancy may be divided into three main parts:

1. The payment of monetary compensation to redundant employees (established in the Redundancy Payments Act (1965) but now incorporated within the Employment Protection (Consolidation) Act (1978)).
2. Protection for the individual employee against unfair selection for redundancy and the provision for time-off to seek work or training (established in the Industrial Relations Act (1971) and Employment

Protection Act (1975) respectively and now incorporated in the Employment Protection (Consolidation) Act (1978)).
3. The requirement for management to consult with recognised independent trade unions prior to redundancies taking place (Employment Protection Act (1975)).

Redundancy payments

It is important to realise that although the Redundancy Payments Act (1965) was introduced at a period of relatively full employment, it followed a number of major company mergers and rationalisations during the early 1960s in which significant numbers of employees had been dismissed with little, if any, notice or compensation. At the same time, few organisations had concluded redundancy agreements and trade union reaction to redundancies was, as Rideout noted, generally 'to attempt to prevent such dismissals ... often by way of work-sharing so that everyone worked less and earned less' which 'was apt to be disastrous, especially if it meant that large contingents of skilled or potentially skilled labour were underemployed in one industry or area, whilst in another expansion was held back for lack of manpower' [15]. Aikin and Reid note that the **intention** of the legislation was therefore 'to compensate a redundant employee for loss of his job, in the same way as he would be compensated for loss of a property right; to foster mobility of labour; and to help employers who were overstaffed to "shake out" excess labour, thus freeing them for more productive work elsewhere' [16]. The legislation was, and is, not intended to provide employees with job security but to relieve the financial hardship associated with the employee's job loss. However, the amount of financial compensation received by the employee varies according to length of service rather than the length of time he/she may be unemployed or the difficulties in finding another job. The organisation's financial burden of redundancy payments was, until 1986, reduced through a state administered **Redundancy Fund** financed by contributions levied from all employers. An organisation could receive reimbursement of part of the payments it made under the legisation. Any payments made in excess of this legal minimum were not reimbursed. The fund was abolished in 1986.

Coverage of the legislation
Certain special groups, such as Crown Servants (including the NHS), are excluded from the provisions relating to redundancy payments although they may be covered by their own compensatory schemes. However, there are other, more general, groups which are also excluded:

1. **Length of service** – any employee with less than two years service after the age of 18 (S.81(4) 1978 Act).

2. **Retirement age** – any employee who, at the date of being made redundant, has reached retirement age (S.82(1) 1978 Act).
3. **Part-time employees** – employees whose contract of employment is for less than 8 hours per week and those whose contract of employment is for between 8 and 16 hours per week and who have less than five years continuous service (Schedule 13(6) 1978 Act).
4. **Fixed-term contracts** – an employee working under a fixed-term contract of two or more years duration if redundancy results only from the non-renewal of the contract and the employee has agreed, in writing, to waive rights to make such a claim (S.142(2) 1978 Act).

Legal definition of redundancy

An employee is entitled to receive redundancy payments where 'dismissal is attributable wholly or mainly to:

(i) the fact that his employer has ceased or intends to cease, to carry on the business for the purposes of which the employee was employed by him, or has ceased, or intends to cease, to carry on that business in the place where the employee was so employed, or

(ii) the fact that the requirements of that business for employees to carry out work of a particular kind, or for employees to carry out work of a particular kind in the place where he was so employed, have ceased or diminished or are expected to cease or diminish' (S.81(2) 1978 Act).

The first part of this definition, which deals with the permanent or temporary cessation of part or all of the employer's business, has, in the main, given rise to few problems of interpretation. However, in the second part, which relates to a reduced level of employment, certain words and phrases are critical in the determination of whether or not an employee is redundant and therefore entitled to receive redundancy payments.

• *'Dismissal'*. Dismisal will only occur if the employer terminates the contract of employment, with or without notice, or the employee terminates it, with or without notice, 'in circumstances such that he is entitled to terminate it without notice by reason of the employer's conduct' (S.83(2)(c) 1978 Act). Thus, if management seeks to impose a unilateral change in the contract of employment because of a change in work requirements, the employee may treat this as repudiation of the contract by the employer and any consequential resignation will not necessarily be a bar to claiming any redundancy. This situation of 'concealed redundancy' may be distinguished from the more general situation of a 'constructive dismissal' under unfair dismissal legislation by applying the test of whether or not the employee would have been made redundant if management's attempt to unilaterally change the contract of employment had not been made. If it appears likely, then the claim will be dealt with under redundancy legislation; if not, the claim will be considered under the normal unfair dismissal legislation.

Aikin and Reid note that dismissal 'involves a unilateral termination of the contract by one party to it, regardless of the wishes of the other' [17]. Thus, if management assists a potentially redundant employee by securing fresh employment with another organisation and then mutually agrees with the employee to terminate the contract of employment so that the employee may commence employment with the new organisation this will not, in legal terms, amount to dismissal. Therefore, the employee will have no statutory right to redundancy payment, although this does not preclude an organisational policy or agreement to make such a payment. Furthermore, if management gives employees **advance warning** that redundancy is likely to take place and an employee resigns, having found alternative work, he/she will have no statutory right to redundancy payments. As far as the Industrial Tribunals are concerned such a management warning, if it does not specify when the redundancy is to take place, merely allows the employee to choose either to stay, receive redundancy payment and then look for other work or to secure alternative work thereby avoiding being unemployed but without the benefit of receiving any compensation for the probable loss of his/her job.

However, once management has given the employee specific notice to terminate the contract of employment, the employee may seek to terminate the contract at an earlier date by giving written notice to that effect. If this is unacceptable, management may respond, again in writing, by stating that it requires the employee to continue until the date on which the notice expires and that it will contest the employee's right to redundancy payment if he/she fails to do so. In this situation an Industrial Tribunal may, having regard to both the reasons for which the employee seeks to leave employment and the reasons for which the employer requires him/her to remain, award all or part of the redundancy payment to which the employee would have been entitled (S.85 1978 Act).

- *'Attributable wholly or mainly to'*. An employee is not entitled to redundancy payment if management can show that the dismissal resulted from misconduct or poor work performance: even though there were at that time redundancies in the organisation amongst the group of workers to which the complainant belonged. This may apply even if the dismissal results from the employee's refusal to agree to or undertake new duties as part of a reorganisation within the workplace. The **presumption in a redundancy case** is that the employee has been dismissed by reason of redundancy and therefore it is for the employer to show that the dismissal resulted from the employee's own conduct, performance or capabilities. The **two aspects of redundancy and unfair dismissal may be linked**. If the Tribunal finds that the employee has been dismissed by reason of redundancy then the dismissal is for a fair reason and the Tribunal will determine whether the employee is entitled to redundancy payment. If, however, the Tribunal finds that the employee has not been dismissed because of redundancy but because of his/her conduct or performance it may then proceed to consider the fairness and reasonableness of the dismissal in the light of unfair dismissal provisions. Generally an employer will be able to demonstrate that an employee is not redundant if the employee's post has been filled by a **replacement**. However, this will not apply if the replacement employee has been moved from another redundant position within the organisation.

- *'Requirements of that business'; 'Work of a particular kind'; 'Place where he was so employed'.* It is important to recognise that the general legal principle underlying the determination of the existence of redundancy, and therefore the statutory right to redundancy payment, is that redundancy only exists if there is a reduction in the requirements of the business as a whole for employees to carry out a particular type of work. Therefore, changes in the type of employee or the skills required to carry out that work or changes in the content of an individual's job consequent upon any reorganisation may not, by themselves, constitute redundancy.

It is necessary to examine the precise **terms of the contract of employment** for, as Rideout noted, if there is 'insufficient work of the contractual kind in the contractual place ... that is plainly redundancy' [18]. Aikin and Reid point out that tribunals have, nevertheless, taken the view that an employee is expected to adapt to new methods and techniques and therefore, in order 'to decide whether a new job has been created or the old one continues, though with varied duties, ... it is necessary to look at the type of work that the employer required before reorganization and compare it with the work required after reorganization. The more different the work is, the more likely there is to be a finding of redundancy' [19]. If an employee's contract of employment designates him/her as a process worker, the employer may be entitled to transfer the employee to any process work or change the duties, particularly if this is achieved through collective agreement, without it being redundancy. Furthermore, whilst a reorganisation of the employee's working time (between part-time and full-time or between day hours and shifts) does not involve a change in the particular kind of work required of him/her, it may constitute redundancy if it involves a reduction in the number of people employed. However, such apparent changes in the employee's contract of employment may, particularly if imposed unilaterally by the employer, constitute grounds for a claim of 'constructive dismissal'; although it may be defended on the grounds of being 'necessary in the best interests of the business'. The ability of the employer to transfer an employee geographically from one location to another without it constituting redundancy will also depend on the employer's contractual rights to require such a move.

Short time working and lay off

The employee's right to claim redundancy payment extends to situations where he/she has not been dismissed but has been laid off or put on short time working because of a shortage of work within the organisation. The legislation defines **lay off** as being a situation in which an employee receives no pay at all from the employer and **short time** as being a situation in which an employee receives less than half a week's pay for that week (S.87 1978 Act). If either situation continues for four consecutive weeks, or for any six weeks out of thirteen, the employee may terminate the contract with due notice and notify the employer that he/she intends to claim redundancy payment (S.88(1) 1978 Act). The employer may serve a counter notice, within seven days of receiving the employee's notification of intent to claim, to contest the claim on the grounds that it is reasonable to expect the work situation to return to normal within four weeks and remain so for at least thirteen weeks (S.88(3) 1978 Act). Obviously in this situation the employee must, when deciding to terminate his/her employment, make a judgement as to whether or not he/she believes the work level is likely to return to normal, and if subsequently this judgement is proved wrong he/she loses any entitlement to redundancy payment.

Offer of alternative employment

An employee will not be entitled to redundancy payment if, before the expiry of the notice period, he/she 'unreasonably' refuses the employer's offer of 'suitable alternative' employment. The suitability of the alternative employment may be assessed on an objective basis by comparing the terms and conditions of the alternative employment with those of the original employment. Thus, it involves examining the wages, hours, status, conditions, etc., of the two jobs. The reasonableness of any refusal to accept the alternative employment has to be judged on more subjective criteria relating to the personal circumstances of the individual employee to whom the job is being offered. It may be reasonable for the employee to refuse an offer of alternative employment if its acceptance might involve excessive personal or domestic difficulties derived from extra travelling time, working shifts, having to move house, etc. The burden of proof in respect of both suitability and reasonableness lies with the employee and clearly the two issues cannot be divorced completely from each other. An offer of alternative employment may be made in respect of the same employer or an associated employer. When the alternative employment entails differences in the terms and conditions of employment the offer should be made in writing so that the employee may assess the difference. In addition, there is a right to a trial period of four weeks under the new employment, at any time during which either the employee or the employer may terminate the contract and the employee will retain the right to claim redundancy payment as if he/she had been made redundant at the original date.

Level of compensation and procedure for claiming
The statutory entitlement to redundancy payment is based on the employee's length of **continuous service** as follows:

Service at age (inclusive)	Payment equivalent to
18–21	½ week's pay
22–40	1 week's pay
41–65 (men)	1½ week's pay
41–60 (women)	1½ week's pay

The calculation of entitlement is subject to a **maximum** of 20 years service and a statutory maximum of a 'week's pay' (in 1990 the maximum redundancy payment was approximately £6,000). Where the employee's level of pay is subject to variation as a result of bonus schemes, etc. or because he/she has no normal hours, a 'week's pay' will be arrived at by averaging over a four or 12 week period prior to the redundancy. In addition, if the employee is in his/her final year preceding the statutory retirement age, the entitlement to redundancy payment will be reduced by $1/_{12}$ for each month. The employer is required, on making any redundancy payment, to provide the employee with a written statement indicating how the amount has been calculated (S.102 1978 Act).

If there is any dispute between the employee and employer regarding the employee's entitlement to redundancy payment or the level of such payment, the employee may take the case to an Industrial Tribunal up to six months after the date of termination.

Other individual rights

Whilst the law does not specify the selection criteria to be used by an employer in a redundancy, it does provide the employee with a degree of protection against an **unfair selection for redundancy**. It is potentially an unfair dismissal, with higher compensation than under redundancy legislation, if the employer selects the employee for redundancy on the basis of either an inadmissible reason or in contravention of a 'customary arrangement or agreed procedure relating to redundancy' (S.59 1978 Act). In this context 'inadmissible reason' relates to either the employee's membership or non-membership of a trade union. Perhaps more importantly, management must follow any policy, arrangement or agreement which can be shown by the employee to have been applied in the past or agreed with the unions. In the absence of any such policy, arrangement or agreement within the organisation the employee may still be able to claim unfair selection for redundancy by citing the existence of a commonly applied practice or agreement within the industry.

An employee who has been given notice of dismissal by reason of redundancy is entitled, before the expiration of the period of notice, to be allowed **reasonable time off during normal working hours to seek new employment** or make arrangements for training (S.31 1978 Act). This right is, however, available only to those employees who have two or more years' service. In addition, the employee is entitled to receive normal pay during the period of absence or, if the employer unreasonably refuses to allow the employee to have the time off, to receive an equivalent payment in lieu. If the employer refuses to allow the time off or to make the payment in lieu, the employee may take a claim before an Industrial Tribunal who may then make an award against the employer not exceeding two-fifths of a week's pay. Thus, whilst the legislation does not define what constitutes 'reasonable time off' by implication the employee is only entitled to two days' paid absence.

Consultation with trade unions

The requirement for management to consult with **independent recognised trade union(s)** representing the group of workers from amongst which redundancies are to be made only applies when it is proposing to dismiss employees and not before. Therefore, whilst it is good practice for management to consult with all independent recognised trade unions as soon as the likelihood of surplus labour is identified, it is only legally required to do so once it has made the decision to cope with the situation by making employees redundant. The **minimum statutory periods** for consultation are:

1. If 10 to 99 employees are to be made redundant in one establishment within a period of 30 days or less, the employer is required to consult at least 30 days before the first dismissal becomes effective.
2. If 100 or more employees are to be made redundant in one establishment within a period of 90 days or less, the employer is required to consult at least 90 days before the first dismissal becomes effective.

In any other situations, for example involving less than 10 employees or the redundancy being spread over longer periods than 30 or 90 days, management is simply required to consult 'at the earliest opportunity' (S.99(3) 1975 Act). This period of consultation may run concurrently with any periods of notice required to be given to the employees concerned.

Management is required to commence the consultation process by disclosing, in writing, to trade union representatives the broad outline of its proposals (S.99(5) 1975 Act). The legislation specifies that the following information should be provided:

1. The reasons for the proposed redundancy.
2. The numbers and types of employees it is proposed to make redundant.

3. The total number of employees of these types employed within the establishment.
4. The proposed method of selecting those employees who are to be made redundant.
5. The proposed method of implementing the redundancy having regard to both any agreed procedure and the period over which the redundancy is to take place.

Following the provision of this information, management is also required to give consideration to any representations made by the union representatives in respect of these proposals and, when replying to them, to state any reasons it may have for rejecting any of their representations. Thus, management's legal obligation is confined to consultation and there is no legal obligation that it should agree any proposals with the trade unions.

If the trade union concerned believes that management has not complied with the statutory requirement to consult, it may make an application to an Industrial Tribunal for a **protective award** (S.101 1975 Act). If the Tribunal finds in favour of the union and employees it may make an award requiring the employer to continue to pay the employees their normal remuneration for a specified period. The period of the protective award may commence from the date of the award or the date of the first dismissal, whichever is the earlier, and will not exceed the length of the statutory consultation period or 28 days where less than 10 employees are involved. The protective award does not reduce the extent of the redundancy, protect the employees indefinitely or ensure that consultation with the trade union is carried out, but simply guarantees that the employees will receive the payment of their wages for a further relatively short period. A protective award will not be made if management can show, in its defence, that there were special reasons which meant that it was not reasonably practicable to comply with the statutory minimum and that it took all reasonably practicable steps to comply with the requirements. For example, tribunals have held that the secrecy required in attempting to sell a company, or the fact that the redundancies had been caused or hastened by the cancellation of a contract, constitute special reasons precluding the necessity to comply with the statutory minimum periods for consultation with trade unions.

21.4 Handling redundancy

There are three main phases in the handling of a redundancy situation (see Figure 21.1):

1. The **preliminary discussion phase** requires management, in consultation or negotiation with appropriate trade unions, to:

(a) establish the need for a redundancy, having considered alternative approaches to alleviating the need to dismiss employees; and

(b) determine the numbers and types of employees to be dismissed and the period of time over which the reduction in the labour force is to be achieved.

2. The **main procedural application phase** is concerned with implementing any previously determined redundancy policy or procedure, particularly in respect of:

(a) the selection of employees to be made redundant;

(b) the level of compensation to be paid; and

(c) the provision of assistance to redundant employees.

If there is no existing policy or procedure on redundancy within the organisation then this main phase will involve both the determination and negotiation of such a policy or procedure as well as its application.

3. The **individual employee phase** involves the notification and counselling of the individual employees to be made redundant.

Redundancy policy and procedure

Perhaps the most important decision to be made by both management and trade unions is **whether to agree a redundancy policy and procedure in advance.** Trade union representatives may, whatever the organisational climate at the time, regard any management proposal for such an advance agreement as a clear indication that management is positively planning for some future redundancy. In their view, any agreement to a redundancy policy and procedure will imply their acceptance of the need for redundancy and a weakening of any opposition they may wish to make when the need for redundancy arises. At the same time, management may feel that they will be equally constrained if they agree to levels of compensation which may prove subsequently to be greater than they can realistically afford. Both sides may also believe that such an agreement could restrict their ability to respond flexibly in the light of the particular redundancy when it arises.

Nevertheless, Mumford argues that in the absence of such an agreement 'there is a greater risk of a redundancy situation's being destructive, anomolous and a cause of contention and bad relations for a long time ahead' [20]. There is little doubt that the advance negotiation of such an agreement can allow both sides to approach the issue in a less emotive and urgent atmosphere than if the agreement has to be both negotiated and applied at the time redundancies are to take place. It allows time to be spent identifying and resolving the conflicting interests of management and employees, thereby resulting in a fairer, more equitable and workable agreement. The

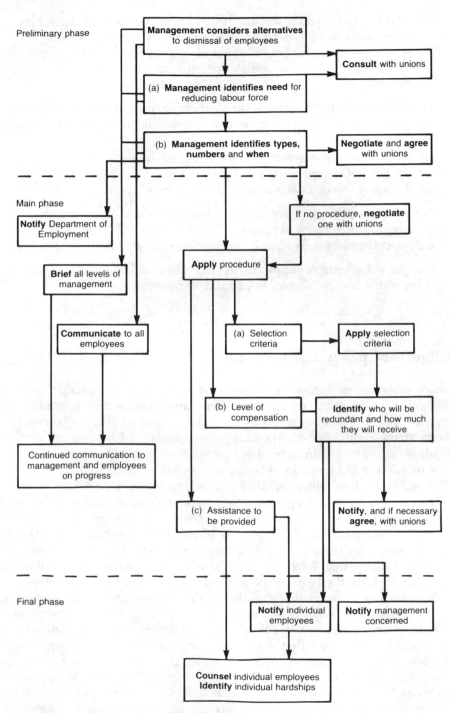

Figure 21.1 *Steps in handling redundancy*

existence of an agreed policy and procedure allows both sides, but particularly management, to formulate their plans more effectively when redundancy arises. A compromise between the desirability of having an advance agreement and the need to respond flexibly to any particular redundancy situation may be achieved by reaching an advance agreement on the **general principles** to be applied in any redundancy situation (including select criteria), whilst leaving **specific details**, such as timing and compensation, to be agreed at the time of the redundancy.

The establishment of an agreed policy and procedure covering redundancy irrespective of when it is negotiated, must involve the reconciliation of differing objectives between management and union. Thus, **management's objectives** in any redundancy situation should be not only to reduce its labour force and costs but also to maintain the morale and goodwill of the remaining employees. The existence of redundancies within an organisation creates a feeling of insecurity even amongst those employees who are not to lose their jobs. There is often a feeling that if redundancy can happen once to some employees then it can easily happen again to other employees. Whilst few organisations can guarantee no further redundancies, management's second objective may be achieved, at least in part, through its handling of the redundancy situation by demonstrating its preparedness to treat employees as fairly as possible consistent with its financial position at the time.

The **trade union's objectives** are primarily to resist, or at the very least minimise, a reduction in the level of the organisation's labour force whilst at the same time securing the best possible terms for those employees likely to be made redundant. Trade unions are generally as concerned to ensure that all alternatives are considered before employees are made redundant as they are to ensure that redundant employees receive the best possible financial compensation for the loss of their jobs. However, within the employees' ranks there is, if the financial compensation is attractive enough, often a divergence in attitudes between the union's desire to resist redundancies and the desire of at least some employees actually to be made redundant.

It may be argued that the negative aspect of redundancy should be closely linked to the more positive concept of **security of employment**. A policy and procedure should emphasis the long-term commitment to, and importance of, effective labour planning, including regular discussions between management and trade unions, and the preparedness of both management and employees to undertake retraining and transfers between different work as a consequence of changes in organisation's demand for labour. It should also detail the more immediate **measures which may be undertaken to avoid a reduction in the labour force**. These may include such measures as a stop on recruitment, the reduction or removal of overtime, a stop on subcontracting work out of the organisation and possibly an increase in subcontracting work in, and the introduction of lay-offs, short time working or other methods of work sharing. Management should be certain, before seeking to establish the need for redundancy with trade union representatives, that the use of such measures will, on its own, be insufficient to generate the required labour cost reductions.

However, the effectiveness of both these short-term and longer-term alternatives in avoiding redundancy will depend not only on the scale and immediacy of the labour cost savings desired by management but also on the size and technology of the organisation. Smaller, single-site organisations may lack the capacity to utilise the transfer of employees between departments and sites whilst short time working is likely to be an inappropriate alternative in continuous process industries. In addition, it should be remembered that even at times of redundancy it may not be possible, or even desirable, for the organisation to stop all recruitment or overtime working. It may still be necessary to maintain the recruitment of certain categories of employees amongst which it is not intended to have redundancies and for which it is not possible to retrain other redundant employees and to continue limited essential overtime working in order to ensure that work is completed on time.

Selection criteria

The first step in selecting employees to be made redundant involves determining the **boundary of the units** within which the selection criteria are to be applied. This is particularly important where management is seeking to implement a proportionate reduction across all or part of its labour force. It must decide whether its selection criteria are to be applied across the organisation as a whole or across each department/section on a segmented basis. The varying effect of these approaches can clearly be seen if the relatively straightforward 'last in – first out' criterion were to be applied. If it were applied across the entire plant as a single unit it could result in an unacceptable level of redundancy in some departments with a high proportion of short service employees. If it were applied on the basis of each department separately it could result in employees being treated unequally with longer-service employees being made redundant in one department whilst shorter-service employees are retained in other departments. The adoption of a plant-wide approach is perhaps most appropriate where the training and skills required in the different departments are relatively similar and employees are therefore capable of quickly adapting to the new work if transferred to fill gaps left by redundant employees. However, in most organisations there is a variation in the product or processes of different departments and therefore selection is often, as Mumford notes, 'carried out on a departmental basis geared to the actual reduction in output of that department or section' [21].

Secondly, the indiscriminate application of any selection criterion can 'result in a workforce incapable of producing anything' [22]. Therefore, most managements will seek to ensure they maintain a **balanced workforce**. This will be reflected not only in different levels of redundancy for different categories of employees so maintaining the right balance within the workforce for future needs, but also in the timing of the redundancies. In order to maintain continuity of production it may be necessary to schedule the redundancy of individual employees to coincide with the availability of another employee, who may require training, to take over. This phasing of redundancies is particularly important where management intends, in spite of a significant reduction in the level of production or even the complete closure of the plant, to complete outstanding orders, dispose of its plant or equipment or transfer it to another location within the company. In some situations a small group of experienced employees, especially maintenance employees, may be required to remain for a period after the shutdown of the plant.

Finally, one, or a combination, of the following approaches may be applied in selecting the particular employees to be made redundant:

Voluntary severance

The principle underlying this approach is that the employee, rather than management, should decide whether he/she is to be made redundant. However, the right to volunteer is generally **restricted** to employees in those grades or departments where a surplus has been identified. Furthermore, management may reserve the right to refuse redundancy to those employees within the specified categories whom it considers to be essential to its future operations by virtue of their skill, work performance or experience. Management may avoid the random impact on the organisation's workforce implicit in the use of this approach by notifying such employees that whilst they may, if they wish, leave the organisation they will not receive redundancy compensation. In order to achieve the necessary volunteers it is usual for management to offer **enhanced redundancy compensation** above the minimum required under the Redundancy Payments legislation. In addition, a provision for older employees to volunteer for early retirement, without loss of pension rights, is generally an integral part of a voluntary severance scheme. Whilst management may regard the introduction of a voluntary severance scheme, with its associated enhanced redundancy compensation, as providing an opportunity to persuade certain employees to leave the organisation, such as the long-term sick or those with poor work records, trade unions will normally insist, as part of their agreement to such a scheme, that no employee is pressurised into volunteering to be made redundant.

It is often suggested that voluntary severance will only work successfully if the **level of required redundancy** is 10–20 per cent of the workforce. Below that level there may be too many volunteers thereby requiring some selection of those to be made redundant with the possible consequence that some volunteers may feel aggrieved that they have not been allowed to leave with compensation; above that level there may be insufficient volunteers thereby requiring additional compulsory redundancies. The major **advantage** with adopting this approach is that the redundancy is likely to be less traumatic for the organisation, trade union and employees involved. However, the main **disadvantages for management** are first, it must offer higher levels of compensation if the necessary level of volunteers is to be achieved, and secondly, it may be the better employees, those most likely to be able to find alternative work, who are most likely to volunteer.

Last in – first out

This approach has traditionally been favoured by most trade unions. The principle underlying this approach is that the longer an employee's service with an organisation the greater his/her implied right to a job, and therefore redundant employees should be selected on the basis of their **seniority of service**. The adoption of such a quantitative criterion based on length of service has the advantage that it avoids the possibility of favouritism or discrimination in the selection of those to be made redundant.

The main **advantages to management** are that first, the organisation is able to retain its longer-service and, by implication, its more skilled and experienced employees, and secondly, it is a relatively low-cost option in that, irrespective of whether or not management offers enhanced compensation terms, short-service employees receive less compensation than longer-service employees. The main **disadvantage to management** stems from the fact that short-service employees are also generally younger employees. Thus, the use of this approach may result in a skewed age profile for the employees remaining in the organisation and create a labour planning problem for the future. Also, the retaining of older, longer-service employees may not allow the organisation to respond as well to the challenge of technological change as retaining younger, more adaptable and more recently trained employees. Thus, the use of this criterion may not result in the type and balance of workforce required for future operations.

At the same time, it can lead, in effect, to a **divided workforce** by creating a relatively protected group of longer-service employees alongside an 'at-risk' group of shorter-service employees. Indeed, its **continual general use** by many employers can easily create a group of employees who are made redundant, or are at risk of being made redundant, more than once because they are unable to build up sufficient service with an employer to move into the more protected group.

Efficiency

Many managements would prefer to select their redundant employees from amongst those employees they consider to be least efficient by reason of their absence, timekeeping, work performance or disciplinary record. However, trade unions generally resist this approach, because they feel it is open to abuse by management, or, when they are prepared to accept its adoption, insist on being provided with the information used by management in its selection decisions and having the right to appeal on their members' behalf if they feel that they have been unfairly included. Obviously the use of this approach is dependent on management having adequate information relating to individual employee performance and conduct.

Social need

It is uncommon for the employee's domestic circumstances to be taken into account in the selection criterion although it may be relevant in the context of determining the compensation or assistance to be provided to redundant employees. However, Mumford [23] does cite one example where domestic circumstances, such as marital status, number of children and whether the employee is the sole family income, were combined with efficiency and length of service criteria on a weighted points basis. Under this scheme domestic circumstances could amount to a maximum of 100 points as against a maximum of only 50 points for length of service.

Level of compensation

Many organisations have in the past agreed to an **enhancement of the statutory levels of redundancy payments** in order to make the redundancy easier to implement and more attractive to the employees concerned. The ability of an organisation to agree to such an arrangement depends, in part, on its technological and financial position. Thus, it is more likely in capital intensive organisations, where labour costs are a relatively small proportion of total costs, or where the redundancy results from technological change rather than recession.

In addition to any general enhancement, the organisation may also agree to make provision for **extra financial compensation** not catered for within the statutory scheme. These may include:

1. **Payment to groups of employees specifically excluded by the statutory scheme,** such as those with less than two years service, those under 18 years of age and part-time employees working less than 16 hours per week.
2. **Assessment of compensation at the employee's full rate of pay** rather than the maximum limit specified in the legislation.
3. **Compensation based on the employee's total service** rather than the 20 year maximum specified in the legislation.
4. Extra payments to those **employees above a particular age or length of service.**

5. **Additional retention payments** for those employees required, by management, to remain beyond the date they wish to leave or beyond the date at which the bulk of employees are to be made redundant.
6. **Payment in lieu of notice** even though the employee has been given prior notification of his dismissal.
7. **Continuing hardship payments** to those employees who, after a specified period, have been unable to secure alternative employment or who have had to accept employment at a significantly lower rate of pay.

Assistance to redundant employees

The 'successful' redundancy is perhaps the one where management is able not only to reduce its labour force but also to ensure that its redundant employees are able to secure alternative employment. Thus, managerial assistance generally centres on aiding the employee's search for such alternative employment. As a **statutory minimum** the employer is required to notify the Department of Employment of any redundancy in excess of ten employees and allow redundant employees reasonable time off to seek work or retraining. However, the employer may be able to provide **additional assistance** by:

1. providing **on-site facilities for the Department of Employment** to attend to advise employees on job opportunities, retraining schemes and facilities, unemployment and other state payments, etc.;
2. **establishing their own 'employment agency'** to contact associated companies or other employers in the locality or elsewhere to try to secure alternative work for their redundant employees;
3. **maintaining a list of redundant employees** who will be given preference for employment should circumstances improve or a vacancy arise.

However, the employer may also go well beyond simply helping the employee to secure new employment. Much of the personnel department's role at a time of redundancy may be taken up with **counselling individual employees**. This may include:

1. discussing with the employee not only possible future careers and retraining but also the question of the individual starting a business;
2. financial guidance on coping with unemployment and making the best use of the redundancy payment;
3. self-appraisal and presentation skills (many employees may not have had to apply and be interviewed for a job for many years); and
4. the psychological aspects of redundancy for both the individual and family.

This work, which will take up a significant amount of time if the number of redundant employees is large, may be undertaken by management itself or the employee may be put in touch with the appropriate organisations which can provide such advice and counselling. Indeed, management may go so far as to provide or pay for redundant employees to attend special courses on any of these topics.

Whilst it may be argued that, at a time of financial stringency for the organisation, this work involves an unnecessary cost in respect of employees who will shortly no longer be the responsibility of the organisation, nevertheless it is this concern for the welfare of redundant employees which is most likely to result in the maintenance of morale and commitment to the organisation amongst the employees who remain. The implementation of a co-ordinated programme of assistance to redundant employees may be facilitated by the establishment of a **special task force**, comprising both line managers and personnel specialists, to undertake this work on a full-time basis for the duration of the redundancy.

Communication, consultation and negotiation

It is possible to identify three distinct groups to whom senior management needs to communicate if a redundancy is to be handled with the minimum of rumours and suspicion: all levels of management, employees and recognised trade unions.

The statutory provisions regarding consultation with recognised independent trade unions provide only a minimum framework for **consultation and negotiation with trade unions** over redundancy. It is important that management should involve trade union representatives at the earliest opportunity. If the cause of the redundancy is technological change within the organisation then the **timing of the initial discussions** with trade unions is entirely within management's control. However, if the cause of the redundancy is economic recession it may become more difficult for management to determine the appropriate point in time at which to commence such discussions. It may be argued that the appropriate time is when the organisation's economic position begins to worsen. Alternatively it may be argued that this would be premature, and unnecessary if the economic position were to improve, and that such discussion should only be undertaken when management believes that an effect on employment is likely. This problem is largely overcome if there are regular discussions on the state of the organisation between senior management and union representatives which may, if necessary, gradually move into discussion concerning redundancy. Management must also decide whether these initial discussions are to be conducted with the full-time officers of the appropriate unions or include the relevant shop stewards. This will be largely determined by the composition of the normal trade union negotiating body within that organisation.

The **content** of the initial discussions will centre on identifying the need for a redundancy and an examination of alternative strategies to the dismissal of employees. Once the need for reducing the labour force has been established, the discussions will then concentrate on identifying the types and numbers of employees to be made redundant and over what time period this is likely to take place. It is at this stage that, in situations of strong unionisation, the discussions are likely to **move from consultation to negotiation** with the trade union representatives seeking to minimise the extent of the proposed dismissals. The other major area of negotiation involves the agreement of a **redundancy procedure**, and in particular the criterion to be applied in the selection of employees to be made redundant and the levels of compensation they are to receive. In some situations trade union representatives may then be involved, jointly with management, in applying the agreed criterion or more normally will be notified by management of the employees selected for redundancy. The trade union representatives may subsequently be involved in **processing grievances** on behalf of their members in respect of their selection for redundancy or the level of compensation they are to receive. Throughout this process of consultation and negotiation management should ensure that it has all necessary information and be in a position to answer questions and consider suggestions or alternatives put forward by the union representatives.

The timing of any **general communication to employees** is as crucial to the successful handling of a redundancy as the timing of the initial discussion with trade union representatives. It may be argued that there is never a 'right' time to tell employees of a potential redundancy in the organisation because this is likely to result in a lowering of employee morale by creating a feeling of insecurity. Some would argue that such information should be delayed for as long as possible. However, it may equally be argued that any unnecessary delay in informing employees can easily lead to distrust and misunderstandings as a result of rumours. Therefore, once management has made the decision to initiate consultations with trade union representatives it should also communicate directly with all employees. It would be unrealistic to expect trade union representatives to enter into discussions on such a sensitive issue in an atmosphere of secrecy from their members. Trade union representatives must be in a position to discuss the issue with their membership if they are both to represent their members' interests and make a realistic contribution in any discussions with management. The direct communication to employees may take the form of a written notice circulated to all employees either at work or at home or a direct briefing by departmental or senior management. The employees should then receive regular communications regarding the progress of discussions with the trade unions and the subsequent implementation of the redundancy programme.

Clearly, trade union representatives and employees should not be told of a potential redundancy before **all levels of management** have been informed. In particular, departmental and supervisory management should, in advance of the general notification to employees, be **sufficiently briefed** by senior management to be able to answer most of the initial questions raised by employees and correct any rumours or misunderstandings. It is of paramount importance that they should not feel that shop stewards have been given more information than themselves. This initial briefing should then be followed by further regular briefings in respect of the management's discussions with trade unions and the implementation of the redundancy programme both generally and specifically in relation to their department or section. At the outset of handling a redundancy senior management must, in a short space of time, brief its management, commence consultations with trade union representatives and communicate to all its employees.

21.5 Summary propositions

- Whilst redundancy at the organisational level may be inevitable, and even desirable, its attendant unemployment may have serious consequences for both the individual and society.
- The legislation relating to redundancy does not give the employee job security but provides only a minimal level of compensation should the employee be made redundant.
- Management's objectives in any redundancy situation are to reduce its labour force whilst maintaining the morale and goodwill of its remaining employees, the union's objectives are to resist, or minimise the extent of, the redundancy whilst securing the best possible financial compensation for those who are made redundant.

Further reading

- P. Mumford, *Redundancy and Security of Employment*, Gower, 1975. This book examines the handling of redundancy within the context of an overall approach to security of employment.
- C. Bourn, *Redundancy Law and Practice*, Butterworth, 1983. A useful examination of redundancy law and its operation.
- *Guide to Redundancy*, Incomes Data Services Ltd., 1980. A very useful survey of many of the practical problems involved in handling a redundancy. It provides many examples drawn from different agreements or policies.
- F. Kemp, B. Buttle and D. Kemp, *Focus on Redundancy*, Kogan Page, 1980. This book looks at redundancy largely from the employee's point

of view in respect of what he/she must do when made redundant and what help is available.

References

1. P. J. White, 'The management of redundancy', *Industrial Relations Journal*, vol. 14, no. 1, 1983, p. 32.
2. R. J. Sutherland, 'Redundancy: perspectives and policies', *Industrial Relations Journal*, vol. 11, no. 4, 1980, p. 17.
3. *ibid.*
4. *ibid.*
5. *ibid.*, p. 23.
6. *ibid.*
7. P. Mumford, *Redundancy and Security of Employment*, Gower, 1975, p. 5.
8. D. Torrington and J. Chapman, *Personnel Management* (2nd edn), Prentice Hall, 1983, p. 473.
9. TUC, *Job Security: A Guide for Negotiators*, 1973, p. 1.
10. TUC *Annual Report*, 1983, p. 245.
11. F. Kemp, B. Buttle and D. Kemp, *Focus on Redundancy*, Kogan Page, 1980, p. 134.
12. Newport and Gwent Industrial Mission, *Redundant? A Personal Survival Kit*, 1975, p. 1.
13. *Unemployment: A new approach for the 80s*, Institute of Employment Consultants & Federation of Personnel Services, 1979, p. 9.
14. Newport and Gwent Industrial Mission, *op. cit.*, Appendix 1.
15. R. W. Rideout, *Trade Unions and the Law*, Allen & Unwin, 1973, p. 212.
16. O. Aikin and J. Reid, *Labour Law: Vol. 1 – Employment, Welfare and Safety at Work*, Penguin, 1971, p. 165. Reprinted by permission of Penguin Books Ltd. ©Olga Aikin and Judith Reid, 1971.
17. *ibid.*, p. 169.
18. R. W. Rideout, *op. cit.*, p. 213.
19. O. Aikin and J. Reid, *op. cit.*, p. 175.
20. P. Mumford, *op. cit.*, pp. 42–3.
21. *ibid.*, p. 47.
22. Incomes Data Services, *Guide to Redundancy*, 1980, p. 42.
23. P. Mumford, *op. cit.*, p. 50.

Appendix 1

Trade union number and membership

Year	Number of unions			Trade union membership				
	A	B		C	D	E		F
				Working	Union	Union		
	Total	TUC		population	membership	density	TUC	
			(%)	(millions)	(millions)	(%)		(%)
					(change p.a.)			
1893	1,279	179	(14)	14.9	1.6 –	11	1.1	(69)
1894	1,314	170	(13)	15.1	1.5 (– 6.2)	10	1.0	(67)
1895	1,340	178	(13)	15.2	1.5 (0.0)	10	1.1	(73)
1896	1,358	180	(13)	15.4	1.6 (+ 6.7)	10	1.1	(69)
1897	1,353	188	(14)	15.5	1.7 (+ 6.2)	11	1.2	(71)
1898	1,326	181	(14)	15.7	1.8 (+ 5.9)	11	1.2	(67)
1899	1,325	184	(14)	15.8	1.9 (+ 5.6)	12	1.3	(68)
1900	1,323	191	(14)	16.0	2.0 (+ 5.3)	13	1.2	(60)
1901	1,322	198	(15)	16.1	2.0 (0.0)	12	1.4	(70)
1902	1,297	204	(16)	16.3	2.0 (0.0)	12	1.5	(75)
1903	1,285	212	(16)	16.4	2.0 (0.0)	12	1.4	(70)
1904	1,256	205	(16)	16.6	2.0 (0.0)	12	1.5	(75)
1905	1,244	226	(18)	16.8	2.0 (0.0)	12	1.6	(80)
1906	1,282	236	(18)	16.9	2.2 (+10.0)	13	1.7	(77)
1907	1,283	214	(17)	17.1	2.5 (+13.6)	15	1.8	(72)
1908	1,268	219	(17)	17.3	2.5 (0.0)	14	1.7	(68)
1909	1,260	212	(17)	17.4	2.5 (0.0)	14	1.6	(64)
1910	1,269	202	(16)	17.6	2.6 (+ 4.0)	15	1.7	(65)
1911	1,290	201	(16)	17.8	3.1 (+19.2)	17	2.0	(65)
1912	1,252	207	(17)	17.8	3.4 (+ 9.7)	19	2.2	(65)
1913	1,269	210	(17)	17.9	4.1 (+20.6)	23	2.4	(59)
1914	1,260	215	(17)	18.0	4.1 (0.0)	23	2.7	(6S)
1915	1,229	227	(18)	18.1	4.4 (+ 7.3)	24	2.9	(66)
1916	1,225	235	(19)	18.2	4.6 (+ 4.5)	25	3.1	(67)
1917	1,241	262	(21)	18.2	5.5 (+19.6)	30	4.5	(82)
1918	1,264	266	(21)	18.3	6.5 (+18.2)	36	5.3	(82)
1919	1,360	215	(16)	18.4	7.9 (+21.5)	43	6.5	(82)
1920	1,384	213	(15)	18.5	8.3 (+ 5.1)	45	6.4	(77)
1921	1,275	206	(16)	18.5	6.6 (–20.5)	36	5.1	(77)

	Number of unions			Trade union membership				
Year	A	B		C	D	E		F
	Total	TUC	(%)	Working population (millions)	Union membership (millions) (change p.a.)	Union density (%)	TUC	(%)
1922	1,232	194	(16)	17.8	5.6 (−15.2)	31	4.4	(79)
1923	1,192	203	(17)	18.0	5.4 (− 3.6)	30	4.3	(80)
1924	1,194	205	(17)	18.1	5.5 (+ 1.9)	30	4.4	(80)
1925	1,176	207	(18)	18.3	5.5 (0.0)	30	4.4	(80)
1926	1,164	204	(18)	18.4	5.2 (− 5.5)	28	4.2	(81)
1927	1,159	196	(17)	18.6	4.9 (− 5.8)	26	3.9	(80)
1928	1,142	202	(18)	18.8	4.9 (0.0)	26	3.7	(76)
1929	1,133	210	(19)	18.9	4.9 (0.0)	26	3.7	(76)
1930	1,121	210	(19)	19.1	4.8 (− 2.0)	25	3.7	(77)
1931	1,108	209	(19)	19.3	4.6 (− 4.2)	24	3.6	(78)
1932	1,081	208	(19)	19.3	4.4 (− 4.3)	23	3.4	(77)
1933	1,081	210	(19)	19.4	4.4 (0.0)	23	3.3	(75)
1934	1,063	211	(20)	19.5	4.6 (+ 4.5)	24	3.4	(74)
1935	1,049	214	(20)	19.6	4.9 (+ 6.5)	25	3.6	(73)
1936	1,036	214	(21)	19.7	5.3 (+ 8.2)	27	4.0	(75)
1937	1,032	216	(21)	19.7	5.8 (+ 9.4)	29	4.5	(78)
1938	1,024	217	(21)	19.8	6.1 (+ 5.2)	31	4.7	(77)
1939	1,019	223	(22)	19.9	6.3 (+ 3.3)	32	4.9	(78)
1940	1,004	223	(22)	20.0	6.6 (+ 4.8)	33	5.1	(77)
1941	996	232	(23)	20.1	7.2 (+ 9.1)	36	5.4	(75)
1942	991	230	(23)	20.2	7.9 (+ 9.7)	39	6.0	(76)
1943	987	190	(19)	20.2	8.2 (+ 3.8)	41	6.6	(80)
1944	963	191	(20)	20.3	8.1 (− 1.2)	40	6.6	(81)
1945	781	192	(25)	20.4	7.9 (− 2.5)	39	6.7	(85)
1946	757	187	(25)	20.5	8.8 (+11.4)	43	7.5	(85)
1947	734	188	(26)	20.6	9.1 (+ 3.4)	44	7.8	(86)
1948	735	187	(25)	20.7	9.3 (+ 2.2)	45	7.9	(85)
1949	726	186	(26)	20.8	9.3 (0.0)	45	7.9	(85)
1950	732	186	(25)	21.1	9.3 (0.0)	44	7.8	(84)
1951	735	183	(25)	21.2	9.6 (+ 3.2)	45	8.0	(83)
1952	719	183	(25)	21.3	9.6 (0.0)	45	8.1	(84)
1953	717	184	(26)	21.4	9.5 (− 1.0)	44	8.1	(85)
1954	703	183	(26)	21.7	9.6 (+ 1.1)	44	8.1	(84)
1955	704	186	(26)	21.9	9.7 (+ 1.0)	44	8.3	(86)
1956	685	185	(27)	22.2	9.8 (+ 1.0)	44	8.3	(85)
1957	685	185	(27)	22.3	9.8 (0.0)	44	8.3	(85)
1958	675	186	(28)	22.3	9.6 (− 2.0)	43	8.2	(85)
1959	668	184	(28)	22.4	9.6 (0.0)	43	8.1	(84)
1960	664	183	(28)	22.8	9.8 (+ 2.1)	43	8.3	(85)
1961	655	182	(28)	23.1	9.9 (+ 1.0)	43	8.3	(84)
1962	649	176	(27)	23.4	10.0 (+ 1.0)	43	8.3	(83)
1963	643	175	(27)	23.6	10.1 (+ 1.0)	43	8.3	(82)
1964	641	172	(27)	23.7	10.2 (+ 1.0)	43	8.7	(85)
1965	630	170	(27)	23.9	10.3 (+ 1.0)	43	8.9	(86)
1966	622	169	(27)	24.1	10.3 (0.0)	43	8.8	(85)
1967	604	110	(18)	23.8	10.2 (− 1.0)	43	8.7	(85)

	Number of unions				Trade union membership			
Year	A	B		C	D	E		F
				Working	Union	Union		
	Total	TUC		population	membership	density	TUC	
			(%)	(millions)	(millions)	(%)		(%)
					(change p.a.)			
1968	586	155	(26)	23.7	10.2 (0.0)	43	8.9	(87)
1969	565	150	(27)	23.6	10.5 (+ 2.9)	44	9.4	(90)
1970	543	142	(26)	23.4	11.2 (+ 6.7)	48	10.0	(89)
1971	525	132	(25)	23.3	11.1 (− 0.9)	48	9.9	(89)
1972	507	126	(25)	23.1	11.4 (+ 2.7)	49	10.0	(88)
1973	519	109	(21)	23.4	11.5 (+ 0.9)	49	10.0	(87)
1974	507	111	(22)	23.6	11.8 (+ 2.6)	50	10.4	(88)
1975	470	113	(24)	23.9	12.0 (+ 1.7)	50	11.0	(92)
1976	473	115	(24)	24.0	12.4 (+ 3.3)	52	11.5	(93)
1977	481	112	(23)	24.3	12.9 (+ 4.0)	53	11.8	(91)
1978	462	112	(24)	24.3	13.1 (+ 1.6)	54	12.1	(92)
1979	453	109	(24)	24.3	13.3 (+ 1.5)	55	12.2	(92)
1980	438	106	(24)	24.2	12.9 (− 3.0)	53	11.6	(90)
1981	414	105	(25)	24.2	12.1 (− 6.2)	50	11.0	(91)
1982	408	102	(25)	24.3	11.6 (− 4.1)	48	10.5	(91)
1983	394	98	(25)	24.3	11.2 (− 2.6)	47	10.1	(89)
1984	375	91	(24)	24.6	11.0 (− 1.8)	45	9.9	(90)
1985	370	88	(24)	24.9	10.8 (− 1.8)	43	9.6	(89)
1986	335	87	(26)	25.0	10.5 (− 2.8)	42	9.2	(88)
1987	330	83	(25)	24.6	10.5 (0.0)	43	9.1	(87)
1988	315	78	(25)	24.8	10.4 (− 1.0)	42	8.7	(84)
1989	309	78	(25)	24.6	10.2 (− 1.9)	41	8.4	(82)

Notes:
1. 1913 figures for TUC (columns B and F) are estimates as no congress was held in 1914.
2. In 1975 31 organisations were no longer deemed to be trade unions (column A).
3. TUC membership figures from 1988 do not include EETPU.

Appendix 2

Britain's strike figures

Year	Number of stoppages	Number of workers (mill.)	Total (millions)	Working Days Lost			
				Per 1,000 working population	Per 1,000 trade unionists	Average per strike	Average per striker
1914	972	0.4	9.4	522	2,293	9,671	23.5
1915	672	0.4	3.0	166	682	4,464	7.5
1916	532	0.3	2.4	132	522	4,511	8.0
1917	730	0.9	5.9	324	1,073	8,082	6.6
1918	1,165	1.2	5.9	322	908	5,064	4.9
1919	1,352	2.6	36.0	1,957	4,557	26,627	13.8
1920	1,607	1.9	28.9	1,562	2,482	17,984	15.2
1921	763	1.8	82.3	4,449	12,470	107,864	45.7
1922	576	0.6	19.7	1,107	3,518	34,201	32.8
1923	628	0.4	11.0	611	2,037	17,516	27.5
1924	710	0.6	8.4	464	1,527	11,831	14.0
1925	603	0.4	8.9	486	1,618	14,760	22.2
1926	323	2.7	161.3	8,766	31,019	499,380	59.7
1927	303	0.1	0.9	48	184	2,970	9.0
1928	302	0.1	1.4	74	286	4,636	14.0
1929	431	0.5	8.3	439	1,694	19,258	16.6
1930	422	0.3	4.5	236	938	10,663	15.0
1931	420	0.5	7.0	363	1,522	16,667	14.0
1932	389	0.4	6.4	332	1,455	16,452	16.0
1933	357	0.1	1.0	52	227	2,801	10.0
1934	474	0.1	1.1	56	239	2,321	11.0
1935	553	0.3	2.0	102	408	3,617	6.7
1936	818	0.3	2.0	102	377	2,445	6.7
1937	1,129	0.6	3.1	157	534	2,746	5.2
1938	875	0.3	1.3	66	213	1,486	4.3
1939	940	0.3	1.4	70	222	1,489	4.7
1940	922	0.3	0.9	45	136	976	3.0
1941	1,251	0.4	1.1	55	153	879	2.7
1942	1,303	0.5	1.5	74	190	1,151	3.0
1943	1,785	0.6	1.8	89	220	1,008	3.0
1944	2,194	0.8	3.7	182	457	1,686	4.6

Year	Number of stoppages	Number of workers (mill.)	Total (millions)	Working Days Lost			
				Per 1,000 working population	Per 1,000 trade unionists	Average per strike	Average per striker
1945	2,293	0.5	2.9	142	367	1,265	5.8
1946	2,205	0.5	2.2	107	250	998	4.4
1947	1,721	0.6	1.4	68	154	813	2.3
1948	1,759	0.4	1.9	92	204	1,080	4.7
1949	1,426	0.5	1.8	87	194	1,262	3.6
1950	1,339	0.3	1.4	66	151	1,046	4.7
1951	1,719	0.4	1.7	80	177	989	4.2
1952	1,717	0.4	1.8	85	188	1,050	4.5
1953	1,746	1.4	2.2	103	232	1,260	1.6
1954	1,989	0.4	2.5	115	260	1,257	6.3
1955	2,419	0.7	3.8	174	392	1,571	5.4
1956	2,648	0.5	2.1	95	214	793	4.2
1957	2,859	1.4	8.4	377	857	2,938	6.0
1958	2,629	0.5	3.5	157	365	1,331	7.0
1959	2,093	0.6	5.3	237	552	2,532	8.8
1960	2,832	0.8	3.1	136	316	1,095	3.9
1961	2,686	0.8	3.0	130	303	1,117	3.8
1962	2,449	4.4	5.8	248	580	2,368	1.3
1963	2,068	0.6	2.0	85	198	967	3.3
1964	2,524	0.9	2.0	84	196	792	2.2
1965	2,354	0.9	2.9	121	282	1,232	3.2
1966	1,937	0.5	2.4	100	233	1,239	4.8
1967	2,832	0.7	2.8	118	275	1,323	4.0
1968	2,378	2.3	4.7	198	461	1,976	2.0
1969	3,116	1.7	6.8	288	648	2,182	4.0
1970	3,906	1.8	10.9	466	973	2,791	6.1
1971	2,228	1.1	13.6	584	1,225	6,104	12.4
1972	2,497	1.7	23.9	1,035	2,096	9,571	14.1
1973	2,873	1.5	7.2	308	626	2,506	4.8
1974	2,922	1.6	14.8	627	1,254	5,065	9.2
1975	2,282	0.8	6.0	251	500	2,629	7.5
1976	2,016	0.7	3.3	137	266	1,637	4.7
1977	2,703	1.1	10.1	416	783	3,737	9.2
1978	2,471	1.0	9.4	387	718	3,804	9.4
1979	2,080	4.6	29.5	1,214	2,218	14,183	6.4
1980	1,330	0.8	11.2	463	868	8,421	14.0
1981	1,338	1.5	4.3	178	355	3,214	2.9
1982	1,528	2.1	5.3	218	457	3,469	2.5
1983	1,352	0.6	3.8	155	336	2,811	6.3
1984	1,221	1.5	27.1	1,102	2,464	22,195	18.1
1985	903	0.8	6.4	257	593	7,087	8.0
1986	1,074	0.7	1.9	76	181	1,769	2.7
1987	1,016	0.9	3.5	142	333	3,445	3.9
1988	781	0.8	3.7	149	356	4,738	4.6
1989	701	0.7	4.1	167	402	5,849	5.9
1990	630	0.3	1.9	77		3,016	6.3

Index